"Come Out, My People!"

"Come Out, My People!"

❦

God's Call out of Empire in the Bible and Beyond

Wes Howard-Brook

ORBIS BOOKS
Maryknoll, New York 10545

Founded in 1970, Orbis Books endeavors to publish works that enlighten the mind, nourish the spirit, and challenge the conscience. The publishing arm of the Maryknoll Fathers and Brothers, Orbis seeks to explore the global dimensions of the Christian faith and mission, to invite dialogue with diverse cultures and religious traditions, and to serve the cause of reconciliation and peace. The books published reflect the views of their authors and do not represent the official position of the Maryknoll Society. To learn more about Maryknoll and Orbis Books, please visit our website at www.maryknollsociety.org.

Library of Congress Cataloging-in-Publication Data

Howard-Brook, Wes.
    Come out, my people! : God's call out of empire in the Bible and beyond / Wes Howard-Brook.
        p.   cm.
    Includes bibliographical references and index.
    ISBN 978-1-57075-892-8 (pbk.)
    1. Bible – Criticism, interpretation, etc. I. Title.
BS511.3.H69 2010
220.6 – dc22   2010015255

In joyous thanksgiving for my beloved metochos, Sue, whose trust in the Risen One inspires me anew each day;

and for the Thursday and Friday John's gospel groups, whose persistent yearning to hear the Word and to do it makes the Word become flesh.

Contents

Preface xiii

Abbreviations xvii

PART I
IN THE BEGINNING

Introduction: "Is God on Our Side?" The Two Religions 3

1. "Then God Said, 'Let there be light!' " (Gen. 1) 13
   The Bible as Story and as History / 13

2. "By the Sweat of Your Face You Shall Eat Bread" (Gen. 2–3) 22

3. "And He Built a City" 30
   East of Eden / 30
   "Am I My Brother's Keeper?" (Gen. 4) / 33
   The Historical Origins of "the City" / 36
   YHWH's Regret (Gen. 5–9) / 43
   The Beginning of Empire (Gen. 10–11) / 45

4. Making One's Name Great 47
   "Let Us Make a Name for Ourselves": The Tower of Babel
      (Gen. 11) / 47
   "I Will Make Your Name Great": YHWH's Call to Abram
      to Come Out of Empire (Gen. 12) / 51

5. The Well-Watered Plain of Sodom 55
   Turning to Egypt for Food (Gen. 12) / 55
   Choosing for Oneself (Gen. 13–14) / 56
   Entertaining Angels ... or Not (Gen. 15–19) / 58

6. Fulfilling YHWH's Promises 66
   Ishmael "yitzchaqing" (Gen. 21) / 67
   The Binding of Isaac (Gen. 22) / 68
   Acquiring a Holding in the Land (Gen. 23) / 70
   Finding a Wife for Isaac (Gen. 24) / 71
   Two Nations Are in Your Womb (Gen. 25) / 73
   Learning to Be a Trickster (Gen. 27–29) / 75
   Wrestling with God and Humans (Gen. 31–32) / 80

7. The Price of Settling Too Soon 83

PART II
FROM EXODUS TO EXILE:
THE TWO RELIGIONS IN CONFLICT
AMID GOD'S PEOPLE

8. Entering the "Exit Story" 93

9. Solomon's Wisdom 98
   Dating Solomon / 104
   Solomon's "Nation Building" / 115
   Not Dividing the Baby / 123

10. Finding the "Way Out" 134
    Jeroboam's Rebellion / 134
    Birthing Israel, the People of YHWH / 140
    The Revenge of the Shilonites / 156

11. Kissing Calves 161
    Elijah, "Troubler of Israel" and His Successor, Elisha / 161
    Amos and Hosea: Calling Israel Back to the Sinai Covenant / 165

12. "I Have Found the Book of the Torah in the House
    of YHWH!" 172
    Hezekiah, Isaiah, and Micah Respond to the Threat of Assyria / 172
    Josiah, the Deuteronomistic History's True Hero / 179
    Monarchy, according to the Compromise Narrative / 187
    Role of Moses and Joshua / 192
    The Destruction of Jerusalem and the End of the Monarchy / 197

13. What Was "Israel" before the Monarchy? 199

PART III
FROM EXILE TO THE EVE OF EASTER:
FALLEN JERUSALEM, FALLEN BABYLON

14. The First Fall of Jerusalem: Jeremiah and Ezekiel 215
    Jeremiah / 215
    Ezekiel / 225

15. "In the Wilderness, Prepare the Way of YHWH":
    Envisioning a Way out of Exile 232
    "Comfort, O Comfort My People": Second Isaiah's Promise of
        Release from the Prison of Exile / 233
    Ezekiel, Part Two: New Jerusalem / 239

16. **The Struggle over Jerusalem's Restoration** 244

Introduction / 244
Haggai-Zechariah / 247
The Law of Your God and the Law of the King: The Imperially
        Sponsored Restoration Project of Ezra-Nehemiah / 249
Military Security, Economic Exploitation, and Oppressive Violence
        against the Poor / 256
"Do Not Let the Foreigner Joined to YHWH say,
        'YHWH Will Surely Separate Me from His People' ":
        The Dissenting Voice of Third Isaiah / 264
Genesis for a New Generation / 268
Second Zechariah and the Beginning of Eschatological Hope / 271
Leviticus: Cosmos, Temple, and Text in Microcosm / 273
Chronicles: David as Patron of the Priesthood and Temple / 278
"The Books of Moses" as Persian-supported "law" for Yehud / 283
Assessing the Range of Visions for the Restored People of God / 285

17. **Seeking "Wisdom" under Greek Rule, Part One:
The Ptolemaic Empire** 287

From Persia to Greece / 287
Wisdom from Above: A Brief Overview of "Royal Wisdom" / 290
Hellenistic Royal Ideology in Ptolemaic Egypt / 293
"I Will Send You the Prophet Elijah": Malachi and the Closure
        of the Era of Prophecy / 296
"All the Earth Was Filled with the Godlessness and Violence That
        Had Befallen It": *First Enoch*'s *Book of the Watchers* / 298
"All Is Vapor": Qoheleth's "Pox" on Both Houses / 309

18. **Seeking "Wisdom" under Greek Rule, Part Two:
The Seleucid Empire** 313

The Shift from Ptolemaic to Seleucid Rule of Judea in 200 BCE / 313
Royal Wisdom on the Eve of Crisis: The Book of Sirach / 315
The Epistle of Enoch: Measuring "Weeks" until the Coming of
        God's Reign / 318
The Crisis under Antiochus IV Epiphanes / 323
The Maccabees: Zealous and Violent Defenders of the Temple
        and of Religious Tradition / 325
"And They Began to Open Their Eyes": Enoch's *Dream Visions* / 330
"And I Saw One Like a Human Being": The Book of Daniel / 335

19. **From Greece to Rome: Longing for God's Reign to Come** 355

The Hasmonean Dynasty: Empire from Within / 355
Cosmos and Calendar: Enoch's *Astronomical Book* and
        the Book of Jubilees / 359
The Qumran Community: Awaiting the
        "End of Days" in the Desert / 362

The Temple Scroll: Envisioning a New Temple and a New King
   for Israel / 366
Psalms of Solomon: Looking for a Messiah to Save Jerusalem / 367
The Reign of Herod the Great, Puppet of Rome / 371
Parables of Enoch: Awaiting the Son of Man / 372

PART IV
FROM EASTER TO THE ESCHATON:
JESUS' FULFILLMENT OF THE RELIGION OF CREATION AND
DEFEAT OF THE RELIGION OF EMPIRE

20. Enlightenment and Empire: Reading Jesus from the *Locus Imperii*
    in the Light of the Resurrection 383

21. The Gospel of Jesus Christ against the Gospel of Empire 393

22. "The Beginning of the Good News of Jesus Christ":
    The Gospel of Mark 399

23. "Strive First for the Kingdom of God": Matthew's Gospel 407

24. Proclaiming Jubilee: Luke's Gospel and Acts of the Apostles 418

25. "Savior of the World": The Gospel of John 435

26. "Christ the Power of God and the Wisdom of God":
    Paul's Counter-imperial Gospel 447

    Paul's "Conversion" / 451
    Forming and Nurturing Communities of the "Called Out"
       (*ekklēsiai*) / 454
    Paul's Gospel of the Victory of the Creator God over the Gods
       of Empire / 457

27. "Come Out, My People": The Book of Revelation 466

Conclusion: Hearing and Responding to God's Call:
"Come Out, My People!" 473

Bibliography 475

Index 517

Tables and Maps

TABLES

Table 1: The Two Religions   6
Table 2: Questions from the Exile   16
Table 3: "Building" (Hebrew, *bnh*) in Genesis   86
Table 4: Comparison of Solomon and Pharaoh   100
Table 5: Comparison between the Torah of the King
      (Deut. 17:14-20)and Solomon's Reign (1 Kings 3–11)   101
Table 6: Exodus to Exile Texts and Their Perspectives   105
Table 7: Mention of Abraham, Isaac, and Jacob from Genesis
      to 2 Kings   118
Table 8: Mention of Moses in Genesis through 2 Kings   120
Table 9: Outline of 1 Kings 3–4   121
Table 10: The Rich Man, Poor Man, Traveler, and Ewe Lamb   127
Table 11: Parallels between Moses and Jeroboam   138
Table 12: Comparison of Glory of YHWH in Temple and
      Wilderness   151
Table 13: Comparison of Temple Dedication and Covenant
      Ceremonies   152
Table 14: Comparison of Isaiah's and Micah's "Swords into
      Plowshares" Prophecies   175
Table 15: Joash and Josiah   181
Table 16: Major Figures in the Collapse of the Monarchy and
      Jerusalem   217
Table 17: Some Links between Ezekiel and Genesis   225
Table 18: Some Links between Ezekiel and Leviticus   226
Table 19: Some Links between Second Isaiah and Genesis   234
Table 20: Biblical Perspectives on the Persian Era Restoration
      of Jerusalem   245
Table 21: Structure of Ezra-Nehemiah (according to
      Tamara Eskenazi)   251
Table 22: The "Microcosm" of the Book of Leviticus
      (following Mary Douglas)   275
Table 23: The Books of *1 Enoch*   299
Table 24: Parallel Imagery in Psalm 97 and *1 Enoch* 1:4–8   304
Table 25: Some Elements Found in both Daniel and Enoch's
      Book of the Watchers and *Dream Visions*   339

Table 26: The "Two Religions" in the Gospels   397
Table 27: Structure of the Sermon on the Mount   413
Table 28: The Seals on the First Scroll   469
Table 29: Babylon and New Jerusalem   472

MAPS

Map 1: Suggested route of Exiles from Judah to Babylon   23
Map 2: Possible routes of Abram's migration   52
Map 3: Jacob's Journey   84
Map 4: Israel in the time of David   112
Map 5: Major worship sites in the divided kingdom   157
Map 6: Seleucid and Ptolemaic empires, c. 200 BCE   314

Preface

There is not, nor has there ever been, such a thing as "Christianity" or "Judaism."

Upon even brief reflection, this perhaps startling statement is obviously true. Whose "Christianity" does one mean when using the term: that of fundamentalists, orthodox Roman Catholics, members of various mainline or evangelical denominations, or that expressed within the realm of countless nondenominational "Christian" communities throughout the world? Similarly for "Judaism": does it refer to Zionists, the ultraorthodox, "secular Jews," or any other place on a wide and broad canvas? To attempt to place meaningful parameters on either term is to face the reality that the words simply have no concrete and specific meaning and never have.[1]

And yet, we find these labels used daily and throughout history as if they did have such concrete and specific meaning. One can take courses in "the history of Christianity" without ever confronting the radically indeterminate nature of the primary terms. One sees the media refer to "conservative" or "progressive" Christians without questioning how either qualifying adjective relates to what Jesus is actually reported to have said and done in the New Testament. We see even cautious and otherwise precise biblical scholars refer to "early Christianity" or "Judaism at the time of Jesus" as if those terms were self-explanatory.

The results of this usage have been disastrous in several ways. *First, it has been a disaster for determining whether being "Christian" can or should have any identifiable content both in terms of worldview and way of life.* People see media reports of "Christians" speaking or acting in certain ways and assume, on the one hand, that this reflects how "Christians" are supposed to act, or, on the other hand, see that "Christians" apparently hold such impossibly paradoxical and irrational views that only the mindless would identify with this label.

Second, it has been a disaster for the understanding of Western history. One surveys the sweep of "Christianity" across Europe and around the globe with its Crusades, colonialism, and conquest and quickly associates it with the power wielded by kings and their elite supporters. It is thus no surprise

---

1. Consider, e.g., Mason, who examines the scholarly confusion over terms such as "Jews" and "Judaism" in the context of the ancient world. Consider also the plethora of recent books challenging the assumption that there was a clear division between "Jews" and "Christians" in the first decades and even centuries of the common era, e.g., Boyarin (2006); Becker and Reed.

that people disgusted by this history of violence, oppression, and exploitation would want nothing to do with the banner under which it has been carried out over the past seventeen hundred years.

Third, it has been a disaster for interreligious dialogue, first between "Jews" and "Christians," but also between Christians and Muslims, Buddhists, Hindus, and others. I will leave it to those who claim one of these other categories as their "religion" to determine whether my claim is equally true for labels such as "Islam" or "Buddhism." We see today how "Islam" has become associated with small factions of violent radicals, when in fact "Islam" refers to a wide range of viewpoints and practices. When the "world religions" are engaged as if they each embody a specific and clear content rather than a spectrum of perspectives, constructive conversation is impossible.

The impetus for this book was not directly to engage interreligious dialogue. Rather, my motivation was to trace the biblical and historical roots of "Christian warfare" and other forms of violence and domination in the name of Jesus. I hope, however, that the lens through which I engage the traditions of ancient Israel may also bear fruit beyond my initial purpose. Coming to see world history as well as current events from the perspective of the ongoing struggle between the "religion of empire" and the "religion of creation" may enable us to find new avenues for conversation among people who appear to embody different "religions" but in fact share a common worldview expressed in different cultural and historical forms. I think of the Vietnam War–era dialogue between the American Catholic monk Thomas Merton and the Vietnamese Buddhist monk Thich Nhat Hanh as a precursor of what is possible.[2]

Further, this lens may enable people who have rejected "Christianity" in particular or even "religion" in general to reconsider the quest for worldviews that bond people in the pursuit of authentic inner and outer peace and justice for humanity and all creation. For example, I shared the manuscript of this book with a friend who had been raised, like me, in a family that was culturally "Jewish" but was not "religious." Now sixty years old, he had never claimed a "religion." Yet his perusal of the opening chapter of this book and Table 1 in particular led him to exclaim, "What you are calling 'the religion of creation' is just what I believe!"

Similarly, my use of the manuscript with undergraduate students at Seattle University has opened minds otherwise closed to "religion." Countless young adults have rejected "Christianity" and "religion" because of the perception that both categories refer to the endless, violent, and hate-filled battle between people who are sure that they are "right" and their opponents are "wrong." Many have retreated either into a vague "personal spirituality" or into a world seemingly apart from "religion" altogether. As a result, they find themselves bereft of resources to engage with others in the work for a more just and humane world. However, when they discover the "religion of

---

2. See, e.g., King (2003).

creation" in the Bible and beyond as presented in this book, there is excitement about a new and hopeful way to understand "religion" that they had not thought possible.

Finally, this new lens has borne fruit in ecumenical dialogue among people whose "religion" is grounded in, one way or another, the New Testament and the person of Jesus Christ. I have discovered an exciting, worldwide circle of discipleship that transcends previous denominational divides, ages, and nationalities in which people are seeking to discover and to live the authentic Way of Jesus, leaving behind the legacy of "Christian" empire. Recognizing how Jesus definitively embraced the "creation" story in the Bible while rejecting the "empire" story provides a new foundation for engaging our scriptural inheritance in service of personal, communal, and global transformation. The path to this place requires a return to "the beginning." The ideas of "Christianity" and "Judaism" have exerted so much power across the centuries that it takes disciplined work to remove the thick layers that have been built up on our perceptions of what the Bible's message is and where Jesus' proclamation of "good news" fits within the larger biblical story. I hope that readers will engage this book not simply as isolated individuals, but also as small groups of people seeking to be bound together in proclaiming and practicing lifeways that are authentic, sustainable, and joyous. I believe with all my being that the Way of Jesus is a path that calls us out of "empire" and into the immediately available beauty and power of the Creator God's realm of overflowing abundance. If this book contributes in some small way to the revealing of this path, I will be deeply grateful.

As with all my books to date, I am grateful for the steadfast and gifted team at Orbis Books with whom I've been privileged to work now for almost two decades, including my wonderful editor and friend, Robert Ellsberg; efficient production manager, Catherine Costello; expert copy editor, John Eagleson; and sharp-eyed proofreader, Chuck John. In addition, I am thrilled to thank a new member of the team, Pony Sheehan, for her beautiful cover design. Each of these talented and experienced people could find greater fame and fortune at "big name" publishers, but chose instead to participate in embodying Orbis's four decades' long commitment to produce books that change the world. In our challenging economic times, they have not only persisted, but have redoubled that commitment.

This book is the result of more than two decades of study, reflection, and experiments in discipleship. I could not begin to name all the people whose ideas and lives have shaped my thoughts and established the foundation on which I am laying my own stones. The list includes not only countless scholars but also friends, colleagues, and companions, both living and dead, who have sought to hear the Good News of Jesus and to do it. I truly thank God for each and every person whose insight, witness, and faith have inspired me. Perhaps this book will, in turn, inspire others to continue the joyous work to which God has called us: to love one another and all creation as we have been loved.

Abbreviations

BA	*Biblical Archaeologist*
BAR	*Biblical Archaeology Review*
BASOR	*Bulletin of the American Schools of Oriental Research*
Bib.Int.	*Biblical Interpretation*
BTB	*Biblical Theology Bulletin*
BZAW	Beihefte zur Zeitschrift für die alttestamentliche Wissenschaft
CBQ	*Catholic Biblical Quarterly*
CBQMS	Catholic Biblical Quarterly Monograph Series
CBR	*Currents in Biblical Research*
CTJ	*Calvin Theological Journal*
CTM	*Currents in Theology and Mission*
DSS	*Dead Sea Scrolls*
HLS	*Holy Land Studies*
HTR	*Harvard Theological Review*
HUCA	*Hebrew Union College Annual*
Int	*Interpretation*
JAR	*Journal of Archaeological Research*
JBL	*Journal of Biblical Literature*
JBS	*Journal of Biblical Studies*
JHC	*Journal of Higher Criticism*
JHS	*Journal of Hebrew Scriptures*
JJS	*Journal of Jewish Studies*
JNES	*Journal of Near Eastern Studies*
JPS	Jewish Publication Society
JSJ	*Journal of the Study of Judaism*

JSNT	*Journal for the Study of the New Testament*
JSOT	*Journal for the Study of the Old Testament*
JSOTSS	Journal for the Study of the Old Testament Supplement Series
JSP	*Journal for the Study of the Pseudepigrapha*
JSPSS	Journal for the Study of the Pseudepigrapha Supplement Series
JTS	*Journal of Theological Studies*
NICNT	New International Commentary on the New Testament
NICOT	New International Commentary on the Old Testament
NTS	*New Testament Studies*
NT	*Novum Testamentum*
OTL	Old Testament Library
PRST	*Perspectives in Religious Studies*
RBL	*Review of Biblical Literature*
SAOC	Studies in Ancient Oriental Civilizations
SBLMS	Society of Biblical Literature Monograph Series
SJOT	*Scandinavian Journal of the Old Testament*
SNTSMS	Society for New Testament Studies Monograph Series
TDNT	*Theological Dictionary of the New Testament*
TMSJ	*The Master's Seminary Journal*
TWOT	*Theological Wordbook of the Old Testament*
VT	*Vetus Testamentum*
WBC	Word Biblical Commentary
WTJ	*Westminster Theological Journal*
ZAW	*Zeitschrift für die alttestamentliche Wissenschaft*

PART I

In the Beginning

Introduction

"Is God on Our Side?"

THE TWO RELIGIONS

"Is God on our side?"

This question has taken center stage in many of the dramas played out on the world stage in recent years. A U.S. president claims God's inspiration for the invasion of Iraq or Afghanistan. Suicide bombers do the will of Allah. Zionist Jews defend the "Holy Land." There is no authority more desired nor controverted than the favor of the divine.

Many people respond to the cacophony of cries claiming God's favor by throwing stones at "religion." One editorial writer in a Seattle newspaper expressed it like this: "Is it any wonder so many of us who were religious and have come to doubt religion or who never were involved in religion dismiss it or harbor suspicion toward it?"[1] Others dig in their heels and substitute rhetoric and "justified violence" for conversation that seeks mutual understanding. Still others, believing in a God of inclusion and love but overwhelmed by the vehement pride of those claiming God's support for their violent cause, withdraw to a "smaller" religion of home and hearth.

Can anything be done besides fighting fire with fire or retreating into private "spirituality"? This book attempts to join clarity of thought and deep faith in the Word claimed by Jesus in response. First, though, we must take a few steps back from the fray and look with a wider lens.

Have you ever walked into a room where people are watching a movie already in progress and tried to get a sense of what's going on in the story? One can leap to all kinds of wild (and false) conclusions about plot and motivation of characters by taking one or two scenes out of their narrative context. Another example: have you found yourself in a foreign land or with people from a different culture and discovered (perhaps after an embarrassing moment) that you had completely misunderstood one another's words or actions? These two kinds of experiences — confusion or misunderstanding as a result of experiences taken out of narrative and/or cultural contexts — are behind much of the failed dialogue around the question of God's partisanship in politics, economics, and war. We already know how to fix the first problem: start the film at the beginning. The solution to the second kind

---

1. John McBride, "Religion Is Not a Primary Need," *Seattle Post-Intelligencer*, July 18, 2006.

of situation is similar: find out how "the others" think and act and why they believe and behave the way they do.

But how do we "start the film at the beginning" when it comes to complex global struggles? One answer is to gain as much understanding as we can about how the situation we're in came to be. In other words, what happened from "the beginning" until we "entered the room"?

We cannot restart the disc of human history. But we can, in a meaningful way, go back "to the beginning" and discover patterns that play themselves out again and again. And this is where, perhaps surprisingly to some, one of our most helpful tools is also the world's most frequently misunderstood book, the Bible. This ancient collection of writings, just like a modern-day film or an experience of a foreign land, can be abused by having its stories told outside of the narrative and cultural contexts in which they were composed and first heard. If you are irreversibly committed to the idea that the Bible proposes simple and straightforward "answers" that can be extracted when needed to "prove" God's support for your views, you are likely to find this book challenging. But if you are willing to approach with an open mind, you may be joyously surprised by the wisdom the Bible contains and the light that wisdom can shed on our struggle to discern God's partisanship in current events.

The Bible does not present a single, unified perspective on what it means to be a "Jew" or a "Christian." Rather, it gathers together witnesses to a passionate, historical *argument* over what it means to be "God's people." It constantly keeps before its audience questions that must be wrestled with before our central question can even be addressed. "Which 'god' are you talking about?" Which 'side' are *you* on?"

The Bible insists that there are no "sidelines" from which to watch others do battle. All people are inevitably and unavoidably drawn into the fray, or at least its consequences, by the fact of sharing this beautiful, abundant, yet fragile and finite planet as our home. We can choose to run away, to be silent, or to hide, but we cannot choose not to *participate*. We may not agree with our neighbor's "religion," but we cannot remain unaffected by it.

This calls us to take our first step back to consider one of the basic terms in this argument: "religion." Ask most people (ask *yourself* right now), "what is religion?" and you're likely to get something like one or more of these responses. Religion is:

+ a system of beliefs and practices associated with labels such as Judaism, Christianity, Islam, Buddhism, or Hinduism;

+ teachings that provide a moral framework for one's life;

+ things you do in a church, synagogue, or mosque;

+ a set of rewards and punishments that motivate people to behave in a certain way;

- answers to questions like, "What happens when we die?" or "What is the purpose of life?"

- a remnant of more primitive times before reason and science when people developed myths to explain natural phenomena such as earthquakes or disease.

For the purpose of this book — and, I'd suggest, for the purpose of any reading of the Bible — I'd like to offer a different meaning, one grounded in the root of the word itself. The Latin *religio* means literally, "to bind again." Even in ancient times, *religio* became associated with some of the specific practices and beliefs associated with "religions." But I invite you to consider throughout this book its broader sense of *the attitudes, beliefs, and/or practices that bind individuals together as a "people."*[2] Seen this way, there are countless "religions" beyond the organized and institutional traditions at the top of the list. Ask yourself: What binds me to other people? Consider some possibilities:

- immediate family;

- ethnicity or race;

- language (formal, such as English; technical, such as "computerese"; or popular, such as slang);

- nationality;

- neighborhood or geographic region;

- common interests, such as sports, music, arts, or hobbies;

- membership in an organization such as a labor union, professional association, or political party;

- concern for social or political issues.

It is obvious that some of these "religions" are stronger than others in that they exert a comparatively more powerful and permanent bonding force. One might scream and cheer with one's fellow football fans, for instance, but one isn't as likely to lay down one's life for them as one might for one's fellow family members or citizens. Similarly, we might feel bound to people whom we see regularly but quickly lose touch if we move away. In contrast, we are likely to stay bound to family or our ethnic group wherever we are.

---

2. Mason argues at length that the term "religion" does not fit any category of collective identity before at least the sixteenth century of our era. I acknowledge that my use herein is heuristic and anachronistic, not "historical." I am not aware of another category that can be used to take into account all of the elements shown in Table 1. Further, he shows definitively that the English words "Jew(s)" and "Judaism" are anachronistic and unwarranted translations of the corresponding Greek words, *Ioudaioi* and *Ioudaismos*. Therefore, throughout this book, I will use various substitutes, depending on context, such as "Israelite," "Judean," or "Jews" with quotation marks. I have left intact the use of forms of the word "Jew" in quotations from other authors.

Table 1: The Two Religions

Feature	Religion of Creation	Religion of Empire
Source of "divine power"	One God, the Creator of Heaven and Earth	Many gods and goddesses
God's "home"	Beyond and within creation and among people	In a temple near the palace in the royal city
Places of sacred encounter	Earth: mountains, rivers, wilderness; direct encounter; table fellowship; human intimacy	Urban temple, mediated by priestly elite; urban royal rituals
Purpose of human life	Praise God with joy in gratitude for the abundant gift of life	Serve the gods through loyalty to "empire"
Basic social structure	Egalitarian kinship	Hierarchical patronage
Basic economic structure	Gift, barter, collaboration amid abundance	Money, debt, competition amid scarcity
Basic social architecture	Village, small town	Urban, megalopolis
Basic political ideology	God alone reigns	Human king reigns as presence of supreme god
Relationship with unknown "others"	Hospitality; love	Suspicion; violence
Religious "obligations"	Love and praise of God and neighbor expressed in "right relationship" (justice)	Rituals expressing loyalty to "patrons," both "divine" and human
Relationship with earth / land	Belongs to God; people are "tenants"	Belongs to king and those who can afford to buy it
Relationship with "enemies"	Love them	Destroy them

Some religions simply express our personal preferences, while others are vigorously passed down across the generations as "truth."

Let's move from this general definition of "religion" to the specific worlds of the Bible. We may presuppose that the Bible is seeking to encourage and support commitment to one of two religions called "Judaism" and "Christianity." There are indeed two religions in the Bible vying for the loyalty of listeners and readers. But to label one as "Judaism" and the other as "Christianity" is to miss the central point.

For example, consider the topic of war. Are "Christians" *for* war or *against* war? We know that people using the label "Christian" to identify their religion fall along the spectrum from absolute pacifism to enthusiastic support for "just war." We'd find a similar spectrum for numerous issues, such as homosexuality, poverty, abortion, the global economy, and so forth. We'd also find "Jews" who are adamant supporters of Israel and justify its defense by any means necessary, while others renounce both nationalism and violence. Yet anywhere on these spectrums, we find people claiming "God is on our side."

This was also true in biblical times, whether within monarchical Israel or among the first communities of Jesus' disciples. But rather than the image of a *spectrum* to portray the range of views on topics that bind or divide people (i.e., *religious* topics such as politics and economics), we can think of the biblical authors speaking in relation to *two opposing magnetic poles* — that is, *two religions* — each pulling on people in opposite directions. The biblical narratives repeatedly show its characters pulled toward one pole and away from the other. Once we can see the Bible Story's big picture — that is, once we start at the beginning and read it in its narrative and cultural contexts — we can see the basic pattern that repeats itself across the generations. What can be especially confusing is when people in the biblical Story gather around the pole that is *away from God* yet claim that God is on their side *in that place.*

To make this clearer, let's jump ahead and look at the features of these "two religions" that will be revealed in our engagement of specific texts. Although this risks oversimplification, let's call them "the religion of creation" and "the religion of empire." That is, we can understand one of the Bible's religions to be grounded in the *experience of and ongoing relationship with the Creator God,* leading to a covenantal bond between that God and God's people for the blessing and abundance of *all* people and *all* creation. The other, while sometimes *claiming* to be grounded in that same God, is actually a human invention used to justify and legitimate attitudes and behaviors that provide blessing and abundance for *some* at the *expense of others.* We'll explore the details as we go. Table 1 provides a schematic overview of these two religions.

One can view all human history — indeed, the very formation of what we call "history" — as the interplay between these two religions. The Bible takes up the story about four thousand years ago, which is, in the big picture, much closer to the "end" than the "beginning" of the roughly two-million-year human existence. But that four thousand year period does give us a sufficiently wide angle with which to view current events rather than simply starting from when we "entered the room."

It might help to pause before we engage the biblical narratives to clarify the use of the term "empire" as a label for the religion at the opposite pole from the religion of creation. Political scientist Herfried Münkler observes that

> the concept of empire has had an arbitrary, often simply denunciatory meaning. Political science has not provided solid definitions and backed them up with examples, but has rather left the field to the whimsical operations of everyday journalism.[3]

---

3. Münkler, 4.

He goes on to remedy this problem by arguing for concrete and specific criteria by which one can distinguish "empire" from other forms of political power, such as "hegemony." For our purposes, we can simply note the major elements he names:

1. *"Imperial boundaries...involve gradations of power and influence"*: that is, there is a structural difference between imperial and nonimperial space.

2. *"Imperiality...dissolves...equality and reduces subordinates to the status of client states or satellites"*: that is, international relations are not between equals, but between a "center" and a "periphery."

3. *"Most empires have owed their existence to a mixture of chance and contingency"*: that is, there need not be a "will to empire" (i.e., "imperialism") or a "grand strategy," but rather, a series of circumstances that lead to increased power and control of people and/or territory.

4. *"The capacity for reform and regeneration...makes an empire independent of the charismatic qualities of its founder (or founding generation)*: that is, there is temporal continuity that transcends the original situation that generated the empire.

5. *"An empire cannot remain neutral in relation to the powers in its sphere of influence"*: that is, it cannot allow either independence or nonparticipation without retaliation.[4]

These elements help us to avoid the risk Münkler names of reducing "empire" to a mere pejorative label.[5] At the same time, it allows us to be inclusive of various historical social orders that were not far-flung geographically yet manifest these elements. Thus, an ancient city-state that exerts long-term authority over its neighboring cities and villages could be understood as the embodiment of the "religion of empire."

We'll attempt in Part I to peer "behind" history to understand where the two religions came from and why. Although we cannot literally see "the beginning," we can make some reasonable hypotheses based on the evidence we do have. Just as astrophysicists posit "the Big Bang" and biologists a theory of evolution to explain the movement from "the beginning" until now, so too the Bible proposes its own story of origins. This Story, while perfectly consistent with the scientists' stories, addresses different questions:

---

4. Ibid., 4–14.

5. Cf. the definition of "empire" offered by Goldstone and Haldon, 18–19: "a territory (continuous or not) ruled from a distinct organizational center (which may be mobile) with clear ideological and political sway over varied elites who in turn exercise political power over a population in which a majority have neither access to nor influence over positions of imperial power." They propose this definition in relation to "state," about which they note that "no agreement has ever been reached on a universally acceptable definition that has any real analytic value.... Too rigid a definition merely acts as a conceptual straitjacket that ignores the fundamentally dynamic and dialectical nature of human social organization" (4–5).

those arising from a people confronted by, but standing in resistance to, the religion of empire. From that original confrontation, the biblical Story unfolds.

This will require not taking the biblical chronology at face value but rather asking questions about when various texts were written, by whom, and why. For example, in the immediately following chapters, we'll consider the book of Genesis. Clearly, the story of creation coming to be in the first chapter of Genesis was not written at the time it narrates. Scholars have been exploring the question of the origins of Genesis for a long time and have proposed various theories. We'll look at how the Genesis stories resonate against a very specific background, during and after the Babylonian Exile in the sixth century BCE.

Similarly, in Part II, we'll take up the texts that narrate the story "from Exodus to Exile," that is, from the call of Moses, through the settlement in the Promised Land, continuing in the time of Israel's and Judah's kings, and ending with the fall of Jerusalem. We may be surprised to discover the likely sequence in which this long narrative came to be, and how different parts of it speak from the perspective of each of the "two religions." This will require unraveling the existing narrative by looking for patterns of "who knew what when." For example, Moses is rarely mentioned in the monarchy narrative. What might this suggest about which story came first? Similarly, Abraham is almost never "remembered" in the narrative of settlement in the Land. Might this suggest that Genesis was written later than the settlement story? By asking these kinds of questions, we'll be able to look "behind" the final version of the narratives and try to discern the order in which they were written. This will also help us to understand what "religion" each text encourages listeners to practice.

In Part III, we'll continue this exploration in the texts written from "Exile to Easter," that is, during the time of the Second Temple in Jerusalem up to the time of Jesus. We'll see how the temple establishment elite encouraged the practice of "royal wisdom" in collaboration with foreign empires (Persian and Greek), while voices from the margins insisted that YHWH stood against such collaboration. Some of these texts speak in the vivid imagery of "apocalyptic" visions and dreams. This will invite us to delve into their symbolic worlds to see what they're "really" trying to say behind their "heavenly" descriptions.

Finally, in Part IV, "from Easter to the Eschaton," we'll engage the New Testament texts. We'll see how Jesus spoke and acted boldly on behalf of the God of Israel proclaimed in the texts of the "religion of creation" and against those who would claim YHWH's authority for the "religion of empire." This bold announcement of "Good News" led the supporters of the religion of empire to persecute and kill Jesus, only to have the Creator God's triumphant power revealed once and for all by raising Jesus from the dead. It was up to Paul, the evangelists, and other disciples to continue to proclaim and to embody this Good News of the victory of the God of creation over the "gods" of empire.

Although the biblical Story will take up most of this book, we'll also explore some texts that were not included in the biblical canon. Perhaps these texts were excluded because they stood in vehement opposition to the prevailing religion of empire. History's "winners" generally do not preserve opposition voices, yet remarkably, some of these can still be heard. They remind us that, as the author of Luke's Gospel shows (Luke 3:1–7), we must listen not only to those upon whom the mainstream media focus, but also to those in "the wilderness" who speak truth that leads to life, for humanity and for all creation.

RELIGION OF EMPIRE: urban/temple-centered; hierarchical patronage social structure; suspicion of outsiders; money/debt economy

David/Solomon story in Samuel-1 Kings 11

Monarchical history to Hezekiah

First Isaiah

Deuteronomy and Joshua (Josiah's "compromise")

Rest of monarchical history

Haggai/First Zechariah Malachi

Ezra/Nehemiah Second Zechariah

1-2 Chronicles

Esther

Third Isaiah

Jeremiah Ezekiel Numbers

Second Isaiah

Leviticus

Genesis

Amos, Hosea, Micah

1000 BCE   900   800   700   600   500

Exodus story

Nonliterate YHWH-based "high place" and "green tree" village worship and social economy

RELIGION OF CREATION: wilderness/village-centered; egalitarian social structure; inclusion of outsiders; gift/barter economy

RELIGION OF EMPIRE: urban/temple-centered; hierarchical patronage social structure; suspicion of outsiders; money/debt economy

[Philo of Alexandria]   [Writings of Josephus]

Sirach

1-2 Maccabees

Tobit

Proverbs, Job, Jonah, Qoheleth

Ruth

"Astronomical Book" (1 Enoch 72-82)

"Book of the Watchers" (1 Enoch 1-36)

Daniel

"Dream Visions" and Epistle of Enoch (1 Enoch 85-105)

Ongoing village-based YHWH-grounded social economy

Other apocalyptic texts

100 CE

"Book of the Parables" (1 Enoch 37-71)

Deutero-Pauline letters

Paul's letters

Gospels/Acts

Hebrews/James

1-2 John/Revelation

400   300   200   100   0   100   200

RELIGION OF CREATION: wilderness/village-centered; egalitarian social structure; inclusion of outsiders; gift/barter economy

Chapter One

"Then God Said, 'Let there be light!'" (Gen. 1)

The Bible as Story and as History

Key to reading any ancient text is placing it in its original context. This process begins by asking two questions:

1. What is the relationship between the *time in the text* and the *time the text was written?*

2. What *questions* are the biblical texts trying to respond to when they tell stories about the past?

The first question rarely has a precise answer. The biblical texts don't come with copyright dates or other precise evidence of the time of their composition. The best we can do is to make reasonable guesses based on clues within the text itself or with the aid of external evidence, such as other texts or archaeology.[1] Over the past two hundred years, scholars have proposed numerous theories, but the more we learn, the weaker scholarly consensus seems to get. As with any field of inquiry, it can become all too easy to pass on theories as if they were proven facts or to make assumptions without actually investigating the evidence.[2]

We can, though, make some reasonable guesses. For instance, as we begin with the story of creation in Genesis 1, we can declare with certainty that it is not an eyewitness account! At the other extreme, we can fairly conclude that texts which quote or refer to earlier texts must be later than the ones being referenced. Again, using an extreme example, since the apostle Paul quotes Genesis in his letters written to early churches in the first century, Genesis must be older than Paul. We've now narrowed the gap to later than the beginning of creation and earlier than the time of Jesus and Paul, two thousand years ago!

This example may seem cartoonishly extreme, yet there are serious biblical scholars who argue that much of the Hebrew Bible was composed much

---

1. See, e.g., Dever (2006).

2. E.g., Sternberg (1999) engages in a painstaking and masterful task of challenging numerous scholarly assumptions about the reference of the word "Hebrews," and, in the process, undermines whole shelves of scholarly work that turn out not to be grounded in careful reading and thought.

closer to the time of Jesus than to the time of the narrated events. These so-called minimalists[3] are, in part, reacting to the exaggerated certainty proclaimed in preceding generations. Many current-day Bible translations make the problem worse by referring in footnotes to theoretical "sources" behind the final biblical texts as if they were facts.[4] The evidence seems clear that both the minimalists and the defenders of earlier source theories have not taken full account of all the available data, as limited as it may be. Thus, we can often provide a solid ballpark figure for a text's time of composition, but some ballparks are bigger than others.

As we'll see in our first few chapters, there is solid evidence that the final form of the first eleven chapters of Genesis — the so-called "Primeval History" — was composed during the time of the Babylonian Exile in the sixth century before the Common Era (BCE).[5]

Linking the text with this specific context enables us to address the second foundational query: What *questions* are the biblical texts responding to when they tell stories about the past? We can declare with absolute certainty that they were *not* asking the same questions that people do today who seek to use Genesis 1–11 in opposition to astrophysics ("How old is the universe?") or geology ("How old is the earth?"). Modern science has been asking its particular sets of questions for perhaps only five hundred years.[6] Whenever we place the composition of Genesis, it was long before the Renaissance.

The urgent questions for God's people in exile in Babylon are clearly and poignantly expressed in Psalm 137:

> By the rivers of Babylon — there we sat down and there we wept
> when we remembered Zion.
> On the willows there we hung up our harps.

---

3. For example, Davies (1995); Lemche.

4. For example, many Bibles refer to Genesis as composed of three "strands," labeled "J," "E" and "P." For a recent adherent's defense of this theory, see Friedman (1999).

5. For one of the best arguments for this dating, see Middleton. This conclusion does not preclude the possibility that there were both oral and earlier written versions of some or all of the stories in Genesis 1–11. For instance, scholars endorsing the theory of a "J" (or Jahwist, from the German name for the Israelites' God, *Jahweh,* also known as "Yahweh") strand often argue that the J author was writing several centuries earlier. For an interpretation of Gen. 1–11 that asks some of the same questions as we are going to explore here while maintaining the assumption that a "J" text can be read apart from "E" and "P" texts, see Hiebert. His assumption necessarily breaks apart the continuity of the Primeval History and fails to place the text in a historical context that makes sense of the "J" narrative's ideological perspective. For instance, he accepts without argument that "J" was composed "early in the monarchy as has customarily been the case," while acknowledging (in a footnote) that scholars differ widely on this point (25–26). As a result, many of his otherwise interesting suggestions about Israel's relationship with "nature" are weakened. For a critique of the concept of "nature" used in today's ecological situation, see McKibben.

6. Barzun traces in fascinating detail the rise and fall of scientific thinking as part of the transformation of Western thought and culture beginning with the Renaissance. See also Taylor (2007).

> For there our captors asked us for songs, and our tormentors asked
>   for mirth, saying, "Sing us one of the songs of Zion!"
> How could we sing the Lord's song in a foreign land?[7]

It is almost unimaginable for people in the United States to comprehend
the enormity of the disruption that was the Exile, although the world's displaced indigenous peoples would easily understand. We must jump ahead
to situate the Exile in the biblical chronology. Consider the following rough
and necessarily approximate timeline of pre-exilic biblical history.

+ **2000–1200 BCE (Middle–Late Bronze Age),[8] Pre-Israel:** the peoples
  who became biblical "Israel" engage the great empires of Babylon and
  Egypt.

+ **1200–1000 BCE (Iron I Age), Settlement:** "Israelites" settle in the
  land of Canaan, mostly in the central and southern highlands as
  family / clan-based villages.

+ **1000–930 BCE (Iron IIA Age), United Monarchy of Judah and Israel:**
  Under David and Solomon, the Israelites are forged into a local imperial
  state with its capital in Jerusalem, built on the model of surrounding
  city-empires, such as Egypt.

+ **930–720s BCE (Iron IIB Age), Monarchies of Judah and Israel:** After
  Solomon, Israel's elders led a movement of secession that resulted in the
  separate and independent monarchical states of Israel in the north and
  Judah in the south. Israel was destroyed by invading Assyrians in the
  720s, while Judah survived — barely.

+ **720s–580s BCE (Iron IIC Age), Monarchy of Judah:** Judah under the
  leadership of King Hezekiah and his advisor, the prophet Isaiah, managed
  to hold off Assyria, but his successors could not hold off the next empire
  to invade, Babylon.

The Babylonian invasion and destruction of Jerusalem and its temple
crushed hundreds of years of hopes and dreams, crystallized around the
belief in the power of their God, YHWH,[9] to protect them from harm. To
conceive of the enormity of this world-shattering event, imagine the Cold
War had turned out differently. Imagine not only Soviet tanks rolling down
the streets of Washington, D.C., but also Soviet bulldozers crushing the
White House and Capitol buildings into rubble. Imagine them then taking
the political and intellectual elite back to Moscow to serve in the capital
of the victorious regime, while ordinary people left behind were expected

---

7. All biblical quotations are from the New Revised Standard Version unless otherwise
indicated.

8. The parenthetical terms refer to the way archaeologists describe these periods,
although the dates listed are controversial and no claim of precision is being made here.

9. We'll look at the role of this name for God in chapter 10 with the encounter at the
burning bush in Exodus 3.

to fend for themselves. What would it mean to be an "American" in such a circumstance? Those taken away might ask, "How can we sing the 'Star Spangled Banner' in Moscow?"

The psalm's lament was only one of many texts to ask this and similar questions during the fifty-year period of Babylonian rule, which ended with the Babylonians' defeat at the hands of the Persians. At the time, though, those in exile did not know how long their banishment would last, any more than Cubans exiled to Florida in the 1950s knew how long Castro would rule their native land. From within this terrible, wrenching experience, a number of questions became central to the identity and future hopes of the exiles. Some of these questions and the biblical texts that addressed them are listed in Table 2.

Table 2: Questions from the Exile

Questions	Texts Addressing Those Questions
1. Why are we here? What went wrong? Did Babylon's gods defeat our God? Or is YHWH trying to teach us a lesson?	The so-called "Deuteronomistic History" (Deuteronomy–2 Kings); Jeremiah
2. Will we ever go back?	Ezekiel, "Second Isaiah" (Isa. 40–55)
3. Are we "Babylonians" now? How do we teach our children who we really are?	Genesis 1–36, especially Genesis 1–11; also Leviticus

We'll look at the first two questions in Parts II and III. We'll now focus on the third question, since it is central to the Bible's opening chapters.

Babylon — more accurately, neo-Babylon or "New Babylon," the second manifestation of empire under that name — was a spectacularly beautiful city. Financed by conquest and tribute, staffed by slaves and the lower classes, it rose from the Mesopotamian desert in unprecedented grandeur. Its Hanging Gardens were renowned as one of the Seven Wonders of the ancient world, and its ziggurats and palaces (see Image 1) were architectural marvels rivaled at the time only by Egypt's pyramids. To be exiled there was hardly to be trapped in the squalor of a prison or refugee camp. On the contrary: for many of God's people, the glory that had been Jerusalem must have paled in comparison. For some, exile may have been experienced as an opportunity, much as German scientists brought to the United States after World War II were grateful to be living in the United States and working on American space and weapons programs. After all, it was the intelligentsia, not the peasantry, that Babylon was interested in bringing home as spoils

Image 1. Reproduction of Nebuchadnezzar's palace in Babyon.

of war. Put to use within the Babylonian royal establishment, some of the exiles may well have accepted their fate and sought to fit in to their new society and its culture.

Central to Babylonian culture was its own story of origins, *Enuma Elish,* the oldest foundational text of "the religion of empire." Its story is filled with powerful, captivating images of titanic battles among the gods.[10] In the beginning, it proclaims, there were two gods, Apsu (male, fresh water) and Tiamet (female, salt water). This couple had numerous god-children, who, as children are wont to do, made lots of noise, preventing the parents from sleeping. In this sleep-deprived state, the parents determined to do away with the noisy offspring, but the young gods got wind of the plot and devised their own scheme in response. One of them, Ea, killed Apsu. Tiamet found a new husband (Kingu) and plotted revenge. Tiamet appeared too strong to be stopped. The young gods sought from among themselves one who would dare to destroy their mother. Marduk asked what his reward would be if successful and was told to ask whatever he wished. His price: a royal city and a royal palace in which to live. The deal was made and the battle joined. The young Marduk got the better of the old mother, in the vivid words of the text, "ripping her body apart like a clamshell." Out of that body (ocean) came forth all the living creatures of the earth. Babylon was built as Marduk's prize and he and his mates took occupancy. But soon they realized that to keep the city clean and running involved tasks below

---

10. The text is accessible in English translation at *www.crivoice.org / enumaelish.html.*

the divine dignity. What to do? Produce a new creature to do the city's tasks: human beings. Marduk killed Tiamet's husband, Kingu, using his blood to fashion the new servants of the gods.

Theologian Walter Wink calls *Enuma Elish* the primal example of "the myth of redemptive violence."[11] Wink clearly and cogently describes how the story enshrines the power of violence to defeat "evil" and to establish "peace," a pattern deeply embedded in the "religion of empire." But *Enuma Elish* does much more than validate and valorize violence. It makes The City the center of the world and the king the embodiment of the chief god, in this case, Marduk. Even more: it equates the structure of hierarchical urban empire with the "divine order." In other words, it inextricably interweaves *religion* (what binds people together) with *politics* (what people do together) and *economics* (how people produce and exchange goods and services together). In Babylon, according to *Enuma Elish,* the gods reside in and the king and his court preside over a social order mandated and maintained by the very gods who built the city in time immemorial.

As we'll see in Part II, the religion that first bound "Israel" contained elements not far removed from *Enuma Elish*. But by the time of the Exile, people had wrestled with YHWH, one another, and their neighbors for centuries. For many, *Enuma Elish*'s version of "creation" was blasphemous. However, it was and remains one thing to criticize someone else's worldview, and quite another to have a clear and coherent vision of one's own.[12]

For many in Babylonian Exile, the first chapters of Genesis offered the beginning of that systemic alternative. At the heart of its stories of origins of the earth and humanity is the question: If the Babylonian story is wrong, how *did* things come to be? Put another way: What stories should we teach our children to keep them from being influenced by the power of *Enuma Elish* and the opulence and might of Babylon that, for now at least, is our home?[13]

Read from this perspective, the majestic and stately account of God's creation "in the beginning" can be heard for what it is: a *counter-narrative* to the Babylonian worldview. Each carefully worded detail expresses with power and beauty the ways of the *true* Creator. For instance, consider the contrast between the means of creating earth's creatures. In *Enuma Elish,* Tiamet's body is ripped open by the violence of her son, bringing forth the species. But in Genesis, it is God's "word" that brings things into being. Both the Hebrew (*'amar*) and Greek[14] (*legō*) verbs for "to speak" imply not simply the physical act of pronouncing words but also the deeper sense of

---

11. Wink (1992), 12–18.

12. As someone who spends a lot of time teaching undergraduates, I've seen repeatedly how much easier it is for them to see how the global corporate economy and its political collaborators are generating massive environmental and human wreckage than it is for them to envision a systemic alternative.

13. Cf. McKeown, 10, 12–14, who also takes the challenge of *Enuma Elish* as the starting point for reading Genesis in its original context.

14. At a much later time, during the period of Hellenistic rule, the Hebrew Scriptures were translated into a Greek version known as the Septuagint, often referred to as LXX in

bringing an intention into being.[15] God's creative word is not in reaction to anything else, as Marduk's violence is. Creation does not arise as a response, but simply because God wills it into being.

Writing in the context of individual work in repairing "damaged identities," Hilde Lindemann Nelson speaks of the healing power of counterstories:

> by uprooting the harmful identity-constituting stories that have shaped a person's own sense of who she is, counterstories aim to alter the person's self-perception. If she replaces the harmful stories with a counterstory, she may come to see herself as worthy of moral respect. . . .
>
> Counterstories, then, are tools designed to repair the damage inflicted on identities by abusive power systems.[16]

Genesis, like other anti-imperial counter-stories we'll engage in this book, functions in this way. They invite hearers to claim the counter-story as more expressive of reality than the imperial story and to form community with others who share this perception. In so doing, people adopt what we are here calling a different "religion."

Other aspects of Genesis 1 also provide a counter-narrative to *Enuma Elish*. Babylon was, like virtually every city in the ancient world, surrounded by a wall. The very name Babylon in the original Akkadian language means "gate of the gods." That is, when you pass through the city gate, you are entering into the divine realm. Conversely, beyond the gate is chaos, wilderness, the realm of wild beasts and even wilder people. One can easily imagine Babylonian parents warning their children never to leave the city unattended. In contrast, Genesis proclaims, *all of creation* is God's realm. The Hebrew of Gen. 1:2, *tohu vebohu*,[17] translated variously as formless void,[18] "welter and waste"[19] or "wild and waste,"[20] most likely expresses the combined state of being unproductive and uninhabited that is the Middle Eastern desert without rain.[21] God's creative Word turns this "pre-creation" into a living, vibrant, abundant realm of goodness and blessing. It tells the children of the Exile, "*Our* God is much bigger and more powerful than what *they* call 'gods.'" For the Babylonians, only the city is sacred ground. But for the people of Genesis, all the heavens and earth are filled with God's creative presence and life.

---

accordance with the story that a group of seventy rabbis produced it. See Simon-Shoshan; Wasserstein and Wasserstein.

15. This is what linguists refer to as a "speech act"; see Austin.

16. Nelson (2001), xiii; see also 6–20 for the role of counterstories in forming "communities of choice."

17. It is a term easily evocative of the mysteriously frightening, as can be experienced by saying it aloud in a spooky voice.

18. NRSV.

19. Alter (1997), 3.

20. Fox, 13.

21. Van Wolde (1996), 20.

Another element of the Babylonian worldview was that sun and moon were divinities to be worshiped. Babylonian astrological lore had developed complex traditions about the sky and its inhabitants. Rather than offer elaborate myths about the sky, Genesis 1 says,

> And God said, "Let there be lights in the dome of the sky to separate the day from the night; and let them be for signs and for seasons and for days and years, and let them be lights in the dome of the sky to give light upon the earth." And it was so. God made the two great lights — the greater light to rule the day and the lesser light to rule the night — and the stars. God set them in the dome of the sky to give light upon the earth, to rule over the day and over the night, and to separate the light from the darkness. And God saw that it was good. (Gen. 1:14–18)

Yes, Genesis proclaims, the lights in the sky serve a divine purpose. But they, like the forests and animals, are merely creatures with no power independent of their Creator. Note that Genesis does not even dignify the "great lights" by naming them "sun" and "moon."[22] The stars are little more than an afterthought, as if mere sky decorations. We can imagine an Israelite parent saying, "No, children, we don't worship the sun, moon, or stars, as the Babylonians do. We only worship the Creator."

Genesis presents "the great sea monsters" as also part of God's good creation. No primal goddess Tiamet, but rather, in Hebrew, the great *tanninim*. They are powerful, but no more so than other divinely made creatures. As Umberto Cassuto points out, the *tanninim* are the only species expressly named in the narrative, and the word itself may be a play on the Akkadian for Tiamet.[23]

Finally, the account reaches its climax with the bringing forth of creatures "in the image of God," human beings (1:26–27). The poetic parallelism is key to what is being claimed:

> Then God said, "Let us make humankind ['*adam*]
> in our image [*tselem*],
> according to our likeness [*demuth*]
> and let them have dominion [*radah*]
> over the fish of the sea,
> and over the birds of the air,
> and over the cattle,
> and over all the wild animals of the earth,
> and over every creeping thing that creeps upon the earth."

22. "Sun" isn't mentioned until Genesis 15:12; every use of the word in Genesis simply marks the boundary between day and night: 15:17; 19:23; 28:11; 32:31; 37:9. The "moon" is mentioned only at 37:9, as part of young Joseph's dream of his family bowing down to him.
23. Cassuto, 49–51.

> So God created humankind [*ha-adam*] in his image [*tselem*],
> in the image [*tselem*] of God he created them;
> male and female he created them.

Hebrew *tselem* generally refers to a statue or other physical representation, such as of a god or goddess.[24] It seems likely that Genesis presents human beings serving a parallel function to Babylonian or other "idols." When you see a human being,[25] you are seeing an "image" of God.[26] As Luise Schottroff powerfully expresses this, following a rabbinical story from the time of Jesus:

> The statues of Caesars in theatres and circuses are cleaned and cared for because they are the images of Roman Caesars. I am God's image, how much more must I be cleaned and cared for. . . . I am the statue of God, God's representative on this earth. The statue of Caesar is nothing compared to me, the child of God.[27]

Genesis refuses to specify *how* human beings represent God. The author knows that this is a truth that cannot be *defined*, but must *be wrestled with*.[28] One thing is clear: humans were not made to be the gods' urban servants but are the climax of God's creation.

The humans are given "dominion" over all the creatures of earth and sky, but *not over each other*. It is a *collective* responsibility. Mark Brett notes that Hebrew *radah* is associated with "royal ideology," and so the use in Genesis here "is best read as a polemical undermining of a role which is otherwise associated primarily with kings." In other words, "the health of the created order does not depend on kings."[29]

And then there is *rest*. The creation is completed. Sabbath is not an external command, but a component of creation.[30] In Genesis 1, God has no opposition, so the completion of God's creation leaves no tension, no conflict, in its wake. All that there is to "do" is to live in it, enjoy it, gather its fruits in gratitude and celebration. But as we know, that is not the world as we experience it, with its violence and power struggles. If Genesis 1 is correct in narrating how it was "in the beginning," how did it turn out the way it is? That is the central question of the Garden story that follows.

---

24. Westermann (1994), 146; cf. Num. 33:52; Ezek. 7:20.
25. Chapter 2 will consider the meaning of *'adam*.
26. Van Wolde (2001), 154–55.
27. Schottroff, 33.
28. For a survey of scholarly opinion, see Wenham (1987), 29–31.
29. Brett (2000), 77, e.g., 1 Kings 4:24; cf. Hos. 4:1–3, which offers a prophetic polemic associating lack of human "faithfulness . . . and knowledge of God" to the practices of "swearing, lying, murder, and stealing . . . bloodshed follows bloodshed" for which "the land mourns . . . together with the wild animals and the birds of the air, even the fish of the sea are perishing." Brett notes how this makes clear that human *radah* over creation must be exercised within the covenant and "knowledge of God" (ibid., 79).
30. Cf. Wallace, 56.

Chapter Two

"By the Sweat of Your Face
You Shall Eat Bread" (Gen. 2–3)

Genesis 1, from the vantage point of exile, looked back to "the beginning" to offer a story counter to that of the Babylonians' own narrative of how the world was made. But, whether in their own land or in exile, God's people Israel experienced life not as pristine harmony, but as struggle for survival. The Exile brought to the fore the question: "Why is life so hard?" Put more theologically, "Why did God allow the Babylonians to destroy Jerusalem and our nation?"

Different biblical authors framed their responses to this question at different places in history. For instance, the authors of the Deuteronomistic History (Deut.–2 Kings, referred to as "DH") tell a story that takes place between Exodus and Exile: from the entrance into the land to the expulsion from it.[1] The DH writers spread their narrative "answer" over a panorama of hundreds of years. The writer of Genesis 2–3, on the other hand, composed a story that takes place "at the beginning" and is over in the blink of an eye.

We saw in our previous chapter how the Genesis 1 creation story was not written to address questions of geology or biology, but rather of meaning and worldview. Similarly, the story of the Garden was not composed to answer historical questions such as "Who were the first people?" or even "Where did 'sin' come from?" In fact, there is no mention of "sin" at all in the text.[2]

Again, imagine yourself among the exiles in Babylon, amid its beauty and splendor. You have walked the hundreds of miles across the desert from the Promised Land to your new "home." Following the "Great River," Euphrates, you saw little food along the way, perhaps recalling the Exodus story of your ancestors' own journey across the harsh southern desert. Of course, your journey was not into freedom but into captivity. Finally, you arrived in the Great City and couldn't help but marvel at its magnificence. At the same time, you wonder, how was all this power and wealth amassed in this place?

---

1. Explored in Part II of this book.
2. Hebrew *chatta't*, "sin," first appears at Gen. 4:7; also in Genesis at 18:20, 31:36, 50:17.

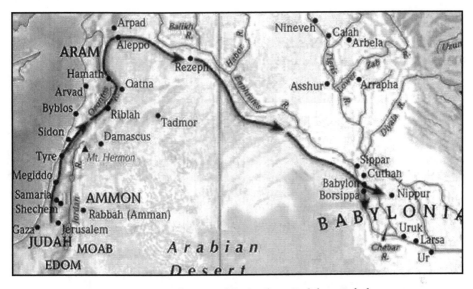

Map 1: Suggested route of Exiles from Judah to Babylon

The location of the city seems no more hospitable than many other locales along the way, although you are now "between the rivers"[3] Euphrates and Tigris, where there is more water. Of course, you know the centrality of water to life. But you see something in the countryside on your way into the city that reveals some of the answer: fields upon fields of grain, fed precious water by an intricate network of canals dug from the rivers out into the dry plain. Unlike the fertile delta of the Nile that flooded enormous quantities of rich, fertile silt down from the mountains each spring, the empires of Mesopotamia survived and prospered on canal irrigation, dug and tended by armies of slaves.[4]

"How did this happen?" you wonder. Not the commonplace reality of a slave-based empire; that you have seen all around you among the Canaanites, and even among your own people. Your questioning goes deeper, back farther, than the most recent powerful nation that happened to defeat your own. How did it all start? In other words, what was the path that led from God's gift of life in harmonious abundance to the seeming endpoint of empire?

The Garden story was written in part to answer this question, again, from the specific vantage point of exile.[5] Obviously, the exiles couldn't personally

---

3. The meaning of "Mesopotamia."

4. For an overview of Mesopotamian economics and social order, see Postgate.

5. Scholars arguing for a "J" authorship for Gen. 2–3 as a "second creation account" pasted together with Genesis 1 don't pay sufficient attention to two basic elements of the story as we find it in its narrative context. First, unlike many other characters and situations from the later chapters of Genesis (such as Abraham's journey and Jacob's family) that are referred to countless times by texts that are certainly pre-exilic (e.g., Mic. 7:20; Isa. 29:22), neither Adam,

"remember" such an ancient time. One possibility is that the core of the story is itself very old, passed down across the generations as oral tradition only to be written in the form we have during the Exile. After all, even before the Exile, life was far from perfect, and people surely imagined possible root causes of human suffering and struggle. But more likely, given the resonance between expulsion from the Garden and exile from the Land, is that the story was composed in exile in response to experience gained along the journey from Israel to Babylon. While the path between the two lands was hardly a "garden," there *were* peoples living in it apart from the power of Babylon or any other empire. Bands of nomadic shepherds plied the desert with sheep and goats, as they also did in the regions of Canaan. But might travelers also have seen people living much like that described in Genesis 2? In other words, might they have encountered tribes of gatherers and hunters engaged in the traditional lifeways that preceded the development of cities and empires?

The question, asked by people in exile, in contrast to people in our world today, would certainly sound very different. When in the 1960s economic anthropologist Marshall Sahlins researched and wrote his now classic book, *Stone Age Economics,* he knew that he would likely be among the last scholars able to do "live" research on his topic. The last tribes who survived in what Sahlins called "the domestic mode of production" were quickly disappearing. Now there are no peoples on the planet not influenced by the global economy and technology.

Sahlins challenged the prejudices of earlier researchers blinded by their own sense of "Protestant work ethic" who saw gatherer/hunters as "lazy" or constantly living on the edge of starvation.[6] He provides voluminous field research data to show that such people needed to work for their daily food an average of five hours a day.[7] They did not gather surplus or plan ahead from one day's food to the next, because storage limited mobility.[8] Rather, as Sahlins observed, they went from feast to feast, eating joyously as much as they could at a time, waiting without anxiety between feasts, even if that meant not eating for several days in a row. When food ran out or seasons changed, they moved on to the next place of abundance. Sahlins notes that far more time was spent and calories gained by simply taking in what hung from trees or waited in the ground than the more energy intensive and dangerous act of hunting wild animals.[9]

Eve, nor the Garden are mentioned in any pre-exilic texts (see Ezek. 28:13 for an example of an exilic text that speaks of "Eden, the garden of God"; also Isa. 51:3). Second, the theme of *expulsion from land given by God* would hardly resonate with people in the heady days of monarchy (the most commonly proposed provenance of "J") as it would during the Exile.

6. Sahlins, 2–9.

7. Ibid., 17. This estimate includes food preparation. Cf. Hayden, 283, who estimates three hours per day for food gathering alone.

8. Sahlins, 31–32.

9. Ibid., 35. Sahlins's "original affluent society" hypothesis has been broadly accepted, although with qualifications, such as those of Bellwood, 19: "Some hunters may indeed have

To point out the simple efficiencies of an ancient form of social economy is not to romanticize the hunter-gatherer way. But it does provide us with a much wider lens with which to observe the choices available to our biblical ancestors. As John Zerzan shows, for over 99 percent of the roughly 2 million years that hominids have walked the earth, agriculture was either unknown or *refused*.[10] It was neither "inevitable" nor an aspect of "progress," but a *choice* to move away from the simple harmony of hunting-gathering and toward a world of stored surplus and its consequences.[11] It was the biggest fork on the road of human existence. It was the cause of the cultural phenomenon we call "history." As Paul Shepard notes, the "rise of centralized authority — monarchies, clerical hierarchies, bureaucracies, trade networks, military units — was the heritage of agriculture."[12]

What did this mean for those on their way to Babylonian Exile? Anthropologists have shown that what we know as the "Near East" was the first place on earth where agriculture was practiced, starting approximately in 9,000 BCE.[13] Over roughly a three-thousand-year period, evidence shows that agriculture waxed and waned with climatic shifts that profoundly affected the availability of sufficient food from foraging and hunting. In times of bounty, however, people returned to more mobile lifeways when possible.[14] The development of family-based agricultural villages became interspersed with more traditional means of food gathering. What is crucial to recognize here is that it was *not for another five thousand years that surplus agriculture had developed villages into city-based empire.*[15]

---

been quite affluent before agriculturalists destroyed their livelihood, but the *earliest* agriculturalists in healthy food-rich environments probably had even more enviable lives from the viewpoint of the many inhabitants, including many hunter-gatherers, of our crowded and starvation-inflicted modern world. True, the rats, diseases, overcrowding, malnutrition, and environmental devastation caught up with the descendents of the first agriculturalists, in some cases very quickly indeed. But the generally low incidence of crowd diseases in hunter-gatherer societies and presumably also in loosely packed earliest agricultural situations, like those on the colonial period temperate-latitude European frontiers in Australasia and the Americas, should make us think instead about 'affluent earliest cultivators' rather than their hunter-gatherer counterparts."

10. Zerzan (1999), 73–87.

11. Bellwood, 36, observes that hunter-gatherer groups enclosed by agriculturalists reveal little eagerness to embrace agriculture.

12. Shepard, 93.

13. For recent discussion of theories of how and why this transition took place in the "Natufian" period, see the collection edited by Delage and the collection edited by Price and Gebauer; also Munro, Bar-Yosef. For some of the methodological issues in overcoming the "nature/culture dichotomy," in exploring these issues, see Boyd. See also Sale, who traces the history of human hunting before agriculture, starting around 70,000 BCE, and its own destructive legacy.

14. See generally Byrd. See also Rowley-Conwy, sharply critiquing "progressivist" views that suggest that agriculture was an inevitable result of a trend toward increasing complexity. Rather, he shows, there is no linear correlation between social complexity and the practice of agriculture.

15. Horden and Purcell, 271–74, distinguish the strategic "normal surplus" of local producers in Mediterranean microecological niches seeking security through limited storage and redistribution from the exploitative surplus generated by large landowners and state control,

Although we cannot know with certainly the extent to which traditional hunter-gatherer societies continued during this period, it seems reasonable to assume that not all people in this area had become settled farmers.[16] It is possible, if not provable, that those people taken from the ruins of Jerusalem to Babylon would have seen such people along the way. Is it this experience that lies behind the vision of God's created order portrayed in Genesis 2? If so, then how to judge the development of surplus agriculture that generated Babylon?

The authors of Genesis 3 name it clearly as *punishment for disobedience* to the divine command issued in the Garden.

> To the woman [*'ishshah*] God said,
> "I will greatly increase your toil [*'itstsavon*] and your pregnancies;[17]
> in pain you shall bring forth children,
> yet your desire shall be for your man [*'ish*], and he shall rule [*mashal*,
>   as Gen. 1:18] over you."
>
> And to the human [*'adam*] God said,
> "Because you have listened to the voice of your woman,
> and have eaten of the tree about which I commanded you, 'You shall
>   not eat of it,'
> cursed is the topsoil [*'adamah*] because of you;
> in painful work [*'itstsavon*] you shall eat of it all the days of your life;
> thorns and thistles it shall bring forth for you;
> and *you shall eat the plants of the field.*
> By the sweat of your face *you shall eat bread* until you return to the
>   topsoil,
> for out of it you were taken; you are dust, and to dust you shall
>   return." (Gen. 3:16–19)

We'll return to the details of the "curse" shortly, but for now let's focus on the "bottom line." The woman's punishment is to have *many childbirths.* Within the context of exile "looking back," we can hear this as a warning about the consequences of surplus agriculture.[18] In nomadic or migratory

---

rejecting "subsistence" as a label derived from a "progressivist" scholarly distancing from the past. See also Sherratt (1997a, 5), arguing that the term "subsistence" "creates a fundamentally misleading dichotomy between the activities of getting food and exchanging items between productive units."

16. "However the people of an area came to be agriculturalists, there would always have remained hunting-gathering populations who would have continued to exist, if allowed, for centuries or perhaps even millennia after agriculture began" (Bellwood, 67); also Layton, studying interactions between modern-day hunter-gatherers and others, observes the ongoing choice to forage and hunt, even while interacting with pastoral and agricultural peoples.

17. Translation of this line is from Meyers (1988), 118; remainder of passage is author's translation.

18. Note how this interpretation makes the story's purpose parallel to that of the warning against having a king, also told in hindsight, 1 Sam. 8:11–20. The warning against monarchy includes the fact that the king will take "one-tenth of your grain and of your vineyards and give it to his officers and his courtiers" (8:15). The passage is discussed further at p. 191.

social groups, nursing was extended as long as possible in order to provide simple "food storage" for one family member. This caused extended periods of nonmenstruation and a natural form of "family planning." In that context, more was not better: the higher number of children, the greater need for food, as well as the risk of danger for those not able to be carried or run fast enough to get away from wild animals.[19] But with agriculture, the family numbers calculus was reversed. There was a need to get children away from the breast and to work in the fields as soon as they were able to offer help.[20]

The "curse" of this was not the "pain of parenting," but the reality that childbearing was the single biggest cause of early death for women until modern medicine.[21] Thus, in a very literal way, the development of surplus agriculture killed countless women.

The second part of the woman's "curse" is the breaking of the egalitarian relationship between herself and the man. No longer will women be "counterparts" (Gen. 2:18, 'ezer kenegdo, sometimes misleadingly translated as "helper" or "helpmate"), but instead, the man will "rule" over the woman. In other words, part of the "curse" is the *establishment of the patriarchal family structure*. Carol Meyers notes, "in light of an understandable reluctance of women to enter into the risks of pregnancy and birth, and because of the social and economic necessity that she do so frequently, the male's will within the realm of sexuality is to be imposed on the will of the female."[22] Eventually, agriculture generated the separation of tasks by gender into "field" (male) and "house/tent" (female).[23]

The text moves on to the curse of the other person, who is called once again 'adam ("human") rather than 'ish ("man"). The punishment is a result of listening to the voice of "your woman" and hence, violating the divinely ordained boundary within the Garden. It is not a condemnation of "women's voices," but of listening to *any* voice other than God's alone.[24] As the woman listened to the snake, so the 'adam has listened to the woman. Now all are cursed. The specific punishment on the man is to wrestle food from the

---

19. Cf. Meyers (1988), 105.

20. See Bellwood, 18, who notes that "sedentary cultivator mothers are able to wean earlier, partly because cereals allow the cooking of gruel/porridge-type foods that can be used for infant foods (as long as one has utensils such as pottery to cook such foods). Thus, they conceive more frequently and have high fertility levels."

21. Note, for instance, the death during childbirth of the matriarch Rachel narrated in Gen. 35:16–19.

22. Meyers (1988), 116.

23. Sherratt (1981), 195, explains how the "secondary products revolution" in agriculture (e.g., shift from the hoe [women's labor] to plow [men's labor] and development of wool-based textiles) put men definitively "in the field" to work animal-drawn, wheeled carts and women "in the house" to spin and weave. Note the implied gender role confusion in the story of the twin boys Esau and Jacob. Esau "rightly" is a hunter and "man of the field [sadeh, as at Gen. 3:18]" under the authority and training of his father, who loves him, while Jacob is found "living in tents," under the authority and training of his mother, who loves him (Gen. 25:27–28).

24. Cf. Gen. 27:13, discussed at pp. 76–78.

cursed ground. Note that the Hebrew word *itstsavon* describes both the woman's pain and the man's pain, although the specific task (childbearing, agriculture) differs.[25] Two details confirm that the focus is the change in mode of food acquisition. First, in 3:18 we hear that "you shall eat the plants of the field" (*'esev hassadeh*). This contrasts explicitly with the gift of *tree fruit* given by God (2:16). Note the parallel use of the same phrase in the plague-curse on Egyptian surplus agriculture:

> YHWH said to Moses, "Stretch out your hand toward heaven so that hail may fall on the whole land of Egypt, on humans and animals and all the *plants of the field* in the land of Egypt." (Exod. 9:22; emphasis added)

The second detail is in the naming of the food that will come from this sweaty, painful work: "you shall eat *bread* [*lechem*] until you return to the ground." Bread is not a "natural" food but one *manufactured* from agricultural grains. Childbirth leading to pain and death, patriarchy, and agricultural labor leading to death: this is the divinely ordained judgment in Genesis on the development of surplus agriculture. As we'll see shortly, it is only one step from this to "the city."

It is often easier to name the curse than the blessing. But the authors of Genesis started there in chapter 2, describing in tender detail the Creator God's molding of the human from the humus (*'adam* from the *'adamah*). It is one clue to the meaning of "in the image of God" in which they were created (1:26–27). We are invited to envision humans as "inspired earth," topsoil animated by the breath of God (2:7). The human *'adam* is given a "counterpart" so that they can now see each other as man and wo-man (which conveys the Hebrew pair, *'ish* and *'ishshah*) and celebrate the gift of life in the abundance of the moist and fruitful Garden they've been given. They are "naked and not ashamed" (2:25). What could be better?

The encounter of the woman and the snake[26] in Genesis 3 is one of the most remarkable episodes ever written, with each detail opening up possibilities but providing tantalizingly few "answers."[27] There is not the slightest concern over the incongruity of a talking snake or the fine-tuned ambiguity of the snake's words. The focus is on the woman's "mistake" in misquoting

---

25. Meyers (1988), 104.

26. Bechtel (1993), 90, notes various ancient understandings and ideas about snakes, including as symbols of wisdom, male sexuality, and so forth, concluding with the observation that a snake is "a wild or uncontrolled animal that is beneficial in cultivated areas, ridding farms of rodents that consume crops and stored grain." However, she does not pursue the implication that arises from the line of interpretation we are following: Could the snake's intention be to evoke the curse so as to provide the snake with a symbiotic relationship to human agriculture? Given the role of women in the development of agriculture, this is a possibility. For how animals have "domesticated" humans to their own ends, see Manning.

27. For excellent close encounters with this text, see Trible, Bechtel (1993), and White (2003).

the divine command by making it *more stringent.* Compare the command and its repetition:

> And YHWH God commanded the *'adam,*
> "You *certainly* may eat of every tree of the garden;
> but of the tree *of the knowledge of good and evil* you shall not eat,
> for in the day that you eat of it you shall die." (2:16–18)

> The woman said to the serpent,
> "We may eat of the fruit of the trees in the garden;
> but God said, 'You shall not eat of the fruit of the tree *that is in the middle of the garden,*
> *nor shall you touch it,* or you shall die.' " (3:2–3)

Throughout the Bible, one can gauge obedience and loyalty by the accuracy of a person's quoting of another, whether of God or people.[28] In this case, the woman both omits from and adds to the divine word, rendering the question of obedience to the command confused and risky. First, she omits the divine *emphasis* on the availability of the tree-food. Second, she omits the name of the one tree expressly prohibited, focusing on its relative location rather than its nature (but you can bet the snake didn't miss that one!). Next, she *adds a prohibition* to God's command: "nor shall you touch it." Finally, she omits the link between the *immediacy* of the consequence of disobedience and death. So what difference does this make? Is God a rigid legalist who issues seemingly arbitrary laws and demands letter-perfect conformity?

The command is not arbitrary nor is the misquotation trivial. By extending the prohibition, the woman runs the risk of concluding (wrongly) that since touching didn't have consequences, she might as well eat. The distinction between "touching" and "eating" is between a *surface* encounter with reality and an *intimate* one. What a different experience it is, after all, merely to touch something (or someone) and to take it (them) into one's body! It is the difference, for instance, between holding hands and sexual intercourse. This is precisely the distinction that God was making that the woman failed to heed. Missing the nature of the tree, she miscalculated the degree of the risk. Missing the boundary of prohibition, she went with the evidence of her senses and mind against the divine Word. And the rest, as they say, is history.

Within this story, we find the biblical authors' attempt to get to the root of the social, economic, and theological situation in which they found themselves in Babylonian Exile. Surrounded by the "success" of canal irrigation agriculture, yet knowing that it was not the will of the Creator God, they compressed their understanding down into an incredibly packed story of paradise-gone-wrong. We'll unpack more of the wisdom in this story in the next chapter as we explore how agriculture leads to the city, and the city to "empire."

---

28. Sternberg (1985).

Chapter Three

"And He Built a City"

East of Eden

Once the man and woman receive their punishment, they are "driven out" (*vayegaresh*) from the Garden (Gen. 3:24). This provides a frame with the following story that concludes with Cain's plaintive cry, "Today you have driven me away [*gerashtta*] from the soil, and I shall be hidden from your face" (4:14). The "driving out" sets up a central theme of the "religion of creation" Story: the divine call to "come out" from a place of empire into a new place to which God will lead.

And although God's people struggle throughout the Bible not to "turn back" to the familiar places of empire (such as Sodom and Egypt), there is no turning back to Eden. Lightning-bearing "cherubim" on the east of the Garden block the way to the tree of life.[1] In this way, the biblical "religion of creation" Story differs from so many world stories, both ancient and modern, in that it denies both an endless, cyclical futility[2] and a nostalgic return to a "golden age" or place. The Genesis authors, of course, did not know their writing would become part of the book we call "the Bible." But they did claim to know that the direction God's people should look from exile was *forward,* not backward. Surplus agriculture and the empires it produced were an undeniable fact of life. There was no longer a "protected" place to which one could return.

So the Story continues with the man and woman, now "Adam and Eve,"[3] in an unspecified locale to "the east" of Eden. From the perspective of Israel, "east" always meant both "away from God" in general and toward Mesopotamia in particular. Having recently made this journey, the original audience understood well the experience of seeking to make a life "east" of God's intended homeland.

Adam's first act is to "know" (*yada'*) his wife, as Cain will do with his own wife (4:17) and Adam will again (4:25). The verb *yada'* is found

---

1. The Lamb will reopen the way to the tree of life when the tree is "transplanted" into New Jerusalem (Rev. 22:2–14).

2. But see the apparent exception, the book of Ecclesiastes, discussed in chapter 17.

3. Although one might also argue that although the woman has been "named" by the man as "Eve," the man remains unnamed until 4:25, when the Hebrew first uses the term *'adam* without the definite article (*"the 'adam"*).

over a thousand times in the Hebrew Bible. It was used three times in the Garden story:

> [The serpent said to the woman]: "God *knows* that when you eat of it your eyes will be opened and you will be like God, *knowing* good and evil." (3:5)

> Then the eyes of both were opened, and they *knew* that they were naked; and they sewed fig leaves together and made loincloths for themselves. (3:7)

> Then YHWH God said, "See, the *'adam* has become like one of us, *knowing* good and evil; and now, he might reach out his hand and take also from the tree of life, and eat, and live forever." (3:22)

In the Garden story, "knowing" is focused on *being like God:* all-knowing and without limits. But instead of God-like knowing, the man and woman discover *shame* that leads to *technology.* That is, they come to "know" that they are "naked." It is a condition that generates a "need" for something that God has not provided and they therefore must make for themselves. The Hebrew verb (*tpr*) rendered "sewed" is quite rare in the Bible,[4] although certainly the act of sewing must have been commonplace. It is one of many times that a biblical author uses an unusual word to draw attention to the uniqueness of the experience being narrated.[5] The story emphasizes that the people have "discovered" their nakedness not by listening to God's voice but rather to a different voice, when God asks pointedly, "*Who* told you that you were naked?" (3:11).

The humans' response to this freshly discovered "nakedness" is to take something God made for one purpose and to use it for another, unintended purpose: "they sewed fig leaves together and made loincloths for themselves." We are not meant to applaud their initiative in coming up with an innovative function for otherwise "useless" fig leaves. But on the other hand, the text is not suggesting that they should have just "done" nothing. Genesis is neither condemning "creativity" nor counseling passivity. Rather, it is showing that the beginning of the path that led directly to Babylon was the *use of the human mind to respond to experiences and "needs" that were not firmly grounded on God's Word alone.* Like parent, like child: it is but a short stretch from fig-leaf loincloth to the City.

So now wearing not fig leaves but God-made skin-clothes (3:21), the humans come to a new kind of knowing: of one another. Adam and Eve are in a liminal space: they are out of the Garden, but still presumably within divine earshot, although Genesis never again presents a conversation between them and God. We are not sure of their relationship with God. Is

---

4. It is found only at Ezek. 13:18, Job 16:15, and Eccles. 3:7.

5. Compare, for example, the virtually unique term *seneh* used to name the "bush" at which Moses encounters the living God, Exodus 3:2.

their knowing of one another a *sacred* experience, or are they *substituting* knowledge of one another for knowledge of God? This distinction is central to the entire biblical journey. God's generous gifts, whether tree fruit or sexual intimacy between human bodies, can take humanity down one of two paths: deeper into relationship with the Creator God or more fully enclosed within a world of our own making.

The Babylonians, like all ancient peoples, knew well the importance of the relationship between human sexuality and the sacred. Within their culture, what scholars call the *hieros gamos* (from the Greek meaning "sacred marriage") was practiced between the king and a woman sometimes misleadingly referred to as a "cult prostitute."[6] Such a role was not like prostitution today, but was a highly honored royal privilege. The annual ritual served to symbolize the union between the Sky (rain as male) and Earth (furrowed soil as female, hence, "Mother Earth") which guaranteed fertility for both land and empire.[7] It also served to coordinate childbearing within the city, as couples imitated the royal ritual and hence were more likely to have children in the relative quiet of winter. Thus, the *hieros gamos* reinforced *Enuma Elish's* view that the royal structure of Babylon was an earthly manifestation of the divine order.

The first narrated sexual union in Genesis stands in direct opposition to this ideology. The earth's fertility and the sky's rain are purely a matter of God's generous concern for God's creatures and need no ritual coaxing. Rather, human sexuality is dually oriented toward each partner's sacred experience of the divine image in the other *and* the bringing forth of the blessing of new life. Hence, we hear Eve's response to the birth of her son, "I have produced [*qaniti,* 'acquired' / 'gained']⁸ a man with [or "from"] YHWH."[9] Yet her response is ambiguous. Is she saying that she and God are co-creators? Or might she be saying that God made the first man, and now she (with her God-like power gained from eating the forbidden fruit) has made the second?[10] The text leaves the question open. The Story simply moves on to the question of the next generation.

We saw in chapter 1 how Genesis acted as a counter-story to *Enuma Elish.* One of the greatest opportunities and challenges throughout human history has been to pass on to one's children the knowledge and wisdom one has gained. But inevitably, each generation must wrestle with reality for itself and decide what ancestral wisdom to retain and what to discard. *Enuma Elish,* through its mythology of Babylon's creation by the gods before humans came to be, conveyed the (false) idea that social reality was stable

6. See, e.g., Deut. 23:17.

7. Kramer (1970).

8. Cf. Gen. 14:19, 22; 25:10; 33:19; 39:1; Wenham (1987), 101.

9. But note the ancient rabbinic midrashic comment on this response: "When a woman sees that she has children she exclaims, 'Behold, my husband is now in my possession' " (*Gen. Rab.* 22:2).

10. Cassuto, 201.

and unchanging. In such a society, rebellion is less likely. The risk, of course, is stagnation and ossification, a situation experienced both in village and city life.[11]

Genesis recognizes that life is not stagnant and unchanging but rather dynamic and transformational. Just as humans cannot go back to the Garden, life cannot be freeze-framed. Each generation — as well as each individual — must discern its own path, even at the risk of harm. This is the situation as Genesis 4 continues.

"Am I My Brother's Keeper?" (Gen. 4)

Two sons are born. Without a word about their childhood, the text jumps to their adult occupations:

> Abel tended flocks, and Cain became a soil servant ['oved 'adamah].[12]

There is mystery here that the author will not explain. Why a division of labor? Why *these* choices? Why aren't the brothers partners with their father? These questions are left completely unaddressed. In the same way, there is no explanation for what follows: each brother's bringing "to YHWH" of the fruit of their work. There has been no command or even a narrated encounter between either brother and YHWH. *How* did they "bring to YHWH"? And despite the numerous, ingenious attempts by commentators to discern a specific difference in the means of presentation,[13] none are given. Rather, it is stated enigmatically that YHWH "gazed" on Abel's offering but "did not gaze" on Cain's. And although some commentators have vehemently denied the possibility that the difference is grounded in a preference for one occupation over another,[14] the only other explanation is that there is no explanation. As Walter Brueggemann concludes: "Life is unfair. God is free."[15]

Perhaps this is what the author is trying to tell us. YHWH is inscrutable and sometimes we guess wrong what will be pleasing and suffer the consequences. But such an interpretation leaves the text dangling both in its narrative and cultural contexts. Between the expulsion from the Garden and the building by Cain of a city (4:17), this story must mean more than "things

---

11. Mumford, 48–50.

12. Author's translation.

13. For instance, Sarna (1970), 29: "Cain's noble purpose was sullied by the intrusion of the self, a defect that blocked the spiritual channels with God." Wittenberg, 107: "The Earth that had been cursed yielded only a meagre harvest.... Cain realized that in spite of his hard labour his harvest was not blessed, while the animals of his younger brother Abel were thriving."

14. Brueggemann (1982), 56: "Like the narrator, we must resist every effort to explain it. There is nothing here of Yahweh preferring cowboys to farmers.... The rejection of Cain is not reasoned." Similarly, Sarna (1970), 28.

15. Brueggemann (1982).

happen." And given the questions asked by the authors in the context of exile, why would they insert such a story here?

The narrative is tightly woven into the fabric of Genesis 1–11: It is not a random thread, but an integral part of a precisely composed story. It *does* convey that it is Cain's *embrace of agriculture* that is at issue. Several factors lead to this conclusion. First, once Genesis shifts from the "primeval history" to the story of the patriarchs and matriarchs in chapter 12, the God-related characters, starting with Abram, are, like Abel, tenders of flocks, not tillers of soil. Second, the authors generate a chain of causation between the disobedience in the Garden in Genesis 3 and the building of Babel in Genesis 11, as we'll see. Third, Cain will become the father of both the first forger of metal tools (4:22) and of the first man to respond to violence with escalating violence (4:23–24), both of which are elements of *Enuma Elish's* worldview, not that of Genesis. But one must admit that the text is sparse, preferring to invite its audience to grapple with the questions than to provide unequivocal answers.

The more familiar elements of the story follow Cain's rejected offering. First is the moment of decision: Cain's encounter with YHWH (4:6–7). God speaks a word of warning to Cain that echoes key terms from the woman's curse (3:16):

> ... sin is lurking at the door; its desire [*teshuqatho*] is for you, but you must master [*timshal*] it.

God's warning presents sin as a seductive, erotic force, with a "desire" parallel to the woman's for the man. Within the context of exile, it evokes the lure of Babylon's wealth and splendor, grounded in "redemptive" violence and surplus agriculture, seducing God's people to allow it control over life. As Umberto Cassuto describes it, sin "wishes to master you and to have dominion over you like the state officials who seek to impose their authority over the people."[16] We'll see this image, fleshed out, so to speak, in Revelation's portrayal of Babylon as a seductive whore dressed in the finest and most beautiful array that empire can provide (Rev. 17–18).

The divine warning includes the opportunity for Cain to "master" sin, parallel to the curse's prediction that the man would master the woman. However, whereas the patriarchal asymmetry is a curse leading to pain and death, the power of humans to master sin moves toward blessing and *shalom*.

In the face of this warning, Cain is silent. He does not speak to YHWH until after the fratricidal deed is done — in a "field," the farmer's domain[17] — and Abel's blood (*dam*) "cries out" to YHWH from the ground (*'adamah*). Blood and soil are intimately connected, but not in the sense we might have expected. The soil, the source of Cain's offering, "betrays" him and allows

16. Cassuto, 211.
17. Myers (forthcoming).

Abel's blood to "speak" directly to God. YHWH asks Cain the question of his brother Abel's whereabouts, which provokes Cain's classically self-justifying reply: "I do not know. Am I my brother's keeper?"(4:9).

With this exchange, Genesis undermines Babylon's claim to divinely authorized violence. As Claus Westermann expresses it,

> The murderer has no escape when faced with this question because there is someone who hears the victim's blood crying out. These words, valid for the whole history of humankind, protect the person as a creature of God from other people.[18]

No "cover story" will justify Cain's act. God hears the cry of the poor, even from the bloody ground. And God acts: it is Cain's turn to discover the consequences of disobedience to the Creator's voice. The would-be agriculturalist is banished from the 'adamah to be a "restless wanderer" over the 'eretz ("land" or "earth"). In a beautifully ambiguous reply, Cain cries out that his iniquity/punishment[19] is more than he can bear. Although in the story world there are as yet no other people on the earth, Cain fears that his new homeless status will make him ready prey for others, since Cain will lack the protective cloak of vengeance that membership in a "people" in a specific place would provide. Yet YHWH will not allow Cain to be subject to such violence, promising divine protection through a "mark" or "sign" ('oth, LXX, semeion). Ched Myers suggests that this "tattoo of taboo" could serve as a warning to other "people of the land" to beware of aggressive farming cultures. It also "cautions the reader against thinking that the problem of Cain can be solved by killing Cain."[20] As Hugh White says, Cain's death

> would have been in accord with a form of objective justice which assumes that absolute evil and good are embodied in dual, opposing, rival personages and groups, and which requires the execution of the evil by the good....[21]

In other words, Cain will not be enslaved by nor enslave others in "the religion of empire." As the cry of the victim Abel was heard by YHWH, so the plight of a murderer is not outside YHWH's purview and care.

What might seem to be the epilogue to the Cain story is in many ways its climax. We hear three key statements that link Cain's action with the story of Babylon's creation. First, we are told that "Cain went away from the face of YHWH" (4:16). One might find a physical place outside the oversight of Marduk or other Babylonian deities, but no reader of Genesis could imagine a "place" where the Creator of heaven and earth could not see or be seen. It

---

18. Westermann (1994), 305.
19. 'awon has both meanings; Westermann (1994), 309.
20. Myers (forthcoming).
21. White (2003), 165.

is *relationship* with YHWH from which Cain has turned. This small detail is central to what follows. *Everything* depends on a direct, personal, ongoing encounter with the living God. Listening and responding to the divine Voice leads to abundance of life and joy. Having turned away from God, Cain and his offspring listen to their own voices and execute their own plans, making life on earth more painful, difficult, and deadly.

Second, in this alienated state, Cain engages in the final actions of his narrated life:

> Cain knew his wife, and she conceived and bore Enoch; and he built a city, and named it Enoch after his son Enoch.

Like father like son, except without the ambiguity we noted in Adam's "knowing" of his wife.[22] Cain's sexuality, like all he does, is apart from God. It does not generate intimacy of relationship between partners who know God in and through one another. Rather, it simply produces offspring. Cain names his son "Enoch," which means either "dedication" (as in the Judean feast of *chanukkah*)[23] or "inauguration." Jacques Ellul notes of the latter meaning

> Inauguration as opposed to creation.... For in Cain's eyes it is not a beginning again, but a beginning. God's creation is seen as nothing.[24]

Third, the son is closely tied by a shared name to Cain's other act of new beginning: "he built a city." One can easily hear this as a satire on *Enuma Elish*. What is "a city" to the first humans? Why would Cain build it? Who is to occupy it? Are we to imagine him building it himself, telling his wife something like, "I'll be back after dinner, dear; I'm going to go build a city"? The absurdity of these questions underscores that the narrative is not trying to convey historical fact, but instead, seeks to establish a primal paradigm: *the first city was built by the first murderer, a person turned away from God.*

It is but a stone's throw from Cain's city, Enoch, to Nimrod's city, Babylon (Gen. 10:8–12). The introduction of the first biblical city invites us to take a step back to explore briefly what we can know about the historical origins of cities. What were the forces, events, and circumstances that led human beings to create and to accept a social world in which some people had power, wealth, and status and others obeyed them?

The Historical Origins of "the City"

Virtually all scholars consider *writing* to be a foundational element of a social organization we call "civilized." The nature of the preliterate evidence

---

22. A question to ask those who would take these stories as literal "history": Where did Cain's wife come from?

23. The festival of *chanukkah* celebrates the Maccabees use of "redemptive violence" to "purify" the temple of imperial influence, discussed in chapter 18.

24. Ellul (1970), 6.

for how and why social power and urbanization developed is limited by this verbal silence. We have ancient pottery and sometimes art to give us clues, but in the era before writing, these fragments lack the context necessary to interpret them with certainty. Beyond this, we have apparent patterns and an ability to make reasonable inferences about how "the city" came to be.

In this regard, we are often in a *weaker* position than the writers of Genesis to know how things were "in the beginning." We can only *imagine* life in an ancient, preliterate tribal village. The Israelites, though, *experienced* such village life all around them. They, like us, had sometimes to speculate about the processes that transformed one form of social life to another. Their speculations, both in the form of the Primeval History of Genesis and throughout the Bible, are fully consonant with the most sophisticated theorizing of modern and postmodern thinkers today.

One such thinker who devoted his lifetime to the question of the city was Lewis Mumford. His *The City in History: Its Origins, Its Transformations, and Its Prospects* was the culmination of his life's research and reflection on the topic. The volume is a rich repository of information and insight. I encourage readers to take up Mumford's full exposition.

The most basic pattern for Mumford is that human "life swings between two poles: movement and settlement."[25] Gatherer families and tribes tended to oscillate between these poles, moving in search of food and space; settling to share resources with others and exchange children for procreation. Mumford notes that

> Thus even before the city is a place of fixed residence, it begins as a meeting place to which people periodically return: the magnet comes before the container, and this ability to attract non-residents to it for intercourse and spiritual stimulus no less than trade remains one of the essential criteria of the city.[26]

Over time, these meeting places became imbued with spiritual power, associated as they were with rituals of birth, death, and life-sustaining trade. As this power grew, the magnetic pull increased. Such places were, of course, not chosen randomly, but in strategic locations, such as water-crossroads. People cleared spaces to accommodate larger groups and domesticated plants and animals to augment food supply. This was not yet agriculture, but simply tending by pruning and cutting indigenous species.

As oscillation between movement and settlement began to swing for extended periods toward the latter pole, the village was born. First as a seasonal settlement, then, where it could be sustained, longer term, the village was the dominant social form until perhaps the twentieth century, when earth's population took its final turn toward urban civilization. The village

---

25. Ibid., 5.
26. Ibid., 10–11.

was largely a woman-centered space in its first formations, focused on rituals of childbearing and childraising. It was women's ways that transformed the magnet into container, as domestication of plants, animals, and humans themselves became dominant activities.

Out of this most basic structure, the process took what Mumford called "the most fundamental step forward in harnessing the sun's energy: not rivaled again until the series of inventions that began with the water mill and reached its climax in nuclear power."[27] Domestication became the intentional gathering of seeds for replanting, which is the essence of agriculture. For the first time in human history, *surplus* might be gathered in a container other than the human belly. For perhaps four or five thousand years, village agriculture developed slowly and steadily, as people discovered successful crop selection and farming methods.[28] Throughout this period, agricultural cultivation of plants and animals was supplemented by the wild food still plentiful beyond, and sometimes right within, the village. It was the *hunter* who dared go beyond the settled bounds of the village to seek such prizes. With each hunting success — and with the development of a division of labor between villages and hunters — the hunter's prowess gained him social status. He began to serve not only as food gainer but as *protector* from both predatory animals and predatory people. For many villages, this meant a shift from the purely egalitarian social structure of a multifamily unit to a *ranked* structure with a "big man" or chief on "top."[29]

With this shift, we turn to another theorist to aid our investigation. Sociologist Michael Mann revolutionized our understanding of how people began to gain and maintain power over other humans with his work *The Sources of Social Power, Volume 1: A History of Power from the Beginning to AD 1760.* Mann systematically critiques previous theories based on *evolutionary* development of social power. He proposes and then tests a theory based instead on the notion of *four overlapping power networks* that emerge from place to place *interstitially.* That is, rather than an entire social structure changing at once, Mann shows how power grows gradually across four networks and sometimes coalesces into the relatively stable social realities of cities, states, and eventually, empires. His four networks are briefly described below.

Ideological power: "Collective and distributive power can be wielded by those who monopolize a claim to meaning" and sustained through *norms* and *aesthetic/ritual practices.* This can take two primary forms. The *transcendent* type "generates a 'sacred' form of authority...set apart from and above more secular authority structures." The *immanent* type "is less dramatically autonomous in its impact, for it largely strengthens whatever is there."[30]

---

27. Ibid., 26.
28. See also Bar-Yosef.
29. Ibid., 21–24; see also Wason.
30. Ibid., 22–24.

Economic power: In addition to the question of wealth, economic power involves the separation of society into *classes* based on ability to gain and use wealth as a means of controlling others. We'll see repeatedly how economic power can combine with ideological power to maintain social control, as it does today in neoliberal rhetoric about the "inevitability" of global capitalism.[31]

Military power: Focused inwardly as defense and outwardly as warmaking, military power is what Mann calls "*sociospatially dual:* a concentrated core in which positive, coerced controls can be exercised, surrounded by an extensive penumbra in which terrorized populations will not normally step beyond certain niceties of compliance but whose behavior cannot be positively controlled."[32]

Political power: As with military power, political power is also *sociospatially dual,* with both a "domestic" and an "international" component. It refers not simply to "politics" in the narrow sense of determining social leaders nor in the universal sense of negotiating differences to reach a common position or course of action. As *power,* Mann is referring to the ability of some people to gain and maintain influence over others through the control of centralized, institutionalized structures.

Lest this sound too abstract, consider the simple example of the domestic village that develops a "big man" hunter-chief.[33] His power might well start *economically,* by gaining control of the distribution of a significant portion of the village's food supply through effective hunting. This might become *political* through the use of a reward system (e.g., providing extra food) for those who develop special loyalty to him or a punishment system (e.g., withholding food) for those perceived as disloyal. The nature of his role as hunter provides *military* power: his expertise with weapons could both defend the village and, with enough loyal followers, attack a neighboring village. It could also be turned against the village in the form of tribute demands or violent repression if resistance to his use of power arose. Across generations, if the hunting power resided in a specific lineage or class of people, rituals and stories could develop to provide *ideological* power in support of a "dynasty" entitled to rule through power derived from "the gods."[34] Over time, the original basis for power is easily forgotten in light of the ability to tell an effective story of "the beginning" of how power came

---

31. See, e.g., Fukuyama.

32. Mann, 26.

33. Wason, 33–66, describes three categories of "non-stratified" but ranked societies: "big man," "ranked," and "chiefdoms," as part of his larger project of exploring the "archaeology of rank." His model provides several helpful criteria beyond our narrower purposes here. See also Shepard, 75, who cites anthropological studies concluding that "better hunters do not 'dominate politics' or play the role of 'big man' in stable hunter-gatherer societies.

34. See also Mumford, 23, who notes without benefit of Mann's later theory: "Yet one must not exaggerate the element of coercion, especially at the beginning: that probably came in only with the further concentration of technical, political, and religious power, which transformed the uncouth, primitive chieftain into the awe-inspiring king."

to be distributed the way it is "now." That is, unless some people chose to tell a *counter-story* that presented the possibility of wresting power away from existing power holders.

Now imagine the village having one or two extra features. For instance, what if the village was in a river flood plain, where soil was regularly replenished with nutrients capable of producing large surpluses? This was the case in two regions where cities and empires developed long ago: Egypt's Nile Delta and Mesopotamia. There are some crucial differences between these two places, as we'll look at later when God's people encounter Egypt in the biblical narrative. For now, let's focus on Mesopotamia, out of which Babylon arose.

Archaeological records indicate that the first irrigation canals were built in the Mesopotamian flood plain about 5500–5000 BCE.[35] The concept probably derived from natural irrigation off the back slopes of natural levees that provided far more abundant food than rain-watered soil could because of rich nutrients in the flood waters. With each step down this road, there are consequences. Mann notes that irrigation meant both increased population and increased constraint. "As soon as improvements began, the inhabitants were territorially caged."[36] The oscillation between movement and settlement collapsed into permanent settlement as people became more and more invested in the work they had done to transform the land. A major canal might take as much as five thousand hours of labor to construct, not including maintenance.

As far as can be determined from the preliterate, material remains, this situation continued with only the most gradual change until around 3000 BCE. Several factors generated the long-term shift from a network of irrigated villages into the formation of cities. All these factors, discussed below, likely originated through what archaeologist Andrew Sherratt has called "the secondary products revolution."[37] That is, domesticated animals, used for thousands of years simply as mobile food storage, began to be used for purposes that did not require killing them, specifically, for traction and for products such as milk and wool. This "revolution" combined with two simultaneous technological developments in the third millennium BCE: the use of the animal-drawn plow (rather than the human-pulled hoe) and the wheeled cart. These changes allowed for transport of "secondary products" across great, arid distances and encouraged both trade and land control by those bearing such products and technologies. This led to tremendous changes in social relationships and structures. We'll focus here on the most important factors.

---

35. The following description is based on Mann, Oppenheim (1977), Kramer (1963), Jacobsen, and Postgate.

36. Mann, 80.

37. Sherratt (1981 and 1983).

First, whereas hoe agriculture had been done mostly by women and encouraged matrilineal descent (i.e., men married into the women's family), plow agriculture reversed this, leading to "arranged marriages in which women, as carriers of property, have to be appropriately matched to maintain the status of the family."[38] This created *family property rights* which fixed inequalities of soil fertility that previously had been shared among the whole community. Animal traction and wheeled carts allowed for "battle-cars" used to defend such property against outsiders.[39]

Second, *strategically located land along a trade route* would give advantages to some over others. In the mineral-poor and other resource-poor Mesopotamian area, control of such routes enabled further advantages by those who could obtain and control access to materials such as metals. Such trade links could extend up to ten thousand miles in any direction.[40]

Third, the *use of outsiders captured in battle as slaves* developed a permanent class of low status persons. Slavery was a key component of urbanization wherever cities formed in the ancient Near East. Slaves were integrated into the fabric of life, working in temples, fields, and various skilled activities.[41]

Finally, the development of formal rituals to express the developing ideological underpinning of the social structure grew, carried out by a *new caste of priests*. The combination of these factors fixed a division of labor, status, and power within the community, transforming the village network into a *political state*. It was out of this increasingly complex structure that the new technology of writing first appeared in the city-state of Sumer.

Although writing eventually developed into a widespread vehicle for sharing culture and ideas, "its first and always its major purpose was to stabilize and institutionalize the two emerging, merging sets of authority relations, private property and the state."[42] That is, writing developed to support and maintain *royal bureaucracy*. A specialized class of workers called "scribes" kept countless lists, mostly involving trade and debt.[43] As Mumford states,

> For a great part of urban history ... the city was primarily a storehouse, a conservator and accumulator. ... It is no accident that the emergence of the city as a self-contained unit, with all its historical organs fully differentiated and active, coincided with the development of the permanent record: with glyphs, ideograms, and script.[44]

---

38. Sherratt (1981), 195.
39. Ibid.
40. Ibid., 192.
41. Mendelsohn, 1–5, 92–117.
42. Mann, 89.
43. See Carr (2005), 18–46, for the educational process that formed young people into royal scribes.
44. Mumford, 97.

Image 2: Reconstruction of ziggurat at Ur (c. 2000 BCE)
by Iraqi Department of Antiquities

This great gathering of goods in taxes, tribute, and war booty, of course, served to enrich only those close to the royal court. The architecture of the Mesopotamian city increasingly reflected a social stratification equating the king and his entourage with the gods. Palace and temple dominated the landscape, especially the structure known as the *ziggurat,* or stepped pyramid (see Image 2). Writing reinforced the social pyramid by making property ownership and status part of the permanent record. In turn, the physical structure of the city further defined social and economic differences by developing neighborhoods or precincts based on occupation and trade.

Eventually, writing grew into an instrument not only of royal list-making, but of "official" story-telling. Both laws and "sacred" narratives (such as *Enuma Elish*) became means by which urban-national identity was established and maintained. One of the most famous examples is the Code of Hammurabi from around 1700 BCE, at least seven hundred years after the first legal texts had been created. Such written texts would never be "read" by ordinary people, but their sheer physical presence on clay tablets underscored the power of the king to organize and maintain the social structure in accordance with "the divine order."

In addition to the imposing presence of ziggurats, the pyramidal social order was also reinforced by stories of how things got to be how they were.

Of course, one of the key elements of *Enuma Elish* that the Genesis narrative seeks to undermine is that the city, and Babylon in particular, was a "gift of the gods" built in time immemorial. Once the notion is established among people that what "is" is what "was," it is a short step to it remaining what "forever will be." A few generations after the building of ancient Babylon (not to be confused with the "New Babylon," which exiled Jerusalem's elite), who would have known how old the city really was? The imposing combination of all four networks of power working together created a Babylon that appeared to its occupants and visitors to be as eternal as the rivers and mountains.

YHWH's Regret (Gen. 5–9)

This brief overview of the radical difference between the Babylon that emerged after thousands of years of human choices and the one presented in *Enuma Elish* prepares us for the next element in the Genesis counternarrative. We left off in Genesis 4:17 with Cain's building of a city. The narrative continues with a genealogy of his offspring. With the naming of the seventh generation, the recital inserts a story about injury and death in the life of Lamech. Translation of 4:23 is notoriously difficult. It is unclear whether it is about vengeance ("I have killed a man for wounding me" [NRSV]) or a growth in violent human power ("as soon as I inflicted a wound or bruise, I killed him").[45] In either case, Lamech's "song" ends with the refrain: "If Cain is avenged sevenfold, truly Lamech seventy-sevenfold." In other words, if the killing of a murderer could evoke sevenfold vengeance (4:15), how much more the death of someone like Lamech who appeared to be "justified" in his lethal response to the initiating violence of another? Of course, Lamech's "logic" requires a huge leap. It was YHWH who promised to avenge the killing of Cain. Lamech, who as far as we know has no relationship with YHWH, derives the principle of escalating vengeance on his own. From the root of Cain's fratricide, Genesis reveals, comes the spiral of human violence. The cycle cannot end until all are dead or people reject vengeance itself.

Genesis narrates the birth of another child (Seth) to Adam and Eve and a genealogy of their descendants. However, this new lineage does not avoid the ongoing, multigenerational effect of the cycle of violence, as we hear: "Now the earth was corrupt in God's sight, and the earth was filled with violence. And God saw that the earth was corrupt; for all flesh had corrupted its ways upon the earth" (6:11–12).

Even before the description of this tragic state of affairs, Genesis makes a sobering observation about the human condition from the Creator's perspective:

---

45. Cassuto (1961–64), 242.

YHWH saw that the wickedness of humankind was great in the earth, and that every inclination of the thoughts of their hearts was only evil continually and YHWH regretted that he had made humankind on the earth and it grieved him to his heart. (6:5–6)[46]

It should give us great pause to hear Genesis announce that the Creator who blessed all of creation and pronounced it "good," declaring humanity "very good," now has decided that the final stage of creation was a mistake. It is a dramatically sweeping judgment on "civilization" and the violence that sustains it.

There was only one human on earth who could prevent humanity from being wiped out altogether. The difference is clear: "Noah was a righteous man, blameless in his generation; Noah walked with God." (6:9). Noah was unique among the humans of his time.[47] We'll explore later the specific meaning of the first two attributes that describe Noah. The third, however, is central to the religion that stands against empire. To "walk with God" is to live each moment in relationship with the truly holy. It is the path opposite that of Cain, who "went away from God's presence." This stark contrast underlies each of "the two religions." One builds a city on one's own initiative and names it after oneself. The other builds an "ark" at God's command to shelter and preserve God's creation.

And so the Flood comes. The story is in many ways a satire of the Sumerian *Gilgamesh Epic.*[48] In that narrative, a future king went off to seek the secret of immortality. After many harrowing experiences — including power acquired by defeating the embodied forces of the natural world and a great flood — he found that he must accept life "as it is." In other words, one can't change the world but must adapt to it. In the Genesis Flood, not only is the hero no king, but the world is utterly transformed as a result of his collaboration with the divine will and power. God makes a "covenant" with Noah and "all flesh" never again to cause widespread destruction by flood (9:9–17).[49]

Noah's reaction to this new development is not narrated, but once he is on dry land, Noah plants a vineyard. What a long time he must wait for that celebratory drink of wine! He, like Cain, is described as a "man of the soil ['adamah]" (9:20). He, too, is a child of agriculture. There was indeed no going back to Eden for Noah and his descendants. From his three sons, Genesis states, "the whole earth was peopled" (9:19). This contrasts starkly with "empire religion," in which peoples are pitted against one another in the ongoing battle for honor and control of resources. But in the religion of

---

46. The enigmatic passage in Gen. 6:1–4 about intercourse between "the sons of God" and human beings will be taken up in chapter 17 with discussion of the book of 1 *Enoch*.

47. Although the rabbinic midrash qualifies this: "in the street of the totally blind, the one-eyed man is called clear-sighted, and the infant is called a scholar" (*Gen. Rab.* 30:9).

48. See Jacobsen, 195–219, for background and themes of the *Gilgamesh Epic.*

49. Apparently reserving the right to cause destruction by other means, such as fire; this will become part of later expectations of divine judgment at "the end of days."

creation, all humanity is one family, creatures of one God, even outside the Garden.

The Beginning of Empire (Gen. 10–11)

The Genesis narrative then shifts its panorama from intimate family relationships to the sweep of world geography and history. Genesis 10 presents the so-called Table of Nations, in which seventy peoples are named as descendants of specific ancestors, stemming from each of Noah's three sons. The line from Ham includes these (in)famous biblical peoples: Egyptians, Canaanites, Philistines, and Sidonians. In the midst of a straightforward listing of these names, the narrative pauses as it did earlier with Cain's descendant, Lamech:

> Cush became the father of Nimrod; he was the first on earth to become a man of power [*gibbor*]. He was a mighty hunter [*gibbor-tsayid*] in the face of YHWH; therefore it is said, "Like Nimrod a mighty hunter in YHWH's face [*lifne YHWH*]." The beginning [*re'shith*] of his empire [*mamlakhto*; LXX, *basileias*] was Babel, Erech, and Accad, all of them in the land of Shinar. From that land he went into Assyria, and built Nineveh, Rehoboth-ir, Calah, and Resen between Nineveh and Calah; that is the great city.[50] (10:8–12)

The passage undermines *Enuma Elish's* claims about Babylon's origin. Nimrod is said to be the first *gibbor*, which "expresses the idea of violent, tyrannical power."[51] He is also a hunter, whether of animals or people is not specified.[52] It is but one step from these occupations to the building not merely of a single city like Cain, but of an *empire*. His relationship "in YHWH's face" is often obscured in translation.[53] Just as we use words such as "confrontation" (literally, "with fronts," i.e., faces) or phrases such as "in your face" to name a hostile encounter, so Genesis characterizes Nimrod's pursuit of violent power. This antagonistic aspect is underscored with the word that starts the next sentence: "the beginning." God made one beginning, and now Nimrod makes another.[54] Nimrod begins a system grounded in violence and shaped into cities that confronts God's created realm. The word translated "empire" is usually rendered "kingdom." Either word fits, but later, the Romans used Greek *basileia* to refer to their own "empire" (Lat. *imperium*). Genesis attacks this claim to imperial authority right from its primal "beginning."

---

50. Author's translation.

51. Westermann (1994), 516.

52. The only other person in Genesis to whom this label is attached is Esau, brother of Jacob, 25:27ff.

53. E.g., "before the LORD" (KJV, NRSV, NIV), following the LXX, *enantion kuriou*; NAB has "by the grace of the LORD" which inexplicably alters both Hebrew and Greek versions.

54. Hebrew *re'shith* is only used elsewhere in Genesis at 49:3.

The cities that form the core of Nimrod's empire are those that first filled the Mesopotamian plain, here known by the ancient name of Shinar.[55] First is Babel itself, the Bible's pejorative label for Babylon. Next is Erech, referring to the first known city, Uruk, about 125 miles southeast of Babylon. Finally is Accad, the first capital of the ancient Sumerian empire.[56]

But in the way of empire, this local network of cities was not enough for Nimrod. The expansion continues, culminating in the naming of one place as "the great city." The Hebrew sentence is ambiguous about the specific city to which this epithet refers, but later in the Bible, Nineveh is given this title (Jon. 1:2; 3:2; 4:11), and eventually, John of Patmos connects it with Babylon (Rev. 17:18–18:2). Regardless of specific original referent, the meaning is clear: a human stance "in YHWH's face" leads to an alternative kingdom/empire and an alternative religion. It is one of the central purposes of Genesis to remind God's people that this kind of empire and its religion have *not* been created by YHWH and do *not* embody the divine order.

---

55. See "Shinar" at Dan. 1:2; Zech. 5:11, clearly referring to Mesopotamia in postexilic texts.

56. Westermann (1994), 517.

Chapter Four

Making One's Name Great

"Let Us Make a Name for Ourselves":
The Tower of Babel (Gen. 11)

After the pause to describe Nimrod's act of city / empire-building, the Genesis 10 genealogy continues through the other descendants of Noah. A narrative and historical tension is set up between what readers already know and what has been told so far. It is no secret that the Israelites come from the Shemite line (hence the term anti-*Semitic*) and Israel's perennial enemies from the Hamite line, with the Japhethites off in the relative distance to the west. One ancestor, Noah, but two ways of being that divide the unity God has made.

This makes all the more astounding the scene that follows in Genesis 11:1–9, naming *all humanity* party to the city- and tower-building project known as Babel. Important to note at the outset is that the passage is as carefully *built of words* as the city is *built of bricks*. Consider, for example, a few ways of viewing the structure of this seemingly simple story. First, as a detailed chiasm:[1]

> A: v. 1: the whole earth had one language
>   B: v. 2: there
>   C: v. 3a: each other
>   D: v. 3b: come let us make bricks
>   E: v. 4a: let us build for ourselves
>   F: v. 4b: a city and a tower
>   G: v. 5a: YHWH came down
>   F[1]: v. 5b: the city and the tower
>   E[1]: v. 5c: which mortals had built
>   D[1]: v. 7: come . . . let us mix
>   C[1]: v. 7b: each other's language
>   B[1] v. 8: from there
> A[1] v. 9: the language of the whole earth[2]

---

1. "Chiasm" refers to a symmetrical textual pattern frequently found in ancient writings, in which a center section is surrounded by paired units joined by word, phrase, and / or theme.
2. Wenham (1987), 235.

Next, as parallel panels:[3]

Panel 1	Panel 2
A: v. 1: one language and one kind of speech	v. 6: one people, one language
B: v. 2: there (*sham*)	v. 7: there
C: v. 3: each other	v. 7: each other
D: v. 4: build a city	v. 8: building a city
E: v. 4: name (*shem*)	v. 9: its name
F: v. 4: lest we are scattered over the face of the earth	vv. 8–9: YHWH scattered them over the face of the earth

Finally, as scenes:

Introduction (v. 1): the situation: one language

Scene 1 (v. 2): Human migration from east, settlement in the plain of Shinar

Scene 2 (vv. 3–4): Human technology leads to a plan for a human-made "name"

scene 3 (v. 5): YHWH as building inspector

Scene 4 (vv. 6–7): YHWH's response

Scene 5 (v. 8): Humanity scattered

Conclusion (v. 9): The meaning of "Babel"[4]

The story parallels communally Cain's individual city-building. As Cain sought to be remembered in the matching name for son and city (Enoch), so now humanity seeks to "make a name for ourselves" (11:4).[5] The people who in v. 1 had "one language and the same words" speak only as a unit. Further, they speak only to themselves: there is no indication that they hear, see, or otherwise know of YHWH's voice or presence. They are humanity collectively seeking to remake creation in the image of the human mind.

The details reveal many satirical elements. The story summarizes as concisely as possible the process of human social development. First, people are on the move, then there is settlement, and finally, urban, technological civilization.[6] The first satirical aspect arises with the words of both people and narrator in v. 3:

---

3. Ibid.
4. Adapted from ibid.
5. Cf. Sirach 40:19, "Children and the building of a city establish a man's name..." and the discussion of the relationship between Sirach and empire, chapter 18.
6. See also Ellul (1967).

And they said to one another, "Come, let us brick bricks [*nilbenah lev-enim*], and burn them burnt [*venisrefah lisrefah*]." And they had brick for stone, and bitumen [*chemar*] for mortar [*chomer*].[7]

The wordplay in our passage would please Lewis Carroll or James Joyce, as the text takes as its building blocks a few very similar sounding words both to name and to mock the action and motivation of the people.[8] Beneath the play, though, is an extremely serious point about the origins of what we call "technology." First the man and woman in the Garden sewed fig leaves to make a loincloth to take care of a false need. Now humanity "bricks bricks" for... what? No need, real or imagined, initiates the process of brick burning. It is like children playing with driftwood on a beach. The urge to stack pieces into a "fort" or house is irresistible. But the act in Genesis is neither innocent or harmless. Rather, we see people making their (our) own substitutes for what God has provided. In place of stones, there are bricks. In place of mud mortar, there is bitumen (asphalt). Indeed, such were the components of Babylonian ziggurats.[9] The substitution of building materials releases humanity from dependence on the limited natural resources available in a locale (stones), and enables them to manufacture a (seemingly) endless supply of building blocks.

And with this discovery, what to build? We hear the new plan in wondrously worded detail:

Then they said, "Come, let us build ourselves a city, and a tower with its top in the heavens, and let us make a name [*shem*] for ourselves; otherwise we shall be scattered abroad upon the face of the whole earth." (11:4)

Note first the numerous self-referential pronouns: "us," "ourselves," (each twice) and "we." No reference either to God or the rest of creation: the brick-building project would enclose humanity in work of its own hands. With bricks and imagination, people reach for the skies in order to "make a name for ourselves." If figleaf-sewing was the beginning of *shame*-based technology, brick-stacking is *shem*-based technology. Like Egypt's pyramids, Babylon's ziggurats extended above earth in order to generate the city and royal elite's sense of divine authority and power. The word "ziggurat" comes from Akkadian *zaqaru*, meaning "to rise up high."[10] "City and tower" express the fullness of what Mumford and Mann have shown us cities were about from the beginning. As Severino Croatto says,

---

7. Author's translation.

8. As Michael Fishbane says, "the tightly coiled acoustical sound track of the text... places back the initial achievements as failures." Fishbane (1998), 38. Gordon Wenham notes further how many of the words used contain as primary consonants the Hebrew letters for N, B, and L, which also spell the implied Hebrew, *nebalah*, "folly." Wenham (1987), 239.

9. Sarna (1970), 70–71.

10. Ibid. (1970), 70.

The name acquired as a result of these great works of architecture...
functions as a cohesive force against dispersion — an ideological theme
that functions as a narrative axe. Thus, the strength of the city is not only
economic, political, cultural, and religious (everything is concentrated
in it), but also ideological, and, as such, appealing. The "name" binds
together, possesses a centripetal power.[11]

This centripetal force is meant to work against what people fear: being
"scattered." We hear not only how the passage satirizes the pretensions of
Babylon to draw all people into its magnet, but also Jerusalem, from which
the Genesis authors *have themselves been scattered.* Our passage, on its own
terms, takes in not only "their" but also "our" attempts to make a name
for ourselves.

It is here that YHWH takes notice and responds: "YHWH came down
to see the city and the tower, which mortals [*beni ha'adam*] had built." The
city and tower, which would be "skyscrapers," are so small that YHWH
cannot see them from where YHWH lives without coming down for a look!
YHWH's response inverts the human goal. If YHWH does not act in the
face of this human project, "nothing that they propose to do will now be
impossible [*lo'-yibbatser*] for them" (11:6). The Hebrew verb translated "be
impossible" also can mean "to fortify," as with a great building or city.[12]
And Jeremiah, likely writing nearly contemporaneously with the authors of
Genesis, uses it to express a closely related point:

> Though Babylon should mount up to heaven, and though she should
> fortify [*tevatstser*] her strong height, from me destroyers would come
> upon her, says YHWH. Listen! — a cry from Babylon! A great crashing
> from the land of the Chaldeans! For YHWH is laying Babylon waste,
> and stilling her loud clamor. (Jer. 51:53–55)

YHWH's response in our story is twofold: to "confuse" (*venavelah*) their
language and to scatter the people "from there" (*misham*). The first response
is described with a word that reverses the main consonants of the word used
by humanity for "bricking." The scattering leads to another wordplay, the
naming of the place as "Babel," punning (in Hebrew) on *balal*, "confused."
But it is also an interlinguistic pun on the Akkadian for "Babylon," meaning
"gate of the gods." Lawrence Turner observes,

> With exquisite irony those who wanted to make a name for themselves
> do indeed receive a name — Babel.... They had wanted to make a name
> by settling down in their city, but the name they receive ... describes their
> scattering.[13]

---

11. Croatto, 210–11.
12. The Hebrew verb stem in Gen. 11:6 is *nifal;* in Jer. 51:53 it is *piel;* cf. Isa. 2:12–18;
25:2.
13. Turner, 60.

The purpose and effect of the confusing of languages is to prevent people from amassing power based on common words and ideas. Jacques Ellul highlights this point:

> By the confusion of tongues, by noncommunication, God keeps man from forming a truth valid for all men. Henceforth, man's truth will only be partial and contested.[14]

One of empire's great powers is to impose a single language that "binds" diverse people. After Babel, speaking a different language becomes a key means of resistance to empire.[15] Part of that "different language" is the telling of a different story, as Genesis does to *Enuma Elish*. "No, children," the parents in exile say, " 'the gods' did not build Babylon, people did. And as YHWH allowed the Babylonians to destroy Jerusalem and scatter us to this place, so YHWH will bring down Babylon."

"I Will Make Your Name Great": YHWH's Call to Abram to Come Out of Empire (Gen. 12)

Having narrated the defeat of the world society united around a human building project, Genesis continues with a genealogy that begins the crossing from primeval time to historical time. From the story of people trying to make a name (*shem*) for themselves, we return to the story of the "descendants [*toledot*] of Shem" in 11:10. After ten generations, we hear of the descendants of a man named Terah (11:27). As with Lamech and Nimrod, the listing of names stops to focus on one specific family whose home is in "Ur of the Chaldeans." Scholarly battles have raged over the relationship between geography and history in this passage.[16] The text is not concerned with such questions, however. Instead, it is setting the stage for a key transition moment in the biblical journey and establishing a paradigm that continues until the Bible's final chapters.

Out of Ur, a city within the Babylonian empire, one family moves. We are not given a reason for Terah's departure. We are told that his destination is "the land of Canaan." How do these urban dwellers know of this distant outpost? What might they expect to find there? The text is silent. Then, having set up this journey, the narrator indicates that it was aborted: "when they came to Haran, they settled there" (11:31). The final words echo 11:2, when the migrants from the east "settled there" in the Shinar plain.[17] Why is the journey ended before the intended destination? We learn nothing about Terah or his motivations.

---

14. Ellul (1970), 18–19.

15. Cf. Halliday's sense of "anti-language" as a means established by those within a society seeking unity in resistance; for how this works in John's Gospel, see Reed.

16. See, e.g., Westermann (1994), 139–40.

17. See also 26:17; 35:1.

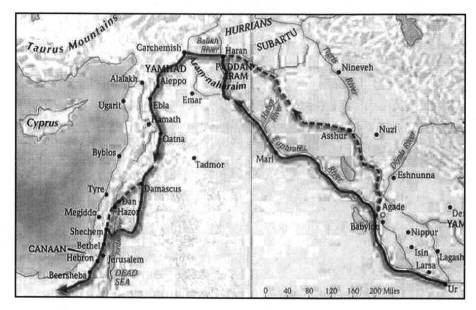

Map 2: Possible routes of Abram's migration

Just when the dramatic tension might seem to have dissipated, we hear this:

> Now YHWH said to Abram, "Go from your country and your kindred and your father's house to the land that I will show you. I will make of you a great nation, and I will bless you, and make your name great, so that you will be a blessing. I will bless those who bless you, and the one who curses you I will curse; and in you all the families [*mishpechoth*] of the earth shall be blessed."
>
> So Abram went, as YHWH had told him; and Lot went with him. Abram was seventy-five years old when he departed from Haran. Abram took his wife, Sarai, and his brother's son Lot, and all the possessions that they had gathered, and the persons whom they had acquired in Haran; and they set forth to go to the land of Canaan. (12:1–5)

These packed verses are the antithesis to the Babel story. In the plain of Shinar, all humanity spoke to one another and paid no attention to the voice of YHWH. But now YHWH speaks and a single human responds with trusting, unquestioning (for now!) obedience. In Shinar, people sought to make a name for themselves. But now, YHWH promises to Abram to "make your name great." In Shinar, people sought to build a city. But now YHWH calls humans out of a city. In Shinar, people sought to settle. But now, YHWH calls humans to be on a journey to an unforeseeable destination.

Questions abound. What would Abram, a man raised amid Babylonian religion, know of a divinity named "YHWH"? How would he recognize the Voice? What kind of experience are we expected to envision in this encounter? Would *we* have heard YHWH's voice if we had been there? Or was it simply an interior sense of clarity that moved Abram to undertake such a radical change at age seventy-five? However it is imagined to have happened, as Sarna says, "the divine silence that persisted for ten generations is shattered."[18]

Was it truly divine silence, or was Abram simply the first human in generations to overcome the cacophony of Babylonian imperial propaganda enough *to listen?* Avivah Gottlieb Zornberg explores some of the rabbinic midrash that considers Abram's motivations. One, from the medieval commentator Rambam (Maimonides), suggests that Abram was dissatisfied with the Babylonian explanation of reality:

> But [Abram's] mind roamed in search of understanding till he achieved the true way and understood out of his own natural intelligence.... Abraham was forty years old when he recognized his Creator. As soon as he achieved this knowledge, he entered into dialogue with the people of Ur of the Chaldeans.... When his arguments prevailed over them, the king sought to kill him and a miracle happened for him, and he left Haran.[19]

Rambam's point is that any person desirous of truth and open to find it would recognize the absurdities in the empire's story and begin the search for another possibility. What Abram found was not an alternative explanation, but *an encounter with Reality itself.* To listen to that Voice necessitated a new start, a great leaving behind of all that inhibited one's ability to commune with the One who is both at the heart of and infinitely beyond the bounds of authentic human knowing and experience.

This is expressed through the divine command in the sequence of "leavings" named in 12:1:

1. your "land" (*'eretz*)
2. your "lineage" (*moledat*)
3. your "father's house" (*bayit 'ab*)

Each of these concentric circles represents a container in which people can become captured by empire and its religion. Each is a component of a social order in which empire is presented as a given, as normal, as the "divine order." Only by *leaving* in response to the Voice of reality can one begin a journey that leads to a completely different way of binding people together, one grounded in *truth* and leading to *blessing* (12:2, *berakhah*).

---

18. Sarna (1989), 88.
19. Quoted at Zornberg (1996), 80–81.

The noun and related verb, used here for the first time in Genesis, are found five times in verses 2–3. The "blessing" is the opposite of the "curse," which brought pain and suffering to humanity. It is the fruit of obedient listening to YHWH: *abundance of life*, not only for Abram, but for all the "families" or "clans" of the earth. In direct contrast to the formation of world-kingdoms by Nimrod and his descendants, Abram's people will be those gathered in *kinship groups* and as such form a "great nation / people" (*goy*).[20]

The Voice of YHWH meets Abram at a decisive crossroad.[21] Two religions beckon humanity from the beginning. In responding to YHWH's Voice, Abram is portrayed as the first "convert" to what emerges as the authentic religion of the Creator God.

Abram is called to leave homeland, lineage, and his own family house. Genesis tells us nothing of what must have been wrenching conversations between Abram and his family in Haran, nor does it hint at how he explained the open-ended journey to his wife, Sarai, and nephew Lot. In a similar way, the gospels portray the response to Jesus' parallel invitation. For example, Mark 1:16–20:

> As Jesus passed along the Sea of Galilee, he saw Simon and his brother Andrew casting a net into the sea — for they were fishermen. And Jesus said to them, "Follow me and I will make you fish for people." And immediately they left their nets and followed him. As he went a little farther, he saw James son of Zebedee and his brother John, who were in their boat mending the nets. Immediately he called them; and they left their father Zebedee in the boat with the hired men, and followed him.

There are always a thousand "reasons" and "arguments" for why one should inhabit the way taught and practiced by nation, ancestors, and family.[22] From the call of Abram to the Bible's final call to "come out" in Revelation 18, God's Voice always presents hearers with a definitive choice to turn from one path to another. The walking of the new path, as the Genesis narrative shows in the stories to follow, is not always easy or obvious. One must constantly discern how to respond to the different religion of people whom one encounters. Abram is not portrayed as plaster saint or flawless hero. But he does what all humans are called to do: leave behind all that is "cursed" and leads to death and move into the way that is blessed and leads to life in abundance.

---

20. We'll return to this theme when we explore the period of Israel's national formation in the Promised Land before the monarchy (chapter 13).

21. Cf. Deut. 11:26–28; 30:19–20, which also express a basic choice in the language of "blessing" and "curse." For the relationship between Deuteronomy and the "two religions," see chapter 12.

22. Cf. Luke 9:59–62.

Chapter Five

The Well-Watered Plain of Sodom

Abram, like the Israelites and all those who seek to do the Creator's will, faces two major challenges. First, his trust in YHWH is tested by the basic needs of daily life: food, water, shelter. Second, he will face the social, political, and economic way of the "Canaanites" already in the land (12:6). Throughout the biblical journey, God's people confront hunger and thirst: starting at Genesis 12:10, running through the wilderness wanderings in Exodus–Deuteronomy, and continuing through the crowds that gather around Jesus (e.g., Mark 6:35–44). This daily reality invites us to reshape the central "religious" question: to whom do we turn when hungry and thirsty? The answer reveals who "god" is for us.[1]

Turning to Egypt for Food (Gen. 12)

In Abram's first testing, he turns directly to Egypt. The story in Genesis 12:10–20 completes the introduction of Abram and Sarai. Apart from it, Abram's faithful response in 12:4–5 is incomplete. First, we note that the word usually translated "famine" in 12:10, Hebrew *ra'av*, means simply "hunger." It does not necessarily imply crop failure. The implication that leads it to be rendered "famine" is that the hunger has been caused by the *failure of agriculture to provide enough for all*. Abram is now a migrant. He knows, as all mobile people do, that food shortages caused "naturally" (i.e., by weather, blight, or infestation) are inherently local. Move on and one will find food elsewhere. When the food supply is dependent upon agriculture, however, local variations in weather or insect populations produce *famine*, i.e., the absence of food "anywhere."

The text acknowledges that Abram knows this well. Rather than sit down and die or pray for a "miracle," Abram comes up with a practical solution: to go to Egypt "to reside there as an alien." How quickly Abram stops seeking YHWH's direction and acts on his own! His choice means both abandoning the land of YHWH's promise and seeking to live amid a people who will see him as "the other," a foreigner. And although we have no

---

1. For an interesting look at this from the perspective of today's free "market as god," see Cox (1999).

reason to imagine that Abram has ever been to Egypt, his Babylonian roots gave him experience of how the world of kings and empires works. He expects that the Egyptians will view his beloved Sarai as an object to be claimed and used, while he himself could be easily disposed of as extraneous (12:11–12). His response is to concoct a plan to protect himself while putting Sarai at great risk: "Please say you are my sister, so that it may go well with me because of you, and that my life may be spared on your account" (12:13). And the plan seems to succeed: the Egyptians, as Abram expected, see Sarai as an object, a "beautiful woman," and take her to Pharaoh, offering Abram a large payment of animals and slaves in exchange for his "sister."

That would seem to be the sad end of the story. But YHWH intervenes on behalf of the promise and against Abram's apparent willingness both to rely on Egypt for food and to profit on the "sale" of his wife to the royal court. With great irony, the text tells us that it is *Pharaoh* who understands that the "great plagues"[2] are a form of punishment inflicted upon the Egyptians. Neither Pharaoh nor Abram seem to perceive YHWH as the source of the punishment. Abram is silent in the face of the king's accusations of dishonesty. And where Abram might now expect to be killed, Pharaoh returns Sarai to him ("your wife").

Here as so often, Genesis teaches through humorous surprise rather than through somber lecturing. The "good pharaoh" has provided a "blessing" to Abram, not only in preserving his life and providing an abundance of goods, but also in the lesson of the story: listening to *YHWH's voice alone* is the only way to life. Pharaoh — and YHWH — have "given" Abram this mistake. He and his descendants will not always have the opportunity to make such a ghastly error and survive.

Choosing for Oneself (Gen. 13–14)

The crisis that follows the departure from Egypt is the inverse of famine, yet the basic choice (this time by Lot) remains the same. We hear that Abram is now "very rich (*kaved me'od*) in livestock, in silver, and in gold" (13:2). Hebrew *kabod* can mean both "heavy" / "weighty" and "honorable" / "glorious." Here it means both. Abram and his entourage weigh heavily on the land because of their abundant possessions, so that the land teeters under the load (13:6). At the same time, the mention of silver and gold — of value only in an exchange between strangers[3] — suggests that Abram is becoming "honorable" among other nomadic peoples

---

2. The Hebrew *nega'* suggests a rampant skin disease; Wenham (1987), 290.

3. See Gen. 23, where Abram negotiates with a stranger a price in silver for a burial plot for Sarah, and Gen. 24, where Abraham's servant woos Rebekah's brother Laban with silver shekels. Tellingly, twenty-six of forty-one references to silver (*kesef*) in Genesis are in the Joseph story (Gen. 42–47), where buying grain from empire is the focus.

as he journeys back from the Negev[4] to the place of his first encounter with YHWH.[5] The qualifier *me'od* is also doubly expressive, meaning both "very" and "powerfully." The extremity of wealth makes Abram powerful among the locals. The traveling band has become what to us seems an oxymoron: wealthy and honored homeless people.

The wealth and power, though, do not make for *shalom* but for *rib,* Hebrew for "strife" or "quarreling." Naomi Steinberg notes, "in Genesis, strife between men concerns wealth and property while the strife between women concerns husbands and children."[6] Westermann highlights the social role of *rib* here: "the quarrel...takes the place of the war in which the larger unions, from tribes on, engage.... [It] is just as serious because it is a question of the very existence of the group."[7] It is a matter of too many people and possessions in too small a space. Someone will have to move on.

Abram magnanimously offers his nephew Lot the choice: you go one way, and I'll go the other. The narrator provides Lot's perspective:

> Lot looked about him, and saw that the plain of the Jordan was well watered everywhere like the garden of YHWH, like the land of Egypt, in the direction of Zoar; this was before YHWH had destroyed Sodom and Gomorrah. So Lot chose for himself all the plain of the Jordan, and Lot journeyed eastward; thus they separated from each other. (13:10–11)

It is our first gaze on the character of Lot, as Lot himself gazes over the land. His choice sets a pattern. As an ancient midrash summarizes, "The whole of this verse connotes immoral desire."[8] When Lot lifts his eyes to look,[9] he sees lush, verdant agricultural land laid out in the Jordan plain. Its attractions parallel the attraction of the woman in the Garden to the fruit of the forbidden tree (3:6). YHWH has not explicitly warned Lot against choosing the rich farmland as the woman was warned against eating the wrong fruit. We are, though, expected to notice that his gaze and decision take place without listening for direction from YHWH. This is underscored by the contrast when YHWH speaks directly to Abram, telling him to "lift your eyes now and look" (13:14). The link with 3:6 is made explicit by the mention in 13:10 of "the garden of YHWH." But there is a difference: it is also "like the land of Egypt." In other words, there is abundant water as in the Garden of Eden, but its ability to produce rich food is like Egypt: it provides not naturally growing tree fruit, but irrigation-produced grain. It is

---

4. There may be a wordplay contrast between "Negev," meaning "dry [place]" and "Eden," meaning "moist [place]." Cf. McKeown, 83.

5. "The narrator is surely suggesting that Abram is trying to recapture his previous experience of God." Wenham (1987), 296.

6. Steinberg (1993), 57, n. 39.

7. Westermann (1995), 176.

8. *Gen. Rab.* 41:7.

9. Compare Gen. 39:7, when the Egyptian official Potiphar's wife "lifts her eyes to look" lustfully on the young "Hebrew," Joseph.

not YHWH's chosen destination at all (creation), but rather, a human-made substitute (empire).

Lest we, with Lot, miss the point, the narrator adds ominously: "this was before YHWH had destroyed Sodom and Gomorrah" (13:10). Lot sees the potential crops, but not their source, and thus, not the dire consequences of his choice. Seeing only what looks good in his own eyes ("chose for himself"), bereft of YHWH's available guidance, Lot's judgment is implicitly cursed. Once the separation between Abram and Lot is complete, the narrator underscores the mistake: "Now the people of Sodom were wicked, great [*me'od*] sinners against YHWH" (13:13). It is a blanket condemnation of the way of life in the "cities of the plain." They are people of the religion of empire, already grounded in Cain, Lamech, Canaan, Nimrod, and the city Babylon. Yes, they have an abundance of food. But how they get it and what they do or don't do with it is central to their status. The *me'od* of their sin contrasts directly with the *me'od* of Abram's wealth in 13:2. Faced with strife, Abram offered "the other" (Lot) the opportunity to make the choice. The Sodomites, as we'll see, act in diametric opposition to Abram's magnanimity.

The first consequence of Lot's choice comes at once. After the narrator tells of Abram's second direct encounter with YHWH and reaffirms the promise of land and descendants, the story seems to turn to a completely different topic in Genesis 14. A rebellion of a royal coalition against their overlord leads to a battle between two alliances. Among the rebels are the kings of Sodom and Gomorrah. They are defeated by falling into bitumen pits, an ironic comment on the previous use of bitumen as ziggurat mortar (11:2). Kings rise by bitumen and also fall by it. But in this case, the defeat of the kings of Sodom and Gomorrah results in the taking captive of Lot and his goods (14:12). Abram's only option seems to be to form a guerrilla force of his own to rescue his nephew. Lot's mistake has forced Abram to risk his life to save him.

After Abram's victory, the king of Sodom offers Abram the spoils if the king can keep the captured Sodomites. But Abram stands firmly before this king (in contrast to his cowering before Pharaoh) and refuses to be made into a mercenary. There is no interaction between Abram and Lot. Abram continues on his journey and Lot, still blind to the nature of urban life, returns to Sodom.

Entertaining Angels... or Not (Gen. 15–19)

The narrative continues in Genesis 15–18 with several stories that continue Abram's journey. In Genesis 15, the old man Abram begins to express doubts that the promise of offspring can actually be fulfilled through his own body and is reassured by a mysterious, nighttime encounter with YHWH. Sarai speaks for the first time in the narrative, struggling with Abram over the slave girl Hagar, part of Pharaoh's gift. Abram concedes to his wife and Hagar runs away. We discover a YHWH whose protective care extends beyond Abram and Sarai, as he appears to Hagar in the wilderness (16:7–13).

YHWH once again appears to Abram in Genesis 17, this time establishing a "covenant" (*berit*). The covenant is marked in two ways. First, YHWH extends his name from Abram (meaning "father of the lofty") to Abraham ("father of many").[10] Laurence Turner says the new name "advertises to all what up to this point had been private knowledge between a man and God."[11] YHWH also changes Sarai's name to "Sarah," meaning "princess," but also closely related to the word later used to describe Jacob's "wrestling" with God and humans, *saritha* (Gen. 32:28).[12] Thus, as YHWH will later name Jacob and his descendants "Israel," now YHWH names Abram's wife the mother of divine/human wrestling.

Second, YHWH commands Abraham and all the males among his people to mark the covenant on the male's fleshly contribution to "blessing" by circumcising their penises. When Abraham says or hears his name and when he engages in the regular acts of elimination and sexual engagement, he is to remember this covenant.

Finally in this section, Abraham and Sarah encounter three visitors as they sit in the shade of the sacred trees of Mamre.[13] Earlier, Abram had "built an altar" there (13:18) as a counter to Babylon's ziggurats. Before that, Abram had also built altars at "the trees of Mamre"[14] and at Bethel. Read from the time of the postexilic audience of Genesis, Abram's altars are also an alternative to the Jerusalem temple. They are precisely the kind of nonurban worship sites destroyed under the centralizing "reform" of Judah's King Josiah (2 Kings 23, discussed in chapter 12). Genesis does not distinguish between the religion of empire practiced by "them" or by "us" in establishing the religion of creation as the authentic means by which to worship YHWH.

The hospitality Abraham and Sarah provide to the visitors is lavish to the point of absurdity. In the midst of the day's heat they hurry to offer a royal banquet. This feast for strangers contrasts with the same visitors' treatment in Sodom in the following story. The conversation that ensues among Abraham, Sarah, and the visitors is itself filled with earthy wordplay.[15] Our

---

10. *TWOT*, 6.

11. Turner, 81. Sarna (1970), 124, adds that the change literally fulfills the promise in 12:2 to make Abram's name "great" by adding a letter to it.

12. See also Hos. 12:4, the only other biblical use of this Hebrew word, also referring to Jacob's wrestling.

13. Given the powerful heat of the region, a shade tree among the palms would be a sacred thing indeed. Both Babylon and later Persia were known for the artificial shade of their landscaped gardens. For the historical development of gardens as a substitute for natural shade and verdancy, see Eisenberg (1999).

14. "Mamre" means "oracle giver," Westermann (1995), 154.

15. One element is the continuation of an ongoing Genesis wordplay, begun in 17:17 over "laughing" (*yitzchaq*, i.e., "Isaac"). See 18:12, 13, 15; 19:14; 21:6, 9; 26:8; 39:14, 17. The word also means "to play with" in the triple sense that is also conveyed by the English: to

focus here is on what follows the departure of the visitors in the direction of Sodom.

For the first time, we hear of an "outcry" (*ze'aqah*) from the people. This time it is against Sodom and Gomorrah; next it will be against the Egyptian taskmasters (Exod. 2:23; 3:7). The word and its closely related cognates express "the anguished cry of the oppressed, the agonized plea of the victim for help in some great injustice."[16] For the second time, YHWH proposes to "go down and see" (as 11:5, 7) the truth of the situation that has come to the divine ears. The narrative presents a shockingly intimate relationship between YHWH and Abraham, establishing a paradigm later embodied between YHWH and Moses and then with prophets like Isaiah and Jeremiah. YHWH informs Abraham in advance of the situation and YHWH's intended response, then Abraham and YHWH engage in a conversation about divine justice. Implicitly recalling the sparing of Noah, a "righteous" man among an evil generation, Abraham argues that it would be unjust to sweep away the righteous with the wicked (18:23). He appeals to "the Judge of all the earth [to] do what is just" (18:25). How radically different this is from *Enuma Elish!* Expecting the gods to act with perfect justice and daring to imagine a mere mortal determining divine behavior are utterly unimaginable to imperial religion. The gods are who they are; they do what they do. There is no point in seeking to change the way things are. But according to Genesis, the Creator God is open to a mutual listening with his creatures.

Abraham's persuasive path moves from the possibility of fifty righteous ones down to the possibility of ten. YHWH is convinced by Abraham's argument, and they both go their own ways to await the outcome of the divine messengers' visit to Sodom. Westermann observes that "there is no event in the whole of Genesis that is mentioned so frequently in the OT as the destruction of Sodom."[17] At the same time, few stories from Genesis have been more radically misunderstood.

Read not only in the cultural and narrative contexts we've been exploring so far, but also in the context of inner-biblical interpretation,[18] the story has nothing to do with condemning "homosexuality." Rather, it condemns, as Ezekiel clearly understood, the lack of hospitality provided in cities to strangers. While Abraham and Sarah lavishly welcomed YHWH's messengers, the people of Sodom radically reject them. Here is Ezekiel's

---

enjoy time together; to mock, and to sexually abuse. So when, for example, we see Ishmael 'yitzchaqing' with Isaac" (21:9), we're not sure which of the three ways to take it. The other wordplay is when Sarah asks whether, given both her and her husband's advanced age and decrepit condition, she is to have "pleasure" (18:12, *'ednah*). Used only here in the Hebrew Bible, the word is cognate with the noun for Eden, meaning "abundant moisture." In other words, she is asking whether her dry old body will become, like Eden, flowing with the (sexual) moisture that leads to fertility.

16. Sarna (1970), 145.
17. Westermann (1995), 298.
18. On "inner-biblical interpretation," see Fishbane (1989).

comment, as he calls upon the memory of Sodom to castigate Jerusalem in his own time:

> This was the guilt of your sister Sodom: she and her daughters had pride, excess of food, and prosperous ease, but did not aid the poor and needy. (Ezek. 16:49)

Not a word about sexuality. Rather, Ezekiel's focus is the same as the narrator of Genesis: the inhospitable and violent stance deemed "normal" by ancient city dwellers. Jesus interprets it the same way, when he compares the judgment on Sodom and Gomorrah to that of cities that reject his disciples.[19]

Although the story does not condemn a particular sexual practice, it does use sexual imagery and innuendo. The first instance is when we hear the two messengers arrive to find Lot "sitting in the gateway of Sodom" (19:1). This parallel's Sarah standing at the "entrance to the tent" (18:10). Both tent and city are "female" in the sense of an open enclosure with life on the inside. As a woman protects her body from unwanted entry, so city people build a wall to protect the body politic from unwanted entry. The Sodomites have real reason to be wary of strangers, given the recent war. This is the very nature of walled cities: to offer protection for those "in" against those "out." This urban raison d'être is necessarily in tension with the hospitality Abraham and Sarah offered. To welcome strangers, from the perspective of the religion of empire, is to risk allowing a virus-like invader into the body, here, akin to a sexually transmitted disease.

So when Lot gets up and begins to invite the strangers into his home for the night, we should not be surprised that the locals immediately and forcefully object. We can imagine Lot's horrified reaction to the visitors' proposal that they "spend the night in the square" (19:2). He "urged them strongly,"[20] a phrase similar to the English idiom, "he twisted their arms." The visitors proceed from the city gateway to the entrance to Lot's house. Is Lot's home a protective "womb" for these strangers? It is a tremendous risk for all involved. As Nahum Sarna says, "Lot, in offering hospitality to the strangers, had violated the norms of the society in which he lived . . . the first example in the literature of the world of the problem of the moral conscience of the individual in opposition to the collective concept of the group."[21]

---

19. Matt. 10:15 and Luke 10:12. Only the New Testament letter of Jude interprets Sodom's evil in sexual terms, although it is likely a metaphor evoking the apocalyptic tradition of *1 Enoch*; Jude 7, see Bauckham (1983), 53–55. The unfortunate translation of the Greek *arsenokoitai* as "sodomites" at 1 Cor. 6:9 and 1 Tim. 1:10 has not helped. This term, understood in the contexts of both Corinthian practice and Paul's letter, refers to men who use younger boys as public sexual status symbols, akin to today's all-too-common practice of transforming wealth into "trophy wives." See, e.g., Witherington (1995), 166. The use in 1 Timothy is simply in a "vice list," so there is no specific context to help understand the usage.

20. The LXX Greek will be echoed in the later urging of urban visitors to accept local hospitality at Luke 24:29 (Jesus to Emmaus) and Acts 16:15 (Paul to Philippi).

21. Sarna (1970), 146.

The feast ensues (one might wonder where Lot's wife is) but immediately, we hear:

> But before they lay down, the men of the city, the men of Sodom, both young and old, all the people to the last man, surrounded the house; and they called to Lot, "Where are the men who came to you tonight? Bring them out to us, so that we may know them."

Note the careful specification of who arrives at Lot's house. First, it is "the men of *the city*." It is as city people that they are intolerant of strangers. Second, it is as "men of *Sodom*": this city in particular is an embodiment of the evils of all cities. Third, they are "both *young and old*": like fathers, like sons, the men come, without the possibility of appealing either to the inexperience of youth or the potential wisdom of age. Finally, they are "*all the people to the last man*": Abraham has "lost" his bargain with YHWH over the fate of Sodom. All the Sodomite men are one in refusing the stranger at the gate, now in Lot's house. Their surrounding of the house forms a human wall outside the house wall and within the city wall from which there seems no escape.

There is great irony in the Sodomites' collective call through the door to Lot. The plea "to know" the visitors would likely provoke a vicious snigger from the gathered crowd. They have no desire to "know" them either in authentic human community or in the tender intimacy of sexual union. Lyn Bechtel comments that the intended rape would accomplish two goals for the Sodomites.

> First, it would intensely shame and dehumanize the messengers, diminish their status . . . sever bonding. . . .
>
> Second, by creating the illusion of power, control, and superiority, it would silence the townsmen's feelings of vulnerability, inferiority or lack of control, feelings generated by the threat of the messengers / spies.[22]

Lot understands all too well what is at stake. He's been living in Sodom for many years and accommodated to the local religion. But the residue of his relationship with Abraham (and with YHWH?) leads him out to dissuade the townsmen. Shutting the door behind him as Noah shut the door of the ark against the deadly floodwaters (Gen. 7:16), Lot makes a proposal certainly as shocking to the original Genesis audience as to us: he offers them his daughters in place of the visitors. Older scholarly claims that sought to justify Lot's behavior as comporting with a supposed greater duty to strangers than to one's own family miss the point. Lot's initial, wrong choice of the "well-watered plain" has led him to this terrible moment. Yet Lot still had an honorable way out. As Laurence Turner notes, "To have offered himself . . . would have maintained his role as a righteous host. . . . But, rather

---

22. Bechtel, 117–18.

than self-sacrifice, he chooses to offer his virgin daughters."[23] The narrative emphasizes the contrast between Lot's response and Abraham's. As Joel Rosenberg points out, "Lot's hospitality...is a poor copy of his kinsman's. His willingness to sacrifice his daughters (and thus his posterity) to the whim of the Sodomites stands in bold contrast to the importance of a posterity to Abraham."[24]

In any event, the city people will have none of it. Their response unveils the terms of the confrontation:

> But they replied, "Stand back!" And they said, "This fellow came here as an alien [*gur*], and he would play the judge! Now we will deal worse with you than with them." Then they pressed hard against the man Lot, and came near the door to break it down. (19:9)

Lot should understand, the Sodomites proclaim, what it means to be an "alien" in the city, having been one himself. The only previous use of Hebrew *gur* was for Abram's temporary (and mistaken) sojourn to Egypt (12:10). Intending only to stay out the famine in the Promised Land, Abram got caught pawning off his wife as his sister and was expelled from Egypt by Pharaoh. Lot, though, has made a permanent home in Sodom. Yet his attempt to appeal to them as "my brothers" (19:7) only further enrages the urbanites. There will be no deal, no compromise, no negotiation. It is one religion against the other in direct and irreconcilable confrontation.

YHWH's messengers act, reaching out to sweep Lot back into the house. We are told that they "struck with blindness" the men at the door. Whether as miraculous blindness (compare 2 Kings 6:18) or as a "sudden, immobilizing, blazing flash of light,"[25] the angelic action prevents the invaders from finding the door. Meir Sternberg points out that, either way, their inability to see the anticipated nakedness of their intended victims serves as a "retributive pun that echoes back all the way to their forefather [Ham] who 'saw the nakedness of his father.' "[26]

The drama now shifts to the question of saving Lot and his family from the destruction about to come. Again, life in Sodom has shaped Lot. His attempt to warn his prospective sons-in-law (were they among the crowd surrounding his house?) is met with ridicule (19:14). The narrator describes their reaction with a form of the verb for "laughing" (*tschq*) heard in the encounter between the YHWH and Sarah (18:10). Here the sexual connotation fits the irony of the entire episode. We might render their response, "he seemed to be screwing around." When morning comes, it is the angels' turn to "urge" Lot to get out of town before it's too late, matching Lot's urging of them the evening before. But unlike his ancestor Noah, who obeyed

---

23. Turner, 87.

24. Rosenberg (1986), 77.

25. Sarna (1989), 136, who notes that the ordinary Hebrew word for blindness is *ivvaron*, not *sanverim* as here and 2 Kings 6:18.

26. Sternberg (1985), 112.

YHWH's command to get away from the impending disaster, Lot "lingered" (19:16). Embodying YHWH's mercy, the messengers take Lot, his wife, and his daughters by the hand and bring him "outside the city." They command him to "flee for your life; do not look back or stop anywhere in the plain; flee to the hills, or else you will be consumed." It is not just a matter of getting out of range of the physical disaster itself, but of finding a home away from the influence of "the plain." Lot and his family (like those in Babylonian Exile) are being offered a fresh start, a chance to learn from their experience and leave city life behind forever. Rather than be grateful, the recalcitrant Lot asks a "favor" of the angels:

> And Lot said to them, "Oh, no, my lords; your servant has found favor with you, and you have shown me great kindness in saving my life; but I cannot flee to the hills, for fear the disaster will overtake me and I die. Look, that city is near enough to flee to, and it is a little one. Let me escape there — is it not a little one? — and my life will be saved!" (19:18–20)

Lot's plea is pathetic and deeply ironic. It seems impossible for one used to city life to even imagine living beyond the urban confines. Lot, rejecting the *difference in kind* between the two religions, suggests as a compromise a *difference in degree*. Might not a "little" city be better than a "big" one like Sodom? The angels accept Lot's offer and the "overthrow" (*hafki*) begins. The verb, literally meaning "turn over," is associated with this story throughout biblical memory.[27] It expresses not simply destruction, but YHWH's just act of crushing back into the earth what humans sought to raise up to heaven to make a name for themselves. The overthrow includes the demolition of the local agriculture upon which urban life was based, the very thing that attracted Lot in the first place (19:25).

Perhaps the most famous detail in the story is the one with which it concludes: Lot's wife looking back and becoming a pillar of salt. There is to be no looking back once one has heeded the divine call to "come out." It will be a repeated temptation, as the Israelites in the wilderness look back to Egypt and Jesus' disciples "look back to the things behind" (John 6:66). But there is also another aspect to Lot's wife's action. She is the only woman in a story of male violence to take independent action. Her absence during the hospitality and confrontation at the house now stands out all the more. She has been silenced by city life, driven into the background except for this one moment. For her, Sodom, despite its evil, was *home*. The salty image of her memorializes the tears that are the "anguish for the women and children of Sodom."[28] While we may celebrate the overthrow of the evil embodied in Sodom, we also are invited to lament the suffering of the innocent victims of empire who so often are destroyed amid the meting out of divine justice.

---

27. E.g., Deut. 29:23, Jer. 49:16; Westermann (1995), 307.
28. Fewell and Gunn, 67.

The Lot story has a brief epilogue that presents the final result of Lot's long-term city dwelling. After the overthrow, he leaves "the little city," Zoar, and takes his daughters to live in a cave in the hills. We are not told why, after his plea was granted, Lot is "afraid to stay [*yshb*] in Zoar" (19:30). The Hebrew verb is used three times in this verse, highlighting the question of where to "settle."[29] Perhaps, seeing the smoke rising across the plain, Lot now understands the fate of those who "settle" in cities, regardless of their size. His retreat makes him the only "caveman" in the Bible.

The cave is "female" space, and Lot's daughters immediately exert authority over it. They are desperate to preserve life and continue the blessing, imagining wrongly that the overthrow has destroyed everyone but them. The following drama is a burlesque on the story of Noah's ark. There is no divine direction or encounter, merely action taken from a myopic perspective. On sequential nights, they get their father drunk enough to impregnate each of them. It caricatures Noah's drunken sleep, when his son Ham saw his nakedness but found his offspring condemned (9:21–25). Here, Lot seems blissfully unaware. Saved from rape by the city folk and removed from their prospective husbands, the daughters' only apparent option is to violate all custom — and an explicit biblical law[30] — to enable a new generation to be born from their lineage. The daughters turn their father into a mere semen donor. The children from this bizarre union are said to be the ancestors of the Moabites and Ammonites, local peoples with an appropriately mixed relationship with the people Israel later in the story.[31]

Genesis has now clearly established the bounds of the "two religions." We will not again see in this biblical book such a stark contrast. From now on, choices will become more subtle, but with no less dire consequences for the wrong choice. It will be up to two twin brothers, grandsons of Abraham and Sarah, to find and to walk the path that YHWH places before them amid people who practice the religion of empire.

---

29. The verb is used over seventy times in Genesis, but the pattern of previous uses highlights this theme: 4:16, 20; 11:2, 31; 13:6 (twice); 13:7, 12 (twice); 13:18; 14:7; 16:3; 18:1; 19:1; 19:25.

30. Lev. 18:6ff. Although Lot's daughters do not know this law, the Genesis audience likely does. See chapter 16 below.

31. Compare, e.g., Deut. 2:9, 2:19 and 23:3–6.

Chapter Six

Fulfilling YHWH's Promises

As we've seen and will continue to see, the "religion of creation" begins with a deep listening to the Word of YHWH and a willingness to obey that Voice wherever it beckons, trusting that it will lead to blessing and abundance of life. The "religion of empire" begins with people listening to themselves and seeking to establish their own greatness apart from intimacy with YHWH. Inevitably, this path leads to violence, domination, and death.

Yet, as anyone who has ever sought to be faithful to the Creator God knows all too well, challenges and temptations continue to abound. Trusting in YHWH does not provide a roadmap for life. Abraham continued to turn to YHWH for further guidance as his journey unfolded and new situations arose. The remaining chapters of the Abraham and Sarah narrative confront them with three basic questions that were important to the people in exile:

1. What does it mean to be a faithful *parent*? In other words, how do God's people relate to and raise their children differently than the parents of "empire"?

2. How are God's people to relate to *"foreigners"*? In other words, as God's people form their own collective identity, how are they to interact with others in the world?

3. How are God's people to negotiate the need for *"outside" wives and husbands* without "losing their religion"?

We'll look briefly at how Genesis portrays Abraham and Sarah wrestling with these questions before turning to the story of Jacob's own wrestling with YHWH.

Abraham and Sarah are soon confronted with what seems to be the undermining of everything that YHWH has promised. After the second "wife/sister" episode in Genesis 20,[1] Abraham experiences the loss of his firstborn, Ishmael, and then what appears to be the loss of his beloved son,

---

1. How interpreters treat this second story of Abraham seeking to fool a king into thinking that Sarah is his sister (and the similar story of Isaac's parallel action in Gen. 26) often says more about the interpreter's own presuppositions than it does about the text itself. For example, for those convinced from the start that Genesis as we have it is a patchwork of sewn together traditions that have left the evidence of stitching plain for all to see, this repeat story represents the "E" (Elohist) version of the wife/sister tradition in parallel to the "J" (Yahwist) version in Gen. 12. For others, for whom Genesis is a coherent, carefully composed narrative

Isaac. Why would YHWH lead Abraham and Sarah out of Babylon with the promise of progeny and blessing only to take it away? Has their journey been completely futile, or is there meaning in the mystery of YHWH?

Ishmael "yitzchaqing" (Gen. 21)

The Ishmael story focuses on Sarah's reaction to the sight of Ishmael "yitzchaqing" (*metsacheq*). While the Septuagint adds a closing phrase, "with her son Isaac," the Hebrew does not, so it remains ambiguous whether what Ishmael is doing is with (or to) Isaac or by himself. It is a crucial moment. Ishmael and Isaac are the first brothers since Abel and Cain. Will one brother again rise up against the other? What is it that Sarah saw Ishmael doing? Whatever it is, it leads her to demand that Abraham "cast out this slave woman with her son; for the son of this slave woman shall not inherit along with my son Isaac" (21:9). Given the multiple connotations of the Hebrew word, there are several overlapping possibilities, each of which suggests a real world problem.

1. *Ishmael might be "playing" with Isaac in the healthy and ordinary way that siblings do.* In this case, Sarah might be rightfully concerned that a growing intimacy between the boys, as well as a deepening affection for both by their father, might put her own, second-born son Isaac in an inferior position in relation to the inheritance, which traditionally went completely to the firstborn.

2. *Ishmael might be "mocking" Isaac as Hagar previously looked down on Sarah* when she had conceived a child prior to her aging mistress (Gen. 16:4). Like mother like son, Sarah might have concluded, leading Sarah for the second time to demand that the usurper be removed.

3. *Ishmael might be "playing" with himself,* in the sense of masturbating (according to the narrative, Ishmael would now be about seventeen years old). In this case, Sarah might be freshly aware of Ishmael's own budding fertility and wish him out of the picture before he fathers his own children in rivalry with Isaac's potential offspring.[2]

4. *Ishmael might be sexually "playing" with Isaac, either consensually or abusively.* In this case, Sarah's reaction is an expression of moral outrage at Ishmael's corrupting influence on her child.[3]

---

in which each story in its narrative context is an essential component, Gen. 20 reveals something about Abraham's character: he continues to struggle with trusting completely in YHWH, despite his experiences.

2. Steinberg (1993), 79–80 and n. 96.

3. Antonelli, 36. The issue would not be "homosexuality" as conceived today, but Ishmael breaking the chain of blessing that YHWH promised would come through Isaac's fertility.

Each of these possibilities reveals how Genesis recognizes the fragile complexity of relationship between one generation and the next. Although cultural contexts change (as they did from the time of the Genesis story world to the authors' world in the Babylonian Exile), the basic struggles remain the same across generations.

The presence of both sons threatens to drive a wedge between the parents. Sarah, fiercely protective of her only child, seeks to assure his future by any means necessary. Abraham, on the other hand, is caught between roles as husband and father. Unlike Sarah, he bears a bodily relationship with both boys. Thus, the text tells us that Sarah's demand "was powerfully evil in his eyes" (21:11). Yet Abraham, apparently unlike Sarah, turns once again to God for guidance. God tells him that *both* boys remain within God's promise of blessing. And so, trusting in the divine Word, Abraham takes his firstborn and the boy's mother and sends them into the barren desert to what seems like certain death.

Genesis powerfully underscores its universal conception of God, as the narrative turns away from the "heroes" to focus on Hagar's anguish as she prepares to see her son die. God is with Hagar and Ishmael as promised. Her own openness to God's voice strongly reinforces the message that the Creator cares for all people, not only those who will become "Israel." This perspective undermines imperial religion's sense of a foundational "holy us" and "unclean them." Whether against Babylon's religion or against the religion of the Second Temple's establishment elite,[4] Genesis insists that anyone and everyone can be part of "God's people." As Joseph Blenkinsopp writes:

> In his dealings with the indigenous peoples Abraham seems to have served for the Judeo-Babylonian immigrants as representative of a "soft" ideology in contrast to the "hard" ideology represented by the tradition of conquest and ethnic cleansing mandated by Deuteronomy and implemented in the book of Joshua.[5]

The Binding of Isaac (Gen. 22)

As far as Abraham is concerned, though, he has seen Ishmael for the last time and must now be consoled with his only remaining son. Yet the final and most difficult test remains to come: God's command to "Take your son, your only son, whom you love, Isaac, and go to the land of Moriah, and offer him there as a burnt offering on one of the mountains that I shall show you" (22:2). The story of the binding of Isaac is one of the Bible's most poignant and challenging stories of faith. We cannot here look at each detail, but we also cannot skip over its mysterious power. Why, generations of readers have asked, would God demand the death of the son who was the

---

4. See chapter 16.
5. Blenkinsopp (2009), 40–41.

long-awaited fruit of the very promise of God in which Abraham had been called repeatedly to trust completely? For some, the story is a scandal: it is impossible to get beyond the inscrutability of God's demand and to trust in a God who appears to call, even for a moment, for child sacrifice. For others, the Abraham saga would not be complete, nor would the Genesis message of what faith truly means, without this testing of an old man's trust.

The text clearly connects the story to YHWH's initial call to Abraham. Only in Genesis 12:1 and 22:2 in the entire Bible do we hear the explicit Hebrew command, "Go!" (*lekh-lekha*). First, it meant leaving behind the concentric circles of personal and social identity that made up Abram's previous life: "your land, your kindred, your father's house." Now, the concentric circles express the levels of love Abraham has for his remaining son: "your son, your only son, whom you love, Isaac." A rabbinic midrash expresses well the increasing intensity and specificity of the demand:

> Said He to him: TAKE, I PRAY THEE — I beg thee — THY SON. "Which son?" he asked. THINE ONLY SON, replied He. "But each is the only one of his mother?" — WHOM THOU LOVEST. — "Is there a limit to the affections?" "EVEN ISAAC"[6]

The midrash also notes something present in Hebrew but often lacking in translation: the divine Voice, upon close examination, issues not a demand but a *request*. There is a "please" ("I pray thee") in God's word that gives Abraham an option. And yet, once again, Abraham obeys without question or comment. This is even more shocking after we have heard him argue at length with YHWH over the fate of the theoretical presence of a handful of guilt-free residents in Sodom. Now, when it comes to the life and death of his beloved son, Abraham offers no argument or resistance.

Each detail of the journey of father and son to the mountain of Moriah enhances the story's power. Son is just as trusting as father. Isaac, who must by now be a teenager, walks faithfully at his father's side. The absence of a sacrificial animal whispers the true plan to him, but he doesn't balk. In fact, he appears to cooperate in his father's effort to bind him to the wood and prepare to slay him with the knife.[7] But, of course, child sacrifice was never part of the religion of the Creator. Rather, the story reveals a perfection of faith that is willing to give up all in obedience to the divine Word. The old man's response to the inexplicable request for child sacrifice will be paralleled in Luke's Gospel by its mirror image: a young girl's response to the inexplicable request for fatherless conception and birth. Neither Abraham nor Mary understands God's Word to them, yet both offer an unconditional "yes" despite their inability to explain the divine Word.

Readers sometimes overlook the final outcome of Genesis 22. Abraham speaks neither to Sarah nor Isaac again in the text. After all, what could

---

6. *Gen. Rab.* 55:7.
7. Wenham (1994a), 109.

have been Sarah's reaction to the event?[8] And what might the future relationship between father and son look like after this? The text answers neither
question, leaving readers simply to ponder possibilities.

The stories of Ishmael and Isaac in Genesis 21–22 form the beginning
of a response to the first question at the beginning of our chapter. God's
people are to raise their children with a deep and abiding trust in God's
available Word. No other Voice can be authoritative: not that of one's own
mind, one's spouse, one's surrounding culture, or one's ancestors. One's own
hopes and expectations for one's children can never allow oneself to refuse
to listen for God's guidance as the ultimate arbiter of what is "best."

Acquiring a Holding in the Land (Gen. 23)

The second question in our opening set presents itself in the two chapters that follow, Genesis 23–24. Many readers have skipped quickly over
the surprisingly detailed account of Abraham's negotiation with Ephron the
Hittite for a place to bury Abraham's dead wife. Meir Sternberg, though,
explicating the story in depth, shows that the key question is how YHWH
will fulfill the *promise of land*.[9] The narrative is the first occasion in which
God's people deal with "outsiders" within the Promised Land. The book of
Joshua[10] presents "sacred" violence as the means for land acquisition. The
response of Abraham, however, is not violence, but *monetary negotiation*.
He neither does battle with the Hittites nor attempts to sneak onto their
land without notice. Rather, despite the painful reality of Sarah's dead body
waiting in the hot sun, he patiently engages the Hittites on their own cultural
terms to buy a burial plot for his wife.

What he seeks and what he, after much struggle, obtains, is not only
a place to lay Sarah's body, but a "permanent holding" (*'achuzzat*) in the
Promised Land. The word is used previously only by God:

> And *I will give to you*, and to your offspring after you, the land where
> you are now an alien, all the land of Canaan, for a perpetual holding
> (*'achuzzat*); and I will be their God. (17:8)

It is used three times in the negotiations with Ephron (Gen. 23:4, 9,
20), then again, with explicit reference to these negotiations, when Jacob
instructs his sons on where to bury him (Gen. 49:29–32). It is used no less
than *thirteen times* in the presentation of the Jubilee law in Leviticus 25:10–
46.[11] A comparison of the use in Genesis with Leviticus reveals the range
of this aspect of God's promise to Israel. On the one hand, God's people

---

8. Zornberg (1996), 124–26, discusses several midrashic suggestions that link her
experience of the binding of Isaac with her own death.

9. Sternberg (1991), 55–57.

10. See chapter 12.

11. It is used a total of sixty-six times in the Hebrew Bible; thus, the Jubilee passage makes
up approximately 20 percent of the Bible's total usage of the term.

are not to be wanderers and wayfarers — like Cain — forever without a home. God's intention is for Israel to become a bountiful people in a place of their own. On the other hand, Leviticus provides divine guidance on how to prevent this promise from eroding because of God's people's own sin. One of the greatest security threats to God's people in the Land came not from outsiders like Canaanites or Babylonians, but from predatory actions of Israelites against one another. The prophets rail repeatedly in God's name against those among God's people who, for example "join house to house, who add field to field, until there is room for no one but you" (Isa. 5:8).

In the immediate situation, Abraham's abundance of silver appears to solve the problem. But two things about the "success" of the negotiations should make us pause. First, we hear *not a word from YHWH* that suggests that this is the divinely chosen means of acquiring a permanent foothold in the land. In fact, we note that YHWH's promise was to "give" the land to Abraham and his seed. How that was to happen, of course, was no more specified than how the old couple were to have a son. Second, *we never hear again of such a negotiation* for the land. It is hard for us today, where not an inch of the planet's surface isn't subject to personal or national claims of ownership, to envision a world where available land lay awaiting people's engagement, whether as temporary sojourners or as longer-term settlers. But there is no reason to think that warfare or purchase were the only possible means of fulfillment of the promise. Neither the acquired holding, the Machpelah[12] Cave, nor the seller, Ephron the Hittite, are ever mentioned outside the book of Genesis.

Finding a Wife for Isaac (Gen. 24)

Money is again the means in the story that follows in Genesis 24, as Abraham faces his final challenge: finding a suitable wife for Isaac. Genesis finessed the question of wives with the first families, conjuring Cain's wife up out of nowhere and leaving the other male descendants' wives unnamed. Now, though, the question is the center of the story. Throughout the Bible, the question of "foreign wives" will recur repeatedly, from the "explanation" for the downfall of Solomon (1 Kings 11) to the reason given in the book of Ezra for the Exile itself (Ezra 10:11ff.). The question, of course, is unavoidable. Given the widespread abhorrence of incest that the Bible shares (Lev. 18), it is obvious that future generations must look "outside" for partners. Abraham is the first character to face this challenge.

The rich old man devises a plan that he enjoins upon his servant to carry out as a sacred obligation:[13] to return to "the old country" and find a wife

---

12. Sternberg (1991), 228–29, discusses the wordplay involved in the meaning of the cave's name: "double" or "fold," indicating multiple layers beyond the surface, both of the cave and of the text.

13. The phrase by which Abraham binds his servant, "put your hand under my thigh (*yarekh*), involves "an oath at the source of life," Westermann (1995), 384. *Yarekh*

for Isaac there. Although YHWH has not said so explicitly, Abraham understands that Isaac's wife is not to come from the local peoples "among whom
I dwell" (24:3). Rather, Abraham (without divine guidance!) makes a calculated gamble. Having been gone now for decades, he pins his hope on his
"country and kindred," the very place and people from which YHWH first
called him. Neither the old man nor his trusted servant are fools. The servant seeks to clarify his commission. What if he can't find a suitable woman
whose family is willing to allow her to head off with a stranger to a foreign and distant land? Should he bring Isaac back "to the land from which
you came?" (24:5). No, Abraham replies: YHWH will guide your search,
as YHWH has guided my own journey. But just to make sure, the servant
embarks on his mission with a huge prize package: ten of his master's camels
and "all kinds of choice gifts from his master" (24:10).

The story unfolds delightfully, as a highly energetic shepherdess who happens to be one of Abraham's family members appears as if out of nowhere at
the well where the servant pauses.[14] The servant's observation of Rebekah's
acts of generous hospitality to a stranger show that she is truly worthy of the
son of a father who has himself exhibited such hospitality. When she identifies herself, the servant blesses YHWH, "the god of my master Abraham,"
for leading him as promised.

But, of course, the key question remains unanswered: will she return
with him? The answer depends on the will of her brother Laban, the man in
charge of the household. The encounter between Laban and the servant at
the well tells us all we need know about Abraham's "nation and kindred":

> As soon as he had seen the nose-ring, and the bracelets on his sister's
> arms, and when he heard the words of his sister Rebekah, "Thus the
> man spoke to me," he went to the man; and there he was, standing by
> the camels at the spring. He said, "Come in, O blessed of YHWH! Why
> do you stand outside when I have prepared the house and a place for
> the camels?" (24:30–31)

Abraham's servant evaluated YHWH's trustworthiness to provide blessing on the experience of abundant hospitality provided by Rebekah.[15]
Laban's eyes, though, are on the gold nose-ring and ten camels. Meir Sternberg comments on Laban's exclamation that the servant is "blessed of
YHWH: "Ignorant of antecedents and identities [22:17, 24:1], Laban twists
this charged phrase into homage to material blessing."[16] As Abraham experienced in his negotiation with Ephron the Hittite, people of the "religion of

---

euphemistically suggests "genitals," cf. Judg. 8:30. Thus, the oath is akin to a temporary
circumcision.

14. Although subtly anticipated by the word to Abraham about the fruitfulness of his kin,
Bethuel (22:23).

15. The question of the servant's own understanding of how YHWH's blessing "works"
is an interesting one, but beyond the scope of our consideration.

16. Sternberg (1985), 144.

empire" equate "the divine order" with *material* "blessing." Laban looks at the servant and sees a very rich master indeed. The ten camels are to him like a fleet of SUVs might be to us: abundance far beyond need or purpose other than to impress.[17] Laban embodies the "other" with which God's people must deal one way or another to survive across the generations. Abraham's strategy seems to be, "better the enemy one knows than one not known." Laban's motivations are no different from the Hittites but at least Abraham can here claim to be "family," where to Ephron he appeared as "a stranger and an alien residing among you" (23:4).

The servant understands the strategy well, and plays right into Laban's assumption as he presents his story of his mission. He begins:

> So he said, "I am Abraham's servant. YHWH has greatly blessed my master, and he has become wealthy; he has given him flocks and herds, silver and gold, male and female slaves, camels and donkeys. And Sarah my master's wife bore a son to my master when she was old; and he has given him all that he has. (24:35–36)

Like an investment consultant reviewing a portfolio with a prospective client, the servant lays out the "reality" to Laban: wealth beyond measure and it all goes to the son whose wife I am here seeking. As the servant continues with what is, by biblical standards, an astoundingly detailed recitation of what readers already know, we hear how he is "spinning" the story to make Laban's response inevitable. Fifteen verses later, Laban quickly agrees to the plan, but with a surprising "admission" of causality: "The thing is from YHWH" (24:50). "YHWH" to Laban is simply the god of Abraham, but the servant's tale sets up this "providential" conclusion. Will Laban now take up Abraham's religion?

This question is buried beneath the prizes: "And the servant brought out jewelry of silver and of gold, and garments, and gave them to Rebekah; he also gave to her brother and to her mother costly ornaments" (24:53). For the second time, Abraham has "succeeded" in moving toward fulfillment of YHWH's promise through the means of gold and silver. Again, though, we must ask: Does this "prove" that Rebekah is indeed the divinely approved choice? With this question hanging, she, like Abram, leaves her country, her kindred, and her father's house to become part of a new people, enabling another generation to grapple with God.

Two Nations Are in Your Womb (Gen. 25)

And grapple they do, right from the womb. Rebekah, like Sarah, is unable to have children, but YHWH hears Isaac's prayer and her womb is opened to receive the seed of promise. In that womb are twins, closing the circle around

---

17. Sarna (1989), 96, notes that a "wealthy man might acquire a few [camels] as a prestige symbol for ornamental rather than utilitarian purposes."

the question of brothers even tighter than with Ishmael and Isaac or if Isaac
and Rebekah were to have two sons in succession. The pregnancy is painful
for Rebekah and programmatic for God's people.[18] Her pain leads her to
"inquire of YHWH," the first woman to do so (25:22). We are not told
what form this "inquiry" took.[19] YHWH's response, however, says more
than appears at first glance:

> Two nations are in your womb, and two peoples born of you shall be
> divided; the one shall be stronger than the other, the elder shall serve
> the younger. (25:23)

It is no mystery to the audience of Genesis who the two nations are. The
text later makes it explicit: they are Israel and its neighbor Edom (25:30;
32:28; 36:1, 8). For now, the divine Word does not name the nations but
simply refers to them as "elder" and "younger" with one (unspecified) as
"stronger." This opens the possibility of a wider narrative and historical
context in which to hear the oracle. The Jacob cycle not only continues
the Genesis story on its own terms, but is also an implicit counter-story, or
at least counter-commentary, on the relationship between the two nations
Israel and Judah, who will be divided for most of their history.

The Word Rebekah receives promises an overturning of cultural practice
regarding *primogeniture,* the firstborn son's right of inheritance. We saw
this process beginning in the giving to the younger son Isaac of "all" that
his father had. But with sons of different mothers, the situation was far
different from that emerging from Rebekah's womb. Esau, the "hairy" one,
is the first to come out. His "younger" brother "came out, with his hand
gripping Esau's heel (*'aqev*); so he was named Jacob (*ya'aqov*)" (25:26).
Jacob is defined by his brother's heel, onto which he seeks to maintain a
tight grip. Jacob is born wrestling for priority with those who "came first,"
just as the Israelites will with the Canaanites (including Edom, e.g., Num.
20:14–21; 1 Sam. 14:47).

The boys grow up in a single verse that expresses the programmatic nature
of the brotherly struggle:

> When the boys grew up, Esau was a skillful hunter [*tsayid*], a man of
> the field [*sadeh*], while Jacob was a quiet man ['*ish tam*], living in tents
> ['*ohalim*]. Isaac loved Esau, because he was fond of game; but Rebekah
> loved Jacob. (25:27–28)

Each of the noted Hebrew words points forward or backward in the biblical story. Esau's hunting vocation echoes Nimrod's, using a term repeated
eight times in Genesis 27 lest readers miss the connection. His place in the
"field" echoes both the curse on the man (3:18) and, more ominously, the

---

18. Cf. Fishbane (1998), 45.

19. Texts that are certainly composed earlier than Genesis suggest a human intermediary
as "seer" or "medium" (1 Sam. 9:9; 28:7; 1 Kings 14:5), but Genesis does not indicate the
means of Rebekah's engagement with YHWH.

place where Cain took his brother Abel to kill him (4:8). Jacob's characterization as a man who is *tam* is more ambiguous.[20] Robert Alter notes that "all the other biblical occurrences of the word...refer to innocence or moral integrity...the choice of an epithet suggesting innocence as an introduction to the episode is bound to give us pause."[21] Jacob immediately will be shown to be anything but innocent. Finally, his dwelling place in "tents" makes him not only a male who occupies female space,[22] but also one who anticipates the rallying call of his eventual namesakes as they announce their secession from the United Monarchy: " 'To your tents, O Israel! Look now to your own house, O David.' So Israel went away to their tents" (1 Kings 12:16).

Thus, we see from the outset that the story of Esau's and Jacob's wrestling with each other and Jacob's with YHWH is about much more than two individuals. Similarly, we hear in Jacob's tricky wresting of the "birthright" (*bekhorah*) from his famished brother more than what first appears. It is no accident that the Hebrew for "birthright" (i.e., the right of primogeniture) is a scrambling of consonants of the word for "blessing" (*berakhah*). We already know from the divine oracle that the birthright means nothing: the elder will serve the younger. Jacob will live not only to regret this "victory," but will desperately seek to "return" what he has taken. Both the taking and return are part of Genesis's parody on success-seeking apart from obedience to the Creator. Jacob has as yet no direct experience of YHWH. His cleverness makes a fool and an enemy out of his brother and the consequences chase him for decades.

The section ends with the narrative note that Esau married two Hittite women — recalling the Hittites with whom Abraham negotiated for Sarah's burial plot — which "made life bitter for Isaac and Rebekah" (26:34). No explanation is given for why Esau would find wives for himself without the consent of his parents or why he chose them from among the Hittites. But his action provides the basis for the only agreement between the parents about their children, and a plan emerges for a better outcome for the younger brother.

Learning to Be a Trickster (Gen. 27–29)

The story of Jacob tricking his father into blessing him under the disguise of his brother, Esau, appears to be a plot between Jacob and his mother against his father. Like all of Genesis, interpretation is rewarded by attention beyond the story's surface. For our purposes, let's consider one aspect often overlooked. The premise of the apparent plot is that Rebekah enlists her

---

20. The word can also mean "complete" or "perfect." Wenham (1987), 177.
21. Alter (1983), 43.
22. Recall Sarah's place in the encounter with the visitors, 18:6, 9, 10, and the discussion in chapter 3.

favored son in a conspiracy that takes advantage of Isaac's dim eyes in order to procure for Jacob the blessing (do the parents know that Jacob has already tricked Esau out of the birthright?). It presupposes a process of transmitting blessing by "magic words," very unlike the perspective in Genesis so far. This suspicious premise might begin to plant a seed of doubt about who is tricking whom and why. Do Isaac and Rebekah really believe that blessing can be passed on by deceit? Perhaps. But other clues in the story seem to reinforce the likelihood that the trickery is oriented another direction and for a different purpose.

Consider Jacob's reticence to go along with his mother's plot (27:11–12). He well knows that he is "smooth" (*halaq*) while Esau is hairy. The self-description conveys the same double entendre in Hebrew as in English: Jacob's "smoothness" is both a matter of absence of body hair and a way of being in the world. His concern is that Isaac knows that Jacob has learned well from his mother the art of using words and situations to overcome power disadvantages. This "smoothness" will appear again in years to come as he engages a master of smoothness, his uncle Laban. So, Jacob wonders, won't my father both know the difference in skin but also the difference in character between my brother and me?

His mother's assurance expresses her willingness to "Let your curse be on me, my son; only obey [*shema'*] my voice [lit, "sound," *qol*], and go" (27:13). Rebekah commands Jacob to listen not to YHWH's voice, but to hers. Both key Hebrew words highlight the shocking imperative. Consider, for example:

> They heard the sound [*qol*] of YHWH God walking in the garden at the time of the evening breeze.   (Gen. 3:8; cf. 1 Kings 19:12)

> Because you have listened [*shama'ta*] to the voice [*qol*] of your wife...
> (Gen. 3:17)

> Hear [*shema'*] O Israel: YHWH is our God, YHWH alone.
> (Deut. 6:4)[23]

The exilic authors of Genesis certainly knew Deuteronomy. The verse known simply as the *Shema* is especially foreboding, read against Rebekah's word as if directly to Jacob. But not yet knowing YHWH's voice as did Adam and Eve, Jacob obeys his mother.

As the ruse unfolds, more clues undermine our surface understanding. Through all five bodily senses, Jacob engages his old father. The first is, fittingly enough, the sound of a son's voice. Immediately, Isaac is suspicious. Is the game over already? After all, we are told that the old man is dim of sight, but not hard of hearing! What will Jacob do under this pressure for which his mother has not specifically prepared him? His response takes us to the test's next stage: he lies directly to Isaac's face and says he is Esau.

---

23. Cf. 4:23; 16:2; 21:12; 22:18; 26:5; 30:6.

But shouldn't this further arouse our suspicions? As the story continues, the initial premise seems to collapse more completely at each turn. Could Isaac not distinguish his beloved son's arms from goat skin? Could he not taste the difference between the wild game around which he and Esau bond and the goat stew Rebekah provides via Jacob?[24] After Isaac gives Jacob the blessing, in comes Esau with the wild game. And when Isaac "learns" that this is truly Esau, we are told that Isaac "trembled with a great trembling" (27:33).[25] The jig is up, but too late. Despite Esau's bitter tears, there is only one paternal blessing, and Jacob now has it.

The story ends with Esau understandably hating Jacob, and Rebekah making hasty plans to get Jacob away before Esau succeeds in "consoling himself" by killing his brother (27:42). Noting to Isaac how she finds her life "sickening"[26] because of Esau's Hittite wives, she easily convinces Isaac to send Jacob back to Laban to find a suitable wife. Isaac sends him away with this word:

> May God Almighty bless you and make you fruitful and numerous, that you may become a company of peoples. May he give to you the blessing of Abraham, to you and to your offspring with you, so that you may take possession of the land where you now live as an alien — land that God gave to Abraham. (28:3–4)

We learn only now that Isaac and Rebekah *know* which blessing really counts: the "blessing of Abraham" that comes from "God Almighty" (*'El Shaddai*).[27] Are we not surprised that Isaac, apparently having been so deceitfully tricked by Jacob, blesses him so graciously? Yet bless him Isaac does, and off Jacob goes to encounter his wily uncle, whom Rebekah knows so well.

Now let's go back and consider all the clues. On the surface, Rebekah's plot leads her to put her beloved son at risk of fratricide and to send him away for his own protection. Somehow he succeeded in tricking the old man but at a high price. But could not Rebekah easily have anticipated what effect her plot would have on Esau? She may have favored Jacob, but Esau was also her son, the other half of the womb wrestling team.

---

24. Both the birthright and blessing transfers involve food illusions. Esau comes in from the hunt and demands some of what appears to him to be Jacob's simmering meat stew, as indicated by his breathless "out of the red, the red," (*min-ha'adom ha'adom hazzeh*) suggesting blood (*dam*). Of course, it is nothing but boiled lentils.

25. Isaac's reaction, if sincere as the text seems to imply, is the strongest — if only — point in favor of the traditional reading of the story as a test of Jacob about which Isaac knows nothing. Bledstein, 289, suggests that Isaac's emotion is a result of being confronted directly with Esau's grief.

26. *BDB* 19.105 notes that the Hebrew *qatsitti* is much stronger than the frequent translation "weary," and connotes "loathing, abhorrence, sickening dread." Cf. Exod. 1:12.

27. Cf. 17:1; 35:11; 43:14; 48:3; and Exod. 6:3, recalling the Genesis references.

What if we turn the story completely over in light of the pain caused by Esau's Hittite wives that initiates the scheming?[28] What if the trick isn't on Isaac by conspirators Jacob and Rebekah, but *on Jacob* by the conspiracy of his parents? On this reading, all the suspicious details fall into place. The purpose of the parents' plot is to see if Jacob is really "smooth" enough to take on his wily old uncle on Laban's home court. Rebekah sets up Jacob to be impaled on his own voice, and then Isaac follows with the accusing question. Will Jacob back down or will he do what needs to be done? Passing the first test by lying directly to his father, Jacob keeps his cool and continues through the rest of the sensory checks on his identity. On this reading, the blessing he gets which "belongs" to Esau is as meaningless as the birthright and both parents know it. From before the boys' birth, Rebekah has known that it was the divine will for the elder to serve the younger. Her plot with Isaac, like Abraham's use of his gold and silver earlier, is an effort to obtain for Jacob not his *father's* blessing, but the "blessing of Abraham" which comes only from God.

Again, hearing the story this way makes sense of why Rebekah seems unperturbed by Esau's hatred and Jacob's imminent departure: *getting Jacob back to Laban to find a suitable wife was the purpose of the plot all along.* With Esau fuming, Jacob has no choice but to embark on a perilous journey to a land he's never seen to deal with a crafty old man. Finally, this explains why Isaac so willingly blesses his trickster son. Rather than being dismayed at Jacob's deceitfulness, he blesses him precisely because he has shown himself capable of taking on Laban.

In the larger narrative, this story continues to explore the means of living out the Genesis premise that those seeking to live among people who practice a different religion must have a strategic plan. Staying within the ambit of YHWH's promise, they must develop ways to maneuver safely toward the goal to which God leads them. But just as with Abraham's efforts to acquire land and a wife with silver and gold, is this kind of intrafamily deceit what YHWH had in mind?

The struggle would certainly resonate with exiles living among worldly wise Babylonians. Like Jacob, their parents would teach them how to find the path away from the "hunter" (Nimrod-Laban / Esau) by evading, rather than confronting, his violence and tendency toward domination. Further

---

28. This interpretation was first suggested to me by Bledstein's essay. She suggests further (293–94) the parallels with the succession of David, with these matching pairs: Isaac/David, Esau/Adonijah, Rebekah/Bathsheba-Nathan, and Jacob/Solomon. Much of the Genesis story can be reread against the "background" of the monarchy as criticism of the Jerusalem-centered imperial religion expressed in the Deuteronomistic History. Such an exploration is beyond the scope of what we can consider here. However, for other examples, consider the "hairy" Esau/Absalom and their broken relationships with their fathers. Also consider the complex allegorical relationships between Jacob, Laban, and the daughters/wives (Leah/Rachel) and the monarchy, with Rachel as Israel and Leah as Judah (of whom she is the mother). For instance, Jacob's seven years married to Leah correspond to David's seven-year reign over Judah, before the "second marriage"; the renunciation formula (Gen. 31:14) by which the daughters leave Laban — who represents the monarchy itself — parallels that at 1 Kings 12:16.

clarification of how "means" and "ends" correspond must await insight gained later in the biblical story.[29]

Of course, Jacob will discover the hard way that Laban is quite capable of taking advantage of his nephew's lack of experience as a trickster. The deal Jacob thinks he's made to work seven years for his uncle for the reward of the beloved Rachel backfires when he arises from the marriage bed to discover not Rachel but her sister Leah (29:25). When he confronts Laban, the answer is telling, not only to Jacob but to the readers of Genesis: "This is not done in our place — giving the younger before the firstborn" (29:26). Jacob is smooth, but he becomes trapped by his unfamiliarity with how things are done in "the old country." What is "not done" is not only receiving Rachel before Leah, but also Jacob becoming stronger than Esau. From the wider narrative perspective, it contrasts with the divine project of making the "younger" people Israel more blessed than the "older" people of both Babylon and Canaan.[30] Laban and the Babylonians are committed to an immutable social structure, in which rigid rules determine a sharply defined hierarchy of social status and power.

Laban finagles fourteen more years of work from his nephew before Jacob can take his two wives and children away. A pair of experiences at sunset and sunrise punctuate Jacob's long journey back from Haran. As he set out, he came to "the place [*maqom*] and stayed there for the night, because the sun had set" (28:11). The word *maqom* is used six times in 28:11–19.[31] The Hebrew word is just as ordinary as the English "place," which is the point of the unfolding scene. Jacob dreams his famous vision of a "ramp"[32] reaching heaven, with angels of God "ascending and descending on it." Jacob's dream recalls what the Babel people intended to build: a tower with its top in the heaven. His dream includes the first encounter the young man has had with "YHWH, the God of Abraham your father and the God of Isaac." YHWH's Word provides the blessing that Isaac prayed his son would gain on the journey: the promise of land, abundant fertility, and YHWH's abiding presence with him "wherever you go" (28:14).

Upon awakening, Jacob proclaims "without doubt,[33] YHWH is in this *place* and I didn't know it!" He continues: "How awesome is this *place!* This is none other than the house of God, and this is the gate of heaven" (28:17). For Genesis, this scene is yet another parody on the Babylonian religion.

---

29. Cf. Jesus' word at Matt. 10:16: "See, I am sending you out like sheep into the midst of wolves; so be wise as serpents and innocent as doves."

30. Of course, the subtle claim of Genesis, by situating its (later) narrative "at the beginning," is that it is "really" the "older" story to empire's "younger" religion. Cf. the struggle in the Hellenistic period to provide "antiquity" to newer ways of being, p. 296.

31. Three times in v. 11, then once each in vv. 16, 17, and 19.

32. Hebrew *sullam,* only here in the Bible, is from the verb meaning, "to heap up," Westermann (1995), 454. Sarna (1989), 198, suggests also a link with Akkadian *simmiltu,* meaning "steps," often used in construction of Babylonian towers and ziggurats.

33. BDB 1.414 notes that Hebrew *'akhen* is very strong as used here, "expressing the reality, in opposition to what had been wrongly imagined."

Recall that Akkadian for "Babylon" means "gate of the gods." According to the religion of empire, divine power and presence reside in *the city*. But Jacob learns, to his evident surprise, that the very One whom his grandfather had encountered in various places could be experienced in *this* place. And, of course, there is nothing about the "place" at all that is important. Jacob's experience was *internal,* in a dream, and had nothing at all to do with the geographic "place."[34] One can experience and know YHWH, Creator of heaven and earth, anywhere and everywhere people are open to receive the Presence. The "this place" readers are expected to understand the text to refer to — even if Jacob himself doesn't yet understand — is not a specific earthly location, but *inside Jacob.*[35] It is Jacob's situation, away from home and in a vulnerable spot, which leads him to be open to the One who was within him all along and now promises to continue to be "wherever you go."

The story, however, concludes ironically. After this powerful experience of YHWH and confirmation of the divine promise, Jacob makes a vow that reveals his trust in YHWH to be far from that of his grandfather:

> *If* God will be with me, *and* will keep me in this way that I go, *and* will give me bread to eat *and* clothing to wear, so that I come again to my father's house in peace, *then* YHWH shall be my God, and this stone, which I have set up for a pillar, shall be God's house;[36] and of all that you give me I will surely give one-tenth to you. (28:20–21)

Jacob puts an astounding series of qualifiers on his commitment to make YHWH his God. His vow says, "*if* God does everything *that I want, I will let* YHWH be my God." It expresses the people Israel's ambivalent attitude throughout their journey with YHWH. Despite the clarity of promise and constancy of YHWH's presence, Israel more often than not failed fully to embody the covenant. Genesis roots this struggle in the eponymous ancestor's own conditional trust.

Wrestling with God and Humans (Gen. 31–32)

As noted, Jacob's journey leads to twenty-one years of servitude under Laban. When he finally escapes (after out-tricking the old trickster himself),

---

34. However, the story's conclusion that Jacob "called the place Bethel" anticipates in the wider biblical narrative — while recalling for Genesis's audience — that "Bethel" was one of the two sites established by Jeroboam as worship locations in place of Jerusalem, and "triumphantly" destroyed by Josiah (1 Kings 12:29–33; 2 Kings 23:15–19. See discussion in chapters 10 and 12.

35. For the audience in and after the Exile, this claim challenges head-on the Deuteronomic tradition continued in Ezra-Nehemiah that *Jerusalem* is "the place" where YHWH is to be encountered; see, e.g., Deut. 12:5–26; Ezra 6:3; Neh. 1:8–9. This theme is discussed in chapter 16. The religion of creation will continue to challenge this sense of a specific "holy place" into the New Testament.

36. Note that Jacob's vow equates "this [single, unhewn] stone" with "the house of God," certainly meant to parody the numerous hewn stones needed to construct the Jerusalem temple (1 Kings 5:17; cf. 2 Kings 12:13; 22:6).

his thoughts return to Esau. Seeking to make peace with his brother after all these years, he sends a messenger, who returns with the ominous word that Esau is "coming to meet you, and four hundred men are with him" (32:6). Jacob is sure this means a private army accompanies Esau. Jacob, "greatly afraid and distressed," divides his company in two and prays hard for YHWH's protection. He seeks to appease Esau by sending three separate advance groups laden with presents. Finally, he sends his family ahead across the Jabbok River and "was left alone" (32:24). And in this state — the mirror image of the one that led to his first experience of YHWH (then fleeing Esau, now approaching him) — Jacob again encounters the divine. This time it is not in a dream, but in "a man" who "wrestled with him until daybreak." When the wrestler sees that he cannot "prevail against Jacob," he strikes him on the upper thigh.[37] The identity of the wrestler threatens to be revealed by the breaking of day, but Jacob insists on being blessed by the stranger. The response is to ask Jacob's name and then to change it to "Israel," "for you have striven with God and with humans, and have prevailed."[38] Jacob then asks the visitor's name but is rebuffed. His proclamation, parallel to his response to the vision in "the place," interprets the encounter: "I have seen God face to face, and yet my life is preserved."

How does Jacob reach this conclusion? His first sense is that "a man" was wrestling with him. And the wrestler tells him that he has striven with God *and with* humans." Who was this wrestler really?

As the story began, Jacob was alone in fear of his brother Esau. After the night wrestling, the "sun rose upon him" as he saw Esau coming toward him. The sunset at the beginning of his journey joins with this dawning of a new day, ending Jacob's "dark night of the soul" and resulting in peace between the two brothers at last. Jacob comes upon Esau and seeks eagerly to "return" the birthright, but Esau refuses, saying "I have enough, my brother; keep what you have for yourself" (33:9). Jacob responds: "No, please; if I find favor with you, then accept my present from my hand; for truly *to see your face is like seeing the face of God. . . .* " Jacob's wrestling has been with God *and with* Esau. As Michael Fishbane says, "The wrestling scene thus appears to be part of Jacob's dream-work, whereby he 'works through' the anticipated struggle with Esau by fusing it with earlier wrestlings with his brother — in the womb and at birth."[39] In other words, in his prayerful solitude, Jacob discovers finally that neither the birthright nor father's blessing mean anything, any more than one "place" is more sacred than another. YHWH has been with both Jacob and Esau; the system of primogeniture

---

37. *yarekh*, recalling 24:2, 9, the place where Abraham's servant placed his hand as a sign of commitment to do his master's will. Here as there, it carries sexual overtones. Sarna notes that the blow does not cause a dislocation as some translations suggest, as that would prevent Jacob from being able to walk at all. Sarna (1989), 227.

38. Compare Gen. 30:8: "Then Rachel said, 'With mighty wrestlings I have wrestled with my sister, and have prevailed.' "

39. Fishbane (1998), 52–53.

itself, along with the social stratification it undergirds and the religion of empire that legitimate both, are shown to be stumbling blocks to the true blessing, which is there for the receiving in creation itself. If "place" was key to Jacob's first encounter with YHWH, "face" is here. The Hebrew *paneh* is used nine times in Genesis 32:17–31 and six times more in 33:10–18. It is in the face-to-face encounter with God — in contrast with Nimrod's "face off" with YHWH — and human beings that one sees that the blessing is not finite and hence in need of controlling, but is abundantly available for all people in all places. Only when Jacob can *see God's own face in the face of his brother Esau* will he be able to face him in peace. This understanding leads directly to the Christian sense of *incarnation,* where people see God's "face" not only in Jesus, but in all who embody the Risen Christ.[40]

Jacob manages both to get away from Laban and safely past his brother. But his journey is not quite complete. YHWH has told him to "return to the land of your ancestors and to your kindred, and I will be with you" (31:3). Jacob will attempt to settle before the journey is complete and will have to learn the hard way the consequences of deciding where to settle without listening for YHWH's guiding Word.

---

40. E.g., John 13:20; see also Matt. 25:31–46.

Chapter Seven

The Price of Settling Too Soon

One of the great challenges for the people Israel throughout their biblical journey was deciding on *the place to settle.* Lot settled in the well-watered Jordan plain and became entrapped in Sodom's evil. Abram listened to YHWH's voice and continued on the move. YHWH's promise, though, included the gift of land. God did not intend, according to Genesis and indeed all of the Hebrew Bible, for Israel to remain forever homeless. The great tension in YHWH's gift of Canaan to Israel was that Israel was the "younger brother." Various peoples already occupied the land upon Abram's arrival (13:7).[1] How would Israel know when and where to claim the fulfillment of the promise of a permanent "place"?

We begin with the story of Jacob's attempt to settle after his departure from Esau.

> But Jacob journeyed to Succoth, and built himself a house [*vayyiven lo bayit*], and made booths for his cattle; therefore the place is called Succoth. Jacob came safely to the city of Shechem,[2] which is in the land of Canaan, on his way from Paddan-aram; and he camped before the city. And from the sons of Hamor, Shechem's father, he bought for one hundred[3] the plot of land on which he had pitched his tent. (33:17–19)

Without any apparent direction from YHWH, Jacob, understandably drained after his life-and-death confrontation with his brother, decides it is time to end the journey. It is clear that this is not simply a rest before completing the return route home to Isaac and Rebekah. He not only builds a house for himself and booths for his animals; he purchases a local plot of land. The only tension left between settling and journeying is that between the "house" and the "tent," which he is said to pitch.

Let's look at the narrative and geographic context to understand Jacob's choice. Jacob began his journey from Beer-sheba, the home established by

---

1. See also the discussion about the historical relationship between "Israel" and the land in chapter 13.

2. The Hebrew text translated "safely to the city of Shechem," *shalem 'ir shechem,* is ambiguous, and can also be translated "Salem, city of Shechem." Either way, there is a hidden irony in Jacob's "safe" arrival in Shechem. Recall that Abram and Sarai passed through, but did not settle there (12:6–9). "Later," it is the site of Joshua's covenant renewal ceremony (Josh. 24), Rehoboam's enthronement, and Israel's rebellion from his rule (1 Kings 12).

3. The Hebrew text is unclear regarding the monetary units involved.

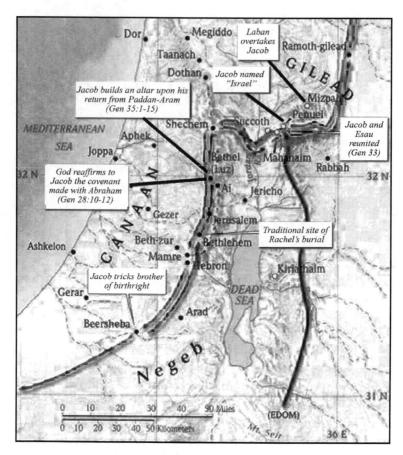

Map 3: Jacob's Journey

Isaac and Rebekah (26:23, 33; 28:10). After his dream, which revealed the presence of YHWH in "this place," he vowed to make YHWH his God if he was brought "in shalom" to his "father's house," i.e., back to Beer-sheba. After the episode we are about to examine (Gen. 34), God tells Jacob to arise and "go up to Bethel and settle there" (35:1). Jacob obeys the divine Voice and goes to Bethel, but then after Rachel dies giving birth to Benjamin, "Israel journeyed on, and pitched his tent beyond the tower of Eder" and lived in that land (35:21). Jacob then returned to Mamre[4] for a last visit

---

4. Mamre is associated here with both the names "Kiriath-arba" and "Hebron"; cf. 13:18; 23:19 (Hebron only). Hebron play an important role in the Deuteronomistic History, in connection with "sacred violence" (Joshua 10), as the inheritance of Caleb, the only survivor of the Exodus (Josh. 14:13–15), as David's settlement place and where his royal reign was first established (2 Sam. 2–5), and as the site of Absalom's rebellion (2 Sam. 15). However, Mamre is not mentioned anywhere in the Bible outside Genesis. As discussed in Part II, the Deuteronomistic History was largely written before the Exile and hence, before Genesis. Does

with the dying Isaac; Esau joins him in burying their father (35:27–29). We next hear the vague, "Jacob settled in the land where his father had lived as an alien, the land of Canaan" (37:1). As the story moves from Jacob to Joseph, the geographic focus shifts to Egypt. It is not until 46:1 that we finally hear that the path has come full circle: "When Israel set out on his journey with all that he had and came to Beer-sheba, he offered sacrifices to the God of his father Isaac."

The point is that with Jacob's settlement in Succoth, near the city of Shechem, he has not completed the journey home. The issue is not legalistic obedience, but listening to YHWH's Word rather than determining for oneself the choice that will truly lead to *shalom*: true "peace" and "safety." YHWH desires people to live in peace and security, but the means and outcome of YHWH's way are the opposite of the "peace and security" which imperial religion offers.[5] Settling in Beer-sheba would mean living away from the most desirable and, hence, most fought over, land in Canaan. Settling in Shechem, on the other hand, will place Jacob in a land ruled by kings in which there is no real *shalom*.

Furthermore, we are told that Jacob "built" a house. Genesis consistently contrasts building projects that respond to the Creator and those that arise from merely human initiative. They are listed in Table 3. Jacob's building project, like those of Cain, Nimrod, and the humans in Shinar, sought to settle his family into a way of life of his own determination. Despite his experiences of YHWH's presence and direction, he has not yet come to complete trust. Jacob, like so many, learns the consequences the hard way.

Some have portrayed the story in Genesis 34 in romantic terms as a love affair between Dinah and Shechem[6] rejected by Dinah's brothers.[7] However, read within its narrative context, it is anything but romantic. Jacob's daughter "went out to visit the women of the land" and was seized and raped by a local prince. There is no ambiguity in the text: Shechem's action is that of a man whose social status "entitles" him to take what he wants. In 1 Samuel, this is "what kings do": they "take your daughters" for their own purposes (1 Sam. 8:13).[8]

Genesis designate Mamre-as-Hebron to comment on Hebron's traditional connection with the Davidic monarchy? The use of the precise phrase in Genesis and Joshua, "Kiriath-arba, that is, Hebron," makes the issue more complex (Gen. 23:2; 35:27; cf. 23:19; Josh. 15:13, 54; 20:7; 21:11). A later editor probably harmonized the texts as part of the construction of the longer narrative, Gen.–2 Kings.

5. Compare 1 Thess. 5:3, where Paul tells the young church, "When they say, 'There is peace and security,' then sudden destruction will come upon them, as labor pains come upon a pregnant woman, and there will be no escape!" In this situation, "peace and security" is the voice of the Roman imperial slogan, *pax et securitas*, Koester (1997), 161–62; see the discussion contrasting the Pax Christi with the Pax Romana throughout Part IV.

6. The eponymous connection between Shechem as son and city recalls Cain's son and city, Enoch (Gen. 4:17), and the violent domination endemic to city life.

7. E.g., Diamant.

8. See p. 191; see also O'Brien.

Table 3: "Building" (Hebrew, *bnh*) in Genesis

Passage	Builder	What Is Built
2:22	God	Humans
4:17	Cain	A city
8:20	Noah	An altar to YHWH
10:11	Nimrod	Nineveh
11:4, 5, 8	Humans	Tower of Babel
12:7–8; 13:18	Abraham	Altars to YHWH
16:2	Sarai/Hagar	Sarai (as a mother)
22:9	Abraham	The altar of sacrifice
26:25	Isaac	An altar to YHWH
30:3	Rachel	Children (family)
33:17	Jacob	A house
35:7	Jacob	An altar to God

The tension is not between a supposed love affair between Dinah and Shechem on one hand and family resistance on the other, but rather, *whether an offer of marriage can excuse rape.* Shechem's father, Hamor, proposes to Jacob and his sons that a marriage alliance join the two peoples (34:9–10). The question of where to find wives continues to challenge the identity of God's people. The proffered solution is to blend two peoples into one.

The seemingly peaceful proposal, though, is not acceptable to Jacob's sons, especially Simeon and Levi, children of Leah (29:33–34) and full brothers of Dinah (30:21). They pretend to go along with the offer by making the "simple" request that the Shechemites be circumcised as a token of good will. The wording of Shechem's proposal to the people of the city reveals where the emphasis lies:

> These people are friendly with us; let them live in the land and trade in it, for the land is large enough for them; let us take their daughters in marriage, and let us give them our daughters. Only on this condition will they agree to live among us, to become one people: that every male among us be circumcised as they are circumcised. Will not their livestock, their property, and all their animals be ours? Only let us agree with them, and they will live among us. (Gen. 34:21–23).

In other words, for a moment of physical pain, all their wealth will be ours! As with Laban, so with the Shechemites: the possibility of added wealth overcomes all other barriers to intermarriage. Simeon and Levi, of course, counted on this urban perspective, as the grim outcome to the "alliance" reveals:

> On the third day, when they were still in pain, two of the sons of Jacob,
> Simeon and Levi, Dinah's brothers, took their swords and came against
> the city unawares, and killed all the males. They killed Hamor and his
> son Shechem with the sword, and took Dinah out of Shechem's house,
> and went away. And the other sons of Jacob came upon the slain, and
> plundered the city, because their sister had been defiled. They took their
> flocks and their herds, their donkeys, and whatever was in the city and
> in the field. All their wealth, all their little ones and their wives, all that
> was in the houses, they captured and made their prey. (34:25–29)

The revenge is as comprehensive as it is grisly. The Genesis authors knew
that the extent of murder and plunder would lead readers to question the
proportionality of crime and punishment. Does one rape justify mass murder
and destruction? Certainly "later" biblical law — already familiar to the
Genesis audience — said a clear "no," as we hear in Deuteronomy:

> If a man meets a virgin who is not engaged, and seizes her and lies with
> her, and they are caught in the act, the man who lay with her shall give
> fifty shekels of silver to the young woman's father, and she shall become
> his wife. (Deut. 22:28–29)

While our own sensibilities might well tilt toward a punishment greater
than a mere fine, the action taken by Simeon and Levi is meant to shock the
audience's conscience.

The final verses reveal that Jacob's *premature settling has caused the entire
situation.* Jacob tells the brothers that their action "had made my name stink
to the inhabitants of the land" (34:30). But the brothers counter, "Should
our sister be treated like a whore?" Beyond the immediate question of pro-
portional punishment lies the deeper issue: the series of bad choices that
occur because of an initial failure to listen to YHWH's Voice. The story
parallels the plight of Lot after he chose to settle near Sodom. The lesson
for the Genesis audience in exile and after is clear: only when guided by the
Creator's Voice will we be led to settle in a place of true safety and peace.

This question continues to resonate when Jacob's youngest son, Joseph,
ends up sold into slavery by his jealous older brothers and the entire family
ends up settling in the land of Goshen in Egypt (45:10).[9] Joseph tells his

---

9. The Joseph story was probably written at a later period, perhaps during the era of
Ptolemaic (Egyptian) rule over Judah. As such, it stands against the Jerusalem elite's collaboration with the Ptolemies to maintain "peace." See discussion in chapter 17. The saga may
also express an allegorical reflection on the David/Solomon story, with Jacob as David (the
patriarch whose sons fall against one another and whose daughter is raped), Joseph as Solomon
(the son of the favored wife (Rachel, Bathsheba), who becomes the strong holder of imperial
power; both have dreams of power and rule over or instead of their elder brothers; both marry
foreign wives, and their excesses of power lead Israel into slavery in foreign lands); Reuben as
Absalom, (both seek to usurp their father's power by lying with the father's concubines), Tamar
as "herself" (in both cases the subject of improper male sexual power over familial women)
and the other brothers as the Israelites (pulled into the orbit of royal authority in Jerusalem).
See chapter 9 for the unraveling of the David/Solomon narrative.

brothers upon their reunion that "it was not you who sent me here, but
God; he has made me a father to Pharaoh, and lord of all his house and
ruler over all the land of Egypt" (45:8) and, then sends them to Jacob with
the invitation to settle in Egypt. But despite what seems to be the happy
ending to the long saga of Joseph's rise to power in Egypt and his father's
joy at discovering his son still alive, readers should not be too quick to
assume that Joseph the theologian has accurately interpreted the signs of
the times.

The young man who began as a dreamer and royal dream interpreter has
now spent many years as an official at Pharaoh's court. In fact, in a moment
of high irony, Genesis tells us that Joseph's rise resulted from his teaching
Pharaoh how to profit off famine (Gen. 41:25–46)![10] Joseph marries an
Egyptian wife and lives as an Egyptian in everything except the Egyptians'
racist refusal to share meals with him (43:32). This should serve as a warning
that sharing royal power is not the same as truly becoming one with the
"other," but Joseph doesn't seem to notice this "small" distinction.[11] By
the reunion, we must ask whether Joseph remains truly in relationship with
YHWH, or whether he, like many "royal theologians" over the centuries,
interprets events according to an imperial sense of the "divine order."

This subversive interpretation of Joseph's role as YHWH's representative
is reinforced by the passage that follows in Genesis 47:13–26. At first glance,
it seems to be an addendum tacked onto an otherwise carefully constructed
tale. It comes immediately after the narrative notice that "Joseph settled his
father and his brothers, and granted them a holding in the land of Egypt, in
the best part of the land, in the land of Rameses, as Pharaoh had instructed"
(47:11). As *Pharaoh*, not YHWH, had instructed. Are we to imagine that
Pharaoh's will and YHWH's are one and the same? If we are inclined in this
direction, Genesis immediately encourages us to reconsider. The passage
expresses forcefully and clearly the nature of Joseph's power in Egypt and
is worth a full hearing:

> Now there was no food in all the land, for the famine was very severe.
> The land of Egypt and the land of Canaan languished because of the
> famine. Joseph collected all the money to be found in the land of Egypt
> and in the land of Canaan, in exchange for the grain that they bought;
> and Joseph brought the money into Pharaoh's house. When the money
> from the land of Egypt and from the land of Canaan was spent, all the
> Egyptians came to Joseph, and said, "Give us food! Why should we

10. Morgenstern, 23, observes that Pharaoh's internal dream narrative places Pharaoh "on
the Nile" (41:1) — as opposed to the story he tells Joseph, "on *the banks* of the Nile" (41:17).
Thus, she notes, "For Pharaoh, the major question to be answered concerns the stability and the
extent of his own power: 'Will I be dominant over the Nile — Egypt's economic and religious
life-force — or, alternatively will the Nile dominate me?'" Joseph's "answer" makes Pharaoh
the master — for now.

11. Note the parallel in how the Sodomites continued to see Lot as an "alien" after his
many years of residence in the city, Gen. 19:9.

die before your eyes? For our money is gone." And Joseph answered, "Give me your livestock, and I will give you food in exchange for your livestock, if your money is gone." So they brought their livestock to Joseph; and Joseph gave them food in exchange for the horses, the flocks, the herds, and the donkeys. That year he supplied them with food in exchange for all their livestock. When that year was ended, they came to him the following year, and said to him, "We can not hide from my lord that our money is all spent; and the herds of cattle are my lord's. There is nothing left in the sight of my lord but our bodies and our lands. Shall we die before your eyes, both we and our land? Buy us and our land in exchange for food. We with our land will become slaves to Pharaoh; just give us seed, so that we may live and not die, and that the land may not become desolate." So Joseph bought all the land of Egypt for Pharaoh. All the Egyptians sold their fields, because the famine was severe upon them; and the land became Pharaoh's. As for the people, he made slaves of them from one end of Egypt to the other. Only the land of the priests he did not buy; for the priests had a fixed allowance from Pharaoh, and lived on the allowance that Pharaoh gave them; therefore they did not sell their land. Then Joseph said to the people, "Now that I have this day bought you and your land for Pharaoh, here is seed for you; sow the land. And at the harvests you shall give one-fifth to Pharaoh, and four-fifths shall be your own, as seed for the field and as food for yourselves and your households, and as food for your little ones." They said, "You have saved our lives; may it please my lord, we will be slaves to Pharaoh." So Joseph made it a statute concerning the land of Egypt, and it stands to this day, that Pharaoh should have the fifth. The land of the priests alone did not become Pharaoh's.

Little commentary is necessary. In control of the food supply, Joseph extracts money, livestock, land, and freedom from the hungry and desperate people, who in the end are grateful to *Pharaoh*, who has "saved our lives." The episode brings full circle Joseph's relationship with Egypt and reveals that beneath the family story of brotherly betrayal and reconciliation is another story that sets up the Exodus and what follows. The text implicitly asks: Can it ever be YHWH's will that we settle in a land of empire? Genesis ends with the possibility that it can, but in the opening verses of Exodus, we discover that it cannot. Immediately, we hear: "Now a new king arose over Egypt, who did not know Joseph" (Exod. 1:8). The deal is off. The Israelites, having grown numerous, will now be dealt with "shrewdly" by the new pharaoh and his people. It will take another act by YHWH and another person's hearing the divine Voice to repair the damage that will befall Israel for settling in Egypt.

PART II

From Exodus to Exile:
The Two Religions
in Conflict amid God's People

Chapter Eight

Entering the "Exit Story"

In the narrative sequence of the biblical canon, the story shifts suddenly after Genesis from family struggles amid surrounding empires to the big screen saga of Moses against Pharaoh. The plot from the books of Exodus through 2 Kings is, on the face of it, straightforward: YHWH calls Moses to lead the Israelites, now a great multitude, out of slavery in Egypt and into the Promised Land. Once in the wilderness, they grumble and complain against Moses and his brother Aaron, yearning to return to the familiar slavery of Egypt. They collectively meet the God of their ancestors at Mount Sinai amid thunder and smoke. While terrified of meeting YHWH up close, they accept YHWH's invitation via Moses to enter into a "covenant": a mutual agreement in which YHWH will be their God and they will be YHWH's chosen people, following the *torah* (instruction) given to Moses on the mountain (found in Exodus and Leviticus). Forty years later (many of the adventures during this period are narrated in the book of Numbers), they finally arrive at the Promised Land's edge, and Moses summarizes and interprets for them their experience in the wilderness (Deuteronomy).

Moses passes the leadership torch to Joshua, who leads them in a series of "holy wars" against the indigenous peoples of the land, known collectively as "Canaanites." The military engagement is only partially successful, and the Israelites settle into tribal areas while the various Canaanite peoples continue to dwell around them (book of Joshua). Once settled, the people face various threats from the surrounding peoples, led in battle by divinely inspired "judges." They are tempted to turn one of these judges (Gideon) into a king who will establish a dynasty, seeking to lock down leadership into a top-down institutional structure like their Canaanite neighbors. But Gideon refuses (Judges 8) and they continue to rely on this occasional form of charismatic leader.

Eventually, however, they tire of the uncertainties and insecurities and approach the last of the judges (Samuel) to seek a king (1 Samuel 8). After consulting with YHWH, Samuel relents and Saul is made king. Quickly, Saul's leadership turns sour, and YHWH picks a replacement: a young shepherd named David. Saul will not give up power easily, though, and a long struggle ensues. Saul remains king of "Israel" (in the north) and David, after many adventures (including a period as a mercenary for the hated Philistines), establishes himself as king of Judah (in the south). Finally, Saul dies in battle and David is made king of both Israel and Judah. He takes the existing city of Jerusalem from the Jebusites and makes it his capital. His court prophet, Nathan, offers an oracle in the name of YHWH making a "covenant" with the "house of David," promising that one of David's sons will always sit on the throne.

Things suddenly turn bad for the new king: David eyes the wife (Bathsheba) of a trusted military officer bathing on the rooftop adjacent to the royal palace, and he "takes" her. When she reveals that she is pregnant, he contrives to have her husband killed in battle as a cover-up. Nathan, though, speaks a parable on YHWH's behalf that recoils on the king: he acknowledges his sin, but too late. YHWH promises that David's house will now turn against him. The remainder of 2 Samuel narrates a sequence of rape, murder, betrayal, and conspiracy that rips David's family apart.

David confronts the popular rebellion of his son Absalom, who is killed by David's chief of staff. When the old king lies on his deathbed, there is a bloody battle for succession, with Bathsheba's son, Solomon, coming out the winner. The dust settles and Solomon, after a dream of being given divine wisdom, builds a grand temple in Jerusalem and becomes a player on the international stage. His reign is summarized ambiguously by the biblical writer, though: he has done great things, but he has also allowed his heart to be turned away from YHWH by his hundreds of foreign wives. As a result, the kingdom will be torn in two, with only a remnant remaining to the Davidic dynasty, because of YHWH's "love" for David.

Sure enough, Solomon's (only?) son,[1] Rehoboam, cannot hold on to power, and Saul's former followers rebel, forming the northern kingdom of Israel. They are first led by Jeroboam, who builds two shrines at the northern and southern ends of his territory to prevent the people's return to Jerusalem. The writer of 1 Kings judges this a terrible sin. The willingness to continue to allow these shrines in Bethel and Dan to exist becomes the focal criterion for judging whether Jeroboam's successors do "good" or "evil" in the sight of YHWH.

Israel and Judah live separate existences for some two hundred years. Sometimes allies and sometimes enemies, they struggle militarily against both their local neighbors and the rising Assyrian empire to the east. The northern kingdom reaches its peak of power and wealth in the eighth century under the Omride dynasty, known most famously for its King Ahab and his wife Queen Jezebel, who are relentlessly opposed by the prophets Elijah and Elisha. Their successors are challenged by the prophets Amos and Hosea.

The writers find holy rule only in the southern kingships of Hezekiah and his great-grandson, Josiah. Hezekiah, supported by the prophet Isaiah, manages to keep the Assyrians from occupying Jerusalem after they have conquered Israel. He is challenged by the prophet Micah (from outside the

---

1. Two daughters are named at 1 Kings 4:11, 15.

text of 2 Kings), but dies peacefully, having been told that Judah's collapse would not happen during his lifetime. The text blames his son Manasseh for the coming catastrophe: the conquest and destruction of Jerusalem by the Assyrians' successor, Babylon. While the Babylonians are gathering strength, the child Josiah is placed on the throne, tutored by the royal elite who seek radical religious reform. Finding a scroll hidden in the temple (likely a form of Deuteronomy), Josiah conducts a devastating campaign against worship sites outside Jerusalem. He celebrates the apparently long forgotten feast of passover in Jerusalem. But just as the renewal is taking shape, Josiah is killed suddenly in battle. The end is near. The prophet Jeremiah arises to warn the people of the consequences of relying on Egypt rather than YHWH against Babylon, but is ignored. As Jeremiah predicts, the Babylonians arrive and crush Jerusalem. They take the elite into exile in Babylon, leaving the "people of the land" to fend for themselves.

YHWH's dream has turned to nightmare. The people have apparently lost everything. The hopes for a life of peace and security in their own land have evaporated. The collapse generates an enormous amount of reflection among the exiles as to how and why it happened and what possibilities might remain for restoration. We will look at these texts in Part III.

For centuries, biblical readers have taken this narrative more or less at face value as a report of historical events that took place over the course of nearly a millennium (roughly 1500–600 BCE). Not until the Enlightenment did people seriously begin to question the relationship between the story and history. As it stands in its canonical order, the story conveys a relatively (and deceivingly) simple message: the shift from a twelve tribe confederacy under YHWH's rule to a human monarchy "like the nations" (1 Sam. 8:5) was a disastrous betrayal of the unique status of Israel as YHWH's "chosen people." In the terms of this book, Israel "converted" from the religion of creation to the religion of empire, with predictable results.

Why not accept this presentation at face value? The notion of a people liberated from empire to forge a truly divinely inspired alternative in their own land fits our overall premise very well. That it went so bad only under-scores the point: Israel's "empire" was no different in kind from that of their neighbors and thus could not really have been an expression of YHWH's will. Biblical Israel never again developed a monarchy to replace the one crushed by Babylon, apparently having learned the lesson.[2]

If this were the end of the story, it might suffice to accept the biblical narrative as presented. However, despite how Israel's biblical history ended, the "monarchy" did not. The promise conveyed by David's prophet Nathan that "your house and your kingdom shall be made sure forever before me; your throne shall be established forever" (2 Sam. 7:16) has remained to this very day an unfulfilled hope for many Jews. Furthermore, the person

---

2. Although the Hasmonean dynasty established by the Maccabees in the second century BCE sought to be recognized as such; see the discussion in chapter 19.

proclaimed as "Lord" and "Savior" by Christians has been understood as the fulfillment of this promise: Jesus the "messiah" (Greek, *Christos*, i.e., "anointed"). The New Testament repeatedly proclaims Jesus of Nazareth as "Christ," "son of David," and "son of God." Since the fourth century when "Christianity" became the official religion of the Roman Empire, wars have been fought repeatedly in the name of a "Christian kingdom."[3] In our own time, U.S. leaders have claimed to be doing the will of Jesus Christ in conducting brutal warfare against the "axis of evil."

The canonical Hebrew Scriptures contain both the story of the wilderness encounter with YHWH at Sinai and the temple encounter with YHWH in Jerusalem (Zion). Recently, Jewish scholar Jon Levenson has argued that what he calls the two traditions of "Sinai" and "Zion" are, in the end, not only compatible but mutually "correcting."[4] If one takes the Hebrew Scriptures as inspired and authoritatively binding on believers, Levenson's position seems the only possible stance. Both stories are in the Jewish Bible. They are either reconcilable or they are not. Taking a stance on behalf of either Sinai *or* Zion would undermine the authority of a major section of the biblical collection. The only other apparent possibility would be to argue that the Zion tradition, having developed later, in effect *replaces* the Sinai tradition.

This latter perspective, although not often stated this explicitly, is the de facto view of many Bible readers, both Jewish and Christian. The Sinai story might convey an ideal, but time moves on and one cannot dwell in that idealistic past any more than one can in Eden.[5] *Realpolitik* requires military might and political compromise to establish national security and prosperity. Relying on "YHWH alone" is a utopian fantasy at best and a dangerous distraction from the "real world" at worst. Thus, the modern state of Israel is protected by a well-armed military. Similarly, Christian "realists" have argued for the "necessity" of worldly power as an "adjunct" to religious faith, or even as the very expression of that faith.[6]

The "inconvenient truth" that Christian exponents of a Zion theology[7] fail to consider, though, is the unequivocal witness throughout the New Testament of Jesus' own perspective on these two traditions. Part IV will show how the gospels, Paul, and John of Patmos stood consistently against the anti-imperial tradition and with the religion of the Creator God.

---

3. How this transformation from the anti-imperial religion of Jesus to the "Christian" imperial religion of Constantine and his successors took place will be the focus of volume 2.

4. Levenson (1985), 208–11.

5. A similar perspective among many Christians sees the life of the early church in Acts 2–5 as a picture of an idealized past that people can no longer live.

6. See, e.g., Lovin. The writings of recent Catholic "neoconservatives" continue this tradition; see, e.g., Weigel. For an argument linking Catholic and Evangelical "neocons" to the Bush II White House foreign policy-making, see Linker.

7. This is not to be confused — although it often overlaps — with Christian evangelical support for the nation of Israel, which is frequently grounded in a particular interpretation of biblical "prophecy" and Jesus' "second coming." See Weber.

What, then, are we to make of the biblical traditions of monarchy and "holy war" against enemies of YHWH? How did the texts that exhort genocide and celebrate royal power end up in the Christian canon? To find an answer, we must look beneath and behind the surface narrative from Exodus to Exile. We will discover some surprising, startling, truths about how the biblical story evolved. To engage this inquiry, we must start not where the story continues at the end of Genesis, but instead, at the "high point" of the story: the royal reign of King Solomon.

Chapter Nine

Solomon's Wisdom

At Gibeon YHWH appeared to Solomon in a dream by night; and God said, "Ask what I should give you."

And Solomon said, "You have shown great and steadfast love to your servant my father David, because he walked before you in faithfulness, in righteousness, and in uprightness of heart toward you; and you have kept for him this great and steadfast love, and have given him a son to sit on his throne today. And now, O YHWH my God, you have made your servant king in place of my father David, although I am only a little child; I do not know how to go out or come in. And your servant is in the midst of the people whom you have chosen, a great people, so numerous they cannot be numbered or counted. Give your servant therefore an understanding mind to govern your people, able to discern **between good and evil**; for who can govern this your great people?"

It pleased YHWH that Solomon had asked this. God said to him, "Because you have asked this, and have not asked for yourself long life or riches, or for the life of your enemies, but have asked for yourself understanding to discern what is right, I now do according to your word. Indeed I give you a wise and discerning mind; no one like you has been before you and no one like you shall arise after you. I give you also what you have not asked, both riches and honor all your life; no other king shall compare with you. If you will walk in my ways, keeping my statutes and my commandments, as your father David walked, then I will lengthen your life."

Then Solomon awoke; it had been a dream. (1 Kings 3:5–15a)

"Was Solomon a good guy or a bad guy?" Ask most people this question and you'll likely get positive responses. If there is one attribute associated with Solomon — and with him perhaps more than anyone who ever lived — it is *wisdom*.[1] The example most offered in support of this claim is his mediation of a dispute between two Jerusalem prostitutes over a baby's maternity, which the king famously resolves by offering to "cut the baby in half." People may associate this wisdom, as the text of 1 Kings does, with

---

1. Neither the Hebrew adjective for "wise" (*chakham*) nor the noun for "wisdom" (*chokhmah*) is used to describe a king after Solomon.

Solomon's supposed authorship of proverbs and songs.[2] They may know that Solomon built the Jerusalem temple, although they might not consider this an expression of his "wisdom." They may even know that Solomon is said to have had over a thousand wives (1 Kings 11:3), but doubt that this was what made him "wise." Beyond this, few people seem to have read the story in 1 Kings 3–11 closely enough to notice how ambiguously the text portrays this most "wise" of Israel's kings.

A close reading of the biblical narrative leads an open-minded reader to wonder: Was the author seeking to praise the king or to bury him?[3] The ambiguity arises both within this account and by comparing Solomon with his father, David. Most remember David as the bold youth who took down the Philistine giant, Goliath, with five smooth stones and went on to become a great warrior-king. Sure, David's behavior wasn't always a model of faithful living, especially in the "matter of Uriah the Hittite," husband of Bathsheba. But, the narrator assures us, "David did what was right in the sight of YHWH, and did not turn aside from anything that he commanded him all the days of his life" (1 Kings 15:5). In contrast, we hear that "Solomon did what was evil in the sight of YHWH, and did not completely follow YHWH, as his father David had done" (1 Kings 11:6).

Reading the text carefully provides much more evidence. The authors give Solomon low marks in comparison with both David and later kings Hezekiah and Josiah. But the portrait gets darker when one compares 1 Kings 3–11 with texts that precede the monarchy in the biblical order of presentation. Let's consider three examples. First, compare the picture (Table 4) of Solomon with that of Pharaoh in Exodus, the quintessential biblical villain.

Can it be a coincidence that the picture of Israel's "wisest" king matches that of its greatest enemy? Why would someone seeking to praise Solomon describe him this way? Before we seek to answer this question, compare the "torah of the king" in Deuteronomy and the nature of Solomon's reign. It is hard to imagine a king of Israel portrayed more systematically in violation of the "torah of the king" than is Solomon.

Finally, consider this connection between Solomon and the Garden of Eden story we considered in chapter 2:

> "Give your servant therefore an understanding mind to govern your people, able to discern between **good and evil**; for who can govern this your great people?" (1 Kings 3:9)

> "but of the tree of the knowledge of **good and evil** you shall not eat, for in the day that you eat of it you shall die." ... So when the woman saw that the tree was good for food, and that it was a delight to the eyes,

---

2. 1 Kings 4:32, traditionally linked with authorship of the biblical books of Proverbs and Song of Songs.

3. E.g., J. Daniel Hays (2003). See also Lasine (1995).

Table 4: Comparison of Solomon and Pharaoh

1 Kings description of Solomon	*Exodus description of Pharaoh*
3:28: they stood in awe of the king, because they perceived that the **wisdom** [*chokmah*] of God was in him (only of Solomon in 1–2 Kings)	1:10: "Come, let us **deal shrewdly** [*nithchakmah*] with them . . . "
4:6: Adoniram son of Abda was **in charge of the forced labor** [*'al-hammas*]. See also 5:27–28; 9:15, 21; 12:18	1:11: "Therefore they set **taskmasters** [*sare missim;* root *mas,* only here in Exodus] over them to oppress them with forced labor."
9:15, 19: "This is the account of the forced labor that King Solomon conscripted to build . . . all of Solomon's **storage cities** [*'arey mamiskenoth*] . . . "	1:11: They built **storage cities** [*'arey mamiskenoth*] (term only in 2 Chronicles elsewhere in Hebrew Bible), Pithom and Rameses, for Pharaoh.
3:16ff: story of women giving birth to boys and question of babies' life and death	1:16ff: story of women giving birth to boys and question of babies' life and death
3:1: Solomon made a marriage alliance with Pharaoh king of Egypt; he took **Pharaoh's daughter** and brought her into the city of David. . . . " See also 7:8; 9:16; 11:1 (No "Pharaoh's daughter" mentioned elsewhere in Hebrew Bible)	2:5–10a: The **daughter of Pharaoh** came down to bathe at the river, while her attendants walked beside the river. She saw the basket among the reeds and sent her maid to bring it. When she opened it, she saw the child. He was crying, and she took pity on him, "This must be one of the Hebrews' children," she said. Then his sister said to Pharaoh's daughter, "Shall I go and get you a nurse from the Hebrew women to nurse the child for you?" Pharaoh's daughter said to her, "Yes." So the girl went and called the child's mother. Pharaoh's daughter said to her, "Take this child and nurse it for me, and I will give you your wages." So the woman took the child and nursed it. When the child grew up, she brought him to Pharaoh's daughter, and she took him as her son.
9:19, 22; 10:26: Solomon gathered together **chariots and horses;** he had fourteen hundred chariots and twelve thousand horses, which he stationed in the chariot cities and with the king in Jerusalem (see also 9:19, 22).	14:9: "The Egyptians pursued them, all Pharaoh's **horses and chariots,** his chariot drivers and his army. . . . " (see also 14:23, 15:19)
12:4: "Your father made our yoke heavy. Now therefore lighten the **hard service** [*qasheh*] of your father and his heavy yoke that he placed on us, and we will serve you."	1:13–14: The Egyptians became ruthless in imposing tasks on the Israelites, and made their lives bitter with **hard service** [*qasheh*] in mortar and brick and in every kind of field labor. They were ruthless in all the tasks that they imposed on them.
3:15: Solomon **awoke, and behold! It had been a dream.** [*vayyiqats shlomoh vehinneh chalom*]	Genesis 41:7: Pharaoh **awoke, and behold! It was a dream.** [*vayyiqats par'oh vehinneh chalom*] (Phrase nowhere else in Hebrew Scriptures)

Table 5: Comparison between the Torah of the King (Deut. 17:14–20) and Solomon's Reign (1 Kings 3–11)

When you have come into the land that YHWH your God is giving you, and have taken possession of it and settled in it, and you say, "I will set a king over me, like all the nations that are around me," **you may indeed set over you a king whom YHWH your God will choose.** One of your own community you may set as king over you; you are not permitted to put a foreigner over you, who is not of your own community.

1:11–14: Then Nathan said to Bathsheba, Solomon's mother, "Have you not heard that Adonijah son of Haggith has become king and our lord David does not know it? Now therefore come, let me give you advice, so that you may save your own life and the life of your son Solomon. **Go in at once to King David, and say to him, 'Did you not, my lord the king, swear to your servant, saying: Your son Solomon shall succeed me as king, and he shall sit on my throne?** Why then is Adonijah king?' Then while you are still there speaking with the king, I will come in after you and confirm your words."

Even so, **he must not acquire many horses for himself, or return the people to Egypt in order to acquire more horses,** since YHWH has said to you, "You must never return that way again."

4:26: Solomon **also had forty thousand stalls of horses for his chariots,** and twelve thousand horsemen.
10:28: **Solomon's import of horses was from Egypt** and Kue, and the king's traders received them from Kue at a price.

And he must not acquire many wives for himself, or else his heart will turn away ...

11:3: **Among his wives were seven hundred princesses and three hundred concubines; and his wives turned away his heart.**

... also silver and gold he must not acquire in great quantity for himself.

10:21–22: All King Solomon's drinking **vessels were of gold, and all the vessels of the House of the Forest of Lebanon were of pure gold; none were of silver** — it was not considered as anything in the days of Solomon. For the king had a fleet of ships of Tarshish at sea with the fleet of Hiram. Once every three years the fleet of ships of Tarshish used to come **bringing gold, silver,** ivory, apes, and peacocks.

When he has taken the throne of his kingdom, he **shall have a copy of *this torah* written for him** in the presence of the levitical priests. It shall remain with him and he shall read in it all the days of his life, so that he may learn to fear YHWH his God, diligently observing all the words of this law and these statutes

2:1–3: "When David's time to die drew near, he charged his son Solomon, saying: 'I am about to go the way of all the earth. Be strong, be courageous, and keep the charge of YHWH your God, walking in his ways and keeping his statutes, his commandments, his ordinances, and his testimonies, as it is **written in the *torah of Moses,*** so that you may prosper in all that you do and wherever you turn.' " (*torah* never again mentioned in relation to Solomon or in 1 Kings)

... neither exalting himself above other members of the community nor **turning aside from the commandment, either to the right** or to the left, so that he and his descendants may reign long over his kingdom in Israel.

9:6–7: [YHWH said to Solomon] "If you **turn aside** from following me, you or your children, and do not keep my commandments and my statutes that I have set before you, but go **and serve other gods and worship them,** then I will cut Israel off from the land that I have given them; and the house that I have consecrated for my name I will cast out of my sight; and Israel will become a proverb and a taunt among all peoples."
11:4: ... when Solomon was old, **his wives turned away his heart after other gods** ...

and that the tree was to be *desired to make one wise*[4] she took of its fruit and ate; and she also gave some to her husband, who was with her, and he ate. Then the eyes of both were opened, and they knew that they were naked; and they sewed fig leaves together and made loincloths for themselves. (Gen. 2:17, 3:6–7)

The only other biblical use of the boldfaced phrase is where the woman of Tekoa describes David as one who can "discern good and evil" (2 Sam. 14:17). Thus, Solomon is overheard praying (in his dream) for exactly what, from the perspective of Genesis, *has been forbidden* to humanity. He rightly deems that only this "forbidden fruit" can enable one to govern "your great people." In other words, with the Genesis text in mind, Solomon's prayer states clearly that only YHWH — or one usurping YHWH's command — can rule YHWH's people.

What are we to make of these biblical texts that cast a series of judgments on Solomon? Did the author of 1 Kings 3–11 intend for readers to hear these "previous" passages? If so, then we must conclude that the author was indeed intending to bury Solomon, not to praise him. But if this is the case, then why such ambiguity in the portrayal within 1 Kings 3–11? Certainly the author of the wider narrative of 1–2 Kings didn't hesitate to condemn utterly most of the royal successors as having done nothing but "evil in the sight of YHWH."[5] Yet Solomon remains "wise" above all others.

What we find in reading the 1 Kings' narrative *on its own* is a carefully balanced account, not a blanket condemnation. Indeed, many recent scholarly readers have concluded that the portrayal starts positively, then turns sour, perhaps based on an editorial judgment from a later period.[6] But in light of the Genesis, Exodus, and Deuteronomy texts, this balance tips so far that Solomon seems to topple completely off his throne.

The juxtaposition of these texts forces us to consider what can seem an impossibly vexed set of questions about authorship and history in the biblical texts. We managed to avoid these questions in Part I by positing a basic version of Genesis from the exilic period as a response to Babylon's own master narratives. Scholars have argued for so many theories and the sometimes extremely subtle distinctions among them that many throw up their hands in despair. One can take a fundamentalist stance to the biblical narrative sequence: "This is the order in which God wrote it." One can take the approach of literary / narrative critics: "This is how the final edition has been composed, regardless of the 'original' pieces and editorial threads that may have been stitched together." One can listen as a naïve participant in

---

4. Gen. 3:6 word for "wise" is Hebrew, *schl,* different from 1 Kings 3:12 word for "wise," *chakham.*

5. The phrase is used thirty times in 1–2 Kings of fifty-three times in the Hebrew Bible.

6. E.g., Knoppers (1993), 113, sees Solomon as a heroic "conservator of beliefs and practices" through which the author "promotes a novel approach to Israelite cult by attributing to royalty a central role in conserving antecedent beliefs and practices." For the "indeterminacy" of the narrative, see Lasine (1995).

synagogue or church: "This is how the story is presented to us in worship." But as noted in the previous chapter, one cannot fully unravel the interwoven threads of the "two religions" without seeking to some degree of certainty to ascertain which narrative blocks came before others.

Traditional scholarship since the eighteenth century has established almost at the level of academic dogma four basic "strands" of composition:

- ◆ **"J," or Jahwist:** found primarily within Genesis and Exodus and composed from within the royal court of Jerusalem, perhaps from the time of Solomon himself.

- ◆ **"E," or Elohist:** also found primarily within Genesis and Exodus and composed from a "northern" perspective sometime after the breakup of the United Monarchy and before the Assyrian conquest (i.e., in the ninth and eighth centuries).

- ◆ **"D" or "DtrH," the Deuteronomist and Deuteronomistic Historian(s):** found in the continuous narrative from Deut.–2 Kings, having been composed and edited at various times, but primarily during the reigns of Hezekiah, Josiah, and, finally, during the Exile.

- ◆ **"P" or Priestly:** found throughout Genesis–Numbers and also in later books such as 1–2 Chronicles and Ezra-Nehemiah: composed after the Exile during the Second Temple period.

Scholars have made passionate arguments for or against including individual verses and sometimes parts of verses within one strand or a strand's "layers" of editing. One quickly suspects that much of this work combines the desire to honor one's predecessors in the academy with a desire to "make a name" for oneself as a scholar by coming up with a novel twist while staying within the "tradition." But does this scholarly consensus have any clothes?

This book is not the place (if such a place could or should exist) to rehearse and rehash the countless nuances of two centuries of scholarly consideration of sources and editorial layers. Instead, one can seek to start fresh, not with an eye toward individual textual "trees" but rather, trying to keep in mind the larger narrative "forest." As we do, we must remember the central query that drives our larger investigation: which "side" is YHWH on, that of Solomon and his successors, or that of his critics? Put another way: Was it YHWH's desire for Israel to embody a *faithful people* or a *powerful empire?*[7] Has that desire "changed" or "evolved" over the centuries? Can we discern a consistent pattern amid the struggles from Exodus to Exile?

We start the quest seemingly in the middle of the story with Solomon for several reasons. First, as we've just seen, it reveals the ambiguity that calls for investigation: is Solomon portrayed to match the pre-existing image of Pharaoh, or might it be the other way around, that *Pharaoh in Exodus*

---

7. Thanks to Joe Hastings for first suggesting this antithesis.

was painted to match Solomon in 1 Kings? Second, Solomon represents the "high point" of Israel's experience of imperial power, wealth and privilege. If Solomon is meant to be "buried," are we to bury just him (and his ilk) or the *monarchy itself?* Third, the Solomon story contains one of the most famous — but rarely carefully read — stories of an ancient king: the two prostitutes and their baby boys. A close look at this familiar passage will teach us a lot about the true nature of "Solomon's wisdom."

Finally, the most important reason for starting with the Solomon saga is that it is *most likely to be the first written piece of the Exodus–Exile narrative.* The details will unfold as we continue through Part II, but Table 6 shows the conclusions that we'll be working toward.

Dating Solomon

One thing all serious readers of Israel's historical narrative agree upon — amid countless disagreements on other points — is that *no written text could predate the Davidic/Solomonic reign.* As we saw above (pp. 41–42), writing and literacy were themselves functions of empire. Apart from and previous to the great city-state powers of the ancient world, there simply were no written texts.[8] The Davidic/Solomonic period is the first moment in which Israel gained access to the imperial technology of writing and vocation of scribe/secretary (*soper*).[9] The first (in terms of narrative sequence) use of *soper* in the Hebrew Bible in this manner[10] is 2 Samuel 8:17, amid the list of David's cabinet officers (as again at 2 Samuel 20:25). The very next use is in the listing of Solomon's own cabinet, 1 Kings 4:3 (Solomon has two *soperim*). Throughout the rest of the Hebrew Bible, the term always applies to such royal officials.[11] This biblical usage is fully consistent with that of other cultures throughout the region. There are not and could not be contemporaneous written narratives of whatever "Israel" was before the monarchy.

Therefore, the scholarly challenge to the David/Solomon written text is in the opposite direction. How *recent* might it be? Various theories proposing answers are fueled by the *absence of any verbal material record of the Solomonic empire whatsoever.* To date, only one shred of evidence has even hinted at the reign of David directly: the so-called "Tel Dan Inscription," which appears (but not without much scholarly controversy) to refer

---

8. See generally Ong and Carr (2005).

9. See Carr (2005), 114–33, for an explanation of how neighboring imperial scribal practices were adapted by the Israelite monarchy.

10. Judg. 5:14 uses it in the phrase *beshebet soper,* variously translated as "the marshal's staff" (NRSV, NAB); "the staff of office" (NASB); "the pen of the writer" (KJV), "the commander's staff" (TNIV). The social and narrative contexts of this verse in Deborah's Song renders the otherwise uniform translation as "scribe" or "secretary" unlikely, so translators struggle to find a suitable alternative.

11. E.g., 2 Kings 12:11; 18:18, 37; 19:2; 22:3–12; 25:19; Isa. 36:3, 22; 37:2; Jer. 8:8; 36:10–32; 37:15, 20; 52:25.

Table 6: Exodus to Exile Texts and Their Perspectives

Time of Composition	Text	Author(s)	Basic Perspective
Tenth century (i.e., during the reign of Solomon)	The David/Solomon story, 1 Sam. 13–1 Kings 10	Royal scribes in Jerusalem	YHWH's promise is with the Davidic monarchy; Solomon is the rightful successor to the throne
Ninth century–eighth century	Exodus	Northern royal scribes	Moses represents true, YHWH-authorized leadership and legitimates the reign of Jeroboam, YHWH's rightful king of the "true" people of God, Israel (not Judah)
Eighth century (i.e., amid the struggle with Assyria)	The bulk of 1–2 Kings up to the time of Hezekiah	Royal scribes in Jerusalem	Hezekiah is YHWH's "chosen" king; the northern kingdom will fall because of its "evil" (= worshiping YHWH outside Jerusalem)
Eighth century (as above)	Isa. 1–39; Judges(?)	Prophetic circles among the royal elite	Hezekiah is YHWH's "chosen" king: peace comes via the true Davidic king reigning in Jerusalem (Zion)
Eighth century (as above)	Amos, Hosea	Southern, Jerusalem-centered prophets and supporters	Northern kingdom of Israel is condemned because of its sins (= injustice against poor and marginalized)
Eighth century	Micah	Southern voices in support of the "people of the land," i.e., the landed gentry	Monarchy itself is condemned
Seventh century (after Assyria conquers Israel and before Babylon arises)	Deuteronomy, Joshua, 1 Samuel 1–12 and version of 1–2 Kings up to Josiah	Royal scribes in Jerusalem working with scribal "refugees" from the north to find a "compromise"	Josiah is the greatest king of all and Moses is the great liberating prophet: together, they express and embody torah and legitimate Jerusalem as the sole "place" at which to worship YHWH
Late seventh–early sixth century	Jeremiah	Southern, Jerusalem-centered prophets and supporters	Even Jerusalem cannot stand in the face of the leaders' deafness to the voice of YHWH
	Zephaniah	Anti-Jerusalem prophet	Josiah's Jerusalem is no better than previous versions[12]

---

12. Knauf, 323–24, suggests that Hosea, Amos, Micah, and Zephaniah were combined sometime after the reign of Josiah to express a collective perspective that "condemns Jerusalem's recent past from the point of view of Bethel's present."

to "House of David" (*bytdwd*).[13] Whatever the "truth" may be about this one artifact tells us nothing about the biblical texts that narrate the David/Solomon story.

It is a truism that "absence of evidence is not itself evidence of absence." That is, the fact of there being no preserved documents or inscriptions that speak of the David/Solomon reign does not thereby reduce the biblical story to "fiction." It simply leaves the question open, seeking guidance from other sources.[14]

The primary nonverbal sources to which biblical historians have looked are forms of material culture, such as art, pottery, and architecture. The field of archaeology concerned with biblical times and places is a contentious and highly political one, in which nonspecialists can quickly become overwhelmed on the one hand by highly technical accounts and on the other by passionate and often personal attacks on those with whom a scholar disagrees.[15] The basic question comes down to this: to what degree does the archaeological record support the existence of the David/Solomon reign? On the one hand, scholars such as Amihai Mazar, William Dever, and Baruch Halpern find ample, if not overwhelming, evidence in support of a tenth-century urban center in Jerusalem befitting a state capital, surrounding fortified cities and related villages consistent with the biblical narrative.[16] On the other hand, such findings are challenged strenuously by Israel Finkelstein and Neil Silberman, who claim that at most there is evidence for a fledgling state-in-formation in the tenth century.[17]

The ambiguous archaeological evidence has generated a field day of scholarly (and not so scholarly) speculations about the relationship between the biblical David/Solomon narrative and the "facts" of history. The so-called "minimalists" have gone so far as to say that the entire David/Solomon story is a fabrication from a much later period. Some of these scholars have suggested that the "refusal" of those who claim to find archaeological evidence in support of the United Monarchy is "really" about the scholars' perspective on current Middle East politics. The "debate" has often erupted in charges of anti-Semitism or anti-Palestinianism.

Some scholars have focused on a much narrower chronological range of possibilities for the relationship between the physical evidence and the composition of the biblical texts at issue. Finkelstein and Silberman, for example, state:

13. For an image of the stele containing the inscription and a bibliography of recent scholarly exchange regarding it, see *www.kchanson.com/ANCDOCS/westsem/teldan.html*.

14. Egyptologist Kenneth A. Kitchen, 115, notes that there are equally large gaps in the material evidence for Egyptian presence in the Levant, hardly "proving" that Egypt was not involved in the region's history. He concludes that it is "the height of ignorance" for scholars to allege that the United Monarchy "did not exist merely because we have no mention of them in external sources."

15. For a summary of the interpersonal polemics, see Shea.

16. Mazar (1992), 375–98; Halpern (2004), 427–78; Dever (1997), 182–86.

17. Finkelstein and Silberman.

Hence the dating of the appearance of historical literature in Israel and the beginning of historiography in the western tradition... to the tenth century BCE in Jerusalem should be dismissed out of hand. In the tenth century BCE, there is no sign of significant scribal activity; Jerusalem was no more than a remote, small village with a population of a few hundred people; and Judah had no more than a few villages with a population of a few thousand people.[18]

They place the composition of our texts in the period of Hezekiah (eighth century). They conclude:

Parallel to the centralization of the Judahite cult in Jerusalem, which included the rejection of the Bethel temple, the Judahite royal family and its entourage had a significant interest in a project of strengthening the power of the dynasty by uniting southerners and northerners around the Davidic king. To that end, they needed to reconcile two conflicting traditions regarding the early days of the Jerusalem dynasty: on the one hand, the upbeat southern traditions about David, the founder of their dynasty, and about Solomon, the builder of their temple, and on the other hand, the critical northern traditions, which preserved memories of the same early period, but from a distinctly Saulide perspective.[19]

I invite readers to be aware of this perspective at the outset, as I show why I side with those who continue to favor a tenth-century composition of the United Monarchy narrative.[20] Clearly, no absolute conclusion can be

---

18. Ibid. (2006), 277.

19. Ibid., 278.

20. Because Finkelstein and Silberman have presented their argument in a popular level book (2007) in addition to scholarly publications, it is important briefly to consider some of the major flaws in their argument. First, they claim repeatedly that "public literacy was obviously the essential precondition for the compilation of the biblical David and Solomon story as a written text intended to influence public opinion in favor of the Davidic Dynasty" (123). However, this condition is by no means "obvious." Mesopotamian imperial literacy was not at all widespread; it was likely that the king himself could not read or write, which was the reason for a scribal cabinet position in the first place. Empires write documents often for the elite alone, just as scholars often write only for other scholars; see Carr (2005), 13. Consider also the role of the Bible as a written text throughout many times and places where literacy was rare. Yet the power of the physical fact of the written text provided both an aura of sacredness and a means of preserving an "official" story for those capable of reading or proclaiming it to others orally. Finkelstein and Silberman admit that the traditions preserved in the David/Solomon story likely do reflect tenth-century realities, which were "presumably conveyed orally" (122). But this presumption only raises numerous other questions (addressed here in the main text), such as why such a highly detailed story of David's exploits would be remembered and conveyed by oral tradition.

Second, they argue that Solomon could not have built the Jerusalem temple because there is no evidence for such a building in "the rugged conditions of tenth-century BCE Jerusalem" (155). However, they admit later that the likeliest location for the temple would be under what is now the Dome of the Rock and hence inaccessible to archaeological surveys. Further, given Herod the Great's first-century building activities on the site, there "is little possibility that Iron Age remains would have survived these immense operations" (171–72). It is a wholly circular argument: there is no archaeological evidence so Solomon wasn't the builder, but there can't

reached given the current state of the evidence. But we cannot avoid the question if we want to determine, as best we can, the relationship between God and empire during Israel's most powerful monarchical moment. In other words, *was YHWH on the side of David and Solomon or not?*

A scholar who has presented a strong counter-argument to Finkelstein and Silberman regarding the consistency of the archaeological evidence with a tenth-century composition of the David/Solomon story is Baruch Halpern. In his 2004 book, *David's Secret Demons,* Halpern challenges the premise that the question turns on whether one finds tenth-century evidence of monumental architecture or widespread literacy in Jerusalem and environs. Rather, he argues, the primary grounds for claiming the existence of centralized state formation in the tenth century is the *strong evidence of trade routes* across Canaan and into neighboring territories. He states:

> ...the boom in trade left a mark in cores into the ice layers of Greenland...starting in the vicinity of 1000....But the start of the intensive trade of the Iron Age stemmed from David's knitting together of the relevant markets and Solomon's exploitation of them. This is why the territorial state, the national state, is first witnessed in Canaan rather than Syria. The territorial state is in fact a minor empire — a monopoly of trade routes — cloaked in the rhetoric of ethnic identity.[21]

Similarly, William Dever's archaeological investigations in the wider region show what he calls a "classic, 'three-tiered,' hierarchically ordered settlement pattern" among villages, small towns and larger cities. This pattern, in combination with "nearly identical" architectural features in cities across various regions, indicates evidence of "centralized planning."[22] He argues further that tenth-century Jerusalem "is a classic example of a 'disembedded capital'...as is Samaria in the ninth–eighth centuries BCE.' " He defines "disembedded capitals" as "administrative centers that develop as relatively compact sites, [and that are] often established de novo, or are

---

be any surviving evidence anyway. Further, they admit that the temple must have been built by Hezekiah's time, but they "simply do not know who built" it (172).

Third, they argue that the portrait of Solomon fits best the seventh-century reality of Manasseh and that the "elaborate descriptions of unimaginable riches and power could be used to show what the future might again hold for Judah" (204). But then they say that the "law of the king" in Deut. 17, written they claim at the same time as the Solomon story itself, "seems to have used Solomon's greatness and opulence to express a message of condemnation about kings who sought majesty above righteousness" and that therefore, "only Solomon's wisdom and his temple were important" (205). Which is it? Was Solomon portrayed as a wealthy, imperial monarch to emulate him or condemn him? If the latter, then why portray his wealth at all in an eighth or seventh-century composition?

Fourth, their entire book makes no mention of the Exodus story at all and its expression of a counter-story to the Solomon story. If the Solomon story was written so late, when was the Exodus story written? Even later? By whom and why? They simply do not address these questions.

    21. Halpern (2004), 354.
    22. Dever (1997), 182–85.

refounded deliberately and are built up of largely public buildings and facilities, but contain relatively few domestic structures."[23]

Thus, Halpern and Dever independently conclude that it is the larger pattern of trade, evidence of centralized planning, and comparison with other "minor empires" of the time and place that support the likelihood of a United Monarchy along the lines described in the biblical narrative.

All this archaeological discussion, however, only creates the *possibility* of a tenth-century composition for the David / Solomon story. There could easily have been such a monarchy in that time and place but with a written account from a much later period, just as we continue today to write histories of times and places long ago. Our investigation must now turn to another source: the biblical story itself.

Several features clearly distinguish the David / Solomon story from the long litany of royal reports that follows in the remainder of 1–2 Kings. First, we are given *an enormous number of names and details* regarding David's rise to power and life as king. We learn about military leaders and battles; shifting alliances between the House of Saul and the House of David; and a whole sequence of individually named advisors, opponents, and family members. In subsequent royal accounts, in contrast, we often hear only bare details of a coup d'état or succession, or learn of a particular event in some detail but hear nothing further about the king, his family, and his friends. If the David / Solomon story was composed two centuries or more after the fact, why would an audience at that time care about such minutiae from the distant past?

Second, there are in the story countless explanations and excuses made for David's behavior (or nonbehavior), including the question of his responsibility for the deaths of numerous people. Halpern shows how the overall pattern protests David's innocence far too much, when the politics of the situation repeatedly suggest David to be the most likely cause (directly or indirectly) of various demises.[24] The narrative directly acknowledges King David's responsibility for a series of disasters, including:

1. *The raising of his son Absalom's ire* at his father when David ignores the rape of Absalom's sister, Tamar, by her half-brother, Amnon, eventually resulting in Absalom's murder of Amnon (2 Sam. 13).

2. *Engendering of Absalom's rebellion* because of David's failure to provide justice to the people, one of the king's responsibilities in traditional Middle Eastern monarchies (2 Sam. 15).

3. *David's demoralization of his own troops* as he grieves the death of Absalom at the close of the rebellion (2 Sam. 19:1–7).

This is not to mention, of course, the "sin" that the narrator claims to be the central flaw in David's otherwise "faithful" loyalty to YHWH: the

---

23. Ibid., 185.
24. Halpern (2004), 73–106, characterizing David as a "serial killer."

death of Uriah the Hittite in an attempt to cover up the king's adulterous relationship with Uriah's wife, Bathsheba (2 Sam. 11–12; cf. 1 Kings 15:5). Furthermore, the text "confesses" numerous questionable aspects of David's behavior *before* he became king, including:

1. *Seeking to extort property through a protection racket* from a wealthy sheepherder named Nabal, whose own wife, Abigail, brings the payoff to David after Nabal refuses to cooperate. We hear David's comment between Nabal's refusal and Abigail's arrival that David and his men "by morning would not leave a single of his men pissing against the wall," i.e., he would have killed Nabal and all his guards (1 Sam. 25:22, au. trans.; cf. Brueggemann [1990a], 178). Nabal suddenly dies mysteriously and David takes Abigail as his wife.

2. When David continues to be pursued by his rival, King Saul of Israel, *he sells himself as a mercenary to the Philistines,* Israel's hated enemy. He then takes his band of six hundred embittered men from the bottom of the social heap (1 Sam. 22:2) on a series of booty raids, killing all witnesses (1 Sam. 27).

Yet the narrator of 1 Kings, after the end of the David/Solomon era, provides this retrospective summary of David's reign:

> David did what was right in the sight of YHWH, and did not turn aside from anything that he commanded him all the days of his life, except in the matter of Uriah the Hittite. (1 Kings 15:5)

Two important questions arise. Why would an author who proclaims David as one who "did what was right in the sight of YHWH" narrate all these mistakes and disasters? Also why would the author present David's killing of Uriah as the sole exception to a life of obedience to YHWH? Was it really worse than causing the deaths of so many innocent victims in his gangster years? What happened to the torah commandment, "Thou shalt not murder"?

Finally, the text portrays Solomon very differently from his father in a number of ways. David is portrayed beginning his long career as a man of action: an avenger of injustice (e.g., the killing of the Philistine giant, Goliath)[25] and a warrior hero (e.g., "And the women sang to one another

---

25. Many scholars have noted the "hidden" overlap between the David and Goliath story in 1 Sam. 17 and this passage tucked in the midst of a final summary of actions during David's time: "Then there was another battle with the Philistines at Gob; and Elhanan son of Jaare-oregim, the Bethlehemite, killed Goliath the Gittite, the shaft of whose spear was like a weaver's beam. There was again war at Gath, where there was a man of great size, who had six fingers on each hand, and six toes on each foot, twenty-four in number; he too was descended from the giants. When he taunted Israel, Jonathan son of David's brother Shimei killed him" (2 Sam. 21:19–21). It is likely that the "official" story in 1 Sam. 17 is a composite of these other encounters, placed as an introduction to the David story by his spinmasters; Halpern (2004), 6–13, 135–37.

as they made merry, 'Saul has killed his thousands, and David his ten thousands,' " 1 Sam. 18:7; again at 21:11). He is passionately loved by many, including his rival Saul's son, Jonathan (1 Sam. 16:21; 18:1; 20:17), daughter, Michal (1 Sam. 18:20, 28), and servants (1 Sam. 18:22); and "all Israel and Judah" (1 Sam. 18:16).[26] David has at least seventeen children, both sons and daughters (2 Sam. 3:2–5; 5:13–16). He shows a wide range of emotions and reactions to the cascade of disasters that befalls him, not unlike a Shakespearean character.[27]

Solomon, in contrast, is a sphinx, an especially fitting epithet given his evident Egyptian engagement (e.g., 1 Kings 3:1). Amazingly, once he takes the reign after his dream, there is no direct Solomonic speaking, except for his temple dedication speech.[28] He never leaves Jerusalem; kings and a queen come to him. He never leads in battle. For all his hundreds of wives, we only hear of one son (and no daughters), his successor Rehoboam, not mentioned during Solomon's lifetime (first at 1 Kings 11:43).

The most apt comparison in modern literature is, it seems to me, that of *The Godfather* saga.[29] David is a near-perfect match with Vito Corleone, who also began his career as an avenger of injustice, gathered around him desperate men for whom "the system" didn't work, and became rich and powerful via extortion and murder. Like the elder Corleone, David settles down in his old age and watches as his "family" comes apart before his mostly helpless eyes. The old godfather and David both manage to hold on to power until the end, but at the cost of the lives of sons and valued colleagues. Like father, like son: Solomon, like Michael Corleone, waits in the wings until the old man is on the edge of death and then is thrust into leadership. Where the fathers were "full" characters and could show both extreme violence ("business") and sentimentality, the sons are utterly ruthless, cold-bloodedly eliminating all opposition in order to secure the "kingdom."

What we see in both the David / Solomon story and *The Godfather* trilogy is the pattern of "redemptive violence" that is the very essence of the religion of empire.[30] What begins with an act (story) of "good" violence becomes a means to acquire wealth and power, which eventually become ends in themselves. It is precisely the path that the United States has taken from the American Revolution through the era of Manifest Destiny to today's global military empire.[31] When this path is claimed to embody the "divine order"

---

26. Although nowhere in the entire narrative does it say that David loved *anyone*, including YHWH.

27. Alter (2000), xx–xxii.

28. Cf. 1 Kings 5:2–6; 10:3, where the narrator notes but does not quote "live" Solomonic speech.

29. For excellent reflections on the social meaning of *The Godfather* saga, see Browne (1999).

30. See generally Wink (1992).

31. I hope to trace "the two religions" throughout United States history in a future volume. For components of this history, see, e.g., Wood (on the early Republic); Stephanson (on Manifest Destiny); and Rosenberg (1982, on late nineteenth and early twentieth-century expansion).

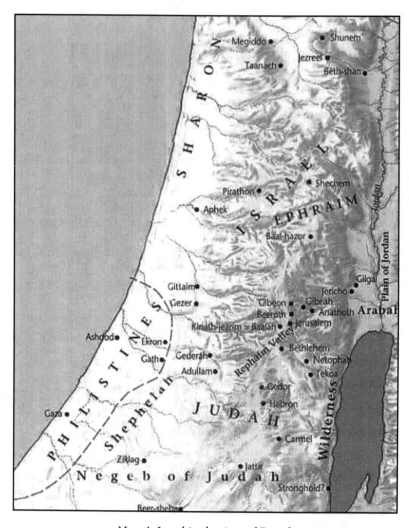

Map 4: Israel in the time of David

or "way of God" (see especially 2 Sam. 7 and 1 Kings 3) it becomes instead yet another expression of imperial religion, the antithesis of the religion of creation.[32]

Whose interests did the David/Solomon story serve? When and why was it composed and presented in the way that we have it?

---

32. It is no coincidence that each of the *Godfather* films begins with an engagement with institutional Roman Catholicism: a wedding, a baptism, and the giving to Michael Corleone of the Vatican's order of San Sebastian. Cf. the more agonized relationship with the Catholic Church and with God evident in the main characters of *The Sopranos* television series, which portrays the next generation's relocation from the city to suburbia.

We turn again to the thorough detective work done by Baruch Halpern in *David's Secret Demons*. Halpern, well aware of the archaeological controversy over a tenth-century date for the saga, reviews every available piece of physical and narrative evidence. He provides detailed links connecting the story with the period within or immediately following the reign of Solomon.[33] Among his conclusions, he says:

> Almost all of David's other warriors and the actors in 1 and 2 Samuel stem from southern Benjamin or southern Judah.... The books of Samuel thus suggest that there were settlers in the Negev and in the vicinity of Jerusalem, but few elements attached themselves to David from the hills of Judah or the Shephelah.... This fits the archaeological situation of the 10th and earlier centuries. It is inconceivable that an author writing later than the ninth century... would have invented such a distribution.[34]

With regard to the story of David in service to the Philistines, he says:

> It is implausible that later denizens of Judah would imagine their king as having been in the service of a king of Gath [one of the primary Philistine cities]. By the late ninth century, Gath was at best a minor site, and by the 8th a dependency either of Judah or of Ashdod, and then of Assyria.[35]

Who in the tenth century would want to portray David this way? Wouldn't Solomon's or David's own scribes be the *least* likely to present such a flawed portrait of their patrons?

Perhaps the best (if imaginary) explanation of this seeming paradox comes from the former East German dissident writer Stephen Heym, in his *King David Report*. Heym, while seeking to maintain his integrity as a writer within the Soviet system, posits a writer hired by Solomon's court to walk the line between the truth and the whole truth: to acknowledge what "everyone knows" about David while producing a piece of imperial propaganda presenting Solomon as "wisest of kings." In the voice of his imagined author:

> I saw that Solomon had thought of practically everything, and that there was no escaping his favour. I also saw that I might end, as some writers did, with my head cut off and my body nailed to the city wall, but that, on the other hand, I might wax fat and prosperous if I guarded my tongue and used my stylus wisely. With some luck and the aid of our Lord Yahveh, I might even insert in the King David Report a word here and a line there by which later generations would perceive what really came to pass in these years and what manner of man David ben Jesse

---

33. Halpern (2004), 57–69.
34. Ibid., 65.
35. Ibid., 69.

was: who served as a whore simultaneously to a king and the king's son and the king's daughter, who fought as a hired soldier against his own blood, who had his own son and his most loyal servants assassinated while loudly bewailing their death, and who forged a people out of a motley of miserable peasants and recalcitrant nomads.[36]

Halpern, approving Heym's basic insight,[37] grounds it in the actual practices of Middle Eastern royal propaganda as well as the specific problems faced by Solomon as David's successor. He states:

> Texts describing the king's accomplishments are primarily directed externally — the unlettered reader will take the claims of the text at face value....
>
> On the other hand, the expectation is that the insider audience, the elite, will analyze the language in detail. The insiders understood the conventions used to amplify achievement.... In other words, members of the elite had to understand how to discount the spin....
>
> One has almost to imagine the insiders applauding the cleverness of the authors who, without falsification, imply the glory and grandeur of their king's accomplishments.[38]

As someone who myself worked as staff counsel to the U.S. Senate Judiciary Committee,[39] I can confirm the ongoing truth of Halpern's insight, as any "system insider" knows. Statements presented for public consumption are well-known by those "inside" to be often half-truths at best, but can be admired by those same insiders for misleading those whose worldview the act of public propaganda is seeking to shape.

In our world, the audience for such public statements is vast, since most people have access to or are influenced by the voice of imperial media. In Solomon's world, however, the creators of the "inside the Beltway" version of history would not expect the attention of ordinary people in scattered small towns and villages. Halpern thus determines the audience to be "at a minimum, the officialdom and army, but even more probably the citizenry of major communities. The texts must have been read or summarized at public events."[40]

Thus, the most likely conclusion is that the David/Solomon story is basically a work of royal propaganda, designed to legitimize and glorify the reign of Solomon as conforming to YHWH's will. As the first written document of what became the Hebrew Bible, it presents a perspective common to the Middle East of its time: the enthroned king embodies the divine will. Wealth, justice, and peace flow from the capital (via the king) out to the

---

36. Heym, 11.
37. Halpern (2004), 5.
38. Ibid., 130.
39. For Sen. Howard Metzenbaum (D. Ohio), 1981–83.
40. Halpern (2004), 129.

provinces. "Zion theology" among written texts is not a betrayal of a pre-existing written tradition of a Sinai covenant. Rather, it is the document that in a very real sense *created* the "nation" of Israel.[41] We'll now explore how David and Solomon can be called Israel's "founding fathers."

Solomon's "Nation Building"

One element common to the David/Solomon story and *The Godfather* was the bloody battle among the sons for the "throne" as the father lay dying. Just as Sonny Corleone seemed the most likely successor, ready to take his "rightful" place, so David's son Adonijah was the heir apparent, at least according to traditional notions of dynasty succession. Sandwiched between two notices of the momentum shifting toward David in the war between the houses of Saul and David, we are told that "sons were born to David at Hebron":

> His firstborn was Amnon, of Ahinoam of Jezreel; his second, Chileab, of Abigail the widow of Nabal of Carmel; the third, Absalom son of Maacah, daughter of King Talmai of Geshur; the fourth, Adonijah son of Haggith; the fifth, Shephatiah son of Abital; and the sixth, Ithream, of David's wife Eglah. (2 Sam. 3:2–5)

The first (Amnon) and third (Absalom) sons die before their father. Chileab, son of Abigail (the wife acquired after her husband Nabal's suspicious demise), is next, but mysteriously, is never mentioned again. This leaves Adonijah in position to replace his father.

We hear later of the sons born to David in Jerusalem, with no link between sons and mothers as with the Hebron brood:

> These are the names of those who were born to him in Jerusalem: Shammua, Shobab, Nathan, Solomon, Ibhar, Elishua, Nepheg, Japhia, Elishama, Eliada, and Eliphelet. (2 Sam. 5:13–16)

A most undistinguished group, biblically speaking, with two exceptions: Solomon, an undistinguished fourth in the list, and the third, Nathan, apparently named for the King's house prophet, the person primarily responsible for pushing Solomon into the royal seat. Why would the tenth son suddenly be the beneficiary of a palace coup d'etat to replace Adonijah?

We find precisely this suspicious sequence in 1 Kings 1. Adonijah gained the political support of Joab, David's longstanding military chief of staff, and Abiathar the priest. Meanwhile, another coalition formed in the wings: Zadok the priest; Benaiah, chief of mercenary forces; Nathan the prophet and two others "did not side with Adonijah" (1 Kings 1:8). Before this group could raise up Solomon, we are told that Adonijah held a ceremonial inauguration party, but "he did not invite the prophet Nathan or Benaiah

---

41. The question of what kind of social entity "Israel" was is addressed in chapter 13.

or the warriors or his brother Solomon" (1:10). The report of Adonijah's snub of this group suggests his awareness that the elite were divided over the succession.

Adonijah, like Sonny Corleone, was bold, but naïve. The wily old court leaders easily outsmarted him and led the apparently senile David into "remembering" that he had promised Solomon the throne. Suddenly, Bathsheba is again part of the story, a character without a previous speaking part. She is Nathan's foil in manipulating the bedridden king. Her own naivete is revealed when, after Solomon is enthroned, Adonijah tries a back-door ploy: asking the queen mother for access to his father's bedwarming partner, the beautiful young Abishag (2:13–17). Bathsheba, astoundingly, seemed utterly unaware of the sexual politics at stake, especially surprising given her own experience in such matters.[42] When Solomon heard of it, he summarily ordered Benaiah to execute Adonijah and banished Abiathar to the local town of Anathoth (2:25–27).[43] Finally, Solomon has Benaiah murder his father's most loyal servant, Joab, for siding with Adonijah and then puts Benaiah in Joab's place. The coup is complete. Solomon, David's tenth born, is the new king. The first dynastic succession in Israel's history has taken place, amid much bloody intrigue.

Why did Solomon win, despite the apparent odds against him? We are reduced largely to speculation, since the writer seems to have assumed that the audience either knew enough about the politics of the Davidic state to understand or would be persuaded by the version presented in what became the biblical text. We'll simply have to leave this mystery unsolved here, as we examine what it was about Solomon's reign that revealed his great "wisdom."[44]

Let's take a step back: Why and how did the monarchy arise in the first place? According to the wider canonical biblical narrative, "Israel" comprised the multigenerational offspring of the eponymous ancestor, Jacob/Israel. The patriarch named his twelve sons as tribal ancestors (Gen. 49).[45] The litany of twelve tribes is repeated in Numbers 1, 10, 13, and 26,

---

42. See also 2 Sam. 16:21–23, where Ahithophel counsels Absalom to "go in to your father's concubines" as a public act of proclaiming himself king; at 2 Sam. 3:6–10, the late King Saul's general, Abner, engages in a similar act with Saul's concubines in an attempt to succeed Saul. When challenged by Saul's son Ishbaal, Abner angrily goes over to David's side and helps secure the combined throne for his former enemy.

43. Anathoth will henceforth be a site of priestly dissent from the royal status quo, breeding such figures as the prophet Jeremiah, as discussed in chapter 14.

44. Halpern (2004), however, presents a detailed theory for why Solomon succeeded David.

45. Genesis 49 is sometimes captioned with the word "blessings," but Jacob certainly does not "bless" Reuben, who is condemned for lying with Jacob's concubine (35:22). Nor does he bless Simeon and Levi, the perpetrators of the Shechem massacre (Gen. 34:25–31), saying "weapons of violence are their swords. May I never come into their council; may I not be joined to their company — for in their anger they killed men, and at their whim they hamstrung oxen. Cursed be their anger, for it is fierce, and their wrath, for it is cruel! I will divide them in Jacob, and scatter them in Israel" (49:5–7). Cf. Zornberg, 363–64. Thus, Genesis distances itself from the "redemptive violence" central to imperial religion.

then again at Deuteronomy 27:12–13. Serial readers will take it as "fact" by the time they reach the Conquest and Settlement narratives in Joshua and accept it as "background" in Judges, even though there is no similar list of all twelve tribes in Judges. When the "elders of Israel" come to Samuel, the old judge/prophet, to "appoint for us, then, a king to govern us, like other nations" (1 Sam. 8:5), the prospective monarchy is presented as if it were the greatest sell-out in Israel's history. That is, the straightforward narrative suggests that the "twelve tribes of Israel" had been united as such for several hundred years, but suddenly, the elders quit on their ancient covenant commitment to be the Chosen People and succumb to the temptation to be "like the nations" from which they were taken and rescued by YHWH. Saul is appointed/anointed by YHWH/Samuel as king over Israel but fails; David is similarly appointed/anointed, but must await Saul's death to take his "rightful" place. Solomon had to struggle to achieve his own "rightful" place, but succeed he did, and under his rule, we are informed:

> Judah and Israel were as numerous as the sand by the sea; they ate and drank and were happy.... During Solomon's lifetime Judah and Israel lived in safety, from Dan even to Beer-sheba, all of them under their vines and fig trees. (1 Kings 4:20, 25)

But beneath and behind this picture of "happy" Judah and Israel reveling in the YHWH-given bounty received via the administration of their beneficent King Solomon lies another story altogether.

To begin to unravel this propagandistic portrait, let's consider the "fact" of "the twelve tribes of Israel" as a sociopolitical unit. Scholars seeking to understand "Israel's" social organization during the period preceding the monarchy have analogized from other cultures for a fitting model. For instance, the idea of an "amphictyony" similar to the Athenian League has been proposed as a lens through which to view tribal Israel.[46] However, later scholarship showed that this model does not fit the picture of biblical Israel.[47] For our purposes, suffice it to recall that, unlike Athens, people living in small cities and villages within the land of Canaan had no writing or long-distance communication. They had little basis before Solomon's establishment and securing of long-distance trade routes for traveling across mountains, deserts, and rivers to establish any kind of relationship with people more than a few days distance, except for occasional trading forays. Whatever "Israel" was before monarchy, it was not a sophisticated "league of nations."

Next, let's consider the question of "twelve tribes." We saw in Part I that the book of Genesis was (mostly) likely written during the period of the Babylonian Exile. Its portrayal of Jacob as father of eleven sons who

---

46. Pioneered by Noth; see also Cross (1973).
47. See the major critique by Gottwald (1979), 345–86.

become the eponymous tribal "fathers" comes from a much later tradition than the David/Solomon saga, as does the wider patriarchal narrative of Abraham/Sarah, Isaac/Rebekah, and Jacob/Rachel–Leah. For instance, note the distribution of the mention of *any* of the primary patriarchs in the Genesis–2 Kings narrative in Table 7.

Table 7: Mention of Abraham, Isaac, and Jacob from Genesis to 2 Kings

Book	*Abraham*	*Isaac*	*Jacob*
Genesis	134 times	82 times	188 times
Exodus	9 times, always as the formula "Abraham, Isaac, and Jacob"		Exod. 1:1, 5; 19:3, "house of Jacob"
Leviticus	Only 26:42: "…then will I remember my covenant with Jacob; I will remember also my covenant with Isaac and also my covenant with Abraham, and I will remember the land."		
Numbers	Only 32:11: "…the land that I swore to give to Abraham, to Isaac, and to Jacob…"		23:7, 10, 21, 23; 24:5, 17, 19; 32:11
Deuteronomy	7 times, always as formula "Abraham, Isaac, and Jacob"		32:9; 33:4, 10, 28
Joshua	24:2–4: a brief summary of the journey from "beyond the River" to Egypt		Also 24:32
Judges	none		
1 Samuel	none		12:8: "When Jacob went into Egypt and the Egyptians oppressed them…"
2 Samuel	none		23:1: "…the God of Jacob…"
1 Kings	18:36: "…YHWH, God of Abraham, Isaac, and Israel…"		18:31: "Elijah took twelve stones, according to the number of the tribes of the sons of Jacob, to whom the word of YHWH came, saying, 'Israel shall be your name.'"
2 Kings	13:23: "…covenant with Abraham, Isaac, and Jacob…"		17:34: "…children of Jacob, whom he named Israel."

There appears but the most minimal of references to the three patriarchs outside Genesis up to 2 Kings other than in the formula "Abraham, Isaac and Jacob," even in texts designated by most scholars as "Priestly" (such as Leviticus) and thus *exilic or postexilic*. But in the section on which we are focused (1 Sam.–2 Kings), there is virtually no reference at all.[48]

Furthermore, the tribal "fathers" are *never* named and listed throughout the books of Samuel and Kings. In fact, the only tribal "fathers" mentioned at all in Samuel–Kings are Benjamin, Dan, Naphtali, Gad, and Asher and among these, only Benjamin and Naphtali as "tribes."[49] The others are simply geographic regions, not specifically linked to Israel's ancestors and not distinguished from neighboring places which are *not* named after Jacob's sons.

The "twelve tribes" are listed only at Deuteronomy 27:12–13 and Joshua 21:[50] By all scholarly accounts, these are seventh-century compositions. Deuteronomy–Joshua forms a continuous unit separate from the monarchical history. Table 8 shows one aspect of this: the focus in these two books on Moses, in contrast with the Samuel/Kings narrative.

What we see is that "after" Joshua, the great liberating hero Moses is basically "forgotten" throughout the monarchy. The passages in 2 Kings that mention Moses are clearly from a later time than the composition of the David/Solomon story, as part of a "compromise" that we'll examine in chapter 12. Only David's passing reference in 1 Kings 2:3 and the three in Solomon's temple dedication speech at 1 Kings 8 break the silence "since" the person of Samuel at 1 Samuel 12.

Let's summarize what we've seen so far. None of the patriarchs, the Jacobic sons, or Moses are part of the monarchic story's "history." The "twelve tribes of Israel" as a form of *national* identity does not predate the David/Solomon period. As historians Maxwell Miller and John Hayes write, "We doubt that such a politically and religiously unified twelve-tribe Israel existed in premonarchical times."[51] We'll explore in chapter 13 the local, tribal, clan, and extended family identity that *did* generate religious and socioeconomic bonds among peoples in the hill country of what became "Judah." For now, the main point is this: *before David and Solomon, there was no such entity as "the twelve tribes of Israel."*

With this in mind, let's look more closely at what 1 Kings tells us about the scope and method of Solomon's reign within "the Land." Our central passage is 1 Kings 3–4. The unit begins with the narrator's announcement in

---

48. The usage in 1 Kings 18:31, 36 is certainly from a period later than the writing of the David/Solomon narrative, perhaps as late as 200 years, as we'll see.

49. Benjamin is called a *shebet* (1 Sam. 9:21, 10:20, 21; 1 Kings 12:1), while Naphtali is called a *matteh* (1 Kings 7:14.) Both terms are used throughout the Hebrew Bible, but infrequently in Samuel/Kings (*shebet* 31 times of 190 total; *matteh* 4 of 252 total). The other uses in Samuel/Kings of either word is as "stick," another meaning of both Hebrew terms translated "tribe."

50. Deut. 33 lists eleven.

51. Miller and Hayes, 78.

Table 8: Mention of Moses in Genesis through 2 Kings

Book	Occurrences
Genesis	None
Exodus	290 times
Leviticus	86 times
Numbers	233 times
Deuteronomy	38 times
Joshua	58 times
Judges	1:16, 20; 3:4; 4:11
1 Samuel	12:6, 8 (Samuel's speech to the people in preparation for the monarchy)
2 Samuel	None
1 Kings	2:3 (David's deathbed speech to Solomon); 8:9, 53, 56 (Solomon's temple dedication speech)
2 Kings	14:6 (re: Amaziah); 18:4, 6, 12 (re: Hezekiah); 21:8 (re: Manasseh); 23:25 (re: Josiah)

the closing verse of the preceding chapter: "So the kingdom was established in the hand of Solomon" (2:46). Table 9 outlines the narrated sequence of events that follows.

Let's observe several aspects of this introduction to Solomon's reign. First, it all seems to happen out of nowhere and all at once. Where Saul and David each struggled with local enemies and with each other over the course of decades, Solomon's tremendous wealth and power seem to appear out of thin air. Suddenly, Solomon has an army of horses and charioteers to rival any empire in the region. Already we can guess that there must be more than meets the eye in the relationship between this account and the "facts on the ground."

Second, we hear that Solomon has organized the region around a twelve-unit administrative structure. If one reads the description of the twelve regions carefully (which the writer lays out in detail), we note that only the "tribes" of Naphtali, Asher, Issachar, and Benjamin are within "Israel," while "Judah" is a separate region outside the twelve-unit body referred to collectively as "all Israel" (4:7). The king does not oversee Judah directly, but has delegated authority to an unnamed royal official (4:19). None of these four "tribes" is referred to *as* a "tribe," nor are the four distinguished from other geographic descriptors within each official's region of authority. There is not a hint that what Solomon has done was to rearrange or destroy "traditional" tribal boundaries, an assumption many scholars make. The reason, as we've seen, is that the biblical descriptions of tribal allotments

Table 9: Outline of 1 Kings 3–4

3:1: The announcement of Solomon's first royal act: a "marriage alliance" with "Pharaoh King of Egypt."

3:2–4: The note that "the people are sacrificing at the high places, however, because no house had yet been built for the name of YHWH"; this includes Solomon, who goes to Gibeon, the "great high place."

3:5–15: The report of Solomon's dream, in which YHWH grants him wisdom

3:16–28: The story of the two prostitute-mothers, whose dispute Solomon resolves

4:1–19: The list of Solomon's royal officers (*sarrim*), divided into two groups:

> vv. 2–4: The cabinet: priests, scribes, recorder, army chief of staff

> vv. 5–19: The *twelve* regional chiefs and the lands over which they have authority

4:20–25: Summary of Solomon's authority, in chiastic form:

> A: (v. 20): "Judah and Israel" are "happy" and numerous
>> B: (v. 21): Solomon's territorial "sovereignty," "from the Euphrates to the land of the Philistines, even to the border of Egypt"
>>> C: (vv. 22–23): the daily provision for the king in grain and animals
>> B¹ (v. 24): Solomon's "dominion" extends "over all the region west of the Euphrates from Tiphsah to Gaza, over all the kings west of the Euphrates; and he had peace on all sides."
> A¹ (v. 25): "During Solomon's lifetime Judah and Israel lived in safety, from Dan even to Beer-sheba, all of them under their vines and fig trees."

4:26: Solomon's 40,000 horse stalls and 12,000 horsemen

4:27–28: the source of the provision in 4:22–23: tribute extracted by the provincial officials named at 4:5–19

4:29–34: Description of Solomon's wisdom

for the "sons of Jacob" all come from a much later period than that of David and Solomon.

The new king's administrative arrangement is presented along with the double notation of Israel and Judah's "happy" and "peaceful" condition. There is no narrative whiff of rebellion or resistance, despite the fact that much resistance to David *had* been narrated (not least of which, his son Absalom's rebellion)[52] and later, Solomon's son Rehoboam will face immediate and definitive resistance that breaks up the sovereignty established under his father.

What we're seeing, therefore, is not a radical rearrangement of a long-standing "national" tribal confederation, but rather a *bold act of nation building.* We noted earlier Halpern's conclusion that the Solomonic reign was founded not so much on monumental architecture and the infrastructure of a huge capital city but instead on a network of trade routes that funneled wealth from local regions into the royal coffers. Solomon's administrative scheme — twelve regions each overseen by officers who assure that huge quantities of grain and animals reach Jerusalem throughout the year — is *the beginning* of the "nation of Israel and Judah."

There is another point to observe about this summary before we look more closely at the "two prostitutes" story. Why does the narrator distinguish "Israel" from "Judah" in the naming of administrative regions and their officials? The text stated earlier that Saul's reign was over "Israel" and David's over "Judah" before Saul's death. With the demise of Israel's king, the following scene unfolds:

> Then all the tribes of Israel came to David at Hebron, and said, "Look, we are your bone and flesh. For some time, while Saul was king over us, it was you who led out Israel and brought it in. YHWH said to you: It is you who shall be shepherd of my people Israel, you who shall be ruler over Israel." So all the elders of Israel came to the king at Hebron; and King David made a covenant with them at Hebron before YHWH, and they anointed David king over Israel. David was thirty years old when he began to reign, and he reigned forty years. At Hebron he reigned over Judah seven years and six months; and at Jerusalem he reigned over all Israel and Judah thirty-three years. (2 Sam. 5:1–5)

From the beginning, "Israel" and "Judah" as monarchical subjects were distinct. The "tribes of Israel" referred to collectively here (but not numbered or named specifically) claim that David is "bone and flesh" with them.[53] At

---

52. E.g., Shimei's public name-calling and stone-throwing at David (2 Sam. 16:5–13) and Sheba's aborted rebellion (2 Sam. 20:1–22), which anticipated the rebellion against Solomon's son, Rehoboam, with the common rallying cry, "We have no portion in David, no share in the son of Jesse! Everyone to your tents, O Israel!" (2 Sam. 20:1; 1 Kings 12:16).

53. The phrase "bone and flesh" is used twice elsewhere in the Hebrew Bible: for Laban's relationship with Jacob (Gen. 29:14) and for Abimelech's rationale for his rule over the "lords of Shechem" (Judg. 9:2); cf. Gen. 2:23. The latter use precedes Jotham's anti-monarchical

the same time, even in their plea that he reign over them (presumably because of their fear that he would now destroy them), they distinguish two *political* entities. There is one "ethnic" group (bone and flesh)[54] that has been formed into two *nations,* each claiming YHWH as the basis of their peoplehood and their kingship. What had begun under David as a two-nation, confederated monarchy has now become a "united" monarchy under the oversight of Solomon's administrative officials.

At the end of the unit we're considering, Solomon's great wisdom is described in familiar ancient Near East terms. He composes proverbs and writes songs. He knows all about plants and animals. His wisdom is so famous that people "came from all the nations to hear" it displayed (4:34). But what does this traditional kind of royal boasting have to do with the dream at Gibeon in 1 Kings 3? And most strangely perhaps, what does it have to do with the *only narrated public act of Solomon's wisdom,* the adjudication of a maternity dispute between two street prostitutes?

Not Dividing the Baby

As we consider "Solomon's wisdom" at the start of his reign, we also must look at the end. In 1 Kings 12:1, the narrator says succinctly that "Solomon slept with his ancestors and was buried in the city of his father David; and his son Rehoboam succeeded him." There is no battle for the throne. Dynasty has been firmly established and Rehoboam is now king.

Immediately, a delegation led by a former Solomonic official named Jeroboam approaches the new king at Shechem:[55]

> "Your father made our yoke heavy. Now therefore lighten the hard service of your father and his heavy yoke that he placed on us, and we will serve you."
> He said to them, "Go away for three days, then come again to me."
> So the people went away.

The truth behind the royal propaganda is revealed: Solomon's reign was not all "happy" and "peaceful," but was in fact a "heavy yoke" and "hard service," "reminiscent" of Pharaoh (see, e.g., Exod. 1:14 and Table 4 above).[56] The new king seeks advice from two groups. First, he asks his father's seasoned veterans, who are now free to speak their minds:

---

parable of the olive, fig, and vine refusing to be anointed as king over the other trees. It is likely that the Judges story is a later reflection on monarchy, perhaps criticizing David's (Abimelech's) supposed "kinship" basis for ruling over Israel. Cf. Schöpflin.

54. See also chapter 13 below on "ethnicity" as a category describing "Israel."

55. Recall that in Gen. 34 Shechem was the site of the rape of Jacob's daughter, Dinah, and the slaughter of the Shechemites. In the wider Deuteronomistic History, it was the site of the "covenant renewal" ceremony led by Joshua (Josh. 24).

56. The passage overflows with words expressing "heavy" and "harsh": 12:4, 10, 11, 13, 14 all repeat the same Hebrew stem *qshh* as a verb or adjective.

They answered him, "If you will be a servant to this people today and serve them, and speak good words to them when you answer them, then they will be your servants forever." (12:7)

But the arrogant young king "disregarded" their advice and turned to "the young men who had grown up with him and now attended him." Their own youthful arrogance reinforces Rehoboam's, as they advise him to respond to the petitioners with an image equating royal authority with male virility:

Thus you should say to this people who spoke to you, "Your father made our yoke heavy, but you must lighten it for us"; thus you should say to them, "My little finger[57] is thicker than my father's loins. Now, whereas my father laid on you a heavy yoke, I will add to your yoke. My father disciplined you with whips, but I will discipline you with scorpions."

Who could misunderstand the meaning of "a thick little finger" in comparison to a "father's loins"? But the young leaders radically miscalculated. Immediately upon hearing the king's answer, "all Israel" replied:

"What share do we have in David? We have no inheritance in the son of Jesse. To your tents, O Israel! Look now to your own house, O David." So Israel went away to their tents. But Rehoboam reigned over the Israelites who were living in the towns of Judah. (12:16b–17)

The alert reader of the biblical narrative will recognize what is now a familiar cry. Soon after David and Joab put down Absalom's rebellion, we were told:

Now a scoundrel named Sheba son of Bichri, a Benjaminite, happened to be there. He sounded the trumpet and cried out, "We have no portion in David, no share in the son of Jesse! Everyone to your tents, O Israel!"
    So all the people of Israel withdrew from David and followed Sheba son of Bichri; but the people of Judah followed their king steadfastly from the Jordan to Jerusalem. (2 Sam. 20:1–2)

The grizzled king David and his military leaders easily put down Sheba's rebellion. But the cry became a political slogan, awaiting the right moment to be proclaimed again. Solomon's tight control squelched resistance. But Rehoboam and his young companions were not as strong, and the "united kingdom" of Israel and Judah came apart. Rehoboam's authority over "Israel" became limited to those "foreigners" dwelling in Judah.

We are now ready to turn to the one story that the author of the David/Solomon saga narrates to convey the essence of Solomon's "wisdom." It is highly ironic that the story of the two prostitutes and their

---

57. The Hebrew text leaves the adjective "little" unattached to an object, allowing readers' imaginations to fill in the sexual image.

babies has become a proverbial call for compromise, under the rubric of "cutting the baby in half." Of course, that is exactly what is *not* possible in the story: a "living son" cannot be divided. The king's wisdom, on the story's surface, was to offer a suggestion that would separate the real mother from the counterfeit, on the assumption that a real mother would not allow the killing even of someone else's baby. Indeed, this is what happened, as the narrator tells us that "compassion for her son burned within her" (3:26).

To get to the deeper meaning of this story, we must pause to see how the writer has "taught us to read" this kind of tale. Consider the story's *narrative placement*: it comes right after Solomon's "dream" and before the listing of his officials, sovereignty, and so forth. How likely is it that the *first and only public act in the king's entire reign* was to resolve a maternity suit between two urban prostitutes? Is this the reason Israel wanted a king? The absurdity of this scenario cries out for readers to ask what's really going on.

Let's look briefly at two similar stories earlier in the David/Solomon saga. The first comes immediately after David's dalliance with Bathsheba, which led David to have her husband, Uriah, killed by telling Joab secretly to put Uriah in the heat of the ongoing battle (2 Sam. 11:14–15, a battle for which the warrior-king stayed home). With Uriah's death and Bathsheba's requisite ritual mourning, the king took her as a wife and she bore the "love child." But, we are told, "the thing that David had done was evil to YHWH" (11:27). YHWH sent the court prophet Nathan to present the king with this parable:

> There were two men in a certain city, the one rich and the other poor. The rich man had very many flocks and herds; but the poor man had nothing but one little ewe lamb, which he had bought. He brought it up, and it grew up with him and with his children; it used to eat of his meager fare, and drink from his cup, and lie in his bosom, and it was like a daughter to him. Now there came a traveler to the rich man, and he was loath to take one of his own flock or herd to prepare for the wayfarer who had come to him, but he took the poor man's lamb, and prepared that for the guest who had come to him. (2 Sam. 12:1–4)

David, as expected, reacts with indignant rage and demands the death of "the man." Nathan, however, tells him "*You* are 'the man'!" Two observations are essential. First, David's strong reaction indicates that he didn't realize that Nathan's story was a parable. His anger only makes sense if he believed that what he was hearing was a "true story." Second, Nathan's response, seemingly clear in its reference, is a masterpiece of multilayered ambiguity; if not in his own mind, then at least in the mind of the writer. "The man" in the most immediate sense was obviously the "rich man" who took "one little ewe lamb," from the poor man to give to the traveler. Nathan's speech confirmed this reading of the parable, as he pronounced YHWH's judgment on the king for his "taking" of Bathsheba, the "ewe lamb," from Uriah, the "poor man." But as Robert Polzin has shown, there is *much* more going on here. He notes that "2 Sam. 12 is the hermeneutic center of the entire royal history" because it can be read from so many perspectives within both the David / Solomon story and the wider historical narrative from Joshua to 2 Kings that has grown up around it.[58] Table 10, adapted and expanded from Polzin's insight, shows many aspects of Israel's narrated history that can be read through the lens of Nathan's parable.

What David heard as a "true story" and Nathan intended as a fiction to get the king to confess to the immediate crime is a kind of prism through which we can see the entire journey from Exodus to Exile.

In case one might think this story is unique, a mere two chapters later we find another example of a multileveled, "real" parable. This time, Joab, the king's military chief of staff, told the tale. The situation at hand is that Absalom had just killed his half-brother Amnon in revenge for Amnon's rape of Absalom's full sister, Tamar. Absalom fled to Geshur, the home of his maternal grandfather. Meanwhile, David, we are told, "mourned for his son day after day.... And the heart of the king went out, yearning for Absalom" (2 Sam. 13:37, 39). Joab, always the political "realist,"[59] saw that the king was distracted from his royal role by his fatherly feelings. On the one hand, the cold-blooded murder of a royal son could not go unheeded. On the other, David was father to both murderer and victim. He was caught between these two roles, paralyzed into inaction. Joab endeavored to break the king's internal stalemate by sending a "wise woman"[60] from the town of Tekoa to David to playact a story of Joab's devising. He told her to "pretend to be a mourner; put on mourning garments, do not anoint yourself with oil, but behave like a woman who has been mourning many days for the dead." Then he "put words into her mouth," which pour out before David:

> When the woman of Tekoa came to the king, she fell on her face to the ground and did obeisance, and said, "Help, O King!"
>
> The king asked her, "What is your trouble?"
>
> She answered, "Alas, I am a widow; my husband is dead. Your servant had two sons, and they fought with one another in the field; there was no one to part them, and one struck the other and killed him.[61] Now the whole family has risen against your servant. They say, 'Give up the man who struck his brother, so that we may kill him for the life of his brother whom he murdered, even if we destroy the heir as well.' Thus they would quench my one remaining ember, and leave to my husband neither name nor remnant on the face of the earth." (2 Sam. 14:4–7)

---

58. Polzin (1993), 120. Abraham's and Sarah's extravagant hospitality to travelers (Gen. 18), offering not a mere ewe-lamb but a tender calf, can be heard as an exilic country-story to Nathan's parable.

59. Political scientist Caleb Henry, 330, argues for Joab as a biblical anti-Machiavellian "warning."

60. Cf. 1 Kings 2:9; 3:12; 5:7, all about Solomon's political "wisdom."

61. Note how the author of Genesis has taken this story and made it the basis for the Cain and Abel narrative in Gen. 4.

Table 10:
The Rich Man, Poor Man, Traveler, and Ewe Lamb

Context in history	Rich man	Poor man	Ewe-lamb	Traveler
Conquest (Josh-Judges)	YHWH	Canaanites	Land of Canaan	Israel
Beginning of monarchy	Israel	Surrounding nations	Monarchy	YHWH/ Samuel
Early days of Saul	Saul	Agag	Sheep(!) (1 Sam. 15:9ff.)	Samuel/ Israelite soldiers
Early days of David	Saul	David	Michal	Palti (1 Sam. 25:44; reversed at 2 Sam 3:15)
Rise of David	YHWH	Palti	Michal	David
The immediate plot	David	Uriah	Bathsheba	Judah (as recipient of David's offspring to be king, i.e., Solomon)
Amnon's rape of Tamar	YHWH	David	Tamar	Amnon
Absalom's rebellion	YHWH	David	David's concubines (2 Sam. 16:22)	Absalom
Adonijah's final plot (the "gift" refused)	Solomon	David	(Abishag 1 Kings 1:2; 2:17–25)	Adonijah
Exile	YHWH	Judah	The Land	Babylon

One might think that the wily David wouldn't fall for such a trick twice, but he did, at least at first. In a few verses, we reach the climax of the story.

> Then she said, "Please, may the king keep YHWH your God in mind, so that the avenger of blood may kill no more, and my son not be destroyed."
> He said, "As YHWH lives, not one hair of your son shall fall to the ground."

Then the woman said, "Please let your servant speak a word to my lord the king." He said, "Speak."

The woman said, "Why then have you planned such a thing against the people of God? For in giving this decision the king convicts himself, inasmuch as the king does not bring his banished one home again." (14:11–13)

When the woman finished her speech, the king finally caught on, and he asked her, "Is the hand of Joab with you in all this?" (14:19) She admitted the truth and then disappeared suddenly as we find the king speaking directly to Joab in v. 21, granting permission to bring Absalom home from exile.

Twice in three chapters, the king is victim of a setup by his closest advisors. Again, even on the surface of the story, the "truth" is parabolic, not literal, but depends on David taking it as "fact." Joab's story of "two sons" can also be understood as a lens through which to read the wider monarchy narrative. To see how, we turn finally to the story of "two sons," which Solomon's "wisdom" resolved.

Perhaps most surprising, in light of these observations, is how the "Solomon's wisdom" story has been taken largely at face value by scholars.[62] We may have laughed at David's expense as we watched him fall into Joab's trap so soon after slipping into Nathan's noose. But are we as readers gullible enough, or inattentive enough, to allow ourselves to be tricked yet again? In other words, is the story of the "two prostitutes" and their two sons any more a "true story" than the one from the mouth of the wise woman of Tekoa?[63]

The narrator has given us all the clues we need to see the tale in 1 Kings 3:16–27 as of the same type as Nathan's and Joab's. Consider first the categorizing of the women as "prostitutes" (*zonoth*). While there are a few references to literal prostitutes in the Hebrew Bible, the overwhelming majority of uses of *zonah* is as a *metaphor for idolatry,* usually that of Israel or Judah. My premise has been that the David/Solomon story is the Bible's first written text, so I cannot argue that our writer is calling upon an already familiar trope. However, the sheer frequency and range of the use of *zonah* as a term expressing religious infidelity to YHWH indicates that it soon became a standard way of speaking, especially among the prophets. Here are a few examples:

YHWH said to Moses, "Soon you will lie down with your ancestors. Then this people will begin to prostitute themselves to the foreign gods

---

62. Hays (2004), 164–65, comes close in stating, "In the context of the upcoming civil war between Judah and Israel, the struggle for the throne, and the immediate lapse into foreign idolatry, this story is rather suggestive." However, he lets the matter drop there and does not pursue what that "suggestive" meaning might be.

63. Note also the "flip side" of the 1 Kings 3 story at 2 Kings 6:24–33, where two mothers argue amid a famine over one's refusal to allow her son to be eaten, as they had agreed, after the first son had been eaten. For the relationship between these two stories, see the exchange between Lasine (1991 and 1993) and Pyper.

in their midst, the gods of the land into which they are going; they will forsake me, breaking my covenant that I have made with them. (Deut. 31:16)

How the faithful city has become a whore! She that was full of justice, righteousness lodged in her — but now murderers! (Isa. 1:21; see also Isa. 23:16; 57:3)

For long ago you broke your yoke and burst your bonds, and you said, "I will not serve!" On every high hill and under every green tree you sprawled and played the whore. (Jer. 2:20; see also Jer. 3:1–8)

But you trusted in your beauty, and played the whore because of your fame, and lavished your whorings on any passer-by. (Ezek. 16:15)

There were two women, the daughters of one mother; they played the whore in Egypt; they played the whore in their youth; their breasts were caressed there, and their virgin bosoms were fondled. Oholah was the name of the elder and Oholibah the name of her sister. They became mine, and they bore sons and daughters. As for their names, Oholah is Samaria, and Oholibah is Jerusalem. (Ezek. 23:2–4)

Note how the final example, from the exilic prophet Ezekiel, speaks of Samaria and Jerusalem, the capital cities of the separated nations of Israel and Judah, as "sisters" who are both whores.

The second clue given us by the writer is that the first woman began her story by claiming that

this woman and I live in the same *house* and I gave birth while she was in the *house*. Then on the third day after I gave birth, this woman also gave birth. We were together; there was no one else with us in the *house*, only the two of us were in the *house*. (3:17–18)

The key term "house" is repeated four times, lest one miss it. "House" is the multivalent word that enabled Nathan to speak the "prophecy" forecasting a dynasty for David at 2 Samuel 7. There, the word is used *fifteen times* in one chapter, as it plays on the double meaning of a physical building and a dynasty, i.e., "the house of David." David had been concerned with the impropriety of his own dwelling in a "house of cedar" while the ark of God's "house" was a mere tent. Nathan took this double entendre and turned it upside down. It is YHWH, not David, who is the builder of houses. And, YHWH added (via Nathan), it will be David's "seed" who will "build a house for my name, and I will establish the throne of his kingdom forever" (2 Sam. 7:13). The central "action" performed by Solomon is indeed the construction of this "house" — the Jerusalem temple — upon which the writer spends several chapters elaborating in great detail. So as we listen to a prostitute tell us repeatedly about how she is "in the house," can we avoid hearing a double reference to the Davidic monarchy and the temple?

Putting these clues together, as well as evidence to follow, we can hear that the story is itself a parable/allegory akin to those of Nathan and Joab. From this perspective, each detail falls into place. The two prostitutes represent the two "peoples," Israel and Judah, each desiring a "son," i.e., their own monarchy that establishes their identity.[64] The first son, we hear, "died in the night" because the mother "lay [*shachbah*] on him." The Hebrew verb *shchb* is used forty times in 1–2 Kings, most often for a king "sleeping with his fathers," i.e., dying. The first son is the "house of Saul," Israel's "son," which is now dead (i.e., has been wiped out by David). The dead son's mother, we are told, then "took" the other son and "laid him at her breast [*becheyqah*]." The Hebrew word here was used twice before in the David/Solomon story: last at 1 Kings 1:2 (Abishag lying at David's "bosom") and before that at 2 Samuel 12:3, 8, in the *midst of the parable of the ewe lamb*. Did it not seem strange in that story that a man is described as keeping a ewe lamb "with him and with his children; it used to eat of his meager fare, and drink from his cup, and *lie in his bosom*, and it was like a daughter to him"? All along, our writer was setting us up for this connection.[65] Israel's monarchy, like the poor man's ewe lamb, has been like a "child" (whether "son" as here or "daughter" as in Nathan's story), growing up with the people and eating what they ate. What a contrast with Solomon, whose daily provision included one hundred *sheep* (4:23).

In place of this dead son/monarchy, Israel has "taken" David as her "son." But when the mother of the living son awakens[66] what she saw was that "it was not the son I had borne." It is the writer's sly reference, intended for "insiders," that Solomon was no David. Indeed, Halpern concludes his detailed study of the David/Solomon story by claiming that the most likely reason the writer had to construct a narrative that admits so much about the protagonists that is unflattering is that *Solomon was not even David's real son*.[67] That is, not only is Solomon "no David" in the sense of being a much flatter character — not being a warrior hero and so forth — he was a *usurper* used by Nathan, Bathsheba, Zadok, and company to "establish" the house of David on a much larger scale. They needed someone moldable, one who wouldn't dare assert his own "personality," lest the position as royal puppet be taken away. Later in the monarchy, we see an insider elite more than once put a puppet of their choosing on the throne: the nursing

---

64. See also the discussion on pp. 189–90 of a similar use of "sons" as symbols of kings in the story of Hannah and Elkanah which serves as prologue to the monarchy story.

65. The word is used twice more in the wider monarchy story, at 1 Kings 17:19 and 22:35.

66. How, in a "factual" reading of the story, could she know what the other woman had done while she was asleep?

67. Halpern (2004), 401–4.

Joash (2 Kings 11:2–12) and the eight-year-old Josiah (2 Kings 21:24).[68] In fact, the setting up of Joash happens in response to this experience:

> Now when Athaliah, Ahaziah's [the current king] mother, *saw that her son was dead*, she set about to destroy all the royal family. (2 Kings 11:1)

The issue in the Ahaziah / Joash transition is the shift from a king of Judah (Ahaziah) from the Omride dynasty of Israel to a king of the Davidic line. Thus, what Athaliah, the queen mother, saw was that the Omride dynasty was "dead," just as the mother in our passage saw that Israel's Saulide dynasty was "dead." Thus, the later writer of the subsequent chapters of the books of Kings understood how to read this story and knew exactly what Solomon's "wisdom" was about: *holding the combined entities of Israel and Judah together under one "son."*

Israel, the mother of the dead son, was willing to say that the "living son" was "neither mine nor yours" and that it could be "divided." Recall that the moment Solomon was dead, it was the "assembly of *all Israel*" that came to Rehoboam with its complaint and plea. When it was refused, they cried, "What share do we have in David? We have no inheritance in the *son* of Jesse! To your tents, O Israel! Look now to *your own house*, O David!" In other words, Israel was never really invested in the "house of David," the "living son." It preferred division over long-term "hard service" under the sons of David. Furthermore, as we'll see in the next chapter, they were willing to accept that their "son" was dead and establish themselves without an imperial monarch at all.

Solomon's "wisdom" was developing an internal system of regional oversight and tribute that would extract wealth from local tribes and clans without leading to "Israel's" departure, supplemented by an elaborate series of international diplomatic arrangements, starting with his marriage alliance with Egypt's Pharaoh. His own son Rehoboam could not hold it together. But during Solomon's lifetime, Israel and Judah were "one," at least from the perspective of Jerusalem.

Was all this the will of YHWH? According to the first part of 1 Kings 3, Solomon's wisdom was given to him by YHWH in a dream. Of course, the only possible source for this story was Solomon himself. The writer left a tantalizing ambiguity in the dream story. It begins: "At Gibeon YHWH appeared to Solomon in a dream by night" (3:5) and concludes: "Then Solomon awoke; it had been a dream" (3:15).[69] We must ask, was it a "real" dream in which Solomon encountered YHWH or was it "only a dream" in

---

68. Note that in Solomon's dream that precedes this story, he acknowledged to YHWH, "I am only a little child; I do not know how to go out or come in" (3:7). "To go out or come in" is a euphemism for leading the people in battle during war, e.g., 1 Sam. 8:20; 17:55; cf. 2 Sam. 11:1. We realize that we don't know how old the new king was when he was put on the throne by his elders. In fact, we are *never* given Solomon's age, although we will be told that Rehoboam was forty-one years old when he began to reign (1 Kings 14:21).

69. Note the last entry in Table 4, showing the identical phrase used regarding Pharaoh and his dream at Gen. 41:7. We saw in chapter 7 that the Joseph story planted strong seeds of

which the young king dreamed of being given great wisdom by God? We cannot answer based on the text alone, certainly a deliberate ambiguity on the writer's part. For those who promoted the "Zion theology" that placed YHWH in the Jerusalem temple and all worship there, Solomon could be understood as truly empowered by YHWH with "wisdom." For those whose experience of YHWH was radically different — what we'll come to see as "Sinai theology" — Solomon's "experience" can be written off as either wishful thinking or simply as propaganda.[70]

To the later authors of Genesis, the received story in the by-then "ancient" books of Kings was taken as an example of supreme arrogance rather than divine authorization. Traditional scholarship has taken the Garden of Eden story to be from the "Yahwist" source and thus an expression of the equation of the Garden with Jerusalem. However, a fresh look at the relationship suggests a different conclusion. The key is in what Solomon "admits" in his dream, as he responds to God's offer to "ask what I should give you":

> Give your servant therefore an understanding mind to govern your people, *able to discern between good and evil;* for who can govern this your great people? (3:9)

Of course, this is exactly what was prohibited to the man and woman in the Garden. The Genesis story could not have been written by people in Solomon's court, since it condemns as primal disobedience succumbing to the desire to know / discern "good and evil," because it would make someone too much like "one of us" (Gen. 3:22). Solomon's dream "admits," especially from the perspective of Genesis, that only one with the knowledge of good and evil is fit to rule YHWH's people. That is, *the only "qualified" king is YHWH.* The Genesis story not only condemns Babylonian claims to embody the divine order within empire, but also those of Solomon and his successors. By placing their text "in the beginning," the Genesis writers (and the Bible's compilers) sought to undermine the pre-existing claim that Solomon's empire was somehow different from those of "the other nations."[71]

As we'll see, that perspective hardly began with the writing of Genesis during exile. Many, if not most, of the people subject to the Davidic monarchy chafed under its "hard service" and "heavy yoke." Much of what follows the David / Solomon saga — and what precedes it within the final biblical sequence — was written within an ambivalent acceptance of the

---

doubt about YHWH's role in maintaining imperial authority, despite Joseph's assurance that it was a divine dream.

70. Cf. Brueggemann (1990b), 118, concluding that the stories in 1 Kings 3:3–14 and 4:29–34 "are rendered imaginatively and function intentionally as propaganda."

71. Recall the note earlier (chapter 6) about how Genesis could be reread with the monarchy as "background" as expressing opposition not only to the "religion of empire" embodied in Babylon but also the one embodied in Jerusalem.

"truth" of Nathan's prophecy, which promised in YHWH's name a permanent holder of the Davidic throne. The writer whose task it was to legitimize the placing of the usurper, Solomon, on the Davidic seat as king over both Israel and Judah had to walk a very narrow line between supporting and undermining his patron. Failure could easily mean instant death, as it did for Adonijah, Joab, and others who refused to accept Solomon's reign. The writer did manage to walk that line. As a result, the written narrative of the Exodus to Exile journey begins with this highly ambiguous "celebration" of the "wisest" of Israel's and Judah's kings.

Chapter Ten

Finding the "Way Out"

Jeroboam's Rebellion

Most people have probably heard of King Solomon, son of David, even if they don't know or can't recall much of his story. But how many know of King Jeroboam, son of Nebat? Yet the Bible mentions the king who led the rebellion against Solomon's son over a hundred times, almost eighty in 1–2 Kings.[1] We hear seventeen subsequent kings condemned for continuing in "the sins of" or "the way of" Jeroboam. What was it about this otherwise obscure leader that became the negative benchmark for royal faithfulness, according to the authors of the later sections of the monarchy story? Jeroboam may be unknown to us, but his narrative portrait is startlingly similar in several key ways to another biblical character familiar to all: Moses.

In chapter 9, we focused on how the text that sought to legitimize Solomon's reign conveys his "wisdom" with subtle ambiguity. But at the conclusion of the Solomon story in 1 Kings 11, the tone suddenly changes. It begins with the revelation that in addition to Pharaoh's daughter (3:1), Solomon also "loved many foreign women." The narrator then for the first time makes a direct (divine) judgment on Solomon's actions:

> YHWH had said to the Israelites, "You shall not enter into marriage with them, neither shall they with you; for they will surely incline your heart to follow their gods"; Solomon clung to these in love. (11:2)

In the final version of the Deuteronomistic History, this quote "recalls" Deuteronomy 7:1–4:

> When YHWH your God brings you into the land that you are about to enter and occupy, and he clears away many nations before you — the Hittites, the Girgashites, the Amorites, the Canaanites, the Perizzites, the Hivites, and the Jebusites, seven nations mightier and more numerous than you — and when YHWH your God gives them over to you and

---

1. The Masoretic Text (Hebrew) version of the Jeroboam narrative differs in substantial ways from the Septuagint (LXX, Greek) version. Furthermore, there are two different LXX traditions of the Jeroboam story. See Sweeney (2007) and Schenker for a discussion of the relationship among these three texts. For our purposes, we consider only the Masoretic version, upon which modern translations are largely based.

you defeat them, then you must utterly destroy them. Make no covenant with them and show them no mercy. Do not intermarry with them, giving your daughters to their sons or taking their daughters for your sons, for that would turn away your children from following me, to serve other gods. Then the anger of YHWH would be kindled against you, and he would destroy you quickly.

The problem is that Deuteronomy is, by all scholarly accounts, a text from the much later period of King Josiah in the seventh century (as we'll see). What we have in 1 Kings 11, then, is a retrospective judgment against Solomon. The Jeroboam narrative that follows is part of this later composition.

The condemnation shifts from the narrator's summary to the direct voice of YHWH to Solomon:

Therefore YHWH said to Solomon, "Since this has been your mind and you have not kept my covenant and my statutes that I have commanded you, *I will surely tear the kingdom from you and give it to your servant.* Yet for the sake of your father David I will not do it in your lifetime; I will tear it out of the hand of your son. I will not, however, tear away the entire kingdom; I will give one tribe to your son, for the sake of my servant David and for the sake of Jerusalem, which I have chosen." (11:11–13)

We next hear of two "adversaries" (*satan*) raised up by God against Solomon, Hadad the Edomite and Rezon, son of Eliada. Hadad is not an important character and never appears after this brief notice. That the text provides the following otherwise irrelevant detail about what Hadad had done to escape from David's avenging "angel," Joab, therefore stands out all the more:

Hadad fled to Egypt with some Edomites who were servants of his father. He was a young boy at that time. They set *out from Midian and came to Paran;* they took people with them from Paran and came to Egypt, to Pharaoh king of Egypt, who gave him a house, assigned him an allowance of food, and gave him land. Hadad found great favor in the sight of Pharaoh, so that he gave him his sister-in-law for a wife, the sister of Queen Tahpenes. The sister of Tahpenes gave birth by him to his son Genubath, whom Tahpenes weaned in Pharaoh's house; Genubath was in Pharaoh's house among the children of Pharaoh. When Hadad heard in Egypt that David slept with his ancestors and that Joab the commander of the army was dead, Hadad said to Pharaoh, "Let me depart, that I may go to my own country." But Pharaoh said to him, "What do you lack with me that you now seek to go to your own country?" And he said, "No, do let me go." (11:17–22)

This is a lot of detail for a story that is completely dropped. Let's consider a few elements. First, the fleeing from Midian to Paran matches the refuges found by Moses, escaping from Pharaoh (to Midian, Exod. 2:15) and David, escaping from Saul (to Paran, 1 Sam. 25:1). Furthermore, Paran frames the geographic reference of the entire book of Deuteronomy (1:1 and 33:2). Second, an Israelite finding favor with Pharaoh and having a half-Egyptian son matches both Joseph (Gen. 41:45–52) and Moses (Exod. 2:19–22).[2] Finally, when Hadad hears that his enemies David and Joab are dead, he asks Pharaoh's permission to leave Egypt, as Moses will do. Like Moses, Hadad is refused permission.

The Hadad scene brings Egypt into the story. Before the chapter is over, Jeroboam will have similarly fled to Egypt, awaiting the death of his own royal enemy, Solomon (11:40–41). Egypt has become a refuge for those standing against the Davidic dynasty. With that notice, the narrator brings the Solomon story to a formal close (11:42–43).

Let's back up a bit to the beginning of the Jeroboam story. We are given several details about him in the first verse:

> Jeroboam son of Nebat, an Ephraimite [*efrati*] of Zeredah, a servant of Solomon, whose mother's name was Zeruah,[3] a widow, rebelled against the king. (11:26)

Mark Leuchter shows how the Hebrew text identifies Jeroboam not as an "Ephraimite" but as an *Ephratite*. This connects him both to David (1 Sam. 17:12; also Ruth 1:2) and Elkanah, the husband of Hannah in the opening scene of 1 Samuel 1:1. Leuchter notes that the prophet Ahijah from Shiloh (where Elkanah went to worship) would celebrate the advent of an Ephratite from Zeredah (in the heart of Ephraim, proximate to Shiloh) within the house of Solomon as a potential replacement for the usurping king. This would hold the promise of restoring Shiloh to its former importance, having been itself usurped by Solomon's temple-building in Jerusalem.[4]

If readers are now thoroughly confused by the politics of place embedded in this network of cross-references, try simply to focus on the big picture. Jeroboam is the perfect candidate for leader of an Israelite rebellion against

---

2. The Midianites who invite Moses to marry into their family perceive him to be an *Egyptian*, Exod. 2:19.

3. Might this make Jeroboam's father, Nebat, a brother of Joab, Abishai, and Asahel, sons of *Zeruiah*, three of David's closest companions, whom he three times claims to be powerless in the face of (2 Sam. 2:18; 3:39; 16:10; 19:22) as they carry out assassinations helpful to David's hold on power? Recall that Joab had sided with Adonijah against Solomon, who then had Joab executed. Why else would Jeroboam's father's mother be named here (the Hebrew word order is more clear than the translation that Zeruah is Nebat's mother, not Jeroboam's)? The father of the sons of Zeruiah is never named, suggesting that she is a widow. If so, then Jeroboam's rebellion took up a struggle otherwise left off at the Solomonic succession. We know nothing else about Nebat and why, if he was a brother of three Davidic soldiers, he appears not to have been involved in David's reign.

4. Leuchter, 61, provides a helpful analysis of the political/theological tugging between Shiloh and Jerusalem, with Jeroboam in the middle.

the House of David. He is from a northern site with ties to a celebrated shrine that has been overshadowed by Jerusalem, *and* he is a trusted servant of Solomon, whom the king has placed in charge of the forced labor from "the house of Joseph,"[5] i.e., *Ephraim* (11:28).[6]

As such, the *Shilonite* prophet Ahijah tracked down Jeroboam beyond Solomon's watchful supporters' eyes and offered him "ten pieces" (of twelve) of the kingdom.[7] Ahijah both repeated the narrator's condemnation of Solomon for worshiping other gods (without blaming the wives, 11:33) and then turned to promise Jeroboam, in YHWH's name, "an enduring house as I built for David" (11:38). Ahijah thus offered to be Jeroboam's Nathan: the mouthpiece for a divine prophecy of dynastic succession into the distant future, if not forever. The initial presentation of Jeroboam is positive: he was chosen by YHWH as an instrument to replace Solomon, much as David was chosen to be the instrument to replace Saul (1 Sam. 15–16).[8]

Like David, Jeroboam must await his predecessor's death. Somehow Solomon got word of the prophecy and sought to kill Jeroboam, who fled to Egypt under the protection of Pharaoh Shishak.[9] It is this very pharaoh who will take the eventual separation of Israel from Judah under Rehoboam as a signal to raid Jerusalem (1 Kings 14:25).

When Solomon died, Jeroboam's supporters sent word to Egypt, and Jeroboam returned to lead the confrontation with Rehoboam. After Rehoboam's misguided reliance on his young advisors turns sour, Jeroboam's moment arrived.

---

5. "House of Joseph" is never mentioned in the torah; this, the only such reference here in 1 Kings, "recalls" 2 Samuel 19:20, where David's former "curser," Shimei, met the king as he fled Jerusalem in the face of Absalom's rebellion. He was identified as a Benjaminite (i.e., Saul's kin) who brought a thousand Benjaminites and a surviving retinue from the "house of Saul" to seek forgiveness for his cursing of David, declaring himself "the first of all *the house of Joseph* to come down to meet my lord the king." Abishai, a "son of Zeruiah," called for Shimei's death, but David distanced himself and promised Shimei, "you shall not die." On his deathbed, though, he reneged, advising Solomon "do not hold him guiltless, for you are a *wise* man; you will know what you ought to do to him, and you must bring his gray head down with blood to Sheol" (1 Kings 2:8–9). The repression of the house of Joseph under Jeroboam's oversight is thus a later expression of the ongoing hostility between the "house of David" and "the house of Saul" (Joseph).

6. Miller and Hayes, 208. First Kings 11:27, which states the reason for Jeroboam's rebellion, is very difficult to translate because of textual ambiguities in the Hebrew. The NRSV says, "Solomon built the Millo, and closed up the gap in the wall of the city of his father David," which explains nothing to the reader. Leuchter offers instead: "Solomon... besieged/surrounded [*sgr*] Perez, the city of David, his father," which would suggest that the king had attacked a city of Ephraim close to Jeroboam's home.

7. The shift from the Solomonic picture in 1 Kings 4 of twelve administrative units to that of a tribal union is another indication that the current text is from a later period.

8. Ash (1998) lists numerous parallels between David and Jeroboam.

9. Egyptian records of Shishak's tenth-century military campaign in Canaan are strong, if indirect, evidence of the historical basis for this section of the Deuteronomistic History; see Master, 122, Stager, 64–67, and Mazar (2003), 92. Further, Kitchen (117) dismisses flatly as "wrong" those who claim that "flight into Egypt is simply a folktale motif.... Real people sought help in Egypt or fled there, not just in stories."

When all Israel heard that Jeroboam had returned, they sent and called him to the assembly and made him king over all Israel. There was no one who followed the house of David, except the tribe of Judah alone. (1 Kings 12:20)

Rehoboam prepared to mount a counterattack, but was warned against it by a "man of God" named Shemaiah, the only time we hear Rehoboam listening to a word of YHWH (12:22–24). The narrative turns again to Jeroboam, now firmly in power outside Judah. We noted earlier that Moses was "in the air" of the Jeroboam story. Table 11 shows these parallels.

Table 11: Parallels between Moses and Jeroboam[10]

Event	*Text*
New king enslaves the population	Exod. 1:8; 1 Kings 2:12
Hero brought into royal court as royal servant to an oppressive "pharaoh"	Exod. 1:22–2:10; 1 Kings 11:26
Hero lives in exile after murder attempt / threat	Exod. 2:15; 1 Kings 11:40
Return after Pharaoh's death	Exod. 4:20; 1 Kings 12:2 Cf. "three days," Exod. 3:18; 5:3; 8:27; 1 Kings 12:5
Successful rebellion and flight	(throughout the Exodus narrative)
In addition: Midian as refuge	Exod. 2:15ff.; 1 Kings 11:18 (just before Jeroboam)
Aaron's sons, Nadab and Abihu (Exod. 6:23)	Jeroboam's sons, Nadab and Abijah (1 Kings 14:1, 20)

The account of Jeroboam's ascendancy to the throne of the new northern kingdom of "Israel" is portrayed by the later author of Kings as parallel to Moses' encounter with Pharaoh. But why would an author who is about to condemn Jeroboam and use that condemnation as the basis for subsequent judgment against other northern kings make Jeroboam look like Israel's greatest hero?

Recall how our inquiry began in chapter 9, as we entered into the contradictions within the portrayal of Solomon. In Table 4, we saw all the ways that Solomon matched Pharaoh. Now we can see the bigger picture: Jeroboam is Moses and Solomon is Pharaoh. Michael Oblath has shown in great detail how many of the specific locations listed as part of Israel's migration in Exodus–Numbers

---

10. From Oblath (2000).

...can be identified in close proximity to known geographical locations. None of these sites are identified in the Hebrew text as located adjacent to, or within, Egypt. It is clear from this data that the geographical perspective of the biblical author(s), as pertains to Exodus events, is toward the southern region of Israel/Judah. The geographical focus is not on Egypt at all. The events described in the Exodus occurred in the far eastern region of the Sinai peninsula, bordering on Edom and the eastern arm of the Red Sea (around present-day Eilat). Therefore, the Israelites did not migrate from the Nile Delta region of Egypt. Our Exodus narrative is dealing with a movement of people within and away from, at least, the southern region of Israel/Judah.[11]

The geographic and textual correlations combine to lead Oblath to conclude:

It is apparent that the Jeroboam narrative is, at the very least, the foundational story upon which the Exodus narrative was based.... The Exodus narrative, in its origin, is simply a literary account, an allegory, of Jeroboam and his relations with Solomon and Rehoboam.[12]

We can now begin to see that the *Exodus story itself was composed in the north as a counter-story to the imperial saga that legitimated Solomon.* Parallel to how Genesis was composed in Babylon as a counter-story to *Enuma Elish*, the central narrative of Exodus[13] arose as an alternative to the David/Solomon story. This paradigm is found throughout the ages across countless cultures, both those influenced by the biblical traditions and those not: a powerful empire uses its control of written media to generate a story of "how things are" that legitimizes a hierarchical structure in which wealth and power flow upward toward the elite. In response, a sacred encounter with the Creator God leads the victims of empire to generate a counter-story, rooted "in the beginning," that empowers their own liberation and the formation of an alternative community.

The Exodus story has empowered the oppressed across time and space to identify with the Israelites as they struggle to break free of Pharaoh's domination.[14] Readers have never felt limited by the specific Israelite/Egyptian historical elements of the story, but have been willing to substitute their own "pharaohs" for the Egyptian ones. This is a fitting response, not least because the original audience already knew that "Pharaoh" was simply a stand-in for their own oppressive monarch. Let's look at how the Exodus

---

11. Oblath, 35.

12. Ibid., 41.

13. Exodus certainly wasn't written in its final form during the ninth century, but included a number of additions over the centuries, not least of which is the Golden Calf story, Exodus 32, discussed below.

14. E.g., the classic interweaving of the Exodus story with that of African Americans, Hurston; cf. Dykstra for how well-off Americans ought more accurately to see ourselves as the Egyptians.

narrative brought about the birth of a new people, called out from empire to serve YHWH, the One who Is.

Birthing Israel, the People of YHWH

A preliminary question that we must address is this: If Exodus arose as a counter-story to extol Jeroboam as rebellion leader against Solomon, why is it couched as a narrative of departure from *Egypt*? Also why create[15] the character of Moses rather than speak directly of Jeroboam? There are many reasons; let's consider two briefly.

First, recall that Solomon's *first act* upon finding the kingdom "established" in his hand was to make a "marriage alliance with Pharaoh king of Egypt" (1 Kings 3:1). He immediately took Pharaoh's daughter (recall that Kings and Exodus are the only biblical texts to mention any "Pharaoh's daughter") and hid her away until both the royal and divine "houses" were completed, i.e., twenty years (1 Kings 9:10). She became a hidden, yet known, symbol of Egypt's "presence" inside "the city of David." This "inside" Egyptian presence was visible in the cherubim with which Solomon ordered the temple decorated (1 Kings 6:23ff.).[16] The author of the Solomon story is not critical of this Egyptian influence. Rather, it is a sign that Solomon's Israel has become a "player" on the world stage, supported by the neighboring powers. Finally, Solomon's "wisdom" was said to have "surpassed the wisdom of all the people of the east, and all the wisdom of Egypt" (4:30). In fact, Halpern argues, Solomon "was probably an Egyptian vassal and protégé, given to emulating his overlord's culture."[17] The Exodus author parodies this theme.

Second, why is "Moses" rather than Jeroboam himself the narrative hero? One of the major differences between the imperial story and its counter-story is the scope with which wisdom, power, and wealth are distributed over time. In the Solomon saga, all reside exclusively within the Davidic king and his court. In the Exodus narrative, however, we are to understand that Jeroboam is merely a vehicle for YHWH's will. Israel held no expectation of a Jeroboam dynasty.[18] Moses' relationship with YHWH and authority are shared among all the covenanted people. By generating a story from

15. Whatever historical truth there may be in an actual person named Moses cannot be determined. While scholars such as Sarna (1991, 1996) make a noble effort at situating the Exodus story within the confines of historical Egypt and thus preserving the historicity of Moses, such attempts don't take full consideration of the countless links between Exodus and 1 Kings, as well as the frequently larger-than-life nature of the Exodus story on its own terms.

16. "Jeroboam's adoption of the antique iconography of the bull-calf was a return to local tradition, as opposed to the Egyptianizing iconography of the ark and cherubim. Cherub iconography is found only in extremely elite contexts, whereas the bull appears in village or countryside settings as well" (Halpern [2003] 420.)

17. Halpern (2004), 397–98.

18. Jeroboam was succeeded by his son, Nadab, who reigned but two years before being killed and replaced by Baasha of the house of Issachar, 1 Kings 15:25–31.

"the distant past" in "Egypt" rather than one expressing realities current to its audience in Judah, the Exodus authors established a paradigm of much greater "antiquity" than the story that they sought to counter.[19]

One overarching biblical characterization of YHWH, grounded in the Exodus narrative, is as the One who led Israel "out of Egypt." It is a refrain that resounds throughout torah and prophets,[20] but is *never* mentioned in the David story. The image is found in the Solomon story, but only in 1 Kings 8:16–9:9 (six times), Solomon's temple dedication speech, and YHWH's return visit to Solomon, texts that express clear Deuteronomic phrasing and thought linked with the seventh-century reign of Josiah.[21] Only with Josiah, nearly three hundred years after Solomon's reign, is the Jerusalem establishment ready to seek a compromise with those who claim Moses as the hero of their sacred story of origins.

In the final form in which the book of Exodus reaches us, it includes a fitting bridge with Genesis: Jacob's sons are named, the Israelites have been "fruitful and prolific," have "multiplied" and grown "strong, yes, strong" (Exod. 1:7). This initial situation symbolizes the relationship between the "house of Joseph" (="house of Saul") and "the house of David" after David has lured Israel to join Judah under his reign in Jerusalem (2 Sam. 5). The "pharaoh who knew Joseph" (i.e., David) has died and another taken his place (i.e., Solomon). All bets are off. The new king looked out and saw, with palpable paranoia, that his "guests" have become a threat:

> He said to his people, "Look, the Israelite people are more numerous and more powerful than we. Come, let us deal shrewdly [*nithchakmah*, lit., "with wisdom/skill"] with them, or they will increase and, in the event of war, join our enemies and fight against us and escape from the land." (1:9–10)

From his first words, this pharaoh *is* Solomon: he calls on royal *chakhmah* in the face of the "Israel" that threatens to "fight against us and escape from the land." His "wisdom" is to "oppress the people with forced labor and have them build "storage cities, Pithom and Rameses, for Pharaoh" (1:11). Although scholar Michael Oblath has found no references in *Egyptian* literature to "storage cities,"[22] he points out that they are referred to in the Deuteronomistic History as belonging to Solomon (1 Kings 9:19). Further-

---

19. Cf. Gruen on how writers in the Hellenistic era (c. fourth–second centuries) continued to "reinvent" "ancient" Israelite traditions in confrontation with the allegedly "newer" Greek traditions, including the notion that Plato and other Greek philosophers learned from the tradition of Moses; see also Hobsbawm and Ranger on this process in other cultural contexts.

20. Nearly a hundred times, although except for Psalms, Egypt is *never mentioned at all* in the Wisdom literature (cf. Prov. 7:16). See discussion of these texts in chapter 17.

21. Cf., e.g., 1 Kings 9:4 and Deut. 26:17, both speaking of "walking" with YHWH and "keeping" YHWH's "statutes and ordinances."

22. Oblath, 37.

more, he notes that the most likely interpretation of the two city names, Pithom and Rameses (Exod. 1:11), is the Egyptian meaning: *pi-Atum,* i.e., "house of Atum," the sun god, and Rameses, *pi-Rameses,* i.e., house of the king. In other words, Israel is forced to build two houses: that of the king and that of the king's god. That, of course, was precisely what Solomon spent twenty years engaging Israel (and others) with forced labor in doing: building his own palace and the Jerusalem temple.[23]

As the threat looms larger, Pharaoh cannot even call the people by their proper name, instead using what became an ethnic/national slur word, "Hebrews" (1:15-16).[24] His fear of this numerous people led him to act irrationally, commanding that only the "Hebrew" baby *boys* — those most valuable for doing hard labor — be killed. The counter-story's first move away from the "wisdom" of empire is embodied in the famous pair of "Hebrew midwives," a term which ambiguously names them either as Egyptian women who deliver "Hebrew" babies (and are thus resisters to Pharaoh from "inside") or as Israelite women who serve their kin (and are resisters from among the oppressed). The ambiguity cannot and is not to be resolved, for among those who also resist Pharaoh is *his own daughter* (2:5-9).[25] The midwives "feared God" and disobeyed the king. In this simple sentence is the very essence of the counter-narrative: *to listen to and thus fear/revere the voice of the true God is necessarily to refuse to listen to voices that stand against God.*[26]

With the midwives' refusal, Pharaoh's command became generalized to "all his people" to throw every Hebrew boy into the Nile. Pharaoh, like all kings, claimed power to command that his will be done. The counter-story, on the other hand, puts such power in the exclusive hand of YHWH, the One about to be revealed to the man saved by Pharaoh's own daughter from drowning.

Four *women* work to oppose Pharaoh: the two midwives, Pharaoh's daughter, and Moses' own mother. Collectively, these resisters embody the combination of forces that makes a movement of social revolution possible. For a counter-narrative that will hereafter focus primarily on male actors, it is an astounding and memorable way to begin.

---

23. Ibid., 39.

24. Sternberg (1999), in a magisterial effort, has taken on and demolished much of the accepted, but ungrounded, scholarly association of "Hebrew" with various names for slaves or other marginal groups in the Near East, such as *'apiru.* Sternberg's dense and erudite work is heavy reading at times, but is also a model for how to separate scholarly "wisdom" from true insight.

25. Might this betrayal by Pharaoh's daughter explain why Solomon took his first wife — *Pharaoh's daughter* — and kept her locked up for years (1 Kings 3:1)? In other words, might Solomon's wife have been a double agent like her Exodus counterpart? We can only speculate, since the Kings text is silent on this point.

26. Dykstra, 163-78; See also the discussion in chapter 12 of the Samuel/YHWH/Israel exchange at 1 Sam. 8.

Once saved, Moses grew up in Pharaoh's court.[27] His ambiguous national identity[28] echoes that of Jeroboam: both saw, from a vantage point of imperial privilege, forced labor imposed upon their own "brothers" (Exod. 2:11; 1 Kings 11:28). Moses killed the Egyptian oppressor and hid the body, but the next day, when he challenged two "Hebrews" fighting each other, they responded by asking, "Who made you a ruler [*sar*] and judge[29] over us?" (2:14). The word *sar* was used previously only for Pharaoh's "taskmasters" (1:11) and echoes the list of Solomon's own *sarrim* (1 Kings 4:2ff.). The question from the enslaved workers, far "below" the man who grew up in Pharaoh's court, expresses one of the central challenges of leadership: can a member of the elite lead the downtrodden without "ruling over" them? *Who* has authorized this attempt to "rule" the people?

At this point, the answer, of course, is "no one," and Moses headed for the hills, landing in Midian[30] and taking up life as a shepherd's son-in-law. The Midianites perceived the stranger to be "Egyptian," but welcomed him (2:19). Moses named his son "Gershom," meaning (in Hebrew) "alien there," a living reminder of his displaced identity. It appears that the murderer-on-the-run had found a place of long-term hiding from his enemies.

Then, for the first time, God enters the narrative. The pharaoh died, only to be replaced by another (Rehoboam). The "groaning" of the Israelites "rose up" and we hear the divine response: "God heard... God remembered... God looked... God knew" (2:24–25). In this sequence of four verbs is expressed the essential relationship that develops at the heart of the liberating religion of creation. Israel will be bound together not by a deity who speaks in royal dreams, but one who hears people's cries of oppression, "knows" the people, and responds to their deepest needs.

Exodus 3 is the foundation upon which this religion was built. Moses encountered YHWH outside of Egypt, outside of empire, in the *wilderness* and at a *mountain*. These two sites are the repeated places in which YHWH encounters Israel.[31] It is "where the authority of the state cannot reach. YHWH's self-disclosure takes place in remote parts rather than within the established and settled cult of the city."[32] The older Exodus story is fully consistent with its younger partner, Genesis, in presenting YHWH as the Creator of heaven and earth, not of urban empire.

---

27. Echoing Genubath, son of Hadad, whose mother is Pharaoh's sister-in-law; 1 Kings 11:20.

28. "Israelite" national identity is the subject of chapter 13.

29. Note how this is echoed in Gen. 19:9, the question asked of Lot by the Sodomites, grounded not in social status based on class, but on "foreignness."

30. Recall the link with 1 Kings 11:8, the "preface" to Jeroboam's rebellion.

31. "Wilderness" (*midbar*) is mentioned twenty-five times in Exod. 3–19; "mountain" (*har*) twenty times in the same text, plus nine more in Exod. 24 (forty-eight times total in Exodus).

32. Levenson (1985), 21.

The text describes the encounter itself with great care and precision: "There the angel of YHWH appeared to him in a flame of fire out of the bush [*hasseneh*]; he looked, and the bush was blazing, yet it was not consumed" (3:2). Jon Levenson notes "two of YHWH's emblems — tree and fire — clash and neither overpowers the other. The two will appear again in tandem in the menora . . . a stylized tree . . . (Exod. 25:31–39)."[33] It is not, as in some translations, "a" bush, but *the* bush. Only here and in Deuteronomy 33:16 is the Hebrew word *seneh* found in the Bible. It is a unique moment, not to be repeated or memorialized with a shrine or pilgrimage site. There can be no "Burning Bush Gift Shop." Like the manna (discussed below), the *seneh* exists only in the story and in Israel's memory. It is not thereby, however, to be understood as any less *real*. Like the location of Abram's call out of Babylon at Genesis 12, Moses' experience expresses both a specific moment of national formation grounded in intimate divine encounter and a paradigm in which all of YHWH's people are expected to participate.

The latter point is underscored by the echo of this scene in the collective encounter of the entire people at Mount *Sinai* in Exodus 19:1ff. Numerous readers have noticed the near identity of the bush and the mountain. Although only Moses is commanded to "go up" the mountain for the most intimate of encounters, all the people experience the tangible presence of YHWH. As we hear, "YHWH will come down upon Mount Sinai in the sight of all the people" (19:11). Moses' experiences, both at the *seneh* and at Sinai, do not authorize him to be a king *over* Israel, but rather, the conveyer of covenant *with* Israel. What is being created by YHWH in the wilderness and at the mountain is "a priestly kingdom and a holy nation" (19:6). Note how these paired terms express the inextricable interweaving of "religion" and "politics." Israel as a "kingdom" and "nation" must also be "priestly" and "holy." As Genesis countered *Enuma Elish*'s Babylonian narrative by proclaiming all individual humans to be expressions of "the divine image" (Gen. 1:26–27), so Exodus proclaims the collective "body" of Israel to be an expression of the essence of the One who is true *essence* itself.[34] This contrasts radically, of course, with the "essence" of imperial religion, where the king alone is said to embody the divine or to do the divine will.

The encounter between YHWH and Moses at the bush is tragicomic. YHWH has "heard" and "remembered" and has now come to get Moses to carry out YHWH's will to liberate "my people who are in Egypt" (3:7). Moses responded to the fire with curiosity and then to the double divine naming, "Moses, Moses," with instant obedience. But as YHWH's will became clear, Moses' responses express only resistance. First, he asked "who am *I*" and then followed with, basically, "who are *you?*" The divine responses parallel the questions: "I will be with you (*'ehyeh*)" and "I am who

---

33. Ibid., 20–21.

34. The English word comes from the Latin *essentia*, from the verb *esse*, "to be," as is the Divine Name itself, YHWH (Greek, *egō eimi*, "I am," Exod. 3:6, 14, 15); see also the absolute "I AM" statements in John's Gospel, e.g., John 8:24, 58; 13:19.

I am" (*'ehyeh asher 'ehyeh*). God went on to add an additional descriptor to help Moses: "the God of your ancestors, the God of Abraham, the God of Isaac, and the God of Jacob, has sent me to you" (3:15).[35] We recall that not one of these ancestral names is mentioned in the entire David / Solomon story. The imperial narrative seeks to root the Davidic dynasty in an abstract cosmic eternity. In contrast, the counter-story roots the call of Moses in *kinship and history:* in the lived experience of ordinary people who have gone before and have already "known" YHWH.

YHWH goes on to name the plan for Moses to carry out, but the liberator-elect continues to balk: "But suppose they do not believe me or listen to me, but say, 'YHWH did not appear to you' " (4:1). It is a fair enough question, both for Moses in the narrative and Jeroboam in rebellion against Solomon. The king in Jerusalem claimed a dream delegated divine authority to him. Why should those considering rebellion against his son trust that Jeroboam was himself divinely authorized?

YHWH performed a pair of "signs" as proof, yet Moses was still reticent. He complained, "O my Lord, I have never been eloquent, neither in the past nor even now that you have spoken to your servant; but I am slow of speech and slow of tongue" (4:10).[36] YHWH, patient so far, said that the One who made speech will be "with your mouth and teach you what you are to speak" (4:12). Finally, Moses said flatly, "please send someone else!" YHWH's "anger" was now aroused, but the deity continued to work with Moses, offering to make Moses' brother Aaron the equivalent of a ventriloquist's dummy.

Moses, out of excuses, relented and the process of liberation began. It should not surprise anyone that Pharaoh considered absurd Moses' proposal to let the people go "so that they may celebrate a festival to me in the wilderness." For Rehoboam's Jerusalem-centered monarchy, celebration of a festival to YHWH "in the wilderness" was equivalent to apostasy.[37] Pharaoh replied, "I do not know YHWH," indicating the absence of relationship between Rehoboam and Israel's God (5:2). Moses' proposal began with the words "thus says YHWH," but was soon countered by "thus says Pharaoh" (5:10). At the core of the tug-of-war that follows is the question: whose word is most powerful, YHWH, the "One who is," or the imperial king (both Egypt's Pharaoh and Judah's Rehoboam)?

---

35. As shown in Table 7 above (p. 118) the tri-patriarchal phrase is used in several biblical texts that otherwise reveal no awareness of detailed traditions about these ancestors. Given our assumption that the core Exodus narrative is several hundred years older than the Genesis patriarchal narratives, we must also assume that there was some ancient tradition associating the three names with Yahwistic faith. Any claim beyond this, though, is mere speculation.

36. Is this perhaps in response to the Jeroboam narrative's "slowness" in providing speech for Jeroboam alone? See 11:26–39, where Ahijah speaks but Jeroboam is silent; cf. 12:3–4, where "Jeroboam and all the assembly of Israel" speak to Rehoboam in a single voice. It is not until 13:4 that Jeroboam speaks on his own.

37. The only character in 1–2 Kings to encounter YHWH in the wilderness is Elijah, 1 Kings 19:4.

"Thus says YHWH" is heard *over 400 times* in the Hebrew Bible — over 350 of those in the prophets — including over 40 in the Deuteronomistic History from Joshua–2 Kings, but *not once* in the Solomon story. The claim that human language expresses divine thought and will is what makes the Bible "inspired." Individual people, for all their flaws — i.e., people like Moses — are claimed to be empowered by their direct encounter with YHWH to become mediators of YHWH's will to the people. In John's Gospel, we hear this claim taken to its conclusion: "the Word became flesh and tented in us" (John 1:14, au. trans.). What is begun here with "Moses" will come to completion with Jesus.

A power battle ensues in the Exodus chapters that follow this first confrontation between Moses and Pharaoh. The Ten Plagues devastate Egypt with bloodied water, frogs, gnats, and other noxious creatures that destroy the "plants of the field" (*'esev sadeh*) (9:22, 25). The plagues express God's creation recoiling against the rampages of empire's agricultural control of natural fertility. Hebrew *'esev sadeh* signifies the product of cultivated land (Gen. 2:5; 3:18).[38] *Sadeh* is first heard in Exodus describing part of the hard labor to which the Israelites are subjected (1:14), but is not heard again until it becomes a refrain in the plague narrative.[39] Each of the plagues reveals the reality beneath Pharaoh's claim to bring goodness to his people. Like the warnings attached to the covenant threatening various similar "punishments" if Israel stubbornly refuses to listen to YHWH (Lev. 26, Deut. 28), the plagues present not a series of arbitrary horrors but are rather a stylized expression of the "natural consequences" of empire. The plagues bring to public awareness what life is really like when Pharaoh and all who side with him (9:34) refuse to listen to YHWH. On the eve of the manna story, YHWH refers back to the plagues as the "diseases [*hammachalah*] that I brought upon the Egyptians" (15:25). That is, the plagues are not only the external manifestations of creation-gone-awry by acts of empire, but also "infect" the people directly.[40] Indeed, we know that surplus-agriculture–based urban life has always generated numerous diseases unknown to people living directly on the land, passed on by insects and rodents drawn to the captive food supply.[41] Once again, the counter-imperial narrative of Genesis resonates with the Exodus image of YHWH the Creator in battle against human-made systems that claim divinely given authority over creation.

---

38. The only other use of the phrase in the torah is Deut. 11:5 as food for livestock; elsewhere in the MT only at 2 Kings 19:26; Isa. 37:27; Jer. 12:4; Zech. 10:1.

39. 8:9; 9:3, 19 (twice); 9:21, 22, 25 (three times); 10:5, 15, then not again until 16:25 (eleven of twenty-two times in Exodus are in the plague narrative).

40. Matthew's Gospel portrays Jesus healing people of "Egypt disease," e.g., Matt. 4:23–24; see pp. 410–11.

41. Shepard (103) observes "if there is a single complex of events responsible for the deterioration of human health and ecology, agricultural civilization is it." See also Price and Gebauer (1995a), 7. Bellwood (18) notes that infant mortality rates were relatively low among early, nonurban agriculturalists.

Each time, Pharaoh momentarily relented, but then with "hardened heart" continued to refuse to obey Moses/YHWH. A "hard heart" to an Egyptian was an asset. As Dorian Coover Cox notes,

> Egyptians prized the ability to appear strong, firm, resolute, and unmoved by events.... Egyptians described it as being 'hard of heart.' A hard heart of this sort was valuable not just at court but at death because the heart needed to declare its owner's innocence.[42]

Thus, to claim that YHWH was actually in charge of Pharaoh's heart was not, as some assume, to take away Pharaoh's "free will," but to underscore that YHWH, not Pharaoh, was ultimately in charge of the cosmic order.[43] The refrain is heard seven times in the plague and pursuit narratives,[44] making clear the totality of YHWH's control.

It was the death of Egypt's own firstborn that finally broke Pharaoh. Any reader who is not totally an Israelite partisan will likely experience shock at this turn of events. Pharaoh was hard-hearted and tyrannical; the "Egyptian" (Jerusalem monarchical) way of life was intolerable and must be escaped. But why should YHWH match Pharaoh in violence against innocent children and one-up Pharaoh by slaughtering firstborn animals as well?

For all the parallels between the stories of Jeroboam's and Moses' rebellions, there is certainly no historical "event" underlying this aspect of the Exodus narrative. It presages the further violence found throughout the torah and historical books: by YHWH directly; by legal commandment; and by seemingly endless warfare, both offensive and defensive. Neither the imperial, Zion theology nor the counter-narrative of Sinai and liberation stand against all violence. The fact of this "divine" violence, at least from a Christian perspective, compromises the witness of the Israelite counter-story, given the imitative violence it has spawned over the centuries. We cannot evade the pervasive presence of texts that accept, justify, or even command massive slaughter of "enemies" in the name of YHWH. However, we can and must pause to distinguish four basic categories of "approved" violence found in the Hebrew Bible from Exodus forward.

First, as here and continuing through Israel's liberation from Egypt across the Red Sea, there is violence *directly from the hand of YHWH*. It is imperative to observe that neither the firstborn nor the Egyptian charioteers die at the hands of Israelite warriors. Israel was told simply to stand back and await YHWH's command to leave. We noted briefly how such violence can often — but not always — be understood as an expression of the "natural consequences" of a people's wrong way of life, narrated in a dramatic and stylized manner to make the story more memorable.

---

42. Cox (2006), 306.
43. Ibid., 307.
44. Exod. 9:12; 10:20, 27; 11:10; 14:4, 8, 17.

Second, there is *violence commanded among Israelites against each other as punishment for violations of torah*. Whether such provisions were ever carried out is impossible to determine. We'll explore in Part IV how the gospels convey Jesus' response to some of these torah injunctions to violence. Given the absence of historical evidence that Israel ever actually practiced the death penalty for the wide range of behaviors that call for it, we may interpret these texts as expressing simply the life-and-death seriousness of living in obedience to torah.

Third, there is *violence commanded against "Canaanites" and other ethnic/national enemies of Israel* during the course of establishing and maintaining an alternative way of life in the Promised Land. The book of Exodus limits divine violence against Canaanites and others in "the land" to YHWH's "driving out" via "pestilence" (*tsir'ah*).[45] It never orders Israelites to engage in divine violence themselves. The texts that present human violence against enemies as YHWH's will are virtually all part of the Deuteronomistic History and others that comprise the collection establishing the "religion of empire" in Jerusalem. This precedent has generated some of the most hideous "holy wars" in Western history, not least of which was that perpetrated by European "settlers" against the indigenous peoples of the Americas, often grounded in a claimed analogy between the newcomers and the Israelites to their respective "Promised Lands." We'll see in Part III how, during the Second Temple period, another dissenting tradition arose in the face of the "official" sanction for YHWH-"inspired" violence against enemies. It will be clearly and decisively on this side that Jesus will stand, to the shock and chagrin of some of his closest followers who were looking to conduct "holy war" against the Romans.

Finally, there is *violence without explicit divine sanction but that suggests divine approval because of its presence in "sacred" texts*. For example, we find the prophet Elijah ordering the mass execution of the priests of Ba'al after a ritual confrontation (1 Kings 18:40). Even more arbitrarily, we see Elijah's successor, Elisha, curse some pesky kids "in the name of YHWH," which appears to cause two bears to emerge from the woods and maul the boys (2 Kings 2:23–24). Such stories perpetuate the notion that not only political enemies of Israel but even minor opponents of individual Israelites can be treated violently "in the name of YHWH." Such texts simply cannot be reconciled with the clear and explicit admonition from Jesus to "love your enemies and pray for those who persecute you" (Matt. 5:44; cf. Luke 6:27). As Exodus challenged the imperial theology of Solomon and his son, so Jesus and his followers will challenge the ongoing tradition of "YHWH empire" violence.

Returning to the Exodus narrative, we find the Israelites struggling to walk the journey into freedom that follows their "birth" via the umbilical

---

45. The word is used elsewhere only as part of the Josianic compromise, Deut. 7:20; Josh. 24:12, with the same reference to the driving out of the previous occupants from the land.

passage through the Red Sea.[46] They are like addicts unable to quit as they recall how in Egypt "we sat by the fleshpots and ate our fill of bread" (16:3). It must have been a major challenge for Jeroboam to gain the trust of people who both suffered under Solomonic "hard service" and yet had become familiar with it. The theme of Israelite "grumbling" in the wilderness as they remember how "good" it was in Egypt expresses both the historical moment of the text's composition as well as a timeless struggle for those who seek to escape imperial tyranny for a more just and sustainable way of life. As it is for the addict, the prospect of freedom is enticing, but the journey is hard and the temptation to "look back"[47] is strong.

YHWH's response in Exodus 16 offers both a unique solution as well as a perennial invitation. "Manna" is a gift from YHWH, "bread from heaven" (16:4; cf. John 6:31ff.). Like the burning bush and Mount Sinai, it is a function of the Exodus (and Numbers)[48] narrative. It (along with YHWH-provided quail) sustains them for the entire wilderness sojourn (16:35). They will find no manna in the Promised Land.

Yet there are hints that there is more to the manna narrative than a once-upon-a-time "miracle" story. First, YHWH's proposition in 16:4–5 calls for the people to "go out and gather [*velaqtu*, from the stem *lqt*] enough for that day. In that way I will test [*'anassennu*, from the stem, *nsh*; LXX, *peirasō*] them, whether they will follow my instruction or not." YHWH's provision of the manna was a "test" or "temptation" of God's people. The "test" actually began a few verses earlier when YHWH "put them to the test" to see if they would listen to the voice of YHWH and obey YHWH's commandments, lest they be inflicted with "Egypt disease" (15:25–26). It parallels YHWH's "test" of Abraham to see if his obedience would include the offering up of his beloved son Isaac (Gen. 22:1).[49] Nowhere outside Genesis–Exodus does YHWH "test" Israel. It has everything to do with whether a new people, obedient to YHWH alone, can be born in the wilderness, leaving all the ways of empire behind.

The Hebrew verb in this passage for "gather" (*lqt*) is used thirty-seven times in the Hebrew Bible, nine of those in Exodus 16:4–27. Although it is occasionally used for "gathering" other things (such as wood or money), when used in relation to food, it is *always about either wild food* (e.g., 2 Kings 4:39) or *gleaning agricultural surplus* (as used twelve times in

---

46. Cf. Pardes, 27–28.

47. Remember Lot's wife in Gen. 19, p. 64 above.

48. The book of Numbers is largely a postexilic combination of earlier wilderness traditions and priestly editing in light of Second Temple concerns. Because the themes overlap those in Exodus and Leviticus, this book will not consider Numbers on its own; for a recent look at Numbers in light of these issues, see Leveen; for a more traditional, Jewish scholarly approach, see Milgrom.

49. The Hebrew verb is, with two exceptions (Ps. 26:2; 2 Chron. 32:31), only used to refer to YHWH's test of Abraham or the wilderness testing of Israel; cf. Deut. 8:2; 13:4; 33:8; Judg. 2:22; 3:1.

Ruth 2:2–23). The test is whether people trust the Creator, not agricultural empire, to provide the "daily bread" needed for survival.

There is another clue in Exodus 16 that manna has to do with resisting the temptation of agriculture: When the people obediently follow the command to put some manna aside rather than gather on the sabbath, Moses tells them, "Eat it today, for today is a sabbath to YHWH; today you will not find it *in the field* [sadeh]" (16:25). Of course, there is no such land in the midst of the wilderness, or the Israelites wouldn't be having such trouble finding food in the first place. "Field food," as we've seen, was found in Egypt. The book of Numbers graphically contrasts the longed-for field food with what YHWH provides:

> The rabble among them had a strong craving; and the Israelites also wept again, and said, "If only we had meat to eat! We remember the fish we used to eat in Egypt for nothing, the cucumbers, the melons, the leeks, the onions, and the garlic; but now our strength is dried up, and there is nothing at all but this manna to look at." (Num. 11:4–6)

The manna story ends with the note: "The Israelites ate manna forty years" (16:35). The path between Egypt and Canaan was not difficult or confusing; in the Joseph story, Jacob's sons repeatedly make the trip without comment (e.g., Gen. 42:1–5). The length of time is a round number symbolizing both a *lifetime* and a *pregnancy*. No one with Egypt in their memory survives the journey;[50] a new generation, weaned away from dependence on empire, is born in the wilderness. Manna, in this sense, is akin to amniotic fluid and mother's milk (cf. Num. 11:12). It comes directly from YHWH's "body," i.e., creation itself, to feed Israel *in utero* and while nursing. Israel will indeed "grow up" and the manna cease. However, mature Israel will continue to be tempted to take up "field food" rather than to trust in what YHWH provides abundantly in creation.

Why would Jeroboam or his supporters want to convey such a message? Was he not also a king like Solomon, if perhaps not quite as ostentatious? The fact is that we know very little about the "real" Jeroboam.[51] The author of 1 Kings tells us little beyond what is relevant to his own agenda, viz., to show Jeroboam as the evil cause of the kingdom's division. There is little archaeological or other evidence, though, to suggest that Jeroboam grew wealthy at the expense of the people of Israel, in sharp contrast with his eighth-century successor, Ahab, who was blasted by the prophets Hosea and Amos for his treatment of the poor while living himself in luxurious comfort. Jeroboam may have sought to lead Israel in a manner more like Moses than like traditional monarchs. Soon after his death, his entire family was killed by a rival, interpreted as fulfillment of the Shilonite Ahijah's

50. Except Caleb, according to Deut. 1:36.
51. Cf. Halpern (2004), 419–20.

prophecy (1 Kings 15:27–29).[52] We will never know whether Jeroboam and his supporters intended texts like Exodus 16 to lead Israel into a way of life that would protect it from reverting to a Solomon-like monarchy. The manna story is not one most kings would embrace as the "divine word," certainly not kings in the Solomonic mold.

With this experience in their minds and bodies, Israel continued its journey away from Egypt to the climax of its collective encounter with YHWH in Exodus 19 and 24. The epiphany available to the eyes and ears of all the people contrasts sharply with that experienced within the Jerusalem temple.

Table 12:
Comparison of Glory of YHWH
in Temple and Wilderness

1 Kings 8:1–3, 10–14	*Exodus 19:16–19; 24:16–17*
Then Solomon assembled the elders of Israel and all the heads of the tribes, the leaders of the fathers' houses of the Israelites, before King Solomon in Jerusalem, to bring up the ark of the covenant of YHWH out of the city of David, which is Zion. *All the people of Israel assembled to King Solomon* at the festival in the month Ethanim, which is the seventh month. *And all the elders of Israel came, and the priests carried the ark....*	On the morning of the third day there was thunder and lightning, as well as a thick cloud on the mountain, and a blast of a trumpet so loud that all the people who were in the camp trembled. *Moses brought the people out of the camp to meet God.* They took their stand at the foot of the mountain. Now Mount Sinai was wrapped in smoke, because YHWH had descended upon it in fire; the smoke went up like the smoke of a kiln, while the whole mountain shook violently. As the blast of the trumpet grew louder and louder, Moses would speak and God would answer him in thunder....
And when the priests came out of the holy place, *a cloud filled the house of YHWH,* so that the priests could not stand to minister because of the cloud; for *the glory of YHWH filled the house of YHWH.* Then Solomon said, "YHWH has said that he would dwell in thick darkness. I have built you an exalted house, a place for you to dwell in forever." Then the *king turned around and blessed all the assembly of Israel,* while all the assembly of Israel stood.	*The glory of YHWH settled on Mount Sinai,* and *the cloud covered it for six days;* on the seventh day he called to Moses out of the cloud. Now the appearance of *the glory of YHWH was like a devouring fire on the top of the mountain in the sight of the people of Israel.*

---

52. It is tempting to speculate whether the complete destruction of the "house of Jeroboam" was engineered by an ancient CIA-like coup, for the sake of preventing his radical alternative social order from coming into fruition. For a hundred years of such overthrows in U.S. history, see Kinzer; see also Douglass for the story of an internal "overthrow" in the assassination of John F. Kennedy.

Table 13:
Comparison of Temple Dedication
and Covenant Ceremonies

1 Kings 8:5, 63–64	*Exodus 24:5–8*
King Solomon and all the congregation of Israel, who had assembled before him, were with him before the ark, *sacrificing so many sheep and oxen that they could not be counted or numbered....* Solomon offered as *sacrifices of well-being* [*zebach shelem*][53] to **YHWH** *twenty-two thousand oxen and one hundred twenty thousand sheep.* So the king and all the people of Israel dedicated the house of YHWH. The same day the king consecrated the middle of the court that was in front of the house of YHWH; for there he offered the burnt offerings and the grain offerings and the fat pieces of the sacrifices of well-being, *because the bronze altar that was before YHWH was too small to receive the burnt offerings and the grain offerings and the fat pieces of the sacrifices of well-being.*	He sent young men of the people of Israel, who offered burnt offerings *and sacrificed oxen as offerings of well-being* [*zebach shelem*] to YHWH. Moses took half of the blood and put it in basins and half of the blood he dashed against the altar. Then he *took the book of the covenant, and read it in the hearing of the people; and they said, "All that YHWH has spoken we will do, and we will be obedient." Moses took the blood and dashed it on the people, and said, "See the blood of the covenant that YHWH has made with you in accordance with all these words."*

In the Solomonic account, YHWH is mediated by king (palace) and priest (temple) to "the assembly of Israel." From the perspective of the royal court, perhaps we are to hear that the presence of elders, tribal heads, and leaders of the fathers' houses represents "all the people." The Solomonic assembly appears to exclude clan (*mishpachah*) leaders, who are never referred to in 1–2 Kings. The "clan" was the basic glue of the network of extended families of rural Israelites.[54] Solomon's empire was constructed to disempower this traditional social unit, working instead only with representatives of "higher level" structures.

In Exodus, however, Moses leads by inviting people to "meet God" directly. They experience the powerful smoke, fire, shaking, and noise in their own bodies, directly from the mountain. This contrast reveals how the

---

53. The phrase is found forty-nine times in the Hebrew Bible, but only here in the monarchy narrative *and* only here in Exodus; cf. Exod. 29:28.

54. *Mishpachah* is used over 300 times in the MT, 185 of those in the torah, of which *only one* is in Deuteronomy. See also Howard-Brook (2001), 75–77, on the role of the *mishpachah* as a key component of Israel's social fabric.

"two religions" convey their claim to announce and to embody "the divine order": one establishes physical and institutional structures that purport to mediate YHWH, while the other calls people to experience YHWH for themselves in creation-grounded, liberated community.

Solomon's ceremony established the Jerusalem temple and the Davidic monarchy as the means by which "Israel" will "know" their God. In Exodus, the people were invited into a committed relationship with YHWH called *covenant*. In Exodus 24, word and blood establish this relationship. All the people speaking "with one voice" freely enter into it (24:3). Note also the sharp contrast between the two biblical stories in the role of animal sacrifice.

Solomon and the gathered elite engage in an obscene orgy of animal bloodshed. Can one even imagine more than a hundred thousand butchered oxen and sheep within the small confines of ancient Jerusalem? There seems to be no particular purpose to this gross spectacle; the newly built altar cannot begin to receive the enormous output of blood and flesh. Certainly there is no suggestion that YHWH demands or even wants such a "feast." Consider, for instance, the comments (in a slightly different context) of the eighth-century prophets Amos and Micah:

> I hate, I despise your festivals, and I take no delight in your solemn assemblies. Even though you offer me your burnt offerings and grain offerings, I will not accept them; and the *offerings of well-being* (*shelem*) *of your fatted animals* I will not look upon. (Amos 5:21–22)

> With what shall I come before YHWH, and bow myself before God on high? Shall I come before him with burnt offerings, with calves a year old? Will YHWH be pleased with *thousands of rams,* with ten thousands of rivers of oil? (Mic. 6:6–7a)

It is hard not to hear these prophetic denunciations recalling the Solomonic assembly.

On the other hand, the blood of the sacrifices offered in Exodus is dashed on altar and people as an expression of the life-and-death nature of the commitment being made at Sinai. No mention is made of quantity. It is simply enough for each person to participate directly in the "blood of the covenant that YHWH has made with you in accordance with all these words" (24:8; cf. Mark 14:24; Heb. 9:20ff.).

Countless scholars and other commentators have reflected on the nature of this "covenant" (*berit*). Comparisons have been made with other ancient forms of commitment between gods/kings and their people.[55] What is important for our purpose is that the Exodus covenant *does not involve a human king*. Even Moses, Joshua, and the elders must step aside as the people speak their assent and receive the ritual blood. This would radically have limited Jeroboam's role in leading the northern "kingdom."

---

55. See, e.g., Albertz (1994), 75.

Here, for the first time, Exodus refers to the people symbolically as "the twelve tribes of Israel" (24:4). The term is repeated and elaborated in the description of the priestly vestment: "There shall be twelve stones with names corresponding to the names of the sons of Israel; they shall be like signets, each engraved with its name, for the twelve tribes" (28:21; also 39:14). Nowhere in Exodus, though (other than in the opening verses bridging Genesis), are the twelve tribal "sons" named as a list. The symbolism of both covenant ritual and priestly vestment transforms the twelve administrative districts established by Solomon *into fictive kinship units.* In the Solomon story, YHWH spoke only of "tribes" (*shebet*) in the temple dedication speech (1 Kings 8:16)[56] and in the final condemnation of the king (1 Kings 11), where it refers to the "tearing" of the kingdom and giving it to Jeroboam. As we'll explore in chapter 13, the envisioning of the "people of Israel" as "twelve tribes" is likely a response to the initiating action of Solomon. In other words, it was Solomon's use of "twelve" to refer to the entirety of his imperial domain that inspired and enabled the Exodus narrative to take up the symbol and reshape it according to a radically different sense of what it is that "binds together" (*religio*) the people of YHWH.

One more theme completes the comparison and contrast of the Solomon story and the counter-story in Exodus. An astounding portion of the book of Exodus (Exod. 25–31; 33–40) is dedicated to YHWH's instructions for and the completion of a series of ritual objects: the priestly vestments and the "tabernacle" (*mishkan),* which will contain various things, including the "ark of the covenant" which itself holds the Tablets brought down by Moses from the mountain. The Mishkan is the Exodus substitute for the Solomonic temple.[57] There are numerous parallels between temple and Mishkan: both are said to contain the "ark of the covenant," both are decorated with cherubim, both are measured in "cubits,"[58] and so forth. But despite the claim that the ark of the covenant rests at the center of the temple, the Mishkan is mentioned only once in the entire monarchical narrative (2 Sam. 7:6). When the ark "arrived" in Jerusalem, there was no Mishkan in sight. Either this YHWH-commanded object simply disappeared without trace or comment, or *it didn't exist at all* (whether as text or physical object) *until after Solomon's reign.* This is further evidence that the Solomon story was written before the Exodus narrative: if the authors of the Solomon saga knew about the Mishkan as they did about the ark, why would they want to omit speaking of it? Wouldn't that assist their attempt to legitimize both Solomon and

---

56. As noted above, its Deuteronomic vocabulary and themes make this likely to be a later composition.

57. Traditional scholarship has seen the Mishkan as a *prototype* of the temple, reading the wider historical narrative as a continuous "progression."

58. Of the 249 uses of the word *'ammah* ("cubit") in the Hebrew Bible, all but 20 are used to measure three things: Noah's ark, the Exodus Mishkan, and Solomon's temple.

Jerusalem as divinely inspired king and holy city? Yet in the biblical narrative as it stands in "chronological order," the final reference to the Mishkan is at Joshua 22:19, 29.

Mishkan and temple are each the physical expression of the theological perspective of their respective textual authors.[59] The temple is *fixed in place,* anchored on Mount Zion, beckoning people to come to meet YHWH there. The Mishkan is a *movable shrine,* traveling with the people as they journey from empire to freedom. The temple was *built by forced labor* from wood, hewn stone, and metal "contributed" by a foreign king and *paid for by massive tribute* (1 Kings 5; 9:11–15). The Mishkan was *built by "all those of wise heart"* (au. trans. *khal-chakham leb*) from *"all the freewill offerings that the Israelites had brought,"* so many offerings that the people must be restrained from bringing too many (Exod. 36:1–8). The temple metalwork was done exclusively by Hiram of Tyre,[60] a man described to be full of "skill, intelligence, and knowledge" (*bitvunah uvda'at uvkhal*). The Mishkan was designed by Bezalel of the tribe of Judah, a man also full of "skill, intelligence, and knowledge" (*bitvunah uvda'at uvkhal*),[61] who inspired "every skillful one" and "everyone whose heart was stirred to come to do the work" (Exod. 35:13–36:1). In each case, the Mishkan takes an imperial form of production and transforms it into a spirit-based, communal activity.

Did Jeroboam know of a Mishkan? The author of 1 Kings tells us not that the rebel leader built a moveable shrine, but rather, that

> ... the king took counsel and *made two calves of gold.* He said to the people, "You have gone up to Jerusalem long enough. *Here are your gods, O Israel, who brought you up out of the land of Egypt."* He set one in Bethel, and the other he put in Dan. And this thing became a sin, for the people went to worship before the one at Bethel and before the other as far as Dan. He also made houses on high places, and appointed priests from among all the people, who were not Levites. Jeroboam appointed a festival on the fifteenth day of the eighth month like the festival that was in Judah, and he offered sacrifices on the altar; so he did in Bethel, sacrificing to the calves that he had made. And he placed in Bethel the priests of the high places that he had made. He went up to the altar that he had made in Bethel on the fifteenth day in the eighth month, in the month that he alone had devised; he appointed a festival for the people of Israel, and he went up to the altar to offer incense. (1 Kings 12:28–33)

---

59. See also chapter 16 below on how the Mishkan became the model for the structure of the book of Leviticus.

60. Can this be the same "Hiram of Tyre" who as king was a major patron of the royal palace and temple construction (e.g., 2 Sam. 5:11; 1 Kings 5:1)? The text refers to the artisan as "son of a widow of the tribe of Naphtali" (1 Kings 7:14). It is at least an odd coincidence.

61. The phrase is found only in these two places in the Hebrew Scriptures.

And then we note that in the *only* chapter in Exodus 25–40 that is *not* about the Mishkan and its related objects, there is a story that includes this passage:

> When the people saw that Moses delayed to come down from the moun-
> tain, the people gathered around Aaron, and said to him, "Come, make
> gods for us, who shall go before us; as for this Moses, the man who
> brought us up out of the land of Egypt, we do not know what has
> become of him." Aaron said to them, "Take off the gold rings that are
> on the ears of your wives, your sons, and your daughters, and bring
> them to me." *So all the people took off the gold rings from their ears,
> and brought them to Aaron. He took the gold from them, formed it in
> a mold, and cast an image of a calf; and they said, "These are your
> gods, O Israel, who brought you up out of the land of Egypt!"* When
> Aaron saw this, he built an altar before it; and Aaron made proclama-
> tion and said, "Tomorrow shall be a festival to YHWH." They rose
> early the next day, and offered burnt offerings and brought sacrifices of
> well-being; and the people sat down to eat and drink, and rose up to
> revel. (Exod. 32:1–6)

What does the infamous "golden calf" in the wilderness have to do with the shrines set up in the towns of Bethel and Dan in Israel? What does "Aaron," brother of Moses, have to do with Jeroboam? Why does the Exodus story seem to have turned around to bite its supposed source and hero, the Moses-like Jeroboam?

The Revenge of the Shilonites

In whichever order one reads these two passages, Jeroboam looks bad. In the Bible's order of presentation, the new leader of Israel appears virtually to have lost his mind: why would one ever want to *imitate* the making of the golden calves, an act more harshly condemned than any other in the entire Exodus narrative?[62] Jeroboam's act — whatever it actually was behind the polemical portrait in 1 Kings — must have taken place before the composition of Exodus 32, a story that intrudes roughly into the center of the Mishkan sequence in Exodus 25–40.

We must also turn the question around and ask: Why would the author of Exodus 32 want to paint Moses' brother, Aaron, as the story's buffoonish goat? It is virtually impossible not to read the Golden Calf tale as a political cartoon. Where did the supposed calf-mold come from in the middle of the desert? Why, when confronted by Moses, would Aaron issue this absurdly feeble reply?

---

62. For an attempt to make intertextual sense of Exodus 32 and 1 Kings 12 from the perspective of an audience in Josiah's time, see Lasine (1992), 133–52.

Map 5: Major worship sites in the divided kingdom

Moses said to Aaron, "What did this people do to you that you have brought so great a sin upon them?" And Aaron said, "Do not let the anger of my lord burn hot; you know the people, that they are bent on evil. They said to me, 'Make us gods, who shall go before us; as for this Moses, the man who brought us up out of the land of Egypt, we do not know what has become of him.' So I said to them, 'Whoever has gold, take it off'; so they gave it to me, and I threw it into the fire, and out came this calf!" (Exod. 32:21–24)

Why would Moses respond with the order to the "sons of Levi" to take up the sword and "each of you kill your brother, your friend and your neighbor" until three thousand lay dead, then proclaim: "Today you have ordained yourselves for the service of YHWH, each one at the cost of a son or a brother, and so have brought a blessing on yourselves this day" (32:29)?

What we find in the interaction between the two stories is a complex ideological battle between groups with differing hopes for the outcome of the

Jeroboam-led rebellion.[63] The core question came down to which locale (and its accompanying priestly leaders) would control worship. The three contenders were Shiloh (claiming "Levi" roots associated with Moses); Bethel (associated with Aaron but also with an indigenous priesthood), and Jerusalem (associated with Zadok, the Davidic priest who sided with Solomon). The map shows the geographic relationship among these competing places.

For our purposes, we need not untangle the political web that generated this harsh mutual polemic found in Exodus 32 and 1 Kings 12, except to the extent that it helps us understand how the imperial story and its counterstory eventually became interwoven into the fabric of biblical narrative. What did Jeroboam do that so upset two out of three of these partisan groups?

The author of 1 Kings 12 tells us that he "made two calves of gold" and set them in Bethel and Dan, at the southernmost and northernmost points in "Israel." He then compounded this with three further acts: (1) "made houses on high places," (2) "appointed priests from among all the people who were not Levites," and (3) "appointed a festival...like the festival that was in Judah [but]...in Bethel," placing the newly ordained priests at the Bethel shrine. Note that Jeroboam was *not* being accused of introducing worship of other gods (such as Ba'al and Astarte, local Canaanite divinities). As Frank Cross notes, "It is inconceivable that the national cult of Jeroboam was other than Yahwistic."[64]

Rather, he is charged with *radical liturgical reform*. Jeroboam replaces worship practices that support an imperial social order with new ones designed to be supportive of his alternative vision for YHWH's people. In choosing Bethel to replace Jerusalem, he sought to root worship in an *older source of communal memory* than that of Davidic/Solomonic Jerusalem.[65] In doing so, however, he made the choice to reject Shiloh, preferred by some members of his coalition. Recall that the prophecy announcing Jeroboam's receipt of most of the Davidic realm was given by Abijah the *Shilonite* (1 Kings 11:29ff.). Furthermore, Jeroboam appointed new priests "from all the people," an act befitting the Exodus opposition to hierarchical or hereditary forms of cultic authority in favor of "a priestly kingdom and holy nation" (Exod. 19:6). In doing so, Jeroboam alienated his Shilonite constituency, who likely hoped that the rebellion would restore Shiloh, not Bethel, to preeminence.[66] Of course, Jeroboam had already turned against the Jerusalem elite, whose Zadokite priesthood would eventually be associated firmly with Aaron.[67]

---

63. See generally Cross (1973), 73–75, 198–200; Halpern (1976); Leuchter, 65–72.
64. Cross (1973), 74.
65. Leuchter, 68–69.
66. Halpern (1976), 38–39.
67. Cross, ibid.; see Ezra 7:1–5, tracing the lineage of the priestly leader of the postexilic restoration of Jerusalem through Zadok and back to Aaron. Blenkinsopp (1998), 34–43, discusses the conflict between "Aaronic" and "Zadokite" priestly lineages during the early part of

The Shilonites, for their part, disgusted with the outcome of the rebellion, turned back to Jerusalem in the hope that eventually, the Bethel shrine would be destroyed and their own authority restored.[68] That, at least, is the way the continuing narrative of 1–2 Kings was written some two hundred years later during the reign of Josiah, the king declared by the author as the greatest ruler of all: "Before him there was no king like him, who turned to YHWH with all his heart, with all his soul, and with all his might, according to all the law of Moses; nor did any like him arise after him" (2 Kings 23:19).

The story in Exodus 32 is the Shilonites' "revenge" on both Jeroboam and the Zadokites. The scene sharply contrasts Moses (their hero) with Aaron (the Zadokite "founding father"), while at the same time ridiculing Jeroboam's attempt to establish an egalitarian priesthood. Note how clearly the passage refers back to the Dan and Bethel shrines, by speaking of a *single* calf that Aaron proclaims to be "your *gods,* O Israel" (32:4, repeated in 32:8). It suggests that Jeroboam's action is more than simply an unpopular (with the Shilonites) liturgical reform, but is actually the establishment of *idolatry.*

Can we see through these partisan perspectives to get a glimpse at what really was going on in Jeroboam's actions? As already noted, one aspect of his proposed alternative was the removal of the priesthood from both the realms of the imperial court and of hereditary lineages. Another is seen in the locations of Bethel and Dan at the extreme northern and southern ends of Israel. Recall the contrast between temple and Mishkan just discussed. The temple's theology proclaimed YHWH as "sitting" enthroned on the cherubim within the confines of the Jerusalem temple (e.g., 2 Kings 19:15; Ps. 80:1; 99:1). In contrast, Jeroboam's shrines suggest that YHWH's presence *extends across the entire land of Israel.* This contrast between a northern, decentralized and a southern, centralized theology will extend over the centuries to the time of Jesus of Nazareth, who grew up and ministered exclusively in the north (according to the synoptic gospel writers) until making his final pilgrimage in confrontation of the Jerusalem establishment.[69] Jeroboam, in other words, sought to enshrine in liturgical practice the theology expressed in Exodus: that YHWH was not a domesticated deity within the ambit of urban empire, but was rather the untamed, uncontrollable, powerful Creator of mountain and wilderness. Such a proclamation has always generated passionate resistance from the holders of imperial religious authority. It should not surprise us that Jeroboam was vilified on all sides by those with control of the media in ancient Israel and Judah.

---

the postexilic era, reaching an eventual compromise as indicated in the genealogy at 1 Chron. 6:1–15. See also chapter 16 below.

68. It is possible that the story in Judges 17–18, in which a shrine is set up in the hill country of Ephraim then appropriated by the Danites, is a "hidden polemic" against Bethel from the same source; cf. Amit. 139–42.

69. See Freyne (2004) and Horsley (1995).

And, unfortunately, even such well-intentioned alternative religious structures run the risk of being taken captive by empire, just as Jesus and the churches established in his Name in order to proclaim and practice his Way became captives of empire after Constantine. In the period following Jeroboam, Bethel became a tool of the dynasty that made Israel a much greater empire than Solomon's Judah, arousing the Yahwistic wrath of a group of outsider prophets who expressed their condemnation in harsh and often bitter words. Elijah and Elisha speak through the pages of 1–2 Kings, while the ire of Amos, Hosea, and Micah is recorded in books bearing their own names.

Chapter Eleven

Kissing Calves

Whatever Jeroboam's true intentions for a separated Israel might have been, it was not long before the northern realm developed its own traditional Middle Eastern monarchical dynasty, the Omrides. The founder, Omri, an army commander, established his own capital city, Samaria (see Map 5, p. 157). Archaeological evidence reveals extensive and elaborate Omride construction in Samaria.[1] It was the willingness of Omri and his son Ahab to become vassals of the newly emerging regional power, Assyria, that made it possible.[2] This placed Israel in the midst of the ninth century BCE "global economy," providing opportunities for trade and economic development that greatly enriched Omri and his supporters.

The Solomonic propaganda presented in 1 Kings 3–10 attests that "Judah and Israel . . . ate and drank and were happy . . . all of them under their vines and fig trees" (4:20, 25). As we saw in chapter 9, there is no protest recorded until after Solomon's death, when the assembly of Israel sought relief from Solomon's "hard service" and "heavy yoke" (12:4). The Omrides, however, did not have as tight a control on the media as did Solomon. We find for the first time in the written record voices speaking on behalf of those oppressed by the royal program, claiming to speak in the name of YHWH. These *prophets* arise in the eighth century, with Samaria well-established and providing luxurious comfort for court denizens and poverty and suffering for others.

Elijah, "Troubler of Israel," and His Successor, Elisha

The written words and deeds of the eighth-century prophets may have been but the tip of an iceberg of resistance to the hijacking of Jeroboam's alternative social order by the Omride monarchs. We hear, for example, that Ahab's infamous wife, Jezebel, "was killing off the prophets of YHWH," leading Ahab's palace chief, Obadiah, to become a double agent, hiding a *hundred* of these prophets in a pair of caves and meeting with Elijah behind

---

1. Mazar (1992), 406–10.
2. "Recent work has modified the view that terror was the primary motivation among vassals for submission to the Assyrian empire. There is evidence that Assyrian policy regarding its periphery included an awareness of 'benefits' that could be extended to vassals and provinces, such as security for local rulers and elites"; Dutcher-Walls (1991), 614; see also Bedford 45.

the king's back (1 Kings 18:3–16). The prophets must have represented an oppressed constituency, akin to how David gathered around him those "in distress, and everyone who was in debt, and everyone who was discontented" (1 Sam. 22:2). The scale of oppression under Ahab was much greater than under Saul or other local tyrants from whose hands David offered salvation. Yet Elijah and his companions did not become a force of military resistance, but instead challenged king and queen with verbal denunciation and confrontational public protest.

The later author of 1 Kings expresses his own basis for denouncing Ahab:

> And as if it had been a light thing for him to walk in the sins of Jeroboam son of Nebat, he took as his wife Jezebel daughter of King Ethbaal of the Sidonians, and went and served Ba'al, and worshiped him. He erected an altar for Ba'al in the house of Ba'al, which he built in Samaria. Ahab also made an Asherah. Ahab did more to provoke the anger of YHWH, the God of Israel, than had all the kings of Israel who were before him. (1 Kings 16:31–33)

It is the earliest reference to worship of the Canaanite deity Ba'al (meaning simply "lord") in the biblical writings. In the canonical sequence, though, the worship of Ba'al had become a temptation in the wilderness (Numbers 25, recalled at Deuteronomy 4:3) and again in the Judges narrative and the introductory section of 1 Samuel (7:4; 12:10). However, in the likely historical order of events, Ba'al and Asherah (Ba'al's female consort, also known as Astarte[3]) worship was introduced to Israel under the influence of Ahab's Sidonian wife, Jezebel.[4] Note how the author distinguishes clearly the "sins of Jeroboam" (i.e., leading people away from exclusive worship in Jerusalem) from the worship of other gods. The "way of the house of Ahab" will become a different criterion for royal evaluation than "the sins of Jeroboam" (e.g., 2 Kings 8:27). A later king of Judah (Manasseh) can be accused of worshiping Ba'al and making Asherahs (2 Kings 21:3), but no southern king is accused of the "sins of Jeroboam."

What is clear from this first confrontation of a king by a prophetic outsider is *that the "religious" charge of worshiping false gods is never separate from the socioeconomic charge of practicing injustice.* Scholars who have attempted to separate "cultic" from "social justice" questions in the prophets have radically misunderstood the integrated perspective that the prophets proclaim. For Ahab to accept the Sidonian Jezebel's god Ba'al is to accept the Sidonian way of life in place of the way of YHWH. We can see this clearly by comparing two adjacent stories in which Elijah takes on Ahab.

---

3. E.g., 1 Sam. 12:10. Note that Solomon is accused of worshiping "Astarte the goddess of the Sidonians" (1 Kings 11:5, 33; see also 2 Kings 23:13) but never Ba'al.

4. That worship of Ba'al is never mentioned between 1 Sam. 12:10 and 1 Kings 16:31 is yet another indication that the David/Solomon portrait was composed earlier than the Deuteronomistic History frame that contains it.

In 1 Kings 18, Elijah is told by "the word of YHWH" to "go, present yourself to Ahab" in the midst of a YHWH-caused drought and resulting famine. We may be surprised to hear Ahab's first spoken words, addressed to Elijah: "Is it you, you troubler of Israel?" (18:17).[5] Elijah may be an "outsider," but the king knows all about him! The prophet responds, "I have not troubled Israel; but you have, and your father's house, because you have forsaken the commandments of YHWH and followed the Ba'als." With this exchange, the battle is on. At stake in this and other stories in the Elijah/Elisha cycle (1 Kings 17–2 Kings 9; also 2 Kings 13) is the question of power and authority. Who truly rules: the king who grounds his claim in worship of Ba'al or YHWH, God of Israel (and his king in Jerusalem)?

Throughout these stories, we find an author supportive of the Davidic dynasty siding with those who resist monarchical authority in Israel. The Deuteronomistic History authors' concern is not monarchy itself, but Israel's separate existence—the "sin of Jeroboam." Thus, the Jerusalem-based writers of the eighth and seventh centuries[6] have common cause with prophets who condemn *Israel's* kings as idolaters and oppressors.

The story in 1 Kings 18 is a political-religious cartoon with an incredibly violent conclusion. Elijah proposes a grand assembly of "all Israel" at Mount Carmel with himself against the 850 prophets of Ba'al and Asherah who "eat at Jezebel's table" (18:19). This does not mean, of course, that the queen serves dinner for them all, but that they are on the royal payroll.[7] The test is as much for the people of Israel as for the king, as Elijah asks them, "How long will you go limping with two different opinions [*hass'ippim*, literally, on 'crutches']? If YHWH is God, follow him; but if Ba'al, then follow him." But "the people did not answer him a word" (18:21). Ahab and Jezebel have either "converted" the people of Israel or cowed them into silence.

Elijah's contest demands that the prophets of Ba'al (the prophets of Asherah apparently didn't show up) call on the name of their god to bring fire to a bull prepared for sacrifice. They cry out "from morning until noon" but "there was no voice and no answer." The narrator and Elijah combine to ridicule their powerlessness. First, the narrator notes that they "limped about the altar that they had made," echoing Elijah's "limping" reference. Then Elijah joins in: "At noon Elijah mocked them, saying, 'Cry aloud! Surely he is a god; either he is occupied, or he has wandered away,[8] or he is

---

5. Cf. 1 Sam. 14:29, where Saul's son Jonathan accuses his own father of having "troubled" the land.

6. It is hard to pin down the origin of the Elijah/Elisha stories. Neither prophet is ever mentioned outside 1–2 Kings in the Hebrew Bible except for one reference in Malachi 4:5, the penultimate verse in the prophetic canon, although Elijah is mentioned twenty-nine times in the New Testament, and even makes a "live" appearance, Mark 9:4 and parallels. However, there are numerous hints that suggest that in their final form, the stories have been integrated into the view expressed in the seventh-century Josianic composition that includes Deut.–Joshua.

7. Cf. 1 Sam. 20:29; 2 Sam. 9:13; Jer. 52:33.

8. The Hebrew, *vekhi-sig*, means literally "or because of a bowel movement."

on a journey, or perhaps he is asleep and must be awakened.' " The narrator then takes a swipe at the prophets of Ba'al:

> Then they cried aloud and, as was their custom, they cut themselves with swords and lances until the blood gushed out over them. As midday passed, they raved on until the time of the offering of the oblation, but there was no voice, no answer, and no response. (18:28–29)

Elijah now went into action. Setting up twelve stones, one for each of the tribes — the only time during the monarchy narrative that the twelve tribes are mentioned (cf. Josh. 4:3–20) — he made a deep trench and ordered it filled with water to cover wood and bull. He then called on YHWH to answer him "so that this people may know that you, O YHWH, are God, and that you have turned their hearts back" (18:37). Immediately, the entire spectacle is consumed in "the fire of YHWH" and the people confess that "YHWH is indeed God." Elijah ordered the entire company of Ba'al prophets seized and killed at the river.

Finally, Elijah, now alone with the king, ordered Ahab to go home to eat and drink because the drought is over. Ahab obeyed and the sky turned black and rain poured down. It is both an amusing and a shocking story, certainly not expected to be taken literally but rather to make an important point in a memorable way. To call on Ba'al (or any other "god") is to render one powerless and to bring about not life but death.

As the king returned home and told his wife, however, Jezebel was equally resolute. She sent this message to Elijah: "So may the gods do to me, and more also, if I do not make your life like the life of one of them by this time tomorrow" (19:2). Elijah became frightened and hid in the wilderness, only to be found and challenged by YHWH. The ensuing experience reveals the other side of YHWH, the all-consuming fire. Elijah was sent to a mountain to await YHWH's coming. He encountered a rock-splitting windstorm, an earthquake, and a fire but YHWH was not in any of these powerful events. Instead, Elijah experienced YHWH in "a sound of thin silence" (19:12). YHWH is not to be encountered only in external events of visible and audible power, but also in utter stillness. Such an experience is unknown to the religion of empire, where elaborate spectacles visibly linked gods and king.

YHWH now gave the prophet new orders, designed to end the reign of Ahab and Jezebel. Meanwhile, we find the king "resentful and sullen" because Naboth, a neighbor to the king's summer palace in Jezreel, would not trade or sell his vineyard to the king (21:1–4). Here we see how the question of social justice is interwoven with "right religion." Naboth's stated reason — repeated by the narrator to make sure we hear it — was that the land was his "ancestral inheritance." The phrase is a technical term and a favorite of the Deuteronomistic History.[9] At issue is not simply a king's

---

9. *Nachalah* is used 222 times in the Hebrew Bible, 95 of which are in the Deuteronomistic History.

greed, but the question of who determines the availability of land: a king's whim or the kinship relations that underlie Israel's existence as a people? Jezebel put it bluntly: "Do you now really hold the kingship in Israel?"[10] She jumped into action, framing the innocent Naboth so that he will be stoned to death.

Marsha White notes a series of parallels between this story and that of David's acquisition of Bathsheba.[11]

1. The object of royal desire is visible from the royal palace.

2. The murders of Uriah and Naboth, the holders of the desired object, are done by stealth, via a letter sent from the palace.

3. A threefold repetition of instructions precedes the deed and a report back to the royal initiator.

4. The king is confronted after-the-fact by a prophet.

5. Punishment is deferred to the king's son as a result of royal repentance.

Clearly, the author seeks to remind the reader of the act that "officially" led to David's downfall. As White says, the "Elijah of the vineyard story is...a second Nathan."[12] The narrative of Ahab's repentance underscores a point central to the Deuteronomic viewpoint that emerges most fully in the seventh-century texts we'll explore in the next chapter: repentance always remains possible. The Word of YHWH can be heard and obeyed, even by the greediest of kings.

The pair of stories we've briefly entered express in microcosm the entire sweep of the Elijah/Elisha cycle embedded within 1–2 Kings. The two prophets, though human and often flawed, pronounce YHWH's powerful judgment on the evils of Israel's monarchy and often embody YHWH's power over life and death as well. Although the Omride dynasty could build palaces and temples and could worship Ba'al and Asherah, they could not silence or exclude the voice of Israel's true God. The more they sought to do so, the more they sealed their own terrible fate.

Amos and Hosea:
Calling Israel Back to the Sinai Covenant

Only once do we hear a link between Elijah and the Sinai tradition we studied in chapter 10. In hiding from the wrath of Jezebel, the prophet twice heard YHWH's word ask what he was doing in hiding. His reply each time is identical:

---

10. Translation from Dutcher-Walls (2004), 42–43.

11. White (1994), 68–69. She notes that the Naboth story is briefly retold at 2 Kings 9:25–26, concluding that the more elaborate version we are examining was written specifically to evoke the comparison with David/Bathsheba, which she presumes was written first.

12. Ibid., 70.

I have been very zealous for YHWH, the God of hosts; for the Israelites have forsaken your covenant, thrown down your altars, and killed your prophets with the sword. I alone am left, and they are seeking my life, to take it away. (1 Kings 19:10, 14)

It is the only time that Israel's evil is linked with violation of *covenant* before the narrator's programmatic summary expressing the reasons for the fall of Israel (2 Kings 17).[13] Once Israel was destroyed late in the eighth century and a river of refugees flowed southward to seek shelter in Jerusalem, the Deuteronomistic History adapted and included northern Exodus traditions. But earlier in the eighth century, with Israel and Judah often at war, it was up to others to challenge Israel's elite in the name of the God of Sinai and the covenant commitment freely entered into in the wilderness.

The prophets Hosea and Amos brought the Word of YHWH into sharp confrontation with Israel's kings and others at the top of the socioeconomic pyramid built with Assyrian support. William Dever notes, "Eighth-century prophetic protest against social injustice was not a new reform movement, but was deeply rooted in the egalitarian traditions of early Israel and its ideal of agrarian reform."[14] Stephen Cook systematically has shown how the "roots of biblical Yahwism" lie in the traditions on which these prophets could ground their protest, i.e., the traditions focused on "Sinai."[15]

Amos was the older of the two prophets. The introductory verse of the book bearing his name situates him in the early eighth century during the reigns of Uzziah of Judah and Jeroboam II of Israel (see 2 Kings 14:23ff.).[16] Amos was "among the shepherds (*noqed*) of Tekoa, a town south of Jerusalem along the edge of the Judean wilderness. The term *noqed* suggests not a hired laborer or nomad, but a flock manager or breeder of sheep (as 2 Kings 3:4).[17] Why would a rancher from south of Jerusalem go north to speak YHWH's word against Israel? Marvin Sweeney offers this explanation:

> As Judah was subservient to Israel during this period, the Judean state would be expected to pay a certain amount of tribute to Israel each year to meet the expenses of the administration, defense, and expansion of the larger Israelite empire. Most of this burden would fall upon the population of Judah.... The need to pay tribute to northern Israel would

---

13. See 2 Kings 17:15, 35, 38; 18:12.
14. Dever (2006), 199.
15. Cook (2004).
16. Sweeney (2001b), 192, states, "The prophet's oracles must be set against the background of the rise of the Israelite state under the rule of Jeroboam ben Joash (786–746 BCE). ... The northern kingdom of Israel was apparently allied with the southern kingdom of Judah under the rule of Uzziah/Azariah ben Amaziah (783–742 BCE), although Judah must be considered as a junior partner in the relationship.... Israel's traditional enemies, Aram and Philistia, were quiet during this period as they lacked the power to challenge the combined Israelite and Judean states. Israel's alliance with Assyria during this period, dating from the reigns of Jeroboam's great-grandfather Jehu (842–815 BCE) and father, Jehoash, no doubt contributed to Israel's security."
17. Birch, 174.

account for Amos' presence in Beth El at the time of the festival of Sukkoth.[18]

Thus, we hear that YHWH has sent Amos to speak against injustice, grounded in false worship, which was taking a huge toll on Amos's friends and neighbors in the south. This protest against the treatment of the victims of Israel's "glory" can be heard in this passage:

> Hear this, you that trample on the needy, and bring to ruin the poor of the land, saying, "When will the new moon be over so that we may sell grain; and the sabbath, so that we may offer wheat for sale? We will make the ephah small and the shekel great, and practice deceit with false balances, buying the poor for silver and the needy for a pair of sandals, and selling the sweepings of the wheat." (Amos 8:4–6; see also 2:6; 4:1; 5:11–12)

His oracles begin with a formulaic blast at each of seven nations that encircle Israel.[19] But the heart of his prophetic word starts in chapter 3 with this announcement:

> Hear this word that YHWH has spoken against you, O people of Israel, against the whole family [*kal-hammishpachah*] that I brought up out of the land of Egypt: You only have I known of all the families [*mishpechot*] of the earth; therefore I will punish you for all your iniquities. (Amos 3:1–2)

Israel's central identity to Amos is as the *mishpachah* YHWH "knows" and has brought out of Egypt. This clearly links his perspective with the Exodus/Sinai tradition. As noted earlier, *mishpachah* is used 166 times in Exodus–Numbers, but *never* in 1–2 Kings. It is not as a monarchy or nation that YHWH knows Israel, but through local, kinship relationships.[20]

At the same time, the wrath of YHWH is directed largely against "Bethel" (the central site of Jeroboam's liturgy) and Samaria (the capital of the Omride and succeeding dynasties). Jeroboam's egalitarian alternative to Jerusalem had become, starting with Ahab and Jezebel, one more empire seeking to provide a "sacred canopy"[21] for its injustice and oppression. We hear Amos's message against Bethel in this representative passage:

> Hear, and testify against the house of Jacob, says Lord YHWH, the God of hosts: On the day I punish Israel for its transgressions, I will punish

---

18. Sweeney (2001b), 192–93.

19. Scholars have long debated the theological implications of Amos 1–2; see, e.g., Hayes, 52–55 (rejecting arguments for compositional layers); Polley, 61–64 (claiming the nations are all part of the former Davidic kingdom); Birch, 181 (claiming it to be expressive of YHWH's universal authority).

20. This theme will be considered in more detail in chapter 13.

21. The term originates with Berger and Luckmann; see also Berger (1990). It was understood long ago, though, as we hear in Isaiah's characterization of this "canopy" as a death shroud, Isa. 25:7.

the altars of Bethel, and the horns of the altar shall be cut off and fall
to the ground. I will tear down the winter house as well as the summer
house; and the houses of ivory shall perish, and the great houses shall
come to an end, says YHWH. (Amos 3:13–15)

The prophet takes his critique a step further later in his oracles. After
YHWH recites all that he has done for Israel, Amos says:

For thus says YHWH to the house of Israel: Seek me and live; but do not
seek Bethel, and do not enter into Gilgal or cross over to Beer-sheba; for
Gilgal shall surely go into exile, and Bethel shall come to nothing. Seek
YHWH and live, or he will break out against the house of Joseph like
fire, and it will devour Bethel, with no one to quench it. (Amos 5:4–6)

Which path should Israel take at this fork in the road? On the one side is
YHWH, the source of life. On the other side are Bethel and Gilgal, on the
road to exile and destruction. Amos's inclusion of Gilgal as a location on
the wrong road likely refers to the source of Israel's own monarchy before
Jeroboam, with the house of Saul. For example, near the end of the section
of 1 Samuel that precedes the David/Solomon story, we are told: "So all
the people went to Gilgal, and there they made Saul king before YHWH
in Gilgal" (1 Sam. 11:15; see also 13:4–15; 15:12, 21, 33). Thus, Amos
condemns not only the specific excesses and injustices of Samaria's elite, but
the very existence of Israel's monarchy.

What is Amos's alternative to "Samaria" and "Bethel"? The closing verses
of the book promise a future restoration through YHWH's own doing:

On that day I will raise up the booth [*sukkah*] of David that is fallen,
and repair its breaches, and raise up its ruins, and rebuild it as in the
days of old; in order that they may possess the remnant of Edom and
all the nations who are called by my name, says YHWH who does this.
The time is surely coming, says YHWH, when the one who plows shall
overtake the one who reaps, and the treader of grapes the one who
sows the seed; the mountains shall drip sweet wine, and all the hills
shall flow with it. I will restore the fortunes of my people Israel, and
they shall rebuild the ruined cities and inhabit them; they shall plant
vineyards and drink their wine, and they shall make gardens and eat
their fruit. I will plant them upon their land, and they shall never again
be plucked up out of the land that I have given them, says YHWH your
God. (Amos 9:11–15; see Acts 15:16–17)

The mention of "the *sukkah* of David" may appear to express a
Jerusalem-centered word on behalf of the Davidic dynasty. However, several factors counsel against this interpretation. First, at the time of Amos,
Judah and Jerusalem were not "fallen" or in "ruins." Further, the oracle
promises a restoration of *Israel*, whose cities would be ruined by the coming of Assyria. Finally, the term *sukkah* doesn't suggest the Jerusalem temple

or other imperial structures, but rather, the "booths" of field and vineyard workers that provide shade and shelter from heat during harvest (e.g., Isa. 1:8; 4:6; Jon. 4:5).[22] Amos concludes not with an image of Israel joining Judah in Jerusalem, but of the restoration of a decentralized people established directly by YHWH's hand. No human king is part of this vision. The direct relationship between YHWH and Israel, as in the Sinai wilderness, will be regenerated.

Hosea, writing later in the eighth century,[23] develops his message within one central image: Israel as the "whoring" wife of a long-suffering yet patient husband, YHWH. This marital metaphor extends the notion of covenant from something between king and people to that between husband and wife. Violation of covenant is not only a political and theological transgression: it is a personal and painful betrayal of an intimate relationship.

Interwoven within the torn fabric of Israel's and YHWH's marriage is Hosea's sharp critique of Israel's monarchy, matching Amos in force and clarity. For instance, Hosea announces:

> Set the trumpet to your lips! One like a vulture is over the house of YHWH, because they have broken my covenant, and transgressed my law. Israel cries to me, "My God, we — Israel — know you!" Israel has spurned the good; the enemy shall pursue him. They made kings, but not through me; they set up princes, but without my knowledge. With their silver and gold they made idols for their own destruction. Your calf is rejected, O Samaria. My anger burns against them. How long will they be incapable of innocence? For it is from Israel, an artisan made it; it is not God. The calf of Samaria shall be broken to pieces. (Hos. 8:1–6)

As Stephen Cook notes, "Monarchy is a form of idolatry for Hosea that has spawned other idolatrous practices."[24]

Like Amos, Hosea condemns Israel's kingship at its historical source:

> Every evil of theirs began at Gilgal; there I came to hate them. Because of the wickedness of their deeds I will drive them out of my house. I will love them no more; all their officials are rebels. Ephraim is stricken, their root is dried up, they shall bear no fruit. Even though they give birth, I will kill the cherished offspring of their womb. (Hos. 9:15–16)

The "cherished offspring of their womb" are not literal children, but the dynastic succession that "began at Gilgal." He cannot even say "Bethel"

---

22. See also Polley, 72–73, interpreting it as a place name in Judah, following 2 Sam. 11:1; 1 Kings 20:12, 16.

23. Sweeney (2001b), 4–5, argues that the book "was written largely in the period following the death of Jeroboam II and prior to the Assyrian assault in 735–732 in an effort to convince Israel to abandon its alliance with Assyria concluded initially by King Jehu and maintained by his successors, Jeohahaz (815–801), Jehoash (801–786), Jeroboam II (786–746), and Zechariah (746), throughout the rule of the Jehu dynasty ... until the emergence of Pekah."

24. Cook (2004), 111.

(meaning, "house of God") but parodies it as "Beth-aven" ("house of evil").[25]

> The inhabitants of Samaria tremble for the calf of Beth-aven. Its people shall mourn for it, and its idolatrous priests shall wail over it, over its glory that has departed from it. (Hos. 10:5; see also 4:15; 5:8)

Hosea's blast at Israel's idolatry is an appeal to the Sinai covenant as the true basis for Israel's existence, not Bethel or the monarchy itself. For example,

> And now they keep on sinning and make a cast image for themselves, idols of silver made according to their understanding, all of them the work of artisans. "Sacrifice to these," they say. People are kissing calves! Therefore they shall be like the morning mist or like the dew that goes away early, like chaff that swirls from the threshing floor or like smoke from a window. Yet I have been YHWH your God *ever since the land of Egypt;* you know no God but me, and besides me there is no savior. It was I who fed you in the wilderness, in the land of drought. When I fed them, they were satisfied; they were satisfied, and their heart was proud; therefore they forgot me.
>
> I will destroy you, O Israel; who can help you? Where now is your king, that he may save you? Where in all your cities are your rulers, of whom you said, "Give me a king and rulers"? I gave you a king in my anger, and I took him away in my wrath. (Hos. 13:2–6, 9–11)

What is Hosea's hope for Israel's future? Older scholars considered Hosea's final chapter to be a postexilic addition. However, Marvin Sweeney sees it as "the rhetorical goal of the prophet's speeches."[26] Again, as with Amos, there is no turning to Jerusalem and its monarchy. Rather, it is the *complete rejection of monarchy* — both their own and that of other nations — that will manifest Israel's "return" to YHWH her God (Hos. 14:1–3). Then and only then will YHWH "heal their disloyalty" and "love them freely" (14:4). The marriage covenant will be restored when Israel comes to know again that YHWH alone is the source of her blessing.

But that future for Israel was a long way off. All the attempts of Israel's kings to generate security against Assyria through successful alliances with its neighbors failed. In 722 BCE, the Assyrian juggernaut crushed Samaria along with the surrounding nations. The victorious empire trumpeted its conquest and its taking of numerous captives back to Nineveh, its capital. According to 2 Kings 17:24–41, the Assyrian king also brought in peoples

---

25. Knauf, 320, notes that there "can be little doubt that the core of Hosea, chapters 4–11, was composed at Bethel after 720...integrated into a single speech by YHWH as a state's attorney, proving Israel's guilt and the justice of his own judgment, ending, however, on a positive note: there will be a future for Israel as YHWH's people but not necessarily for a state of Israel (Hos. 11)."

26. Sweeney (2001b), 136.

from other lands to Samaria and the surrounding region, presumably to dilute the sense of national identity (see chapter 13). But many Israelites — especially those in southern Samaria close to Bethel — sought to escape Assyrian control by moving south to Judah, not yet under Assyrian control.[27] Israel's loss was Judah's gain: in the late eighth and through the seventh centuries, Judah became the center of conflicting hopes: of those who held Davidic dreams of renewed empire as well as of those rooted in encounter with a YHWH whose power was manifest in liberation *from* kings and empires.

---

27. Finkelstein and Silberman, 263–69.

Chapter Twelve

"I Have Found the Book of the Torah in the House of YHWH!"

Hezekiah, Isaiah, and Micah
Respond to the Threat of Assyria

King Hezekiah reigned over Judah as Assyria took control of Israel. One of his closest advisors was the prophet Isaiah, who counseled the king not to worry about Assyria because YHWH would protect Jerusalem (Isa. 37:33–36 = 2 Kings 19:32–35).[1] But from the king's vantage point, things were not quite that simple. He was concerned with two groups of people: Judah's landed nobility and the Israelite refugees. As Israel Finkelstein and Neil Silberman say with regard to the latter group:

> The presence of substantial numbers of northern immigrants in Judah — and the new demographic situation it created — must have presented a challenge to the southern leadership and created an urgent need to unite the two segments of the new Judahite society — Judahites and Israelites — into a single national entity. In other words, there must have been a necessity to re-format Judah into a new nation. And the main problems that needed to be addressed were ideological: particularly the different — not to say alien and hostile — cult and royal traditions of the northerners who came to settle in Judah.[2]

Hezekiah had come into power with tremendous hope placed on his shoulders. His father, Ahaz, had cowered in the face of an alliance between Israel and its neighbor, Aram, which threatened Jerusalem around 730 BCE (2 Kings 16:5; Isa. 7:1–2). Second Kings tells us that Ahaz sought security in an alliance with Assyria's King Tiglath-Pileser, which cost much silver and gold from the temple and led Ahaz to build an altar in the temple that matched that of the Assyrian king in Damascus (2 Kings 16:8–18). Such an alliance conformed to Assyria's "religion of empire" in which the king,

---

1. Isa. 36–39 is the same (with small variations) as 2 Kings 18:13–20:19, indicating the close connection between Isaiah and Hezekiah. There is much scholarly debate over the nature of this connection, however; see, e.g., Hogenhaven.
2. Finkelstein and Silberman, 269.

through the chief Assyrian deity Ashur, was empowered to "extend the borders" of the empire to achieve "order" throughout the earth.[3] Thus, the new altar expressed Ahaz's acceptance of Ashur's (Assyria's) rule.

Isaiah looked beyond Ahaz's political compromise, in prophesying a royal successor who would turns things around:

> Therefore YHWH himself will give you a sign. Look, the young woman is with child and shall bear a son, and shall name him Immanuel. He shall eat curds and honey by the time he knows how to refuse the evil and choose the good. For before the child knows how to refuse the evil and choose the good, the land before whose two kings you are in dread will be deserted. (Isa. 7:14–16)

Thus, in its context, the famous Immanuel prophecy anticipated the coming to the throne not of Jesus of Nazareth, but Hezekiah.

Eight years after Samaria's capture, Hezekiah faced an attack from Assyria's King Sennacherib in which the fortified cities of Judah were captured.[4] After Hezekiah offered an enormous tribute in gold and silver, Sennacherib sent a delegation to persuade Hezekiah and all the people of Jerusalem to give up completely. His representatives mocked Hezekiah's trust in YHWH and urged the king and people to practice *Realpolitik* and accept Assyrian power and authority.

The speech begins:

> The Rabshakeh [one of Sennacherib's officials] said to them, "Say to Hezekiah: Thus says the great king, the king of Assyria: On what do you base this confidence of yours? Do you think that mere words are strategy and power for war? On whom do you now rely, that you have rebelled against me? See, you are relying now on Egypt, that broken reed of a staff, which will pierce the hand of anyone who leans on it. Such is Pharaoh king of Egypt to all who rely on him.
>
> But if you say to me, "We rely on YHWH our God," is it not he whose high places and altars Hezekiah has removed, saying to Judah and to Jerusalem, "You shall worship before this altar in Jerusalem"? (2 Kings 18:19–22)

The Rabshakeh makes reference to Hezekiah's earlier actions that the Deuteronomistic History (DH) author had stated were "right in the sight of YHWH":

> He removed the high places, broke down the pillars, and cut down the sacred pole. He broke in pieces the bronze serpent that Moses had made, for until those days the people of Israel had made offerings to it; it was called Nehushtan. He trusted in YHWH the God of Israel; so that there

---

3. Bedford, 48.
4. 2 Kings 18:13; Isa. 36:1; this is where the Isaiah/2 Kings texts coincide.

was no one like him among all the kings of Judah after him, or among those who were before him. (2 Kings 18:4–5)[5]

The Assyrian speech challenges what the DH author praises: the removal of the "high places and altars," it suggests, is evident of Hezekiah's *lack* of trust in YHWH, and the Assyrian invasion is YHWH's punishment on Judah.[6] Why else would he tear down *altars to YHWH* outside Jerusalem?

Why else indeed? Note that the DH author does not claim that the removed shrines expressed worship of other gods. Baruch Halpern, after analyzing Assyrian inscriptions, archaeological remains, and the biblical text, concludes that Hezekiah's "reform" was part of his adaptation of a "hedgehog" strategy. In short, in the face of imminent Assyrian attack, Hezekiah sought to protect the walled city of Jerusalem by giving up the cities and towns in the Judean countryside.[7] This meant centralizing authority in the monarchy at the expense of local kinship-based leadership. It also had the effect of distancing the Israelites from their last vestige of independence: the old shrine at Bethel established by Jeroboam some two hundred years earlier, only seventeen miles from Jerusalem.[8]

Hezekiah had the prophet Isaiah's support in the plan to centralize worship in Jerusalem. Throughout Isaiah 1–39,[9] we hear oracles supporting Zion as "the place of the name of YHWH of hosts" (Isa. 18:7; also 24:23; 33:20). Furthermore, the Assyrian speech invites comparison between two prophetic responses. The speech includes this key offer:

> Do not listen to Hezekiah; for thus says the king of Assyria: 'Make your peace with me and come out to me; then *every one of you will eat from your own vine and your own fig tree,* and drink water from your own cistern, until I come and take you away to a land like your own land, a land of grain and wine, a land of bread and vineyards, a land of olive oil and honey, that you may live and not die. (2 Kings 18:31–32)

Let's now take a side-by-side look at two similar, yet also profoundly differing, prophecies, regarding both Zion and "vine and fig tree."

Isaiah's "swords into plowshares" prophecy comes near the very start of his book, seemingly detached from a specific sociopolitical situation. It

---

5. There are a number of other fascinating questions that this passage raises, which we cannot engage here, such as: (1) Why would the author specify a bronze serpent "made by Moses" as the object of Hezekiah's destruction? Put another way, what might the "people of Israel's" veneration of this object say about the persistence of Jeroboam's anti-Jerusalem movement two hundred years earlier? (2) Why would this one object be named (the meaning of the name is unclear)? Cf. Num. 21:4–9, likely an elaboration of this reference as part of Numbers' internecine struggle among priestly groups in the Second Temple period. See also John 3:14–15.

6. Ben Zvi, 86.

7. Halpern (1991), 26–27.

8. Finkelstein and Silberman, 274–75.

9. Sometimes known as "First Isaiah," distinguished from "Second Isaiah," the voice behind Isa. 40–55 from the time of the Exile; and "Third Isaiah," the voice behind Isa. 56–66, from the period of Persian restoration of Jerusalem.

Table 14:
Comparison of Isaiah's and Micah's
"Swords into Plowshares" Prophecies

Isaiah 2:1–4	*Micah 3:9–4:5*
The word that Isaiah son of Amoz saw concerning Judah and Jerusalem: *In days to come the mountain of YHWH's house shall be established as the highest of the mountains, and shall be raised above the hills; all the nations shall stream to it. Many peoples shall come and say, "Come, let us go up to the mountain of YHWH, to the house of the God of Jacob; that he may teach us his ways and that we may walk in his paths." For out of Zion shall go forth instruction, and the word of YHWH from Jerusalem.* *He shall judge between the nations, and shall arbitrate for many peoples; they shall beat their swords into plowshares, and their spears into pruning hooks; nation shall not lift up sword against nation, neither shall they learn war any more.*	Hear this, you rulers of the house of Jacob and chiefs of the house of Israel, who abhor justice and pervert all equity, who build Zion with bloodshed and Jerusalem with wrong! Its rulers give judgment for a bribe, its priests teach for a price, its prophets give oracles for money; yet they lean upon YHWH and say, "Surely YHWH is with us! No harm shall come upon us." Therefore **because of you Zion shall be plowed as a field; Jerusalem shall become a heap of ruins, and the mountain of the house a wooded height.** *In days to come the mountain of YHWH's house shall be established as the highest of the mountains, and shall be raised up above the hills. Peoples shall stream to it, and many nations shall come and say: "Come, let us go up to the mountain of YHWH, to the house of the God of Jacob; that he may teach us his ways and that we may walk in his paths." For out of Zion shall go forth instruction, and the word of YHWH from Jerusalem.* *He shall judge between many peoples, and shall arbitrate between strong nations far away; they shall beat their swords into plowshares, and their spears into pruning hooks; nation shall not lift up sword against nation, neither shall they learn war any more;* **but they shall all sit under their own vines and under their own fig trees, and no one shall make them afraid; for the mouth of YHWH of hosts has spoken.** For all the peoples walk, each in the name of its god, but we will walk in the name of YHWH our God forever and ever.

offers an overarching hope for "days to come," a time in the who-knows-when future when Zion will be the destination of "all the nations" and "many peoples" and war will be abolished. It provides a cosmic perspective from which events "on the ground" can be judged.

Micah, on the other hand, situates his identical prophecy deeply within a harsh critique of the social and economic injustices of "the rulers of the house of Jacob" who "build Zion with bloodshed[10] and Jerusalem with wrong!" A look further back in Micah 3 reveals the prophet's bitter condemnation of the elite leadership:

> Listen, you heads of Jacob and rulers of the house of Israel! Should you not know justice? — you who hate the good and love the evil, who tear the skin off my people, and the flesh off their bones; who eat the flesh of my people, flay their skin off them, break their bones in pieces, and chop them up like meat in a kettle, like flesh in a caldron. Then they will cry to YHWH, but he will not answer them; he will hide his face from them at that time, because they have acted wickedly. (Mic. 3:1–4)

Just before Micah's version of the "swords into plowshares" prophecy, he concludes his condemnation by announcing that the sins of the elite will cause Jerusalem to become a "heap of ruins." This bold prediction was remembered a hundred years later, where it is used to save Jeremiah's life: since Hezekiah didn't put Micah to death for saying this, neither should Jeremiah be executed as a traitor (Jer. 26:18). It is no accident that those who recall Micah in speaking up for Jeremiah are the "elders of the land," i.e., the same clan-based, landed gentry pushed aside by Hezekiah's centralizing "reform."

Micah's version comes to a very different conclusion from Isaiah's. It echoes the Assyrian offer.[11] Not only will war come to an end, but all will sit "under their own vines and under their own fig trees." It is an image of *local, self-sufficient agriculture that will be the basis for authentic security.* In presenting this vision of "days to come," Micah takes an old tradition and turns it around. Recall the verse that officially summarized Solomon's "wisdom": "During Solomon's lifetime Judah and Israel lived in safety, from Dan even to Beer-sheba, *all of them under their vines and fig trees*" (1 Kings 4:25). Solomon's propaganda imagined *national* bounty for Judah and Israel grounded in military security. Micah, on the other hand, projects a time when the end of war will mean that *all nations* will experience *locally* the

---

10. *bedamim,* lit, "with bloods," a frequent euphemism for "bloodshed," e.g., Gen. 4:10–11; 1 Kings 2:5; Hos. 4:2. LXX has *aimatōn,* matched at John 1:13.

11. Scholars generally hold that Mic. 4:1–5, with its pro-Zion perspective, was inserted later. As Stephen Cook (2004), 133, writes, "Micah and his followers simply would not have authored such a text, which embodies a centralized, hierarchical administration of power." However, Cook shows that "Micah's group has grafted an insertion into the passage at this point [viz., 4:4] that places a critical *spin* on its pro-Zion vision." (Ibid., emphasis in original.) It is on this basis that I read it as we have it, inserted in an eighth-century context speaking to the Assyrian situation.

bounty flowing from true peace. As Stephen Cook writes, "in contrast to royal, ruling-class ideology, [Micah] ... sounds a powerful note of solidarity with those who live close to the land, especially with all whom the powerful have evicted from their land and exploited as day laborers."[12]

What we see in Micah, in other words, is *a creation-oriented alternative* to Isaiah. Micah is not among the king's advisors. He is instead a voice for those exploited and excluded by Hezekiah's "hedgehog" defense of Jerusalem. His vision is not, like Isaiah's, intended for a king who will listen to YHWH's voice through the mouth of prophets. Rather, he stands *against monarchy altogether*. Micah, although apparently a Judahite, speaks on behalf of the Sinai covenant tradition.[13]

This Sinai tradition is at stake in the perspectives of both the DH and the prophets. Recall how the Assyrian "promise" of vines and fig trees continued with a description "a land of grain and wine, a land of bread and vineyards, a land of olive oil and honey...." Dominic Rudman comments,

> What is promised to Jerusalem's inhabitants is nothing less than a new Exodus with the Assyrian king usurping the place of Yahweh.... In effect, Sennacherib is offering a new covenant to supersede that already in force between Yahweh and Israel, with similar blessings attached to it.[14]

This passage is part of the DH authors' incorporation of the "counter-story" into a new version that they hope will appeal both to Judahites and to Israelites.

Within 2 Kings, Hezekiah responded by sending his own delegation to Isaiah for advice (2 Kings 19:1–5). The prophet predicted that YHWH would cause Sennacherib to hear a rumor that would send him back to Assyria. When the Assyrian delegation responded with further threats, Hezekiah turned in prayer to YHWH, which was answered through Isaiah (2 Kings 19:20ff.). The outcome was that "the angel of YHWH set out and struck down 185,000 in the camp of the Assyrians.... Then King Sennacherib of Assyria left, went home, and lived at Nineveh" (2 Kings 19:35–36). The outcome echoes YHWH's destruction of Egyptians in the Exodus story, now likely found within Jerusalem because of the influx of Israelite refugees.

Micah, on the other hand, offers another response.

> Now you are walled around with a wall; siege is laid against us; with a rod they strike the ruler of Israel upon the cheek. But you, O Bethlehem of Ephrathah, who are one of the little clans of Judah, from you shall come forth for me one who is to rule in Israel, whose origin is from of old, from ancient days. Therefore he shall give them up until the time

---

12. Ibid., 134.
13. Ibid.
14. Rudman, 106, 108.

when she who is in labor has brought forth; then the rest of his kindred shall return to the people of Israel. And he shall stand and feed his flock in the strength of YHWH, in the majesty of the name of YHWH his God. And they shall live secure, for now he shall be great to the ends of the earth; and he shall be the one of peace. If the Assyrians come into our land and tread upon our soil, we will raise against them seven shepherds and eight installed as rulers. (Mic. 5:1–5)

This passage is often understood to be predicting a Davidic messiah, under the influence of Matthew's Gospel, where it is (mis)quoted by the "chief priests and scribes of the people" to King Herod in response to his question of "where the messiah was to be born" (Matt. 2:4–6). But in its own context, Micah is expressing a *counter*-David hope. Several details make this clear. First, the threat of Assyria frames the passage. Second, although Bethlehem was clearly associated with the memory of David, naming it rather than Jerusalem as the source of the coming ruler "would seem to imply the continued vitality of the relations among clans in Judah."[15] Third, the one who is predicted to come forth is not named as a king, but simply as one who "is to rule" (*mashal*), a term applied to Israelite or Judahite kings only at 1 Kings 5:1 (Solomon's "rule"). It is used a number of times, though, for *rejection of human rule in favor of YHWH's rule*. For example, Judges 8:22–23 says:

Then the Israelites said to Gideon, "Rule over us, you and your son and your grandson also; for you have delivered us out of the hand of Midian." Gideon said to them, "I will not rule over you, and my son will not rule over you; YHWH will rule over you."

Finally, the one to come is "from of old, from ancient days." Cook notes that in this context, the term likely refers back not to the promise of Davidic dynasty in 2 Samuel 7 but to the time *before the monarchy altogether.*[16]

The continuation in Micah 6 confirms this reading. The passage has long been recognized to be in the form of a "covenant lawsuit" in which YHWH calls upon the people to "plead their case" before the jury of mountains and hills. In YHWH's opening statement, he claims, "I brought you up from the land of Egypt, and redeemed you from the house of slavery; and I sent before you Moses, Aaron, and Miriam"[17] (Mic. 6:4). The Sinai, not Davidic, covenant, is the basis for the people's divinely provided salvation.

When the people respond by proposing huge numbers of offerings,[18] another voice (Micah's?) responds by reminding the people that they already have been told "what is good" and what "YHWH requires": to do justice,

---

15. Levenson (1985), 198.
16. Cook (2004), 124.
17. Only here outside Exodus and Numbers is Miriam remembered positively as a leader.
18. The "thousands of rams" recall Solomon's temple dedication ceremony, which contrasted with the simple sacrifices provided to seal the Sinai covenant.

love kindness, and to walk humbly with your God" (6:8). No royal priestly establishment is necessary to restore right relationship with YHWH. Micah rejects imperial religious sacrifices in favor of the practice of justice befitting the covenant commitment to be a "priestly kingdom and a holy nation" (Exod. 19:6).

In sum, Isaiah's vision is one that imagines a renewed kingship and a restored Jerusalem in which YHWH's peace will be found.[19] Micah, on the other hand, foresees *revolution*: an utter rejection of monarchy as the basis for the end of war and the establishment of justice on Zion.[20]

Within the DH, Hezekiah grew old while Assyria remained at a distance. As Assyria weakened, the neighboring kingdom of Babylon began to grow strong. The Babylonian king sent a delegation to Hezekiah, apparently in peace. Hezekiah led the king on a tour of Jerusalem's wealth, presumably in the hope of buying off the Assyrians. Isaiah confronted him, offering a word from YHWH that anticipated the coming exile. We are given both a public and private glimpse of the king's response:

> Then Hezekiah said to Isaiah, "The word of YHWH that you have spoken is good." For he thought, "Why not, if there will be peace and security in my days?" (2 Kings 20:19)

The story of Hezekiah ends on a realistic note: why should a politician care if the nation will collapse under someone else's watch? Hezekiah is satisfied that his record will be clean for history. Of course, that his inner thoughts are reported undermines this hope. Regardless of how history remembered Hezekiah, the future of the nation was in the hands of his successors.

Josiah, the Deuteronomistic History's True Hero

With Assyria on the decline and Israel in ruins, Judah began to flourish again in the seventh century BCE under its new king, Manasseh.[21] The countryside was repopulated; new shrines and other buildings were constructed, and trade was established with neighboring nations. But for the DH author, none of this mattered. Manasseh, the longest reigning king in either Israel's or Judah's history, is systematically condemned as someone nearly purely evil (2 Kings 21:1–9). He is even blamed for the worst disaster imaginable: the Babylonian Exile.[22] YHWH announces this condemnation through "his

---

19. Nakanose, 84–86.
20. Pixley, 56–58.
21. Finkelstein and Silberman, 155–59.
22. The DH judgment on Manasseh may reflect, in part, his lucrative alliance with Assyria; see Parpola, 104.

servants the prophets," but not to anyone within the narrative itself (21:10–16).[23] This passage has long been understood to be part of a postexilic "rewrite" of the DH, which otherwise had its culmination in the "happy ending" of the reign of Josiah, Manasseh's grandson. After all, if Josiah was the great hero (as we'll see), why were Jerusalem and the Davidic dynasty destroyed, contrary to the unconditional promise at 2 Samuel 7?[24]

The DH authors had to face this theological challenge along with a bigger one that had been looming for decades: how to compose a story of national identity and history that included *both* the Sinai and Zion covenants together so as to include the Israelite refugees within Judah's Jerusalem temple state? We saw but a hint of this in the Hezekiah/Isaiah narrative. The solution lay in the composition of the Josiah narrative.

We recall that Josiah was first mentioned as the subject of a prophecy made to Jeroboam's altar, which predicted that "A son shall be born to the house of David, Josiah by name; and he shall sacrifice on you the priests of the high places who offer incense on you, and human bones shall be burned on you" (1 Kings 13:2). The authors thus present Josiah's appearance as the fulfillment of "ancient" prophecy, not simply the ascension of one more king.

Josiah became king at the age of eight after "the people of the land" had put a violent halt to an attempted coup by the servants of Amon, Manasseh's son and Josiah's father (2 Kings 21:19–26). This is the first of a tightly constructed series of parallels between the child-king and a distant predecessor, Joash, as shown in Table 15.

The theme of both passages is the priestly collection of money and hiring of workers for "repairs to the house of YHWH." Furthermore, in each narrative, this is the first issue addressed by the king. Why construct this elaborate parallel? The key is in seeing the theme as a *metaphor for the "repairing" of the division between Israel and Judah, between the Sinai and Zion covenants, and between the different ways of life that they represent.* As the first story in Solomon's reign displayed his "wisdom" in holding together Israel and Judah, so the test for Joash and Josiah is: can they repair the "breach" between the two separated peoples?

We hear in the Joash version that, despite the abundance of donations and the availability of workers, "the priests had made no repairs on the house" (2 Kings 12:6). The king challenged them and demanded that they take no more donations unless they were used for "repair of the house." We then hear what may seem a strange outcome: "So the priests agreed that they would neither accept more money from the people nor repair the house" (12:8). Why would the priests refuse to engage the "repair of the house"? Patricia Dutcher-Walls comments that it "can possibly be understood as their resistance to what they considered meddling in the financial administration

---

23. For "his servants the prophets," see also 2 Kings 17:23; 24:2; cf. "my servants the prophets," 9:17; 17:13.

24. See, e.g., Halpern (1998a).

Table 15: Joash and Josiah

Parallel	Place in Joash Story	Place in Josiah Story
Name similarity in Hebrew	*yeho'ash* = Jehoash / Joash	*yo'shiyyahu* = Josiah[25]
Installed by "people of the land"	11:1–3, 12–20	21:24
Young age at beginning of reign	seven years old (12:1)	eight years old (22:1)
"did what was right in the sight of YHWH"	12:2	22:2
Mention of "high priest"	12:10	22:4, 8; 23:4
Mention of king's "secretary" (*sofer*)	12:10	22:3, 8, 9, 10, 12
"repair" (*bedeq*) the "house of YHWH"	12:5–9	22:5
Accounting of temple funds	12:4ff.	22:7
"they dealt honestly" (*be'emunah*)	12:16	22:7
Carpenters, masons, builders, timber	12:11	22:6

of the temple."[26] She is correct to point out that the problem is priestly resistance to "meddling" by the king, but the issue is much bigger (for the author) than temple finances. Why is the DH telling a story about what appears to be an ancient administrative conflict? Why the parallel Josiah version of the story?

The real question is whether the priests will participate in the "repairing" of the split between Israel and Judah. Note that Joash takes the throne in place of a half-Omride, half-Davidic king, Ahaziah, who had been killed, along with virtually everyone linked with the house of Omri (2 Kings 11:1–12). The kingdoms had thus been "united," but from a DH perspective, in the totally wrong way: with an *Israelite* dynast overseeing both kingdoms. The only remaining Omride was Athaliah, the queen mother, who jumped into action when she *"saw that her son was dead"* (2 Kings 11:1). Recall the almost identical statement of the prostitute in the Solomon "wisdom" story, "When I rose in the morning to nurse *my son, I saw that he was dead*" (1 Kings 3:21). Nowhere else in the Hebrew Bible do we hear about anyone seeing that their son is dead.[27]

Before Athaliah can engage her plan to kill "all the seed of the kingdom" (2 Kings 11:1), the Davidic, infant son of Ahaziah, Joash, is stolen away for

---

25. Note also "Joshua" is *yehoshua'*, as discussed below.
26. Dutcher-Walls (1996), 164.
27. Compare David, who only *hears* that his son Absalom is dead, but never "sees" it; 2 Sam. 18:32–33.

six years while Athaliah reigns. With her death and the kingship of Joash, the first order of business was the ongoing DH agenda of restoring unity under a Davidic monarchy with Jerusalem at the center.

But Joash's priests — not said to be appointed by him — refused to cooperate. Even Jehioiada, the young king's guardian and tutor, would not participate. At issue were the interests of "the people of the land," those who arranged for Joash's kingship and whose descendants arrange for Josiah's (2 Kings 11:14–20; 21:24). For, as we are told, despite "doing what was right in the sight of YHWH...nevertheless the high places were not taken away; the people continued to sacrifice and make offerings on the high places" (2 Kings 12:2–3).

These "high places" were the rural shrines of the "people of the land." The persistence of the high places is a refrain the DH author repeats in criticizing Joash's successors (e.g., 2 Kings 14:4; 15:4; 15:35; 16:4). It was Hezekiah who finally got this job done (18:4), only to have them rebuilt by his son, Manasseh (21:3). Halpern describes how Manasseh's project was done under Assyrian supervision to enable highly lucrative trade in wine, oil, and spices. The high places reunited Jerusalem with the landed gentry who profited on the processing of these goods. With this project, "Judah crossed over from a traditional economy based in extensive agriculture to a cash-cropping, industrial economy."[28]

Joash was unable to get the priests to engage the "repair of the house of YHWH" because it would have meant *destroying the high places cherished by his own supporters*. The resistance to Joash was strong enough that he was assassinated by a conspiracy of his own servants (12:20–21).

What made Josiah more successful at the project of "repairing the house of YHWH"? The key difference was the presence of the numerous Israelite refugees in Judah. For close to a hundred years, those displaced by the Assyrian conquest had found a home in Jerusalem and Judah. They were resistant to the Davidic monarchy, but not invested in the local Judahite shrines. It was not *their* family lineages that were found among the "people of the land." They were apparently willing to form a coalition with Josiah that forced the people of the land to compromise, just as they needed to compromise in order to consider Jerusalem and Judah "home." The symbolic story of Josiah's successful repair of the house of YHWH expresses his successful program of uniting the imperial religion and the religion of creation into a single national narrative in the name of YHWH: the book of Deuteronomy and the wider Deuteronomistic History.[29]

Shigeyuki Nakanose helpfully explores the economic motivations underlying Josiah's "repair" program. He writes:

---

28. Halpern (1991), 63–64.

29. Nakanose, 76, speculates why ordinary peasants would go along with Josiah's project, suggesting such factors as increased employment in a mercenary army, improved labor and trade opportunities in Jerusalem, and perhaps social programs in support of the landless to reduce pressure for revolutionary resistance.

What faces Josiah is an excruciating contradiction. The attempts to rebuild Israel's empire required economic resources, for instance, for an effective military establishment that was highly expensive in itself. Yet the evidence shows the Josianic economy to be limited, because his actual taxation system was in a deadlock due to the ever widening impoverishment of the populace, and the luxuried life of the ruling elite drained disproportionate resources, as well.

Not able to raise taxes, but facing an elite unwilling to give up their profits, Josiah had one further option:

> The last alternative for increasing the state's income would have been to improve somehow the efficiency of extracting "agricultural surpluses" from the peasants. In other words, the court would have to increase the income from the free southern peasants and later reintroduce taxation on northern peasants. From that point on, Josiah undertook his bloody campaign to abolish all the local shrines to which the peasants had been making their offerings and paying the religious tithe.... Consequently, the peasants were forced to bring their surpluses to the Jerusalem temple.[30]

Josiah needed a "religious" justification that would mask this raw economic motivation. Thus, it is no change of subject when the story shifts from the account of the repair project to the high priest Hilkiah's report that "I have found the book of the torah[31] in the house of YHWH" (2 Kings 22:8). In case readers have trouble putting the pieces together, the narrator helps by interweaving the report of Hilkiah's announcement to Shaphan the secretary about the finding of the book and that of Shaphan to the king regarding both the fate of the repair money *and* the finding of the book (22:8–10). They *are the same story:* the finding of the book in that specific place is the basis for the "repair" of the "house of YHWH." The exact phrase "book of the torah" (*sefer hattorah*) is found among pre-exilic writings exclusively in the DH.[32] That it is found *in the house of YHWH* expresses the coming together *in one place* of the central symbols of the Zion and Sinai stories.

Scholars are virtually unanimous in understanding the specific book found to be a form of Deuteronomy. The meaning of the narrative is broader than whatever the historical facts may be about the sudden "finding" of a particular book.[33] The text claims that what was found was the book of the *torah.* This certainly doesn't imply the final version of Genesis-Deuteronomy as we now have them, or even some earlier form of this collection. What it

---

30. Nakanose, 50.
31. *hassofer sefer hattorah,* literally, "the book, book of the torah."
32. Deut. 28:61; 29:20; 30:10; 31:26; Josh. 1:8; 8:31, 34; 23:6; 24:26; 2 Kings 14:6; 22:8, 11; in postexilic material, Neh. 8:1, 3, 8, 18; 9:3; 2 Chron. 17:9; 34:14, 15 (last two are parallel to our current passage).
33. The sudden finding has been understood as a "pious fiction" or, putting it more bluntly, an act of propaganda; e.g., Blenkinsopp (1995), 159.

does mean is that the counter-story featuring Moses as YHWH's appointed agent of imperial liberation has been taken up within the monarchy, its priesthood, and its own story of YHWH-promised, Davidic dynasty.

The bringing of the *torah* directly into the narrative is yet another piece of evidence for the earlier composition of the David/Solomon story. *Torah* is mentioned forty-three times in the entire Deuteronomistic History, distributed as follows:

Deuteronomy:	22
Joshua:	9
Judges:	0
1 Samuel:	0
2 Samuel:	1 (7:19)
1 Kings:	1 (2:3)
2 Kings	10 (10:31; 14:6; 17:13, 34, 37; 21:8; 22:8, 11; 23:24, 25)

It is mentioned twice in the entire David/Solomon story. The second use, in 1 Kings 2:3, is clearly a later insertion by a DH editor: it expresses a much used Deuteronomic formula and interrupts David's dying directions to Solomon about "cleaning up" (i.e., killing) the remaining obstacles to Solomonic rule. The other is worth our attention. It comes from David's mouth in response to Nathan's pronouncement that YHWH has promised an eternal dynasty for the house of David:

> And yet this was a small thing in your eyes, O Lord YHWH; you have spoken also of your servant's house for a great while to come. May this be *torah* for the people, O Lord YHWH! (2 Sam. 7:19)

David prays that the *Davidic covenant* "be *torah* for the people." From the perspective of the Israelite audience and other supporters (such as Micah and his people) of the Sinai story, this is blasphemy.

If the David/Solomon narrative was a composition from the eighth or even seventh century, why would the role of torah not be included in the portrait of the heroic ancestor who is the model for all future kings? The only reason is that, as we've shown, the David/Solomon story was written *before* the Exodus story. Once established as "official history," later editors rarely tampered with it.

From Josiah's perspective, the finding of the book of the torah is occasion both for lament and for public action in accordance with the "new" word from YHWH. After sending his advisors to consult with the prophetess Huldah, he "discovers" YHWH's wrath against "this place" and "its inhabitants." Huldah's word, though, promises that Josiah, like Hezekiah, will not experience the curse directly (2 Kings 22:15–20).[34]

---

34. For a deep exploration of the place of Huldah's prophecy in the Deuteronomistic History, see Halpern (1998a).

Josiah, on receiving this reprieve, jumped into action. After reading "all the words of the book of the covenant that had been found in the house of YHWH," he made his own covenant "to follow YHWH, keeping his commandments, his decrees, and his statutes, with all his heart and all his soul, to perform the words of *this* covenant that were written in *this* book." Immediately, "all the people joined in the covenant" (2 Kings 23:2–3). He then launched a "reform," each component of which established the Jerusalem-centered, YHWH-alone basis for the reconstitution of YHWH's people. The following actions provide clues about the true nature of Josiah's "reform":

1. He had the priests "bring out of the temple of YHWH all the vessels made for Ba'al, for Asherah, and for all the host of heaven; he burned them outside Jerusalem in the fields of the Kidron, and *carried their ashes to Bethel.*"

2. "He deposed the idolatrous priests"[35] whom the kings of Judah had ordained to make offerings *in the high places, at the cities of Judah and around Jerusalem;* those also who made offerings to Ba'al, to the sun, the moon, the constellations, and all the host of the heavens."

3. "He brought out the image of Asherah from the house of YHWH, outside Jerusalem, to the Wadi Kidron, burned it at the Wadi Kidron, *beat it to dust [dqq] and threw the dust of it upon the graves of the common people.*"

4. "He *brought all the priests out of the towns of Judah, and defiled the high places where the priests had made offerings,* from Geba to Beer-sheba; he broke down the high places of the gates that were at the entrance of the gate of Joshua the governor of the city, which were on the left at the gate of the city. *The priests of the high places, however, did not come up to the altar of YHWH in Jerusalem, but ate unleavened bread among their kindred.*"

5. "The altars on the roof of the upper chamber of Ahaz, which the kings of Judah had made, and *the altars that Manasseh had made* in the two courts of the house of YHWH, he pulled down from there and broke in pieces, and threw the rubble into the Wadi Kidron."

6. "The king defiled the high places that were east of Jerusalem, to the south of the Mount of Destruction, *which King Solomon of Israel had built* for Astarte the abomination of the Sidonians, for Chemosh the abomination of Moab, and for Milcom the abomination of the

---

35. The Hebrew *hakkemarim* is found elsewhere in the Hebrew Bible only at Hos. 10:5 and Zeph. 1:4; it may be an Assyrian loan word used to label priests not of other gods but of other places of worship; Sweeney (2001b), 105.

Ammonites. He broke the pillars in pieces, cut down the sacred poles [or, 'Asherahs'[36]], and covered the sites with human bones."

7. "Moreover, *the altar at Bethel, the high place erected by Jeroboam son of Nebat, who caused Israel to sin—* he pulled down that altar along with the high place. He burned the high place, *crushing it to dust (dqq)*; he also burned the sacred pole."

8. "Josiah removed all the *shrines of the high places that were in the towns of Samaria, which kings of Israel had made,* provoking YHWH to anger; he did to them *just as he had done at Bethel.* He *slaughtered on the altars all the priests of the high places who were there, and burned human bones on them.* Then he returned to Jerusalem."

The sequence reveals a relentless, systematic determination to destroy and defile any possible remnant of a separate "Israelite" identity outside Jerusalem. Altars, high places, and priests are treated with equal violence. The acts of both Israelite and Judahite kings are targeted: all that remained was the house of YHWH in Jerusalem and priests loyal to Josiah. The specific wording of Josiah's disposal of the rubble makes a key link: "[Moses] took the calf that they had made, burned it with fire, *ground it to powder [dqq],* scattered it on the water" (Exod. 32:20). Moses' crushing of the golden calf is almost identical to Josiah's crushing of both the Asherah (2 Kings 23:6) and, more importantly, the high place at Bethel erected by Jeroboam, i.e., the location of the calf shrine condemned by both Amos and Hosea. This connection is made by "Moses" as he recalls the Exodus incident at Deuteronomy 9:21:[37]

Then I took the sinful thing you had made, the calf, and burned it with fire and crushed it, grinding it thoroughly, until it was reduced to dust [*dqq*]; and I threw the dust of it into the stream that runs down the mountain.

The "reduce to dust" references link Josiah to two traditions. First, Josiah is the one who was to fulfill the DH prophecy of the "man of God" (1 Kings 13:2). Second, Josiah is like *Moses,* the destroyer of Israel's "idolatrous" calves in Exodus. But the crushing of religious objects was only the first act in Josiah's campaign.

It is one thing to destroy what are claimed to be "idolatrous" altars and shrines.[38] It is another to establish alternative forms of worship that bind people together. Josiah's next step was to command that the "passover to

---

36. Hebrew *'asherah* can refer to the specific fertility goddess by that name or to the object by which she was revered ("sacred pole"). In the second half of 2 Kings, it is a major expression of "idolatry": 13:6; 17:10, 16; 18:4; 21:3, 7; 23:4, 6, 7, 14, 15.

37. The Hebrew verb stem, *dqq,* is found elsewhere in pre-exilic texts only at Exod. 30:36; 2 Sam. 22:43; Isa. 28:28; 41:5 and Mic. 4:13.

38. Despite Josiah's destruction of the Bethel altar, however, the site remained after the Babylonian destruction of Jerusalem; see Zech. 7:3, Blenkinsopp (1998 and 2003) and Knauf.

YHWH your God *as prescribed in this book* of the covenant" be kept *in Jerusalem*. The author acknowledges that "*No such passover* had been kept since the days of the judges who judged Israel, or during all the days of the kings of Israel or of the kings of Judah" (2 Kings 23:22). This bold move could only have worked with the collaboration of those committed to the Sinai tradition. For in Exodus 12, the passover was mandated as a *family* feast, with *no specific location commanded* at which to celebrate it. In Deuteronomy 16, though, it is "remembered" differently. Amid the historical recollection of the exodus experience, Moses says:

> You shall offer the passover sacrifice for YHWH your God, from the flock and the herd, *at the place that YHWH will choose as a dwelling for his name.* . . . You are *not permitted to offer the passover sacrifice within any of your towns* that YHWH your God is giving you. *But at the place that YHWH your God will choose as a dwelling for his name, only there shall you offer the passover sacrifice,* in the evening at sunset, the time of day when you departed from Egypt. (Deut. 16:2, 5–6)

That "place," of course, was Jerusalem.[39] What had once been a local kinship-based Israelite feast in celebration of their liberation by YHWH from Pharaoh/Solomon was now transformed into a national cultic occasion celebrated in the royal capital. It would be something like celebrating the Fourth of July in Buckingham Palace.

The outcome of this "finding of the book of the torah in the house of YHWH" was a new "constitution of the monarchy."[40] It consisted of a document — a form of Deuteronomy and the DH up to Josiah — and a public feast — passover — that together established the long elusive goal of the DH authors: restoration of the people of YHWH under a Jerusalem-centered monarchy and temple. Each side gained and lost something in the compromise.

Monarchy, according to the Compromise Narrative

Let's look briefly at several aspects of how Josiah and his collaborators interwove the imperial and Exodus stories into what became the central narrative of Israel from Exodus to Exile. We will probably never know the actual historical events that moved Israel to make Saul a "king." We perhaps have some inkling of how David became Judah's king, embedded within the propagandistic document produced to support Solomon's succession. As we saw in chapter 3, social power throughout the world developed through the combination of several factors. The "facts" about Saul and David were probably not much different from the wider historical pattern. But the DH

---

39. Although the open-ended expression allowed the Samaritan Pentateuch to claim that the temple at Mount Gerizim was also supported by this text; Josephus, *Ant.* 13.3:4.

40. Halpern (1981).

authors made several important points as they completed the monarchy narrative.

First, Saul, Jeroboam, and Solomon were all condemned. David's mixed history was partially covered over by the refrain — belied by the actual narrative — that he did "what was right in the sight of YHWH" (1 Kings 11:33, 38; 15:5, 11; 2 Kings 14:3; 16:2; 18:3; 22:2). The Davidic dynasty covenant promise (2 Sam. 7) was retained, but qualified in later places, as, for example, in this address to Solomon inserted into the narrative:

> As for you, *if you will walk before me,* as David your father walked, with integrity of heart and uprightness, doing according to all that I have commanded you, and keeping my statutes and my ordinances, *then I will establish your royal throne over Israel forever, as I promised your father David,* saying, "There shall not fail you a successor on the throne of Israel." (1 Kings 9:4–5; see also 11:38)

Second, the scope and purpose of monarchy are transformed from the normal justification (providing military-based "peace and security") to the keeping of the "*torah* of the king" (Deut. 17:14–20). We saw earlier how the "*torah* of the king" expressed a point-by-point condemnation of Solomon (pp. 99–101). Now we can see that it also provided *a blueprint for the monarchy of Josiah.*

Finally, the monarchical history was prefaced not only with the "second torah" (the meaning of the Greek-based title, "Deuteronomy"), but also with the books of Joshua / Judges, and the introductory section of 1 Samuel, chapters 1–12. We'll look briefly at Joshua below and at Judges in chapter 13. For the moment, let's focus on the core of the message in the story of Samuel: prophet, judge, and reluctant kingmaker.

The biblical canon maintains an artificial division of Deuteronomy– 2 Kings into a series of individual books. David Jobling argues that, instead of the books of Judges and 1–2 Samuel, we should think of two narratives: Judges 2:11 through 1 Samuel 12 as "The Extended Book of Judges," and 1 Samuel 13 through 2 Samuel 7 as "The Book of the Everlasting Covenant."[41] Jobling's proposed division helps focus on how 1 Samuel 1–12 fits with what precedes it more than what follows. He comments that "Extended Judges"

> presents a sort of debate over the merits of governmental systems. It has two aims: to present judgeship as a divine dispensation and as in some sense ideal, and to explain how it gave way to kingship. These goals are pursued by two contradictory strategies. From one point of view, the book chronicles a fall from an ideal and tries to assign blame for this

---

41. Jobling (1998), 29–34.

fall. From another it tries to persuade itself that there really was no fall, that kingship can be brought within the ideal.[42]

Jobling is perhaps more correct than he intended in calling the presentation a *"sort* of debate," for the debate was over before the text was written. Included within the narrative are both perspectives on monarchy, now woven into a single story.

1 Samuel picks up where Judges ends:[43]

> So the Israelites departed from there at that time by tribes and families, and they went out from there to their own territories. In those days there was no king in Israel; all the people did what was right in their own eyes. (Judg. 21:25)

Kinship is the basis for Israel's social order, but it is qualified by the implication that it was the absence of *kingship* that left the people without divine direction. First Samuel starts immediately with an allegorical story (in the canonical sequence, the *first* in the DH's monarchy narrative). It is, as are the "later" ones we've examined, about mothers and sons. In this case, it is a family fight between two wives over one of their as-yet unconceived sons. Robert Polzin has shown how this story symbolizes the request for a king, made later in the narrative at 1 Samuel 8.[44] Allegorically, Elkanah the husband is YHWH; Peninnah, the wife with sons, is the "other nations"; and Hannah, the wife with no sons, is Israel. Hannah's desire for a son mirrors Israel's desire for a king, to which Elkanah replies, "Hannah, why do you weep? Why do you not eat? Why is your heart sad? Am I not more to you than ten sons?" (1 Sam. 1:8). In other words, is not the love of YHWH greater than having a monarchic dynasty?

Hannah takes her lament to Shiloh, the place to which Elkanah went each year to worship. Recall that Shiloh will be "later" the home of the prophets and priests who made Jeroboam king in place of Solomon, then turned on him when he "betrayed" them by appointing priests from "all the people." In this final version of the larger DH, Shiloh is also criticized. Hannah comes to the priest Eli, who is "sitting on the seat" (*kisse'*). Polzin comments that Eli

> is presented to us as a *royal figure* as well as a priest... *kisse'* is first and foremost a royal seat, the throne.... The intimate connection between judgship and kingship is the appropriate ideological zone for this first

---

42. Ibid., 43. Given our reading here of 1 Sam. 13 through 1 Kings 10 as "the David–Solomon succession" narrative (see Table 6), we consider here only Jobling's reconfiguration of the first narrative unit.

43. The canonical sequence interposes the book of Ruth between Judges and 1 Samuel, presumably to show David's ancestry, Ruth 4:17–22. There are many interesting themes in the book of Ruth, not least of which is the closing claim that David's mother was a *Moabite;* cf. Matt. 1:5. I do not address Ruth in this book, but see Kates and Twersky Reimer; Doob Sakenfeld.

44. Polzin (1989), 20–38.

chapter which forges a link between the subject matter of the book of Judges and that of Samuel/Kings.[45]

Eli confused the silent prayer of Hannah with drunkenness. This is an apt metaphor for the yearning for a king. Is it prayer or "drunkenness" to ask YHWH for "sons"? The question hung while Hannah returned home and conceived her desired son, Samuel. The naming itself is a wonderful pun that expresses the conflict latent in the question of monarchy. Eli's dismissal of Hannah includes his comment, "the God of Israel grant the petition [*sha'alte,* from *sh'l*] you have made to him" (1 Sam. 1:17). When Hannah bears her son, we hear, "She named him Samuel, for she said, 'I have asked (*she'iltti,* from *sh'l*) him of YHWH.'" The name "Samuel" is explained in relation to "asking," but suggests the name of the first king: *Saul* (*sha'ul*).

Once Samuel was weaned, Hannah fulfilled her vow to offer him to YHWH, and he became an apprentice to the aging Eli. Her song in 1 Samuel 2[46] is a perfect amalgam of both the imperial and liberating stories. It proclaims a YHWH who "raises up the poor from the dust," gives "strength to his king," and exalts "the power of his anointed" (1 Sam. 2:8, 10). Of course, the affirmation of both "king" and "anointed" (*meshiyach,* i.e., "messiah") are pronounced long in advance of the request for a king. This underscores how this entire section is actually a reflection on monarchy from the Josiah era.

The allegory concludes with the shift of symbolic characters from Elkanah and his wives to Eli and his sons. They are described as "scoundrels" (*beliya'al*), a Deuteronomic term that expresses unfaithfulness to YHWH.[47] In different words, Samuel's own two sons are also named as unsuitable successors to their father (1 Sam. 8:1–3). Both priest and prophet/judge have sons who reveal the central flaw of dynastic succession: son is not necessarily like father. Of course, this also implicates Solomon, who in the end was not deemed a worthy successor to David: his altars are among those torn down by Josiah. So before the request for a king was made, we have heard implied that even if *monarchy* is deemed the will of YHWH, *dynasty* is another question. That point was "already" established in Deuteronomy 17:15, the torah of the king, where we heard that a king must be one "whom YHWH your God will choose." YHWH has chosen Samuel, but not his sons. The inference is that YHWH may have chosen David (a point conceded by the Sinai group in the compromise narrative), but one can question whether YHWH also chose Solomon. For generations of DH readers, the final text leaves the question open enough for both sides to make their argument.

First Samuel continues with another satirical, symbolic story (1 Sam. 4–6). It involves the journeys of the "ark of the covenant" of YHWH, a term

---

45. Ibid., 23, emphasis in original.
46. Her song is echoed in Mary's Magnificat at Luke 1:46–55.
47. See, e.g., Deut. 13:14; 15:9; Judg. 19:22; 20:13; 1 Sam. 10:27.

clearly borrowed from Exodus 25–40.[48] After these chapters, it is not mentioned again until it is escorted out of Jerusalem by the priests and "all the Levites" during Absalom's rebellion (2 Sam. 15:24). Here, however, it needs no escort: it travels by itself, led by a pair of milk-cows, after giving its possessors, the Philistines, a bad case of hemorrhoids (1 Sam. 5:1–6:12). The message is again clear: YHWH's power does not require human control or guidance. The monarchy is no more necessary for protection against the Philistines than for escape from the Egyptians.

This anti-monarchical voice reaches its clearest expression in the exchange between the elders of Israel, Samuel, and YHWH (1 Sam. 8). The request is explicit; the Josiah group must have swallowed hard before accepting it into the compromise text:

> Then all the elders of Israel gathered together and came to Samuel at Ramah, and said to him, "You are old and your sons do not follow in your ways; appoint for us, then, a king to govern us, like other nations."

To have a king at all is to be "like other nations": to give up the call to be a "priestly kingdom and a holy nation." YHWH's response to the angry Samuel clarifies the matter:

> YHWH said to Samuel, "Listen to the voice of the people in all that they say to you; for they have not rejected you, but *they have rejected me from being king over them. Just as they have done to me, from the day I brought them up out of Egypt to this day, forsaking me and serving other gods,* so also they are doing to you."

YHWH then charges Samuel to warn the people about the "justice of the king" (*mishpat hammelek*). As Walter Brueggemann has pointed out, the "governing verb of Samuel's characterization of monarchy" is *take,* used six times in 8:11–17.[49] This royal taking is echoed in the later narrative of Joseph's "taking" on behalf of Pharaoh in Gen. 47:13–26 (discussed in chapter 7). The king will take sons, daughters, fields, vineyards, grain, slaves, cattle, donkey, and flocks. "And in that day you will cry out because of your king, whom you have chosen for yourselves; but YHWH will not answer you in that day" (1 Sam. 8:18).

But, of course, "the people refused to listen" and the Saulide monarchy was established. This powerful warning about the reality of empire echoes throughout the ages, beyond the bounds of the DH and the Bible itself. The

---

48. Exodus uses the Hebrew term, *'aron ha'edot,* literally, "ark of the testimony," 25:22; 26:33, 34; 30:6, 26; 31:7; 39:35; 40:3, 5, 21; also Num. 4:5; 7:89; only once in the DH at Josh. 4:16. First Samuel uses the DH variation, *'aron berit,* "ark of the covenant," 1 Sam. 4:3–5. The term's distribution in DH underscores that Deut.–1 Sam. 12 is a later addition to the monarchy narrative: Deut. three times; Josh. thirteen times (all in Josh. 3–8); Judges once; 1 Sam., three times (all this scene); 2 Sam. once (15:24); 1 Kings, five times (insertions into the Solomon story); 2 Kings, none; see also Jer. 3:16. The only other biblical uses are at Num. 10:33; 14:44; and in the postexilic revisionist history 1–2 Chronicles thirteen times.

49. Brueggemann (1990), 63; see also O'Brien.

only way it could be included within a narrative proclaiming the Davidic dynasty to be the eternal will of YHWH is by portraying Josiah in conformity with the torah of the king (Deut. 17:14–20) and not with 1 Samuel 8:11–17. It is a "perfect" compromise between the two sides of the "debate," one that has left centuries of Jews and Christians utterly confused as to whether human kingship is or isn't YHWH's will. This should not be a question for Christians at all given what we'll see in the New Testament (Part IV). But for Jews who accept the entire Hebrew Bible as the Word of YHWH, the contradictions within the narrative remain.

Role of Moses and Joshua

If the DH compromise leaves open the question of monarchy, what about other forms of human leadership among YHWH's people? Deuteronomy makes Moses, hero of the Sinai tradition, the voice of the "book of the torah" found "in the house of YHWH." Deuteronomy establishes a series of "offices" that accompany and, in theory, temper monarchy, including judges and "officials," Levitical priests, and prophets (Deut. 16:18–18:22). It expresses a kind of ancient "balance of powers." But towering over all of the offices is the figure of Moses himself, a once-in-history leader. The inclusion of a Moses'-voiced Deuteronomy allows for the inclusion of Exodus, just as the inclusion of the anti-monarchical 1 Samuel 1–12 allows for the inclusion of the David/Solomon story. Each side got its "founding story" along with a commentary on it provided by the other side.

Moses' role in Deuteronomy is to speak in the voices of both Zion and Sinai in alternating rhythm. We saw above how Moses was said to change the passover observance from the local family feast in Exodus to the urban royal ritual in 2 Kings. He legitimizes monarchy, but limits it to a Josiah-like form. His words form the substance of the "book of the torah" read and proclaimed by Josiah. And yet, the Sinai contingent managed to retain a key component of "creation religion" that stands in tension with the Jerusalem-centered religious establishment:

> Surely, this commandment that I am commanding you today is not too hard for you, nor is it too far away. It is not in heaven, that you should say, "Who will go up to heaven for us, and get it for us so that we may hear it and observe it?" Neither is it beyond the sea, that you should say, "Who will cross to the other side of the sea for us, and get it for us so that we may hear it and observe it?" No, the word is very near to you; it is in your mouth and in your heart for you to observe. (Deut. 30:11–14)

It is of the essence of the religion of creation that *all* people have access to the Word of YHWH, without mediating institutions that claim to be "closer" to YHWH. Moses, although put partially in service of a centralizing religious establishment, remains the advocate for all YHWH's people who yearn to know the Lord.

What about Moses' successor, Joshua? Deuteronomy, starring Moses, and the book of Joshua, featuring the eponymous hero, are thickly intertwined. For example, Moses is mentioned fifty-nine times in Joshua, compared with only seventeen total in Judges–2 Kings. We have already seen why Moses was not mentioned in the David/Solomon story: because the writers of the imperial propaganda did not know of "Moses." Each mention of Moses in Judges–2 Kings interrupts the narrative context to insert the Sinai hero and his torah at strategic points. In Joshua, however, Moses, although dead, is everywhere. Every move Joshua makes is an expression of the fulfillment of the torah of Moses. YHWH's opening programmatic speech expresses the perspective of the entire book of Joshua:

> Every place that the sole of your foot will tread upon I have given to you, *as I promised to Moses.* From the wilderness and the Lebanon as far as the great river, the river Euphrates, all the land of the Hittites, to the Great Sea in the west shall be your territory. No one shall be able to stand against you all the days of your life. *As I was with Moses, so I will be with you;* I will not fail you or forsake you. Be strong and courageous; for you shall put this people in possession of the land that I swore to their ancestors to give them. Only be strong and very courageous, being careful to act *in accordance with all the law that my servant Moses commanded you;* do not turn from it to the right hand or to the left, so that you may be successful wherever you go. *This book of the law* (torah) *shall not depart out of your mouth; you shall meditate on it day and night, so that you may be careful to act in accordance with all that is written in it.* For then you shall make your way prosperous, and then you shall be successful. I hereby command you: Be strong and courageous; do not be frightened or dismayed, for YHWH your God is with you wherever you go. (Josh. 1:3–9)

Not only is the name of Moses everywhere, but also Moses' Deuteronomic voice is heard throughout the book of Joshua. It is a matter of command-and-response: what Moses heard YHWH say, Joshua now carries out.

But the text also looks the other direction at the same time. As Richard Nelson has shown, Joshua "prefigures" the Deuteronomistic History's true hero of divine obedience, Josiah.[50] In the passage above, he is called to practice daily torah reading, in fulfillment of the torah of the king (Deut. 17:18–19), just as Josiah will read the entire book of the torah before the people. The only passover celebrated from Exodus to Exile before Josiah's is the one Joshua led (5:10–11). Even their Hebrew names are very close. But the character of Josiah also recalls Moses, as we saw above (Exod. 32

---

50. Nelson (1981).

and 2 Kings 23). Josiah embodies *both* Moses *and* his successor, according to the DH. The replacement of Jeroboam with Josiah was something that the Sinai people had to accept in order for the compromise to work.

At least one section of the book of Joshua, however, was designed to placate the Sinai group. The ritual crossing of the Jordan to enter the Promised Land includes the taking of twelve stones, one for each of the "tribes of Israel," from the river and placing them in the camp. Joshua explains the ritual this way:

> When your children ask in time to come, "What do those stones mean to you?" then you shall tell them that the waters of the Jordan were cut off in front of the ark of the covenant of YHWH. When it crossed over the Jordan, the waters of the Jordan were cut off. So these stones shall be to the Israelites a memorial forever. (Josh. 4:6–7)

The key initiating phrase, "when your children ask," has been borrowed from Exodus 12:26, the explanation of the passover. It is repeated in Deuteronomy to explain the meaning of the torah itself, where Moses tells them,

> When your children ask you in time to come, "What is the meaning of the decrees and the statutes and the ordinances that YHWH our God has commanded you?" you shall say to your children, "We were Pharaoh's slaves in Egypt, but YHWH brought us out of Egypt with a mighty hand. YHWH displayed before our eyes great and awesome signs and wonders against Egypt, against Pharaoh and all his household. He brought us out from there in order to bring us in, to give us the land that he promised on oath to our ancestors. Then YHWH commanded us to observe all these statutes, to fear YHWH our God, for our lasting good, so as to keep us alive, as is now the case. If we diligently observe this entire commandment before YHWH our God, as he has commanded us, we will be in the right." (Deut. 6:20–25)

Moses' explanation of passover and torah — which "now" includes Deuteronomy — is thus linked to Joshua's explanation of a water-crossing ritual that recalls the crossing of the Red Sea. The compromise arranges these two events as a divinely planned sequence: first Moses acts as YHWH's agent to lead the people out of Egyptian slavery, and then Joshua acts as YHWH's agent to lead the people out of the wilderness and into the Promised Land. The Sinai group is "given" the "ancient" memory of the people as a *tribal* confederation, something never mentioned throughout the monarchy except by Elijah, in another story of twelve stones symbolizing the twelve tribes (1 Kings 18:31).[51]

---

51. The twelve-stone symbolism is taken from the jewels set in the priestly vestment (Exod. 28:21 and 39:14).

Through this adaptation of the Sinai narrative, the "memory" of Israel's "origin" is transformed from that of Solomonic subjects to a community of twelve tribes, each with their own territory. The result seeks to balance centralization and decentralization. Solomon's ancient twelve administrative districts become specified tribal and clan territories, the details of which are laid out in Joshua 13–21. There is no archaeological or other evidence that these tribal and clan allotments existed before the time of Josiah. As we'll explore in chapter 13, the question of what "Israel" "really" was before the monarchy is not easy to answer. Whatever the historical reality of a pre-monarchical division of land according to tribes may have been, the book of Joshua is clearly the earliest *written* record of such an allocation. Although the notion of Israel as twelve tribes survived into New Testament times and was an important symbol in Jesus' selection and empowerment of twelve apostles,[52] it is never mentioned again in the Hebrew Bible, except at Ezekiel 47:13–48:35, clearly meant to recall the Joshua allocation.

A final aspect of the two perspectives that meets in the combined narrative is that of "holy war." Nowhere in the book of Exodus does YHWH command the Israelites to engage in warfare.[53] However, Joshua has an encounter with YHWH that recalls Moses' burning bush experience and transforms it to fit DH's perspective:

> Once when Joshua was by Jericho, he looked up and saw a man standing before him with a drawn sword in his hand. Joshua went to him and said to him, "Are you one of us, or one of our adversaries?" He replied, "Neither; but as commander of the army of YHWH I have now come." And Joshua fell on his face to the earth and worshiped, and he said to him, "What do you command your servant, my lord?" The commander of the army of YHWH said to Joshua, "Remove the sandals from your feet, for the place where you stand is holy." (Josh. 5:13–15)

Moses' experience led to the appointment of Moses as leader of the Exodus in which YHWH alone engaged the Egyptian army. But Joshua's encounter continues with YHWH's command to encircle Jericho, and after the walls come tumbling down, he and the people "devoted to destruction [*chrm*] by the edge of the sword all in the city, both men and women, young and old, oxen, sheep, and donkeys" (6:21). The Hebrew *chrm* refers to "holy war" against the enemies of YHWH. It is used only once in Exodus to refer

---

52. E.g., Matt. 19:28; Luke 22:30; cf. Rev. 7, where the image of twelve thousand from each of the twelve tribes is transformed into a countless multitude "from every nation, from all tribes and peoples and languages" (7:9).

53. Exodus' only war episode is the encounter with Amalek, in which Moses commands Joshua to fight with the sword (17:9–13). This seems to be an insertion meant to harmonize with the Num-Deut-Josh tradition. In the Golden Calf story, Moses called upon "YHWH, the God of Israel" as legitimation for fratricidal slaughter, but the narrator says the "sons of Levi did *as Moses commanded* . . . " (Exod. 32:27), leaving open the question whether YHWH truly authorized this violence. Since Exod. 32 is clearly an insertion on behalf of the Shilonite Levites, it also stands outside the main Exodus narrative. See also pp. 156–59.

to the consequence of an Israelite sacrificing to a god other than YHWH (22:19 [Eng, 22:20]). In Deuteronomy-Joshua, however, it is found *twenty-two times*. It is a refrain looking both directions in time. It is in Moses' mouth "recalling" destruction of peoples in the name of YHWH during the wilderness period (e.g., Deut. 2:34; 3:6) and commanding similar destruction of those Israel will encounter in the Land (e.g., Deut. 7:2; 13:15–17; 20:17). The book of Joshua narrates the fulfillment of these "Mosaic" commands (e.g., Josh. 8:26; 10:28, 39). For example, we hear:

> And all the towns of those kings, and all their kings, Joshua took, and struck them with the edge of the sword, utterly destroying them, as Moses the servant of YHWH had commanded. (11:12)

The tradition of "sacred violence" was, as we've seen, central to Josiah's "reform." René Girard has argued that it is part of the secret "hidden since the foundation of the world" that Jesus came to reveal.[54] The bonding of a people — i.e., forming a "religion" that undergirds a social organization — through the scapegoating and destruction of "the other" and the establishment of shrines to celebrate that "victory" is of the essence of "imperial religion."[55] In stark contrast, Exodus narrated a story of Israel's communal bonding around the mountain at which they encountered YHWH, with no need for "sacrifice" of animals or enemies.

The "success" of Josiah and his group in imposing this element on the Exodus partisans was certainly a matter of power politics, not theological persuasion. The biblical result has been to provide grounds for the people of God to justify war in the name of YHWH ever since. As we'll see in Part IV, however, *Christians have no basis for calling upon Joshua to justify "holy war" in the name of Jesus*, who stood in adamant opposition to this tradition, despite his disciples' continual resistance to his stance.[56] The command to "love your enemies" sides with the religion of creation within which all humanity is part of a single, divinely generated family.[57]

We can only imagine the negotiations that led both the Sinai and Zion groups to accept this compromise.[58] In the end, however, what did it accomplish? Where was the will of YHWH in the finished product that became

---

54. Girard (1987; also 1979 and 1989); see also Bailie, 153–66, on the use of sacred violence in Joshua.

55. Joshua 8:29 narrates the ritual execution of the king of Ai and the raising over his dead body of "a great heap of stones, which stands there to this day."

56. E.g., Luke 9:52–54; John 18:36.

57. Cf. Shepard, 91, who notes that in ancient hunting cultures, "Winning and losing are transient phenomena — some small part of the whole. Opponents are essential. One loves one's enemies. To destroy them in any final sense is unthinkable."

58. In its seventh-century context, Deuteronomy contains many aspects that challenged Assyrian imperial claims of divine legitimation just as Genesis challenged Babylonian claims; see, e.g., Deut. 13 and the judgment of Porpola, 105: "In the mind of the writer of Deuteronomy 13, the God of Israel has taken the place previously occupied in the collective mind of the nation by the feared, almighty king of Assyria.... The conclusion seems inescapable that the Deuteronomic concept of God... is heavily indebted to Assyrian religion and royal ideology."

the continuous narrative of YHWH's people from Exodus to Exile? What did it mean when soon Babylon came and destroyed Jerusalem?

The Destruction of Jerusalem and the End of the Monarchy

The DH underwent at least one post-Josiah revision to include the final chapters of Judah's history. Josiah's sudden and violent death seemed to cast doubt over the holiness of the king's "reform" and the written compromise that it produced. The DH's "answer" is that Manasseh, Josiah's grandfather, was so evil that there was no possibility of even Josiah's pious obedience compensating for it.

The prophet Zephaniah provided a voice of strong dissent against the entire Josianic program. His verdict is sharp and clear:

Ah, soiled, defiled, oppressing city! It has listened to no voice; it has accepted no correction. It has not trusted in YHWH; it has not drawn near to its God. The officials within it are roaring lions; its judges are evening wolves that leave nothing until the morning. Its prophets are reckless, faithless persons; its priests have profaned what is sacred, they have done violence to the law. (Zeph. 3:1–4)

Only YHWH "within" Jerusalem is righteous. The prophet rejects the "reform" and, implicitly, the compromise, counseling instead that people wait for YHWH to act with judgment and then transformation (3:8–20). Ernst Knauf writes that it is "wholly unlikely that such a text could have been uttered, preserved, and transmitted while Josiah was actually ruling."[59] He suggests that it was collected, along with Hosea, Amos, and Micah, after the Exile proved the prophetic condemnation of Jerusalem to be correct.

The prophet Jeremiah offered his own interpretation. While agreeing that Manasseh was the central villain, he also blamed Jerusalem as a whole. For example, we hear:

I will make them a horror to all the kingdoms of the earth because of what King Manasseh son of Hezekiah of Judah did in Jerusalem. Who will have pity on you, O Jerusalem, or who will bemoan you? Who will turn aside to ask about your welfare? You have rejected me, says YHWH, you are going backward; so I have stretched out my hand against you and destroyed you—I am weary of relenting. (Jer. 15:4–6)

Note how this last statement resonates with YHWH's word via Samuel: in seeking a king, the people had rejected YHWH (1 Sam. 8). Jeremiah, while a strong supporter of the DH program,[60] leaves room for accepting

---

59. Knauf, 323.

60. See, e.g., Friedman (1989), for the argument that Jeremiah or someone from his circle was the DH author.

a future restoration centralized in Jerusalem but without a king. We'll look more at Jeremiah in Part III, when YHWH's people reflect on the disaster of the Exile and how YHWH might act to restore them to the land.

Within a decade or so of Josiah's death, the Babylonian king Nebuchad-nezzar took control of Jerusalem away from Pharaoh Neco, who took over after killing Josiah.[61] Jerusalem was now subject to an external power it could not resist. Before long, Jerusalem was besieged, then destroyed, and the elite taken captive and brought to Babylon.

What is the legacy of this long struggle regarding the kind of social order that truly expresses the will of YHWH? Some readers, seeking to fit the pieces of the canonical puzzle together into a coherent picture — in order to preserve the sense that all of the Bible is truly "God's Word" — have seen monarchy and / or a centralized Jerusalem as an "evolutionary" step away from the "primitive" tribal, kinship-based Exodus story.[62] This view, of course, fits well with an Enlightenment model of urban "civilization" "pro-gressing" away from a "prehistoric" way of life. It is only one step from this to seeing today's globalized, capitalist countries as "developed" and local economies and social structures seen as "backward" or "undeveloped."

As we've seen, the view that results from reading the biblical narrative in its linear, final form through the lens of such an evolutionary model does a great injustice to the "war of myths"[63] in which the Hebrew Bible is engaged. But it is also understandable why people would be inclined to read it that way, especially readers situated amid nations and empires vying over the centuries to justify their power over one another and over their own peoples as "divinely inspired."

For hundreds of years after the fall of Jerusalem, the people of YHWH searched the Scriptures for guidance as to how to live within the vari-ous imperial regimes that followed: Babylonian, Persian, Greek and finally, Roman. If the result of this search was much conflict and division among YHWH's people, it is because the legacy left by the literary compromise negotiated under Josiah's reign made the "answer" anything but clear to future generations.

---

61. Halpern (1998) helpfully explores the politics of this confrontation and why the 2 Kings text tells the story as it does.

62. Cf. Levinson (1985).

63. E.g., Myers (1988), 14–17, for this term in the context of Mark's Gospel.

Chapter Thirteen

What Was "Israel" before the Monarchy?

As we've seen in the preceding chapters, "Israel" and "Judah" were names throughout the monarchy for two different sociopolitical entities, each claiming YHWH as partner to its own covenant. "Israel," however, carries other biblical connotations. Throughout the torah, it refers to the entire people of YHWH. It is also used collectively to refer to the entire Promised Land, i.e., "the land of Israel" (e.g., Ezek. 40:2). This last use, of course, remains bitterly disputed in the Middle East today.

A straightforward reading of the narrative from Genesis–Kings has long implied that "Israel" was the name for the descendants of the eponymous ancestor Jacob/Israel, first as extended family (e.g., Exod. 1), then as a tribal confederation and its divinely allocated land (e.g., Joshua 3, 13–21), next as the northern monarchy (separated from the southern monarchy), and ultimately, as the restored, theonational people after the Exile. We have seen, however, that the canonical chronology has a questionable relationship with the actual sequence of historical events. In particular, we have explored the likelihood that the David/Solomon royal accession/succession narrative is the oldest written text in the Bible. Further, we have shown how the myth of the "twelve tribes of Israel" first arose as a subversion of Solomon's royal division of the land into twelve administrative districts under Jerusalem's control (pp. 116-22 above).

And yet, there *was something* called "Israel" that predated the tenth-century monarchy. The thirteenth century BCE Egyptian "Merneptah stele" refers to those over whom the Egyptian king had been triumphant:

> Ashekon has been overcome;
> Gezes has been captured;
> Yano'am is made non-existent.
> *Israel is laid waste and his seed [or "grain"[1]] is not:*
> Hurru is become a widow because of Egypt.[2]

---

1. Hasel, 52–54, argues that Egyptian *prt* refers to "seed" as in "grain," and writes, "This implies that *Israel* is a socioethnic entity with a sociopolitical structure distinguished from that of city-states and other entities mentioned in this unit....The phrase 'its grain is not' appears to communicate the destruction or removal of this entity's life support system, its security mechanism for an entity without a city-state support system....Thus, we may perceive *Israel* within the context and information of the Merneptah stela to be a rural sedentary group of agriculturalists without its own urban city-state support system" (emphasis in original).

2. Quoted at, e.g., Sparks (1998), 96 (emphasis added); for discussion, see 94–124; also e.g., Faust (2007), 159–68; Hasel.

Was Merneptah's "Israel" the same as premonarchical, biblical "Israel"? Taken alone, the Egyptian artifact provides little help in answering this question. Countless archaeologists and anthropologists have argued the case for and against some correlation between all available material remains, including the Merneptah stele, and the Bible's textual claims about "Israel's" origin.[3] Our purpose, fortunately, does not require reaching a definitive conclusion about this question. We can reduce our inquiry to simpler questions. First, was "Israel" before the monarchy an "ethnic" or other entity uniting families and clans into a single identity? If so, what factors might have caused this "ethnogenesis"? Second, how was this collective identity supported or subverted by the texts we've explored so far?

An initial challenge is to clarify terms. Although there is no one "correct" definition of "ethnicity,"[4] the one offered by Elizabeth Bloch-Smith will suffice:

> An *ethnos* is a group of people larger than a clan or lineage claiming common ancestry. While cultural or biological kinship may reinforce the bond, a fabricated "collective memory of a former unity" or "putative myth of shared descent and kinship" ultimately conjoins the various lineages.[5]

Bloch-Smith notes further two types of ethnic "traits": *primordial* and *circumstantial*. "Primordial features are perceived by the group to have existed from the beginning.... Kinship, territory, or select traditions, including religion, often define the group's origins." Circumstantial factors "are variously activated in response to changing situations," in an ongoing struggle to distinguish "us" from "them." Examples include material culture (e.g., pottery or architectural styles) or relationships with other groups (e.g., alliances by marriage or treaty). She claims that the "quest for early Israel is a study of ethnogenesis."[6]

This latter term finds a helpful definition in the work of anthropologist Jonathan D. Hill. He writes:

> Ethnogenesis is ... a concept encompassing peoples' simultaneously cultural and political struggles to create enduring identities in general contexts of radical change and discontinuity.... Ethnogenesis can be understood as a creative adaptation to a general history of violent changes — including demographic collapse, forced relocations, enslavement, ethnic soldiering, ethnocide and genocide.[7]

---

3. For recent summaries and arguments, see, e.g., Bloch-Smith, Dever (2003), Mazar (2003), Miller (2004), Killebrew and Faust (2007).

4. See Emberling for discussion of the problems and challenges of defining "ethnicity" in a way both useful and precise.

5. Bloch-Smith, 402; internal quotes from Emberling, 301–4, and Hall.

6. Ibid., 403. See also Killebrew, 8.

7. Hill (1996b) 1.

Writing in the context of ethnogenesis among indigenous peoples in the Americas, Hill notes that the "importance of African, indigenous American, and European religions as cornerstones in the building of new ethnic identities emerges as one of the central themes."[8] That is — as we explored in Part I regarding the relationship between Genesis and the Babylonian creation story *Enuma Elish* — religious narrative has always been a primary means by which oppressed people bond. The Genesis narrative of "in the beginning" is an expression of what Bloch-Smith called "primordial ethnic traits." Similarly, we saw in chapter 10 how Exodus served a similar function in the face of Solomonic enslavement "in the name of YHWH."

Anthony Smith writes that "there must also emerge a strong sense of belonging and an active solidarity, which in time of stress and danger can override class, factional or regional divisions within the community."[9] Smith provides a detailed taxonomy of ways in which premodern ethnic communities can develop and maintain collective identity. He describes an "optimal sequence for the maintenance and activation of ethnic consciousness in a population over the long term":

1. "[The] emergence of a population in a given area ... with certain initial common cultural characteristics"

2. "[They are] gradually united from a congerie of tribes, usually through intermittent warfare with neighbouring confederations or city-states, and would then undergo some degree of political centralization either of itself, or through external conquest."

3. "[They] attain to a state of cultural achievement and political self-rule ... which would then become a model for subsequent development."

4. "Even in decline and exile, the memories, myths and values of the homeland would continue to operate as guarantors of ethnic survival in the absence of any hope of restored sovereignty or autonomy."[10]

This pattern fits well the development of "Israel" according to the biblical narrative we have explored. But beyond the story itself, what evidence is there that this is what actually happened? Numerous archaeologists have interpreted the assemblages of pottery, the remains of buildings, and the composition of soil found amid the land we call "Israel." Earlier generations often engaged in this activity to "prove" the historicity of the Bible by seeking to correlate archaeological findings with biblical events, especially the stories of Conquest and Settlement in Joshua–Judges.

More recent work has taken into account changes in archaeological method and "read" the remains without being prejudiced by the Bible. One

---

8. Ibid., 3.
9. Smith (1988), 30.
10. Ibid., 95.

such scholar is Avraham Faust, who begins with a nuanced archaeological exploration of Israel's ethnogenesis before turning to the Bible.[11] Faust concludes that the following cluster of factors distinguish "Israel" ethnically from, most especially, the Philistines, before the monarchy:

1. **Plain pottery:** as opposed to the Philistines' decorated pottery

2. **Lack of imported pottery:** "It is likely that interaction with the Philistines resulted in negative attitudes toward their highly symbolic pottery."

3. **Limited pottery forms:** "The limited repertoire of the Iron I[12] pottery reflects an ethos of simplicity and egalitarianism."

4. **Prevalence of "four room house" architecture:** possibly expressing, among other things, Israel's purity concerns.

5. **Circumcision:** "It is quite clear that the term 'uncircumcised' is used in the Bible mainly as an ethnic marker, and since most of the local population of the region practiced circumcision, the trait could have served as a marker only in relation to the Philistines.... In other words, circumcision may have been practiced earlier then became ethnically significant only as a result of relations with the Philistines."

6. **Absence of temples and royal inscriptions and presence of simple burials:** all suggesting an "ethos of equality."[13]

Faust's analysis correlates "Israel" in the thirteenth century Merneptah stele with this archaeological evidence to conclude that the people who occupied rural village sites in the Canaan highlands in the twelfth century and exhibiting these six characteristics were the "Israel" named in the stele and the Bible. Slightly more cautiously, William Dever calls them "proto-Israelites": "the ancestors — the authentic and direct progenitors — of those who later became the biblical Israelites."[14] Importantly, he warns against too quickly equating the entire hill country population with biblical "Israel," because of the heterogeneous nature of that population. The *"Israel of the Hebrew Bible...comes into existence only with the Divided Monarchy in the tenth century."*[15]

What happened between the thirteenth and tenth centuries — between the time of the Merneptah stele and the time of David and Solomon — that generated both the Jerusalem-based monarchy with its imperial religion and the resistance movement that became the northern kingdom of Israel with its more creation-centered religion, both in the name of YHWH?

---

11. Faust (2007). For helpful, critical reviews of Faust's work, see Sparks (2008) and Pfoh (2008).

12. See p. 15 for a correlation of archaeological chronological terms, such as "Iron I," and the biblical narrative chronology.

13. Faust (2007), 48, 64, 70, 82–83, 91, 97–98.

14. Dever (2006), 194.

15. Ibid., emphasis added.

A brief outline can help us to envision the complex events in this crucial period. We will use the work of scholar Anne Killebrew, who applies the "world-systems theory" of Immanuel Wallerstein to understand this period.[16] Wallerstein's key insight is to comprehend social, economic, and political dynamics in terms of "world-systems" consisting of relations among "core," "semiperiphery," and "periphery" areas. As he states, the hyphen in "world-systems" is important:

> we are talking not about systems, economies, empires *of the* (whole) world, but about systems, economies, empires *that are* a world (but quite possibly, and indeed usually, not encompassing the entire globe).... We are dealing with a spatial/temporal zone which cuts across many political and cultural units.[17]

Within a world-system, relationships are unequal: some actors (core) have the power to control others (periphery), while some are caught in the middle (semiperiphery).[18]

Killebrew states that in the thirteenth century the region we call "Israel" was part of two world-systems with Egypt and the Hittite empire as "cores" and Syro-Palestine as part of the periphery. She writes,

> Throughout the Eastern Mediterranean region, the palace served as the administrative center and seat of the local ruler in an urban settlement. In the case of the "small kings," the palaces' control extended to the respective surrounding hinterland.... Economically, monopolistic production and intensive interregional trade characterized the palace system.
>
> ...in the Syro-Palestinian region, the double level of political rule was particularly evident because of the numerous small, semiautonomous city-states, each with local dynasties. Greater Canaan was divided between the two major core powers in the region....Hittite authority extended over parts of northern Levant (Syria), while the Egyptians viewed southern Levant (Palestine) as part of their sphere of influence....The administrative style of the two major powers differed. The Egyptian vassal states had well-defined obligations, while the pharaoh had few. The goal of the Egyptians was the extraction of tribute, control over the major routes crossing Canaan, and the prevention of rebellion.[19]

It was within this context that the Merneptah stele celebrated the Egyptian defeat of "Israel." Killebrew adds,

---

16. Killebrew, 21–22; Wallerstein (1974); for a brief and lucid overview of his theory and its application to today's world-system, see Wallerstein (2004).

17. Wallerstein (2004), 16–17, emphasis in original. Wallerstein's secular concept dovetails nicely with the use of "world" (*kosmos*) in John's Gospel; see chapter 25.

18. Cf. Münkler's criteria of "empire" at pp. 7–8.

19. Killebrew, 24–25.

The relative homogeneity of Canaanite culture, which was clearly on the periphery of the Egyptian center, was a result of Egyptian imperialist policy in Canaan and the region's role during the age of internationalism.... The role of Egypt was not to colonize Canaan but rather to administer the collection of tribute and to impose minimal security arrangements and a semblance of order on the fractious and quarrelsome Canaanite rulers. The goal was to promote and oversee Egypt and imperial interests and to guarantee the loyalty of the local Canaanite elite.[20]

However, for reasons about which scholars continue to debate, this system was radically transformed in the twelfth century and "created a multicultural mosaic of cultures and ideologies that resulted in the rise and development of the first-millennium biblical world."[21] The immediate effect was a total transformation of the region. Killebrew notes that "international lines of communication between the empires" were

replaced by more local contacts, which resulted in the fragmentation of Canaan into smaller regionally defined units.... The political situation seems to be volatile, with Canaanite rulers frequently requesting Egyptian intervention to settle disputes between the various urban centers. This type of political structure is often referred to as a "city-state system."[22]

During this power vacuum, the Sea Peoples known as the Philistines swept in to claim regional hegemony. Virtually all scholars agree that the Jerusalem-centered monarchy was a reaction against Philistine expansion. Here the archaeological and biblical data coincide in distinguishing two groups of people. But this simply sharpens the central question of our chapter: What was "Israel" in the period between the Egyptian-centered world-system of the thirteenth century and the emergence of the Davidic monarchy in Jerusalem?

We return to Dever's analysis of the twelfth-century archaeological evidence. He notes that "in contrast to other areas of Canaan, the *hill country*... witnessed a population explosion in the twelfth century BC," as evidenced by an increase in the total number of settled sites from 58 to around 350.[23] He continues: "These areas constituted the frontier — the margins of urban Canaanite society. Why this pattern of settlement, unless a military confrontation was precisely what the highland colonizers wished *to avoid?*"[24]

---

20. Ibid., 51, 83.
21. Ibid., 22; 33–37 reviews various theories explaining the changes, concluding that "no one theoretical model outlined above fully takes into consideration the host of complex forces that transformed the thirteenth and twelfth centuries BCE."
22. Ibid., 28, 33.
23. Dever (2006), 98, emphasis in original.
24. Ibid., 99, emphasis in original.

Dever's question leads him — and us — to consider the biblical traditions that purport to describe this time period, i.e., the book of Judges. Dever analyzes the tribal names given in Judges as evidence of "a loose alliance of tribes" (i.e., primarily Ephraim and Benjamin) that "was the premonarchical 'Israel' to which the Merneptah inscription refers."[25] However, most biblical scholars have discounted the "history" in Judges, which is clearly a narrative shaped by a Deuteronomic, Jerusalem-centered perspective. Its central theological purpose is to show that without a king, the people "did what was right in their own eyes" (Judg. 17:6; 21:25).[26] Its canonical place between the Josiah-era book of Joshua and opening chapters of 1 Samuel (see chapter 12 above) highlights this function. It is no more valuable as a window into twelfth-tenth century "Israel" than Joshua is to the preceding period.

The reality is that apart from anonymous archaeological remains, we have no direct evidence at all of "Israel" before the monarchy apart from the Merneptah stele. The most one can truly claim is that the archaeological evidence suggests something like a *resistance movement* against the Philistines, among which may have been people who identified themselves as "Israel."

Anthropologists show many examples of *ethnogenesis* as an expression of resistance to the incursion of a military or economic power.[27] It can also happen when people voluntarily or coercively migrate. As Geoff Emberling notes, "Whereas they may not have formed a particularly distinctive group before moving, in their new context they become more distinctive."[28] The development of the Jamaican Maroon ethnic communities from escaped plantation slaves in the seventeenth century offers an instructive parallel to what might have happened when the Philistines gained strength in Canaan.[29] Kenneth Bilby describes how Maroon ethnogenesis "unfolded through a number of interdependent processes." First, new group identities developed out of bonds formed among formal slaves for mutual survival. Actual kinship joined fictive kinship relationships to generate new, extended family units. This process was linked with new territorial claims and boundaries. Later, political relationships developed that superseded kin-based groupings. Finally, religious ideology, derived from African models, "constituted a powerful cement."[30] Thus, *ethnicity was forged through shared resistance to empire, centered on claims of kinship, land, and religion.*

The biblical Genesis and Exodus narratives reveal a nearly identical pattern. However, as we've seen, these texts are certainly from much later than the premonarchical period. In their own times of composition, they represent what Eric Hobsbawm has called "invention of tradition."[31] They

---

25. Ibid., 97.
26. See Schneider, xii–xv; cf. Brettler, 1–9.
27. Emberling, 308.
28. Ibid.
29. Bilby.
30. Ibid., 122.
31. Hobsbawm and Ranger.

were designed to provide "ancient" legitimation for the understandings and behavior of people in later periods, viz., the Israelite break with the Jerusalem monarchy (Exodus) and the exiles' resistance to Babylonian worldviews and social structures (Genesis). New ("old") understandings of kinship, land, and religion serve as alternatives to dominant narratives. Again, the biblical texts simply do not answer the question of the premonarchical formation of "Israel."

We are led back full circle to where Part II began: to the time of David and Solomon. Perhaps we can shed some light by asking the question another way: If "Israel" was an expression of social/cultural identity formed in resistance to either or both Egyptian or Philistine hegemony, why would the narrative seeking to legitimate David's reign and Solomon's succession claim "*YHWH, the God of Israel*," as its authority? Consider: forms of the phrase, "YHWH, God of Israel," are found over 160 times in the Hebrew Scriptures, virtually all in the Deuteronomistic History, 1–2 Chronicles and Ezra, and the Jerusalem-centered prophets Isaiah and Jeremiah.[32] In other words, nearly all texts referring to the God of *Israel* were written in *Judah* after the split between the two kingdoms.

The answer is perhaps obvious, yet still surprising: the specification of YHWH as "God of Israel" is necessary only when referring to *someone else's god*. The first of two uses in Exodus illustrates this point. When the name YHWH is revealed to Moses (in the wilderness), it is qualified as "the God of your father, the God of Abraham, the God of Isaac, and the God of Jacob" (Exod. 3:6). However, the qualifier, "God of Israel" is required at Exodus 5:1 because Moses is addressing his words *to Pharaoh*. Of the nearly four hundred uses of YHWH in Exodus, this qualifier is found only one other time. The context is Moses' response to the Golden Calf built by Aaron. Recall that the story is the "revenge of the Shilonites" on Jeroboam for not putting them in charge of the new cult apparatus at the northern sites of Dan and Bethel (see pp. 156–59). Moses says to the Levites (representing the Shiloh priests), "Thus says YHWH, the *God of Israel*, 'Put your sword on your side, each of you! Go back and forth from gate to gate throughout the camp, and each of you kill your brother, your friend, and your neighbor'" (32:27). In other words, it is the Shilonites attempt to undermine Jeroboam's claim that "YHWH, the God of Israel" has authorized his rebellion and new religious institution.

Apart from these two instances, throughout the torah and in the prophets who address Israel directly, the name YHWH needs and receives no geographic (ethnic) qualifier. Note that the Bible *never* uses the term "YHWH, God of *Judah*," despite the centrality of Judah and Jerusalem both before and after the Exile. I suggest that whatever the ethnic origins of the label

---

32. My search found other uses at Exod. 5:1; 32:27; Ps. 41:3; 71:22; 72:18; 78:41; 89:18; Ezek. 44:2; Mal. 2:16.

"Israel" might have been, it became a term irrevocably associated with the *deity YHWH* identified with the *people Israel.*

A few brief examples of how the term "YHWH, God of Israel" is used in the David/Solomon story reveal a key implication of this association between "YHWH" and "Israel." At 1 Samuel 23, David is being pursued by Saul and invokes "YHWH, the God of Israel" for the first time to determine whether Saul intends to destroy the city of Keilah (in Judah) because of David. When the response is that Saul will come and that the people of Keilah will betray David to Saul, David remains in the "hill country of the wilderness of Ziph," i.e., in *Judah.* David calls on *Saul's God* to find out what Saul will do and then *remains outside Israel.*

Another text links this title with Saul, king of Israel. At 2 Samuel 12, Nathan tricks King David about the Bathsheba affair with the parable of the rich man, poor man, ewe-lamb, and traveler (see pp. 125–27 above). At the moment of confrontation, Nathan says this:

> "You are the man! Thus says *YHWH, the God of Israel:* I anointed you king over *Israel,* and I rescued you from the hand of Saul; I gave you your master's house, and your master's wives into your bosom, and gave you the house[33] of *Israel and of Judah* . . . (2 Sam. 12:7–8)

The point is that David was made king not only over Judah, but also over Israel, and given his "master's [Saul's] house," i.e., both the royal, dynastic authority *and* Saul's daughter (Michal, one form of the "ewe lamb") and son (Jonathan, David's best friend). The "God of Israel" took this "foreigner"[34] and made him king in place of the "native son," Saul. It is this very God who now confronts David for his having "done evil" in YHWH's sight.

Another important example is Solomon's use of the term as a refrain in his blessing-prayer over Israel during the temple consecration ceremony. Five times in 1 Kings 8:15–25, Solomon triumphantly invokes "YHWH, God of Israel." Given our exploration of the true nature of the Solomon story, we should not be taken in by this blatantly self-serving piece of theo-political propaganda from Solomon's mouth. It is a typical, royal claim of divine authorization, linking Solomon's urban, temple-centered empire with all those before and after it in the Middle East and beyond. The speech is all about David, Solomon, Jerusalem, the temple, and the dynastic promise (2 Sam. 7), and not at all about the people themselves or their *shalom.* Paying close attention to each detail of this carefully crafted statement would be highly instructive. For our purpose, however, it should suffice to see that what is at its core is the claim that Jerusalem and its temple are now the "home" of the "God of Israel."

---

33. Note the singular "house" modifying the combination of Israel *and* Judah.

34. See 1 Sam. 17:12, where David is called "the son of an Ephrathite of Bethlehem in Judah"; also the book of Ruth agrees with this paternity while attributing *Moabite* ancestry to David's great-grandmother Naomi.

The speech seals what was begun by David in his battle with and defeat of Saul: the control of Israel by outsiders. Only by successfully claiming YHWH, God of Israel, as the legitimating authority for the Jerusalem monarchy could the house of David reign over Israel as Israel's "protection"[35] from the Philistines. The first step, taken by a "mixed multitude,"[36] was away from the lowland cities and into new rural settlements in the hills, enabled by the technologies of lime-plastered cisterns and terrace farming.[37] As the Philistines' threat increased,[38] the pressure to develop at least a defensive military capacity increased, leading to Saul's establishment as Israel's first king in the name of YHWH. A combination of Saul's ineffectiveness and David's bold actions and powerful bonding with disaffected men from the countryside led the pendulum to shift toward David. Eventually, Saul and his entire family were defeated, leading the now even more desperate Israelites to take up their last option: alliance with David.

The specific terms of the alliance are telling for our current inquiry:

> Then *all the tribes of Israel* came to David at Hebron, and said, "Look, *we are your bone and flesh.* For some time, while Saul was king over us, it was you who led out Israel and brought it in. YHWH said to you: It is you who shall be shepherd of *my people Israel,* you who shall be ruler over Israel." So all the elders of Israel came to the king at Hebron; and King David made a covenant with them at Hebron before YHWH, and they anointed David king over Israel. (2 Sam. 5:1–3)

The "tribes of Israel" offer "ethnic" solidarity with David in exchange for "national security." It is highly likely that this reference to the "tribes of Israel" is a function of the DH's perspective. As noted, these tribes are never listed in the monarchy story. It is the author's way of highlighting the shift from an independent, decentralized "Israel" to the new alliance of "Israel and Judah," which immediately became centered in Jerusalem. That they remain two-in-one rather than a truly integrated entity is underscored in the following verse: "and at Jerusalem he reigned over all Israel and Judah" (2 Sam. 5:5).

Once Solomon's reign is over, "all the assembly of Israel" came to his son, Rehoboam, to complain about the harsh treatment they received under his father. The "national security" deal has gone sour. Life under Judah's king turned out to be no better than it might have under the "lords of the Philistines." It is as "Israel" that the people come to seek relief from

---

35. The double meaning of "protection" as legitimate security and as an organized racket to extract tribute with threats of violence is intended, given David's history, e.g., 1 Sam. 25, 27. For an example of this same double meaning in U.S. history, see Butler.

36. Killebrew, 249, uses this term from Exod. 12:38 to describe the composition of those who sought a new way of life in the hill country, away from the Philistines.

37. E.g., Miller and Hayes, 83; Dever (2006), 114–17.

38. 1 Sam. 13:19–22 claims that the Philistines controlled access to iron tool and weapon sharpening, but Mirau, 108, shows that there is no evidence to support this.

oppression and as "Israel" that they proclaim the end of the alliance with the king of Judah (1 Kings 12:16–20). As the narrator sums it up: "There was no one who followed the house of David, except the tribe of Judah alone" (1 Kings 12:20).

Thus, even the Jerusalem-centered perspective of the DH acknowledges that "Israel" was originally and remained a reality separate from Judah and Jerusalem. Solomon, seeking to consolidate the power achieved by his father through acts of cunning and bloodshed, quickly made two important political moves. First, to reaffirm the alliance made by his father with Israel, he claims Israel's God, YHWH, as his own. Second, Solomon made a "marriage alliance" with Pharaoh, king of Egypt.[39] Despite Egypt's receding power, Solomon knew that Egypt remained a key regional player.[40] Of course, Jeroboam, leader of Israel's rebellion, understood this too: his flight from Solomon took him to Egypt's King Shishak, who attacked Jerusalem once Jeroboam had led Israel away (1 Kings 11:40; 14:25).[41]

As noted, marriage alliances are a common "circumstantial trait" of ethnicity.[42] Through these acts (and his hundreds of other such alliances, 1 Kings 11:1–3), Solomon acted as a typical king, seeking to create human bonds that embodied political power, while claiming the authority of as many gods as possible. The DH author admits that for Solomon YHWH was simply one god among many.

Before Solomon, Israel was likely the name for a loose association of people who claimed YHWH as their God and lived in simple, egalitarian, hill country villages. Whether the organization of this premonarchical Israel was based only on local kinship relationships (i.e., "father's houses" [*bayit 'ab*] and "clan" [*mishpachah*]) or included "tribes" (*shevet* or *matteh*) cannot be answered as a matter of history. Similarly, we cannot answer "yes" or "no" to the question of whether premonarchical Israel was what we would call an "ethnic group." All the evidence for "Israel" comes through the perspective of others, whether Egypt's stele or Judah's royal writings.

What does seem clear, though, is that whatever Israel was before David and Solomon, the actions of empire generated a much stronger sense of

---

39. Kitchen, 118–21, shows that the pharaoh at the time was Siamun, predecessor of Shishak, who sheltered Jeroboam. Shishak "favored a radically different policy in nearby Canaan. His actions with regard to Jeroboam imply that he viewed the Solomonic realm as a hindrance to his own possible aims for expansion" (123).

40. Halpern (2004), 401–6, suggests that Solomon himself may have been an Egyptian usurper, hence the need for the formal legitimation of his reign that the biblical story provides. If so, then Solomon would have simply been making a "family" alliance with Egypt. Kitchen notes that the "reasons for an Egypto-Israelite alliance against Philistia can only be surmised," while blasting scholars who dismiss this narrative as historically unfounded, showing instead the plausibility of this marriage alliance given twenty-first Dynasty Egyptian policy (119–20).

41. Kitchen (123) suggests several factors that would have motivated Shishak's military campaign.

42. See also Anderson, 20: "antique monarchical states expanded not only by warfare but by sexual politics.... Dynastic marriages brought together diverse populations under new auspices."

mutual identity than had previously existed. As Anthony Smith writes, "Ethnicism is fundamentally defensive. It is a response to outside threats and divisions within."[43] Similarly, Faust notes:

> Defining oneself in resistance to pressure from the outside is therefore clearly a major mechanism of ethnogenesis.... The two mechanisms of resistance and state activity are by no means contradictory and can very well operate together.... The activity of a central government can both "impose" an identity on a group of people, even if they did not have this identity before, and also promote the emergence of an identity as a form of resistance to its activities; these could very well be the "same" identity. The two processes can at times be one.[44]

This, it seems, is what happened with Israel under Solomon. What had been rural village solidarity in a small region of the hill country was expanded and consolidated into a larger identity.[45] Solomon's imposition of twelve administrative districts upon a wider geographic region than had previously encompassed "Israel" facilitated this process. Empires always require transportation and communication networks. Whether Rome's establishment of paved roads throughout the Mediterranean or the U.S. interstate highway system,[46] such pathways are essential to movement of trade and armies. The movement of tribute demanded by Solomon from throughout Israel required such a highway network (1 Kings 4:7–18). The apostle Paul took advantage of Rome's road system to share his "Good News" throughout the empire, seeking to establish a house church network as a renewed "Israel" serving as an alternative "ethnic" solidarity to Roman citizenship (see chapter 26). Solomon's imperial structure similarly enabled locals to communicate and to bond in new ways.

An example from more recent times illustrates this process of imperially generated ethnogenesis. Before Spain's conquest, the islands later known as "the Philippines" contained peoples of countless local ethnicities and languages.[47] The name "Philippines" is itself a function of imperial Spain's control. What had previously been a loose trade network among many

---

43. Smith (1988), 55.

44. Faust (2007), 136–37.

45. I have avoided using the word "state" to describe Solomon's kingdom as inappropriate to the kind of ancient social organization at issue; see Master (2001) for a systemic critique of traditional evolutionary models (succession of kin, clan, chiefdom, state) in interpreting tenth-century Israel, suggesting instead a Weberian "patrimonial model," taken up also by Stager.

46. "Eisenhower had first realized the value of good highways in 1919, when he participated in the U.S. Army's first transcontinental motor convoy from Washington, D.C., to San Francisco. Again, during World War II, Eisenhower saw the German advantage that resulted from their autobahn highway network, and he also noted the enhanced mobility of the Allies, on those same highways, when they fought their way into Germany. These experiences significantly shaped Eisenhower's views on highways and their role in national defense." *www.ourdocuments.gov/doc.php?flash=old&doc=88*.

47. For a popularly accessible account, see Karnow 26–47.

different peoples, however, became the ethnicity "Filipino" under Spanish rule.[48] Once established, "Filipino" became a rallying point, first for resistance to Spain and then for resistance to the United States. A similar process occurred in the archipelago now known as "Indonesia," another European naming that eventually established an ethnic identity among formerly local, disparate peoples.[49]

"Israel," unlike "Filipino" or "Indonesian," was a name apparently generated and claimed first by the people themselves. But under Solomon, this name developed a stronger sense of shared identity, history and purpose. We cannot know how "ordinary Israelites" saw and thought of themselves during this period. Seeking their self-understanding from the biblical text is no more revealing than seeking to know what twenty-first century Christians are "really like" by reading institutional church documents.

We can only suggest that the solidarity generated in resistance to Solomon created "Israel" as what Benedict Anderson has called an "imagined community." Although certainly not a "nation" in the modern sense,[50] "Israel" became a symbol of a people joined by trust in the Creator God who led them out of empire and into a place of freedom and equality. Whatever "ethnic" diversity may have previously existed (Egyptian, "Canaanite," and so forth) became subsumed within an identity envisioned as "family" and "people" in "covenant" with YHWH. It is to this sense of shared identity and purpose to which the prophets continually called the people to return.

As we've seen, this identity merged with that of Jerusalem / Judah again after Assyria's eighth-century invasion. Never again would "Israel" stand on its own as the people of YHWH in their own land. Those who sought, with imperial authorization, to rebuild Jerusalem and the temple after the Exile claimed the name "Israel" and the authority of YHWH, Israel's God, for their project. For centuries to come, this name would be wrestled over by those seeking to establish and those seeking to resist empire in the name of YHWH.

---

48. Kramer (2006), 35–86, describes how this process created an elite identity (*illustrados*) with whom the Spanish could negotiate, separate from the "savages" in rural and forest regions. This process of imperial segregation of "civilized" people from "savage natives" has been repeated throughout history.

49. See generally Taylor (2003).

50. Anderson, 37–46, discusses the sixteenth-century origins of "national consciousness" as a result of the "coalition between Protestantism and print capitalism" (40).

PART III

From Exile
to the Eve of Easter:
Fallen Jerusalem,
Fallen Babylon

Chapter Fourteen

The First Fall of Jerusalem

JEREMIAH AND EZEKIEL

Jeremiah

Jeremiah saw it coming:

> Declare in Judah, and proclaim in Jerusalem, and say: Blow the trumpet through the land; shout aloud and say, "Gather together, and let us go into the fortified cities!" Raise a standard toward Zion, flee for safety, do not delay, for I am bringing evil from the north, and a great destruction. A lion has gone up from its thicket, a destroyer of nations has set out; he has gone out from his place to make your land a waste; your cities will be ruins without inhabitant. Because of this put on sackcloth, lament and wail: "The fierce anger of YHWH has not turned away from us." On that day, says YHWH, courage shall fail the king and the officials; the priests shall be appalled and the prophets astounded. (Jer. 4:5–9)

The storm that was Babylon was brewing in the distance. Jeremiah, a priest from Anathoth — the ancient home of Abiathar, David's priest who had sided against Solomon (1 Kings 2:26–27) — was one of Jerusalem's elite in the generation following Josiah. Within the sprawling book that bears his name is a section scholars call "the Baruch Narrative" (Jer. 36–45).[1] In style and content, it is in many ways a continuation of the DH account of the monarchy's and Jerusalem's collapse.[2] And yet, within the larger framework of "Jeremiah," it also offers a passionate critique of the establishment perspective, a critique that threatens Jeremiah's life. As Walter Brueggemann says,

> Jeremiah's reading is not shaped by power politics but by the categories of Israel's covenantal traditions of faith.
>
> ... the severity of covenant sanctions and the power of God's yearning pathos are set in deep tension. This deep tension forms the central

---

1. Stulman, 297, as some others, sees Jer. 37–44 as the Baruch Narrative with chapters 36 and 45 as "bookends." The final form of Jeremiah is likely a complex mix of pre-exilic and postexilic perspectives on YHWH's judgment on Judah and eventually on Babylon; for an in-depth analysis of the relationships between these two perspectives, see Seitz (1989).

2. For example, Jer. 39:1–10 follows almost verbatim the narrative of 2 Kings 25:1–12; see also Jer. 52:4–16.

interest, theological significance, and literary power of the book of Jeremiah. This yearning pathos that is presented as God's fundamental inclination toward Judah is a departure from and critique of the primary inclination of Deuteronomic theology.[3]

In other words, Jeremiah, while fully immersed in the politics of the Jerusalem elite's struggle to respond to the twin threats of Egypt and Babylon, *offers not prudent advice but the Word of YHWH.* Not surprisingly, those in power largely ignored or repressed that Word. In the end, it was Jeremiah's diagnosis of Judah's disease and his prescription for a cure that became the canonical truth that would purport to guide future generations in their relationships with both YHWH and foreign empires. Jeremiah's task was to discern how the Josianic compromise — the combination of both Sinai/creation and Zion/royal "religions" — played out in the biggest crisis to face YHWH's people since the Philistines and their iron-wheeled chariots.

Table 16 will help us gain our bearings amid the many unfamiliar names and political contexts. I encourage readers to take the time to follow the details of the story, because in understanding the politics of the situation, we can understand more clearly Jeremiah's role and the message he offered as the Word of YHWH.

The basic sequence of events is straightforward. After Josiah's death, Pharaoh Neco appointed Josiah's son, Eliakim, as king and renamed him "Jehoiakim." Jehoiakim served as an Egyptian vassal until Nebuchadnezzar took Jerusalem; he then became a Babylonian vassal for three years. During this time, we are told that Jeremiah received a word from YHWH that was written down by his scribe Baruch and was then proclaimed in the "hearing of all the people" in the chamber of Gemariah son of Shaphan the secretary. As Louis Stulman comments, "The reading of the word is a dangerous and compelling act. It subverts, unsettles, and triggers a flurry of activity and culminates in a confrontation with the king."[4] The scene is clearly intended to recall Gemariah's father, Shaphan, finding the scroll in the "house of YHWH," which was brought to Josiah and proclaimed in his presence. Josiah tore his garments and called for public obedience to the Word of YHWH (2 Kings 22:3ff.). Gemariah's own son, Micaiah, reported Baruch's words to the king.[5] In sharp contrast to his own father, however, Jehoiakim cut the scroll into strips and then burned them in the company of his cabinet officials. The Baruch Narrative's judgment is clear: "Yet neither the king, nor any of his servants who heard all these words, was alarmed, nor did they tear their garments" (Jer. 36:24).[6] Jehoiakim was not a king who heeded prophets.

---

3. Brueggemann (1998), 3, 5.

4. Stulman, 299.

5. For the literary and historical relationships within this scribal family, see Dearman.

6. The Hebrew text contains a three-way pun (via the roots, qr' and qr') linking the words "read" and "cut" (the scroll) with "tear" of the garments, inviting readers to meditate on the relationship between the three acts.

Table 16: Major Figures
in the Collapse of the Monarchy and Jerusalem

Character (in Alphabetical Order)	Primary Relationships	Key Biblical References, Especially within the "Baruch Narrative" (Jer. 36–45)
Baruch son of Neriah	Jeremiah's scribe	Jer. 32:12–16; 36:4–32; 43:1–6
Ebed-melech the Ethiopian	"Servant to the king" (the meaning of his name) who befriended Jeremiah.	Jer. 38:7–12; 39:15–18
Gedaliah son of Ahikam son of Shaphan	Josiah's scribe, Shaphan's grandson, appointed governor of the "people of the land" in Judah by King Nebuchadnezzar of Babylon; Jeremiah is put in his care by the Babylonian military leader. Gedaliah advises the people of the land to stay and serve the Chaldeans (=Babylonians). He was killed in a rebellion by the people of the land.	Jer. 39:14; 40–41
Gemariah son of Shaphan	Son of Shaphan, who "found" the book identified with Deuteronomy (2 Kings 22).	Jer. 36:10–12
Hananiah, son of Azzur, from Gibeon	Prophesies that Babylon's power will be broken in two years; he confronts Jeremiah and his own prophecy of long-term exile. Jeremiah correctly prophesies Hananiah's death.	Jer. 28
Ishmael son of Nethaniah	Leader of a rebellion against Gedaliah, whom he assassinated.	Jer. 40–41
Jehoiakim (formerly Eliakim), son of Josiah	Vassal of Pharaoh Neco, then a servant of Nebuchadnezzar for three years. He later rebelled. When given a scroll dictated by Jeremiah and transcribed by Baruch, he burned it in front of his officials.	Jer. 1:3; 22:18–19; 36; 2 Kings 23:34–24:5
Jehoiachin, son of Jehoiakim	Succeeded his father as king, then surrendered to Nebuchadnezzar and was taken to Babylon with family, officials and "the elite of the land."	2 Kings 24:8–15; Jer. 52:31–33 (= 2 Kings 25:27–29); Ezek. 1:2
Johanan son of Kareah	Leader of a group who escaped the Babylonians by fleeing to Egypt, after rejecting Jeremiah's "word of YHWH" as a lie.	Jer. 40:9–16; 41:11–16; 42:1–8; 43:2–5
Micaiah son of Gemariah son of Shaphan	Another of Shaphan's grandsons; he responded to Baruch's reading of Jeremiah's words and reported it to the king's cabinet	Jer. 36:11–13
Nebuchadrezzar, aka Nebuchadnezzar	King of Babylon	Jer. 21ff.; 2 Kings 24–25
Pharaoh Neco, king of Egypt	Defeated Josiah in battle and appointed Jehoiakim, Josiah's son, in his place	Jer. 46:2; 2 Kings 23:29–35
Zedekiah (formerly Mattaniah) son of Josiah and brother of Jehoiakim	Made king by Nebuchadnezzar in place of Jehoiachin. He rebelled, only to have his sons slaughtered before him and his own eyes blinded before being taken to Babylon. Caught between the Word from Jeremiah calling for submission to Babylon and the people looking to Egypt to support a rebellion.	Jer. 21; 27, 32; 34; 37–39; 2 Kings 24:17–25:7

The scroll's message was simple and clear: "the king of Babylon will certainly come and destroy this land" (Jer. 36:29). Politically, though, this outcome was far from obvious. Egypt remained strong and pundits were divided on the question of who would win the superpower struggle. Throughout the Baruch Narrative and the wider book of Jeremiah, the prophet expresses the view of the "pro-Babylonian" party among the Judahite elite. Babylon will win, and resistance is not only futile, but against YHWH's will. Babylon's invasion is Jerusalem's punishment for its consistent violation of the covenant. The people must accept YHWH's judgment if there is to be hope for the future.

Meanwhile, Jehoiakim died and was replaced by his son, Jehoiachin, who immediately surrendered to Nebuchadnezzar and was taken to Babylon with his family, officials, and "the elite of the land" (2 Kings 24:15). Nebuchadnezzar replaced Jehoiachin with another of Josiah's sons, Jehoiachin's uncle, Zedekiah. For the people in exile (including Ezekiel), Jehoiachin is the "real" king. Gabriele Boccaccini explains the prophet's task: "While preaching submission to Nebuchadnezzar (Jer. 27), Jeremiah had to dismiss and ridicule any hope related to Jehoiachin (22:24–30; 28:5–16)."[7]

The Baruch Narrative's judgment follows at once: "But neither he [Zedekiah] nor his servants nor the people of the land listened to the words of YHWH that he spoke through the prophet Jeremiah" (Jer. 37:2). Zedekiah found himself politically caught between a rock and a hard place. On the one hand was a faction seeking a security alliance with Egypt; on the other, those like Jeremiah urging surrender to Babylon. Jeremiah was accused of treason and not supporting the troops, which he denied, but he was arrested, beaten, and imprisoned (Jer. 37:13–15; 38:2–4). Zedekiah arranged a secret meeting with him[8] in which he hoped for a word from YHWH. The Word again was clear: "You shall be handed over to the king of Babylon." Zedekiah waffled: he reduced the prophet's punishment to house arrest, from where the people continued to hear his proclamation of doom. The officials clamored for Jeremiah to be put to death. Zedekiah acknowledged his powerlessness and allowed for Jeremiah to be thrown into a cistern with no water. Stulman notes: "Zedekiah lacks the moral courage or political prowess to deliver Judah during its darkest hour. The last king of Judah proved to be a tragic figure: cautious, inept, and compromised. His ambivalence is the ultimate complicity."[9]

Jeremiah was rescued by an unlikely savior, Ebed-melech the Ethiopian. Jeremiah was then brought once again before Zedekiah. The king confessed his "fear of the Judeans"[10] who had gone over to Babylon. He

---

7. Boccaccini (2002), 46.

8. Cf. the secret meeting between Jesus and Nicodemus, John 3.

9. Stulman, 312.

10. Fear of the Judeans is a theme that runs throughout John's Gospel as an expression of unwillingness to do what one knows is God's will, 7:13; 9:22; 19:38; 20:19. Note also the parallels between the portraits of Zedekiah here and of Pontius Pilate in the gospel.

made Jeremiah commit to a false cover story to prevent word getting out of the covert meeting between king and prophet. Eventually, Nebuchadnezzar returned and the city was besieged, with Zedekiah and his soldiers fleeing for their lives, only to be caught and brought before Nebuchadnezzar. The Babylonian monarch punished Zedekiah by making him watch his sons be slaughtered before his eyes as the last thing he would ever see, after which Zedekiah was blinded, the king's house and other houses were burned, and the elite were exiled to Babylon (Jer. 39:1–9). Only "the poor people who owned nothing" were left to tend vineyards and fields.

Jeremiah, for his part, was protected by the Babylonian military commander, a response that would seem to lend credence to the view of those who saw Jeremiah as a traitor. He was entrusted to Gedaliah, grandson of the scribe Shaphan, who had been appointed by the Babylonians as governor of those remaining in Judah. Gedaliah gathered the people and promised that if they cooperated with the Babylonians, there would be peace. Many accepted this offer and life seemed to return to normal.

However, a rebellion arose under the leadership of Ishmael son of Nethaniah, a vehement nationalist who refused to accept this accommodation to empire. Gedaliah was warned about the rebellion by Johanan son of Kareah, one of his officials, but refused to believe that Ishmael was a rebel. He should have, though: Ishmael and his supporters assassinated the Babylonian appointee and continued on a rampage. Johanan confronted Ishmael and freed those whom Ishmael had taken captive, but Ishmael escaped. Fearing that they would be accused of being part of Ishmael's rebellion, Johanan and his supporters tried to flee to Egypt. As they went, they sought a word from Jeremiah. The prophet's message from YHWH is key to the theological understanding of the impending division among the Judeans who were not exiled and worth quoting in full:

> Thus says YHWH, the God of Israel, to whom you sent me to present your plea before him: If you will only remain in this land, then I will build you up and not pull you down; I will plant you, and not pluck you up; for I regret [cf. Gen. 6:7; 1 Sam. 15:11] the disaster that I have brought upon you. Do not be afraid of the king of Babylon, as you have been; do not be afraid of him, says YHWH, for I am with you, to save you and to rescue you from his hand. I will grant you mercy, and he will have mercy on you and restore you to your native soil. But if you continue to say, "We will not stay in this land," thus disobeying the voice of YHWH your God and saying, "No, we will go to the land of Egypt, where we shall not see war, or hear the sound of the trumpet, or be hungry for bread, and there we will stay," then hear the word of YHWH, O remnant of Judah. Thus says YHWH of hosts, the God of Israel: If you are determined to enter Egypt and go to settle there, then the sword that you fear shall overtake you there, in the land of Egypt; and the famine that you dread shall follow close after you into

Egypt; and there you shall die. All the people who have determined to go to Egypt to settle there shall die by the sword, by famine, and by pestilence; they shall have no remnant or survivor from the disaster that I am bringing upon them. "For thus says YHWH of hosts, the God of Israel: Just as my anger and my wrath were poured out on the inhabitants of Jerusalem, so my wrath will be poured out on you when you go to Egypt. You shall become an object of execration and horror, of cursing and ridicule. You shall see this place no more. YHWH has said to you, O remnant of Judah, Do not go to Egypt. Be well aware that I have warned you today that you have made a fatal mistake. For you yourselves sent me to YHWH your God, saying, 'Pray for us to YHWH our God, and whatever YHWH our God says, tell us and we will do it.' So I have told you today, but you have not obeyed the voice of YHWH your God in anything that he sent me to tell you. Be well aware, then, that you shall die by the sword, by famine, and by pestilence in the place where you desire to go and settle." (Jer. 42:9–22)

Jeremiah's word claims, without hesitation or doubt, that YHWH's will is for the people to remain in the land rather than go to Egypt. However, no specific reason is given why, in the choice of empires, Babylon is favored by YHWH and Egypt rejected as the place of *shalom* for YHWH's people. The people's response is equally adamant:

Azariah son of Hoshaiah and Johanan son of Kareah and all the other insolent men said to Jeremiah, "You are telling a lie. YHWH our God did not send you to say, 'Do not go to Egypt to settle there'; but Baruch son of Neriah is inciting you against us, to hand us over to the Chaldeans, in order that they may kill us or take us into exile in Babylon." (Jer. 43:2–3)

At stake in this confrontation is whether Jeremiah's message is truly YHWH's Word.[11] We are told that the people continued with their plan to go to Egypt and took Jeremiah and Baruch with them. In Egypt, Jeremiah prophesied both that Nebuchadnezzar would come and break up Egypt, and that the "Judeans living in the land of Egypt" were bringing disaster on themselves, not only for being in Egypt, but for rampant idolatry (Jer. 44). In the passage quoted above, though, nothing was said about idolatry. Jeremiah's word to those heading for Egypt is simply the theological judgment that political and economic security will best be attained by staying and submitting to Babylon rather than going to Egypt. Idolatry does not enter the picture until *after* the people have settled in Egypt.

---

11. Brueggemann (1994) considers the relationships among Jeremiah the "poet," Baruch the "politician," and the Shaphan families as a "middle ground" that "apply" the prophet's poetry to the situation. Thus, the opponents see Baruch "using" Jeremiah to accomplish a political result and name Baruch, not Jeremiah, as the source of the "lie." Brueggemann criticizes the opponents' perspective as "simplistic and excessively cynical, for the interface between serious faith and serious politics is never so one-dimensional" (415).

A number of key questions arise from these events. First, why would Judeans be more tempted by idolatry in Egypt than in Babylon, where, according to Jeremiah, the exiles were to "seek the *shalom* of the city" (Jer. 29:7)? Both Babylon and Egypt had established systems of religious stories and practices in support of their empires. There appears to be no reason why the threat of idolatry would point the people to one empire rather than the other.

Second, the accusation of *lying* arises three times in the Baruch Narrative,[12] putting in readers' minds the question of whose voice to trust and on what basis. Here are the two other passages:

> A sentinel there named Irijah son of Shelemiah son of Hananiah[13] arrested the prophet Jeremiah saying, "You are deserting to the Chaldeans." And Jeremiah said, "That is a lie; I am not deserting to the Chaldeans." But Irijah would not listen to him, and arrested Jeremiah and brought him to the officials. (Jer. 37:13–14)

> Gedaliah son of Ahikam said to Johanan son of Kareah, "Do not do such a thing, for you are telling a lie about Ishmael." (40:16)

In the case of Gedaliah's distrust of Johanan, events proved Johanan to be truthful despite the governor's doubt, at the cost of Gedaliah's life. In the case of Jeremiah's being charged with deserting to the Chaldeans (Babylonians), the text surprisingly leaves the question open. We hear that after Jeremiah has been rescued from the well into which he had been thrown, the Babylonian military commander appears to offer him a friendly choice of futures:

> The captain of the guard took Jeremiah and said to him, "YHWH your God threatened this place with this disaster; and now YHWH has brought it about, and has done as he said, because all of you sinned against YHWH and did not obey his voice. Therefore this thing has come upon you. Now look, I have just released you today from the fetters on your hands. If you wish to come with me to Babylon, come, and I will take good care of you; but if you do not wish to come with me to Babylon, you need not come. See, the whole land is before you;[14] go wherever you think it good and right [Heb, lit., "what is right in your eyes"] to go. If you remain, then return to Gedaliah son of Ahikam son of Shaphan, whom the king of Babylon appointed governor of the towns

---

12. Hebrew *sheqer*, "a lie," is used thirty-seven times in Jeremiah of fifty-four in all the prophets combined.

13. Irijah's grandfather, Hananiah, had challenged Jeremiah's prediction of a long exile by offering his own prophecy that it would be over in two years. Jeremiah repeatedly accused Hananiah of telling and encouraging the people to trust in "a lie" (27:10, 14, 15, 16; 28:15). See also the confrontation between Jeremiah's word of YHWH and that of other prophets, Jer. 29:21–32.

14. Recall Abram's identically worded offer, Gen. 13:9, the only other use of this phrase in the Hebrew Scriptures; cf. Gen. 20:15; 47:6.

of Judah, and stay with him among the people; or go wherever you think it right to go." So the captain of the guard gave him an allowance of food and a present, and let him go. (Jer. 40:2–5)

Doesn't it sound like Jeremiah established a relationship with the invaders that would support the accusation that he was a deserter? Also note that a phrase twice-used by the Babylonian commander — "what is right in your eyes" — is a Deuteronomistic term, found twenty-seven times combined in Deuteronomy–2 Kings and Jeremiah, but only in 2 Chronicles elsewhere in the Bible. In other words, this speech has clearly been *composed* by the author of the Baruch Narrative. Why would a pro-Jeremiah author want to support the suggestion that Jeremiah was collaborating with the Babylonians?

Third, recall the false cover story that Zedekiah asked Jeremiah to agree to in order to prevent word of their meeting from getting out. We are told that "the officials did come to Jeremiah and questioned him; and he answered them in the very words the king had commanded" (Jer. 38:24–27). In other words, Jeremiah deliberately *lied* to them! Is a person willing to lie to protect a king from his internal opponents to be absolutely trusted in his claim to speak the Word of YHWH?

Fourth, although Jeremiah repeatedly claims that those who go to Egypt will be utterly destroyed by YHWH as punishment for refusing to listen, there is little historical evidence to support this outcome. In fact, in subsequent centuries, a thriving Judean community was established in Egypt, spawning luminaries such as Philo of Alexandria, a Judean philosopher contemporaneous with the apostle Paul. In other words, if the test of a prophet is whether his words are shown to have been true,[15] Jeremiah's credibility was left wanting.

Finally, after accusing Jeremiah of lying, those bound for Egypt took Jeremiah and Baruch with them, where he prophesied publicly and vehemently against the entire Judean community in Egypt. Why would they want to take the prophet and his scribe with them? Earlier in the book, Jeremiah *sent a letter* to the exiles in Babylon telling them to build families there and to "seek the shalom of the city," but the prophet himself did *not* go to the very place he prophesied that YHWH wanted the people to remain for now. Why would Jeremiah *go to Egypt* but only *write to Babylon*?[16]

The reason for raising these questions is that Jeremiah, both in the Baruch Narrative and the wider canonical book, is the *first biblical voice to proclaim YHWH's will to be subservience to a foreign empire.* In other words, is Jeremiah a prophet in YHWH's name for the religion of empire or the religion of creation? Why has a pro-Jeremiah narrative planted these seeds

---

15. This was Jeremiah's basis for why he, and not Hananiah, was speaking YHWH's Word, Jer. 28:15–17.
16. See Jer. 29:1ff.; also 51:59–64.

of doubt in readers' minds about Jeremiah's pro-Babylonian motives and stance?

Of course, in the overall message of the book, Jeremiah is hardly "pro-Babylonian." He offers as YHWH's Word that the people should accept exile or Babylonian colonial rule in Judah for a time. But as the book comes to a close, the prophet scathingly denounces Babylon and prophesies its impending collapse, in language taken up centuries later by John of Patmos,[17] author of the Bible's final book. He tells "Israel and Judah" to "flee from the midst of Babylon.... Do not perish because of her guilt.... Come out of her, my people! Save your lives, each of you, from the fierce anger of YHWH!" (Jer. 51:6, 45). What YHWH has done to Jerusalem will also befall Babylon: "The land trembles and writhes, for YHWH's purposes against Babylon stand, to make the land of Babylon a desolation, without inhabitant" (Jer. 51:29).

The key may be in the implicit role of the exiles to be what Second Isaiah called a "light to the nations."[18] We noted that Jeremiah's letter to the exiles called for them to "seek the shalom of the city where I have sent you into exile, and pray to YHWH on its behalf, for in its shalom you will find your shalom" (Jer. 29:7). Given Jeremiah's eventual condemnation of Babylon for its oppressive, imperial behavior, this cannot mean that the exiles' shalom is found in conforming to Babylon on Babylon's own terms. Rather, it suggests that the exiles, living according to the covenant between YHWH and the people that burned so strongly in Jeremiah's heart,[19] might be the source of a healing transformation of the imperial city. From this perspective, we can hear the cry of the exiles proclaimed amid the oracle of judgment: "We tried to heal Babylon, but she could not be healed. Forsake her, and let each of us go to our own country; for her judgment has reached up to heaven and has been lifted up even to the skies" (Jer. 51:9).

Thus, Jeremiah's command to accept exile is not lending divine support to empire, but transforming the purpose of exile from punishment of YHWH's people to hope for Babylon's conversion.[20] Sadly, the Babylonians proved to be as stiff-necked as the Jerusalemites; their city, too, fell as the consequence of its divine disorientation.

We can only guess why Jeremiah accompanied the Judeans to Egypt rather than joining the exiles in Babylon. We learn nothing further about his motives or his fate. We can also only hazard guesses as to why he so adamantly insisted that Babylon rather than Egypt would be the place of at

---

17. See chapter 27.

18. Isa. 42:6; 49:6; cf. 51:4; later, Matt. 5:4; John 8:12; 9:5 adapt this role to apply to Jesus' disciples, as discussed in chapters 23 and 25.

19. E.g., Jer. 11:2–10; 22:8–9.

20. Compare the prophetic satire in the book of Jonah, as the prophet resentfully, after much resistance, goes to Nineveh to seek its conversion. The book of Jonah may well have been meant to ridicule the notion that empires repent rather than collapse. Cf. Miles (1975); more generally see Jernielity.

least temporary shalom. Perhaps Egypt had already become a larger-than-life symbol, given the Deuteronomic trajectory: the thought of returning to Egypt for security seemed the utter undoing of YHWH's bursting of the bonds of slavery associated with the place.[21] Perhaps, for those in a later period who gathered the prophet's writings into the book bearing his name, only those who yearned to return to the Promised Land could be called the people of YHWH, a theme central to the tradition in Ezra-Nehemiah, as we'll see shortly. For these later editors and collectors of Scripture, only the exiles in Babylon who returned to the land truly "heard the voice of YHWH," while those who went to Egypt without plans to return had become a different people, unwilling to listen to the Word of YHWH.[22] Jeremiah certainly understood the eventual return from Babylon as a new Exodus:

> Therefore, the days are surely coming, says YHWH, when it shall no longer be said, "As YHWH lives who brought the people of Israel up out of the land of Egypt," but "As YHWH lives who brought the people of Israel up out of the land of the north and out of all the lands where he had driven them." For I will bring them back to their own land that I gave to their ancestors. (Jer. 16:14–15)

In the end, Jeremiah was not pro-Babylonian, but *pro-Jerusalem*. As a priest-prophet from Anathoth, he represented a longstanding tradition of loyal dissent. Fully urban and urbane, Jeremiah could garner both the attention and the ire of the highest among Jerusalem's elite. He was no John the Baptist in the wilderness. His stinging critique of social injustice demanded conformity to the covenant vision contained in Deuteronomy, a book composed in his youth. Thus, Jeremiah insisted on urban centralization as the basis of national unity. If Jerusalem was condemned, it was not because it was a *city*, but because it was an *unfaithful* city. According to this vision, YHWH's love for the people meant enduring love for Jerusalem. If the city was destroyed because of YHWH's righteous wrath, it would also eventually be rebuilt because of YHWH's enduring *chesed*, i.e., "covenant love/loyalty."

If he had lived, Josiah would have embraced Jeremiah's word in a way his royal successors were unwilling to do. Josiah, like Jeremiah, stood for a Jerusalem-centered, YHWH-focused monarchy that would hold Israel and Judah together under the Deuteronomic covenant. But in the aftermath of Jerusalem's destruction and exile, other voices arose that envisioned a covenant community in which humans did not dominate one another at all, even as benevolent kings. The book of Genesis, as we saw in Part I, expressed the views of one of these voices. Another, with very close ties to Genesis, came from Jeremiah's younger contemporary priest-prophet Ezekiel.

---

21. Compare, e.g., Jer. 2:6 and 2:17–18.
22. Thanks to Stuart Scadron-Wattles for this suggestion.

Ezekiel

Reading the book of Ezekiel can provoke strong reactions. The prophetic word begins with and is punctuated by what may seem to many moderns to be psychotic or perhaps drug-induced visions of bizarre beasts and spiraling wheels within wheels. Ezekiel's condemnation of Jerusalem as a wife who has become a whore is unsparing and violent; to some it is misogynistic. His language is at times wild and impolite, at least to our ears. But for all of Ezekiel's undomesticated speech, he grounds the vision he presents to the exilic community in the same soil as the much calmer Genesis narrative, as well as the orderly legal provisions of Leviticus. Tables 17 and 18 show some of the many links.

Table 17: Some Links between Ezekiel and Genesis

Image / Word in Ezekiel	*Image / Word in Genesis*	*Comment*
1:4: "seated above the likeness of a throne was something that seemed like [*demut*] a human form."	1:26: "Let us make humankind . . . in our likeness" (*demut*)	*Demut*: of twenty-five times in Hebrew Bible, sixteen times in Ezek.; plus Gen. 1:26; 5:1, 3
1:22: "Over the heads of the living creatures there was something like a dome" (*raqqi'a*)	1:6: And God said, "Let there be a dome (*raqqi'a*) in the midst of the waters . . . "	Of seventeen times in Hebrew Bible, thirteen times in Gen. 1 and Ezek. 1 (also Ezek. 10:1)
28:13: "You were in Eden, the garden of God" (also Ezek. 31:9–18; 36:35)	2:8: "God planted a garden in Eden"	*Eden* only Joel 2:3; Isa. 51:3 elsewhere; Ezek. 28 has numerous echoes / parallels with Gen. 2–3
28:16: "the guardian cherub drove you out from among the stones of fire"	3:24: "He drove out the man; and . . . he placed the cherubim, and a sword flaming and turning to guard the way"	
38:22: " . . . and I will pour down torrential rains and hailstones, fire and sulfur, upon him"	19:24: "Then YHWH rained on Sodom and Gomorrah sulfur and fire from YHWH out of heaven"	*Rain of fire and sulfur* only Psalm 11:6 elsewhere in Hebrew Bible.

Table 18: Some Links between Ezekiel and Leviticus

Image / Word in Ezekiel	Image / Word in Leviticus	Comment
4:16: "I am going to break the staff of bread in Jerusalem" (also Ezek. 5:16; 14:13)	26:26: "When I break your staff of bread"	Not elsewhere in Hebrew Bible
5:2: "and I will unsheathe the sword after them" (also Ezek. 5:12; 12:14)	26:33: "and I will unsheathe the sword against you"	Not elsewhere in Hebrew Bible
5:10: "Surely, parents shall eat their children in your midst"	26:29: "You shall eat the flesh of your sons, and you shall eat the flesh of your daughters"	See also Jer. 19:9
5:17: "I will send famine and wild animals against you, and they will rob you of your children; pestilence and bloodshed shall pass through you; and I will bring the sword upon you. I, YHWH, have spoken"	6:22: "I will let loose wild animals against you ... I will bring the sword against you ... I will send pestilence among you"	See also Exod. 23:28–29; Deut. 7:20–22; Jer. 15:2–3; 27:6–8
6:4: "and I will throw down your slain in front of your idols"	26:30: "I will heap your carcasses on the carcasses of your idols"	Not elsewhere in Hebrew Bible
20:5: "I am YHWH your God."	11:44: "I am YHWH your God."	Of thirty-seven times in Hebrew Bible, twice in Ezek. and twenty-one times in Lev.
22:7: "Father and mother are treated with contempt in you"	19:3: "You shall each revere your mother and father"	Treat with contempt: also Mic. 7:6 Revere: also Exod. 20:12; Deut. 5:16
22:10: "they uncover their fathers' nakedness ('*erevah*)"	18:7: "You shall not uncover the nakedness ('*erevah*) of your father"	Cf. Gen. 9:22–23; '*erevah*, fifty-four times in Hebrew Bible, thirty-two times in Lev.; six times in Ezek.
34:4: "with force and harshness (*perek*) you have ruled (*radah*) them."	25:43, 46: "You shall not rule (*radah*) over them with harshness (*perek*) ... no one shall rule over the other with harshness."	Combination not elsewhere in Hebrew Bible
34:25, 27: "and I will send down the showers in their season.... The trees of the field shall yield their fruit, and the earth shall yield its increase."	26:4: "I will give you your rains in their season, and the land shall yield its produce, and the trees of the field shall yield their fruit."	Ezek. 34:25–31 and 36:8–15 closely parallel Lev. 26:3–14

These numerous parallels show that the three books share a common vision of creation, the invitation to human existence in God's presence, and the consequences of humanity choosing to "play God." For now, we note what Ezekiel does and doesn't share with Jeremiah as a prophet of Jerusalem's doom, and what that implies for the future of God's people amid the empires of the world. In the next chapter, we will see how Ezekiel's vision of restoration is part of a chorus of biblical voices challenging the embrace of Persian colonial rule over the "New Jerusalem."

The mystical vision with which the book begins is not mere fireworks or decoration placed on top of standard prophetic speech. Rather, Ezekiel, living among the exiles, describes his experience to establish the central premise of his book: that YHWH, the God of Israel, is truly the God who created and who rules over all of heaven and earth. In doing so, he takes up what to his audience would have been familiar Assyrian royal propaganda and subverts it. Assyria, of course, was the empire that conquered Israel, the northern kingdom of YHWH's people, in 722 BCE, and threatened Judah for a century until finally falling to Babylon. Many of the former Israelites who had sought refuge in Jerusalem under King Hezekiah knew this imperial propagandistic imagery well. Ezekiel, as a Jerusalem priest taken into exile, would certainly also have been familiar with Assyrian imagery. As Margaret Odell states,

> Ezekiel's use of this propaganda undermines its credibility. Assyrian royal ideology had long been employed to assert the powerlessness of the God of Israel against the awe-inspiring power of the Assyrian king [e.g., Isa. 36]....
>
> In appropriating this political imagery, Ezekiel asserts that the only effective power in the lives of the people of Israel is Yahweh.[23]

The vision of the voice and throne from above the dome of the sky forcefully claims that the One who speaks and whose presence is perceived in fiery glory is truly king over all peoples. As such, he is creator and judge. Roughly the first half of the book reveals the judgment; the latter half envisions the re-creation of Israel.

Politically, Ezekiel was in a very different place from Jeremiah. Jeremiah struggled mightily to present the will of YHWH as surrender to Babylon and waiting for eventual release. He tells them to

> not let the prophets and the diviners who are among you deceive you, and do not listen to the dreams that they dream, for it is a lie that they are prophesying to you in my name; I did not send them, says YHWH. For thus says YHWH: Only when Babylon's seventy years are completed will I visit you, and I will fulfill to you my promise and bring you back to this place. (Jer. 29:8–10)

---

23. Odell, 35–36.

Ezekiel, on the other hand, pointed his vision back to Jerusalem and the reign of YHWH, not identifying the exiles' welfare with Babylon's. Ezekiel distanced himself from Jeremiah and his Deuteronomistic perspective. Whereas Jeremiah first put his hopes, unsuccessfully as it turned out, on the Babylonian puppet-king, Zedekiah, Ezekiel's initial hope was upon the exiled king, Jehoiachin, as we hear from the dating of his first oracle at Ezekiel 1:2: " ... the fifth year of the exile of King Jehoiachin." However, just as Zedekiah buckled under pressure, so Jehoiachin accepted Babylonian honor and thus, control. Gabriele Boccaccini writes, the "exiled priests who are behind the tradition of Ezekiel had many good reasons to be upset at King Jehoiachin.... From their vantage point, the Davidic king, with his prophets and Levitical priests, was a quisling who had deserted them and sided with the enemy."[24]

Ezekiel's visions, symbolic actions and oracles grew out of this experience. The result was a program with three goals. First, he sought to separate YHWH's reign as Creator from the reign of any human king, including any Davidic successor. Second, he hoped to separate monarchy from priesthood, delegitimizing the king's right to appoint priests. Third, he sought to focus hope on a restored Jerusalem that would embody YHWH's glory and abundance. Ezekiel did not seek to persuade kings to follow his advice. Rather, he listened to and presented the Word of YHWH from his own direct experience to an unspecified and hence, unlimited, audience.[25]

The Voice of YHWH commanded that Ezekiel engage in a series of public acts that symbolized his renunciation of the Jerusalem priesthood and his movement into deeper solidarity with the people.[26] The priest must defile himself by cooking food on dung, an expression of desperation during famine (Ezek. 4:9–17), then he must shave his head and beard. In doing so, Odell notes that "Ezekiel has now fully relinquished his role as a priest. The act of shaving his head was associated with mourning rites forbidden to priests ... and in doing so, subjects himself to the waves of death that will wash over his people."[27]

Among the most difficult of Ezekiel's judgment oracles is chapter 16, in which Jerusalem is characterized as a young woman abandoned by her parents but adopted by YHWH. The woman is bathed, clothed, and adorned by YHWH and becomes famous "among the nations on account of your beauty, for it was perfect," says YHWH, "because of my splendor that I had bestowed on you" (16:14). However, things immediately turn bad: the young woman Jerusalem "trusted in [her] beauty and played the whore," sacrificing her own children and "offering [herself] to every passer-by" (16:15, 25).

---

24. Boccaccini (2002), 48.

25. Of course, as a priest writing from within the Exile, Ezekiel's audience, at least initially, was limited to those with him in Babylon.

26. Odell, 56.

27. Ibid., 67–68. See Ezek. 44:20.

As we'll explore in chapter 27, the imagery of city-as-whore is taken up again in the Bible's final book: Revelation's portrait of fallen Babylon. Ezekiel's imagery is not condemning women; it is not about women at all. It is the *male leadership* of Jerusalem that is portrayed as "whore" for its infidelity to YHWH. Ezekiel's judgment scene uses sexuality as a metaphor for the practice of both *idolatry* and *economic injustice*, which, theologically, are two sides of the same coin.[28] The prophetic condemnation is not about sexual behavior as such, but rather "intercourse" that is exploitative or self-focused.

Once we comprehend the biblical use of the sexual metaphor, many oft-misunderstood passages are clarified, including the sin of Jerusalem's "sister" city, Sodom. As the prophet proclaims: "This was the guilt of your sister Sodom: she and her daughters had pride, excess of food, and prosperous ease, but did not aid the poor and needy" (Ezek. 16:49). The true crime of "sodomy," as was discussed in detail in chapter 5, is not "homosexuality" but greed and inhospitality to the stranger. Sodom, like Jerusalem, was *condemned for practicing the religion of empire* rather than the religion of the Creator. The city has become "unclean" with idolatry, i.e., the worship of her own power over others.

A few chapters later, Ezekiel specifies the cause of Jerusalem's sad slide from beloved wife to wretched whore. It is the priesthood of Jerusalem that was unclean, along with other leadership groups and therefore the people themselves:

> Mortal, say to it: You are a land that is not cleansed, not rained upon in the day of indignation. Its *princes* within it are like a roaring lion tearing the prey; they have devoured human lives; they have taken treasure and precious things; they have made many widows within it. Its *priests* have done violence to my teaching and have profaned my holy things; they have made no distinction between the holy and the common, neither have they taught the difference between the unclean and the clean, and they have disregarded my sabbaths, so that I am profaned among them. Its *officials* within it are like wolves tearing the prey, shedding blood, destroying lives to get dishonest gain. Its *prophets* have smeared white-wash on their behalf, seeing false visions and divining lies for them, saying, "Thus says YHWH GOD," when YHWH has not spoken. The *people of the land* have practiced extortion and committed robbery; they have oppressed the poor and needy, and have extorted from the alien without redress. (Ezek. 22:24–29)

It is a portrait of *empire embodied in what was to be a holy city.*[29] That Ezekiel sees Jerusalem's crimes as examples of imperial archetypes is revealed

---

28. Cf. Rev. 9:20–21.

29. See also Neh. 11:1 and chapter 16 on the postexilic designation of Jerusalem as "holy city."

in his oracles against Tyre (Ezek. 26–28) and Egypt (which is in turn compared to Assyria; Ezek. 29–32, especially chapter 31). There can be no thought that the actual people of these places were the intended audience of the prophet's words. Rather, the oracles express the reality that YHWH is the judge of *all* nations, and the criteria by which YHWH judges are universal.

The lament over the seafaring trading city of Tyre in Ezekiel 27–28 is a prime example of the message that permeates the entire book. In chapter 27, we hear a litany of nations who traded with Tyre, an ancient global economy, in goods such as silver, iron, tin, and lead; human slaves; war horses; ivory and ebony; purple, linen, coral, and rubies; honey, oil and balm; lamb, rams and goats; wine and wool; spices and gold; carpets and embroidered cloth.[30] It is because of being the center of this global trading network that the prince of Tyre can say, "I am a god; I sit in the seat of the gods, in the heart of the seas." However, YHWH's response is equally adamant: "you are but a mortal, and no god,[31] though you have *made* your mind *like* the divine mind" (Ezek. 28:2). Dexter Callender suggests that this recalls Genesis 3:22, "the *'adam* has become *like one of us.*"[32]

The second clause of the previous quote is repeated four verses later (28:6), framing YHWH's reason for attributing this divine mind-making to the city: "By your great wisdom in trade you have increased your wealth, and your heart has become proud in your wealth" (28:5). The final section of the oracles against Tyre makes the connection with Genesis 3 even more explicit: YHWH says that Tyre was "in Eden, the garden of God" (28:13). Further, Tyre had as a "covering" a series of precious stones that match those of the priestly breastplate in Exodus 28:15–18.[33] However, Tyre's abundance of violence-based trade led to the expulsion of the city from "the mountain of God" and "from among the stones of fire" by the "guardian cherub." It is the *relationship between international trade and violence/injustice* that is labeled "sin" and "profanity" (28:16, 18).[34]

The parallels with Genesis 3 reveal that what the Garden of Eden story presented as the first human act of seeking to be like God is portrayed in Ezekiel 27–28 as a *collective* overreaching. Ezekiel paints the prince of Tyre as "the Primal Human," an originating image of divine/human synthesis common in ancient imperial propaganda.[35] Genesis, on the other hand,

---

30. Cf. Rev. 18:12–14.

31. See also Isa. 31:3, where the same phrase is used about the Egyptians.

32. Callender 187; the second quoted clause is from Callender's suggested translation.

33. The LXX list is a precise match between Exod. 28 and Ezek. 28; the Hebrew differs slightly.

34. Callender, 122, n. 276 notes that the "reference to trade and violence is considered by most critical scholars a later explanatory gloss." However, this begs both the questions of "later" *when* and *who* would make this link between the portrayal of Tyre as the Primal Human and the practice of unjust and violent trade. Cf. the textual chain linking Nimrod as founder of Babylon with similar behavior, Gen. 10:8–12; Hab. 2; Rev. 17–18.

35. Callender, 87–135; 179–89.

claims that *all humanity*, as male and female, are created in the image of God. Both Genesis and Ezekiel challenge the central claim of every manifestation of imperial religion: that a human king who stands above all others is the means through which people experience the divine made flesh.

Similarly, Ezekiel's oracle against Egypt in chapter 31, like Genesis 2, counters the ancient imperial iconography of "the cosmic tree." In condemning the divine pretensions of pharaonic Egypt, Ezekiel again draws on Assyrian imagery that compared its monarchy and power to a tall cedar tree.[36] After describing its towering size and sheltering branches and shade, the prophet turns the intent of the image upside down: "*I* made it beautiful with its mass of branches" (31:9).[37] Odell notes "it is Yahweh, not the Assyrian god, who allows the tree to flourish."[38] Yet like the prince of Tyre, the Assyrian cedar's "heart was proud of its height," and so YHWH "gave it into the hand of the prince of the nations; he has dealt with it as its wickedness deserves" (31:11).

Ezekiel, in contrast to Jeremiah, never suggests that the exiles can have a beneficial effect on Babylon. He does not announce Babylon's fall directly, but the relentless oracles against self-divinizing and whoring city-states leave no doubt as to Babylon's eventual fate. For Ezekiel, the pattern is universal and cosmic: YHWH alone is creator and judge; any who would rebel against this reality will inevitably face the harsh and deadly consequences of their actions. Jerusalem is condemned not as an empire itself, but for prostituting itself to the imperial power of others. Until Jerusalem arises from the valley of dry bones, it can be of no value to anyone else (Ezek. 37). The only hope is YHWH's sovereign power to bring life out of barrenness and death.[39]

---

36. Compare the similar imagery drawn upon in the parable of the trees choosing one among themselves to reign over them as king, Judg. 9:7–21, as well as the subversive overturning of this tradition in the parable of the mustard seed at Mark 4:31–32.

37. Note the numerous parallels to Gen. 2 in Ezek. 31, including the second mention of Eden, the "garden of God," and the rivers that flow out from around the tree.

38. Odell, 393.

39. The brief book of Habakkuk shares in the divine condemnation of Babylon, using traditional prophetic imagery denouncing wealth and status gained by violence (*hamas*, six times), bloodshed (*dam*, three times) and economic injustice. However, it does not take up the more cosmic perspective of YHWH as Creator nor in its three chapters does it look toward a future restoration.

Chapter Fifteen

"In the Wilderness, Prepare the Way of YHWH"

ENVISIONING A WAY OUT OF EXILE

One of the most important reasons for meditating on history theologically is to help discern the direction in which YHWH calls God's people to go. Jeremiah's and Ezekiel's message about the past was clear: Jerusalem was destroyed and the elite exiled not because YHWH was weak, but because of the city's unfaithfulness to the covenant love relationship with YHWH. Not until this was fully accepted could Jerusalem be forgiven and reborn. Yet if the people truly returned to YHWH, what form would a new Jerusalem take?

The Bible contains a range of responses to this question. We have seen the Genesis story of nonurban, extended family life as an alternative to urban monarchy. For Genesis, it is the city itself, grounded in violence and domination, that embodied the evil from which the people must turn. But for many — then and now — this prescription was too radical. How could we turn away from "civilization" and all its "benefits"?[1]

Second Isaiah, Ezekiel, Leviticus, 1–2 Chronicles each offer a perspective on the question of how a new Jerusalem would be organized in obedience to YHWH. The first two of these present their visions from within the experience of exile, anticipating release. The latter texts offer alternatives to what in fact became the basis for the reestablishment of Jerusalem: the ethnically "pure" accommodation with imperial Persia narrated in the books of Ezra and Nehemiah. At stake was the relationship between the people of Israel, their God, and the peoples and way of the "nations." 1 Samuel had long ago condemned yearning for a king "like the nations" as a rejection of YHWH's exclusive sovereignty. In the absence of their own king, how *should* the people of God live amid the way of empire that surrounded them?

---

1. For examples of today's burgeoning anti-civilization literature, see Glendinning, Jensen (2006a, 2006b, and 2008), Quinn, Shepard, and Zerzan (1999 and 2008); see also Myers (2005) on "anarcho-primitivism and the Bible." There is also a growing online conversation at fora such as Jesus Radicals (*www.jesusradicals.com*), Jesus Manifesto (*www.jesusmanifesto.com*), and In the Land of the Living: a journal of anarcho-primitivism and Christianity (*www.inthelandoftheliving.org/Home*).

"Comfort, O Comfort My People":
Second Isaiah's Promise of Release from the Prison of Exile

Before they could reflect on how to live once they were restored to their land, though, the exiled people of YHWH had truly to believe that their time of punishment had come to an end. An anonymous prophet working in the tradition of Isaiah[2] generated some of the most powerful and influential imagery in the Hebrew Bible. Like Ezekiel and Genesis, Second Isaiah's YHWH is the Creator of heaven and earth, under whom all the nations are judged. But judgment was not this prophet's primary concern. Instead, his concern is that people recognize that the time for judgment and punishment had passed. It was now time for a word of comfort that would encourage people to take the long journey into the unknown, out of Babylon and back to the Promised Land. And so we hear in the book's opening verses:

> Comfort, O comfort my people, says your God. Speak tenderly to Jerusalem, and cry to her that she has served her term, that her penalty is paid, that she has received from YHWH's hand double for all her sins. A voice cries out: "In the wilderness prepare the way of YHWH, make straight in the desert a highway for our God. Every valley shall be lifted up, and every mountain and hill be made low; the uneven ground shall become level, and the rough places a plain. Then the glory of YHWH shall be revealed, and all people shall see it together, for the mouth of YHWH has spoken." (Isa. 40:1–5)

For Christians, of course, portions of these familiar words echo from the beginning of the synoptic gospels.[3] For now, let us hear Second Isaiah in his own context, announcing the Word of YHWH to a people in exile, calling them home.

As we saw in chapter 14, Ezekiel and Genesis have much common imagery and language, befitting their shared origination during exile as well as their overlapping theological viewpoint. Similarly, Second Isaiah has many connection points with what became the Bible's first book, especially with the opening narrative in Genesis of God's creation of heaven and earth. Table 19 shows some of the many links between Genesis and Second Isaiah.

---

2. Scholars have long debated the relationship between parts and whole in the canonical book of Isaiah. It is clear that the sixty-six chapters were written over a long period of time. Earlier form critics not only separated the book into three sections ("Isaiah": chapters 1–39; "Second Isaiah": chapters 40–55 and "Third Isaiah": chapters 56–66), but further subdivided each section into numerous smaller units. More recently, many scholars have begun to reread Isaiah as a unit, regardless of how and when the various parts were composed. I accept that Isa. 40–55 is an exilic composition within the tradition of Isa. 1–39 and that Isa. 56–66 (see below) is a similar composition from the time of Persian restoration. However, Christopher Seitz (2004) shows convincingly the importance of interpreting "Second Isaiah" within the wider narrative of canonical Isaiah, especially for Christians. For Second Isaiah's use of Isaiah as well as Jeremiah, see Sommer.

3. Mark 1:3; Luke 3:4–6; Matt. 3:3. See chapters 22–24.

Table 19:
Some Links between Second Isaiah and Genesis

Image/Word in Second Isaiah	Image/Word in Genesis	Comment
God as creator/creating (*br'*)	1:1: In the beginning when God created (*br'*)	Of forty-eight uses of *br'* in Hebrew Bible, eleven in Gen. 1–5; sixteen in Second Isaiah (and five in Third Isaiah)
42:5: God, YHWH, who created the heavens	1:1: Created the heavens and the earth	*Created heavens:* Isa. 45:18; 65:17; not elsewhere in Hebrew Bible
40:17: Creation contrasted with "nothing" [*tohu*]	1:2: the earth was a formless void [*tohu vebohu*] and darkness covered the face of the deep, while a wind from God swept over the face of the waters.	*Tohu* also at Isa. 40:23; 41:29; 44:9; 45:18; 49:4
45:7: "I form light and create darkness"	1:3: Then God said, "Let there be light" ... God separated the light from the darkness.	
41:10: "I am with you" (also 43:5)	26:24: "I am with you" (also 28:15)	Nineteen times in Hebrew Bible (five in Jeremiah)
48:19: "your offspring [*zera'*, "seed"] would have been like the sand" (also 33:12)	22:17: "I will make your offspring [*zera'*] as numerous as the stars of heaven and as the sand that is on the seashore."	*Seed like sand:* Only Jer. 33:22 elsewhere
51:2: "Look to Abraham your father and to Sarah who bore you; for he was but one when I called him, but I blessed him and made him many."	12:2: "I will make of you [Abram] a great nation, and I will bless you 17:2: and will make you exceedingly numerous." (also 22:17)	Only mention of Abraham and Sarah together outside Gen. in Hebrew Bible.
54:9: "This is like the days of Noah to me: Just as I swore that the waters of Noah would never again go over the earth, so I have sworn that I will not be angry with you and will not rebuke you."	9:15: "I will remember my covenant that is between me and you and every living creature of all flesh; and the waters shall never again become a flood to destroy all flesh."	Noah and flood not elsewhere in Hebrew Bible; cf. *1 En.* 10; 60; 65; 106–7

Central to the provision of hope for the exiles is instilling trust that the God of Israel is the Creator of all that is. This may seem obvious to us, having inherited the canonical order of the Bible. However, the image of YHWH as Creator is primarily exilic and postexilic. In the days of monarchy, it was enough for kings to claim YHWH as God of Israel, just as other peoples claimed their chief god as a national deity who reigned via the king. For the Exodus traditions seeking to lead people away from Jerusalem and its kings, YHWH was primarily experienced as liberator.[4] But with the Exile, Judeans in Babylon needed to know whether their God was truly more powerful than Marduk and his cohort.[5] As Leo Perdue notes,

> [Second Isaiah's] attack on cult images points to his concerted efforts to subvert the authenticity of Babylonian cosmology and imperial greatness that, among other things, pointed to Babylon as the center of the cosmos. By contrast, Second Isaiah argues against the animation and knowledge of crafted idols and asserts that Yahweh alone is creator, director of history, and determiner of human destinies.[6]

Many would argue that both true monotheism and the claim that YHWH was Creator crystallized in this exilic period for the first time.[7] We see both claims strongly presented in Second Isaiah. For this author, other "gods" are mere wood and stone. Isaiah 44 presents a classic satire on these "gods." A few excerpts convey the theme:

> Do not fear, or be afraid; have I not told you from of old and declared it? You are my witnesses! Is there any god besides me? There is no other rock; I know not one.
>
> The carpenter stretches a line, marks it out with a stylus, fashions it with planes, and marks it with a compass; he makes it in human form, with human beauty, to be set up in a shrine. He cuts down cedars or chooses a holm tree or an oak and lets it grow strong among the trees of the forest. He plants a cedar and the rain nourishes it. Then it can be used as fuel. Part of it he takes and warms himself; he kindles a fire and bakes bread. Then he makes a god and worships it, makes it a carved image and bows down before it. Half of it he burns in the fire; over this half he roasts meat, eats it, and is satisfied. He also warms himself

---

4. Second Isaiah (LXX) does connect with the Exodus tradition, though, in rendering Hebrew "YHWH" as Greek *egō eimi* (following Exod. 3:6). The phrase is found twenty-one times in the book of Isaiah, all but one (56:3) in Second Isaiah. This use is taken up in John's Gospel to refer to Jesus.

5. Recall the discussion in chapter 1 on the questions arising from the experience of exile.

6. Perdue (2008), 146.

7. Halpern (1998b), 632, shows that while Second Isaiah was the "ablest, most self-conscious, and logically most consistent exponent" of monotheism, it is expressed earlier in the pre-exilic texts of Jer. 1:16; 2:11, 27. Halpern dismisses views that these are postexilic additions to Jeremiah to conform his book to the later perspective as "highly improbable" (ibid.). See also Smith (2002), 82–193, who takes a very different approach to Israel's history than I do in this book, but reaches the same result on this point.

and says, "Ah, I am warm, I can feel the fire!" The rest of it he makes
into a god, his idol, bows down to it and worships it; he prays to it and
says, "Save me, for you are my god!" They do not know, nor do they
comprehend; for their eyes are shut, so that they cannot see, and their
minds as well, so that they cannot understand. No one considers, nor is
there knowledge or discernment to say, "Half of it I burned in the fire; I
also baked bread on its coals, I roasted meat and have eaten. Now shall
I make the rest of it an abomination? Shall I fall down before a block of
wood?" He feeds on ashes; a deluded mind has led him astray, and he
cannot save himself or say, "Is not this thing in my right hand a fraud?"
Remember these things, O Jacob, and Israel, for you are my servant; I
formed you, you are my servant; O Israel, you will not be forgotten by
me. (41:8–9; 13–21)

The image of worshiping barbeque briquettes powerfully mocks imperial
religious symbolism. YHWH's people have both nothing to gain from practicing idolatry and nothing to fear from those who do. The evidence of the
Creator's power, in sharp contrast, is all around: in the stars and rain of the
sky (41:26; 55:10); the sea and mountains (40:12); and the breath of life
within each human being (42:5). It is this God who loves them and will lead
them out of exile back to their homeland. Joining with Jeremiah 51, Second
Isaiah calls the people to "come out" of Babylon and walk the new path
through the wilderness that YHWH is forging (49:9; 52:11). The one who
announces that "your God reigns" brings "good news"[8] to those who sit in
the darkness of the Exile.

How is this to happen? Unlike the captivity in Egypt, the people of
YHWH will not be released by the direct power of the hand of YHWH.
Rather, Israel's God will use a startling instrument to accomplish the task:

Thus says YHWH, your Redeemer, who formed you in the womb: I
am YHWH, who made all things, who alone stretched out the heavens,
who by myself spread out the earth ... who says of Cyrus, "He is my
shepherd, and he shall carry out all my purpose"; and who says of
Jerusalem, "It shall be rebuilt," and of the temple, "Your foundation
shall be laid." Thus says YHWH to his anointed [*mashiyach*; LXX,
christos), to Cyrus, whose right hand I have grasped to subdue nations
before him and strip kings of their robes, to open doors before him —
and the gates shall not be closed ... (Isa. 44:24, 44:28–45:1)

This "shepherd" and "anointed" one is none other than the *king of Persia*. This unlikely "messiah" and "Christ," however, is merely an instrument.
YHWH says to Cyrus, "I arm you, though you do not know me" (45:5).

---

8. Isa. 52:7; the LXX uses *euangelizō* for "good news," a verb key to the New Testament's
proclamation of Jesus; see chapter 22.

Second Isaiah does not bless the Persian king or nation.[9] Cyrus is simply a means to an end, a tool to break down Babylon's bars and allow the prisoners to go free. For YHWH, all kings and human powers "are like a drop from a bucket, and are accounted as dust on the scales.... All the nations are as nothing before him; they are accounted by him as less than nothing and emptiness" (40:15, 17). YHWH's use of Cyrus does not lead to Cyrus's own exaltation or the people's subservience to Persia. Once the people are out of their prison and on the way home, their allegiance is to YHWH alone, their Creator and their "husband" (54:5).[10] Persia, just another drop in the bucket of nations, can quickly be forgotten in the joy of returning home.

Second Isaiah includes a set of poems that, taken both as a unit among themselves and as integrated into the wider narrative of Isaiah 40–55, convey the great challenge of getting the people in exile to accept this call to "come out." There is an enormous scholarly literature on these four so-called "Servant Songs" (Isa. 42:1–4; 49:1–6; 50:4–9; 52:13–53:12).[11] The poems were so central to the gospel writers' portrayal of Jesus' suffering and death that it is almost impossible for Christian readers to hear them in their original context and not as "about" Jesus. For instance, consider this familiar passage:

> He was despised and rejected by others; a man of suffering and acquainted with infirmity; and as one from whom others hide their faces he was despised, and we held him of no account. Surely he has borne our infirmities and carried our diseases; yet we accounted him stricken, struck down by God, and afflicted. But he was wounded for our transgressions, crushed for our iniquities; upon him was the punishment that made us whole, and by his bruises we are healed. (Isa. 53:3–5)

What was, according to the New Testament, fulfilled in Jesus, was already an important message during the Exile. Just as we saw how the Isaian prophecy of a "son" to be born who would be called "Prince of Peace" referred in the first instance to King Hezekiah, so here, Second Isaiah's "Servant" was not simply an anticipation of a centuries-later individual. It is only by listening to these passages in their original context that we can truly understand Jesus' own mission and why the evangelists rely so heavily on these powerful images to explain Jesus' own death and resurrection.

One of the key questions that scholars have grappled with — with no clear "answer" — is the identity of the "servant of YHWH." The wider narrative of Second Isaiah identifies *Israel* as YHWH's servant, as we hear near the very beginning: "But you, Israel, my servant (*'eved*), Jacob, whom I have chosen, the offspring of Abraham, my beloved" (41:8). Hebrew *'eved* is

---

9. Cf. Fried (2002), who argues that Second Isaiah intended to transfer all the authority of the Davidic messiah to Cyrus to facilitate acceptance of Persian rule.

10. The Hebrew, *b'l*, is more literally translated "lord."

11. For a recent collection of helpful essays, see Janowski and Stuhlmacher. For a detailed comparison of the Masoretic (Hebrew) and Septuagint (Greek) versions, see Ekblad (1999).

used forty times in the entire book of Isaiah, twenty-two of those in Second Isaiah (six times in the Servant Songs). The initial message to Servant Israel is clear: "You are my servant, I have chosen you and not cast you off"; do not fear, for I am with you, do not be afraid, for I am your God; I will strengthen you, I will help you" (41:9b–10). The refrain "do not be afraid" resounds repeatedly in Second Isaiah,[12] underscoring what it is that prevents the people from responding with joy to YHWH's call to "come out."

Somewhere along the way through Second Isaiah, though, it seems that the Servant was transformed from Israel to a specific individual. Is it the voice of the prophet himself? Another anonymous figure? A symbolic person? We cannot and do not need to answer this question. What is important for our purpose is *how* it is that the Servant is eventually successful in getting the people to respond to the call out of exile.

The first Servant Song (42:1–4) claims that the means of bringing "justice to the nations" and establishing "justice in the earth" is through gentle, persistent obedience to the Word of YHWH, not the violence of empire (see also 53:9). Justice is for the "nations" and "the earth" rather than only for Israel. This perspective flows out of Second Isaiah's understanding of who YHWH is and what Israel's vocation as YHWH's Servant has always been. The invocation of "Abraham, my beloved" underscores the connection between Genesis and Second Isaiah. Just as the call of Abram out of Babylon was intended to be a blessing for "all the families of the earth," so now Israel collectively is to embody that promise.[13]

Israel is "blind" to the way out, but YHWH promises to "open the eyes that are blind, to bring out the prisoners from the dungeon, from the prison those who sit in darkness" (42:7). Throughout the chapters that follow, YHWH pleads with Israel to see and to hear, to respond with joy, not to be afraid, to leave the prison of the Exile behind. But the people refuse to listen to the Voice of their Creator. YHWH no longer pleads directly with Servant Israel. Christopher Seitz shows how 48:16 is the turning point in Second Isaiah: "And now the Lord YHWH has sent me. . . . " He writes, "at the juncture where final tribute is paid to Cyrus, a first-person voice appears . . . [that] will dominate the following presentation."[14] Now *this individual* will embody Israel's vocation, so that others will be inspired to join in. Again, we hear in the second Servant Song (49:1–6) that this vocation has a universal purpose: "It is too light a thing that you should be my servant to raise up the tribes of Jacob and to restore the survivors of Israel; I will give you as a light to the nations, that my salvation may reach to the end of the earth" (49:6).

---

12. Isa. 40:9; 41:10, 13, 14; 43:1, 5; 44:2, 8; 51:7; 54:4.
13. Cf. Isa. 51:2: "Look to Abraham your father and to Sarah who bore you; for he was but one when I called him, but I blessed him and made him many."
14. Seitz (2004), 126.

The people's response, however, is not joyous imitation of the Servant, but derision. The third Servant Song (50:4–9) expresses the Servant's determination to carry out his mission despite the people's response:

> I gave my back to those who struck me, and my cheeks to those who pulled out the beard; I did not hide my face from insult and spitting. The Lord YHWH helps me; therefore I have not been disgraced; therefore I have set my face like flint, and I know that I shall not be put to shame; he who vindicates me is near. Who will contend with me? Let us stand up together. Who are my adversaries? Let them confront me. (50:6–8)

In the final Servant Song (52:13–53:12) we hear of the Servant's success. The people come to a startling recognition as they gaze on the Servant's suffering. They *had* assumed that his suffering was a result of *his own* sins, a punishment from God: "We accounted him stricken, struck down by God" (53:4b).[15] But now their long-blinded eyes are suddenly opened: "Surely he has borne *our* infirmities and carried *our* diseases... he was wounded for *our* transgressions, crushed for *our* iniquities!" (53:4a, 5). The people then confess that they are "like sheep who have gone astray, we have all turned to our own way and YHWH has laid on him the iniquity of us all" (53:6).

It is not clear whether the Servant's fate was actually to die or simply to be relegated to a place among the wicked.[16] Either way, the people's eventual recognition of the truth results from seeing their own sins embodied in the Servant. In other words, in observing the Servant, they become aware of the consequences of their own refusal to trust in YHWH and come out of exile. As a result, the Servant is "exalted and lifted up, and shall be very high" (52:13). As Martin Hengel notes, this echoes ironically First Isaiah's oracle about the fall from on high of Babylon at Isaiah 14:19.[17] As Babylon is brought down, YHWH's Servant is lifted up high.[18] With this exaltation, the people have finally overcome their blindness and fear and are ready to "come out" into the place of restoration and comfort with which Second Isaiah began.

Ezekiel, Part Two: New Jerusalem

After chapter upon chapter of scathing denunciation of Jerusalem and the surrounding imperial nations, Ezekiel's prophetic heart, like that of Second Isaiah, began to soften and express YHWH's turning back toward YHWH's own people. The transition takes place in chapter 34. Ezekiel begins by condemning the "shepherds of Israel": "You have not strengthened the weak, you have not healed the sick, you have not bound up the injured, you have

---

15. Hermisson, 36.
16. See Barré, 20–21, for discussion of the interpretative options.
17. Hengel, 97.
18. Echoed at, e.g., Luke 1:52–54.

not brought back the strayed, you have not sought the lost, but with force and harshness you have ruled[19] them" (34:4). Margaret Odell suggests that contrary to the common interpretation of the "shepherds" as the former Jerusalem nobility, the international context suggests "that the chapter is more specifically concerned with the political domination of Israel by foreign overlords and its plundering by neighboring nations, which are depicted in the oracle as fat sheep, rams, and goats" (34:17–22).[20]

In place of these exploitative shepherds, YHWH proclaims,

> I myself will search for my sheep, and will seek them out...will rescue them from all the places to which they have been scattered on a day of clouds and thick darkness. I will bring them out from the peoples and gather them from the countries, and will bring them into their own land; and I will feed them on the mountains of Israel, by the watercourses, and in all the inhabited parts of the land....I will seek the lost, and I will bring back the strayed, and I will bind up the injured, and I will strengthen the weak, but the fat and the strong I will destroy. I will feed them with justice. (34:11–16)

YHWH thus promises to replace imperial domination over YHWH's people with direct, divine rule in the Promised Land. A few chapters later, Ezekiel's vision takes him to a valley filled with dry bones (Ezek. 37). YHWH tells the prophet to "prophesy to these bones" and say to them: "I will cause breath/spirit [*ruach*] to enter you, and you shall live!" (37:5). The bones are "the whole house of Israel," who have given up hope. But YHWH assures them that God's power can bring life out of death, even the death of exile.

> "And you shall know that I am YHWH, when I open your graves, and bring you up from your graves, O my people. I will put my spirit within you, and you shall live, and I will place you on your own soil; then you shall know that I, YHWH, have spoken and will act," says YHWH. (37:13–14)

Like Second Isaiah, Ezekiel's first restorative task is to replant the Spirit of YHWH within the people. Thus strengthened and revived, they can begin to imagine a new life in the Land.

Ezekiel's book closes with a lengthy vision of a restored temple in Jerusalem, which he sees from "a very high mountain" (40:2). While some scholars question whether Ezekiel 40–48 is from the same person as the earlier part of the book,[21] the vision is a fitting conclusion to the exilic prophecy

---

19. Note the combined use of Hebrew *radah*, "rule" (as in Gen. 1:26, 28) and *prk*, "violence/harshness" (as in Exod. 1:13–14, pharaoh).

20. Odell, 423–25, noting that the title "shepherd" is used about Israel's leaders only for David and Joshua, and then only for leading the people in and out of battle, e.g., 2 Sam. 5:2; Num. 24:17; cf. Jer. 6:3; 12:10, interpreted by 22:22; 25:34; see also Zech. 11 and Zech. 10:3, which refers back to Ezekiel. The concern of Zechariah "is thus not to purge Judah of corrupt leadership, but to restore self-rule."

21. See, e.g., the discussion below about the role of Zadokite priests.

of judgment and restoration. Much of the vision describes in great detail the physical structure of the temple Ezekiel sees. Three themes are important. First, the envisioned temple, unlike its Solomonic predecessor, is not the legitimizing structure of a human monarchy, but is the center of a *restored community in which YHWH alone is sovereign* (43:1–8). Second, the temple is to be the basis for *renewed purity of the people as a whole*. This purity is not simply a matter of rituals and sacrifice, but of communal social justice. For example, we hear in the midst of what one might characterize as "priestly" requirements this Word from YHWH:

> Enough, O princes of Israel! Put away violence and oppression, and do what is just and right. Cease your evictions of my people, says Lord YHWH. You shall have honest balances, an honest ephah, and an honest bath [i.e., measures of grain]. (45:9–10)

As we'll explore more below, the *torah* that undergirds Ezekiel's sense of justice is not Deuteronomy, central to Jeremiah, but a new "holiness code" found in the book of Leviticus.

Finally, the temple vision anticipates a specific priesthood serving as leaders: the Zadokites.[22] The specification of this group as authorized ministers of the new temple is one of the main elements that leads some scholars to question the authorship of Ezekiel 40–48.[23] Nowhere else does Ezekiel address priestly authority. In fact, priests are not mentioned at all in chapters 1–39, except to identify Ezekiel himself (a status that he then ritually disclaimed) and to denounce the priestly leadership of Jerusalem (7:26; 22:26). In contrast, priests are mentioned twenty-two times in the closing vision. We recall from our chapter 10 the discussion of the Zadokites in relation to the struggle between Solomon's successors in Jerusalem and those gathered around Jeroboam and his successors in the northern kingdom of Israel. Zadok himself, according to the Deuteronomistic History, sided with Solomon over Adonijah at the succession after David's death.[24] The politics of priesthood were deeply intertwined with those of the monarchy. However, Ezekiel's reference to the "sons of Zadok" is the first mention of such a group. As we'll soon see, though, the label "Zadokite" was to carry a tremendous theological and political weight over the coming centuries. At stake is nothing less than the relationship between priesthood and empire.

---

22. See Ezek. 40:46; 43:19; 44:15; 48:11.

23. Blenkinsopp (1998), 41, suggests that the Zadokite passages are "probably interpolated" into the Ezekiel text. See the extensive discussion in Cook (1995b), regarding the relationship between the wider Ezekiel trajectory and the role of the Zadokites in Ezek. 44; Cook notes, "Ezekiel 44's positive presentation of the Zadokites represents a radically different view of them than that in Ezekiel 1–24" (204).

24. This is not to suggest an actual historical succession between the Zadok of 2 Samuel and Ezekiel's "Zadokites"; see, e.g., Blenkinsopp (2009), 148–49.

Ezekiel distinguishes "Zadokites" from "Levites" who "went astray" along with the people (48:11; cf. 44:10–14).[25] At the heart of the matter is the question of the admittance of foreigners to the envisioned temple:

> Say to the rebellious house, to the house of Israel, Thus says Lord YHWH: O house of Israel, let there be an end to all your abominations in admitting foreigners, uncircumcised in heart and flesh, to be in my sanctuary, profaning my temple when you offer to me my food, the fat and the blood.... Thus says the Lord YHWH: No foreigner, uncircumcised in heart and flesh, of all the foreigners who are among the people of Israel, shall enter my sanctuary. But the Levites who went far from me, going astray from me after their idols when Israel went astray, shall bear their punishment. (44:6–10)

As we'll see in chapter 16, the question of excluding "foreigners" deeply divided biblical authors throughout the Second Temple period. Stephen Cook sees this passage "countering" the positive view of foreigners found in Isaiah 56–66.[26] That the people at issue are "uncircumcised in heart and flesh" indicates that they are not simply "Israelites" who, through intermarriage, are considered "foreigners" by the Ezra-Nehemiah group (discussed in the following chapter).[27] Given the book of Ezekiel's consistent condemnation of empire and empire's arrogation of priestly authority, might there be another way to read this exclusionary passage? Rather than suddenly changing course and betraying the earlier vision of YHWH as Creator of all, might Ezekiel 44 and the temple vision be condemning not "foreigners" coming to YHWH to worship, but foreigners *as priests and participants in the leadership* of the restored temple? In other words, might Ezekiel's vision here not be one that offers a narrow sense of who is an "Israelite," but the *exclusion of foreign empire* from participating in a renewed Jerusalem cult? As we'll see in chapter 17, later visionaries within the Enoch tradition were to condemn altogether the Second Temple as "impure" because of its priestly intercourse with empire. Perhaps Ezekiel is a direct ancestor of this emerging tradition.[28]

Ezekiel's vision ends without resolution. As far as we know, the prophet died in Babylon, with his vision but a future hope. However, the time

---

25. Cook (1995b) shows the intricate connection between Ezek. 44 and the narrative of "Korah's rebellion" at Numbers 16–18. He argues, following Michael Fishbane (1985), 138–43], that Ezek. 44 is seeking to undermine the "P" text in Numbers, which was itself part of the process of "invented tradition" underlying the association of the postexilic Jerusalem priesthood with the line of Moses' brother, Aaron. This battle was one in a long line of priestly fights over legitimacy, extending over many centuries to come. Scholars have long sought to unravel the historical referents associated with these texts. For another view, see Boccaccini (2002).

26. Cook (1995b), 207.

27. See also Blenkinsopp (2009), 137.

28. This is counter to Boccaccini's view, which sees Ezekiel as the ancestor of "Zadokite Judaism" which he systematically contrasts with "Enochic Judaism." This question is addressed in chapter 17.

anticipated by Jeremiah, Ezekiel, and Second Isaiah was soon approaching. Babylon would fall to the Persians, and the exiled elite sent back to their ancestral land. How were they to begin the process of rebuilding? And not unimportantly, who would pay for it and why? Finally, what of the "people of the land" who had remained during the Exile: what part would they play in the new community of YHWH's people? These were the questions fought over among those who found themselves in the Land after the fall of Babylon.

Chapter Sixteen

The Struggle over Jerusalem's Restoration

Introduction

The Persian king Cyrus's defeat of the Babylonian king Nabonidus in 539 did not draw nearly as sharp a line between the periods of "Exile" and "Restoration" as some historical schemas might suggest. Rather, it began a complex shift in political power dynamics that had a long, slow, influence on those people who already lived in or who moved to the former environs of Jerusalem. A wide range of perspectives developed over the decades and centuries to follow regarding YHWH's will in relationship to Jerusalem, to the temple, and to the Persians. Some of the biblical texts (Haggai, Zechariah, Ezra/Nehemiah, Esther) explicitly address themselves to the Persian situation. Others (1–2 Chronicles, Leviticus, Third Isaiah, Ruth) offer an implicit viewpoint.

The complex, sometimes deceptive relationship between the biblical texts' internal timeline and external evidence from archaeology, Persian inscriptions, and other documents can confuse understanding of events and theological perspectives in the sixth–fourth centuries. However, the effort is essential in order to comprehend the shift from the First Temple monarchy to the Second Temple social order, in which YHWH's people no longer governed themselves but were subject to the power of foreign empires. During this period, the "two religions" began to crystallize into the forms experienced in the time of Jesus.

Table 20 shows the basic viewpoint of each text on the central questions after the Persian defeat of Babylon.

What were the general circumstances of the former Judah under Persian colonial rule into which these biblical voices spoke? As noted in chapter 14, Jeremiah witnesses to the ongoing presence of people in Judah during the Exile. After Jerusalem's destruction, the elite were removed, but peasant farming villages continued. Although there is no direct evidence, it is reasonable to infer that the destruction of the temple and its debt records resulted in a kind of "jubilee" (see Lev. 25) for those remaining. With the removal of those whom Isaiah castigated as "you who join house to house, who add field to field, until there is room for no one but you" (Isa. 5:8), ordinary people could return to their ancestral land and live in peace.

Table 20: Biblical Perspectives on
the Persian Era Restoration of Jerusalem

Text (and approximate time)	*Rebuilding the Temple*	*The Persians*	*The "People of the Land" and Question of Intermarriage*
Haggai (520)	Redemption depends on rebuilding the temple. It is to be the collective project of all the people.	Not mentioned, except for dating the oracle by regnal year.	Included within YHWH's people.
First Zechariah (Zech. 1–8) (520–518)	YHWH will "comfort Zion and again choose Jerusalem" (1:19); rebuilding is YHWH's will.	Not required to enable the project to be carried out.	Included within YHWH's people.
Ezra / Nehemiah (mid-fifth to early fourth centuries)	YHWH has led the former exiles to begin the rebuilding.	Persian sponsorship / patronage of temple and economic reconstruction, as well as legal framework of daily life, are the will of YHWH.	Excluded from people of YHWH; intermarriage absolutely prohibited.
Third Isaiah (Isa. 56–66) (mid-fifth century)	Rebuilding itself isn't as important as practicing inclusive justice and relying on YHWH alone; creation is YHWH's "throne" and "footstool."	Not mentioned, but implicitly irrelevant to YHWH's plan.	Included within YHWH's people.
Leviticus (from exile?)	Implicit in structure of book itself.	Not mentioned.	Included; intermarriage not prohibited.
1–2 Chronicles (fourth century?)	Temple is central to restoration.	Not mentioned. "Israel" includes everyone in the Land.	
Ruth	Not an issue.	Setting is pre-monarchy.	David is half-Moabite.
Esther	Not relevant to "diaspora" context.	Persian royal support protects Judeans throughout the empire.	The Judean, Esther, can be married to the Persian king!

Small village farming was (and remains) a family affair. The work of the local economy fully involved women and children. This will be important to keep in mind when we consider Ezra-Nehemiah's ban on "foreign" wives. Daily life in Judah would thus have reverted to an earthy rhythm, more akin to the way of YHWH the Creator than the socially stratified, urban-centered life under monarchy.

The immediate effects of Persian rule, beginning in the 530s, would have included levying of taxes. Imperial territory — including the "Province beyond the River" in which Judah was located — was largely an opportunity for gathering wealth from the locals.[1] This required developing local leadership that could work with the empire to assure a steady flow of revenue. As we'll see momentarily, this often involved an imperially appointed governor along with priestly leadership to provide "divine authority" to the arrangement.

Persia introduced a money economy into what had been a more traditional barter-exchange society.[2] We hear this in Nehemiah 5, where working people protest having to borrow money to pay the king's tax. The money economy generated a scramble for advancement. The Persian system of "royal grants" of property to favored individuals re-created a highly stratified society. This in turn led to enormous anxiety and competition among people seeking access to privilege and favor of those "above," a pattern that we will see again under the Roman Empire.[3]

To the north, the former region of Israel, especially around the city of Samaria, was more prosperous than the southern region, now labeled "Yehud" by the Persians. Both superior farmland and proximity to the wealthy island cities of Sidon and Tyre (recall Ezekiel's oracles against them) would have benefited the north. This would have made the coastal region a more desirable resettlement locale than the more arid and mountainous region around Jerusalem.[4]

Contrary to the idealized (and propagandistic) view presented in Ezra of a mass migration of exiles from Babylon back to the Promised Land, the actual resettlement would likely have been more of a sporadic trickle over decades, if not longer. Lester Grabbe comments,

> On the contrary [to Ezra's picture], the end of the sixth and beginning of the fifth century saw significant reduction in population, especially in the Benjamin area. The returnees are likely to have been a few thousand at most, probably over a period of time. Jerusalem may have been resettled after perhaps a long gap of no inhabitants, but it was only a small settlement early in the Persian period.[5]

---

1. On Persian rule in general in the province of Yehud, see Grabbe (2004a) and Berquist (1995 and 2007).
2. Seow (2008), 193–99.
3. Ibid., 199–217.
4. Grabbe (2004a), 156–62.
5. Ibid., 274.

Haggai-Zechariah

Haggai and Zechariah began to proclaim their prophecies in 520 under the reign of King Darius, successor to the "messiah" Cyrus. The mission of both prophets was to inspire the people of Judah into rebuilding the "house of YHWH." Their task, however, was much like being promoters of a church capital campaign in the midst of a depression. The people were convinced that "the time has not yet come," i.e., that the economic circumstances made a massive rebuilding project imprudent (Hag. 1:2).[6] Haggai attempted to rouse the people by likening their situation to King David's, living in "paneled houses" while the temple lay in ruins (Hag. 1:4; cf. 2 Sam. 7:2–7). His theological interpretation of the situation the people faced reversed the common assumption: it was the failure to build YHWH's house that was the *cause* of the economic hard times (1:9–11).

Haggai's plea drew a response:

> Then Zerubbabel son of Shealtiel, and Joshua son of Jehozadak, the high priest, with all the remnant of the people, obeyed the voice of YHWH their God, and the words of the prophet Haggai, as YHWH their God had sent him; and the people feared YHWH. Then Haggai, the messenger of YHWH, spoke to the people with YHWH's message, saying, I am with you, says YHWH. And YHWH stirred up the spirit of Zerubbabel son of Shealtiel, governor of Judah, and the spirit of Joshua son of Jehozadak, the high priest, and the spirit of all the remnant of the people; and they came and worked on the house of YHWH of hosts, their God. (Hag. 1:12–14)

The two named persons expressed continuity with the old monarchy. The Persian-appointed governor, Zerubbabel, was of Davidic lineage, a great-grandson of King Josiah, according to 1 Chronicles 3:17.[7] Although Haggai doesn't name this genealogy, he implies it with a combination of terms reminiscent of the Davidic reign (2:20–23).[8] His companion, the high priest Joshua,[9] was of Zadokite lineage, according to 1 Chronicles 6:14–15. Together, they embody a typical Persian colonial arrangement.[10] Haggai portrayed them as inspired leaders who in turn inspired the people to overcome their reticence to initiate the building process.

Zechariah 1–8 offers a more complex picture, conveyed through a series of visionary experiences of YHWH Sabaoth, i.e., "Lord of Hosts."[11] Mark

---

6. Kessler (2002), 244–48 shows how the common interpretation of Hag. 1:2 as referring to a "divinely appointed time" misunderstands both the Hebrew wording and the way "such a prophetic text may be used to reconstruct an historical context."

7. We'll explore below the ideological perspective of 1–2 Chronicles.

8. Boda (2000–2001).

9. Known in Ezra-Nehemiah as "Jeshua."

10. Grabbe (2004a), 147–48.

11. Zechariah uses this cosmic-military term for God 53 times (of 286 times in the Hebrew Scriptures).

Boda unravels the mystery of why the setting of the book is, like Haggai, in the second year of the reign of the Persian king Darius, while in Zechariah 1–6, the named opponent is Babylon. He notes that, contrary to biblical prophetic hopes, the reign of Cyrus led to Babylon's defeat, but not its destruction. In 522–521, there were two Babylonian uprisings against Persian rule preceding Darius's acquisition of full control. This led to Darius's administrative-financial reforms, creating a stable administration with firm authority over its occupied territories. Boda states,

> Zechariah 1:7–6:15 finds in the recent upheaval of the Persian empire significant progress toward the Persian fulfillment of prophetic expectations.... Although Cyrus had begun the process in 539 B.C., in the Zecharian tradition it was Darius who displayed greater progress in the fulfillment of the prophetic hope.[12]

Thus, we find in the prophet's visions the ongoing hope for the complete destruction of Babylon that would cause a stream of refugees to return to the Promised Land. This future event would allow various groups to converge in joining the remnant in the rebuilding of Jerusalem and the temple. John Kessler shows that Zechariah's vision is one generated by the remnant community yearning to be rejoined by their families. He notes that

> ... from the Zecharian perspective, the return of the Diaspora members is in some sense contingent upon the faithfulness of the remnant community already in Yehud; ... the return of the exiles and the resumption of normal existence in the land, a situation for which the tiny community longs, are thereby made conditional upon their own fidelity.[13]

Most important for our current purpose is to see that Zechariah's vision is of a wide diversity of YHWH's people coming together in a joyful project of reestablishing a place of worship and communal life under YHWH's reign. It is open to those Egyptian immigrants from Judah whom Jeremiah condemned; to those from the wider geography of the former Israel, and even to those of the nations (e.g., Zech. 2:15; 7:7; 8:7).[14] Throughout Zechariah's visions, Kessler concludes,

> There is no evidence of priestly disputes or competition, no conflict between political and religious authorities, and no heterodox and ethnically suspect worshipers of Yahweh from whom to keep separate.... Rather, the twin criteria of the correct worship of Yahweh and commensurate ethical behavior form the defining features of the community.[15]

---

12. Boda (2005), 36–40; quote at 40.
13. Kessler (2007), 163.
14. Ibid., 158–59.
15. Ibid., 165.

In other words, Zechariah hopes for a restoration of the religion of YHWH the Creator, somehow possible despite Persian hegemony.

This is not what happened. Instead, a combination of priestly, scribal, and royal elite worked out a deal with Persia and claimed it to be YHWH's will. That not all agreed with this elite theological evaluation is seen in the strong dissent and hope for an authentic, future restoration found in Zechariah 9–14 (known as "Second Zechariah"), as well as from the anonymous prophet known as Third Isaiah. To understand their dissent, we must take a close look at the ideological program of the historical winners.

The Law of Your God and the Law of the King: the Imperially Sponsored Restoration Project of Ezra-Nehemiah

The books of Ezra-Nehemiah,[16] on first reading, appear to continue the story at the end of the Baruch Narrative. Indeed, the first verse of Ezra claims this continuity: "In the first year of King Cyrus of Persia, in order that the word of YHWH by the mouth of Jeremiah might be accomplished, YHWH stirred up the spirit of King Cyrus of Persia." Sara Japhet writes,

> The starting point refers back, with no intermittence, to the destruction of the temple.... Although the author is certainly aware of the time gap... — the gap of 70 years being the essence of Jeremiah's prophecy — there is no consequence in his account of this gap, either historical or theological. Historical time moves from destruction to restoration, from prophecy to fulfillment.... The history of Judah is seen from the perspective of those who left it and are now to return.[17]

It is not at all clear to which "word of YHWH" from Jeremiah the author is referring. Jeremiah, unlike Second Isaiah, never mentions Cyrus or Persia. The verse claims the authority (and theology?) of Jeremiah and announces the fulfillment of "the word of YHWH." These are powerful claims with which to begin a book.

We must note, though, that YHWH *never once speaks directly in the entire narrative*. Similarly, there is no "glory of YHWH" as in Ezekiel or

---

16. Ancient Hebrew texts contained both Ezra and Nehemiah as a single book. Modern scholars have argued that this unity was editorially forged from a variety of different, older texts; see, e.g., Grabbe (1998), 104–5. However, such approaches generally have created more problems then they've solved, including questions of chronology, authorship, historical accuracy, and so forth. These problems demonstrate the futility of seeking to look "behind" these canonical texts for some earlier documents that might provide keys to the historical truth value of the narrative. Instead, I largely follow Eskenazi's (1988) narrative reading, at least insofar as it provides a clear, coherent interpretation of the combined book. See also Japhet (2003 and 2006) for a programmatic reconsideration of the chronology as a "periodization": Ezra 1–6, "the story of the rebuilding of the temple," and Ezra 7–Neh. 13, the "combined Acts of Ezra and Nehemiah" (2006), 496.

17. Japhet (2003), 80–81.

visionary account as in Zechariah. Rather, the focal point of the Ezra-Nehemiah story is the authority of *written texts that claim divine authority*. This is established from the immediately following verses, which report the words of a "written edict"[18] in which Cyrus announces authority from "YHWH, the God of heaven." From the start, we have a king proclaiming divine legitimation for his commandments, a universal element of imperial religion. But biblically, this is something new: a *foreign* king claiming the explicit authority of the God of Israel, but under a more universal (and exalted) epithet (cf. 1:3).

As a text in both the Jewish and Christian canons, Ezra-Nehemiah carries the presumption of being what it purports to be, i.e., an authentic, "inspired" Word.[19] However, given the paradigm we have been exploring throughout this book, Ezra-Nehemiah manifests the "religion of empire" opposed by prophets and others for centuries. And, as we'll see, it was opposed by other canonical voices on just these grounds.[20]

Sara Japhet explains how the overall structure of the book parallels a previous biblical pattern:

> The picture of the Restoration as a time span of two consecutive generations, with a political system characterized by the leadership of two leaders, a layman and a priest, follows a venerable historical and literary model: the Exodus from Egypt, followed by conquest and settlement in the land of Israel.... The first generation of the Restoration is conceived as parallel to the departure from Egypt. The people of Israel left the Babylonian Exile to go back to Jerusalem, with the pronounced purpose of building the temple, similar to the Exodus from Egypt to worship YHWH (Exod. 5:1–3) and build the tabernacle. The second generation is parallel to that of settlement, when Israel consolidated its hold on the land, withstood the temptations represented by the local population, and strove to create a pure and holy community.[21]

This is a highly ideological claim by the writers of Ezra-Nehemiah. It builds on the Josianic compromise that linked Israel's Moses with Jerusalem's Joshua (Josiah) to produce the First Temple state. This "second Exodus" story seeks now to legitimate the building of a new temple state. In this model, the Persian Cyrus is the antithesis of the Egyptian Pharaoh: whereas the latter's "heart was hardened," the former's "spirit is roused"

---

18. *miktav,* used at Exod. 32:16 and Deut. 10:4 for the "tablets" of the Ten Commandments. Also see Isa. 38:9 (Hezekiah); 2 Chron. 21:2; 35:4; 36:22.

19. Although "inspiration" is often named as an attribute of all biblical texts, it was not, in fact, a criterion for inclusion or exclusion of books from the newly official, Christian canon at the Council of Nicaea in 325; see Dungan, 89–90.

20. As far as I have determined, Ezra-Nehemiah is never quoted or referred to anywhere in the New Testament. Neither main character is ever referenced outside the combined book in another canonical text, although "Ezra" becomes the personification of a revelatory message in New Testament times; for an overview of the "Ezra tradition," see Kratz.

21. Japhet (2006), 502–3; see also (1994), 208–16.

Table 21: Structure of Ezra-Nehemiah (according to Tamara Eskenazi)

I. Decree to the community to build the house of God (Ezra 1:1–4)

II. The community builds the house of God according to the decree (Ezra 1:5–Neh. 7:72)

    A. Introduction (Ezra 1:5–6)

    B. First movement: the altar (under King Cyrus) and temple (under King Darius) are built (Ezra 1:7–6:22)

    C. Second movement: the community is built (under King Arta-xerxes) (Ezra 7:1–10:44)

    D. Third movement: "house of God" is built by restoring walls (under King Artaxerxes) (Neh. 1:1–7:5)

    E. Recapitulation: list of returnees (Neh. 7:6–72)

III. The community celebrates the completion of the house of God according to torah (Neh. 8:1–13:31)

---

by YHWH.[22] Further, as shown below, the "people of the land" in both cases are shunned as "foreigners." We can now hear Jeremiah's word as the "inspiration" for this analogy:

> Therefore, the days are surely coming, says YHWH, when it shall no longer be said, "As YHWH lives who brought the people of Israel up out of the land of Egypt," but "As YHWH lives who brought the people of Israel up out of the land of the north and out of all the lands where he had driven them." For I will bring them back to their own land that I gave to their ancestors. (Jer. 16:14–15; again, 23:7–8)

Tamara Cohn Eskenazi has marked a path (Table 21) through the interwoven written documents and first and third person narratives that comprise the essential "plot."[23] YHWH has, through the combined agencies of Persian kings and the former exiles, reestablished "the house of YHWH."

It is a steady progression (although opponents must be overcome) from royal decree to altar, temple, community, and, finally, the establishment of Jerusalem as "house of YHWH"[24] and "holy city" (Neh. 11:1). And just as steadily, the combined authority of YHWH and Persian king advances the action. In fact, the combination might well bring to mind another, earlier

---

22. Ibid., 503–4.

23. Eskenazi (1988), 38–42.

24. In Ezra-Nehemiah, we find the following usage: "house of YHWH" (nine times); "house of God" (thirty-five times), "house of our God" (fourteen times), "house of your/their God" (four times).

combination: that of YHWH and *Judah's* king, Josiah. What we'll find after some closer examination is that Ezra-Nehemiah was designed to be a successor to Deuteronomy, serving a closely parallel function: *the "purification" of Jerusalem and the people via obedience to a written text which presents a compromise between YHWH and empire as divinely given Word.*

As we saw in chapter 12, Josiah's "reform" was grounded in the "finding" of a "book" that established a compromise between the "two religions" of empire and creation/liberation, i.e., a form of Deuteronomy. Moses was the servant of the YHWH who was experienced "outside" Jerusalem (representative of the former northern people of Israel) who was brought into alignment with Jerusalem-centered unity of worship and social practice under the "YHWH-inspired" reign of Josiah (representative of the southern people of Judah). In a similar way, the priest-scribe Ezra came from the exilic community in Babylon to join with the royal governor Nehemiah who comes from the Persian capital, Susa, to combine forces in a way that sought to unite as one people the exiles and the remnant of Judah.

The "successful" outcome of Ezra-Nehemiah is a "holy city" in which everything "inside" is sacred/pure and everything outside is profane/impure. Thus, the ironic result of this narrative journey is *a Jerusalem whose relationship with the surrounding region is precisely the same as that of Babylon.* The routes to the outcome are, of course, very different. Ezra-Nehemiah is no *Enuma Elish*. Yet there are sufficient similarities for Mark Brett to suggest that the final form of Genesis, edited and read during this post-exilic period, expresses a counter-story not only to *Enuma Elish,* but also to Ezra-Nehemiah.[25]

We can only explore a few of the ways in which Ezra-Nehemiah was an imperially supported compromise document. Readers unfamiliar with the text are encouraged to read the entire narrative with sufficient care to be able to discern how these main themes are reinforced in many of the smaller textual details.

Ethnic Exclusion

Eskenazi astutely notes that the primary character in the book is the people of God. Ezra and Nehemiah are not ends in themselves. They are merely instruments for accomplishing what the text presents as YHWH's purpose: the reunification of the holy people in the house of YHWH. The key passage is Ezra 9–10. The altar and temple have been built; it is now time to build the community itself. Ezra enters the story in chapter 7. He arrives with a royal letter of recommendation and high authority from the Persian king, Artaxerxes. The text provides a detailed list of those exiles who accompanied him from Babylon. Immediately thereafter, Ezra is approached by the officials, who inform him:

---

25. Brett (2000), 5; his specific premise is that Genesis throughout opposes Ezra-Nehemiah's ideology of "the holy seed" (Ezra 9:2) as the basis for determining membership in the people of YHWH.

The people of Israel, the priests, and the Levites have not separated themselves from the peoples of the lands with their abominations, from the Canaanites, the Hittites, the Perizzites, the Jebusites, the Ammonites, the Moabites, the Egyptians, and the Amorites. For they have taken some of their daughters as wives for themselves and for their sons. Thus the holy seed has mixed itself with the peoples of the lands, and in this faithlessness the officials and leaders have led the way. (Ezra 9:1–2)

Eskenazi and Judd note elsewhere that the Hebrew is more ambiguous at a key point than the quoted NRSV text, presenting a *simile* rather than *identification:* "the peoples of the land whose abhorrent practices are *like* those of the Canaanites...." This renders much more ambiguous the "ethnicity" of those excluded.[26] As we explored in chapter 13, "ethnicity" is a concept with very soft edges; "Israelite" identity in particular can be defined from many different perspectives. Whoever these people are, Ezra is called upon to respond to their "otherness," characterized here as "abominations" without further specification.

Cultural anthropologist Mary Douglas offers a clear rationale for the existence of these mixed marriages between the former exiles and the locals:

The returnees from Babylon...would have needed to establish kinship links in order to make a claim on their ancestral lands....Without well-established rights to land they would soon run out of funds and perhaps even be reduced to working as labourers....Marriage is the obvious way for the new arrivals to insert themselves into the farming economy.

On the side of the local inhabitants...it would have been a great inducement to a poverty-stricken family to marry one of their daughters to a returned exile claiming to be a cousin, rich, and offering to take care of the family's debts. In those dangerous times he could also provide them with a useful link with the Persian authorities.[27]

Ezra's response to this "news" is to tear his garments, declare a fast, and utter a prayer to YHWH. His words echo throughout with Deuteronomistic phrases and theology.[28] For example, Ezra quotes a commandment from "your [i.e., YHWH's] servants the prophets": "The land that you are entering to possess is a land unclean with the pollutions of the peoples of the lands, with their abominations. They have filled it from end to end with

---

26. Eskenazi and Judd (1994), 268–71.

27. Douglas, 75–76. Note how a similar strategy is adopted in the book of Ruth.

28. Note the parallel Deuteronomic flavor of Ezra's summary of salvation history at Neh. 9:6–31. The highly selective retelling interweaves references to Exodus and Deuteronomy, much as one would expect from a revised compromise text. However, it omits altogether the monarchy, with not a single reference to David or Solomon. The reason, shown below, is that the Davidic covenant has been replaced by reliance on Persian imperial oversight. Ezra-Nehemiah has little interest in reminding people of the eternal promise of an occupant on the throne of David, 2 Sam. 7.

their uncleanness" (9:11). The phrase "entering to possess" is found twenty-four times in the Hebrew Bible: seventeen in Deuteronomy and all but three others in the Deuteronomistic History or here and Nehemiah 9:15, 23. Ezra's next sentence appears to continue v. 11: "Therefore do not give your daughters to their sons, neither take their daughters for your sons, and never seek their peace or prosperity, so that you may be strong and eat the good of the land and leave it for an inheritance to your children forever." However, it almost directly quotes Deuteronomy 7:3: "Do not intermarry with them, giving your daughters to their sons or taking their daughters for your sons." Two verses later in Deuteronomy, we hear how Israel is told to deal with these "peoples of the land": "...break down their altars, smash their pillars, hew down their sacred poles, and burn their idols with fire." This, of course, was precisely what *Josiah* did: "He broke the pillars in pieces, cut down the sacred poles, and covered the sites with human bones" (2 Kings 23:14).

Ezra's "solution" is less violent than that of Deuteronomy or Josiah. Having completed his prayer, he is approached by Shecaniah,[29] who counsels:

> So now let us make a covenant with our God to send away all these wives and their children, according to the counsel of my lord and of those who tremble at the commandment of our God; and let it be done according to the law. Take action, for it is your duty, and we are with you; be strong, and do it. (10:3–4)

However, even Deuteronomy does not support this particular measure. For example, we hear: "You shall *not* abhor any of the Egyptians, because you were an alien residing in their land. The children of the third generation that are born to them may be admitted to the assembly of YHWH" (Deut. 23:7–8). Ezra's condemnation of "foreign" marriages includes Judean-Egyptian families, against Deuteronomy. Ezra nonetheless goes to the returned exiles with the proposal and it is accepted.[30] The blaming of the problem on the foreign wives recalls the Deuteronomistic History's judgment on Solomon. It was not for being a self-aggrandizing empire builder, but for allowing his foreign wives to "turn away his heart" that the narrator claimed the kingdom would be torn away from his descendants (1 Kings 11).

---

29. Douglas, 77, observing Shecaniah's relative youth (his father was still alive to sign the pledge document, Ezra 10:26), states "Ezra's constituency would have been the younger, the men of the future." In this way, they parallel Rehoboam's supporters, 1 Kings 12:10–14.

30. Smith-Christopher (1994), 264, argues from sociological theory that the Persians may have had reasons to encourage mixed marriages (as practiced by their elite) and thus, Ezra's "breakup of foreign marriages must be understood as an act of political defiance." However, the article does not directly address the question of Persian control of the province's leadership for their economic and political advantage.

We might pause where the text does not to imagine the depth and breadth of human suffering occasioned by this action. Whole families were broken up, leaving defenseless women and children bereft and abandoned. An apparently integrated, multicultural social fabric was torn in shreds; and for what? Was this truly the will of YHWH? As Douglas notes, many of the priests "would be on the side of assimilation and toleration of foreigners. Though it was all in ruins, their tradition taught them how much the prosperity of Judah and the wealth of the temple had depended on Jerusalem's cosmopolitan status."[31] The patriarch Joseph was said to have an Egyptian wife, with no hint of criticism.[32] In fact, Joseph's half-Egyptian sons become the tribal ancestors, Manasseh and Ephraim (Gen. 41:50–52), of the territory known in Ezra-Nehemiah's time as "Samaria." As always, however, the religion of empire reaches "peace" and "unity" at the expense of the suffering of those excluded. Voices of protest abound, though directly from within the Bible.[33]

The Ezra-Nehemiah perspective also excluded people of the former northern kingdom of Israel who had become integrated with the peoples brought in by the Assyrians to dilute local solidarity (2 Kings 17:24–41).[34] We are expected to recall the Deuteronomistic editorial evaluation of these people: "these nations worshiped YHWH, but also served their carved images; to this day their children and their children's children continue to do as their ancestors did" (2 Kings 17:41).

Not surprisingly, given this background, the narrator introduces these people as "the adversaries of Judah and Benjamin" (Ezra 4:1).[35] Yet they come south not as troublemakers, but desiring to participate in the project: "They approached Zerubbabel and the heads of families and said to them, 'Let us build with you, for we worship your God as you do, and we have been sacrificing to him ever since the days of King Esar-haddon of Assyria who brought us here'" (4:2). The visit generates the only direct speech from Zerubbabel: "You shall have no part with us in building a house to our God; but we alone will build to YHWH, the God of Israel, as King Cyrus of Persia has commanded us." Note that Zerubbabel grounds his position not on torah, a Word from YHWH or even a charge of idolatry against the visitors, but on the *command of the Persian king.*

The short-term result is that what could have been a joyously communal building project became an occasion for building hostility and creating enemies. The petitioners engaged in a campaign to oppose the building of

31. Douglas, 65.
32. However, the Joseph story may well have been composed in the Hellenistic era, after the fall of the Persian empire, and therefore have been unknown to the authors of Ezra-Nehemiah.
33. Cf. Blenkinsopp (2009), 114–15.
34. Bedford, 53–56.
35. Fried (2006) points out that these people have been appointed by Persia as officials of the neighboring satrapy; cf. Neh. 4:7–13. See also Knoppers (2007) for an extensive discussion of whether these "enemies" are from "without" or "within."

the temple that included bribery of local officials and a letter written to King Artaxerxes[36] that warned the Persians that the temple, if rebuilt, would become a site of nationalistic rebellion against the Persians (Ezra 4:4–16). The campaign successfully convinced the king to put a stop to the project, which, predictably, turned short-term hostility into long-term ethnic hatred.

According to Ezra-Nehemiah, it was at this point that Haggai and Zechariah began to preach to inspire the people into rebuilding. How different is this putative context from what we heard in the canonical books of the prophets themselves. Instead of a question simply of prudent financial timing, Ezra-Nehemiah presents an ethnic battle, interpreted politically by the Persian king, as the reason for the delay in construction.

In Nehemiah 2, we find an incident structurally parallel to Ezra 4.[37] The newly arrived Nehemiah, supposedly coming to his former homeland as an act of piety to help construct the city walls, was mocked and ridiculed by a coalition of Sanballat the Horonite, Tobiah the Ammonite, and Geshem the Arab. They came to Nehemiah and asked him a question that takes up the theme from Ezra 4: "Are you rebelling against the king?" Nehemiah's response echoes Ezra's: "The God of heaven is the one who will give us success, and we his servants are going to start building; but you have no share or claim or historic right in Jerusalem" (Neh. 2:19–20). This coalition did not seek to participate in the building project, but rather to stop it in order to prevent Jerusalem from becoming a local, rival power backed by Persia. They continue to threaten the construction workers by enlisting the support of the Samaritan army. This led Nehemiah to post military guards and prepare the people for the possibility of war (4:16–23). Thus, the claim of divine (royal) authority to exclude has generated both ethnic tensions and international saber-rattling.

Military Security, Economic Exploitation, and Oppressive Violence against the Poor

Amid this tense situation, Nehemiah became aware of an "outcry [*tsa'aqat*] of the people" expressing a litany of protests against rampant social injustice, including the need to borrow money at interest to pay the king's tax (5:4), from which the temple elite have been expressly exempted by imperial edict (Ezra 7:24). Their children are being enslaved and raped,[38] their property mortgaged, and then foreclosed on to pay debt to the elite. The Hebrew *tsa'aqat* expresses a plea for YHWH's help against oppression.[39] However, it is not YHWH who responds but Nehemiah. He does not pray

---

36. Scholars note that the text appears chronologically confused at this point, given that Darius preceded Artaxerxes. See, e.g., Grabbe (1998), 21.

37. Eskenazi (1988), 79.

38. Hebrew, *nikbashot* (nifal), is otherwise used for "subduing" the land, Num. 32:22, 29; Josh. 18:1; 1 Chron. 22:18.

39. E.g., Gen. 18:21, 19:13; Exod. 3:7, 9.

for guidance, but, "thinking it over," calls together the "nobles and officials" and upbraids them for "taking interest from your own people." As Kenneth Hoglund notes,

> Nehemiah's response was not to exempt the population from the burden of these imperial obligations in consideration of the circumstances but to alleviate the short-term impact of this economic crisis by forcing lenders, including himself (5:10), to forgo the demand of interest payments and pledges.[40]

Nehemiah then singled out the priests to take an oath promising compliance with his orders, probably because their imperial tax-exemption had implicated them in the economic suffering of their own kin.[41] Furthermore, Nehemiah does and says nothing about the sexual violence against and enslavement of Judean children. Those injustices apparently come with the imperial territory, and seem of little moral concern to Nehemiah and those he represents.

The text sequence allows us to infer a direct relationship between this newly revealed systemic injustice and the threat of war resulting from the exclusion of neighboring peoples. Yet we are certainly expected by the authors to read Nehemiah's actions positively.[42] It is only by recognizing that his behavior embodies the religion of empire that we can see the social and economic havoc that Nehemiah's project entails.

In the passages we have examined, it appears characters are acting on their own to exclude and to exploit others. Zerubbabel, Ezra, and Nehemiah each seem only to consult other locals in reaching their decisions. If we take a step back to look at the big picture, however, we can see that *the entire Ezra-Nehemiah project is a Persian-sponsored and supported program.* A few examples illustrate systemic Persian involvement in the project from beginning to end, not out of Persian benevolence, but rather, out of imperial self-interest.

Persia's Motivation for Rebuilding Jerusalem

We have already seen that the book of Ezra opens with an announcement of King Cyrus's edict allowing the project to begin. Zerubbabel serves as the Persian provincial governor, even if some people may hope that his Davidic roots express YHWH's will for an eventual war of independence from Persia. The narrator summarizes the successful completion of the first movement of the project by stating: "So the elders of the Judeans built and prospered, through the prophesying of the prophet Haggai and Zechariah son of Iddo. They finished their building by command of the God of Israel and by decree

---

40. Hoglund, 214.
41. Blenkinsopp (2009), 114.
42. Nehemiah 5 has often been cited as an example of people in official positions responding favorably to the cries of the oppressed for social justice, as well as for a surprisingly wide variety of positive pastoral applications; see generally Williams (2002).

of Cyrus, Darius, and King Artaxerxes of Persia" (6:14). The "decree" is singular although the kings are plural, because we are to understand the series of monarchs embodying Persian support over time.[43]

Ezra appears in chapter 7 with a "pedigree"[44] of fourteen generations.[45] However, as Eskenazi observes, naming "Ezra first in conjunction with the king of Persia (Ezra 7:1) and then in conjunction with Aaron the first priest (Ezra 7:5b–6a), the book literally flanks Ezra and his mission by the Persian king and the first priest."[46] Ezra is a "scribe skilled in the torah of Moses that YHWH the God of Israel had given." Thus, he is both priest and scribe.

This description echoes a previous Deuteronomic juxtaposition of priest and scribe: Shaphan the scribe and Hilkiah the priest who "found" a book of the torah in "the house of YHWH" during Josiah's reign (2 Kings 22:8–13). The occasion for this finding, we recall, was the transfer of funds to enable the repair of "the house of YHWH" (22:5–7). The money was given to general contractors and specific craftsmen, including carpenters and masons. Earlier in the book of Ezra, we were told that the foundation for the new "house of YHWH" was built by money provided by King Cyrus of Persia and given to *masons and carpenters* (Ezra 3:7). The only other mention of masons and carpenters in the Bible outside of 1–2 Chronicles[47] is just after David consolidated royal power over Israel and Judah: "King Hiram of Tyre sent messengers to David, along with cedar trees, and *carpenters and masons* who built David a house" (2 Sam. 5:11). Later, this same Hiram supported Solomon's temple building project, promising, "I will fulfill all your needs in the matter of cedar.... There was peace between Hiram and Solomon; and the two of them cut a covenant" (1 Kings 5:8, 12). And sure enough, Ezra states that money was given to "the *Tyrians* to bring cedar trees" (3:7). Thus, all four "house building/repair" projects are connected, not only to each other via "carpenters and masons," but to royal sponsorship. All but Josiah's are linked to *foreign* sponsorship. Ezra, as combined priest-scribe, is rightly situated to cut an implied covenant with King Artaxerxes to continue Persian imperial support.

Indeed, Ezra arrived in Yehud with a glowing letter of introduction from Artaxerxes, granting him "all the silver and gold that you shall find in the whole province of Babylonia" for sacrifices at the temple and "whatever else is required for the house of your God" (7:16, 20). The king gave Ezra and his colleagues carte blanche to spend this imperial grant in "whatever way seems good to you... according to the will of your God" (7:18). Ezra was authorized to appoint magistrates and judges to assure that all the people

---

43. Eskenazi (1988), 41.

44. Ibid., 62, notes how this word is more appropriate to describe the list of Ezra's ancestors in Ezra 7:1–5 than "genealogy" because it is a matter of establishing his credentials as one who will lead the project at this point.

45. Cf. Matt. 1, the "pedigree" of Jesus in three times fourteen generations.

46. Ibid., 63.

47. Cf. 1 Chron. 14:1; 22:15; 2 Chron. 24:12.

"obey the law [*dat*] of your God and the law [*dat*] of the king," under penalty of imprisonment, banishment, confiscation of goods, or even death (7:26).

In other words, Artaxerxes sets up the priest-scribe Ezra as the king's own man in the province. All the people have to do is "obey the law of the king" along with the law of God. It is not torah, however, that Artaxerxes enjoins as binding under penalty of death, but the king's *dat*.[48] Josef Wiesehöfer explains that *dat* is:

> not...a kind of "imperial law" or an imperial collection of royally authorized local regulations but has to be taken as a term for every royal decision, every order published by the king. The personal character of this royal law or ordinance is stressed time and again, and it even seems to replace the concept of a divine law.[49]

As Eskenazi states, "Ezra-Nehemiah envisions no tension between the two.... Heavenly ruler and earthly ruler collaborate for the sake of the house of God."[50] But is there really no conflict between YHWH's law and the commands of an imperial monarch? The religion of empire is always grounded in precisely this principle: that royal edict *is* divine law.

Our final illustration of the Persian-Judean collaboration is the scene conveying the impetus for Nehemiah's arrival in the province. We have observed Nehemiah exercising authority over the nobles and other Jerusalem elite, organizing the wall building project, establishing military security, and demanding that the elite relent from at least some of their oppressive practices. Who was this Nehemiah? What was the basis of his authority? How, within the wider narrative of Ezra-Nehemiah, was he related to the priest-scribe Ezra?

The book of Nehemiah opens in the first person, with Nehemiah speaking from his home in the Persian capital of Susa.[51] Joseph Blenkinsopp notes that such ancient first-person narratives were

> for the most part, propagandistic and apologetic, and only occasionally anecdotal. The best-known examples are Mesopotamian royal inscriptions in the first person dealing with military campaigns, the building and dedicating of temples, and the like.[52]

Nehemiah was cupbearer to the Persian king, i.e., a member of the royal cabinet.[53] A Judean delegation arrived in Susa for unstated reasons, and

---

48. See also Esther 3:8.
49. Wiesehöfer, 87.
50. Eskenazi (1988), 77.
51. Cf. Esther 1:2; Dan. 8:2, which also locate their protagonists in the Persian capital city.
52. Blenkinsopp (2009), 93.
53. Although Grabbe (2004a), 295, suggests that Nehemiah is "a glorified waiter," the textual evidence is strongly against this conclusion. Nehemiah's achieving an audience with the king and demanding substantial authority (and funding) and his eventual appointment as

Nehemiah asked his "brothers" about Jerusalem. They report that "the survivors there in the province who escaped captivity are in great trouble and shame; the wall of Jerusalem is broken down, and its gates have been destroyed by fire" (1:3). This came as surprising bad news to Nehemiah, who apparently was unaware of conditions in his ancestral homeland. After praying aloud,[54] he approached the king with a bold proposal: that he be allowed leave to go to Judah to "rebuild it" (2:5). The king granted his request and, as with Ezra, provided a letter authorizing imperial resources for the project. Nehemiah's travels were accompanied by an imperial military escort. When this stranger arrived in Jerusalem, he made a night inspection of the city and then gathered the elite to urge upon them a commitment to the building project. They immediately agreed (2:13–18).

Why would a Persian king sponsor this building project and send a trusted member of his cabinet to oversee it? The answer, despite the superficial ruse of Nehemiah's pious petition, should be clear: the *reconstruction of Jerusalem was a Persian-sponsored project all along*. Kenneth Hoglund provides powerful historical and archaeological evidence showing Persia's motivations for initiating and supporting this project through to the end, despite the opposition of local peoples. As we have seen, in the time of Haggai and Zechariah under the reign of the Persian king Darius, the empire had just begun to stabilize its control over its distant territories. However, such imperial control rarely remains stable for long, as people yearning for freedom and self-rule seek ways, covert[55] or overt, to loosen the imperial hold. By the mid-fifth century, the status quo had been badly shaken. Eric Meyers summarizes the situation:

> As Darius set his political ambitions more and more to the north ... the Greek cities of Ionia and Cyprus declared their intention to block him. Athens soon joined.... In 490 Darius was defeated at the battle of Marathon, and in 480 his son Xerxes I and the Persians were defeated at the battle of Salamis in Cyprus. In 478 the Delian League was established to liberate many Greek cities from Persian control. Against this backdrop, therefore, it is not surprising that Babylonia and Egypt sought to regain their independence.... It is thus not surprising that all of this had repercussions in Palestine.[56]

Hoglund shows how the Egyptian Revolt led to the Persian decision to establish a strong military base in Jerusalem.[57] He states:

---

governor of the province hardly suggest his original role was as menial servant. See also the only other biblical cupbearer, whose dream Joseph interpreted in Pharaoh's court, who is referred to as an "official," Gen. 40:2.

54. Nehemiah frequently prays aloud, but we never hear YHWH respond.

55. See Scott (1987 and 1992) for the often unnoticed yet effective forms of hidden resistance to empire over the centuries.

56. Meyers (1995), 715.

57. Hoglund 97–205.

Nehemiah's request relates to the use of timber supplies for the construction of a fortress or citadel to be located adjacent to the temple to the north of the most concentrated portion of the city. Presumably manned by imperial troops, the citadel not only would serve to protect a vulnerable portion of the city, but also would place a concentration of imperial force just outside the city where it would be noticed by the inhabitants of Jerusalem.... The rarity of such urban fortification systems in the mid-fifth century should serve to highlight the unusual nature of Nehemiah's request and the imperial court's willingness to permit the refortification of Jerusalem.[58]

In other words, it was *Persia's own strategic military needs* that led the empire to finance, oversee, and carry out the rebuilding of Jerusalem. Much like the United States establishing a naval base at Pearl Harbor in the occupied territory of Hawaii against the potential threat of Japan,[59] the Persians had their own incentive to support the reestablishment of both Jerusalem and the authority of the temple elite. Hoglund observes,

One of the hallmarks of the Achaemenid [i.e., the reigning Persian dynasty] imperial administration was its flexibility in the face of established local customs. Rather than superimposing a rigid set of imperial laws over a subject territory, the imperial system sought to work within the legal structures already in place. This process required a class of imperial functionaries possessing legal expertise, a group that appears in various documents as the "royal judges" who are charged with the application of the imperial law within more localized settings.[60]

The episodes we've explored fit within this context. Nehemiah's show of ancestral piety masked his imperial commission to oversee the completion of Jerusalem's fortifications for Persia's military advantage. The text, having initially suggested Nehemiah's "religious" motivation, acknowledges that, sometime along the way, he became the Persian-appointed governor of the province (Neh. 5:14). Eskenazi notes, "One senses a sleight of hand not unlike that in the Bathsheba-Nathan scene in 1 Kings 1."[61] Nehemiah claimed his authority precisely when the wall-building threatened to come to a halt due to rebellion of the oppressed construction workers. Nehemiah's response was not to establish torah justice, but rather to assure that the imperial project would be completed. The elite general contractors understood what was at stake and immediately agreed to Nehemiah's demand to stop

---

58. Ibid., 209–11. He also notes that the letter written by the Samaritans in opposition to an unauthorized rebuilding project, recorded at Ezra 4:7–23, underscores the unusual nature of Nehemiah's request (211–12).

59. Herring, 317; see also Kinzer, 9–30, for the larger story of the U.S. overthrow of the indigenous Hawaiian government.

60. Hoglund, 234–35. See also Wiesehöfer, 86.

61. Eskenazi (1988), 149.

taking interest. Their long-term commitment to Persian largesse outweighed their interest in short-term exploitation of local workers.

Ezra, for his part, was also a key component of the imperial project. His appointment of judges and magistrates served the Persian goal of building up a local trusted elite to maintain order so that taxes could be collected.[62] Joachim Shaper states,

> The Jerusalem temple administration acted as the interface between the tax-paying population of Judah and the Persian government.... The collaboration between the central authorities and the temple hierarchy seems to have been smooth and efficient; the needs of both partners were duly catered for.[63]

Ezra's commission included establishing obedience to Persian law. Behind his façade of collaborative leadership, Ezra oversaw an imperial policy of exclusion of ethnic outsiders and privileged, tax-exempt status for the temple elite, all backed up by the threat of extreme punishment, including death, to lawbreakers and resisters.

One of Ezra's most dramatic and oppressive actions was to demand the break-up of ethnically mixed marriages among the returned exiles.[64] We also see within Ezra-Nehemiah detailed lists of the acceptable returnee families (Ezra 7 and Neh. 2), which serve as "citizenship" documentation for the members of the new community. Why would Persia want to establish ethnic purity within Jerusalem? Again, Hoglund provides the answer:

> Among the administrative requirements of an imperial system is the need to integrate various groups within a subject territory into the imperial structure. This could be done by utilizing pre-existent group denominators such as kinship, cult or trade, or it could be accomplished by groups that transcended existing denominators. Often such groups possessed an economic role within the imperial system, ensuring the group perception that their self-interest was bound up in the well-being of the empire.... This requirement for group identity was more pressing when an imperial system was engaged in the use of deportation and resettlement as a means of political control over a subject region.... Banishment from the group as a penalty would deny the possibility of regaining access to the rights and privileges enjoyed by the group as a unit.... There is clear evidence from Mesopotamia that the

---

62. Hoglund, 236.

63. Shaper, 537.

64. Williamson, 479, discusses the extent to which the Ezra-Nehemiah regime reorganized the foundations of social life away from the ancient "father's houses" (*bayit 'abot*), concluding that "the social structure of early Persian period Judah was more mixed than has generally been thought, representing within the single community elements whose social orientation was based on the developed 'fathers' house,' as well as elements who continued to reckon themselves by households grouped according to locality." However, he does note that the clan-solidarity of the *mishpachot* seems to have been lost between the "fathers' houses" and the "combination of regional authority and social hierarchy" (480).

Achaemenid court practiced a form of imperial domain, treating land gained by conquest as imperial territory and disposing of it to courtiers and various officials.... Thus any group of returning exiles ... were not reclaiming a right to land tenure based on past land allotment systems but were being allowed to reside in a homeland by the graciousness of the empire.

Such systems of allocating territories to dependent populations will work as long as the imperial system is capable of maintaining some clarity as to who is allowed access to a particular region and who is not. Intermarriage among various groups would tend to smudge the demarcation between the groups.

In this light, the concerns expressed by Ezra and Nehemiah over the practice of intermarriage within the community would be in keeping with the effort of the imperial court to enhance a degree of control over the Levantine region. Ezra's legal reforms and Nehemiah's anger over the continuing presence of intermarriage would represent a perception of the danger such activity presented to the continuation of the *qahal* [Heb. for "assembly"] in Yehud.[65]

Ezra-Nehemiah does not deny imperial involvement in the building of "the house of YHWH." Rather, it not only acknowledges it from the beginning, but claims that Persian authority is an expression of YHWH's will. Note Hoglund's characterization of the Persian understanding of the relationship between the people of Yehud and the land: it is not theirs because of a claim to right but because of "the graciousness of the empire." This perspective is far from the understanding in Genesis of the land as YHWH's gift via the covenant with Abraham. But within the "religion of empire," the Ezra-Nehemiah viewpoint makes perfect sense. It is, as we've seen, in deep continuity with the imperial projects of David, Solomon, and Josiah. Its "holy city" has no local king and little interest in the Davidic covenant because the Persian monarch serves as a divinely authorized substitute. Its seemingly inclusive and even "democratic"[66] society is such only within the systemic exclusion of whole populations and the legally privileged status of some groups over others even within the society, much like the American Founders intoned that "all men are created equal" while excluding most of the population from political participation.

Ezra and Nehemiah represent the two groups collaborating to facilitate the compromise with empire. Ezra, priest, scribe, and member of the

---

65. Hoglund, 237–40. Cf. Smith-Christopher (1994), 262–64, who argues that the Persians, and the Greeks after them, practiced mixed marriages and encouraged subject peoples to imitate them, in which case "the breakup of foreign marriages must be understood ... as an act of political defiance" (264). However, Ezra's other actions hardly seem in defiance of Persia's goals. See also Blenkinsopp (2009), 68, 144–45, who sees Ezra's policy as an elaboration of Ezek. 44:9's call for ritual ethnic purity among participants in the temple cult.

66. Eskenazi (1988), 70, praises the "democratic" leadership of Ezra.

exilic community in Babylon, embodied the temple elite. Their roots, as we've seen, were in the First Temple monarchy. Their role was to establish YHWH's approval for the compromise. Nehemiah, royal cupbearer and attendant to the Persian king in Susa, embodied the Persian side. He carried the imperial fist hidden within Ezra's velvet glove. His immediate root is the tradition of previous imperially appointed governors such as the Babylonian Gedaliah. His role was to translate Persia's program into relationships "on the ground" in Yehud.[67] The book of Revelation extrapolates these representative roles into the seductive "whore" and the violent "beast" that together embody empire.

Ezra-Nehemiah expresses the official view of the new Jerusalem elite at the time of the restoration.[68] However, the text is never recalled within Hebrew Scripture or the New Testament. The final editors of the biblical canon included several other narratives, however, that would allow readers to hear Ezra-Nehemiah's claims within a framework of widespread resistance in YHWH's name.

"Do Not Let the Foreigner Joined to YHWH say, 'YHWH Will Surely Separate Me from His People'": The Dissenting Voice of Third Isaiah

After Ezra-Nehemiah's claim to YHWH's authority for a system grounded in violence, exploitation of the poor, and ethnic exclusion, the voice of the anonymous prophet known as Third Isaiah comes as a breath of fresh air. Isaiah 56–66 takes on the Ezra-Nehemiah program point-by-point. We find in these chapters an utterly different way of being bound as a people. It proclaims a religion in the name of YHWH with roots deep in creation and the exodus covenant and branches extending to the gospels of the New Testament.[69]

Norman Gottwald has shown how the entire unit forms an extended chiasm (see the following page). It is a tightly structured, systemic critique of the Ezra-Nehemiah accommodation to empire. Examination of a few passages illustrates how Third Isaiah claimed the direct authority of YHWH for its support of a social order opposite the one imposed by Ezra-Nehemiah.

---

67. Blenkinsopp (2009), 83–85 suggests, based on the likely ethnicity of names listed in Ezra 2, that the "exilic" group may in fact have not been descendants of previous generations of Judahites, but were part of an imperially sanctioned "process of colonization" that sought "an adopted homeland rather than a return."

68. Although the final canonical form may have continued to develop until Hasmonean times; see, e.g., Blenkinsopp (2009), 89–90.

69. Cohen (2006), 142, refers to the group behind Third Isaiah as a "proto-sect," anticipating the full-blown sectarian groups that developed during the Hasmonean period: Pharisees, Sadducees, and Essenes.

A: 56:1–8: salvation to foreigners
  B: 56:9–57:13: indictment of wicked leaders
    C: 57:14–21: salvation for the people
      D: 58:1–14: indictment of corrupt worship
        E: 59:1–15a: lament / confession over sins of the people
          F: 59:15b–20: theophany of judgment / redemption
            G: 60–62: proclamation of redemption
          F^1: 63:1–6: theophany of judgment / redemption
        E^1: 63:7–64:12: lament / confession over sins of the people
      D^1: 65:1–16: indictment of corrupt worship
    C^1: 65:17–25: salvation for the people (plus new heavens / earth)
  B^1: 66:1–6: indictment of wicked leaders and exclusion of faithful
    from cult
A^1: 66:7–24: salvation to foreigners[70]

Ethnic Inclusion

Ezra-Nehemiah sought to *exclude* those who could not formally prove their heritage as members of the exiled community; Third Isaiah begins by *including any* who seek to "join themselves to YHWH":

> Do not let the foreigner joined to YHWH say, "YHWH will surely separate me from his people," ... For thus says YHWH ... the foreigners who join themselves to YHWH, to minister to him, to love the name of YHWH, and to be his servants, all who keep the sabbath, and do not profane it, and hold fast my covenant — these I will bring to my holy mountain, and make them joyful in my house of prayer; their burnt offerings and their sacrifices will be accepted on my altar; for my house shall be called a house of prayer for all peoples. (Isa. 56:3–6)

The inclusion of "foreigners" is a refrain throughout Third Isaiah.[71] For example, "Foreigners shall build up your walls, and their kings shall minister to you" (60:10), and "Strangers shall stand and feed your flocks, foreigners shall till your land and dress your vines" (61:5). The specific Hebrew term *ben-nakhar*, literally, "sons of foreignness," is found only nineteen times in the Hebrew Bible, five in Third Isaiah, but also at Nehemiah 9:2: "Then those of Israelite descent separated themselves from all foreigners."

Third Isaiah anticipates a time when the house of YHWH will be a "house of prayer for all peoples," a text "fulfilled" explicitly at Mark 11:17 and implicitly throughout the multicultural vision of the book of Revelation.[72]

---

70. Gottwald (1985), 508.
71. See Mayer for the fascinating story of the decades-long resistance to the exclusion of African Americans and women from participation in American "democracy" led by William Lloyd Garrison on biblical grounds, especially focused on Isaiah 56.
72. E.g., Rev. 5:9; 14:6.

The criteria for inclusion will not be ethnic, but *covenantal*. Unlike the wrenching break-up of families mandated in Ezra-Nehemiah, Third Isaiah's vision leads to joy for all.

True Worship: The End of Social Injustice

Ezra-Nehemiah includes several scenes of individual and communal prayer and worship. What stands out, however, is that it is all one-directional. YHWH *never is heard responding* to these entreaties and celebrations. As we'll see, Ezra-Nehemiah was the leading edge of a movement away from direct experience of YHWH's Voice in favor of study of written texts. Third Isaiah, however, not only claims to be the direct expression of YHWH's Voice, but proposes a *dialogue* between YHWH and worshipers who are not hearing YHWH's response to their prayers and fasting (Isa. 58). The juxtaposition is immediate and sharp:

> "Why do we fast, but you do not see? Why humble ourselves, but you do not notice?" Look, you serve your own interest on your fast day, and oppress all your workers. Look, you fast only to quarrel and to fight and to strike with a wicked fist. Such fasting as you do today will not make your voice heard on high.... Is not this the fast that I choose: to loose the bonds of injustice, to undo the thongs of the yoke, to let the oppressed go free, and to break every yoke? Is it not to share your bread with the hungry, and bring the homeless poor into your house; when you see the naked, to cover them, and not to hide yourself from your own kin? Then your light shall break forth like the dawn, and your healing shall spring up quickly; your vindicator shall go before you, the glory of YHWH shall be your rear guard. Then you shall call, and YHWH will answer; you shall cry for help, and he will say, "Here I am." (Isa. 58:3–9)

The situation described here correlates with Nehemiah 5: workers systematically oppressed by those who claim to be "pure" and "holy." The passage goes on to connect the practice of social justice with successful rebuilding of the temple:

> Your ancient ruins shall be rebuilt; you shall raise up the foundations of many generations; you shall be called the repairer of the breach, the restorer of streets to live in. If you refrain from trampling the sabbath, from pursuing your own interests on my holy day; if you call the sabbath a delight and the holy day of YHWH honorable; if you honor it, not going your own ways, serving your own interests, or pursuing your own affairs. (Isa. 58:12–13)

The rebuilding is explicitly conditioned on the practice of *true* holiness. In place of Ezra, Nehemiah and other imperially appointed officials in authority over Yehud, Third Isaiah says, in YHWH's Voice: "I will appoint Peace as your overseer and Righteousness as your taskmaster" (60:17).[73] Instead of the outcry of oppressed workers and their families, "Violence shall no more be heard in your land, devastation or destruction within your borders; you shall call your walls Salvation, and your gates Praise" (60:18).

A few verses later at the chiastic center of Third Isaiah's proclamation, the narrative shifts from the Voice of YHWH to the voice of an unnamed person upon whom the spirit of Lord YHWH has come. We hear:

> YHWH has anointed me; he has sent me to bring good news to the oppressed, to bind up the brokenhearted, to proclaim liberty to the captives, and release to the prisoners; to proclaim the year of YHWH's favor, and the day of vengeance of our God; to comfort all who mourn; to provide for those who mourn in Zion — to give them a garland instead of ashes, the oil of gladness instead of mourning, the mantle of praise instead of a faint spirit. They will be called oaks of righteousness, the planting of YHWH, to display his glory. They shall build up the ancient ruins, they shall raise up the former devastations; they shall repair the ruined cities, the devastations of many generations. (Isa. 61:1–4)

It is to this text that Jesus turns, according to Luke, to proclaim his "mission statement" (Luke 4:16–21).[74] Its promise of comfort to the afflicted and joy to the mourning echoes throughout Third Isaiah, where words for "joy," "gladness," and "rejoicing" are a constant refrain, in place of the sadness one can imagine the Ezra-Nehemiah regime evoked.[75]

In a remarkable passage, the prophet directly confronts the supporters of the imperial compromise:

> Hear the word of YHWH, *you who tremble at his word* [*hacharedim 'el-debarov*]: Your own people who hate you and reject you for my name's sake have said, "Let YHWH be glorified, so that we may see your joy"; but it is they who shall be put to shame. Listen, an uproar from the city! A voice from the temple! The voice of YHWH, dealing retribution to his enemies! (Isa. 66:5–6)

"Those who tremble" at the word are mentioned elsewhere in the Hebrew Bible only in Ezra:

> So now let us make a covenant with our God to send away all these wives and their children, according to the counsel of my lord and of

---

73. Hebrew *pequddah,* "overseer," recalls the Levites serving in this function, Ezek. 44:9; Third Isaiah never mentions priestly or Levitical offices, referring to the people liberated from oppression as "priests of YHWH" (Isa. 61:6). Hebrew *ngs,* "taskmaster," recalls and contrasts with Pharaoh's taskmasters, Exod. 3:7; 5:6–14.

74. Luke omits the prophetic announcement of the building up of ancient ruins, however, because for Luke, as for the other evangelists, the time of Jerusalem and the temple has passed. Jesus himself embodies the "house of YHWH"; cf. John 2:13–22.

75. E.g., Isa. 60:5; 61:10; 62:5; 65:13–19; 66:5–14.

those who tremble at the commandment [*hacharedim bemitsvat*] of our God; and let it be done according to the law. (Ezra 10:3; see also 9:4)

The prophet proclaims that "those who tremble" in support of the imperial program are the "enemies" of YHWH, who will put *them* to shame for their oppression of the poor and exclusion of" foreigners."[76]

Third Isaiah's voice, of course, did not prevail. The Ezra-Nehemiah coalition successfully oversaw the imperial project and established themselves as the new temple elite. Third Isaiah's lack of immediate success, though, did not break his spirit or his trust in YHWH. Instead, he envisioned a time in which YHWH's will would truly be done. Taking up the cosmic imagery of Second Isaiah, he proclaimed a God whose reign extends far beyond mere earthly Jerusalem: "Heaven is my throne and the earth is my footstool; what is the house that you would build for me?" (66:1). This Creator God and King will himself generate a much greater building project:

> For I am about to create new heavens and a new earth; the former things shall not be remembered or come to mind. But be glad and rejoice forever in what I am creating; for I am about to create Jerusalem as a joy, and its people as a delight. I will rejoice in Jerusalem, and delight in my people; no more shall the sound of weeping be heard in it, or the cry of distress. (65:17–19)

Third Isaiah's vision of a divinely built New Jerusalem is one of many in which seers, in deep, intimate relationship with YHWH and solidarity with YHWH's suffering people, express trust that a time will indeed come when YHWH's will *is* done, on earth as it is in heaven.[77]

Genesis for a New Generation

Texts are written primarily for their immediate audiences. Over time, as situations change, most texts become obsolete, valuable only as artifacts of an increasingly distant past. However, some texts continue to speak across generations, either because their themes transcend their immediate circumstances of origin or because people see new situations to be analogous to the text's original context. Theologian David Tracy describes the qualities of "classic" texts that continue to speak across time and cultural distance.[78] *Religious* classic texts generate *knowing of YHWH* in new cultural settings. The book of Genesis fits within this category.

---

76. Cf. Blenkinsopp (2009), 199–200, who reads Third Isaiah's *charedim* as a different group from Ezra's. This interpretation does not take account of how Third Isaiah systematically attacks the Ezra-Nehemiah perspective and its supporters in the Name of YHWH.

77. For the Jeremian roots of Third Isaiah's "new heavens" vision, see Halpern (1998), 635–36.

78. Tracy.

We saw in Part I how Genesis narrated a "counter-story" for its original audience in Babylonian Exile. We cannot know with certainty when Genesis reached its final canonical form. It is likely, though, that it continued to be a living text well into the Persian period, if not beyond. Whether freshly edited for a new situation or resonating in new ways for a succeeding generation, many of the Genesis stories counter Ezra-Nehemiah as much as Babylon's *Enuma Elish*.

Key is the consistent message in Genesis of YHWH's blessed relationship with foreigners. A few examples illustrate how Genesis might have been heard within Persian Yehud.

At the conclusion of the Garden of Eden story, the narrator explains the social consequence of humanity as male and female: "Therefore a man leaves his father and his mother and clings to his wife, and they become one flesh" (Gen. 2:24). Mark Brett comments:

> In a context where men were being urged to leave their foreign wives, however, the peculiar strength of this language may well be explained by reading the verse as suggesting a priority of commitments: the kinship bond with the wife stands above that of the parents, and in this sense, marriage comes before bloodlines. The notion of the "holy seed" [in Ezra 9:2] suggests the reverse — that marriage has to conform to the bloodlines.[79]

Repeatedly, Genesis dramatizes the dominant ideology that blood ("holy seed") trumps marriage only to undermine it. An example is the relationships among Sarai, Abram, Hagar, and Ishmael (Gen. 16; explored briefly in chapter 6). Hagar was an Egyptian, yet was living with Israel's first matriarch and patriarch. Sarai sought to be "built up" through her "slave girl."[80] Neither Sarai nor Abram ever used her name, speaking only in terms of her subservient role. The narrator and YHWH's messenger, however, consistently call her by name. She was not simply a foreigner slaving for "us," but was, from YHWH's perspective, a human being in need of divine protection.

That the narrative follows Hagar in her escape from Sarai is itself a strong statement. Whereas the "people of the land" in Ezra-Nehemiah are generally only spoken about by others, Genesis leads readers to empathize with Hagar's plight by narrating her personal experience of being treated "harshly" (Gen. 16:6). Further, we find that Hagar had her own relationship with YHWH "in the wilderness" (16:7). The encounter led to a direct promise to her that paralleled the promise to Abra(ha)m: "I will so greatly multiply your offspring that they cannot be counted for multitude" (cf. 17:2; 22:17). YHWH's messenger then proclaimed a naming oracle parallel to the one about Sarai: "Now you have conceived and shall bear a son; you shall

---

79. Brett (2000), 31.
80. *bnh*, "built," as the Tower of Babel; see also chapter 7, Table 3, p. 86.

call him Ishmael" (cf. 17:19).[81] Finally, in response, Hagar named YHWH
as "El-roi," i.e., "the God who sees me."[82] Each element of this encounter
places Hagar and Ishmael fully within YHWH's blessing, even if not part of
the specific lineage of "Israel."

But the narrative is not done with Hagar and Ishmael. In Genesis 21,
Isaac was born, and Sarah saw Ishmael "yitzchaqing" with her child.[83] Sarah
demanded that Abraham "cast out" both mother and child, and Abraham
dutifully obeyed the command to expel the foreign "wife."[84] Once again, the
story and YHWH's angel follow Hagar into the wilderness. With great irony,
Genesis speaks of an *Egyptian* and her son who found themselves in the
wilderness as a result of oppression at the hands of Israel's matriarch, only to
be rescued by God.[85] Not only does the narrative "ethnically" reverse Israel's
central liberation story; it also undermines Ezra-Nehemiah's condemnation
of "foreign wives" and their offspring. Away from the eyes of the dominant
people (here, Abraham and Sarah) — but not the eyes of readers — God
is with those who would be expelled because of their foreignness, blessing
them and their children.

Genesis continues to challenge Ezra-Nehemiah's ideology in the stories of
obtaining wives for Isaac and Jacob (Gen. 24 and 29). In its original context, Laban and his family represent the "old country," i.e., Babylon, from
which Abram was first called. But within the Persian context, we can hear
these stories putting into question the wisdom of limiting marriage partners
to one's "own" people. For example, in neither Genesis 24 nor 29 do we
hear YHWH bless the choice of wives for Isaac or Jacob. Further, Isaac's
warning to Jacob to "not marry one of the Canaanite women" as Esau has
done (26:34; 28:1; cf. Gen. 24:3) is undermined by Esau gaining bountiful
blessing just as Ishmael did (Gen. 25:12–18; 36:1ff.). Jacob's attempt to keep
his distance from Esau is countered by his brother's running to embrace and
kiss him (33:4). Throughout these passages, Genesis subverts the idea that
"we" are blessed by staying separate from "them."

Perhaps the most direct challenge of Genesis to this anti-foreign-women
ideology is in the encounter between Judah and Tamar (Gen. 38). The narrator has repeatedly noted that characters represent the nations that carry
their name (e.g., "Esau is Edom," 36:1, 8, 16, 43). In this story, Jacob's son
represents the people of Judah in the time of the text's audience. The foreign
daughter-in-law, Tamar, is assumed by Judah to be a death threat to his sons,
although the narrator has explicitly named YHWH as the cause of the sons'
demise because of their evil (38:7, 10). Judah thus withholds his remaining
son from Tamar. The foreign woman "covers herself" and is taken by Judah

---

81. For similar naming oracles see Judg. 13:3–7; Isa. 7:14–17; Luke 1:28–32.
82. Westermann (1995), 247.
83. See pp. 67–68 above.
84. Gen. 16:3 refers to Hagar as Abram's "wife" or "woman" (*'ishshah*).
85. "Wilderness" (*midbar*) is used four of seven times in Genesis in relation to Hagar and
Ishmael: 16:7; 21:4, 20, 21; cf. 14:6; 36:24; 27:22.

as a prostitute.[86] Judah makes her pregnant, but the word comes back to him that "Your daughter-in-law Tamar has played the whore; moreover she is pregnant as a result of whoredom" (38:24). Judah's response is immediate: "Bring her out and let her be burned," a shocking verdict made without the slightest investigation or opportunity for Tamar to speak. The story thus holds up for examination the Ezra-Nehemiah group's willingness to banish foreign wives without considering whether they are actually a danger or threat to Judah's security.

The story ends with a twist: Tamar sends back to Judah the symbols of identity which he had provided as a pledge against his future payment for the "prostitute's" services. He acknowledges that they are his and announces "She is more in the right than I, since I did not give her to my son Shelah" (38:26). The postexilic Judahite community is thereby challenged to hear that the foreign women they have withheld from their sons were more "in the right" than they were in rushing to judgment against them.

Another key component of the Genesis perspective that confronts Ezra-Nehemiah ideology is its consistent anti-urban perspective. As we saw in Part I, Genesis associates cities with murder and oppression. The divine judgment on the Sodomites' rejection of the "alien" (19:9) would certainly put in question the Jerusalem elite's similar behavior.[87] Likewise, that Jacob experiences YHWH in a "place" other than Jerusalem undermines the centralization regime of both the monarchy and Ezra-Nehemiah's program (Gen. 28:16; Deut. 12:5, 11, etc.).

Throughout the Second Temple period and beyond, the powerful Genesis stories continued to challenge proponents of the religion of empire. Jesus, in Matthew's Gospel, speaks of *palingenesia*— "genesis again"[88]— in connection with his vision of the Kingdom of God (Matt. 19:28). The Bible's eventual first book, whose inclusive religion was rejected by the temple builders, became a foundation stone for the Good News of Jesus.[89]

Second Zechariah
and the Beginning of Eschatological Hope

The materials found in Zechariah 9–14 likely represent a range of perspectives from voices outside the Ezra-Nehemiah establishment sometime within the fifth century. Unfortunately, it has been very difficult for scholars to

---

86. The text contrasts his perception that Tamar is a "prostitute" (*zonah*) with the possibility that she is a "consecrated woman" (*qadeshah*, often mistranslated as "cult prostitute").

87. Pharaoh's willingness to use the foreign "Hebrew" Joseph to serve his own imperial goals while refusing to eat with him (43:32), would also tear at the "sacred canopy" Ezra-Nehemiah sought to put over their restoration strategy. However, as noted in Part I, the Joseph narrative may well have been composed after Ezra-Nehemiah.

88. NRSV: "renewal of all things." This is discussed in chapter 23.

89. Cf. Ps. 118:22; Mark 12:10; Matt. 21:42; Luke 20:17; Acts 4:11; 1 Pet 2:7.

agree on much about these passages because of the diversity of viewpoints expressed.[90] One thing is clear: whoever put the pieces together was deeply dissatisfied with the Jerusalem status quo. Eric Meyers states,

> The disappointment of not participating in the new prosperity of the Persian Era and the disappointment of having only limited autonomy, coupled with an anxiety over the limited growth of the population of Yehud, created considerable anxiety in the minds of the later prophets, especially Second Zechariah (chapters 9–14).[91]

These passages project hope to a future when YHWH will act to make things right. This deferral expresses a movement toward *eschatology,* consideration of the "times of the end." Third Isaiah's vision of New Jerusalem is within this perspective, along with the later Isaiah 24–27.[92] In a context when the religion of empire held a tight control over Jerusalem institutions, those holding to the YHWH religion of creation and liberation faced the choice to quit altogether, accommodate to those in power, or hold on to hope that someday YHWH would make things right. Second Zechariah ends with the latter vision in chapter 14:

> See, a day is coming for YHWH.... YHWH will go forth and fight against those nations as when he fights on a day of battle. On that day his feet shall stand on the Mount of Olives.... On that day there shall not be either cold or frost;... that day living waters shall flow out from Jerusalem.... And YHWH will become king over all the earth; on that day YHWH will be one and his name one. (Zech. 14:1, 4, 6, 8–9)

For Ezra-Nehemiah, that "day" had already come, as we hear in the threefold repetition of "on that day" amid the celebration of the completion of "the house of YHWH" (Neh. 12:43, 44; 13:1). For Second Zechariah, as for Third Isaiah and the later prophet Joel,[93] "that day" would not happen as a result of collaboration with empire, but by YHWH's direct reign becoming manifest for all to see and to know. As Joel says:

> YHWH roars from Zion, and utters his voice from Jerusalem, and the heavens and the earth shake. But YHWH is a refuge for his people, a stronghold for the people of Israel. So you shall know that I, YHWH your God, dwell in Zion, my holy mountain.... In that day the mountains shall drip sweet wine, the hills shall flow with milk, and all the stream beds of Judah shall flow with water; a fountain shall come forth from the house of YHWH and water the Wadi Shittim. (Joel 3:16–18)

Eschatological prophecy was not, however, the only way the elite dissented from the harshness of the Ezra-Nehemiah regime. The book of

---

90. On the challenge of dating Zech. 9–14, see Redditt (1994).
91. Meyers (1995), 718.
92. See, e.g., Albertz (1994), 570–74, who dates Isa. 24–27 to the third century BCE.
93. E.g., Joel 1:15; 2:1; 3:14, 18.

Leviticus presents a more egalitarian and creation-inclusive (if urban-centered) version of torah than Deuteronomy. The books of Chronicles retell the history of monarchy with a more inclusive sense of "Israel" than the Deuteronomistic History. Through these alternative texts, groups among the Jerusalem elite sought to engage the temple establishment from the "inside." They provided what one might call a "kinder, gentler" version of the religion of the Second Temple. It would not be for at least another century that written texts would challenge the establishment's foundational premises.

Leviticus: Cosmos, Temple, and Text in Microcosm

Leviticus is one of the most challenging books in the Bible for readers in our world to engage. Its litanies of now obsolete rules and its lack of narrative action make it seem boring and irrelevant. But when understood within its own historical moment as an alternative to Ezra-Nehemiah, we can better appreciate the importance of its message.

Leviticus was likely an exilic and postexilic composition.[94] Its perspective is certainly "priestly," but not at all that of the priest-scribe Ezra. If Ezra-Nehemiah followed the line from Deuteronomy through the Deuteronomistic History and Jeremiah, the path of Leviticus went through Exodus and Ezekiel.

Mary Douglas has brilliantly penetrated the veil that separates modern readers from the logic of Leviticus by revealing its structure to be a multi-leveled "microcosm" modeled on the tabernacle (*mishkan*) described in Exodus 25–27.[95] She observes:

> It was no accident that Solomon's magnificent temple was not copied. The model for the book was the little portable tabernacle described in the book of Exodus. Solomon's temple would suggest gross pretension of power and authority.... The desert tabernacle was the obvious choice for a new religion, which rejects pomp and outward show. But the people who returned from exile with Ezra were not touched by those considerations.[96]

---

94. Table 18, p. 226 shows some of the parallels between Leviticus and the exilic Ezekiel. For a judicious review of critical theories of Leviticus's date of composition, see Wenham (1994b), 8–13. For a more detailed examination of this question that reveals the limits of redaction criticism, see the essays in Kugler and Rendtorff (2006).

95. Her view challenges the traditional scholarly perspective, that Leviticus consists of two parts, the supposed "P" section (chapters 1–16) and the "H" or "Holiness Code" (chapters 17–27). Rolf Rendtorff (1996) shows, however, that the traditional view was always more assumed than proven, and concludes: "the so-called Holiness Code cannot be taken any longer as a basic structural element for Leviticus in general" (28).

96. Douglas, 154.

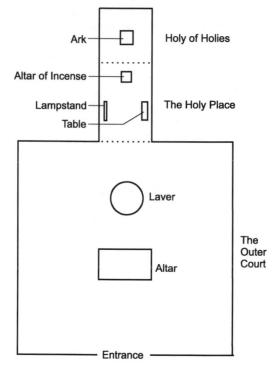

Diagram 1: The Body/House Cosmogram

The proportions of the Mishkan shown in Diagram 1[97] correspond to the chapters and sections of the book of Leviticus.[98] Furthermore, they also correspond in general relationship with the three levels of Mount Sinai and with the three sections of a sacrificial animal (see Table 22).

The book — like Mount Sinai, an animal, and the Mishkan — has a pair of "screens" that separate the three parts. This divides the book into three segments, each of which has, according to Douglas, a "solemn triad," the center of which is the focal point of the segment. The topics of each segment correspond to what was to take place in the corresponding section of the Mishkan.

These correspondences allow us to see more clearly both the literary focal points of the book as well as the larger theological perspective of the Leviticus editors. The *starting point is Exodus.* Everything in Leviticus corresponds to the people's wilderness experience of YHWH, transferred to an urban context. Those in exile "would be able to hold the book in their

---

97. Recall the discussion in chapter 10 above.
98. Diagram from Douglas, 151.

Table 22: The "Microcosm" of the Book of Leviticus (following Mary Douglas)

Component	Leviticus	Mount Sinai	Sacrificial Animal	Mishkan
Large section at starting point	chapters 1–16 SOLEMN TRIAD: chapters 8–10, with chapter 9 focus: Aaron's offerings lead to the people experiencing the glory of YHWH.	Lower slopes: open to all	Head/meat	Court of Sacrifice: open to all
First "screen"	10:10–23: violent death of Aaron's sons	Dense cloud	Fat covering kidneys	first curtain
Middle section	chapters 17–24 SOLEMN TRIAD: chapters 18–20, with chapter 19 focus: "love your neighbor as yourself"	Edge of cloud: open to Aaron, sons and seventy elders	Midriff area	Holy Place: Only priests allowed; furnished with table and lampstand
Second "screen"	Lev. 24:10–23: violent death of a blasphemer	Cloud like smoke	Hard suet	Second curtain
Inner section	chapters 25–27 SOLEMN TRIAD: chapters 25–27, with chapter 26 focus: blessings/curses for following jubilee or not	Summit: Moses and YHWH only	Entrails, genitals	Holy of Holies: priest and YHWH only; furnished with cherubim, ark and tablets of Covenant

hands, and, reading it, they could perform a virtual walk around a virtual tabernacle."[99]

Second, the center passages of each section combine to express an integrated vision of worship and the practice of social justice that includes all the people *and* the land. A look at each focal passage illustrates this principle.

Leviticus 9 follows the opening chapters that describe YHWH's will for offering various sacrifices. The "solemn triad" begins with Moses' anointing of Aaron and his sons as priests. The triad center narrates Aaron and his sons offering the sacrifices named in the previous chapters. The ritual embodies an equality between the priests' and the people's sacrifices. When the offerings are completed, Moses and Aaron bless the people, "and the glory of YHWH appeared to all the people" (Lev. 9:23). We see a priesthood deeply involved with serving both YHWH and the people. There is blessing and the experience of divine glory for everyone together.

99. Douglas, 153.

We move from the "outer court" to the Holy Place. The framing chapters of the solemn triad contain many parallels concerned with illicit sexual union, especially incest.[100] The center is chapter 19, a litany of social justice provisions. The focus is on the wealthy providing for the poor by allowing for gleaning of harvests, fair relationships with laborers, and honest business dealings. One passage in particular is important for our purpose:

> When an alien resides with you in your land, you shall not oppress the alien. The alien who resides with you shall be to you as the citizen among you; you shall love the alien as yourself, for you were aliens in the land of Egypt: I am YHWH your God. (19:33–34)

This passage is verbally parallel with one earlier in the chapter that is more familiar to most readers:

> You shall not hate in your heart anyone of your kin; you shall reprove your neighbor, or you will incur guilt yourself. You shall not take vengeance or bear a grudge against any of your people, but you shall love your neighbor as yourself: I am YHWH. (Lev. 19:17–18)

Taken together, the texts equate "alien" and "neighbor." It is a stark contrast with the Ezra-Nehemiah view. It is to this passage, along with the Shema (Deut. 6:4–5), that Jesus went when asked by a *scribe* what the greatest commandment was (Mark 12:28–31).[101] In Luke's Gospel, however, the question is turned around: Jesus asks a lawyer, who wonders about the requirements for inheriting eternal life, what he "reads" in the law (Luke 10:25–28). The lawyer gives the "right answer," but then, "seeking to justify himself," asks, "and who is my neighbor?" Jesus responds with one of his most famous stories, in which the embodiment of neighborliness is none other than a *Samaritan,* precisely one of those excluded by the Ezra-Nehemiah scribal-priestly-royal coalition and its successors. The synoptic gospels all underscore the centrality to Jesus of the Leviticus vision of inclusive, justice-practicing community gathered around worship of YHWH.

Our walk through Leviticus ends with the Holy of Holies in chapters 25–27. We find here provisions for sabbatical and jubilee years. A tremendous outpouring of literature in recent years has explored the biblical understanding of jubilee, as presented in Leviticus and reinterpreted in the New Testament, as we'll see especially in chapter 24.[102] Central for our current consideration, though, is simply how these chapters serve as the sacred climax to the book of Leviticus.

---

100. E.g., all thirty-two uses of the word "nakedness" in Leviticus are in these two chapters; also the prohibition on sacrificing children to Molech is only at Lev. 18:21 and 20:2–5.

101. Matthew's version has a Pharisee lawyer asking the question, Matt. 22:34–40.

102. See, e.g., resources gathered at the website of the Sabbath Economics Collaborative, *www.sabbatheconomics.org/content/page.php?section=1,* especially Myers (2001), Lowery, and Kinsler and Kinsler.

The basic purpose of the sabbatical and jubilee is to assure that no long-term structural injustices and inequalities become entrenched within the community of YHWH's people. Every seven years, debts are to be released while fields and animals are allowed a year of rest. Then, every fifty years (a sabbatical of sabbaticals), there is to be a great "homebringing," the literal meaning of the Hebrew, *yovel*.[103] Everyone is to return to their ancestral, YHWH-given land. All debts are to be forgiven and liberty to all is to be declared. It envisions a great "fresh start"[104] that levels the social and economic playing field for each family and for the earth itself. The economic vision of Leviticus is thus deeply egalitarian and communitarian, a far cry from the exploitative, imperial economy supported by Ezra-Nehemiah, despite Nehemiah's one-time relief measure (Neh. 5). It is also a prescription against the exploitative imperial social and economic structure we saw condemned so strongly by Ezekiel.

As with the previous section, parallels between chapters 25 and 27 form the frame for chapter 26.[105] The central chapter describes blessings for living in accordance with the statutes and commandments of the entire book and curses for failure to do so. Leviticus does not portray YHWH promising arbitrary rewards and punishments for following a set of random rules. Rather, YHWH teaches them *the natural consequences of living in obedience or disobedience to the Creator's ways.* Obedience leads to "peace in the land," the absence of fear, and plenty of food. Repeated disobedience leads to increasingly oppressive circumstances, culminating in *exile* (26:33). In other words, the chapter looks both backward and forward: the failure to obey YHWH was both the cause of the Exile and a warning for future generations.[106] The closing verses of the chapter offer a thread of hope, held out as a lifeline to Leviticus's exilic and postexilic audience:

> Yet for all that, when they are in the land of their enemies, I will not spurn them, or abhor them so as to destroy them utterly and break my covenant with them; for I am YHWH their God; but I will remember in their favor the covenant with their ancestors whom I brought out of the land of Egypt in the sight of the nations, to be their God: I am YHWH. (26:44–45)

Under the regime of Ezra-Nehemiah and their Persian overlords, Leviticus became a shadow of its former self. Douglas concludes: "For the politicians [the evil of intermarriage] was a much more immediate and powerful concern than the representation of the whole Covenant and of the Law in the dimensions of the tabernacle."[107] The powerful microcosmic structure of Leviticus was apparently forgotten amid the practice of the religion of

---

103. Fox, 628 n. 10.
104. See Acts 3:19–20 and discussion at p. 423.
105. E.g., *yovel* is found twenty times in Leviticus, all in chapters 25 and 27.
106. Cf. Deut. 28, a parallel set of consequences for obedience or disobedience.
107. Douglas, 155.

empire. However, the inclusive, peaceful, and just vision remained a part of the temple's sacred Scriptures, awaiting another moment to be proclaimed as the Word of YHWH to be made flesh in the people.

Chronicles: David as Patron
of the Priesthood and Temple

The books of Chronicles offer a revisionist version of Israel's history, from Creation to Exile and beyond. Modern scholars have understood them to be part either of the sweeping "Priestly" writing or more narrowly part of the Ezra-Nehemiah tradition. Sara Japhet, however, has shown how Chronicles expresses its own unique perspective on who Israel and YHWH were and are to be.[108] It draws upon previous texts while generating its own ideology. It goes farther than any other biblical text to establish the notion of "sacred kingship," established exclusively in Jerusalem. Yet it suggests a more inclusive sense of "Israel" that seems to challenge the radically exclusivist view of Ezra-Nehemiah. Its David and Solomon are immaculately clean versions of the characters we saw in the Deuteronomistic History. Gone are idolatry, adultery, and murder. Instead, we find kings who embody YHWH's will for Israel faithfully and completely. Chronicles thus moves away from historical events and toward a schematized model of YHWH's eternal and everlasting relationship with Israel in Jerusalem.

A quick overview of the first verses of the opening chapters of 1 Chronicles conveys how the work is structured:

1:1: "Adam, Seth, Enosh..."

2:1: "These are the sons of Israel:..." (continuing through David, 2:15, and beyond)

3:1: "These are the sons of David who were born to him in Hebron:..."

4:1: "The sons of Judah:..." (continuing to the time of King Hezekiah)

5:1: "The sons of Reuben the firstborn of Israel..." (continuing until the Assyrian conquest)

6:1: "The sons of Levi:..." (continuing to the priestly service of Aaron and his sons, 6:49)

7:1: "The sons of Issachar:..." (continuing through Joshua, as tenth generation son of Ephraim, 7:27)

8:1: "Benjamin became the father of Bela his firstborn..."

---

108. E.g., Japhet (1989, 1993, 2003) and the articles collected in her 2006 volume. This brief overview of the place of Chronicles amid the biblical texts originating in the Persian period relies heavily on her work. For a nuanced criticism of Japhet's view, see Blenkinsopp (2009), 164–67.

9:1: "So all Israel was enrolled by genealogies; and these are written in the Book of the Kings of Israel. And Judah was taken into exile in Babylon because of their unfaithfulness."

Chronicles thus moves from Adam to Exile in eight chapters of genealogies. After this, it circles back to narrate Saul's death, and hence, the "inevitability" of a united monarchy under David. First Chronicles 11:1–3 echoes nearly verbatim 2 Samuel 5:1–3.[109] There are no stories of conquest and settlement (Joshua–Judges) or of the long struggle between Saul and David.[110] Gone also are the troubles within David's family and the battle for succession. Instead, there is a smooth and steady movement — allegedly reflecting YHWH's will — leading from Creation to the establishment of monarchy and temple.

Also omitted are the stories of matriarchs and patriarchs that situated the origin of "Israel" within a struggle to find God's will in a landscape littered with urban empires.[111] Gone, too, is the entire Exodus tradition, with its years of wilderness wanderings that expressed the people's ambivalent response to YHWH's call to be covenant partners. Japhet writes: "The bond between the people and the land, like the bond between the people and its god, is described as something continuous and abiding. This bond cannot be associated with a particular moment in history, for it has existed since the beginning of time."[112]

And so it is with the Jerusalem institutions. All has been established with the original act of Creation. Japhet continues:

> Time does not produce change, nor does the future hold any surprises for [humanity]. Time merely provides illustrations of unchanging principles. By the same token, the possibility of change or innovation is almost nonexistent, for everything in the world comes from God, who is eternal and, by definition, unchanging.[113]

---

109. Scholars who link Chronicles to the so-called "Priestly" redaction of Genesis often take the lengthy quotation of genealogies as "proof" of common authorship. However, Chronicles also quotes or paraphrases the Deuteronomistic History in many places without the scholarly suggestion of common authorship between the two historical accounts. Part I above attempted to show how the book of Genesis, especially the Primeval History (Gen. 1–11), is perfectly coherent as a unified narrative from the time of the Babylonian Exile, rather than as a pastiche of sources from different periods. Given Chronicles' radically different perspective on YHWH's plan for Israel from that of Genesis, it will be read here as a text independent of both Ezra-Nehemiah (following Japhet) and the "Priestly source" of the Pentateuch.

110. Japhet (1989), 379.

111. However, Chronicles goes out of its way to associate the Jerusalem temple mount with Mount Moriah, the place to which YHWH sent Abraham to offer up Isaac; 2 Chron. 3:1; Gen. 22:2, the only places in the Bible where "Moriah" is mentioned. Cf. the LXX version of Gen. 22, which substitutes *gēn tēn hupsēlēn,* "the high land / earth," abstracting from the specific location, "Moriah," that would have been meaningless to an audience in Alexandria where the LXX was generated.

112. Ibid., 386.

113. Ibid., 501.

All that can happen "historically" is people choosing to act according to or against this unchanging, eternal will. From this perspective, the very existence of a northern kingdom of Israel is a grotesque aberration. Chronicles takes little time to tell the story of Jeroboam and his successors, because nothing good or even worth knowing can come from cutting oneself off from Jerusalem.[114]

All that matters is the movement toward Jerusalem, the monarchy, and the temple. Here is where we find the most explicit connection with long-standing, imperial notions of divine kingship. The Deuteronomistic History in its final form reflects deep ambivalence about monarchy. Its hero is Josiah, but Josiah's "found" text presents a "torah of the kingship" (Deut. 17:14–20) that few kings could fulfill, and that kept YHWH as true king, separate from YHWH's human anointed one. David and Solomon are founders, yet are deeply flawed. The very conception of human kingship was presented as an abandonment of YHWH's direct rule (1 Sam. 8).

But Chronicles reflects none of this ambivalence. As Japhet expresses it:

> "The throne of YHWH" constitutes an abstract expression referring to Yahweh's dominion over Israel, which is put into concrete political practice by means of David and Solomon. In a metaphorical, and clearly non-mythological sense, it may be said that Solomon ascends the throne of YHWH; his very kingship over Israel is equivalent to sitting on YHWH's throne "as king for YHWH." In these verses [1 Chron. 29:23–25], we find the clearest biblical expression of the idea that Israel's monarchy — the actual political institution — is none other than divine kingship; the king is God's representative and the executor of the functions of kingship.[115]

Three times, we hear YHWH proclaim that he will be a "father" to his "son," Solomon (1 Chron. 17:13; 22:10; 28:6). This portrayal of Solomon as "son of God" resonates through the ages, from Babylon, through Greece, and to Rome, with the deification of kings. However, there are two major difference between Chronicles' theology of divine kingship and that of other empires. First, Solomon — and his successors — are bound by the same torah as the rest of Israel.

Second, Chronicles is not *ultimately* interested in the monarchy at all, given its composition under Persian rule. Rather, the purpose of "good kings" like David and Solomon is to *build a temple and establish the priesthood*. We see this connection in the juxtaposition of the "father / son" proclamation noted above (1 Chron. 28) and what follows a few verses later, beginning with the conclusion of David's speech to his son, the king-in-waiting:

---

114. Ibid., 310.
115. Ibid., 400.

"Take heed now, for YHWH has chosen you to build a house as the sanctuary; be strong, and act."

Then David gave his son Solomon the plan of the vestibule of the temple, and of its houses, its treasuries, its upper rooms, and its inner chambers, and of the room for the mercy seat; and the plan of all that he had in mind: for the courts of the house of YHWH, all the surrounding chambers, the treasuries of the house of God, and the treasuries for dedicated gifts; for the divisions of the priests and of the Levites. (28:10–13a)

David then made a blessing-speech before the people, after which the narrator concludes: "and they ate and drank before YHWH on that day with great joy. They made David's son Solomon king a second time; they anointed him as YHWH's prince, and Zadok as priest" (1 Chron. 29:22). It is the very Zadok who "becomes" the ancestor, first for the Ezekiel group during the Exile, and then for their successors under Persian rule.

This royal temple priesthood and its supporters are to become, for Chronicles, the leaders of the Second Temple. In Chronicles, "commanders" (*sare*) of the people are partners with Solomon in building the temple (e.g., 1 Chron. 22:17). The term for "commanders" expresses a hierarchical role, in contrast to the "elders" who mediate between king and people in other traditions.[116] In contrast, *zaqen* ("elder," literally, "gray [beard]") reflects decentralized, kinship-based authority. In Exodus, the "elders of Israel" (3:16) are direct counterparts of the "taskmasters" of Egypt. "Elders" are mentioned 180 times in the Hebrew Bible: 78 times in the Deuteronomistic History,[117] but only ten times in Chronicles. It is a long way down from the throne to the people in this vision of YHWH's reign.

The Deuteronomistic History ends with King Jehoiachin exiled in Babylon, dining at the king's table. In stark contrast, 2 Chronicles ends with fulfillment of prophecy and a royal invitation:

In the first year of King Cyrus of Persia, in fulfillment of the word of YHWH spoken by Jeremiah, YHWH stirred up the spirit of King Cyrus of Persia so that he sent a herald throughout all his kingdom and also declared in a written edict: "Thus says King Cyrus of Persia: YHWH, the God of heaven, has given me all the kingdoms of the earth, and he has charged me to build him a house at Jerusalem, which is in Judah. Whoever is among you of all his people, may YHWH his God be with him! Let him go up." (2 Chron. 36:22–23)

---

116. The *sar* (leader) is mentioned 98 times in 1–2 Chronicles of 421 times in the Hebrew Bible, with many of these other uses referring to imperial representatives (e.g., Pharaoh's men, Gen. 40:2ff.; Exod. 1:11; 2:14).

117. *Zaqen* is used twelve times in Exodus, all but one referring to Israel's "elders."

The quote is virtually identical to the starting verses of Ezra 1. What distinguishes Chronicles from Ezra-Nehemiah is not its sense that the Persian sponsorship of the restoration is YHWH's doing, but the scope of who is to be invited to participate in the new Jerusalem. Chronicles is not, like Third Isaiah, opening the gates of Jerusalem to foreigners. Rather, it is suggesting that *there have never been foreigners in Israel at all!* Japhet says that in Chronicles

> ... the entire historical narrative, from beginning to end, makes no mention of the presence of foreign peoples in the land of Israel. ... Hezekiah sends messengers throughout the land of Israel, calling for the Israelites to celebrate passover in Jerusalem (1 Chron. 30:1, 5, 6, etc.). ... According to the Chronistic outlook, the population's composition remained completely unchanged following the downfall of the northern kingdom and the exile.[118]

The corollary of this fiction is that "everyone who lives in the land of Israel, whatever his status, belongs to the people of Israel." Japhet concludes,

> this portrayal betrays the writer's view of his own period and expresses his attitude towards the Samaritan problem in his time. ... The Chronicler did not consider the Samaritans a separate community. The inhabitants of Samaria were, along with the "resident aliens," descendants of Israelite tribes, the Judeans' brothers and an organic part of the people of Israel. We may say that the Chronicler calls for an end to tension and hatred between segments of the people and summons all Israel to unite in worshiping YHWH in Jerusalem.[119]

Another implication of this perspective is a reversal of Ezra-Nehemiah's view on intermarriage. Rather than the "foreign" wife (and children) being seen as polluting threats to Israel's purity, Chronicles sees that marriage to an Israelite transforms the foreigner into one of "us." It is this same perspective that will animate the apostle Paul's advice about "mixed marriages" within the church at Corinth: "For the unbelieving husband is made holy through his wife, and the unbelieving wife is made holy through her husband" (1 Cor. 7:14).[120]

This more inclusive sense of who constitutes "Israel" distinguishes Chronicles from Ezra-Nehemiah, but it barely moves it off the far end of the spectrum of "the two religions." It should not surprise us that this perspective is never heard from in the New Testament as part of the "Good News" of Jesus.

---

118. Japhet (1989), 329.
119. Ibid., 333–34.
120. See Baumert, 58–59; also Thiselton, 530.

"The Books of Moses"
as Persian-supported "Law" for Yehud

We have so far examined some of the individual books that eventually became part of what we know now as the "Old Testament" or "Hebrew Scriptures." While the final process of canonization remained in the distant future, the Persian period likely established one set of these writings as a formal unit, known collectively as the *torah* or "Five Books of Moses." We find the first reference at Nehemiah 8:1: "all the people gathered together into the square before the Water Gate. They told the scribe Ezra to bring the book of the torah of Moses, which YHWH had given to Israel." The actual text almost certainly continued to be edited for several centuries. But we find here the first suggestion that separate texts, written from diverse theological perspectives, were being combined under Persian authority and Ezra's priestly leadership and presented as collectively derived from "Moses."[121] As we will see in the next chapters, this establishment of the "torah of Moses" as, in essence, the constitution of the Second Temple, was extremely controversial. We have seen how narratives like Genesis and the core of Exodus are radically subversive of the religion of empire. Once these texts became incorporated into a longer narrative of Genesis-Deuteronomy, though, their radicality became subverted to the voice within Deuteronomy which closes the collection. In other words, the anti-urban and anti-monarchy perspective was transformed into something like a "primitive" tradition that led (inevitably, with divine approval) to the establishment of Jerusalem and the temple as the center of YHWH religion. Most readers today take the "movement" from nomadic family, through wilderness wanderings, to settlement in the Land as a "natural" progression. This perspective began with the establishment of the sequence of books as a narrative unit during the Persian "restoration."

The establishment under Emperor Constantine in the fourth century CE of an official canonical collection we call the "New Testament" functioned similarly to that of the Persian-era gathering of the "book of Moses" into a single unit.[122] Both imperial acts generated an "official" religious perspective from which all variations were branded "heresy" or at least what might be called "dissent." For the first time, YHWH's people were presented with a written tradition that was deemed to be "the torah of God" (Neh. 8:8). Carol Newsom observes that the narrative of the "reading of the book of the torah of Moses" in Nehemiah 8 includes a description of the physical

---

121. Watts gathers a collection of essays reviewing the theory of Peter Frei, claiming explicit Persian authorization of the Pentateuch. Most of the authors are critical of Frei's theory for a variety of reasons. For our purpose, it is sufficient to note that (1) the Persians were in political and economic control of the province of Yehud and (2) Ezra was working under Persian authority when he presented "the book of the torah of Moses" to the people.

122. See Dungan.

scene which reveals the "ideology of knowledge of torah that characterizes Ezra-Nehemiah":

> a priest/scribe, authorized by the Persian king, stands on a raised platform, flanked by prominent lay members of the community. He reads from a written book of torah as a group of expert interpreters mediates the knowledge to the assembled community, who hear, understand, and respond. Knowledge of torah forms and unites the community; but it also articulates it in a hierarchical manner.[123]

The official view was that the era of prophecy was now over. YHWH would no longer speak directly to the people, but rather, through the "magisterium" of the temple. Leo Perdue summarizes the situation:

> The significant differences of religious understanding found... in the Second Temple period... proved to be an obstacle to religious conformity. This concern for homogeneity emerged not only internally from the Jewish religious authorities in Jerusalem, in particular the Zadokite priestly hierarchy, but also externally as part of the Persian political policy for ruling the vast empire they conquered. The codification of socioreligious law among the vassal nations and colonies was one means for achieving stability among the multiple ethnicities and cultures of the empire. Thus the efforts of Ezra... point to the desire of the Persian rulers and the Jewish authorities in Jerusalem who were loyal to the Achaemenid court to create a common expression of Judaism and brand as illegitimate other forms.... Monotheism, the temple in Jerusalem, the Torah, and the authority of the Zadokite priesthood became a unified articulation of state and provincial legitimated Judaism. Competing shrines, religious understandings of deity, and law codes... were deemed illicit.[124]

Ezra-Nehemiah records the people responding to this action with obedient "amens," worship, and rejoicing (Neh. 8:6, 12). The text clearly implies that this torah was not ancient, but was in fact, a new creation, being heard for the first time (with, of course, "official" interpretation; 8:8). We hear that the people found written in the torah the command to live in *sukkot*, i.e., "booths," in the seventh month. After the people responded obediently by constructing booths throughout the region, we are told that "from the days of Jeshua [i.e., Joshua] son of Nun to that day the people of Israel had not done so" (Neh 8:14–17). The text offers no explanation for this failure. Unlike the story of the uncelebrated passover restored under Josiah by the book "found" in the house of YHWH (2 Kings 22), Ezra-Nehemiah simply presents the command to celebrate the festival of Booths as one heard and

---

123. Newsom, 34.
124. Perdue (2008), 192–93.

performed for the first time.[125] As the Second Temple period continued, the "book of Moses" was gradually transformed from a torah established under foreign, imperial authority to an "ancestral" torah.

Not all accepted this story, however. With "Moses" now claimed by the upholders of the religion of empire, those committed to the direct rule of the Creator, YHWH, developed their own sacred texts in direct confrontation with those of the temple elite. A potential "counter-torah" of five "books" eventually developed under the even more ancient authority of Enoch, seventh generation descendant from Adam. We will explore this crucial, yet little known, collection in the following chapters.

Assessing the Range of Visions for the Restored People of God

For people used to thinking of the Bible as providing a linear, consistent message about God and God's people, this survey of Restoration visions can be bewildering and confusing. But a glance at the range of "theologies" offered in the name of Jesus today reveals an even more complex mix of perspectives than we've seen in this chapter. What is the "Christian" stance today on "God and empire"? Now as then, it depends on who one asks.

This need not lead us to reduce the question to a matter of "opinion," as is so common in a postmodern world where "truth" seems simply a matter of perspective. We will see that Jesus and the New Testament writers cut sharply through the range of positions and stood together with those Restoration-era writers who experienced and described YHWH standing apart from and against human-made systems of oppression and exclusion.

What did this all mean for the people of Yehud and the wider region during the period of Persian rule? First, we must acknowledge that we have no idea what "ordinary people" believed or practiced. In our highly literate, online world, we have access to a multitude of documents from official church institutions and office holders, academics, activists, and just plain folks with a webpage. What would reading a range of those texts tell us about what "ordinary people" believe or practice today? Imagining the daily faith lives of people from the ancient past is virtually impossible.

Our biblical texts narrate the hopes, dreams, and actions of the elite. We cannot "hear" the voices of those "below." Ziony Zevit sorts through the confusion often found in the writing of scholars who purport to separate "popular" from "elite" religion in the ancient world. He concludes:

> There was no state or elite or official or popular religion in ancient Israel. There was a political body that we may label "state"; there were social and economic elites; there were sacerdotal and royal officials; there was

---

125. For an effort to recover the practice of the "Festival of Shelters" for Christian discipleship, see Loring.

a populace; and there was the so-called "man in the street." But data do not support the proposition that a particular type of pattern of credo or praxis may be associated with them.[126]

What we have is not a portrayal of what "people believed" in the early Second Temple period, but what various elites sought to persuade or coerce people into accepting as YHWH's truth. The voices are priestly and scribal, people with not only the ability to write and the leisure to do it, but also with access to the structures of ideological preservation that led their writings to be retained over the long haul. We are sealed off from the historical debates or conversations that must have taken place among the promoters of the various visions we have explored. We have no equivalent of ancient TV talk shows or political blogs to reveal how the Ezra-Nehemiah group responded to the Third Isaiah group, or how Chronicles was preserved as a "counter-story" to the Deuteronomistic History. For the period of Persian control of Judea — in contrast to the Hellenistic period which followed (discussed in the next chapters) — we have no extra-biblical sources expressing viewpoints beyond those that made the canonical "cut" (a decision not finally made for centuries to come). All we know is that the biblical narratives contain the range of perspectives later deemed to be close enough to one another, despite their differences, to be collected into a single set of sacred texts.

Given this range, we find a uniform acceptance of both Jerusalem and the temple as essential elements of the Restoration. The argument took place within these parameters. The central themes of debate were the degree of inclusivity allowed among "the people of YHWH" and the relationship between YHWH's rule and the rule of Persia. As we've seen, Ezra-Nehemiah expressed one extreme: a very narrow definition of "us" and explicit union between the "law of YHWH" and the "law of the king." Third Isaiah and Genesis were at the other end of the spectrum, explicitly including "foreigners" and hoping for "new heavens and a new earth" in which YHWH's reign would be completely independent from the reign of human kings and human oppression. Between were texts like Leviticus and Chronicles, calling people to live justly within a Jerusalem that remained subject to external, imperial authority: Leviticus with its emphasis on the practices of love of neighbor and jubilee, and Chronicles focusing on a priestly monarchy.

Persia controlled the region for some two hundred years. Its own religion, Zoroastrianism, seeped into Yehud and contributed to new expressions of the increasingly ancient religions centered on YHWH, as we'll see in the next chapter. But with the sweep of a brash young military leader across the Mediterranean in the fourth century, everything changed. The cultural milieu known as "Hellenism" followed Alexander the Great's military triumph and became the "way things were" for centuries to come.

---

126. Zevit, 132.

Chapter Seventeen

Seeking "Wisdom" under Greek Rule

PART ONE: THE PTOLEMAIC EMPIRE

From Persia to Greece

The Persian Empire ruled over Israel for two hundred years. Given our sweep across more than three millennia, this might seem like a mere blip in the continuum of biblical and Christian history. But when we consider that the United States is only a little more than two hundred years old, we might pause to consider how much can happen over such a span.

Persia did not impose its culture or religious tradition of Zoroastrianism on its conquered peoples. Yet it would be foolish to imagine that there was no lasting influence of Persian ideas and practices on the people of Yehud. Scholars continue to debate the scope and degree of that influence,[1] but virtually all accept that certain features of the Persian worldview came to be part of later Israelite/Judean writings. For example, the perception that history unfolds in relatively fixed, sequential blocks was a basic element of Zoroastrianism, and is also found in numerous apocalyptic texts. Zoroastrianism's idea of a heavenly competition for the hearts and minds of people between a good deity (Ahura Mazda) and an evil deity (Angra Mainyu) is also echoed in apocalyptic texts. Finally, a movement of history toward a definitive conclusion where evil is finally eradicated has its roots in Persian thought.[2]

This does not mean, however, that the writers who took up these Persian ideas were supportive of either the Persian Empire specifically or of empire in general. To the contrary, Persian influence was a major component in what developed into one of the most powerful and long-lasting written forms of resistance to empire in the Name of YHWH: *apocalyptic literature,* both "Jewish" and "Christian." For the next four hundred years, apocalyptic became a vessel for protest against accommodation to empire and for the proclamation of YHWH's alternative vision of harmonious life on earth among people and between people and creation.

The event that planted the seeds of this movement was the astonishingly rapid conquest of the eastern Mediterranean by the Macedonian warrior

---

1. E.g., Cohn, 220–26, and Grabbe (2004a), 363–64.
2. Collins (1998), 31–33.

known as Alexander the Great. His virtually unchallenged march swept through Yehud in 332, putting an abrupt end to Persian authority, and ushering in over two hundred years of Greek rule. His conquest continued on into Egypt, where he immediately ordered the founding of the city in his name that would become central later both to Romans and Christians.[3]

From the start of his reign, Alexander sought to establish his divine credentials. In Egypt, this meant harmonizing his claim to be descended from Zeus with a claim to be a pharaoh as "son of Re," the sun god. This action "gave legitimacy to the idea that the king was divine and a representative of the gods on earth."[4]

Upon Alexander's death in 323, the kingdom was divided into four parts among his successors, known as the *Diadochoi*. Egypt was the prize, given to one of the conqueror's best and most loyal friends, Ptolemy. Thus began the Ptolemaic Dynasty, which included the province of Coele Syria, in which lay Jerusalem. Within a few years, another portion of Alexander's empire was under the control of his friend Seleucus, the founder of the Seleucid Dynasty. Seleucus built his capital city of Antioch on the model of Alexandria. For nearly two hundred years, the two dynasties battled each other, with control of Jerusalem first in the hands of the Ptolemies and later the Seleucids, before the indigenous Hasmonean Dynasty took control in the mid-second century until defeated by Rome in 63 BCE. It has been estimated that between Alexander's conquest and the Roman takeover, "some 200 military campaigns were fought in or around Palestine."[5]

Amid seemingly endless wars and intrigues, the people of Jerusalem and the surrounding region struggled to discern where to place their loyalty. Where were prophets to offer a Word from YHWH? What *was* YHWH's will in this tumultuous time?

While the era of prophets was at least officially over, there are numerous extant Israelite texts from this period. They convey a wide range of approaches to the reality of Greek rule and the sweep of Hellenistic culture across the Mediterranean. There is a risk of over-simplification if we attempt to categorize them as either pro- or anti-empire.[6] Instead, I suggest considering the variety of views from within three broad categories of "wisdom."

1. **Royal, establishment wisdom:** in support of temple, Mosaic torah, and imperial control of Jerusalem as the embodiment of YHWH's order or, in the Diaspora, in support of Hellenistic monarchy and Greek philosophy alongside torah, *grounded in* reasoned study of

---

3. Hölbl, 9–10.

4. Ibid., 11.

5. Smith-Christopher (1996), 26, referencing the work of Morton Smith.

6. Boccaccini (1998 and 2001) divides these texts into "Zadokite" or "Enochian" Judaism. We will benefit greatly from Boccaccini's insights, while being aware of the caution of VanderKam (2007a), 16, that this division is too neat and clean in a very complex situation, and does not take full account of the voluminous material from the Diaspora.

torah and creation; *texts include* Proverbs and later, Sirach, *Letter of Aristeas.*

2. **Subversive wisdom:** in opposition to some or all of the above, and in support of YHWH's direct rule, which will take place in the future, *grounded in* direct revelation; *texts include* the material gathered in *1 Enoch, Jubilees,* and Daniel.

3. **Skeptical / ironic wisdom:** in opposition both to royal wisdom's claim to be embodied in the temple establishment and to subversive wisdom's claim to direct revelation, yet not directly confrontational with the status quo, *grounded in* (often philosophical) reason and reflection on human nature; *texts include* Job, Qoheleth (Ecclesiastes), and Diaspora literature such as *3 Maccabees,* Greek additions to Esther, and retellings of Exodus and other biblical texts.

The eventual, canonization of Hebrew Scriptures placed biblical books into three categories: torah, prophets, and "writings," the latter sometimes also known as "wisdom literature."[7] The books that were included express only some of the perspectives known from this period. Those excluded — especially *1 Enoch* — were deemed too radical to make the canonical cut. But as we'll see, it was more often the texts unpalatable to the temple elite and their later successors that lie at the roots of the Gospel of Jesus than those deemed acceptable in their collaboration with empire.

One point of clarification may be necessary before considering specific texts. In earlier scholarship, an opposition was sometimes presented between "Judaism" and "Hellenism." This perspective has been thoroughly discredited in a number of ways, several of which are important here. First, the label "Judaism" is both anachronistic and over-schematized. As Shaye Cohen and Steve Mason have shown convincingly, the term "Jew" and category "Judaism" come from a much later period and carried a wide range of meanings, much as they continue to today.[8] Does "Jew" refer to a member of an "ethnic" group, a holder of a certain worldview, a resident of a particular place? Is "Judaism" what royal scribes say, what later rabbis say, or whatever one claims it to be? The attempt by writers like E. P. Sanders[9] to extract a core Judaism (which he called "covenantal nomism") has been strenuously refuted in the face of strong evidence of irreconcilable differences among various expressions of what might be considered "Judaisms."[10] In other words, what we've seen at the root of Israelite religion remained true

---

7. Sometimes referred to by the Hebrew acronym, Tanak: Torah, Nebiim (prophets), and Ketuvim (writings).

8. Cohen (2001); Mason. Cf. Blenkinsopp (2009), 27–28, who argues from usage in Esther and Zechariah for an earlier sense of "Jewish" identity.

9. Sanders (1977).

10. E.g., Neusner (1990), Collins (1999), and Elliott (2000). This is discussed further in chapter 26.

throughout history. There have *always* been multiple and often opposing expressions of religion in the Name of YHWH.

Second, the supposed conflict between the religion of "Jews" and the ways of life labeled "Hellenism" has been shown to be both overstated and misleading. For instance, Erich S. Gruen has shown in great detail how the supposed anti-Hellenistic campaign of the Maccabees was in fact opposed not to "Hellenism" but to "consorting with the enemy," i.e., the Seleucid king.[11] Older scholarship assumed that *Palestinian* Yahwism was somehow less "tainted" by Hellenism than forms embodied in the Diaspora, but this, too, has been shown not to be the case. Just as American Christians take completely for granted the cultural milieu of the English language, democracy, and individual rights, while continuing to argue about specific elements of that culture (e.g., consumerism, the "American dream"), so "Jews" throughout the Mediterranean accepted the general environment of Greek culture, reserving argument for specific components.[12]

Thus, to understand the vehemence with which our texts express their perspectives, we must be clear on what the issues *weren't* before we can see what they *were*. They are not positing a pure and sacred "Judaism" against an impure and profane "Hellenism."[13] Similarly, they are not promoting the Jerusalem-centered community over against the communities scattered throughout the Mediterranean under Greek rule. What they *were* doing was promoting or resisting, to varying degrees, collaboration with the Greek empire as a means for faithful obedience to YHWH.

Wisdom from Above: A Brief Overview of "Royal Wisdom"

We saw in Part II that Solomon's "dream" for the gift of God's wisdom sounded more like royal propaganda than authentic divine revelation. The first "counter-story" to challenge the claim to divine authorization for Solomon's "wisdom" was Genesis 2, in which the "knowledge of good and evil" — precisely the content of Solomon's dream-desire[14] — was *forbidden* to humans.[15] Possession of such "wisdom" led not to human flourishing but to expulsion from YHWH's original "place" for humanity, within the

---

11. Gruen, 6. This is discussed further in chapter 19.
12. Collins (2005b), 25–26.
13. However, as we'll see in chapter 19, the Hasmoneans, who ruled from Jerusalem after the Maccabees' victory, *presented* themselves as engaged in such a struggle against "Hellenism," even while they embodied much of what they purported to resist.
14. Gen. 2:9, 17; 3:5; 1 Kings 3:9; 4:28; cf. 2 Sam. 14:17.
15. Although, as we explored in chapter 10, the Exodus narrative was the first written counter-story to the reign of Solomon, it didn't challenge directly his claim to divine wisdom. Rather, it presented divine wisdom *distributed among the people* rather than lodged exclusively in the king.

Garden of creation. From a political perspective, it led not to "vine and fig trees" for all, but rather the expulsion from the land via exile.

Royal "wisdom" was a standard measure throughout the ancient Near East for a king's worthiness to hold office. The Deuteronomistic History, as we saw, portrays Solomon's personal wisdom with stereotypical royal imagery (e.g., 1 Kings 4:29–34; 10:4–9). The Exodus counter-story portrayed a paranoid, oppressive pharaoh who was anything but "wise" in his treatment of the Israelites or his own people.

Yet in the Hellenistic era — and perhaps already within the previous Babylonian and Persian eras[16] — Israelite writers again took up the genre of royal wisdom. This resurgence sought to legitimize the imperial status quo. As Leo Perdue writes,

> Wisdom was a product of the empires, which required savants to write court annals, teachings of moral virtues to the elite and professionals who held important posts, ... and a crafted ideology that provided the legitimation of reigning kings and dynasties. ... Indeed, the important components of sapiential doctrines of justifying kings and their rule included what one finds in later Western European political systems: the rule by divine right in which rulers and dynasties were chosen by the nation's supreme deity, the political order that was based on sacred and revealed law, the extraordinary virtues possessed by the king (justice, beneficence, strength, glory, charity, wisdom, and mercy), and the incomparable intelligence of chosen kings.[17]

James Crenshaw explains how "foreign" this perspective was to the Creation / Exodus biblical paradigm:

> Within Proverbs, Job and Ecclesiastes one looks in vain for the dominant themes of Yahwistic thought: the exodus from Egypt, election of Israel, the Davidic covenant, the Mosaic legislation, the patriarchal narratives, the divine control of history and movement toward a glorious moment when right will triumph. ... When concern for justice surfaces in their teachings, it either registers a protest to God or merely observes the harsh facts of life. The slightest hint of prophetic outcry is wholly lacking in proverbs and maxims.[18]

As these authors show, royal wisdom was all about supporting and preserving "the way things are." Monarchy and the wider socioeconomic hierarchies are simply "givens." A faithful life, from this perspective, does not engage questions of social justice. Instead, it concerns itself with achieving "the good life" for oneself and one's family. Crenshaw notes some of the virtues enshrined in the book of Proverbs:

---

16. Perdue (2008), 117–23, situates at least the core of Job in the Babylonian Exile.
17. Ibid., 1, 13.
18. Crenshaw, 29, 31.

- Obedience to parents
- Self-control, especially of one's words in front of one's social superiors
- Subordination of the passions
- Prudent, calculated actions
- Generosity with one's personal (God-given) wealth[19]

One might compare some of the chapter titles of the 1997 bestseller by former Reagan Secretary of Education William Bennett,[20] *The Book of Virtues:*

- Self-discipline
- Compassion
- Responsibility
- Work
- Perseverance
- Honesty
- Loyalty

Elite wisdom has not changed much over the centuries. The problem, of course, is not these virtues in themselves, but rather, what they omit. Missing is YHWH's empowerment of people to protest injustice or to care for widows, orphans, and other persons on the social margins. Perdue writes, "The sages of Proverbs had little place for radicals who demanded a more just society."[21] One can develop one's "moral character" while one's food and clothing are produced by slaves or children in sweatshops without raising an eyebrow.

Such wisdom purports to be ahistorical, culled from "universal" principles independent of the specific situation "on the ground."[22] Not surprisingly, wisdom from the Hellenistic era imagines a YHWH far removed from the struggle for justice. Perdue notes that this YHWH "is neither the eschatological God who draws history to its culmination nor YHWH of Israel's salvation history."[23] No wonder the great themes of biblical narrative are virtually never mentioned in royal wisdom. They are not relevant to the expression of "transcendent" truths in an unchanging and unchangeable world.

---

19. Ibid., 81–85.
20. Bennett himself is a perfect expression of the social location that produces such wisdom. As his bookcover proclaims, in addition to serving within the Cabinet, he has a Ph.D. and law degree from top universities and is a Fellow with the elite conservative Heritage Foundation and a senior editor of the neoconservative journal *National Review.*
21. Perdue (2008), 114.
22. Crenshaw, 55.
23. Perdue (2008), 7.

Royal wisdom claimed to be deducible from human observations of nature and the social world, without any kind of active, personal relationship with YHWH. Indeed, it was openly suspicious of such claims, as elite wisdom continues to be today. An exclusively transcendent God does not communicate directly with people, but can be known only indirectly. People build up wisdom over the generations rather than having it revealed in a flash of divine inspiration or revelation.

It was the realm of people with elite credentials. Its audience was not everyday folk, but the children of the privileged. Perdue notes that the purveyors of royal wisdom served "as scribes and sages in these [royal] administrations, as advisors to rulers, and as teachers in wisdom schools that primarily prepared young men for scribal and official positions in the government (royal or colonial) and temple."[24]

Finally, royal wisdom was openly international in scope, borrowing freely from various national traditions. For example, much of the book of Proverbs echoes ancient Egyptian traditions, as well as newer traditions developed under Alexander the Great and his successors.[25]

Hellenistic Royal Ideology in Ptolemaic Egypt

This hospitable cross-cultural mingling enabled Alexander and the Ptolemaic Dynasty to interweave Greek and Egyptian traditions in establishing their monarchies as the divine order. Although royal wisdom purported to be universal and ahistorical, priests and politicians knew better: each local people had specific traditions that bound them together. These had to be taken into account by royal propagandists for their message to "stick." It is generally more effective — and much cheaper — to *seduce* people into accepting control by a foreign empire than to bully them violently into submission.[26] It will be instructive to look briefly at how the Ptolemies did it. This will enable us better to understand the dissenting view expressed in *1 Enoch's Book of the Watchers*.

Alexander and his successors faced two major ideological challenges. First, as Gunther Hölbl writes, he "had to distance himself from his Persian predecessors so as to appear as a liberator of the land and not yet another conqueror."[27] The Egyptians had greatly detested Persian rule. Alexander presented himself as anti-Persian by, among other acts, offering sacrifice to the fertility god Apis. This stance enabled the Ptolemies to gain the support of the Egyptian priesthoods for the stringent economic policy necessary to

---

24. Ibid., 101.
25. Crenshaw, 98; Perdue (2008), 14.
26. Note the portrayal in the book of Revelation of empire as both violent "beast" and seductive "whore."
27. Hölbl, 78.

carry out the seemingly endless wars with the rival Seleucids over the next hundred years.[28]

Second, he had to gain the support and loyalty of the same priests for his assumption of the dual roles of Greek king and Egyptian pharaoh. The Greek royal cult had developed as people's belief in the traditional gods of Olympus waned. The key element was the king's "charismatic invincibility, which was upheld by the gods and which had to be proven if recognition by the kingdom's subjects was to be secured." The kingship "transformed him into a saviour, liberator (especially of Greek cities), protector and begetter and guarantor of fertility and affluence."[29] In contrast, the invincibility of the pharaoh was "affirmed in his role as the victorious [god] Horus. . . . It was of little consequence whether he fulfilled the obligations of this role on campaign outside Egypt or in a temple ritual with a priest acting as his representative."[30]

The Ptolemies carefully crafted a strategy to accomplish this goal. Beginning with Ptolemy I, the dynasty itself was deified as a matter of state policy. The dead Alexander was elevated to the level of a state god and the priest of the cult named for him became the highest state priest in the land.[31] He was declared the "New Dionysus" and thus associated with the triumphal return of Dionysus from the East.[32] This set not just individual kings but the entire Ptolemaic dynasty among the gods.

Next, they sought to establish worship of divinities that would unite not only Greeks and Egyptians, but all the peoples they had conquered. One of these gods was Zeus-Ammon, who was of Egyptian origin and had sites dedicated to him in Greece and Macedonia. Another was the new god Serapis, connected with both Isis (mother of Horus) and Osiris (god of the dead, but also known as Horus's father). A temple to Serapis, the Serapeum, was built in Alexandria in the mid-third century, and was a center of urban life until destroyed by a Christian mob in 391 CE.[33] As Hölbl writes,

> On the one hand, Isis and Serapis were seen as Hellenistic gods integrated into the Greek world but, on the other, they were also viewed as ancient Egyptian divinities. Their dual nature thus corresponded nicely to the twofold aspect of the Ptolemaic king. . . . The religion of Isis and Serapis spread quickly throughout the eastern Mediterranean from the end of the fourth century onward.[34]

Finally, the Ptolemies developed an annual synod of Egyptian priests, meeting at the king's court to discuss cultic and economic matters. The

---

28. Ibid., 81.
29. Ibid., 91.
30. Ibid.
31. Ibid., 94.
32. Pàmias, 192–93.
33. For the events that led to this destruction, see Haas, 159–69.
34. Ibid., 100–101.

Ptolemies "encouraged the clergy to express its loyalty openly as a means to gain support for their regime and to counteract the resentment of the native population toward a foreign dynasty.... The priests, for their part, increasingly came to expect concessions from the king during this period."[35] Poets and other scholars were enlisted in the generation of royal propaganda connecting the dynasty with its supposed divine ancestors.[36]

However, beneath the surface of this public synthesis of Hellenistic and Egyptian religions, turmoil was brewing. A series of Egyptian texts express outrage at and condemnation of Greek rule. Consider two examples. The "Demotic Chronicle" was likely produced in the first half of the Ptolemaic dynasty, no later than the reign of 246–21.[37] Its "fundamental theme ... is that only those kings will endure who live in accordance with the will of the gods," known as *ma'at* in Egyptian.[38] It reflects a theology not unlike that of the Deuteronomistic History: harmony with divine will is revealed through worldly success of all kinds. It attributes the failures of the preceding three centuries — including Persian and Greek invasions — to the rulers being out of such divine harmony. It envisions the expulsion of foreigners and the resuscitation of an Egyptian national state.[39]

Another text with even more explicit criticism of the accommodation to foreign empire is the "Potter's Oracle," perhaps from the late second century BCE.[40] It prophesied a series of troubles destined to befall Egypt, including a bad king who would found a new city and introduce a new god: Alexander and Serapis are clearly in mind. This would generate not blessing but misfortune on a grand scale, including "famine, murder, the collapse of the moral order, and oppression" leading to civil war among the Greeks.[41] The disaster would end with the coming of a new king, with the assistance of Isis, who would inaugurate a golden age of justice and harmony.[42]

These documents were accompanied by increasingly widespread revolt among the lower classes that lasted until the coming of Rome, including strikes and mass flights into the desert.[43] The priesthoods were divided, some collaborating with the Ptolemies to their own enrichment and others seeking to inspire the natives to resistance and maintenance of their ancestral religious traditions.

Jerusalem and its surrounding area were subject to these same Ptolemies. As we've seen, "royal wisdom" texts supported the status quo, reducing faithfulness to YHWH to a matter of personal virtue. But as in Egypt, not

---

35. Ibid., 106.
36. Pàmias, 193.
37. Lloyd, 41.
38. Ibid.
39. Ibid., 44.
40. Ibid., 51.
41. Ibid.
42. Ibid.
43. Ibid., 36; Hölbl, 153.

all of Israel's priests and scribes were imperial collaborators.[44] A powerful tradition began in this period if not earlier. If not for the Dead Sea Scrolls, we might still not know about the resistance movement that became part of the foundation for the biblical book of Daniel and, in many ways, for the Gospel of Jesus Christ. That tradition is gathered in the book known today as *1 Enoch*, as we'll see. Its claim to authority from a source earlier than Moses enabled it to fight for a hearing at a time when the Jerusalem temple scribes had determined, at least implicitly, that the "era of prophecy" had ended.

"I Will Send You the Prophet Elijah": *Malachi and the Closure of the Era of Prophecy*

People identifying themselves as, in one way or another, part of the family of Abraham who worshiped YHWH were scattered all around the Mediterranean. Erich S. Gruen has shown how numerous texts from these people made enormous efforts to root their beliefs and practices in ancient revelation and experience.[45] Extremely creative stories were told to show, for example, that the Greeks were dependent on Moses for their wisdom. Part of the impetus for these ingenious narratives was the desire to root personal identity in an "ancient" collective narrative.

For the Jerusalem elite, this led to the shaping of the collection of disparate pieces of Scripture into what purported — for the first time — to be a continuous, divinely inspired narrative: the torah and the prophets.

This was not yet a "canon" in the sense of a closed set of "books" that one might call a "Bible." We'll see in chapter 19 that it was most likely under Hasmonean rule that something like an "official" collection was promulgated.[46] During the period of Ptolemaic rule, though, scribes took one major step in this direction. They claimed that the "era of prophecy" had ended under the Persian authority of Ezra. This had huge implications for texts yet to be written, especially those, such as *1 Enoch* and Daniel, that challenged the official view of what God was doing during Hellenistic rule.

One key passage undergirding this claim is the conclusion of what is now the book of Malachi:

> Remember the teaching of my servant Moses, the statutes and ordinances that I commanded him at Horeb for all Israel. Lo, I will send you the prophet Elijah before the great and terrible day of YHWH comes. (Eng. 4:3–4; Heb. 3:22–24)

The name "Malachi" is Hebrew, meaning "my messenger." There was not a person called "Malachi" whose words are in this book; rather, the

---

44. For the religious and sociological bases for scribal resistance, see Horsley (2010), 9–17.
45. Gruen.
46. Carr (2005), 253–76.

book is a composition of three separate pronouncements plus this editorial conclusion.[47] The book was likely composed in the early Persian period, after the temple reconstruction.[48] Its function was to create a twelfth unit in the scroll of what we call the "minor prophets," beginning with Hosea. This "completed" the scroll, the Prophets and the wider collection of "prophetic" (i.e., "inspired") texts. Karel Van Der Toorn explains the purpose of the editorial closing verses:

> The double edge of the epilogue reflects the two major concerns of the editors. The Torah of Moses is the ultimate source of authority they acknowledge; attributed to Moses in his capacity as "servant" of YHWH, it contains the "decrees and verdicts..." for every Israelite. But the tenor and the phraseology are strongly reminiscent of the Book of Deuteronomy. The scribal editors imply that the publication of the Prophets is not meant to take the place of the Torah but to serve as a reminder of its importance.
>
> The second part of the epilogue has a Deuteronomic flavor as well. Since the era of the prophets has come to a close, the editors do not predict the coming of a new prophet but the return of a famous prophet of old. Their source of inspiration is Deuteronomy 18:15–18, where God announces that He will raise up a prophet like Moses.... The Jerusalem editors of the Minor Prophets identify this Restorer with Elijah; he would restore... the heart of the fathers to the sons and vice versa.[49]

We'll see that this "closure" was ripped open at the beginning of Mark's Gospel. But for the Hellenistic, Jerusalem scribes, the closure of the "prophetic era" meant that from their time forward, no new "word of YHWH" would be proclaimed, although it was still possible to "discover" previous such words that had somehow been "lost." This era was clearly defined: "Moses stands at its beginning and Ezra at its end. Everything written that is holy and inspired can have come only from their time."[50] This helps to explain what we find in all the subsequent texts until the New Testament: the "author" must be someone from within this Moses-Ezra frame.

The other important outcome of this "closure" was the rejection of any new revelation claimed to flow from a living relationship with YHWH. Now one can, according to this scribal ideology, only "know" YHWH from study of past revelations. Jesus of Nazareth boldly confronted this ideology, claiming a direct relationship with the living YHWH as the source of his wisdom. For now, those who took issue had to present their "wisdom" through the mouths of prophets of old, such as the primordial patriarch, Enoch, seventh generation son of Adam.

---

47. Van Der Toorn, 252–54. Cf. Sweeney (2000b), 714, who argues that the closing verses "are integral to the prophet's speech and argument in Mal. 3:13–24 [NRSV: 3:13–4:6]."

48. Sweeney (2000b), 715, 719.

49. Van Der Toorn, 253–54.

50. Ibid., 256.

"All the Earth Was Filled
with the Godlessness and Violence That Had Befallen It":
First Enoch's "Book of the Watchers"

The biblical texts we have considered so far come in forms relatively "user friendly" to today's readers. We have heard historical narratives and prophetic speeches speak about events that may be unfamiliar to us, but about which we can relatively easily come to an understanding with a bit of background about names, dates, and sociopolitical circumstances.

But when we turn to *1 Enoch,* we enter a different realm. George Nickelsburg, one of the foremost students of this literature, explains:

> In a "postmodern" twenty-first century, the Enochic world seems strange, fantastic, and even weird: fallen angels mating with mortal women, the ghosts of dead giants roaming the earth, flights to heaven, and bizarre visions about sheep and wild beasts. One should not be deceived, however. When read with care and empathy, the unfamiliar imagery comes alive to reveal a humanity much like our own. They struggle with violence, lies, disappointment, and lack of meaning, and they are pulled in opposite directions by hope and despair and the competing forces of high religious symbols and explosive human emotions.[51]

For most Christians today, *1 Enoch* is not only strange in language and imagery; it is totally unknown. I hope that readers will be willing to become familiar enough with this collection to note two things. First, we will explore how it radically opposes in the name of YHWH the royal wisdom we have just explored. Second, we will see how it bridges the tradition of anti-imperial resistance between the prophets and the New Testament. To engage *1 Enoch,* we must first comprehend what the book is and where it came from.

Wisdom from on High: An Overview of 1 Enoch

For centuries, the only manuscripts of *1 Enoch* available were those contained within the Ethiopic Bible, copies of which are extant from the fifteenth-nineteenth centuries CE, and fragments in Greek from the fourth to the sixth centuries CE. With the discovery of the Dead Sea Scrolls, however, a treasury of portions of *1 Enoch* in Aramaic was added to the Ethiopic manuscripts. The Aramaic manuscripts widened the scope of available texts

---

51. Nickelsburg (2001), 1. This volume is the first of two by Nickelsburg offering a detailed exploration of the origins, language and themes in *1 Enoch* along with a detailed commentary. All quotations from *1 Enoch* are from Nickelsburg and VanderKam (2004), which is a companion to the 2001 volume.

Table 23: The Books of *1 Enoch*

Title	Chapters	Date of Composition	Historical Context
Astronomical Book	72–82	?	Persian era?
Book of the Watchers	1–36	Third century BCE	Advent of Ptolemaic rule
Dream Visions, including the *Apocalypse of Weeks*	83–90	160s BCE	Antiochus IV Epiphanes and Maccabean revolt
Epistle of Enoch, including the *Animal Apocalypse*[52]	91–107	Mid–late second century BCE	Hasmonean dynasty
Parables of Enoch	37–71	Mid-first century CE	Roman occupation of Palestine

and allowed scholars to situate more specifically the origins and development of what is now a 108 chapter collection.[53]

Most scholars understand the collection to consist of five "books" written over at least 250 and perhaps as many as 500 years. Table 23 provides an overview.

First Enoch is thus a composite tradition much like the canonical book of Isaiah, itself written over the course of some three hundred years. But unlike Isaiah, its voice is an ancient figure with little connection to actual history: Enoch, seventh generation son of Adam (Gen. 5:18–24). What are we to make of the purported authorship of these writings by a person from the primordial past?

We are dealing here with a phenomenon scholars refer to as *pseud-epigrapha*: the "false attribution" of authorship, especially to persons from the distant past or who may not have been historical persons at all. John J. Collins notes that the phenomenon was widespread in the Hellenistic age, found in Babylonian, Persian, and Egyptian prophecy, along with the "Jew-ish" texts we'll be considering such as *1 Enoch*.[54] Of course, texts from the Hellenistic era are no more pseudepigraphal than earlier texts such as Deuteronomy and the other "books of Moses." Is authorship of *any* of the books in the canon of Hebrew Scripture attributed to the "real" writer(s)?

Collins continues by claiming that "the effectiveness of the device pre-supposes the credulity of the masses" who would be taken in by what the actual authors know is a "false" claim to authorship.[55] Mark Adam Elliott has challenged this perspective:

---

52. Boccaccini (1998), 104–12, argues for a "proto-Epistle" from the mid-second century that was then added onto later; see also Nickelsburg (2003a) and Boccaccini (2003) for further debate on this point.

53. Nickelsburg and VanderKam, 13; more detailed explanation is provided at Nickels-burg (2001), 9–20. I encourage readers to obtain a copy of this new translation of *1 Enoch* by Nickelsburg and VanderKam, which renders the original languages in accessible and exciting English. All quotations from *1 Enoch* herein are from that translation.

54. Collins (1998), 39.

55. Ibid., 40.

...not enough attention has been given to how improbable this is, inasmuch as a discovery or even suspicion of falsification would automatically override any authority the message may have wished to project, just the opposite of what was intended.... Far more likely is that works presented under the names of ancient worthies either contained traditional material whose origins were lost to antiquity or, alternatively, that the material was believed to have been transmitted in more mystical ways.[56]

Collins assumes that the authors are being deceptive, claiming false authority to enhance their credibility.[57] Elliott, on the other hand, assumes that these texts are from sincere people who are engaged in an authentic search for God's will in their time. Although we cannot "know" the intentions of ancient authors, especially those hidden behind pseudepigraphal texts, the following discussion sides with Elliott on this question. *First Enoch* was most likely written by people seeking to wake up their audiences to the deeper reality of sociopolitical events and God's relationship to those events. The authors were not trying to pull a fast one on a credible audience, but seeking to convince their hearers to reject "royal wisdom" and the imperial status quo it supported.

The opening quote from Nickelsburg prepares us to encounter within *1 Enoch* imagery far different from ordinary experience, then or now. That imagery, contained within purported dreams and tours of heaven under angelic guidance, has been traditionally labeled "apocalyptic." There are at least two major challenges to readers today in applying this label. First, the term is used in popular culture, both religious and secular, to refer to "end of the world" violence and destruction.[58] In fact, the word comes from the Greek *apokaluptō*, meaning "to lift the veil," i.e., to reveal something otherwise hidden from human view. It is essential that readers put aside pop culture and "rapture"-related presuppositions in order to hear what our ancient authors were trying to convey in "apocalyptic" texts.

Second, scholars have argued seemingly endlessly about definitions of the terms "apocalypse" (a kind/genre of text), "apocalyptic" (a worldview expressed in writing) and "apocalypticism" (a historical movement).[59] The purpose of the search for a precise definition of a supposed genre called "apocalypse" was to distinguish it from other genres, such as "wisdom." This project was itself a function of an older way of conceiving of biblical texts known as "form criticism," in which determining the "form" (genre) of a text was the first step in understanding its historical context and hence its meaning.

---

56. Elliott (2000), 463.

57. Note the similar argument made by New Testament scholars about "deutero-Pauline" epistles such as 1–2 Timothy and Titus.

58. For a history of this use within premillennialism, see Howard-Brook and Gwyther, 3–18.

59. See generally Collins (1998), 1–42.

However, more recent understandings of texts in general and of the ancient world in particular have challenged many of the presuppositions underlying this project. Scholars are increasingly coming to recognize that categories such as "apocalypse" and "wisdom" as labels for texts are functions of the modern scholarly mind, not of the ancient authors or of their worlds.[60] No definition completely separates one of these supposed genres from the other, nor are the worldviews of "wisdom" and "apocalyptic" sealed off from each other.

First Enoch, no less than texts traditionally understood as "wisdom literature" such as Proverbs or Qoheleth, is a search for "wisdom" written by members of the scribal elite.[61] The section we are about to engage, the *Book of the Watchers* (*BW*), claims to be the voice of Enoch, "righteous scribe" (*1 En.* 12:4). It is not the *goal* that differs between royal wisdom texts and *1 Enoch;* it is, among other things, the *sources* of "wisdom" that each text claims as the means to know YHWH's will. To obtain royal wisdom, one must use one's rational mind, oriented around the "fear of YHWH," to examine torah texts and creation itself. For *1 Enoch,* on the other hand, the primary source is a *direct, revelatory experience* of "heaven," i.e., the "other side of the veil" separating the part of creation ordinarily experienced by human beings from the wider realm of YHWH's power and authority.[62]

This basic distinction in wisdom sources will continue to be asserted, in both directions, for hundreds of years, from the beginning of the Ptolemaic empire in the third century BCE through the first century CE Roman Empire. That is, upholders of royal wisdom — such as Sadducees — will reject claims to revelatory insight (e.g., Mark 12:18; Acts 23:8), while Jesus, Paul, and others gifted with apocalyptic visions will castigate those who deny the power of YHWH to reveal truth directly to people (e.g., Mark 12:24; 1 Cor. 1–2). *First Enoch* is thus the beginning of over four hundred years of confrontation between what we've been calling "the two religions" in a new arena: the search for wisdom.

The Anti-Imperial Thrust of the Entire Corpus of 1 Enoch

Scholars have long recognized that *1 Enoch* is "dissent literature," vehemently challenging the status quo of Hellenistic and Roman Judea. It has been more difficult, though, to specify what exactly the argument is about.

---

60. See the programmatic volume ed. Wright and Wills growing out of the Society of Biblical Literature's Wisdom and Apocalypticism Group; see also Horsley (2007), esp. 2–13, wherein he summarizes the insights of the Wright and Wills volume and proposes a new methodology for reading texts such as *1 Enoch,* Sirach and Daniel; and also Horsley (2010), 1–8.

61. E.g., Horsley (2010), 48.

62. Post-Enlightenment thinking has, under the influence of Greek philosophy, spoken in terms of "natural" and "supernatural" realms. For people oriented exclusively around scientific ways of knowing, "supernatural" is often simply a polite term for "imaginary" or more polemically, "illusory." For biblically oriented people, however, "creation" was not divided into such spheres but instead is collectively designated "heaven(s) and earth," e.g., Gen. 1:1. From this perspective, communication from or visions of "heaven" are no more strange than rain or snow moving between heaven and earth; e.g., Isa. 55:8–11.

Some have suggested that it was primarily a matter of priestly prerogatives: the establishment "Zadokites" excluding those who became identified as "Enochians," who responded to this priestly exclusion by seeing the world not as orderly but as "chaotic."[63] But as we'll see, throughout the collection, criticism is not so much of priests themselves (although *1 Enoch* is certainly critical of the Jerusalem temple and its priestly supporters), as of those named as "giants" (in *Book of the Watchers*) and "the kings, the mighty and exalted who possess the earth" (in *Parables*). *First Enoch* expresses a *sustained protest, in the Name of YHWH, against Judea's priestly, royal, and scribal elites for their collaboration with foreign empires.* Its purpose and message parallel the Egyptian protest literature we considered in the preceding section.

This should not surprise us, given how deeply *1 Enoch* is grounded in the Primeval History of Genesis. We saw in Part I how the opening chapters of the Hebrew Scriptures parody the Babylonian *Enuma Elish* and offer a counter-narrative of YHWH as peaceful and benevolent Creator of all that is, including the earth, its animals, and all its peoples. *First Enoch* offers what one might call a "midrash" or commentary on Genesis 1–11, from the perspective of Israelites living first under Ptolemaic and then Seleucid rule.[64] Its critique is as radical as that of Exodus against the imperial story of David and Solomon, and of the prophets against the kings and wealthy elite of both Israel and Judah.

Why was *1 Enoch* not included within the biblical canon? It was definitely understood as an inspired book at the time of Jesus, as we see by its quotation in the New Testament book of Jude:

> It was also about these [evildoers] that Enoch, in the seventh generation from Adam, prophesied, saying, "See, YHWH is coming with ten thousands of his holy ones, to execute judgment on all, and to convict everyone of all the deeds of ungodliness that they have committed in such an ungodly way, and of all the harsh things that ungodly sinners have spoken against him." (Jude 14–15)

References to *1 Enoch* abound in early Christian writers such as Origen.[65] We'll look in the next chapter at how the apocalyptic book of Daniel differed from *1 Enoch* and why it, but not *1 Enoch,* made the "cut" of the Hebrew Scriptures. But it should not be too surprising that a text that characterized the entire Second Temple as "impure," rejects (at least initially) the torah of Moses as authoritative and castigates relentlessly the elite collaborators with empire, would not be enshrined as "inspired" by that same elite. Much as the

---

63. E.g., Boccaccini (1998), 99–100 and (2002), 77.

64. "Midrash" refers to the largely postbiblical Jewish tradition of interpreting biblical texts by imaginative retellings that fill in "missing" details of event or intention; see, e.g., Neusner (1994 and 2004). For an engagement between midrash and intertextuality, see Boyarin (1994a).

65. VanderKam (1995); Nickelsburg (2001), 86–94.

writings of some twentieth-century liberation theologians were condemned by church officials for their alleged association with "Marxism" and other "sins," so *1 Enoch* was rejected by writers such as Sirach, Qoheleth, and other purveyors of elite wisdom. But for others, *1 Enoch,* more than royal wisdom texts, conveyed an inspired Word of YHWH to guide them through difficult times.

Book of the Watchers *as Anti-imperial Counter-Wisdom*

The *Book of the Watchers* (*BW*) begins with an introduction (chapters 1–5), which many believe was added later to the narrative in chapters 11–36.[66] The opening chapters consist of three parts: the introduction of Enoch (1:1–3), a theophany of God's coming in judgment (1:4–9), and an indictment and judgment against the wicked and for the "chosen" (2:1–5:9).

Enoch presents himself as "a righteous man whose eyes were opened by God" (1:2). Genesis says that Enoch "walked with God, then he was no more, because God took him" (Gen. 5:24). This enigmatic passage is the basis for claiming Enoch as the source of ancient revelation. His description here as "a righteous man" matches that of his grandson, Noah (Gen. 6:9; 7:1). Noah is the only person in Genesis said to be "righteous," just as Enoch is the only named individual with that attribution in *1 Enoch.* The term "righteous," though, is used throughout all of *1 Enoch,* with reference to God, God's chosen people, and the coming Righteous One. It carries legal connotations, befitting the context of judgment with which the book opens and with which it is suffused.

Richard Horsley sees these opening verses resembling the oracles of Balaam in Numbers 22–24. He comments, "This clearly suggests a political role of Enoch scribes: they saw themselves as the heirs of diviner-prophets such as Balaam, and as constrained by God to prophesy against their aristocratic patrons, the heads of the Judean temple-state."[67]

The theophany that follows closely parallels Psalm 97, a celebration of the kingship of YHWH, as shown in Table 24.

The tradition underlying this psalm's powerful revelation of YHWH-the-Creator's rule (e.g., Mic. 1:2–7; Jer. 25:30–38) "was sharply political, pronouncing condemnation of oppressive domestic or foreign rulers and their defeat by God acting as divine Warrior with heavenly armies."[68]

First Enoch regularly refers to Hebrew Scripture, but a thorough examination reveals that it is highly selective. One can hear in *1 Enoch* echoes of Genesis, Psalms, and prophets like Isaiah and Ezekiel, but other parts are conspicuously absent, especially the name of Moses and the books of "his" torah. For the author of *BW*, the Mosaic torah had become corrupted in the hands of the temple elite. Before Moses, though, YHWH's wisdom was

66. Nickelsburg (2001), 25.
67. Horsley (2007), 157; also (2010), 51.
68. Horsley (2007), 158.

Table 24: Parallel Imagery in Psalm 97 and *1 Enoch* 1:4–8

Excerpts from Psalm 97	*Excerpts from 1 Enoch 1:4–8*
YHWH is king!	The Great Holy One will come forth from his dwelling,
Righteousness and justice are the foundation of his throne.	and the eternal God will tread from thence upon Mount Sinai.
Fire goes before him, and consumes his adversaries on every side. His lightnings light up the world; **the earth sees and trembles.**	**All the ends of the earth will be shaken, and trembling** and great fear will seize them until the ends of the earth.
The **mountains melt like wax before YHWH,** The heavens proclaim his righteousness; and all the peoples behold his glory. All worshipers of images are put to shame, those who make their boast in worthless idols; all gods bow down before him.	The high mountains will be shaken and fall and break apart, and the **high hills will be made low and melt like wax before the fire.** The earth will be wholly rent asunder, and everything on the earth will perish, and there will be judgment on all.
YHWH loves those who hate evil; he guards the lives of his faithful; he rescues them from the hand of the wicked.	**With the righteous he will make peace, and over the chosen there will be protection, and upon them will be mercy.**
Light dawns for the righteous, and joy for the upright in heart.	**Light will shine upon them,** and he will make peace with them.

revealed to Enoch. Although Genesis became part of the Second Temple's torah, its story precedes Moses and the giving of "the law," a point that will be taken up hundreds of years later by the apostle Paul. *First Enoch* is thus thoroughly grounded in the Word of YHWH, but stands, as have its dissenting predecessors, over against the texts claimed by Jerusalem's Ptolemaic collaborators.

The final part of the introductory chapters begins with a call to contemplate God's works in nature, a theme fully at home in the royal wisdom tradition. The point is to observe the constancy of earth, seasons, and trees, which "carry out and do not alter their works from his words" (4:3). In contrast are "you" who have "not stood firm...but you have turned aside" (4:4). These will be cursed, while the "chosen" will rejoice, receiving "forgiveness of sins and all mercy and peace and clemency" (4:6). After the judgment on sinners, "wisdom will be given to all the chosen and they will all live" (4:8). The benediction on the chosen echoes Third Isaiah, where rejoicing and fullness of days accompany "my chosen" (Isa. 65:13–25), with one enormous difference. The biblical prophet foresees a renewed Jerusalem in which YHWH dwells, although without a human-made "house" (66:1). The author of *BW*, though, does not specify where the chosen will find their joy and peace. Jerusalem is never mentioned in the entire book of *1 Enoch*. As with his foundational text of Genesis 1–11, our author has nothing good to say about human cities.

The narrative that follows in *1 En.* 6–16 combines two stories of the fallen "Watchers," one in which the evil chief is named Shemihazah, and the other in which he is named Asael. The combined story symbolically denounces the effect of rule under the successors of Alexander. It takes as a template the brief story in Genesis 6:1–4 of the "sons of God" taking wives from among humans and bearing children through them. The anti-imperial thrust of the Genesis story is clear:

> Nephilim [LXX, *gigantes*, "giants"] were on the earth in those days — and also afterward — when the sons of God went in to the daughters of humans, who bore children to them. These were the heroes [*haggiborim*, like Nimrod, Gen. 10:8] that were of old, men of the name [anticipating Gen. 11:4, the Tower of Babel builders]. (Gen. 6:4)

The verses that follow immediately link these "giant men of the name" with the "wickedness of humankind...on the earth" that causes the Flood. It is here that we learn that Noah, Enoch's grandson, is the "righteous man" who will be saved from the judgment. Genesis 6:1–4 describes the intrusion into God's creation of those perceived to be "sons of God," a title commonly taken by imperial rulers. *BW* fertilizes this story-seed until it blossoms into a full narrative.

Those referred to in Genesis 6 as "sons of God" are called in *BW* "sons of heaven" and then later, Watchers. The children of the union of "two hundred" of these sons of heaven and human wives are described as "great giants," who in turn bore Nephilim (*1 En.* 7:2). We then hear the result of this new generation:

> They were devouring the labor of all the sons of men, and men were not able to supply them. And the giants began to kill men and to devour them.... Asael taught men to make swords of iron and weapons and shields and breastplates and every instrument of war. (7:3, 8:1)

It presents the origins of imperial exploitation of the labor of ordinary people — a theme flowing from Exodus 1–2 through Nehemiah 5 in earlier biblical narratives — and how that economic exploitation leads to surpluses that enable a war economy.[69]

The text continues by describing how they taught people spells, sorcery, and astrology, after which "as men were perishing, the cry went up to

---

69. Cf. Ibid., 160.

heaven" (8:4). This garners the attention in heaven of four angels: Michael, Sariel, Raphael, and Gabriel, who "saw much bloodshed on the earth. All the earth was filled with the godlessness and violence that had befallen it" (9:1). Nickelsburg comments:

> This emphasis suggests a setting in the wars of the Diadochi (323–302 BCE). A large cast of Macedonian chieftains corresponds to the giants. These two decades are a period of continued war, bloodshed, and assassination.... The image of divine beginning is reminiscent of claims that some of the Diadochi had gods as their fathers.... The myth would be an answer to these claims in the form of a kind of parody. The author would be saying, "Yes, their fathers were divine; however, they were not gods, but demons — angels who rebelled against the authority of God."[70]

The angels gather around the throne of the "Most High," whom they address:

> You are the God of gods and Lord of lords and King of kings and God of the age. And the throne of your glory (exists) for every generation of the generations that are from of old. And your name (is) holy and great and blessed for all the ages. For you have made all things and have authority over all. And all things are manifest and uncovered before you, and you see all things, and there is nothing that can be hidden from you. (9:4–5)

Nickelsburg notes that this imagery of God as king on his throne permeates the entire book:

> By depicting God as king, the Enochic authors provide their readers or audience with a familiar point of reference; they lived in a world that was ruled by earthly kings. At the same time, the terminology made it possible to assert God's status as the *unique* king.[71]

Thus, the angels appeal to this King of kings to act according to his power and to judge those who have filled the earth with violence and blood.[72] The response is a command to go to Noah to prepare for the judgment, in harmony with the Genesis narrative. However, *BW* continues with the command to "bind Asael hand and foot, and cast him into the darkness...and let him dwell there for an exceedingly long time" (10:4–5).[73] A similar command follows to each angel to bind or destroy those now called "Watchers"

---

70. Nickelsburg (2001), 170; also Tiller (2007), 253, and Collins (2005a), 42. Cf. Horsley (2010), 56, who notes that the "actions of the giants, however, need not be confined to the Diadochoi. They might rather pertain generally to the effects of Hellenistic rule on the people of Judea."

71. Nickelsburg (2001), 43, emphasis in original.

72. Cf. Rev. 6:9–10.

73. Cf. Rev. 20:1–3.

until all evil is destroyed and "the earth will be tilled in righteousness" (10:18).

The second part of the story begins in *1 En.* 12 with a command directly to Enoch to go to Asael and announce God's judgment. The Watchers ask Enoch to write a petition seeking forgiveness for their deeds, which he does; he then falls asleep. He has dreams and visions that begin with the rejection of the Watchers' petition and lead to his ascent to the heavenly "great house" (14:10). In imagery reminiscent of Ezekiel 1, Enoch sees the throne with "wheels like the shining sun" and below which are "rivers of flaming fire" (14:18). The throne is surrounded by "ten thousand times ten thousand."[74]

YHWH speaks to Enoch from the heavenly throne the words he is to tell the rebellious Watchers, whose bodies are destroyed but whose spirits now roam the earth to "do violence" and "make desolate" (15:9–11). The concept of disembodied spirits that occupy people and thereby cause destruction and lead humanity astray continues, of course, in the New Testament tradition. Jesus has power over these evil spirits and shares that power with his disciples (e.g., Mark 6:7). In *BW*'s own time, this imagery offers an explanation of the Judeans' sufferings under ongoing Ptolemaic rule:

> with its rigorous economic exploitation of the peoples it controlled, . . . its periodic warfare in Syria-Palestine against the rival Seleucids, . . . its seduction of the indigenous elite to compromise a traditional Judean way of life, . . . and the debilitating effects of all of these on Judean social-economic and personal life. . . . The spirits of the giants are driving imperial kings to the same destructive actions that the giants perpetrated in Enoch's time.[75]

Enoch is then taken on a heavenly tour, which revealed the places of punishment for the rebellious Watchers and the abode of the dead, separated into places for the wicked and the righteous. He then saw a menorah of mountains: seven in a row, three to each side, and a center one that rose above the others. This mountain had "fragrant trees encircling it" with one "such as I had never smelled" which had "a fragrance sweeter smelling than all spices, and its leaves and its blossom and the tree never wither" (24:2–4). Michael then told Enoch that this mountain is "like the throne of God" and that the tree "will be given to the righteous" after it is "transplanted to the holy place, by the house of God, the King of eternity"; its "fragrances will be in their bones and they will live a long life on the earth" (24:3–5). Enoch's journey concludes with a vision of "the paradise of righteousness" in which "the tree of wisdom" stands, and of "whose fruit the holy ones eat and learn great wisdom" (32:3).

This scenario may seem at least partially familiar to readers today who have been raised with images of God's final judgment in which people are

---

74. Cf. Rev. 5:11.
75. Horsley (2007), 161; also (2010), 59.

sent either to a glorious heavenly reward or sentenced to an eternal, fiery hell. But it is essential to note that *this passage is the earliest expression of this imagery*. It stands diametrically opposed to the presuppositions and theology of the Jerusalem temple elite. Gabriele Boccaccini summarizes the contrast:

> Against the Zadokite idea of stability and order, Enochic Judaism introduced the concept of the "end of days" as the time of final judgment and vindication beyond death and history. What in the prophetic tradition was the announcement of some indeterminate future event of God's intervention became the expectation of a final cataclysmic event that will mark the end of God's first creation and the beginning of a second creation — a new world qualitatively different from, and discontinuous with, what was before.... The concept of new creation implies that something went wrong in the first creation — a disturbing and quite embarrassing idea that the Zadokites could not accept without denying the very foundations of their theology and power.[76]

Never before had a Yahwistic writer envisioned God's power of judgment being expressed after death. The Deuteronomistic theology presented a one-to-one correspondence between earthly behavior and earthly outcome: when Israel was obedient, all would be well; when it was disobedient, life on earth would be hell. The purveyors of royal wisdom took up this perspective and presented it as the official theology of the Second Temple, embedded as it was in the torah of Moses. Against this, *BW* presented a shocking alternative: God's judgment was not visible on earth, but would become manifest only after death. And that judgment would fall heavily and irrevocably on those powerful ones, the "giants" and their successors, who taught warfare, shed blood, and disregarded God's righteousness.

Who comprised the "righteous," the "holy ones" who would be saved? Biblical prophets had understood and proclaimed that salvation was for "Israel" as a people. No matter how evil some of the Israelites had been, the fate of one was the fate of all. Destruction of Jerusalem and the Exile were the consequence for YHWH's covenant people — even if the "people of the land" remained and continued their lives while their leaders went to Babylon. The exilic and postexilic visions of Second and Third Isaiah had similarly anticipated the restoration of the whole people of God.

BW, though, does not mention Israel at all. Its presentation of Noah as the "righteous man" offers a pre-"Israelite" conception. "Righteousness" was not a matter of a specific national or ethnic identity, but of living according to the authentic ways of God. As Mark Adam Elliott shows, *BW* is the first in a long series of texts that envision the salvation not of "Israel" but of

---

76. Boccaccini (2002), 91–92.

the "*survivors* of Israel."[77] The conception of survivors of Israel who will
be saved, rather than the nation as a whole, continues through the rest of
the Enochic corpus and into its many branches, including the texts of those
who left Jerusalem to establish a new community in the desert at Qumran.
It will culminate in that group of "survivors of Israel" who will see this
vision through to the end: those followers of Jesus who will become known
as "Christians."

"All Is Vapor": Qoheleth's "Pox" on Both Houses

Then as now, rational minds tend to respond to claims of apocalyptic vision
with skepticism. As the author of Ecclesiastes, also known as Qoheleth,
states: "However much they may toil in seeking, they will not find it out;
even though those who are wise claim to know, they cannot find it out"
(Eccl 8:17).

Qoheleth is a book at least as strange in its own way as *1 Enoch,* but
for very different reasons.[78] Its deity "is not the God of the patriarchs, who
cares for them, or of the Exodus, where he delivers his people out of bondage
and makes a covenant with them, or of the Davidic kings, who blesses them
when they are obedient."[79] It is equally suspicious of torah piety among
practitioners of royal wisdom and of the hope for God's radical reversal of
injustice in *1 Enoch.*[80] It offers no vision of salvation, either for Israel or
the individual. Instead, it counsels, "This is what I have seen to be good: it
is fitting to eat and drink and find enjoyment in all the toil with which one
toils under the sun the few days of the life God gives us; for this is our lot"
(5:18).

Whose voice is this, and from when? The surface claims the voice of Solomon, but the linguistic evidence makes this impossible.[81] Choon-Leong Seow
argues for a date under Persian rule of Yehud, where the money economy
became widespread and drew people into the pursuit of monetary wealth.[82]
Others argue for the Ptolemaic era, sometime in the late third century.[83]

---

77. Elliott (2000), emphasis added. *BW* does not ask the question of whether "the nations"
would be among the survivors. Cf. Isa. 49:6; Mic. 2:12.

78. For a detailed survey of scholarly views on Qoheleth, concluding that the book is
intentionally ambiguous, see Ingram. For a Qoheleth-like assault on the vanity of much scholarly analysis of Qoheleth, see Ellul (1990). For our purposes, we need not resolve the numerous
questions of paradox and meaning within this book, but can focus simply on its relationship
with other third-century BCE forms of "wisdom."

79. Sneed, 4.

80. Perdue (2003), 251.

81. For a detailed analysis of the linguistic evidence relevant to dating, see Seow (1996).
However, Ellul (1990), 20–21, notes the important symbolic role of Solomon as the first person
voice of the book. Given the interpretation of Solomon in chapter 9 of this book, that role
becomes perhaps more ironic than Qoheleth's author intended.

82. Ibid., and Seow (2008).

83. Harrison, 162–65; Perdue (2003), 245 and (2008), 221–24; Boccaccini (2002), 120.

Although Seow shows a strong correlation between the text and social circumstances of the late Achaemenid Persian Empire, the determining factor the other direction may be Qoheleth's opposition to claims of revelatory experience.

If it was not written specifically to oppose, in part, *B W*, it surely serves that purpose well. As Leo Perdue comments, the "most plausible theory for the interpretation of Qoheleth's opponents is that they were primarily apocalyptic sages who are active in the third century BCE and combined apocalyptic language and thought with traditional wisdom and the Torah."[84] Its rejection of *B W's* perspective is clear and consistent. Consider these verses in the context of Enoch's dream-generated tour of heaven:

> God is in heaven, and you upon earth; therefore let your words be
>   few.
> With many dreams come vanities and a multitude of words; but fear
>   God. (5:2, 7)

Similarly, we can hear the opposition to the claim that post-mortem judgment corresponds to one's earthly life:

> For the fate of humans and the fate of animals is the same; as one dies,
> so dies the other. They all have the same breath, and humans have no
> advantage over the animals; for all is vapor. All go to one place; all
> are from the dust, and all turn to dust again. Who knows whether the
> human spirit goes upward and the spirit of animals goes downward to
> the earth? (3:19–21)

At the same time, though, the text resists the claims of royal wisdom that the imperial order corresponds to God's order. For instance, consider this word of what we might call *realpolitik:*

> Keep the king's command because of your sacred oath. Do not be terri-
> fied; go from his presence, do not delay when the matter is unpleasant,
> for he does whatever he pleases. For the word of the king is powerful,
> and who can say to him, "What are you doing?" (8:2–4)

> Do not curse the king, even in your thoughts, or curse the rich, even
> in your bedroom; for a bird of the air may carry your voice, or some
> winged creature tell the matter. (10:20)

In other words, obey the king not because he is doing God's will, but because disobedience will get you in trouble! As Boccaccini comments, "A very convenient political ideology in support of the absolute power of the Hellenistic king and his wealthy allies is turned by Qoheleth into a revelation of God's power."[85]

---

84. Perdue (2003), 245.
85. Boccaccini (2002), 122.

Similarly, Qoheleth is suspicious of Deuteronomistic (royal) theology's claim that wealth and good health are signs of a righteous life. It suggests a "middle way" between pious righteousness and foolish wickedness:

> I have seen everything; there are righteous people who perish in their righteousness, and there are wicked people who prolong their life in their evil-doing. Do not be too righteous, and do not act too wise; why should you destroy yourself? Do not be too wicked, and do not be a fool; why should you die before your time? (7:15–17)

What social location would lead one to stand in opposition to both royal and apocalyptic wisdom? What are the social and political consequences of Qoheleth's rejection of both wisdom perspectives? First, that the author has the leisure and training to observe life and to reflect on it in polished prose places him among the elite. Mark Sneed notes, the "legitimation of a moderate Hellenistic Judean upper class is subtle but strong in the book."[86] Qoheleth sees injustice and poverty around him, but neither involves himself nor offers a vision of a solution. He "appears to be totally oblivious to the fact that his leisure lifestyle of study and writing is dependent on the back-breaking labour of Judean peasants."[87]

His perspective is like many elite intellectuals throughout the ages, who have the ability to see how the world really is, but take no risks to improve it. Rather, his counsel is simply to enjoy what one can while one can: food, spouse, friends, comfort. Such an attitude turns its back on injustice and the possibility of God's passionate concern for the victims of empire. What about those whose daily toil consists in struggling for enough food merely to survive? Boccaccini observes that the Greeks replaced the Persian office of governor with a system of "tax farming," in which bribery and corruption were rampant. "The system enhanced the power of the wealthiest families in various districts of the Ptolemaic kingdom. . . . The gap between the few and the many, between the city and the countryside deepened. Judah was no exception."[88] But Qoheleth has little to say to "the many" whose lives were becoming increasingly desperate. In Egypt, as we saw, conditions deteriorated into street revolt and labor strikes. Qoheleth's response is a shrug: what can one do? Its distance from the prophetic and emerging apocalyptic tradition is obvious in its never being quoted in the New Testament and only rarely in the first centuries of Christianity.[89]

Qoheleth's perspective is important for us to consider. It expresses the view of many who reject "too much religion" at either end of the spectrum, either in an effort to legitimize an unjust status quo or to inspire a movement in opposition to it. It is easy for those with plenty of food and leisure to sit

---

86. Sneed, 7.
87. Ibid., 8.
88. Boccaccini (2002), 119. That same system continued under the Romans as we'll see.
89. Longman, 30.

back and observe the struggle from a safe distance, cynically rejecting the call to enter the fray. This perspective will continue to remain an option for those who are neither invested in the system nor the victims of it. Meanwhile, as the political winds shifted away from the Ptolemies and toward their rivals, the Seleucids, adherents of both royal wisdom and its apocalyptic alternative continued to do battle.

Chapter Eighteen

Seeking "Wisdom" under Greek Rule

PART TWO: THE SELEUCID EMPIRE

The Shift from Ptolemaic to Seleucid Rule
of Judea in 200 BCE

The Ptolemaic and Seleucid empires fought a long series of wars during the third century BCE, with Judea almost always in the middle. Finally, in what is known as the Fifth Syrian War, the Seleucid king, Antiochus III, took control of the region in 200 BCE. The history of this battle for control is complex in its names and details of events, yet simple in its basic pattern. Like empires that preceded and those to follow, the Ptolemies became overstretched militarily and economically, burdened by an elaborate royal apparatus and an inability to exact sufficient taxes and tribute to support it. In the words of historian Günther Hölbl befitting the imagery of Daniel 2, "the Ptolemaic empire began to totter on its feet like a colossus unsure of its step."[1]

The long period of inter-empire struggle generated an extreme insecurity among local elites. Richard Horsley notes that it was "simple political-economic realism for local rulers and other magnates to gauge the winds of imperial political fortune, and to be prepared to shift loyalties with changes in imperial regimes." The advent of Antiochus III led many in Jerusalem's own aristocracy to move from Ptolemaic to Seleucid support.[2] Of course, it was just such political "realism" that the Enoch tradition saw as pollution and idolatry. Jeremiah had long ago castigated the Jerusalem elite for calculating political advantage between pagan empires. It would be up to new prophets to denounce collaboration with the Seleucids as no different from collaboration with any other human-made empire.

We have three primary sources for Seleucid rule in Judea: 1 Maccabees, 2 Maccabees, and Josephus's *Antiquities of the Jews*. None of these offers

---

1. Hölbl, 134.
2. Horsley (2007), 41 notes, in contrast to Boccaccini (whom he does not cite), that there is "no evidence of well-defined parties before the events of the Seleucid takeover ... much less that they were driven by distinctive ideologies."

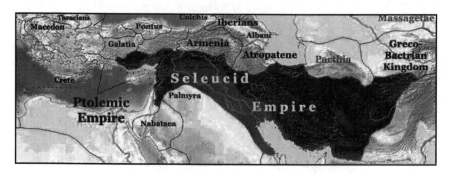

Map 6: Seleucid and Ptolemaic empires, c. 200 BCE

an "objective" perspective. First Maccabees is a highly charged polemical text in support of the Maccabees' revolt and their successors, the Hasmoneans, who ruled Judea in semi-independence between the Seleucids and the Romans. Second Maccabees is an epitome of what purports to be a five-volume work (2 Macc. 2:19–23). John Collins summarizes its purpose:

> [It is a] history which in effect separated the temple and the story of the revolt from the Hasmonean priest-kings [and thus] could avoid party dissension and enable the Jews of the Diaspora to affirm both the temple and the independent Jewish state without acknowledging the legitimacy of the Hasmoneans.... The ideal of Judaism which is held forth is not primarily political but is based on the pious observance of the law, and includes the hope of the martyrs for resurrection. The law-abiding Jew is content to live in peace and give no offense to his neighbor.[3]

The final source is the historian Josephus, a member of the Jerusalem aristocracy who found comfortable retirement writing under Roman sponsorship after the Jewish-Roman War of 66–70 CE. Josephus's multiple accounts, including the "Tobiad Romance" within his *Antiquities,* must be carefully sifted in order to separate legend from historical events.[4]

Fortunately for our purpose, we need not sort out all the details.[5] Rather, we can focus simply on three major movements that set up the crisis in the 170s BCE under the reign of the Seleucid king, Antiochus IV Epiphanes.

---

3. Collins (1999), 82–83.

4. Gruen, 102–4; VanderKam (2004), 197–226, painstakingly sifts Josephus and 1–2 Maccabees to present a "plausible historical reconstruction" (219) of events in the crucial period of 175–162.

5. For a more detailed narrative summary, see Horsley (2007), 33–51; Boccaccini (2002), 151–63; see also VanderKam (2004) for discussion of each in the sequence of Jerusalem high priests during the Second Temple, and 112–239 for the Ptolemaic/Seleucid periods.

First, though, it will be helpful to consider the state of "wisdom" in the immediate aftermath of the transition from Ptolemaic to Seleucid rule.

Royal Wisdom on the Eve of Crisis:
The Book of Sirach

The first of the major changes under Seleucid rule was the reversion "to the Persian practice of explicit support for the Jerusalem temple-state as the principal instrument of imperial rule."[6] Boccaccini comments,

> As the Seleucid king restored the political supremacy of the high priesthood, the accumulation of economic and religious power gave unprecedented strength to the Zadokites. The beginning of the Seleucid period was truly the golden age of the Zadokite priesthood, the peak of their power and influence.[7]

The local Jerusalem council (Gk., *gerousia*) was empowered by the Seleucids to render local legal decisions based on *torah*. The high priest may have presided over this council, although he would have been accountable to the Seleucids.[8] The high priest was "a sort of secular prince, having the authority to collect not only tithes for the temple but also the tributes and taxes owed to the king and to retain part of them."[9]

This high priesthood would have been supported by a class of specialized "retainers," i.e., experts hired to grease the local wheels of the imperial machine. These retainers would have included literate scribes trained in torah but also conversant with Greek traditions, including philosophy and literature. Such scribes would have faced the daunting challenge of remaining true to torah's insistence on exclusive loyalty to YHWH, the God of Israel, while also faithfully serving the Seleucid king.

We considered a similar context under Persian rule, where Ezra, priest and scribe, admonished the people of restored Jerusalem to "obey the law of your God and the law of the king" (Ezra 7:26). Now under Seleucid authority, that role fell to scribes such as Joshua Ben Sira.

The book of Sirach, like 1–2 Maccabees, is part of the deuterocanonical collection, having been written in Greek as part of the Septuagint rather than the Hebrew Scriptures. For Catholics, portions are heard within the three-year lectionary cycle of Scripture readings. But few read it as a whole or within the specific historical context — named directly in the book — in which it was written. Heard in this way, Ben Sira's writing opens a window into the struggle such a scribe must have experienced.

---

6. Horsley (2007), 44.
7. Boccaccini (2002), 133.
8. Perdue (2008), 262.
9. Boccaccini (2002), 133.

The book begins with a first-person prologue by Ben Sira's grandson, writing after a time of residence in Egypt beginning in 132 BCE. He notes that the work was originally written in Hebrew, and "does not have exactly the same sense when translated into another language" (0.15). However, he offers it "for those living abroad who wished to gain learning, being prepared in character to live according to the law" (0.27). Thus, we can infer that the original text was composed sometime between the Seleucid conquest of Jerusalem in 200 and the advent of Antiochus IV Epiphanes in 175, when relative quiet reigned.[10]

As with earlier examples of royal wisdom that we've engaged, the central theological stance found within the book of Sirach is "fear of YHWH." It runs like a refrain between verses of prudential, aristocratic wisdom. What that means in practice is to honor those "above" oneself in power and authority while remaining compassionate to those "below."

Sirach is written for an audience of the privileged young men of Judea being formed to serve the temple-state, as we hear explicitly:

> Do not slight the discourse of the sages,
> but busy yourself with their maxims;
> because from them you will gain instruction
> and learn how to serve great men. (8:8)

Sirach presents himself as the teacher of a *bet-midrash,* a "house of [torah] study" (51:23). His students received the "conventional wisdom" that would enable them to do their jobs well for the rewards of gold and honor. Above all, prudence and measured behavior are valued as expressions of "fear of YHWH." A few brief quotations give the flavor of this conventionality:

With all your soul fear YHWH, and honor his priests. (7:29)

Riches are good if they are free from sin. (13:24)

Wakefulness over wealth wastes away one's flesh, and anxiety about it removes sleep. (31:1)

If you will, you can keep the commandments, and to act faithfully is a matter of your own choice. (15:15)

He who speaks wisely will advance himself, and a sensible man will please great men. (20:27)

He who loves his son will whip him often, in order that he may rejoice at the way he turns out. (30:1)

As we see in the "Wisdom Hymn" (Sir. 24), the temple-state is understood to be the expression of the divine order. This excerpt focuses this theme:

---

10. Perdue (2008), 260.

> Then the Creator of all things gave me [Wisdom] a commandment, and the one who created me assigned a place for my tent. And he said, "Make your dwelling in Jacob, and in Israel receive your inheritance." From eternity, in the beginning, he created me, and for eternity I shall not cease to exist. In the holy tabernacle I ministered before him, and so I was established in Zion. In the beloved city likewise he gave me a resting place, and in Jerusalem was my dominion. (24:8–11)

Horsley comments, "It would be difficult to find a stronger statement of the absolute authority of the Jerusalem temple-state as a way of legitimating the established political order."[11] He adds,

> The declaration that divine Wisdom had been established in authority in the temple seems all the more remarkable when we juxtapose it with the historical context.... Factions of the priestly aristocracy... would have been under no illusion about the concrete political power arrangements under which the temple-state operated.[12]

Sirach is not, though, oblivious of the poverty and suffering around him. He counsels, in accordance with torah, constant response to people's basic needs. For example,

> Do not reject an afflicted suppliant, nor turn your face away from the poor. (4:4)

> Stretch forth your hand to the poor, so that your blessing may be complete. (7:32)

> Do not shrink from visiting a sick man, because for such deeds you will be loved. (7:35)

Through these and other admonitions, Sirach trained his students to practice an ancient form of *noblesse oblige*. Horsley notes that Sirach's wisdom in this regard "served the interests of the wealthy as well, in so far as the scribal circles that defended the interests of the poor may have provided a legitimate (but non-threatening) outlet for the frustration that may have developed among the impoverished peasantry."[13]

Sirach was also a man of his time and social station in his attitude about women and slaves:

> Do not give yourself to a woman so that she gains mastery over your strength. (9:2)

> Better is the wickedness of a man than a woman who does good; and it is a woman who brings shame and disgrace. (42:14)

---

11. Horsley (2007), 147.
12. Ibid.
13. Ibid. (2007), 69.

Set your slave to work, and you will find rest; leave his hands idle, and he will seek liberty.... If he does not obey, make his fetters heavy. (35:25, 28)

It should be clear that Sirach's wisdom inculcates service to the status quo in the name of the God of Israel. Slaves, women, children, and laborers all have their "place," generally apart from and socially "below" those whom Sirach is addressing.

This support for the status quo kept Sirach silent on the imperial and priestly politics that surrounded him. Sirach's livelihood, like that of many *literati* throughout the ages, depended on not biting too hard the hand that feeds him.[14] He was a consummate insider whose concern for the poor did not risk his own security and status.

Further, Sirach appears to have been a vehement opponent of those whose writings claimed divine authority for a more radical social critique, such as found in *1 Enoch*.[15] Like Qoheleth, he rejected the possibility of wisdom being attained through visions and dreams: "dreams give wings to fools" (34:2). His presentation of God's Wisdom established in Jerusalem was the opposite of what we'll see in Enoch's *Dream Visions*. He taught that death is the final end: "when a man is dead, he will inherit creeping things, and wild beasts, and worms" (10:11) and "From the dead...thanksgiving has ceased" (17:28).

Sirach's "wisdom" would feel right at home in many circles of biblical scholarship and established church ministry today. Fear God, but accept the status of the world's mighty ones. Prayer is good, but do not claim visionary insight. Life is more than money, but honor those who have it. Be kind to those below you, but do what you can to stay above them. Sirach's students, in other words, may well have been the central targets for those whose revelatory insights provided a much more radical, anti-imperial perspective on the collaboration between the temple-state aristocracy and the Seleucids, especially once the major crisis hit.[16]

The Epistle of Enoch:
Measuring "Weeks" until the Coming of God's Reign

Roughly contemporaneous with the imperially supportive wisdom of Ben Sira was another piece of Enoch tradition, known as *The Epistle of Enoch*

---

14. Cf. Horsley (2010), 9–10.

15. Boccaccini (2002), 137–50, lays out this opposition in helpful detail.

16. An important example of "royal wisdom" is the *Letter of Aristeas,* which presents the legendary story of how the Septuagint translation of the Hebrew Scriptures was commissioned by the Ptolemaic king of Egypt. See generally Wasserstein and Wasserstein. Because this text's provenance is Alexandria rather than Israel/Judah, I will not discuss it in this volume, but in volume 2, where Alexandria will be a major locus of the transformation of the Gospel of Jesus into imperial Christianity. For a helpful investigation of the cultural politics of translation in relation to the Septuagint, see Simon-Shoshan.

(*1 En.* 91–105). The section consists of three basic units: (1) an introduction from Enoch to his son, Methuselah; (2) a review of history known as the "Apocalypse of Weeks" (*Ap.Weeks*); and (3) a series of discourses by Enoch that offer a sharp rebuke to social and economic injustice. Scholars have argued at length about both the unity of this section and its date of composition.[17] Michael Knibb argues that the different forms of writing "reflect a common purpose: to encourage the righteous to persevere in right conduct in the face of oppressive circumstances, and to reinforce this message by the assurance of the certainty of punishment that awaits the sinners at judgment and of the blessed state that awaits the righteous."[18] Given that the *Ap.Weeks* does not refer to the crisis under Antiochus IV Epiphanes which is the focus of Enoch's *Dream Visions* and the book of Daniel, it seems best to date the Epistle to the time just before the crisis.[19]

The *Epistle of Enoch* reads like an anti-imperial response to Sirach from beginning to end. In the introduction, Enoch says:

> The vision of heaven was shown to me, and from the words of the watchers and holy ones I have learned everything, and in the heavenly tablets I read everything and I understood. (93:1)

The reference to "heavenly tablets" will recur both later in the *Epistle* (103:1) and in the book of *Jubilees,* discussed in chapter 19. It challenged the claim of the Jerusalem temple establishment that "their" revelation in the torah given by Moses was complete in itself. Rather, the Enochians claimed that it was from *their* revelation that one could learn "everything."

The *Ap.Weeks* follows, presenting in a single verse each "week" of history. Enoch's, the first week, is the only one in which "righteousness endured." Starting in the second week, "deceit and violence will spring up" (93:4). God is not mentioned directly in this section but is present passively in "righteousness" and "truth," which correspond to the pair "deceit" and "violence." The opposing pairs compete for supremacy.[20] This pattern will also be manifested in the Dead Sea Scrolls, especially the *Rule of the Community* (1QS 3:16–4:26), transformed into the opposition between the "sons

---

17. See, e.g., Nickelsburg (2001), 24, 336–37, 426; Stuckenbruck, 5–16, 60–62. Boccaccini (1998), 104–13, argues for *Ap.Weeks* as separate from the rest of the Epistle, and after *Dream Visions,* based on its similarities in outlook with *Jubilees,* which is clearly from after the Antiochus IV Epiphanes crisis, a thesis sharply rejected by Stuckenbruck, 213–14. This question, difficult to answer with certainty, is not central for our purposes.

18. Knibb (2005), 216; cf. Nickelsburg's response to Knibb (2005b), 236, noting the term "chosen" repeatedly used in *Ap.Weeks* but not in the main body of the Epistle, but concluding, "the apocalypse is integrated into the Epistle and that, in a way, it provides not only a time referent but also a polarized conceptual framework for the Epistle."

19. Horsley (2007), 167.

20. Klaus Koch, 191–92, notes the double meaning of the Aramaic *qushta* as both "righteousness" and "truth," contrasting with the Aramaic pair *shiqra* (deceit) and *hamsa* (violence). He suggests the possibility that these opposing pairs are derived from Persian Zoroastrianism, as seen in the text *Bhaman Yasht.* Of course, in Zoroastrianism, history unfolds with an open question of whether good or evil will triumph, whereas in the Enochic texts, as in other apocalyptic texts (e.g., Revelation), God's victory is assured.

of light / truth" and those of darkness / lies. Later, it will be taken up in New Testament texts such as John's Gospel.[21]

The only "law" in the *Ap. Weeks* is that given to Noah; the torah of Moses goes unmentioned. Similarly, the monarchy is omitted, and with it the Davidic covenant. The Second Temple period, in the seventh week, is described simply as one in which "there will arise a perverse generation, and many will be its deeds, and all its deeds will be perverse" (93:9), nearly precisely opposite Sirach's vision of YHWH's eternal Wisdom dwelling in Jerusalem and the temple.

It is only at the end of this seventh week that "the chosen will be chosen as witnesses of righteousness . . . to whom will be given sevenfold wisdom and knowledge." Their task, which will be successful, will be to "uproot the foundations of violence, and the structure of deceit in it, to execute judgment" (93:10–11). Horsley reads this as an expression of resistance against the temple-state by the Enochians already begun before the crisis under Antiochus IV Epiphanes.[22]

From this point forward, the *Ap. Weeks* anticipates events in its original audience's future. The envisioned world transformation was to unfold in three stages: (1) the restoration of Israel and rebuilding of a new temple (week 8), (2) the restoration of all humankind (week 9), and (3) the great judgment and new heaven and earth (week 10).[23] It will thus require enduring faithfulness among those to whom God's wisdom has been given.

Helge Kvanvig argues that the presentation in *Ap. Weeks* of Israel's (and the world's) history acts as a "counter-story" to the temple's "master narrative" as recited in Nehemiah 8–10.[24] Although the story world of Ezra-Nehemiah is the Persian period before the Hellenistic empires of Ptolemies and Seleucids, the final canonical form of the book likely continued to evolve into the later period.[25] As with all interpretations of the past, the Ezra-Nehemiah "remembrance" was highly selective and directed toward the legitimation of the new temple and its imperial sponsorship. Both Nehemiah 8–10 and *Ap. Weeks* feature Abraham as a key figure, but, as noted, *Ap. Weeks* omits any mention of Moses and the Mosaic torah upon which the Second Temple was grounded. Further, *Ap. Weeks* highlights the "chosen" nature of a subgroup of God's people, who will "uproot the foundations of violence," *only after* which will there be a new temple. The *Ap. Weeks* is thus engaged in a battle with the temple establishment for the "truth" of the story of God's people, both looking back to the beginning

21. E.g., John 1:5; 12:35 (light / dark); 8:40–46 (truth vs. deceit and violence); see also Eph. 5:8–14; 1 Thess. 5:4–5.

22. Horsley (2007), 167.

23. Boccaccini (1998), 109. The concluding stage of judgment and the revealing of a new heaven and earth are taken up at Rev. 20–22, although Revelation's New Jerusalem has no temple.

24. Kvanvig (2009), 177.

25. Ibid., 165.

and forward to the end. At all points, it stands against the collaboration of God and empire.

The *Epistle of Enoch* continues with a series of prophetic discourses. They are astoundingly concrete, unlike the symbolic language of so much of the Enochic corpus. They respond to the injustice of Jerusalem's collaboration with empire by boldly denouncing the wealthy and powerful, something Sirach was apparently afraid to do. The form throughout is alternating woes and blessings, which we'll see again in the Gospel of Luke's Sermon on the Plain (Luke 6:21–26). The message of the Enochic and the Lucan expressions are very close,[26] as a sample from the *Epistle* reveals:

> Woe to those who build iniquity and violence, and lay deceit as a foundation; for quickly they will be overthrown, and they will have no peace. (94:6)

> Woe to you, rich, for in your riches you have trusted; from your riches you will depart, because you have not remembered the Most High in the days of your riches. (94:8)

> Woe to you, sinners, for your riches make you appear to be righteous, but your heart convicts you of being sinners; and this word will be a testimony against you. (96:4)

> Woe to you, mighty, who with might oppress the righteous one; for the day of your destruction will come. (96:8)

> Woe to you, fool; for you will be destroyed because of your folly. You did not listen to the wise; and good things will not happen to you, but evils will surround you. (98:9)

> Be hopeful, O righteous; for quickly the sinners will perish before you, and you will have authority over them as you desire. (96:1)

> Blessed will be all who listen to the words of the wise, and learn to do the commandments of the Most High; and walk in the paths of his righteousness, and do not err with the erring; for they will be saved. (99:10)

The "woes" come as warnings to those still living, i.e., the aristocracy of the early second century BCE. The final chapters of the *Epistle,* though, speak to those who have already died. Sirach's traditional royal wisdom perspective, that death is the end, is radically challenged. The viewpoint of the oppressive elite is taken up directly, as we hear:

> Woe to you, dead sinners. When you die in your sinful wealth, those who are like you say about you, "Blessed are the sinners all their days that they had seen. And now they have died with goods and wealth, and

---

26. Nickelsburg (2003d) explores in depth the parallels between *Epistle of Enoch* and Luke; see also Kloppenborg.

affliction and murder they have not seen in their life. They have died in splendor, and judgment was not executed on them in their life." Know that down to Sheol they will lead your souls;[27] and there they will be in great distress, and darkness and in a snare and in a flaming fire. Into great judgment your souls will enter, and the great judgment will be for all the generations of eternity. Woe to you, you will have no peace. (103:5–8)

Similarly, those who were "righteous and pious in life" are told not to complain, but to expect to be justly rewarded:

Do not say ... "In the days of our tribulation, we toiled laboriously, and every tribulation we saw, and many evils we found. We were consumed and became few, and our spirits, small; and we were destroyed and there was no one to help us with word and deed; we were powerless and found nothing. We complained to the rulers in our tribulation, and cried out against those who struck us down and oppressed us; and our complaints they did not receive, nor did they wish to give a hearing to our voice. They did not help us, they did not find (anything) against those who oppressed us and devoured us." (103:9–10, 14–15)

I swear to you that the angels in heaven make mention of you for good before the glory of the Great One, and your names are written before the glory of the Great One. Take courage, then; for formerly you were worn out by evils and tribulations, but now you will shine like the luminaries of heaven; you will shine and appear, and the portals of heaven will be open for you. Your cry will be heard and the judgment for which you cry will also appear to you. (104:1–3)

Whether in anticipation of Daniel 12's similar reversal or echoing it, the *Epistle* insists that God's justice does not cease at the grave.

Finally, the *Epistle* takes on the question of Scripture and its authority. In the face of Sirach's praise of the temple scribal establishment and its role in interpreting torah, the *Epistle* claims that the Enochic books are the source of truth and wisdom:

Would that they would write[28] all my words in truth, and neither remove nor alter these words, but write in truth all that I testify to them. And again I know a second mystery, that to the righteous and pious and wise my books will be given for the joy of righteousness and much wisdom.

---

27. Greek *ai psuchai humōn,* "your souls" or "your lives"; Ethiopic, *manfaskemu,* "your spirit"; Stuckenbruck, 530. As elsewhere in the *Epistle of Enoch,* it is not clear what this aspect of the human person is that the author imagines to continue after death.

28. For the role of writing in establishing authority in this period, especially in the book of *Jubilees,* see Najman, 381–88.

Indeed, to them the books will be given, and they will believe in them, and in them all the righteous will rejoice and be glad, to learn from them all the paths of truth. (104:11–13)[29]

Horsley observes that this promise of joy, truth, and wisdom coming from alternative book collections is a "new and distinctive" aspect of the Enochic perspective.[30] This perspective will continue over coming centuries, leading to the canonizing of a completely separate collection of texts known as the New Testament.

The Crisis under Antiochus IV Epiphanes

Although there was relative calm between the two imperial dynasties in the early second century BCE, tension remained within Jerusalem. Horsley notes,

> Judea was ruled by the Jerusalem aristocracy, mainly priestly, and headed by a chief priest, only now with less rivalry from a powerful tax-farmer in charge of imperial revenues. But within the Jerusalem aristocracy there were still other powerful figures, besides the high priest and competing factions, who understood the contingencies of competing and internally conflicted imperial regimes.[31]

One of these other figures was the "temple-captain,"[32] Simon, who plotted an intrigue against the high priest, Onias III, sometime in the early second century. Both parties sought the support of the Seleucid government. Horsley criticizes older views that see this conflict as an expression of either inter-family rivalry (between Oniads and Tobiads) or factional rivalry (between pro-Ptolemaic and pro-Seleucid groups). Rather, this episode reveals the struggle for power among local elites in Jerusalem and the dependence of both groups on imperial support.[33]

The second major event following the shift from Ptolemaic to Seleucid rule was the rise of Antiochus IV Epiphanes as Seleucid king in 175 BCE. The new king was desperately in need of revenue. Onias's brother, Jason, offered the king a deal: If Jason was given the high priesthood, he would

---

29. Note also "Woe to you who alter the true words and pervert the everlasting covenant and consider themselves to be without sin; they will be swallowed up in the earth" (99:2). Horsley (2007), 171, notes how this verse echoes Num. 16:23–35, where erring priests and their families are swallowed up by the earth.

30. Ibid., 170.

31. Ibid., 45.

32. VanderKam (2004), 191, notes that "nothing is said in the context to help the reader understand what the position involved."

33. Horsley (2007), 46; also (2010), 25–28. Briant, 55–61, shows how the Seleucids continued the Persian policy of creating ties to local elites to maintain imperial control.

commit to increasing the amount of Judean tribute to the Seleucids. The king agreed to Jason's proposal. Thus, the Jerusalem high priest became a Seleucid imperial official (2 Macc. 4:8–10). The deal also involved the establishment in Jerusalem of a gymnasium, which "was the fundamental educational organ in a Greek city."[34] Horsley notes that these changes did not totally displace the temple, but "would have posed a particular threat to the regular priests, Levites, scribes, and others whose lifework and livelihood were tied up with the temple."[35]

The final event leading to the crisis was a series of intrigues after Menelaus — the brother of Simon who had earlier opposed Onias III — replaced Jason as high priest in 172, having secured the post by outbidding Jason by three hundred silver talents, a huge sum (2 Macc. 4:24). However, as Gabriele Boccaccini comments, Menelaus "had offered the Seleucid king a higher bid, but it was the people, and the poorest among the people, who had to pay for it. As the burden of taxation increased, so did the popular discontent."[36] Second Maccabees characterizes Menelaus as "possessing no qualification for the high-priesthood, but having the hot temper of a cruel tyrant and the rage of a savage wild beast" (2 Macc. 4:25). When the retired Onias returned to expose Menelaus's schemes, Menelaus had Onias treacherously assassinated (2 Macc. 4:34).

The transition from Ptolemaic to Seleucid rule was thus accompanied by a seemingly endless series of intrigues, betrayals, and shifting loyalties, as various people, whether out of self-interest or some sense of common good, strategized and conspired. Where was YHWH in all this? We can see in the texts that survive evidence of continuity with older traditions — both of the pro- and anti-empire perspectives — and of innovation, as new circumstances led to new insights on how YHWH would save his people from oppression.

The books of Maccabees present a relatively straightforward narrative of zealous, justified violence in defense of ancestral tradition. The next section of *1 Enoch,* the book of *Dream Visions (1 En.* 83–90), responds with a symbolic portrayal of all of history up to the time of Antiochus IV Epiphanes. The book of Daniel offers a series of anti-imperial court tales and an apocalyptic perspective akin to *Dream Visions,* but with a different understanding of how YHWH's justice would be achieved. A look at each of these perspectives will continue to prepare us for the most radical response of all: the Gospel of Jesus.

---

34. VanderKam (2004), 199. Jason also established an *ephebeion,* the vehicle for acculturation of youth into the ideals of Greek citizenship. Gruen, 4, notes that the author of 2 Maccabees makes no objection to these Hellenistic institutions per se, but objects to Jason for his collaboration with the enemy; see also VanderKam (2004), 202.

35. Horsley (2007), 48.

36. Boccaccini (2002), 156.

The Maccabees: Zealous and Violent Defenders of the Temple and of Religious Tradition

Our sources differ greatly on the circumstances of and reasons for the crisis. The executed Onias may well be referred to in both Daniel (9:26) and *1 En.* (90:8). His death was a major event for all who wrote in response to the reign of Antiochus IV Epiphanes.

Several things seem clear. First, Antiochus supported Menelaus throughout this period. Second, Antiochus twice invaded Egypt in his ongoing battle with the Ptolemies. During the second invasion, the former high priest, Jason, having heard rumors of the king's death, used the opportunity to attack what he thought was the now unprotected Menelaus and his local supporters in Jerusalem (2 Macc. 5:5–7). However, his attack failed and Jason fled, dying in exile.

Meanwhile, word of Jason's revolt reached the still living Antiochus, who interpreted it as a general rebellion against Seleucid rule. The king returned to Jerusalem in 169 with a huge force and slaughtered massive numbers of inhabitants while raiding the temple sanctuary for its gold and treasures (2 Macc. 5:15–18; 1 Macc. 1:20–24). He then issued decrees banning traditional Judean practices, including circumcision, temple sacrifices, observance of Sabbath and other festivals, and perhaps even possession of a torah scroll. Second Maccabees names this as a local decree; 1 Maccabees presents it as part of an empire-wide effort to establish cultural unity (cf. 1 Macc. 1:45–50; 2 Macc. 6:2–6, 10–11). If we follow the 2 Maccabees portrayal as a local action, we can see that it supported both the king's and Menelaus's goals:

> Antiochus had a strategic interest in strengthening his military presence in Jerusalem and avoiding the coalescence of any opposition that could be used by the Ptolemies.... Menelaus needed a sign of discontinuity that would definitively affirm his power and the legitimacy of his priesthood.[37]

Scholars offer a range of explanations for Antiochus's repression.[38] Regardless of whatever the "facts" might be, the turmoil and repression led to the rising of Mattathias and his sons (led by Judas), known as the Maccabees, from the town of Modein. Boccaccini comments that the "unexpected opposition came... from those who, mostly in the countryside outside Jerusalem, more heavily had to bear the burden of taxation while being excluded from the benefits of Hellenistic economy and culture."[39] They escaped to the wilderness, where they gathered together a guerrilla army in resistance to Antiochus IV Epiphanes and his supporters. Boccaccini adds, the "genius of the Maccabees was to present themselves not as the leaders of just another rival priestly family seeking power, as they were,

---

37. Ibid., 160.
38. E.g., VanderKam (2004), 213; Boccaccini (2002), 161–62.
39. Boccaccini (2002), 162.

but as the champions of the national tradition against the Greeks, and to turn the civil war into a war of liberation against foreign oppressors."[40]

A key moment came as the enemy prepared to do battle with Mattathias and his companions on the Sabbath. The first response of Mattathias and his supporters was to obey the torah, even at the risk of death (1 Macc. 2:34–37). However, when the attack led to the death of a thousand persons, the people resolved instead to fight on the Sabbath rather than to die as martyrs (2:41). The very torah being defended had to be broken in order to protect it.

Mattathias' "zeal for the torah" is compared to that of Phinehas, son of Aaron, who, according to the book of Numbers, killed those who "yoked themselves to the Ba'al of Peor" during the wilderness sojourn (Num. 25:7ff.). This identification clearly placed the Maccabee narrative within the tradition of the book of Joshua and other narratives of "holy war" in the name of YHWH.[41] First Maccabees continues to strengthen this characterization by presenting a deathbed speech by Mattathias that calls his children to "show zeal for the torah and give your lives for the covenant of our fathers" and to "remember the deeds of the fathers... [to] receive great honor and an everlasting name" (2:50–51). Mattathias' list of "the fathers" is highly selective and quite revealing of what constitutes "great honor and an everlasting name":

> Was not Abraham found faithful when tested, and it was reckoned to him as righteousness [cf. Rom. 4:3–22; Gal. 3:6]? Joseph in the time of his distress kept the commandment, and became lord of Egypt. Phinehas our father, because he was deeply zealous, received the covenant of everlasting priesthood. Joshua, because he fulfilled the command, became a judge in Israel. Caleb, because he testified in the assembly, received an inheritance in the land. David, because he was merciful, inherited the throne of the kingdom forever. Elijah because of great zeal for the torah was taken up into heaven. Hannaniah, Azariah, and Mishael [see Dan. 1:6–19] believed and were saved from the flame [Dan. 3]. Daniel because of his innocence was delivered from the mouth of the lions [Dan. 6]. (1 Macc. 2:52–60)

Among those not named: Jacob, Moses, and nearly all the prophets. And among those named, the specific deed and reward given to each illumines the Maccabean perspective. For example, Joseph is noted for becoming "lord of Egypt," Joshua for becoming a "judge" (a claim found nowhere else in the Hebrew Scriptures); David for "inheriting the throne forever," and so forth. Elijah, the only prophet named, is revered for his own "great zeal

---

40. Ibid.

41. Phinehas is clearly a hero to the supporters of the pro-empire religion; see Josh. 22:13ff.; Judg. 20:28; 1 Chron. 9:20; Ezra 7:5; cf. Ps. 106:30, which says that Phinehas "stood up and interceded" rather than slaughtering the supporters of the Ba'al of Peor. Cf. Phil. 3:6, where Paul refers to his church-persecuting "zeal" before his coming to know Christ; see also, Acts 22:3; Rom. 10:2.

for the torah," a likely reference to his mass execution of the prophets of Ba'al (1 Kings 18). The naming of key characters in the book of Daniel highlights what we'll see to be the competing viewpoints between Maccabees and Daniel. Together, the names, deeds, and rewards establish a model for the Hasmonean dynasty that follows the Maccabees' victory. And yet, there is no mention at all of "YHWH" or "God" in this speech. It is not a sermon but a pep talk by a dying military commander. It ends with this command: "Pay back the nations in full, and heed what the law commands" (1 Macc. 2:68). Similarly, as authority is passed to his son, Judas, the new leader is praised as a powerful warrior who was "renowned to the ends of the earth," but still no mention is made of YHWH (3:1–8).

First Maccabees portrays the Maccabees' revolt as a time of national pride and strength in which they "struck down sinners in their anger" and "rescued the torah out of the hands of nations and kings" (1 Macc. 2:44, 48), rededicating the temple and establishing the feast of Chanukah (1 Macc. 4:56–59).

First Maccabees can be read superficially as presenting a battle between "Judaism" and "Gentile customs," with the Maccabees as defenders of a "pure" Judaism (e.g., 1 Macc. 1:10–15). However, as Erich S. Gruen has shown, the specific language used later in 1 Maccabees presents the enemy not as an abstraction called "Hellenism," but as "the surrounding nations" (e.g., 1 Macc. 3:25, Greek, *ta ethne ta kuklō*), a term in the pro-empire biblical tradition that refers to local peoples such as Canaanites and Ammonites.[42] In other words, 1 Maccabees deliberately links the actions of Judas and his brothers to those of the "holy wars" of the past. Throughout its narrative, we hear echoes of the violent Conquest tradition found in the book of Joshua. First Maccabees became the celebrated statement of national independence from foreign empire after three hundred years of colonial captivity. Its highest moment is the "purification" of the Jerusalem temple and the reestablishment of traditional sacrifices in that place. But does it express the will of YHWH for Israel? On that question, the book is utterly silent.

Second Maccabees, while also celebrating the victory over the Seleucids and the establishment of Chanukah (2 Macc. 10:1–8), offers a somewhat different perspective on what it meant to be faithful. In 2 Maccabees 6–7, we hear two stories of nonviolent martyrdom for refusing to obey the imperial command to violate torah by eating pork. The first story is of an old

---

42. Gruen, 5; Josh. 23:1. Gruen, 6, notes the use in 1 Maccabees of terms such as *allophuloi*, people of "a different tribe," 1 Macc. 5:15. The term is found 317 times in the LXX, overwhelmingly in the Deuteronomistic History (239 times), Chronicles (35 times), and 1–2 Maccabees (12 times), only once in Gen.–Exod. (Exod. 34:15). More broadly, Neil Elliott (2008), 46, notes that despite common English translations, "to speak of 'Jewish-*Gentile* conflicts' in antiquity is to confuse social analysis with ideology" (emphasis in original). The apostle Paul's contrasting pair is consistently *Ioudaios* ("Judean") and *Hellēn* ("Greek") (e.g., Gal. 3:28; 1 Cor. 1:24; 10:32; Rom. 3:9; 10:12). I consistently use "the nations" rather than "the Gentiles" to render the plural forms of *ho ethnos*.

scribe named Eleazar who welcomes "death with honor rather than life with pollution, [and] went up to the rack of his own accord" (2 Macc. 6:19). His dying words proclaim his reason: "Therefore, by manfully giving up my life now, I will show myself worthy of my old age and leave to the young a noble example (LXX, *hupodeigma*) of how to die a good death willingly and nobly for the revered and holy laws" (6:27–28). *Hupodeigma* is a word rarely used in the Bible,[43] but will be taken up by Jesus when he offers a different "example of how to die a good death willingly and nobly" (John 13:15; cf. Jam. 5:10).

The second story is a gruesome narrative of seven brothers and their mother who are each tortured and killed in the sight of those who remain. The mother "encouraged each of them...[with] her woman's reasoning and a man's courage, offering this wisdom: 'the Creator of the world, who shaped human birth and devised the origin of all things, will in his mercy give life and breath back to you again, since you now forget yourselves for the sake of his laws' " (7:23). It is the first narrative claim of life after death in a "Jewish" text apart from *Book of the Watchers'* apocalyptic vision.[44] It is presented as if it was an already familiar belief, which the sons were expected to know, and of which the mother was simply reminding them. All of them are killed, including the last one, "putting his whole trust in YHWH" (7:40).

This hope in resurrection returns later in 2 Maccabees in a story about Judas's prayer and financial collection for a sin offering for fallen Judean soldiers who were found to have borne idolatrous tokens under their tunics. The narrator concludes the story:

> In doing this he acted very well and honorably, taking account of the resurrection [LXX, *anastasis*]. For if he were not expecting that those who had fallen would rise again, it would have been superfluous and foolish to pray for the dead. (2 Macc. 12:43–44)

The hope for "resurrection" was also voiced by the fourth of the sons to die in the previous story (2 Macc. 7:14), but is nowhere else found in the Septuagint using this key Greek term.[45] With these stories, 2 Maccabees combines the traditions of holy war with the expectation of God's post-mortem gift of restored life. What specific form that restored life might have been understood to take is anyone's guess,[46] but it will echo, of course, into the New Testament.

---

43. Only Ezek. 42:15 (different meaning); 4 Macc. 17:23 (same as 2 Macc.); cf. Sir. 44:16 (Enoch as an example of "repentance to all generations").

44. See Levenson (2006) for a comprehensive and helpful review of "intimations of immortality" in the Hebrew Bible.

45. *Anastasis* is used in the LXX elsewhere only to refer to ordinary "rising" from sitting, Lam. 3:63; Dan. 11:20; Zeph. 3:8.

46. Levenson (2006), 112, notes: "However distant the resurrection of the dead may be from the understanding of death and life in ancient Israel, the concept of immortality in the sense of a soul that survives death is even more distant."

Two other elements of 2 Maccabees' perspective are worth our attention. In the following story, we hear of the anger of "the King of kings" aroused against the high priest Menelaus, the arch-villain of the entire book. This specific title for God had been used in previous texts to refer to the Persian king, Artaxerxes, and the Babylonian king, Nebuchadnezzar (Ezra 7:12; Ezek. 26:7). Only in Daniel (2:37) is it used elsewhere in Hebrew Scriptures to refer to the God of Israel, as it will in the New Testament (1 Tim. 6:15; Rev. 17:14; 19:16). However, we recall that it was already a part of the Enoch tradition in the *Book of the Watchers* (*1 En.* 9:4), as it will be again in *Dream Visions* (*1 En.* 84:2). Thus, 2 Maccabees joins with the emerging apocalyptic tradition in portraying the God of Israel as the supreme ruler of all, above every human authority.

Finally, near the end of 2 Maccabees, a visionary encounter with the prophet Jeremiah is narrated (2 Macc. 15:13–17). Nothing in the tradition would have anticipated the living appearance of a long-dead prophet, but again, 2 Maccabees presents this without any sense of surprise or shock.[47] In the vision, Jeremiah gives a golden sword to Judas, saying, "Take this holy sword, a gift from God, with which you will strike down your adversaries." The vision of a man with a sacred sword recalls Joshua's reported encounter (Josh. 5:13), which in turn transformed Moses' encounter with YHWH (Exod. 3) from a call to obey YHWH the liberator into a call to liberation by holy war. In 2 Maccabees, the association of the sacred sword with Jeremiah portrays the Maccabees' own war of liberation as the fulfillment of the prophet's word about the end of the Exile (Jer. 25:12; 29:10), already claimed to be fulfilled at Ezra 1:1, and taken up again in Daniel as seventy weeks of years (Dan. 9:2, 24). Thus, in these few verses, the author of 2 Maccabees associates the Maccabees' war backward with Joshua and Jeremiah, and forward in tension with Daniel's perspective.

In each of these additions to the tradition of 1 Maccabees — the hope of resurrection as reward for martyrdom, the naming of God as "King of kings," and the vision of Jeremiah — 2 Maccabees takes up themes that are central to *1 Enoch's "Dream Visions"* as well as to the viewpoint of Daniel. In the crisis generated by the collaboration of the high priest Menelaus with the Seleucid king Antiochus IV Epiphanes, three groups expressed in writing radically different understandings of how to be faithful. The Maccabees opted for holy war, claiming that God was on their side. Meanwhile, two other authors urged people to understand and to respond to the crisis differently. At stake was the future of Israel amid the empires of the world.

---

47. In light of this report, we can understand Jesus' disciples' response at Matt. 16:14 to Jesus' question, "Who do people say that the Son of Man is?" "And they said, 'Some say John the Baptist, but others Elijah, and still others *Jeremiah* or one of the prophets.'"

"And They Began to Open Their Eyes":
Enoch's "Dream Visions"

First Enoch 83–90 consists of two visions narrated by Enoch to his son Methuselah. The first, in chapters 83–84, is a vision of the Flood. The second, in chapters 85–90, is frequently referred to as the "Animal Apocalypse" (*An.Apoc.*) and consists of a dream in which Israel's history from the beginning is presented with a series of animals symbolizing various biblical characters. Patrick Tiller, the only person to have written a book-length commentary on *Dream Visions* (*DV*), suggests that the first vision was added later, perhaps by a different author. He writes: "The function of the *An.Apoc.* seems to be to promote a certain political stance and to encourage those that already adhere to it. The function of the first dream-vision seems to be to legitimate the heirs of the Enochic traditions over against other possibly competing groups."[48] Our focus will thus be on *An.Apoc.* and its counsel to faithful "sheep" in the midst of the crisis.

Much of the symbolism in *An.Apoc.* is relatively easy to unravel for one familiar with the biblical story, which by this time period, was well established. For example, consider the opening paragraph:

> ...and look, a bull came forth from the earth, and that bull was white. And after it a young heifer came forth. And with her two bull calves came forth; one of them was black and one was red. And that black calf struck the red one and pursued it over the earth. And from then on I could not see that red calf. But that black calf grew up, and a young heifer came to it. And I saw that many cattle came forth from it, that were like it and were following after it. (*1 En.* 85:3–5)

The "bull" is Adam, the "heifer" is Eve, the black calf is Cain and the red calf is Abel. The narrative continues in this fashion. Chapter 86, though, breaks into the animal symbolism by borrowing imagery that links it with the earlier Enochic *Book of the Watchers*:

> I saw the heaven above, and look, a star fell from heaven, and it arose and was eating and pasturing among those cattle....I saw many stars descend and cast themselves down from heaven to that first star. And in the midst of those calves they became bulls, and they were pasturing with them in their midst...and they began to mount the cows of the bulls, and they all conceived and bore elephants and camels and asses. And all the bulls feared them and were terrified before them, and they began to bite with their teeth and devour and gore with their horns. (*1 En.* 86:1, 3–5)

The angelic Watchers are now portrayed as "stars" who mate with the "cows of the bulls," producing animals symbolic of imperial chaos. The

---

48. Tiller (1993), 99.

imagery in *BW* presented the Watchers as stand-ins for the Hellenistic kings of the author's own time. Now, a hundred years later, another Enochic author takes up the story, but here the fallen stars represent the advent of empire at the beginning of history. Only later in the *An.Apoc.* will we see specific representations of the imperial forces of the new author's own time.

The allegory continues through the generations of the Genesis patriarchs and into the captivity in Egypt. Moses is portrayed as a "sheep that had escaped safely from the wolves" (89:16). His call and confrontation with Pharaoh follows the Exodus story, but no passover is mentioned. The other sheep accompany Moses to "the summit of a high rock" (i.e., Mount Sinai), but they are afraid to encounter the "Lord of the sheep," and "began to be blinded and to stray from the path that it had shown them," a reference to the Golden Calf incident (89:29–32). There is no mention at all of a covenant being made in the wilderness. Andreas Bedenbender explains, "Without covenant and without a special act of divine legislation, the fact that so many Jews had subordinated themselves to the new order of Menelaus becomes more understandable."[49] Of course, it also expresses the Enochic view that the Mosaic torah has been taken captive by the aristocratic leadership aligned with Menelaus and the Seleucids.

After this, Enoch sees "that sheep became a man and built a house for the Lord of the sheep and made all the sheep stand in that house" (89:36). Tiller shows, contrary to earlier interpretations that saw this "house" as the wilderness tabernacle, it actually represents the desert camp. It is not "the Lord of the sheep" but the sheep themselves who occupy the house. Tiller adds:

> The second clue is that the house later comes to represent the city of Jerusalem, which implies some symbolic continuity between the two houses. An altogether new sign, the tower, is introduced to represent the temple. In keeping with this symbolic discontinuity between the first house and the later tower, none of the language that identifies the tower as a cultic place is used of this house; there is no table, it is not lofty, and the owner of the sheep does not stand on or in it. Thus the house stands in symbolic and functional continuity with Jerusalem but not with the temple.[50]

The use of "tower" to refer to the temple recalls the Tower of Babel (Gen. 11). The sheep are not in the "tower," however, but in "the house." This is central to *An.Apoc.*'s perspective: its closing vision presents no restored temple, as with the Maccabees, but rather, "the owner of the sheep now dwells together with the sheep."[51] This idea distinguishes *An.Apoc.* from Daniel, but links it with the New Testament's book of Revelation, in which

---

49. Bedenbender (2007), 77.
50. Tiller (1993), 42–43.
51. Ibid., 47.

New Jerusalem similarly has no temple (Rev. 21:22). It is the desert camp
that represents Israel's idealized past, "in which Israel and God live together
in peace and goodness."[52] It is this vision that became central to those who
left Jerusalem and Judea to settle in the desert at Qumran by the Dead Sea,
preserving *DV* as part of their library, while they awaited YHWH's act of
redemption.[53]

The story proceeds through the period of the judges and the monarchy,
including the sending of prophets by the Lord of the sheep "to testify and
lament over them" (89:53). No preference is expressed for the Jerusalem-
centered kingdom; rather, all "went astray in everything, and their eyes were
blinded," which leads to being abandoned "into the hands of the lions and
the leopards... and to all the beasts; and those wild beasts began to tear
those sheep to pieces" (89:54–55). With that, the Exile began.

The allegory now shifts to the Second Temple period, over which God
"summoned seventy shepherds, and he left those sheep to them, that they
might pasture them" (89:59). The time of the oversight of these seventy
shepherds is arranged as follows:

Babylonian period: 12

Persian period: 23

Ptolemaic period: 23

Seleucid period: 12[54]

Tiller shows that these seventy shepherds do not correspond to the seventy
nations of Genesis 10, but rather are "70 angelic patrons of Israel, each
appointed for a particular period of time, both to care for and to punish
Israel."[55] In other words, they express an apocalyptic perspective on the
reigns of the foreign empires that have controlled Israel since the Exile.
Tiller concludes,

> The real rulers of Judah, however, are not the local chieftains, priests or
> elders... or even the foreign representatives of the imperial court, but
> angelic beings whom God has commissioned to take his place in the
> care of his people. This assessment turns the imperial claim to divine
> descent on its head. Yes, there is something other-worldly behind the
> empire, but it is demonic, not divine.[56]

The angel/shepherds are symbolized by animals that would not have
been "kosher" under the laws of Leviticus. Tiller points out that this

---

52. Ibid., 36; also 48–50.
53. Although the Qumran community certainly did anticipate a renewed Jerusalem with
a purified temple, as discussed below.
54. Tiller (1993), 55.
55. Ibid., 54.
56. Tiller (2005), 117.

symbolism marks the foreign rulers as disordered, unnatural, and unclean-unfit for mixing with the Judean faithful. With this symbolic expression the allegory denies the claim that imperial rule is somehow benevolent; whatever benefactions it may bestow bring only disorder and chaos.[57]

This understanding clarifies *An.Apoc.*'s view that, from the beginning, the Second Temple was not a holy place: "all the bread on [the table] was polluted and not pure" (89:73). In other words, the Ezra-Nehemiah compromise with Persia was condemned as not the will of YHWH at all; *the Exile had not yet truly ended* but continued right up through the author's own time. As long as foreign powers were in control of YHWH's people, the punishment that led to the Exile was not complete. Gabriele Boccaccini comments, "the entire history of Israel in the postexilic period unfolds under demonic influence... until God comes to the earth and the new creation is inaugurated. In an era of corruption and decline, the Zadokite temple is no exception: it is a contaminated sanctuary."[58] Thus, Jeremiah's prophecy of an exile of "seventy years" was rejected in favor of an exile that endured for the reign of seventy shepherds.[59]

The Ptolemaic period is passed over in a single paragraph, as the "eagles and vultures and kites and ravens... began to devour those sheep and peck out their eyes and devour their flesh... and the sheep became few" (90:2, 4). Things begin to change, however, under the reign of the final twelve shepherds: "lambs were born of those white sheep, and they began to open their eyes and to see and to cry out to the sheep. But they did not listen to them nor attend to their words, but they were extremely deaf and their eyes were extremely and excessively blinded" (90:6–7).[60] The sheep who "began to open their eyes" are the Enoch group, pleading with the Jerusalem aristocracy to cease its collaboration with Antiochus IV Epiphanes and his priestly puppets, Jason and Menelaus. They were hoping that their kinsmen would come to see, as they have, that

> The foreign emperor falsely claims legitimacy on the grounds that the conqueror has the right to rule and that he can trace his ancestry to the gods. The true basis for his rule over Israel is that God has abandoned his people into the care of false shepherds. They are illegitimate rulers, whose place has been secured by disobedient angels. Fellow Judeans are called to spiritual vision and military resistance.[61]

But these sheep remained "extremely deaf" and "excessively blind." The Maccabees now enter the picture, portrayed as "rams," who received the

---

57. Ibid., 118.
58. Boccaccini (1998), 83.
59. Tiller (2005), 118.
60. Albertz (2001), 191, linking this passage with Dan. 11:4, suggests that both witness to the failure of an earlier apocalyptic movement in the winter of 201/200 under Antiochus III.
61. Tiller (2005), 119.

help of the Lord of the sheep in a battle against the shepherds and beasts. But immediately after this,

> The Lord of the sheep came to them and took in his hand the staff of his wrath and struck the earth, and the earth was split, and all the beasts and all the birds of heaven fell (away) from among those sheep and sank in the earth, and it covered over them. And I saw until a large sword was given to those sheep, and the sheep went out against all the wild beasts to kill them, and all the beasts and the birds of heaven fled before them. (90:18–19)

The *An.Apoc.* presents the Maccabees' military campaign as part of God's response to empire. But as Tiller states, "It is impossible to imagine that any of the claimants to power during the postexilic period could have won the loyalty of the allegorist.... The Maccabees are supported, however, not as national rulers, but as rebels."[62] This will be clear in subsequent Enochic texts, which express strong condemnation of the Hasmonean kings and high priests who reigned when the Maccabean war was completed.

The vision ends with a portrayal of God's judgment and the unfolding of a new age of true peace. The "stars" and the shepherds are condemned and thrown into a fiery abyss, along with the blinded sheep. The basis for judgment is not "the nations" vs. "Jews," nor is God's salvation for Israel as a nation or a people. Rather, it is only for sheep who had "opened their eyes" and became "white, and their wool was thick and pure" (90:32, 35). Nothing in *An.Apoc.* suggests that those saved are of a single ethnicity or any other specific identity other than having purity of insight and behavior. This perspective takes up the tradition of Third Isaiah, in which foreigners and eunuchs were welcome among YHWH's people. Also like Third Isaiah, the author of *An.Apoc.* envisions a new creation in which God's rule is manifest and authentic peace and justice reign, without interference from human empire falsely claiming divine authority. Tiller concludes that in the presence of the viewpoints calling for faithful torah observance (as expressed in Sirach) or the adoption of Hellenism, the "books of Enoch display a third, more radical way. The goal of history is an end to all political divisions. No longer will one people rule another. Rather the God of Israel will personally rule a unified people without the need for temple or king."[63]

The final paragraphs of *An.Apoc.* present the birth of a "white bull," whom some have taken as a messianic figure. However, the "white bull" played no part either in the opening of the eyes of the sheep or in the decisive battle that brought peace. Rather, it is "an eschatological counterpart to Adam...and all humanity is transformed into his image,"[64] as we hear: "all their species were changed, and they all became white cattle" (90:38).

---

62. Ibid., 120.
63. Ibid., 121.
64. Kvanvig, 109; also Elliott (2000), 470.

The author's vision has no need for an individual human savior; Enoch has provided the vision and it is up to each person to "open their eyes" and ears and to respond to it.

Whose perspective did *An.Apoc.* and the wider *Dream Visions* express? Horsley suggests a dissenting scribal circle.[65] However, this "does not imply the existence of a social group" with a specific structure, as at Qumran.[66] All we can reasonably infer is that there was enough of a social context for the text to be written and retained over several centuries and to be referred to by another text from this time period, the book of *Jubilees*.[67] Finally, it is not difficult to image a passionate dispute between the scribal circle gathered around *DV* and those who produced a competing narrative of resistance to Seleucid oppression, those for whom the book of Daniel provided the "true" way to respond to the crisis.

"And I Saw One like a Human Being": The Book of Daniel

The book of Daniel, like the Enochic material and other texts that we'll look at in the next chapter, was written at a very different time than that of events within the narrative. This basic fact offers no challenge: amost all the historical books of the Bible from Genesis to 2 Kings were also written much later than the events within them. Daniel, though, like Enoch, is, in part, a pseudepigraphal work. Its first half (Dan. 1–6) presents a series of tales placed within the court of the Babylonian king, Nebuchadnezzar (chapters 1–4), and his successors (chapters 5–6).[68] They may include anti-empire traditions that extend as far back as the Exile.[69] The second half (Dan. 7–12) presents a first-person narrative of "Daniel's" dream visions that bear a strong resemblance to the Enochian *Dream Visions* we've just explored. It has been understood since the third century CE, though, that these visions were not predictions made hundreds of years in advance, but rather, were written during the time of Antiochus IV Epiphanes to explain events current to the author.[70]

---

65. Horsley (2007), 165; (2010), 72.

66. Tiller (2007), 254.

67. On *Jubilees,* see generally VanderKam (2001); Endres; and Boccaccini and Ibba. For the "chain of documents" linking the sections of *1 Enoch* with texts such as Daniel, Jubilees, and the Dead Sea Scrolls, see Boccaccini (1998 and 2002).

68. The named successors are not historically accurate, but are chosen to correspond to the traditional "four kingdoms" schema that forms the framework of both parts of the book; see Collins (1998); see also Veleta on how this is part of Daniel 1–6's use of the categories of "Menippean satire."

69. Smith-Christopher (2001b), 289.

70. Casey is the classic work on this point.

Complicating matters further is the fact that part of the book is written in Hebrew (1:1–2:4a; chapters 8–12) and part in Aramaic (2:4b–7:28).[71] Yet the linguistic separation does not directly match the shift between court tales and apocalyptic visions.[72] Gabriele Boccaccini suggests that Daniel 1 was originally written in Aramaic and then translated into Hebrew to provide a binding frame.[73] Daniel 7 is the bridge that holds the two sections together: its Aramaic language connects it to what precedes; its "four kingdoms" theme connects with Daniel 2; and its apocalyptic perspective connects it to what follows.[74] This results in a threefold structure.

Daniel 1 (*Hebrew:*) introduction

Daniel 2–7 (*Aramaic*)

Theme: sovereignty belongs to God
chiastic internal structure:
> 2: succession of four kingdoms (king's dream of giant statue)
>> 3: trust in YHWH under imperial threat (lions' den)
>>> 4–5: God punishes imperial pride (cosmic tree and handwriting on wall)
>> 6: trust in YHWH under imperial threat (fiery furnace)
> 7: succession of four kingdoms (Daniel's vision of beasts and "human one")

Daniel 8–12 (*(Hebrew*)

Theme: cause of historical degeneration is breaking of Mosaic (Deuteronomic) covenant
chiastic internal structure:
> 8: the fourth kingdom
>> 9: Daniel's Deuteronomic prayer of repentance on behalf of Jerusalem and its people[75]
> 10–12: the fourth kingdom

---

71. Albertz (2001), 187–91, argues that the Hebrew Dan. 8–12 is older than the Aramaic Dan. 2–7, and "testifies to the existence of an earlier apocalyptic movement in Judah at the end of the third century BC under the reign of Antiochus III. This earlier movement is probably also meant in *1 En.* 90:6–7."

72. Cf. Albertz (2001), who sees the each linguistic unit as comprising a separate "apocalypse" from a different time of composition, the Aramaic from near the end of the third century, and the Hebrew from the time of the Maccabean crisis. He notes further that the Greek (LXX) version of Dan. 2–7 "represents an independent shape of the Daniel stories.... The LXX... almost completely lacks the main topic of the Aramaic apocalypse: the praise and establishment of God's kingdom" (180–81). The authors of the Septuagint were not faced directly with the crisis of Antiochus IV Epiphanes, so were free to reshape the tradition to serve the goals of the Jewish elite in Alexandria (ibid., 181–82). We will focus here on the Aramaic / Hebrew version.

73. Boccaccini (2002), 171.

74. Albertz (2001), 177–79.

75. Ibid., 171–72.

The form and style of the opening chapters have roots in widespread patterns of folktale, especially the genre known as "wisdom court legends."[76] They have been adapted, though, for a specific context and purpose. As Richard Horsley writes, "The genre of court legend has been combined and transformed with several other forms that all revolve around political conflict. The tales have creatively combined the traditional Israelite and/or ancient Near Eastern forms to present prophetic criticism of arrogant imperial rule from the Judean perspective of the universal rule of God."[77] Marvin Sweeney and Daniel Smith-Christopher have both sharply criticized earlier scholarly views that interpret Daniel 1–6 as strategies for *accommodation,* rather than resistance, to empire.[78] Sweeney notes the irony that such interpretation "presupposes an Enlightenment hermeneutical perspective, derived ultimately from the universal worldview of Hellenism" that the stories are seeking to resist.[79] He shows that "the political and religious aims of the Hasmonean revolt permeate the entire book, not only the visions of Daniel 7–12, and...they must be taken seriously in theological interpretation. The book of Daniel does not seek to escape this world; it is actively engaged in it."[80] It will thus be worth our while to consider the *entire* book of Daniel, not just the more obviously anti-imperial apocalyptic chapters, to see its consistent stance.

Recently, David M. Valeta has shown how the court tales fit within the literary genre known as "Menippean satire."[81] This ancient form has long been used by the oppressed to tell stories that humorously undermine entrenched powers. Characteristics include, according to Valeta:

1. comic elements;

2. a freedom of plot and philosophical inventiveness;

3. a use of extraordinary, fantastic situations or wild parodic displays of learning to test the truth;

4. some combination of both crude and lofty imagery, settings, and themes;

5. a concern for ultimate questions;

6. scenes and dialogue from the earthly, heavenly, and netherworldly realms;

7. observation of behavior from an unusual vantage point;

---

76. Wills (1990) provides many examples of the underlying story pattern; see also Van Der Toorn (2002).

77. Horsley (2007), 175.

78. Sweeney (2001a); Smith-Christopher (1996); see also Horsley (2010), 35; cf. Nolan Fewell (1991) who interprets the stories as a combination of resistance and acceptance of the rewards offered for exhibiting wisdom useful to the empire.

79. Sweeney (2001a), 125.

80. Ibid., 126–27.

81. Valeta, relying on the work of Mikhail Bakhtin; see also Weinbrot for a survey of the use of this genre from the Romans to the eighteenth century.

8. characters who experience unusual, abnormal states;

9. characters who participate in scandals, eccentric behavior, and/or inappropriate speech;

10. sharp contrasts and oxymoronic combinations;

11. elements of social utopia.

All of these characteristics are found in the Daniel stories. This categorization dissipates the need for scholarly anxiety over elements of these tales, including their "incorrect" history. As Sweeney shows, each of the tales uses a setting from the past to lampoon the behavior of the king with whom the author is truly concerned: Antiochus IV Epiphanes.

We saw earlier that 2 Maccabees contains several very specific elements common to Daniel. The overlap between the early Enoch material (*BW* and *DV*) and Daniel is even more extensive, as Table 25 shows.

These parallels reflect general principles that unite the two books, including: (1) God is universal "king of kings," (2) true knowledge includes revelation by divinely inspired dream-visions, (3) human empires are destined to fall by God's judgment against them, and (4) the Exile is not yet over; rather, the Second Temple continues under YHWH's punishment, as evidenced by its collaboration with foreign empires.

There are also substantial differences between them that set their adherents on separate paths: Enoch on the way to "Essenism" (and Qumran), and Daniel on the way to "Pharisaism."[82] The core difference is their attitude toward Jerusalem and its temple, and the "Zadokite" (Deuteronomic) theology that prevailed among its elite supporters. As we've seen, previous Enoch writings rejected both Jerusalem and its elite as hopelessly under the influence of the evil spirits who were the legacy of the fallen angelic Watchers. Daniel, on the other hand, although deeply critical of Jerusalem's sinfulness, accepts in principle the core Deuteronomic theology and the possibility of a purified temple (although no restoration is mentioned). Thus, for the Enochic *Dream Visions,* redemption requires a "new house" for God's people, whether that is on earth "in the end" or after death "in heaven." Daniel, though, envisions an end to the reign of "the beasts" and the rising from the dust of the earth of those who are "wise." Finally, *Dream Visions* supports the Maccabees' revolt as at least contributing to the execution of God's judgment against Antiochus IV Epiphanes and the Seleucid empire. Daniel, on the other hand, counsels the wisdom of simply allowing the battle to take place "in heaven," knowing that God's victory is assured.

Daniel 1: Resisting Empire in Daily Life

The opening verses of Daniel place the narrative in the "third year of the reign of King Jehoiakim of Judah" when "King Nebuchadnezzar of Babylon

---

82. Boccaccini (1998).

Table 25: Some Elements Found in both Daniel and Enoch's *Book of the Watchers* and *Dream Visions*

Image	Daniel	Enoch
Angelic "watchers"	4:13, 17, 23	chapters 1–16
Kings and their court as beasts	7:1–12	chapters 89–90
Horn appeared on a beast	7:8	90:9
God's throne with rivers of fire	7:9–10	14:19
God as wool-haired	7:9	46:1
Myriads serving God	7:10	14:22
Heavenly court in judgment	7:10, 26	90:20
Heavenly books opened	7:10	89:70; 90:20
Burned with fire as judgment	7:11	10:6; 18:11; 21:7–10
Host of heaven	8:10	18:14
Angel Gabriel	8:16 etc.	9:1; chapter 20
Visionary frightened and falls prostrate	8:17	14:14, 24
Angel's restorative touch	8:18	60:4
Flying angel	9:21	61:1
Jeremiah's prophecy of 70 years / weeks	9:24	10:11–12; 89:59
Angel Michael	10:13 etc.	9:1; 10:11; 20:5
Book of truth	10:21	Cf. 93:2
Judea as "beautiful land"	11:16	89:40; 90:20
Eternal life	12:2	10:10
Righteous shall shine	12:3	104:2–6

came to Jerusalem and besieged it." This specific detail, though, does not match the evidence for the final years of Jerusalem before the Babylonian Exile.[83] In fact, Daniel's data generally do not match what we otherwise know about the sequence of empires during the Second Temple period, except for the detailed narrative of Hellenistic rule in Daniel 11. The point of establishing this initial context in Daniel 1 is not accurate history, though, but rather, a paradigm about how Israelites are to respond to the seemingly unending presence of foreign imperial powers.

The immediate opening of the story reveals its anti-imperial standpoint. Time is measured by Judean, not Babylonian, regnal years. Also we are informed that it is Daniel's, not Nebuchadnezzar's, God, who is in charge.[84] The foreign king's actions unfold against this backdrop.

The story continues with the bringing of young men from Israel's elite nobility to "the land of Shinar" (recalling Gen. 10:10; 11:2) for three-

83. Collins (1994), 131; cf. 2 Kings 24:1; 25:1.
84. Valeta, 319; Fewell (1991), 14–15.

years' training as servants in the Babylonian royal court.[85] We learn of their Israelite names — Daniel, Hananiah, Mishael, and Azariah — which were also mentioned at 1 Macc. 2:59–60. The imperial chief of eunuchs, Ashpenaz,[86] renames them to confirm their new identity: Belteshazzar, Shadrach, Meshach, and Abednego. The question then becomes: how deeply does this new identity penetrate? In other words, does the sheer fact of imperial political control mean the end of Israelite identity and loyalty to YHWH?

The story focuses on Daniel, who the narrator tells us "resolved that he would not defile himself with the royal rations of food and wine" (1:8). Danna Nolan Fewell notes that the royal food and wine are "symbols of political patronage; to consume them would be tantamount to declaring complete political allegiance."[87] Perhaps to our surprise, it is Ashpenaz who was afraid of Nebuchadnezzar, not Daniel. But rather than turn Daniel in, we hear that "God allowed Daniel to receive favor and compassion from the chief of eunuchs." Daniel Smith-Christopher writes, "The friendship between Daniel and Ashpenaz, therefore, is the solidarity of the oppressed, both of whom served the imperial will under threat of death; and the solidarity crosses ethnic lines."[88] We recall Pharaoh's midwives — also minor characters with names — whose earlier solidarity with the "Hebrew" women risked imperial retaliation. Behind and under the attention of kings, the oppressed across the ages have often found surprising supporters in high places.[89]

Much like the situation of Joseph in Pharaoh's court in Genesis, the narrative reveals the God of Israel to be in control despite the imperial façade. After ten days on a diet of vegetables, Daniel and his companions "appeared better and fatter than all the young men who had been eating the royal rations" (1:15).

There is certainly humor within this simple tale, which Erich S. Gruen has shown prevailed in much Israelite literature of the Hellenistic age.[90] Unlike the grim story in 2 Maccabees 7 of the brothers and their mother standing firm under torture for refusing to eat pork, we hear nothing specific in Daniel 1 about the "royal rations"[91] that suggest it is a matter of following torah-based kosher rules. Israelites were not principled vegetarians, either.[92] But

---

85. Fewell (1991), 17–18, writes: "The young men are to learn the Babylonian way of life, adopt a Babylonian profession, and confess Babylonian allegiance. Such a transformation benefits the king; the captives must be made to see that such a transformation benefits them as well."

86. That this relatively minor figure is himself named highlights his humanity and hence his own choice of how to serve or to resist empire.

87. Ibid., 19.

88. Smith-Christopher (1996), 42; also Valeta, 320.

89. Cf. Luke 8:3, where we hear that Jesus' mission was supported by Johanna, wife of Herod's chief steward, Chuza. See also Acts 17:12.

90. Gruen.

91. Hebrew *patbag* ("royal rations") is a Persian loanword, used only in Dan. 1 and 11:26.

92. But compare Gen. 2:16 and 9:1–3, making human meat-eating a concession to human violence rather than a part of God's original plan.

one can easily imagine the original audience chuckling at the young Israelites fattening up more than their imperial counterparts on a diet of roots and leaves.

The story is not really about food as such, but about maintaining an identity separate from that defined by the imperial elite in ordinary circumstances. It is certainly meant to contrast with the closing verses of the Deuteronomistic History, where we hear:

> So Jehoiachin [Jehoiakim's son] put aside his prison clothes. Every day of his life he dined regularly in the king's presence. For his allowance, a regular allowance was given him by the king, a portion every day, as long as he lived. (2 Kings 25:29–30)[93]

At the conclusion of the story in Daniel 1, our hero is also found "stationed in the king's court," but not, apparently, sharing in the king's table fellowship. It is the other side of the Joseph-Pharaoh relationship, where Egyptian racism kept the king from sharing meals with his "Hebrew" viceroy (Gen. 43:32). Whereas Joseph did his best to become united with his imperial overlords but was not fully accepted, Daniel resists imperially imposed assimilation. Later in Daniel, the angelic visionary explains to him that Antiochus IV Epiphanes will be betrayed by "those who eat of the royal rations" (11:26), explained further in the next verse as "two kings, their minds bent on evil, shall sit at one table and exchange lies." But from the start, Daniel will have no part in imperial politics. It is a fitting introduction to a book in which the challenge of empire's authority quickly becomes a matter of life and death.

Daniel 2–7: Interpreting Imperial Dreams

The stories that follow this introduction are tightly intertwined. We have already noted the concentric structure that links chapters 2/7, 3/6 and 4/5 as pairs. The narrative is also built around a thematic sequence. Chapter 2 tells of the king's *dream of a great statue,* followed in chapter 3 by the king's (absurd) *building of a great statue.*[94] Chapter 4 connects back to chapter 2 via the theme of a royal dream vision — this time, of a great tree, which leads to Nebuchadnezzar's transformation into an ox — followed in chapter 5 by his royal son's vision of the "handwriting on the wall" that leads to his death. Finally, the conclusions of both chapters 5 and 6 present Daniel elevated by the king, while chapter 6 is connected by "lions" to the narrative in chapter 7.[95] Both the parallel and sequential links reinforce the

---

93. Cf. 1 Sam. 20:30–34, where Jonathan, son of Saul, leaves his father's royal table in solidarity with David against his father.

94. The stories are also linked by the unique use of the phrase, "torn limb from limb and your/their houses laid in ruins," Dan. 2:5; 3:29.

95. Lions are mentioned only in Daniel in chapters 6–7; the stories are also linked by the proclamation that God's "kingdom shall never be destroyed, and his dominion has no end," 6:26; 7:14.

central theme of this section of the book: imperial pride and power, not being grounded in the wisdom that comes directly from God, are doomed to fall. Resisting empire is thus justified and will be rewarded.

The first pair of stories in Daniel 2 and 7 share the "four kingdoms" historical schema common in the ancient world.[96] In Daniel 2, Nebuchadnezzar has a troubling dream of which no one knows the content. The king utterly irrationally challenges his own spirit-world experts to tell both the dream and its interpretation under threat of being "torn limb from limb and your houses... laid in ruins" (2:5).[97] For what conceivable reason would a king make such an impossible demand on his own elite? When they protest, the king "flew into a violent rage and commanded that all the wise men of Babylon be destroyed" (2:12). The king is thus portrayed not as a thinking human being, but as a wild beast, matching the dream vision in chapter 7.

Of course, Daniel can do the impossible task of interpreting the dream because of the "wisdom and power" of his God. His motivation is to save the Babylonian wise men from the king's wrath (2:19–24).[98] He precedes the revelation of his wisdom with praise of God, making clear that the dream interpretation is not a result of his own ability. Smith-Christopher writes that "Daniel is mustering spiritual power for warfare."[99] The dream is of a huge and brilliant statue, of which the head "was of fine gold, its chest and arms of silver, its middle and thighs of bronze, its legs of iron, its feet partly of iron and partly of clay." A stone was cut out, "not by human hands," which broke the statue to pieces that were carried away by the wind like chaff. The stone in turn became a "great mountain and filled the whole earth." Daniel explained that the various components, of descending value, symbolized a series of kingdoms, all of which will fall. But Smith-Christopher asks cogently:

> To whom is gold and silver of more value than iron and clay? To the common person, iron and clay are the materials of daily living and useful materials, whether they be plows or bowls. Who possesses gold but the powerful (cf. Job 3:15)? Gold and silver have their main value as monetary units, or decoration for religious idols or temple vessels.... In short, in the context of the exile, the head of gold was hardly a sign of admiration, but a sign of a Near Eastern empire's insatiable drive to hoard precious metals.[100]

The statue was destroyed by a stone "cut out, not by human hands," which "became a great mountain" (2:34–35). The contrast is clearly between the fragile and temporary, human-made statue and the powerful, permanent "kingdom that shall never be destroyed," established directly by

---

96. Collins (1994), 166–70.
97. Smith-Christopher (1996), 51, notes that this is a technical, legal phrase.
98. Note the phrase "vision of the night," linking 2:19 and 7:2.
99. Ibid., 52.
100. Ibid., 54.

God (2:44). As Richard Horsley writes, the "mystery of the dream . . . is that God's kingdom will finally destroy all the empires."[101]

The story ends with Nebuchadnezzar's further irrationality: he falls down to worship Daniel and then promotes him to rule over Babylon after Daniel has told him that his kingdom is doomed (2:46–48).[102] This irrationality will continue in the chapters that follow.

The series of collapsing kingdoms followed by a divinely generated eternal one is paralleled in Daniel's own vision in 7:1–14, which is interpreted to Daniel by a heavenly being. This vision adds one key detail to Daniel 2. In one of the most important and most studied passages of the Hebrew Scriptures, we hear that Daniel saw

> one like a human being [or, "a son of man"] coming with the clouds of heaven. And he came to the Ancient One and was presented before him. To him was given dominion and glory and kingship, that all peoples, nations, and languages should serve him. His dominion is an everlasting dominion that shall not pass away, and his kingship is one that shall never be destroyed. (7:13–14)

We cannot begin to engage here the mountain of scholarly reflection that has attempted to unravel the linguistic, narrative, and theological questions. Is the being an angel, such as Michael, described in Daniel as "the prince of your people" (10:21; 12:1)? A heavenly "messiah"? Is the dominion presented on earth, in heaven, or both? When and how is it to be manifest? All we can say for now is that Daniel's vision anticipates God's authority being shared in some mysterious way, and that it will embody an indestructible alternative to all human empires. As Walter Wink writes, "Daniel is reaffirming faith that God intends to replace the bestiality of conquest states with a more humane arrangement: nations will be ruled by human principles and humane leaders rather than by the predatory empires that so long held sway."[103] The form, "*the* son of man," will, of course, be applied in the New Testament to Jesus,[104] where its meaning will be the subject of much discussion, confrontation and confusion, both within the text and among modern scholars.

The interpretation of Daniel's vision that follows in chapter 7 clearly links the "fourth beast" with the Hellenistic kingdoms, and its "horns" with the kings leading up to and including Antiochus IV Epiphanes. Daniel's vision

---

101. Horsley (2010), 37.

102. However, cf. Fewell (1991), 33, 36 who suggests that the prediction of a *future* collapse is enough to satisfy the king in the present, akin to Hezekiah (2 Kings 20:19). From this perspective, he worships the divine-like person who can interpret his dream.

103. Wink (2001), 53; see also Albertz (2001), 185.

104. The term is used in the New Testament eighty-two times in the gospels, once in Acts (7:56), and at Rev. 1:13; 14:14. Wink (2001), 19–22, notes that the specification, "*the* son of [*the*] man" used in the gospels is unprecedented in Hebrew or Aramaic texts, raising questions about the meaning of the New Testament term in relation to Daniel.

conveys the divinely revealed message that this kingdom, like all before it, is doomed to collapse, despite its momentary possession of rapacious power. No Maccabean "holy war" is required to produce this result. It is God's power alone that takes away its dominion and leads to its destruction.

With this frame in place, the stories in Daniel 3–6 simply illustrate the basic theological principle. Daniel 3 narrates the ongoing absurdity of Nebuchadnezzar, who, having just been told that his dream of a great statue expressed the fate of his own and subsequent kingdoms, proceeded to build a great, golden statue. By so doing, "the empire establishes gold as a God of the whole world."[105] The statue attempts to "correct" the dream by eliminating the "feet of clay" that represented the unstable foundation of the empire.[106] The narrator's description that "all the peoples, nations, and languages fell down and worshiped the golden statue" indicates that the event was intended to generate political solidarity among conquered peoples, akin to the Hellenistic political-religious rituals of the author's time, not least of which were those of Antiochus IV Epiphanes.[107]

The narrative caricatures the Babylonian king and his minions by repeatedly reciting lists of officials and musical instruments in a cartoonish way, while the king issues a decree calling for the death penalty by fiery furnace for anyone who does not fall down and worship the statue. The Chaldeans, expressing residual envy from their being bested by Daniel's dream powers, tattled on his three companions. When confronted by the king, who was again in a "furious rage" (3:13), they calmly refused to defend themselves, expressing their trust in their God. Smith-Christopher writes, "This is a statement of faith against the appearance of defeat. The most infuriating aspect of radical faith is its adamant refusal to be impressed with the obvious — namely, the subordinated status and powerlessness of the Jews before the mighty emperor — and their steadfast adherence to an alternative reality: God reigns."[108] With the king "so filled with rage...that his face was distorted" (3:19),[109] the three are thrown into the furnace but are protected by an angel. As with Daniel in the previous chapter, the king responds by rewarding the three with a promotion. Valeta notes that the "rewards for Daniel and his friends are wildly extravagant and parody the royal policy of spoils for the wise and victorious."[110]

---

105. Smith-Christopher (1996), 61, translating and quoting Ton Veerkamp.

106. Fewell (1991), 38.

107. Cf. Ibid., 40–41. The phrase "all peoples, nations, and languages" is a refrain in this section of Daniel: 3:4, 7, 29; 4:1; 5:19; 6:25; 7:14; cf. Rev. 5:9; 10:11; 13:7; 14:6; 17:15.

108. Smith-Christopher (1996), 64.

109. Aramaic, *utselem 'anpohi*, lit, "the image of his face," linking him with the statue, *tselem* (used seventeen times in Daniel, all in Dan. 2–3, only here for other than the statue). Cf. the related Hebrew at Gen. 1:26–27 as "image." The king has created the statue in his own image, paralleling God's creation of humanity.

110. Valeta, 320.

This story is paralleled in Daniel 6 by the tattling on Daniel by a conspiracy of royal officers serving "Darius the Mede,"[111] for violating a law against praying to "anyone, divine or human, for thirty days, except to you, O king" (6:7).[112] We hear that "athough Daniel knew that the document had been signed, he continued to go to his house, which had windows in its upper room open toward Jerusalem, and to get down on his knees three times a day to pray to his God and praise him, just as he had done previously" (6:10). It was a blatant act of civil disobedience against the king's law.[113]

Unlike Nebuchadnezzar, though, Darius is portrayed as "much distressed" and "determined to save Daniel" (6:14). His hand forced by the manipulation of his courtiers, he sent Daniel into the lions' den, but with this word, "May your God, whom you faithfully serve, deliver you!" Smith-Christopher comments, "The court of Darius is a kangaroo court, the kind of justice system that is always suspect in the eyes of the subordinated sections of society. Daniel was innocent; yet Persian law threw him to the lions quite legally and properly."[114]

Daniel, like his companions in the previous story, was saved by an angel, and the conspirators instead are thrown to the lions. Darius then issued a decree demanding "fear before the God of Daniel: For he is the living God, enduring forever. His kingdom shall never be destroyed, and his dominion has no end" (6:26, matching 7:14). The variation on the theme of the two parallel stories is in the portrayal of Darius. He is not a raging fool like Nebuchadnezzar; rather, he is a powerless pawn of his own imperial system, easily tricked and trapped by his own subordinates. The message is clear: empire isn't simply the personal rule of the emperor, but is a *social order* standing against the will of God, which will come back to bite all who seek to succeed within its realm.

The stories at the center of this section focus on the chastisement of royal pride that falsely imagines that empire is invincible. Daniel 4 takes up elements from Ezekiel's story of the cosmic tree (Ezek. 31), considered earlier.[115] Nebuchadnezzar calls upon Daniel / Belteshazzar to interpret another dream: of "a tree at the center of the earth... its top reached to heaven... and it provided food for all. The animals of the field found shade under it, the birds of the air nested in its branches" (4:11–12).[116] The "animals of the field" represent the peoples who have been taken captive by the empire, and

---

111. Darius was a Persian, not a Mede, but the satirical nature of the story is not concerned with historical accuracy of this kind.

112. The writing of this law stands over against God's writing on the wall in the previous chapter; Polaski, 661.

113. Smith-Christopher (1996), 91, notes that the Aramaic text is passive ("the windows were open") but the Old Greek translation renders it actively ("he opened the windows"), emphasizing Daniel's willful disobedience.

114. Ibid., 94.

115. p. 231.

116. Cf. Jesus' parable at Mark 4:32 (parallels at Matt. 13:32; Luke 13:19).

among whom Nebuchadnezzar will be sentenced, in order to "identify with the victims of his own rule."[117]

Like the statue, the tree was cut down and destroyed, but then there is a further detail: "he" was given the mind[118] of a beast. That Nebuchadnezzar needs help to understand the dream continues to underscore the satirical nature of his characterization. The tree, of course, is himself, doomed to be brought low. The king, though, is given an escape hatch to avoid this fate: "atone for your sins with righteousness, and your iniquities with mercy to the oppressed, so that your prosperity may be prolonged" (4:27). As Smith-Christopher notes, "the Babylonian emperor must no longer behave like a Babylonian emperor."[119] But we hear nothing in response: not repentance or even a word from the king. A year passes with no change, the king speaking aloud to himself from his royal roof, "Is this not Babylon the great,[120] which I have built as a royal capital by my mighty power and for my glorious majesty?"[121] Immediately, "while the words were still in the king's mouth, a voice came from heaven" to pronounce the fulfillment of the dream vision: the king "was driven away from human society, ate grass like oxen, and his body was bathed with the dew of heaven, until his hair grew as long as eagles' feathers and his nails became like birds' claws" (4:33). Horsley comments, "The king is transformed into the most docile and obedient of his previous subjects, eating grass like an ox (a beast who labors under the lash in agriculture and in construction of royal buildings).... Nebuchadnezzar's transformation into a beast turns the Mesopotamian myth of a primordial human figure [as seen in Ezekiel 31] on its head."[122]

The transformation of the king into ox nearly completes the theopolitical cartoon portrait of Nebuchadnezzar in these chapters. But surprisingly, the king was given one more chance. He lifted his eyes to heaven, blessing and praising "the Most High," and his kingdom was restored to him. John Collins observes, in contrast to the stories in the final section of Daniel, this "story expresses a stubborn hope for the reclamation of even the most arrogant tyrant and for universal recognition of the Most High God."[123] But from another angle, it fits the story of the Assyrian king's repentance in the book of Jonah: no such repentance ever happened historically, nor could it seriously be imagined to be possible. These stories are tragicomedies, not sober moral lessons. Empires and their rulers, in real life, do not

---

117. Smith-Christopher (1996), 73, 75.

118. Aramaic, *lebab*, "heart."

119. Smith-Christopher (1996), 75.

120. The title, "Babylon the great," returns at Rev. 14:8; 16:19; 18:2.

121. Note how this boast also serves as a "confession" that Babylon is indeed a human building project, in contradiction to *Enuma Elish*'s claim that it was built by the gods for Marduk, and in accordance with Genesis 11's Tower of Babel story; see above pp. 47–50

122. Horsley (2007), 178. Horsley (2010), 41, also notes that this reverses Jeremiah's declaration that God had "given [Nebuchadnezzar] even the wild animals of the field to serve him" (Jer. 27:6).

123. Collins (1994), 234.

repent; rather, they collapse and are destroyed. Even in the king's supposed restoration, he speaks only of "*my* majesty . . . *my* kingdom . . . greatness was added to *me*" (4:36).

The final story in this section is the other half of the matching pair in Daniel 5. A new king, Belshazzar, portrayed as son of Nebuchadnezzar,[124] gets drunk at a huge feast with a "thousand of his lords" and brings out the gold and silver vessels taken by Nebuchadnezzar from the Jerusalem temple. Donald Polaski writes that

> these vessels . . . define Belshazzar's own power over against that of Nebuchadnezzar, who seized them from the temple with power derived from God (1:2). . . . They serve as a clear description of royal authority: kings use whatever is at their disposal, be it cultic equipment, women, or the bureaucracy.[125]

We are told that they "drank the wine and praised the gods of gold and silver, bronze, iron, wood, and stone" (5:4).[126] At once, they saw mysterious fingers writing on the palace wall. The king was now terrified, "his knees knocking together" (5:6). None of his "wise men" could solve the mystery, leaving the king "greatly terrified" (5:9). Daniel was again summoned, and offered a royal reward of a purple robe, a gold chain, and the third rank in the kingdom. But unlike his biblical parallel, Joseph, who accepts nearly identical items from Pharaoh,[127] Daniel tells the king, "Keep your gifts!"[128] Instead, Daniel interprets the writing on the wall for the sake of God's glory. After recalling the previous story of Nebuchadnezzar's downfall, he boldly told the king "even though you knew all this, you have exalted yourself against the Lord of heaven!" (5:22–23). The specific writing ("MENE, MENE, TEKEL, PARSIN") is symbolic of royal finances,[129] and means that the king and his empire will be brought to an end. Rainer Albertz notes, in "casting down Belshazzar the blasphemer, God demonstrated that he could establish his rule against a world empire."[130] With absurdity matching that of his "father," Belshazzar gives the royal reward to Daniel anyway, despite his having predicted his demise and Daniel's disclaimer of desire for it. The story closes with this word: "That very night Belshazzar, the Chaldean king, was killed" (5:30).

---

124. Historically, he was son of Nabonidus, and served as vice-regent under his father (Collins [1994], 243).

125. Polaski, 651.

126. Cf. Rev. 9:20.

127. Gen. 41:42–45.

128. Cf. Abraham at Gen. 14:21–24, who refuses the gifts of King Melchizedek. Fewell (1991), 96, notes that Daniel was willing to accept gifts in chapter 2; it is not the reward that is the problem here, but the giver: the son has learned nothing from his father's prideful downfall.

129. Smith-Christopher (1996), 84, comments that the "judgment takes place not so much in the courtroom as in the bank lobby!"

130. Albertz (2001), 184.

Each of these stories adds its own facet to the gem displayed in Daniel 2–7. The lessons are loud, clear, and laughably obvious: for all their claims to divine status, the world's kings are actually not even truly human. They are more like dumb and enraged beasts, charging around acting as if they are in authority, but, in fact, they are hardly rational. The portrait recalls Pharaoh at the beginning of Exodus, paranoid and hard-hearted despite numerous opportunities to see how things really are and who the true source of power is. All that God's people can do is to stay faithful to who they truly are and to try to stay out of the way of the "beasts." Valeta writes, "The hidden transcripts of these stories help readers understand that true power resides not in the empires of the world but in those persons who choose to follow God and remain faithful no matter what happens."[131] Albertz adds that the

> Aramaic apocalypse...calls for a clear and public resistance against the totalitarian claim of the state, including public consequences such as martyrdom. It announces the destruction of the Hellenistic empire in the near future and draws up an ideal form of political government instead, in which the pious audience of the apocalypse will participate.[132]

But, in the meantime, those enraged beasts can do tremendous harm. What are God's people to do when faced not simply with individual commands of arbitrary and obtuse tyrants, but with systemic imperial violence? It is to this question that the final section of Daniel turns.

Daniel 8–12: Revealing the True End of Exile

The final section of Daniel contains visions that expand on the initial one in chapter 7, providing numerous details that describe the events of Ptolemaic and Seleucid control of Jerusalem and Judea.[133] Like Enoch's *Dream Visions,* this section portrays imperial agents and their victims as animals attacking one another. *Dream Visions* is easily "decoded" as an allegory; it does not suggest an actual correspondence between the reality of, say, Adam and Eve, and the white bulls that symbolize them. But Daniel's visions are claiming more than this, which we can see given the "beastly" characterization of imperial kings in Daniel 2–7. John J. Collins points us in the right direction:

> In modern thinking we assume the priority of human experience and see the mythological world of the gods as a projection. In the ancient world, in contrast, the priority of the world of the gods is assumed, and earthly affairs are regarded as reflections of this greater reality.[134]

That is, Daniel's visions do not simply offer a fantastic allegory of the "real" world on earth, but rather, *reveal how things appear from the perspective of "heaven,"* where the Ancient One reigns. This distinction is

---

131. Valeta, 323–24.
132. Albertz (2001), 186.
133. E.g., Collins (1994), 377–90, correlates the details of Dan. 11 with historical events.
134. Collins (1998), 105.

important not only for understanding Daniel's visions in these chapters, but for the entire sweep of apocalyptic writing up through the book of Revelation in the New Testament. Readers and hearers "on earth" amid the crisis of Antiochus IV Epiphanes are being shown a God's-eye view of historical events, which provides hope and guidance on how they are to respond.

The narrative insists repeatedly that what is revealed to Daniel is both troubling and incomprehensible without heavenly interpretation.[135] One of the heavenly interpreters, although unnamed, is described in vivid detail:

> I looked up and saw a man clothed in linen, with a belt of gold from Uphaz around his waist. His body was like beryl, his face like lightning, his eyes like flaming torches, his arms and legs like the gleam of burnished bronze, and the sound of his words like the roar of a multitude. (Dan. 10:5–6)

Smith-Christopher observes, "This image lives in a way that Nebuchadnezzar's vision of his kingdom does not."[136] Many of these details look back to Ezekiel's visionary accounts. But they also look forward from the perspective of the entire Christian canon in a very specific way, especially when combined with the imagery we've already seen at Daniel 7:9–13:

> I saw one like the Son of Man, clothed with a long robe and with a golden sash across his chest. His head and his hair were white as white wool, white as snow; his eyes were like a flame of fire, his feet were like burnished bronze, refined as in a furnace, and his voice was like the sound of many waters. In his right hand he held seven stars, and from his mouth came a sharp, two-edged sword, and his face was like the sun shining with full force. (Rev. 1:13–16)

The authors of Daniel were not "predicting" Jesus in any way. Rather, John of Patmos, like Saul of Tarsus and the gospel writers, read Daniel in light of their experience and understanding of Jesus' death and resurrection and saw the full embodiment of Daniel's vision in Jesus. We'll come back to this theme in chapter 20. What is important for now is to recognize that the visions conveyed in Daniel 7–12 are not mere allegories, but seek to express in words the experience of the revelation of God's realm to human beings.

The vision moves through the details of imperial history over several centuries. Smith-Christopher notes that the author "takes little comfort in the change of powers from Persian to Greek. There is no consideration here that one world power's policies are better than another's."[137] Near the end of the visions, Daniel is told of Antiochus IV Epiphanes' abolishing of the regular temple sacrifices and the setting up of "the abomination that desolates" in the temple (11:31, also 9:27; 12:11; cf. Mark 13:14). We can only guess

---

135. E.g., 7:15–16, 28; 8:17–19, 27; 10:7–12.

136. Smith-Christopher (1996), 137.

137. Ibid., 138.

what specific idolatrous image or statue was placed in the temple.[138] We saw earlier that for the author of *Dream Visions,* the entire period of the Second Temple was polluted, its sacrifices made unclean by the ongoing compromise between the priestly and scribal elite and their imperial overlords. For Daniel, although evil has run rampant for centuries under the reigns of the "beasts," it is the specific action by Antiochus IV Epiphanes that marks a turning point.

The author sought to show how people responded to the presence of a Hellenistic cult object in the Jerusalem temple and what that expresses in terms of God's sovereignty. First, we hear that "he shall seduce with intrigue those who violate the covenant" (11:32), referring to the aristocratic allies of Menelaus. Next, we hear that "the people who know their God will become strong and act." This cannot be the Maccabees, whose violence Daniel opposed. It may refer to the scribes behind *Dream Visions,* whose view is closer to Daniel's, despite their differences.[139] Finally, we hear

> The wise [*maskilim*] among the people shall give understanding to many; for some days, however, they shall fall by sword and flame, and suffer captivity and plunder. When they fall victim, few will help,[140] and many shall join them insincerely. Some of the wise shall stumble,[141] so that they may be refined, purified, and cleansed, until the time of the end, for there is still an interval until the time appointed. (11:33–35)

The *maskilim* are the author's heroes.[142] Collins notes, "There can be little doubt that the author of Daniel belonged to this circle and that the instruction they impart corresponds to the apocalyptic wisdom of the book."[143] The term itself refers back to the Fourth Servant Song at Isaiah 52:13–53:12.[144] Daniel's brief story of the *maskilim* presents Second Isaiah's Suffering Servant taking flesh in the context of the Maccabean crisis. Just as the Servant's hardships were revealed to be the embodiment of the sins of God's people, so now Daniel's *maskilim* suffer because of the sins of those who have violated the covenant by accommodating to the Seleucid Empire. Both the Servant

---

138. Collins (1994), 357–58, reviews the many options.

139. Ibid., 385.

140. NRSV: "they shall receive a little help." This and similar translations have led many to interpret the "little help" as the author's grudging reference to the role of the Maccabean revolt. However, Horsley (2010), 98, notes that the Maccabean revolt may well not have started yet, and that a more precise translation would be "they will receive little help from anyone."

141. Albertz (2001), 193–95, says this "cannot mean that some...will die or even suffer martyrdom as is often interpreted on the basis of v. 33b"; rather, referring back to Dan. 11:4, "the failure of the previous apocalypticists is meant," some who had formed a coalition with the Maccabees, i.e., those associated with 1 *Enoch*'s *Animal Apocalypse.*

142. For a recent exploration of the possible social milieu of the *maskilim,* see Beyerle.

143. Ibid., 66.

144. The word *maskilim* is from the Hebrew verb root *skl,* translated at Isa. 52:13 as "shall prosper" (NRSV), but which can also mean "shall give instruction." The Servant Song is discussed above at p. 239.

and *maskilim* accept unjust suffering rather than inflicting it on others, trusting in God's power to exalt them in the end. This exaltation is expressed in Daniel 12:2–3:

> Many of those who sleep in the dust of the earth shall awake, some to eternal life (*chayye 'olam;* LXX, *zōē aiōnion*), and some to shame and everlasting contempt. The *maskilim* shall shine like the brightness of the sky, and those who make many righteous,[145] like the stars forever and ever.

Daniel's *maskilim* continue to embody the Suffering Servant, who "shall make many righteous" (Isa. 53:11). Their vindication will take the form of "awakening" from "the dust of the earth" to "eternal life," while others will awake to "eternal contempt/shame."[146] It is impossible to know exactly what this meant to Daniel and his audience. Horsley suggests that rather than jumping to fit Daniel into later, Christian understandings of "resurrection," the text belongs "in a long-established tradition of prophetic hope that God would restore the people of Judea."[147] It is clearly not a "spiritual," but an embodied restoration that is envisioned. The term translated "eternal life" or "everlasting life" is found only here in the Hebrew Bible. The Greek, meaning literally "life of the age," became a common expression for the fullness of life given by God in the messianic age, especially in the New Testament, where it is used thirty-seven times.[148] Daniel's vision offers the promise of God's restoration of the fullness of life to the righteous, but not until they are "purified, cleansed and refined" (11:35; 12:10) by suffering through all the evil that empire can pour out, just as the Servant saw light after receiving the contempt of his contemporaries (Isa. 53:11). Jon Levenson notes that "eternal life" "corresponds to — indeed, it is inseparable from — the prediction earlier in Daniel that 'the God of heaven will set up a kingdom that shall never be destroyed, a kingdom that shall not be transferred to another people. It will crush and wipe out all these kingdoms, but shall itself last forever.'"[149] Daniel's vision promises a divine reversal of the status quo accepted by the purveyors of royal wisdom.[150]

---

145. Following Horsley (2007), 188; NRSV has "lead many to righteousness."

146. Cf. Isa. 66:24.

147. Ibid., 190, against Collins's (1994), 386, understanding of this passage as leaning toward individual salvation; see also Elliott (2000) for the developing sense within this period of the salvation of a "righteous remnant" rather than the nation/people of Israel. An example of a prophetic text expecting the restoration of Judah in imagery of restored life is Ezek. 37's vision of dry bones. For a discussion of Dan. 12:1–3 in the context of biblical precedent for a hope of postmortem survival, especially Isa. 26, see Levenson (2006), 181–200, who notes much "is lost when the resurrection of the dead is treated as a free-floating concept whose essence remains constant no matter what the culture in which it appears or to which it migrates" (185).

148. It is found only once elsewhere in the LXX, at *PsSol* 3:12.

149. Levenson (2006), 187.

150. See, e.g., ibid., 194: "Ben Sira's disbelief in resurrection is so explicit that one might surmise that he was acquainted with the new belief and wanted to refute it," citing Sir. 28:19–23.

When and how would this take place? At the center of Daniel 8–12 is what might seem at first an anomalous "insertion" into the series of visions, wherein Daniel turns to YHWH with prayer and fasting (Dan. 9:4–19).[151] Its language and style suggest that it was composed by a different writer than the rest of the book, perhaps at another time.[152] However, a closer look reveals that this prayer is an integral part of both this section and the entire book of Daniel.[153] It places at the center of Daniel 8–12 the theological perspective that both informs the entire book and distinguishes it most clearly from Enoch's *Dream Visions*.[154] It provides the theological explanation for the historical events that unfold in the surrounding vision narratives: the prophecy of "seventy years" of exile in Jeremiah 25 was being fulfilled.

We saw that 2 Maccabees 15's vision of Jeremiah himself presenting a sacred, golden sword to Judas Maccabee was that book's expression of the completion of the time of exile predicted by the prophet. *Dream Visions,* in contrast, presented its own narrative of seventy shepherds who would continue to enforce exilic conditions on God's people in Jerusalem until "the end." Daniel presents yet another perspective on Jeremiah's prophecy: that the seventy years would become "seventy weeks" of years, i.e., ten jubilees. Despite many writers' attempts to correlate this period of 490 years to the literal period from Babylonian captivity to the Maccabees' victory, it seems clear that these numbers, like the others in Daniel, are meant theologically, not chronologically.[155] The expansion of the expected 70 years to seven times that length is one of several clear references in Daniel 9 to another "prophetic" prediction: the punishment of God's people "sevenfold for your sins" as a result of the failure to practice jubilee (Lev. 26:23–24).[156]

Daniel 9 interweaves fulfillment of Jeremiah 25 and Leviticus 26 from the beginning, as the very reason that Daniel turns to YHWH in prayer: "I, Daniel, perceived in the books the number of years that, according to the word of YHWH to the prophet Jeremiah, must be fulfilled for the devastation [*charbah*] of Jerusalem, namely, seventy years" (9:2). Hebrew *charbah*

---

151. Smith-Christopher (1996), 127, compares this prayer with those at Ezra 9; 1 Kings 8 and 2 *Baruch* 1–3. He further explains the true purpose of fasting in postexilic texts: "Fasting was not merely a rite used to ask for forgiveness, but was an act of spiritual warfare that was presumed to have material results — to invite the direct intervention of God" (126).

152. See, e.g., Redditt (2000), 239–40, 242, who suggests "that it was a previously existing liturgical document in Hebrew."

153. Boccaccini (2002), 181–88, argues the case in detail; see also Redditt (2000), 240–41.

154. Against Collins (1994), 360, who argues that its theology "does not represent" that of the wider book.

155. Meadowcroft, 433.

156. Scholars have debated the historical identities of the "anointed prince" (9:25) and "anointed one" (9:26) whose time would mean the end of the seventy weeks. Meadowcroft argues for the interesting possibility that Daniel 9 does not envision specific individuals, but a communal embodiment of the "holy of holies" anointed in 9:24, which links the passage forward to the Christian understanding of the relationship between people, city, and sanctuary in Rev. 21.

is virtually a technical term for the ruin of Jerusalem, found in the torah only at Leviticus 26:31, 33, and three times in Jeremiah (25:9, 11, 18).[157]

There are several important implications of this connection. First, although Daniel 9, like the visions that surround it, comes to focus on the "desolation" of the temple by Antiochus IV Epiphanes (9:27), the *entire Second Temple period is revealed to be the time of YHWH's punishment of Jerusalem.* This distinguishes Daniel from *Dream Visions,* which roots the current crisis in the original act of human empire-building named in Genesis. Daniel does not address the question of the connection between earlier history and human sinfulness, but keeps the focus on the time of ongoing exile.

Second, Daniel's linking of Jeremiah and Leviticus *separates the sinfulness of the elite's collaboration with empire from the goodness of the torah texts* in themselves, which have become the constitution of the Second Temple. We have seen how the Enoch tradition rejected the temple and Mosaic torah along with the priests and scribes who have embodied those institutions. Daniel, in contrast, accepts the basic Zadokite premise of a covenant between YHWH and Israel, upheld by prophets like Jeremiah, which determines the fate of God's people:

> I prayed to YHWH my God and made confession, saying, "Ah, Lord, great and awesome God, keeping covenant [*berit*] and steadfast love [*chesed*] with those who love you and keep your commandments, we have sinned and done wrong, acted wickedly and rebelled, turning aside from your commandments and ordinances. We have not listened to your servants the prophets, who spoke in your name to our kings, our princes, and our ancestors, and to all the people of the land. (9:4–6)

The key Hebrew terms noted are in Daniel almost only here[158] as part of this classic summary of Zadokite theology. If the people had kept covenant and listened to the prophets, the power of empire would not have produced the ongoing punishment of exile. Again, this contrasts sharply with *Dream Visions,* which does not accept the correspondence between history and the keeping or breaking of covenant by Israel as a whole. The Exile is simply one episode in the much longer history of the influence of the fallen "Watchers" on humanity.

---

157. Of forty-two times in the Hebrew Scriptures, *charbah* is used thirty-three times in Isaiah-Ezekiel; of nine times in Isaiah, all but one are in Second–Third Isaiah, e.g., Isa. 44:26; 61:4; cf. Ezra 9:9, where it is used as part of the Ezra-Nehemiah claim that Persian rule equals the end of exile.

Daniel has two Greek manuscript traditions, "Old Greek" (OG) and Theodotion (Th), which match in most cases but in 9:2, use different words to translate *charbah*: OG, *oneidismos,* "insult" or "disgrace" (elsewhere in OG at 9:16; 11:8; 12:2, matched by Th in each case); Th, *eremōsis,* "desolation" or "destruction" (elsewhere in Th at 8:13; 9:27; 12:11, matched by OG in each case, and also used in OG at 9:18; 11:31). Both words express elements of Jerusalem's suffering as a result of breaking the covenant: the physical devastation and the insults of "the nations."

158. *Chesed* is also used at 1:4.

Third, the specification of failure to keep the Leviticus jubilee provisions as the cause for the Exile points toward the means by which the Exile can finally be ended by YHWH's "mercy and forgiveness" (Dan. 9:9). It is not a matter of purity of temple sacrificial practice or other "priestly" law, but of the overarching pattern of right relationship among YHWH, people, and the earth expressed in Leviticus 25. The sinfulness is a function of not only "the people of Judah" and the "inhabitants of Jerusalem" but of "all Israel" turning aside (9:7, 11). The visions show that it was the collaboration of the temple elite that caused this national disaster, but here, the ordinary people are also implicated. Living covenant righteousness for Daniel was a matter not exclusively of individual piety but of communal commitment and practice. Just as the Suffering Servant's exaltation was meant to lead to the repentance of the entire people of YHWH, so Daniel's "many" who arise from the dust of the earth were intended to bring about righteousness for all the people. This will happen when people collectively live in shalom-harmony with the Creator and all of creation in accordance with Jubilee. Again this contrasts with *Dream Visions,* which speaks generally about blind and deaf sheep that are judged and cast into a fiery abyss versus those who "opened their eyes" and "returned to the house." No specific provisions of torah are named as the cause of or solution to the crisis.

Fourth, Daniel affirms the centrality of Jerusalem and the temple for the future of God's people. Jerusalem is a city that bears God's name (9:18–19) and is God's "holy mountain" (9:16, 20; 11:45; cf. 2:35, 45). Just as Jeremiah had been sharply critical of Jerusalem's elite yet maintained a Jerusalem-centered perspective, so now Daniel prays on behalf of the city that has turned away but continues to belong to YHWH. *Dream Visions* never mentions Jerusalem at all, and in the new creation, there is no "tower" (i.e., temple). Boccaccini comments, "It is no surprise, therefore, that the covenantal Daniel would be canonized by Rabbinic Judaism, while the Enochic literature, including *Dream Visions,* would not."[159]

Finally, the prayer in Daniel 9 presents the possibility of reversal as wholly a matter of *God's own* "righteousness," not the people's (9:7, 16, 18). Only the sheer gift of mercy from a just God could break the yoke of imperial slavery that resulted from the people rebelling against God. Neither personal repentance nor priestly offerings in the temple could compensate for such sinfulness. Daniel's and the *maskilim's* wisdom is itself a gift (9:22), grounded as it is in the apocalyptic inbreaking that results in the visions and the book of Daniel itself. In this, Daniel and *Dream Visions* agree: it is God's righteousness and generosity that provide salvation from the sinful ways of empire. Whether at the end of seventy weeks of years or the time of seventy shepherds, the reign of the God of Israel, the King of kings, will become manifest, in a world utterly transformed into true justice and shalom.

---

159. Boccaccini (1998), 84.

Chapter Nineteen

From Greece to Rome

LONGING FOR GOD'S REIGN TO COME

The Hasmonean Dynasty: Empire from Within

The Maccabees' victory over Antiochus IV Epiphanes was a watershed event. It began the first period of a semi-independent Judea since the Babylonian Exile. We've seen how, as the battle raged, the writers behind *1 Enoch's Dream Visions* and the book of Daniel envisioned a more complete victory than the Maccabees could gain. They sought the unhindered and definitive presence of YHWH's reign of true justice and peace.

Instead, they got the Hasmonean dynasty. From its inception, the Hasmonean reign was fraught with inner struggle, corruption, and compromise with the newest Mediterranean power, Rome.[1] Throughout this period until Rome's conquest of Palestine[2] in 63 BCE, Judean[3] writers struggled to make sense of this situation. The ongoing ideological battle between "the two religions" continued, some supporting the dynastic reign while others looked beyond and "above" it for hope. Some left Jerusalem altogether, founding a community in the Dead Sea desert, eventually leaving behind caches of scrolls in the caves at Khirbet Qumran. Others settled into Hellenistic life in cities such as Alexandria, reducing faithfulness to YHWH to the most minimal of practices while accepting the imperial order without question. Still others wrote apocalyptic texts that challenged empire in various ways.

We need not, for our purposes, follow the hundred years of Hasmonean rule in detail. What is important is that we comprehend the aspects of that reign that led many in Judah to continue in the name of YHWH to resist the Jerusalem aristocracy. What was proclaimed as a great victory soon was perceived by many as simply another manifestation of the deceit and violence condemned in the *Epistle of Enoch*.

---

1. The ideology of kingship from 165 to 63 BCE is summarized at Mendels, 55–79; monarchy's relationship with Jerusalem and the priesthood at Mendels, 131–59; the history of the high priesthood in the Hasmonean era is studied in detail by VanderKam (2004), 240–393.

2. "Palestine" was the Roman name for the province that included Jerusalem.

3. Although it is common to refer to these writers as "Jews," it is anachronistic to use this term before, at the earliest, the fall of the Jerusalem temple and the collapse of national identity grounded in Judah/Judea. See discussion at pp. 5–289.

The Hasmoneans took up the Zadokite-supported "torah and prophets" trumpeted by Ben Sira and made it the key to their regime's claim to divine legitimation. Seth Schwartz notes that its "authority rested not simply, initially perhaps not at all, on the consensus of the Jews, but on the might of the imperial and native rulers of Palestine."[4] The "torah and prophets" as a scriptural collection became a central instrument in an elite educational curriculum.[5] The scribes who promoted this system of "God, torah, and temple" were not, of course, representatives of "the people," but "had a professional interest in promoting their institutions' ideologies."[6] As part of this educational process, they "stylized their own monarchy as an anti-Hellenizing construct."[7] We see this in 1 Maccabees 1, where the "lawless" are defined by their desire to conform to Hellenistic ways.

However, a closer reading of the entire book of 1 Maccabees, along with Josephus's account and the available material evidence, reveals that the Hasmonean anti-Hellenistic stance was more of a pose for political purposes than a reality. For example, inscriptions and coins of the Hasmonean regime regularly displayed Hellenistic symbols. Many leading Judean figures bore Greek names. The gymnasium, presented in 1 Maccabees 1 as the arch-symbol of foreign influence, remained standing without protest after the Seleucids were defeated.[8] "Hellenism," as such, was not the issue for the Hasmoneans or for their eventual opponents.

The real issue was the legitimacy of the Jerusalem temple. Shaye Cohen summarizes the situation:

> The desecration of the temple and the persecution of Judaism by Epiphanes, the overt corruption of the high priesthood, the Maccabean revolt and the reclamation of the temple through force of arms, and the usurpation of the high priesthood by Jonathan the Hasmonean, all these highlighted the problematic status of the temple. Was it legitimate? Was it the real house of God? Even if the temple had been legitimate before, how could one be sure that its purification was efficacious in the eyes of God? ... Through vigorous propaganda the Maccabees sought to legitimate both themselves and the temple they had regained, but many Jews were not convinced. Those who were least convinced formed sects.[9]

Josephus, tantalizingly, gives us but the briefest description of three groups in his own time that emerged during the Hasmonean period.[10] The *Sadducees,* claiming themselves to be descendants of the Zadokites (from

---

4. Schwartz, 56.
5. Carr (2005), 253–54.
6. Schwartz, 63.
7. Ibid., 257.
8. Gruen, 6–40. Collins (2005b) notes that the gymnasium was never really the issue: "It was quite possible to have a gymnasium in Jerusalem without posing a threat to monotheism."
9. Cohen (2006), 161.
10. *Ant.* 13.5.9; 18.1.2–5. See generally Saldarini; however, his book repeatedly confesses how little information there is about the Pharisees and Sadducees.

which their name is derived), were among the aristocratic class. They fit well the perspective we saw in Sirach, rejecting resurrection, dream revelations, and the possibility of social transformation. They supported the temple and its engagement with Hellenism, including relationships with Seleucid kings.

The *Pharisees,* well known from the gospels, stood in opposition to the Sadducees and had strong support among the Jerusalem populace. Josephus reports: "These have so great a power over the multitude that when they say anything against the king, or against the high priest, they are presently believed."[11] There is conflicting evidence about whether the Pharisees, like the later rabbis who likely descended from the Pharisees, believed in an "oral torah" that supplemented the torah of Moses.[12] They seem to have accepted the potential legitimacy of the temple, but were apparently willing to use their popular support to challenge high priests whom they found troublesome. They saw their practice of purity in table fellowship as a substitute for the impurity of the temple. Unfortunately, the limited available evidence makes it very difficult to distinguish the "real" Pharisees of this period from both their descendants in Jesus' time and the polemical characterization of them in the gospels.

The *Essenes* were the third group named by Josephus. Here we enter into an incredibly complicated topic, important, yet far beyond the scope of what we can consider. The key point is that the Essenes were almost certainly the root of those who rejected both the Sadducees and the Pharisees and established their own desert camp community by the Dead Sea at Qumran. The Essenes and their ancestors were likely the source of the Enochic texts and the "sectarian" texts among the Dead Sea Scrolls.[13] We'll see below how these texts express conflicting views about the relationship between YHWH's will and the temple.

Each of these groups responded in its own way to the Hasmonean reign, which itself faced the ongoing challenge of the relationship with the Seleucids, who, although expelled from Jerusalem, were not totally defeated. A few highlights illustrate the nature of the struggle.

As the quote from Cohen above indicates, the Hasmonean leaders took up the title of "high priest." We saw earlier that Menelaus, high priest during the reign of Antiochus IV Epiphanes, was willing to manipulate the system for his own personal advantage. The Maccabees' victory and the establishment of a "purified" temple did not eliminate the political and economic aspects of the high priesthood that were subject to personal ambition and gain. The next named high priest after Menelaus was Jonathan, who held

---

11. *Ant.* 13.10.5.

12. Cohen (1984), 37; for the relationship between Pharisees and rabbis, see Cohen (1984) and (2006), 154–59; Schwartz, 110–11.

13. The literature is enormous; see, e.g., Boccaccini (1998 and 2005), VanderKam (2002), 242–50, and Nickelsburg (2003a). The "sectarian" texts are those which reflect the specific theology of the Qumran community, in contrast with biblical texts also found among the Dead Sea Scrolls.

the office from 152 to 142.[14] This leaves a mysterious gap from 159 to 152 in which our sources provide no named officeholder. This has led to speculation over whether the leader of the Qumran community, called within their documents the "Teacher of Righteousness," had been a high priest during this time, whose conflict with Jonathan led to the Teacher and his supporters' complete rejection of Jerusalem and the temple. Unfortunately, as James VanderKam notes, there is "no secure evidence in favor" of this reconstruction.[15]

What is clear, though, at least from the evidence of 1 Maccabees, is that Jonathan, the youngest son of Mattathias, manipulated competing Seleucid royal claimants into a bidding war over his appointment to the high priesthood in exchange for his loyalty to them (1 Macc. 9–10). As a result, Jonathan carried, in addition to the title of high priest, the titles of *archonta* ("ruler") and *hegoumenon* ("governor"). He continued to work the Seleucids' political instability to his own advantage during the decade of his reign. It is likely that he is the mysterious person referred to in the Dead Sea Scrolls as the "Wicked Priest."[16]

The early Hasmonean rulers did not take the title "king" to avoid exacerbating the resistance of groups like the Essenes.[17] As we saw in chapter 17, Alexander the Great and his Ptolemaic successors went to great length to convey the notion that their reigns were approved of by the gods. The Hasmoneans well knew that Judah's own pre-exilic monarchy had made a similar claim in the story of Saul's and David's selection by YHWH. The Deuteronomic tradition, which they had taken up as part of the official Scripture of the regime, included the "torah of the king" (Deut. 17:14–20), which required that the king abide strictly by the torah and not act as typical kings did.[18] Hasmonean claims to legitimacy were shaky enough when it came to the high priesthood; adding "king" would further polarize those suspicious of their authority.

Jonathan's reign was followed by that of Simon III, during which independence was first declared (1 Macc. 13:41–42). First Maccabees suggests that his investiture as high priest was performed by "the people," but VanderKam shows that this account manipulates the evidence in Simon's favor. "The people" at issue were likely the members of the Maccabean army; the real legitimation came from a letter from the Seleucid king, Demetrius II.[19] "Independence" still required that the high priest be approved of by a foreign monarch.

---

14. Whether the Hasmoneans were actually from the genealogical line of Zadok (and thus, whether they were legitimate holders of the office of high priest) is much disputed; see Schofield and VanderKam, who conclude that "we have considerable reason to believe that the Hasmoneans were a Zadokite family and no evidence to the contrary" (87).

15. VanderKam (2004), 246–50.

16. Ibid., 267–69.

17. Mendels, 60.

18. See discussion above at pp. 188–92.

19. VanderKam (2004), 278–82.

The next high priest was John Hyrcanus, reigning from 134 to 104. Josephus tells us that John had been a Pharisee, but switched to the Sadducees after being confronted by one Eleazar over the legitimacy of John's holding of the high priesthood.[20] Given the popular power held by the Pharisees, after this event, Josephus says, "grew the hatred of the masses for him and his sons."[21] There was a sharp divide between the Hasmoneans and the people from this point forward.

Finally, we must consider the rule, just before the Roman conquest, of the infamous high priest Alexander Jannaeus (103–76). He followed in the footsteps of his short-termed predecessor, Aristobulus, in taking up the long-avoided title of "king." Alexander engaged in near constant wars of expansion, which, although partially successful, generated "massive drains on human and economic resources [and] sparked violent protests,"[22] including Alexander being pelted with citrons at the Feast of Booths. His desperate Judean opponents sought support from the Seleucid king, Demetrius III, who invaded Jerusalem and defeated Alexander, but whose own brutality led the Judeans to withdraw from him. Seeing an opening, Alexander sought revenge, crucifying eight hundred men and butchering their wives and children while he drunkenly watched, along with his concubines, from the sidelines.[23] Scholars debate whether the eight hundred were themselves Pharisees or simply their supporters.[24] In either case, the Hasmonean approval rating was certainly at low ebb.

The many texts composed during this period reflect the passion of opposition that developed under the Hasmoneans. A glimpse at a few provides a bridge linking the earlier struggles between "the two religions" we've been considering throughout this book and the revolutionary event soon to come in the Gospel of Jesus Christ.

Cosmos and Calendar:
Enoch's Astronomical Book *and the* Book of Jubilees

One of the earliest sections of *1 Enoch* is known as the "Astronomical Book" (1 *En.* 72–82). Its focus probably sounds hopelessly obscure to a reader today, occupied as it is with details about the relationships among earth, moon, sun, and stars. That "cosmic" concern, though, is taken up by another book, one written during the Hasmonean era, *Jubilees*. The question in both is about the *calendar*: Should God's people be governed by the lunar or solar year?

---

20. Saldarini, 85–89, interprets this episode in terms of patron/client relations: when the Pharisees' challenged their patron, Hyrcanus, he shifted his patronage to the Saduccees.

21. *Ant.* 13.10.6.

22. VanderKam (2004), 319.

23. *Ant.* 13.14.2.

24. VanderKam (2004), 362–30; Schiffman, 265.

Before our eyes and minds glaze over, we must be aware that at stake is *control of time.* Who has authority over it, God or the king? Is it a function, in other words, of creation or empire? Mark Adam Elliott comments: "Control of the calendar implied control of the cultic life of a community, and rejection of the 'official' calendar implied a challenge to the established authority."[25] Consider some simple examples from our own experience of calendar control. "TGIF" expresses popular celebration of the *weekend,* a unit of "free time" over which countless union members battled before it became a standard part of the American rhythm.[26] Yet now, the more familiar refrain is "24/7," the antithetical expression meaning "no-time-is-free." "Summer vacation" similarly offers an accepted space in which individuals and families can leave work and school behind. But a strong movement has formed in the United States for school all-year-round.[27] Battles over control of time have always been about justice and power.[28] Enoch's *Astronomical Book* and *Jubilees* took up this challenge in their own era.

The Seleucids used a 354-day, *lunar* calendar, continued by the Hasmoneans. The *Astronomical Book,* however, presents God's creation moving to the rhythm of a 364–day, *solar* calendar (*1 En.* 72:33).[29] This calendar was revealed to Enoch by God via "heavenly tablets," which contained all that Enoch was to share with humanity (81:1–2). The *Astronomical Book* is referred to in *Jubilees* in the latter's own historical review, where Enoch is praised as "the first among men that are born on earth who learned writing and knowledge and wisdom and who wrote down the signs of heaven according to the order of their months in a book, that men might know the seasons of the years" (*Jub.* 4:17–18). Further, *Jubilees* repeatedly emphasizes its own reliance on the "heavenly tablets" as the source of knowledge.[30]

Where the *Astronomical Book* simply presents the solar calendar as a given, *Jubilees* makes it part of "an explicit polemic against the lunar calendar.... Jubilees attributes the calendrical change to the influence of the Gentiles and presents it as a new phenomenon to be corrected with the greatest urgency."[31] The narrative has Enoch declare that this "is not of my own devising; for the book (lies) written before me, and on the heavenly tablets the division of days is ordained, lest they forget the feasts of the

---

25. Elliott (2000), 161.
26. E.g., Rayback.
27. E.g., the National Association for Year-Round Education, which presents its mission as "calendar reform," *www.nayre.org/.*
28. Consider, for example, the struggle over the sixteenth-century Gregorian calendar reform; for a popular presentation of this and related calendrical controversies, see Duncan.
29. The 364-day calendar obviously does not correspond to physical reality. Its structure is of a symmetry of 52 weeks, such that feasts always fall on the same day, as befits a sense of the permanence and regularity of God's creation and the place of religious feasts within it. The 354-day calendar, on the other hand, does not have an exact number of weeks, so feasts and other memorials shift dates over time, highlighting the "human" aspect of such a calendar.
30. Starting at *Jub.* 3:10 and mentioned, by my count, some thirty-one times.
31. Boccaccini (1998), 96.

covenant and walk according to the feasts of the nations after their error and after their ignorance" (*Jub.* 6:35–36).

The calendar question is itself part of *Jubilees'* larger narrative of resistance to "the nations." The text is structured as a retelling of the story from Genesis to Exodus 12.[32] Within this framework, Moses is acknowledged as one who received commands from YHWH. *Jubilees* is thus not as flatly opposed to the Mosaic torah as was Enoch's *Book of the Watchers* and *Dream Visions*. However, the revelation to Moses is simply part of the more expansive revelation to Enoch from the heavenly tablets. Both are ultimately incomplete: "No writing, Enochic or Mosaic, is the exact transcript of the heavenly tablets."[33]

Jubilees takes a big step toward acceptance of the "Zadokite" torah used by the Hasmoneans.[34] But *Jubilees* does this as part of its own program, which is sharply critical of the temple elite's collaboration with "the nations," i.e., the Seleucids. The Zadokite priesthood is rejected: "Levi," not "Aaron," is the source of priestly lineage (*Jub.* 30:18).[35] Only a "pure" priesthood, i.e., one not dependent on the legitimation of "the nations," was acceptable.

Throughout *Jubilees,* the emphasis is on "purity" in many forms. Jonathan Klawans shows that, beyond "ritual" impurity, *Jubilees* is primarily concerned with "moral" purity, i.e., murder, bloodshed, idolatry, and "sexual transgression."[36] Citing a series of passages, Klawans notes that the similarities between *Jubilees* and the "Holiness Code" in Leviticus are "overwhelming."[37] Yet there are also differences. The key one is that in Leviticus, as in Ezra-Nehemiah, intermarriage or sexual contact with "foreigners" is a matter of pure *lineage*. In *Jubilees,* though, "the nations" are condemned not as a non-Israelite ethnicity, but because of *their way of life,* which includes the sins noted above.

Just as *Book of the Watchers* built on the Genesis 6 story to explain the "root" of imperial violence under the Ptolemies, now *Jubilees* establishes that "the nations'" violence in the Seleucid-Hasmonean era is built into the very structure of creation itself.[38] Israel's "election" is also built-in

---

32. Earlier scholarship referred to this as part of a specific genre, "rewritten Bible," but more recent work has critiqued the anachronistic sense of a clear distinction at this time between "the Bible" and non-"biblical" texts such as *1 Enoch* and *Jubilees;* see, e.g., Horsley (2007), 117.

33. Boccaccini (1998), 89.

34. Najman observes that *Jubilees'* Mosaic grounding is one of four distinct authority claims made in the book, including access to the heavenly tablets, the angelic voice who dictates the torah to Moses, and the claim to provide divinely revealed interpretation of previous texts (Genesis and Exodus). The range of claims is a function of the struggle for religious authority and clarity of YHWH's will under Hasmonean rule.

35. VanderKam (2008), 418.

36. Klawans, 47.

37. Ibid.

38. Boccaccini (1998), 94. See also Henze (2009), who helpfully contrasts *Jubilees'* orientation to the past with Daniel's future orientation.

and irrevocable. The nations are not to be evangelized; they cannot repent. Unlike *Dream Visions, Jubilees* does not present a way of "righteousness" that all human beings could choose to follow. What is required is absolute separation of "Israel" from "the nations."

Whether this was meant to be taken literally in the multicultural world of the Hasmoneans cannot be determined. It does, though, make clear that the people of Israel are to live according to a torah that is diametrically opposed to that of all other peoples' way of life. And at the heart of that "other way" was violence and idolatry, i.e., the way of "empire." Thus, *Jubilees* understands opposition to empire as part of Israel's original vocation, even if it envisions an Israel that is saved while "the nations" are doomed to destruction.

The Qumran Community: Awaiting the "End of Days" in the Desert

Scholarship on the Dead Sea Scrolls is a world unto itself. In the years since their discovery in 1947, the huge collection of documents and fragments has gradually been translated and published.[39] It was not until the end of 1991 that all the texts became widely available; thus, scholarship from before that date was working with very limited evidence. Questions abound: To whom did they belong? How were the biblical and nonbiblical texts related? When were they written? When were they put in the caves and why? What was the relationship between these documents, the ruins at Qumran, and the Essenes referred to by Josephus? Did John the Baptist or Jesus know these texts or the people who made them?

Scholarship and popular culture have grappled with these and many other queries. It can quickly becoming overwhelming to try to distinguish well-grounded thinking from sensationalist exaggeration from politically motivated propaganda.[40] We will simply focus on two issues. First, what was the Qumranians' response to the Hasmonean dynasty? Second, how did the sectarians relate to other resistance groups of the time, e.g., the Enochians or the Pharisees?

One of the most difficult, yet necessary, questions about the Dead Sea Scrolls that must be addressed is the relationship among the scrolls themselves. Some are what we know as "biblical" texts, which provide ancient Hebrew language versions of these books. The majority of the scrolls, though, are nonbiblical.[41] These latter include texts we've already explored, such as Sirach and *1 Enoch*. But they also include a large number of scrolls

---

39. For the story of their discovery and the international politics at issue, see VanderKam and Flint, 3–19.

40. Two solid surveys are VanderKam (1994) and VanderKam and Flint.

41. VanderKam and Flint, 103, note that 222 scrolls or fragments are biblical; 670 are nonbiblical.

not otherwise known. Are all these remaining scrolls of the same group? The same time? Imagine someone discovering *your church's* library two thousand years from now, and trying to discern which of these books expressed "your congregation's worldview." Maybe some of your books express older theology that reflects the thoughts of your grandparents' generation. Perhaps some books were kept because you wanted to know and remember what "opponents" thought on a given topic or you wanted to engage in an interreligious or ecumenical dialogue. It would be very easy to make serious mistakes when seeking to reconstruct your congregation's thinking from its books.

But your church library might also contain parish bulletins, mission statements, committee reports, and other texts that one could accurately conclude were internally generated. Similarly, some of the Dead Sea Scrolls speak directly to an audience about events that correlate with the Hasmonean (and subsequent Roman) period. Scholars refer to these as the "sectarian" scrolls, much like those within a parish that are about the congregation's own history and life. It is from these, in relation to the biblical and other nonbiblical texts, that we can tentatively piece together the Qumran community's perspective on the burning issues of their time.

Our first question is easy to answer: the Qumran community was radically opposed to the Hasmoneans and their collaboration with the Seleucids. The ongoing failure of the Maccabean rebellion to result in a truly "purified" temple and community led them to take the radical step of moving to the desert sometime in the late second century.[42] We have seen that the first Hasmonean high priest, Jonathan, was likely the one to whom the Qumran texts refer as the "Wicked Priest." The hostility extended beyond whatever evils Jonathan may have been thought personally to embody. As Nickelsburg writes, the Qumran community thought that

> Israel as a whole is in a state of apostasy, here explicitly following the Babylonian Exile. This situation...is underscored by the recitation of rebellions against God, whose origins are ascribed to the Watchers (CD 2:17–3:12). The exceptions of Abraham, Isaac, and Jacob (3:2–4) and, by implication, Noah prepare for a reference to the remnant with whom God established his covenant (in Damascus) (3:12–19). Thus, we are thrust into a polarized world — a small covenant community in the midst of a wicked and perverse nation (and world).[43]

The community itself had entered into a covenant with YHWH; *they* were the temple, not the building in Jerusalem. *They* will serve as God's agents of judgment on sinners who are not part of the community.[44] The *Rule of the Community* (1QS) describes the process of entering into this

---

42. Scholars dispute the exact time of origin of the Qumran community; most settle for sometime in the mid- to late second century.

43. Nickelsburg (2003b), 147.

44. Ibid., 141–42.

covenant. The community was modeled not on Jerusalem but on the Exodus wilderness camp, with leaders appointed to oversee individual member's choices (cf. Exod. 18:25).[45] Each member was to merge his property with that of the community as they separated from "the congregation of the men of deceit" (1QS 5:2). This placed the Qumran covenanters firmly in line with the creation-based, resistance religion of Israel going back to its foundation as a rebellion against Solomon and his temple.

The purpose of the community was not, though, to remain self-enclosed, but to "prepare a way" for God to come in judgment and restoration, echoing Second Isaiah (40:3). It envisioned a time when all Israel would live in accordance with the ways revealed to the Qumran community. This would take place in the "end of days" in which "there shall come the prophet and the messiahs of Aaron and Israel" (1QS 9:11). There has been much debate about the exact nature of the "messianic expectations" at Qumran expressed by this passage.[46] We have seen little evidence of messianic expectation in texts such as 1 Enoch or Jubilees. Collins suggests that the reference here is "likely to be a reaction to the combination of royal and priestly offices of the Hasmoneans."[47] However, certainty is impossible. The "end of days" did not imply the conclusion of the space-time continuum, but as with the pre-exilic prophets, a time of Israel's definitive transformation (e.g., Isa. 2; Mic. 4). The term is used more than thirty times in the Dead Sea Scrolls. "It is a time of testing, and it is a time of at least incipient salvation.... It includes the dawn of the messianic age."[48]

What would mark the coming of the messianic age and the end of days? The War Scroll is a preparation manual for a final war between "the sons of darkness" and the "sons of light." Collins states, "The preparation of such an elaborate War Rule strongly suggests that the community was prepared to implement it, if the members believed that the appointed time had arrived. That time may very well have arrived in the war against Rome."[49] What part members of the community might have had in the Judean-Roman War of 66–70 CE is impossible to say, but it is clear that the Romans destroyed the Qumran site in 68 CE, right in the midst of the war. If the Dead Sea Scrolls community was not involved, there would seem to be no reason for the Romans to travel to this distant outpost to demolish it.

What was the relationship between the Qumran community and other resistance groups? The Dead Sea Scrolls are, as previously noted, one of our prime sources for copies of parts of 1 Enoch. Yet not all of the five "books" of 1 Enoch were found at Qumran.[50] As we'll see, the final unit, the Parables

---

45. Collins (2003), 100.
46. See generally Collins (1995).
47. Collins (1997b), 78.
48. Ibid., 56–57.
49. Ibid., 108.
50. Absent were the full Epistle of Enoch, the Parables, and the Enochic document collected apart from 1 Enoch, the Testaments of the Twelve Patriarchs.

of Enoch, was probably written near the end of the Qumran site's existence. The theology of *Parables* moves a different direction from both the earlier Enoch material and the sectarian texts from Qumran.

A plethora of theories has sought to explain these relationships. Gabriele Boccaccini's *Beyond the Essene Hypothesis* has laid out a "document chain" that shows "family relationships" among all of these late Second Temple resistance texts. He argues that the sectarian texts express a break between the Qumran people and the rest of the Enochic group, the beginnings of which can be seen in the "Damascus Document" (referred to as "CD").[51] CD "aimed to promote a stricter separation from the rest of Israel than the previous Enochic tradition had claimed." It followed *Jubilees* in calling for strict separation from the nations, which was taken literally with the move into the desert some time after CD was written. Boccaccini writes: "Damascus Document was a pre-Qumranic document written by a sectarian elite within Enochic Judaism, addressing the larger Enochic communities in an attempt to gain the leadership of the movement."[52]

Boccaccini argues that one of the central causes of the split that followed between Enochic and Qumranic traditions was the question of human responsibility for evil. The *Epistle of Enoch,* while accepting the earlier Enochic perspective that evil was in the world because of the presence of the spirits of the descendants of the fallen Watchers, also maintained that each person remained responsible for choosing whether or not to submit to that evil. The Qumran community, though, developed a thoroughly predestinarian perspective, in which people belonged either to the "sons of darkness" or the "sons of light."[53] There would not be a movement of repentance and reconciliation; there would only be a final war of judgment. The Qumran path became a dead end; the Enochic path led to the form of "Judaism" we now call "Christianity."[54] Boccaccini, however, treats this as if it were largely an abstract, theological debate, rather than a matter of "evil" embodied specifically in the Hasmoneans and the Romans. Thus, the Enoch tradition claimed that people should actively resist succumbing to empire, while the Qumran community saw themselves as having been "saved" from "the beginning."

The Qumran community also positioned itself in opposition to the Pharisees. In the sectarian texts, Pharisees are referred to with coded names such as the "seekers of smooth things" and the "builders of the wall," whom God hates (CD 4:19–5:11; 8:18).[55] One text refers to a "man of lies" who was likely a Pharisaic teacher (4QpHab 2:1–2).[56]

---

51. Boccaccini (1998), 119–62, presents the specific causes of the schism.

52. Ibid., 127.

53. Ibid. See the helpful exchange between Nickelsburg (2003a) and Boccaccini (2003) on this topic.

54. Boccaccini (2005) gathers scholarly responses to this theory, with specific responses to this portion of Boccaccini's theory at 329–45.

55. VanderKam (2003); Schiffman, 265.

56. Schiffman, 266.

The cause for this name-calling was the split over the claim to authority for their respective interpretations of torah. This was not simply an ancient and obscure power battle among theologians; it also involved a key question on which Jesus' later confrontation with the Pharisees turned: What role would the Jerusalem temple have in the coming of God's kingdom? The Pharisees were the inheritors of the Danielic tradition, itself an offshoot from the Enochic tradition, as we've seen. Daniel 9 presents an impassioned prayer of repentance and hope for God's mercy on the "holy city" and "holy place." The Exile may not be over, but when it was, Jerusalem and the temple would become truly purified and renewed as the center of God's kingdom. At Qumran, though, we've seen that there was no hope for such purification. Rather, God's judgment would come in the final war. On this point, the gospels show Jesus closer to the viewpoint of Qumran than of the Pharisees. Of course, the Enochians also did not place hope in a restored Jerusalem, but rather in a new creation in which there was no temple at all. Jerusalem's ongoing collaboration with empire — as in Solomon's time, "our" empire — generated the passionate argument that lasted until Rome ended it by destroying both the city and the temple.

The Temple Scroll:
Envisioning a New Temple and a New King for Israel

The longest text found at Qumran was a document not composed by the sect itself: the *Temple Scroll*.[57] Like *Jubilees,* it rewrote existing scriptural narrative. It took parts of Deuteronomy, especially the "torah of the king" in Deuteronomy 17, and reformulated it. Scholars differ widely in determining its date of composition, with estimates ranging from as far back as early in the Second Temple period to the middle of the Hasmonean dynasty.[58] Sidnie White Crawford argues that, regardless of its original date of composition, there was an "upsurge of interest" in it at Qumran that "may have been brought about by contemporary events: the excesses of the Hasmonean and Herodian kings, the ascendancy of the Pharisees in matters of cult and purity regulations and the subsequent sharpening of the conflict with the Qumran Essenes, and above all the rebuilding of the temple by Herod."[59] We'll look at the advent of Herod below. The reason for considering the *Temple Scroll* at this point is to recognize its portrait of a rebuilt temple in the present and a final, eschatological temple built by God.

Regardless of when during the Second Temple period the *Temple Scroll* was written, it conveys a deep dissatisfaction with the temple as it was. The dimensions of its envisioned temple would make the building and environs

---

57. For an interactive view of the actual scroll, see *www.imj.org.il/shrine_center/temple _Scrolling/index.html.*
58. Crawford (2000), 23–31.
59. Crawford (2008), 88.

as big as the entire second-century BCE city of Jerusalem.[60] Crawford writes that the

> goal of the plan for the temple and its [three] courts is to create a compound of concentric zones of holiness, in which the holiness emanating from that Divine Presence in the center, the temple itself, radiates outward across the entire land of Israel. As the holiness radiates outward, so the levels of ritual purity progress inward, with each court demanding a higher degree of purity.[61]

The *Temple Scroll* sought to establish the authority of YHWH within a purified temple, city and people. At the same time, it envisioned the restoration of a human king of Israel who would be unlike the Hasmoneans.[62] The king would be clearly subordinated to the priesthood.[63] He was not to make decisions apart from a council of twelve representatives from each group of the "leaders of the people," the priests, and the Levites. For all the qualifications surrounding the king's authority, the *Temple Scroll* took for granted that there would be a monarchy even in an idealized Jerusalem. As Steven Fraade writes, the "king was too central to the narrative sacred history of Israel, extending to the author's own day, to permit his exclusion."[64] The question, then, wasn't a king, yes or no, but *what kind* of king could do YHWH's will in leading the people.

Psalms of Solomon:
Looking for a Messiah to Save Jerusalem

As the Romans were gaining strength, the Hasmonean throne was being fought over between two rival brothers: Aristobulus II and Hyrcanus II. Their mother, Salome Alexandra, was the widow of Alexander Jannaeus, who, we recall, had butchered hundreds of Judeans who had sided with his opponent. Josephus reports that after her husband's death, Alexandra gained the public support of the Pharisees. A woman could not be high priest, so she appointed the elder — and quieter — son, Hyrcanus, to that post. She attempted to rid herself of the younger son, the hotheaded Aristobulus, by sending him to fight against the Ptolemies. Instead, he returned and attempted to seize the throne from his mother to prevent the Pharisees

---

60. Crawford (2000), 39.
61. Ibid., 34.
62. Scholars are divided on whether the Temple Scroll's "law of the king" is a direct polemic against the Hasmonean Alexander Jannaeus; cf. Hengel, Charlesworth, and Mendels with Wise (1990); also Fraade (2003), 38, who writes, "While the Temple Scroll's law of the king should be viewed in the historical context of sectarian discontent with the Hasmonean rulers and their successors, it should not be reduced to a simple polemical response to the specific behaviors of particular kings."
63. Fraade (2003), 35.
64. Ibid., 39.

from taking over at her death.[65] Hyrcanus urged her to resist the takeover attempt, but she died before putting a stop to Aristobulus's plan. The two brothers reached a truce, with Aristobulus taking the throne and Hyrcanus serving as high priest.

Things were not to end so quickly or smoothly. A friend of Hyrcanus — Antipater, the Idumean father of Herod the Great — aroused him to oppose Aristobulus. As the Roman general Pompey moved closer, both sent ambassadors to him to seek Roman support against the other. Josephus notes that Pompey also heard from another group that the people of Judea

> did not desire to be under kingly government, because the form of government they received from their forefathers was that of subjection to the priests of that God whom they worshipped; and [they complained], that though these two were the posterity of priests, yet did they seek to change the government of their nation to another form, in order to enslave them.[66]

Pompey told the ambassadors that he would resolve the matter upon his arrival. Meanwhile, though, Aristobulus organized a resistance army, arousing Pompey's anger. Hyrcanus, recognizing which way things would go, offered to assist Pompey against Aristobulus. As the Romans arrived, Aristobulus's men shut the city gates, seized the temple, and cut off the bridge between the temple and the city. When Pompey's offer of a peaceful takeover was refused, the general laid siege to the city. The predictable, horrifying scenario of death and famine unfolded. Hyrcanus was rewarded for his cooperation with the high priesthood, but as Josephus notes in concluding the episode,

> now we lost our liberty, and became subject to the Romans, and were deprived of that country which we had gained by our arms from the Syrians [i.e., Seleucids], and were compelled to restore it to the Syrians. Moreover, the Romans exacted of us, in a little time, above ten thousand talents.[67]

In the midst of these events, an anonymous poet composed a series of psalms expressing sorrow, anger, and hope for God's deliverance. Several of the texts, known collectively as the *Psalms of Solomon (Pss.Sol.),* describe events that correlate with Pompey's siege and takeover of Jerusalem.[68] Other psalms are more general cries for God's help in the face of corrupt leaders. Recently, Brad Embry has suggested that the entire sequence of psalms forms "a thematically and structurally coherent composition" composed by a member of the anonymous "third group" who went to Pompey to protest

---

65. *Ant.* 13.16.5.

66. *Ant.* 14.3.2

67. *Ant.* 14.4.5.

68. Questions of language, provenance, and dating of *Pss.Sol.* are engaged by Atkinson, 1–13. Quotations used here are from Atkinson's translation.

the Hasmonean monarchy as a whole.[69] We need not resolve this question for our purposes.

Most important is that within the *Psalms of Solomon* is *the earliest written expression of hope for a Davidic messiah who will save Jerusalem from the Romans.* This is found in *Ps.Sol.* 17, near the end of the collection. Embry notes that this hope is not the center of the author's perspective on historical events, but the *culmination.*[70] The earlier psalms express a theological understanding of Pompey's invasion grounded in the Mosaic covenant and, specifically, the Deuteronomistic perspective. Just as Jeremiah interpreted the Babylonian invasion as the consequence of Jerusalem's sinfulness, now this author similarly understands the Roman invasion. We hear this in an excerpt from *Ps.Sol.* 2:

> When the sinner became proud he struck down the fortified walls
> with a battering ram,
> and you did not restrain him.
> Foreign nations went up to your altar,
> in pride they trampled it with their sandals;
> because the sons of Jerusalem had defiled the Lord's sanctuary,
> they profaned the offerings to God with lawlessness. (2:1–3)

Here the Romans are portrayed as God's instrument of punishment for the "lawlessness" of the priests and people. The Romans, however, act beyond their commission, "not out of zeal" but "in lust of soul." The first stage of God's punishment of Rome comes immediately with the poetic description of Pompey's sudden assassination in Egypt. He is referred to as a "dragon," echoing Ezekiel 32's reference to Pharaoh as a dragon, and anticipating John of Patmos's use of dragon imagery in the book of Revelation for the source of all imperial evil (e.g., Rev. 12–13). The psalm concludes with the poet's confident hope that the Lord, "a great and righteous king, judging what is under heaven," will "separate righteous and sinner" and will "have mercy on the righteous, [delivering him] from the humiliation of the sinner, and...repay the sinner for what he has done to the righteous" (2:32, 34–35).

The psalms continue to reject both Hasmonean and Roman reigns as impure and sinful. When we reach *Ps.Sol.* 17, we hear of the coming of a messiah who will complete the process of purification. The poet draws on biblical imagery that will also be used by the New Testament writers, including Isaiah 11, Psalm 2, and Psalm 110. An excerpt reveals the tone and message:

> O Lord, you are our king forever and ever,
> for in you, O God, shall our soul boast (v. 1)

---

69. Embry 102, 118.
70. Ibid., 111.

You, O Lord, you chose David king over Israel,
and you swore to him concerning his offspring forever,
that his kind would never fail before you.
But, because of our sins, sinners rose up against us,
they attacked us and thrust us out, [those] to whom you did not
　　　promise,
they took possession with violence and they did not glorify your
　　　honorable name (vv. 4–5)

[a detailed description of Pompey's invasion follows in vv. 6–20]

See, O Lord, and raise up for them their king, the son of David,
at the time which you chose, O God, to rule over Israel your servant.
And gird him with strength to shatter in pieces unrighteous rulers,
to purge Jerusalem from nations that trample her down in destruction.
In wisdom of righteousness, to drive out sinners from the inheritance,
to smash the arrogance of the sinner like a potter's vessel.
So that he should shatter all their substance with an iron rod,
[and] should destroy the lawless nations by the word of his mouth,
and he should reprove sinners with the thought of their hearts.
And he shall gather a holy people, whom he shall lead in righteousness,
and he shall judge the tribes of the people that have been sanctified
　　　by YHWH his God. (vv. 21–26)

And he shall be a righteous king, taught by God, over them,
and there shall be no injustice in his days in their midst,
for all shall be holy, and their king the Lord's Messiah.
For he shall not put his hope in horse and rider and bow,
nor shall he multiply for himself gold and silver for war,
nor shall he gather hopes from a multitude of people for the day of
　　　battle. (vv. 32–33)

This expectation of a Davidic messiah echoes also in several Qumran texts,[71] where the *Psalms of Solomon* were not found, suggesting a common tradition of using earlier Scripture texts to describe a future, divinely appointed king.[72] This yearning sounds familiar, of course, to Christian readers. However, in the five hundred years since the Exile, this was the first written expression of such a hope.

A key question was the means by which this messiah would purify and restore Jerusalem. Both Kenneth Atkinson and John Collins seem to believe it to be self-evident that a violent conquest was envisioned.[73] Collins notes that the fact that the destruction was to be "by the word of his mouth" is

---

71. See Collins (1995), 65–74; Atkinson, 144–75.
72. Atkinson, 143.
73. Atkinson, 141–42, but see n. 25 revealing a wide range of opposing views; Collins (1995), 55.

"none the less destruction" and hence, a result of military violence.[74] However, the above excerpt highlights that the messiah's power will *not* be by "horse and rider and bow" nor will he "multiply for himself silver and gold for war" (cf. Deut. 17:17). The reference that he "should shatter...with an iron rod" is to canonical Psalm 2:9, which certainly *does* envision a traditional use of royal military power. However, *Ps.Sol.* 17 follows immediately — unlike the canonical psalm — with the parallel line,[75] "should destroy the lawless nations by the word of his mouth." This pair ("rod" and "word") is reused at Rev. 19:15, describing the reign of the Lamb, a.k.a., "the Word of God." In context, as we'll see, Revelation's violent imagery is part of empire's (Babylon's) defeat by the sacrificial love of the Lamb, not military power. In other words, the violent imagery is used paradoxically to unmask the real nature of God's reign in which the disciples of Jesus share. Whether the author of *Ps.Sol.* 17 had such a concept in mind cannot be definitively determined, but the language certainly leaves the question of messianic violence more open than some scholars would suggest.[76] It certainly claims that the messiah's royal authority will not be grounded in the kind of taxation and militarism that was endemic to Hasmonean and Roman rule.

We only know of the *Psalms of Solomon* from texts not discovered until the seventeenth century.[77] Like the Dead Sea Scrolls, they were part of a minority movement that disappeared from history until being fortuitously found long after the fact. Boccaccini notes that the *Psalms,* unlike the Qumran texts, have left the "Enochic paradigm" behind and taken up again the "covenantal paradigm" in their seeking of divine wisdom.[78] In common, though, they express both deep dissatisfaction with Jerusalem's accommodation with empire and an abiding hope for God's inbreaking salvation.

The Reign of Herod the Great, Puppet of Rome

Pompey's conquest of Jerusalem began a period of turmoil and transition in Judea. Rome underwent a chaotic civil war before the Battle of Actium in 31 BCE, at which Octavian defeated Mark Antony and Cleopatra and was declared emperor, taking the name Augustus. In the meantime, decisions had to be made about how Roman authority would be represented in Judea.

We saw earlier how the Hasmonean friend-of-Rome Hyrcanus II had been aided by the Idumean Antipater, who became Rome's local strong man. He

---

74. Collins (1995), 55.

75. For the nature of biblical poetic parallelism, see Alter (1987 and 2007).

76. See also Capper, 113 and n. 83, who takes issue with Atkinson and believes that *Ps.Sol.* 17 envisioned a "nonmilitant Davidic Messiah...who will rule over Israel as the ideally pious and obedient king."

77. Atkinson, 4.

78. Boccaccini (2007a), 274.

appointed his son, Herod, to be governor of Galilee in 47. Antipater was poisoned in 43, leaving his son the most powerful man in Palestine. As the civil war raged, the Parthians (the former Persians) filled a brief vacuum by appointing their own Hasmonean puppet, Antigonus, and Herod was forced to flee. Accepting Parthian patronage made the Hasmoneans enemies of Rome. Herod saw this as his chance. He allied with Mark Antony and was proclaimed "king of the Judeans" by the Roman Senate, with a celebration in the temple of Jupiter in Rome. With Rome's backing, Herod returned to Palestine to claim his throne.

It was then his turn to lay siege to Jerusalem. After four bitter months, he succeeded in capturing the city and having all remaining Hasmoneans killed. When Octavian defeated Herod's patron, Antony, Herod quickly proclaimed his loyalty to the new emperor, who affirmed his kingship over Judea. His loyalty was, literally, monumental: he embarked on a tremendous building campaign, naming everything he could after his new patrons, including the new cities, Sebaste (Greek for Augustus) in Samaria and the Judean port, Caesarea. Most famously, starting in 18 BCE, he embarked on a seemingly endless "remodeling campaign" of the Jerusalem temple. His building projects also included temples to Roma and Augustus and numerous palaces throughout the land. They were the best that imperial money and skill could buy and produce. Rome was very happy with its client in Palestine.

It should come as no surprise, though, that Herod was deeply hated by the locals. His bloodline was Edomite (the Idumeans' ancestors) a group hated by many Judeans.[79] His thirty year reign (34–4) was characterized by brutal violence, which he visited with equal force on his own family. And perhaps most of all, he expressed in the most opulent way imaginable the blasphemous claim that the Roman Empire embodied the divine order. It was not long before texts and rebellions developed in resistance to him and his successors.

Parables of Enoch: *Awaiting the Son of Man*

Ordinary people's sense that the biblical canon includes all or at least most of the texts written about God and Israel is shattered when one considers the enormous number of documents contained in the so-called Pseudepigrapha. The two-volume standard set is comprised of over two thousand pages of ancient texts, with brief introductions to each.[80] Although it is often impossible to pin down exact dates of composition, most of these texts are from the first centuries BCE and CE. Many of these texts are apocalyptic visions or heavenly tours that purported to offer a God's-eye perspective on current events. Some were probably edited and added to over a long period,

---

79. Recall how the Jacob cycle in Genesis 25–36 sought to replace the ancient hostility between Israel and Edom with a peaceful sharing of YHWH's blessing on the descendants of both "brothers."

80. Charlesworth (1983 and 1985).

as we've seen with the "book" of *1 Enoch*. Examples of texts that took on the question of God's will amid Roman authority over Jerusalem are the *Testaments of the Twelve Patriarchs*[81] and the *Sibylline Oracles*. The latter collection likely originated in Alexandria, which also produced the *Wisdom of Solomon* contained in the Septuagint.[82]

Our focus here will be on one example of this vast material, the final portion of the Enochic corpus, known as the *Parables* or *Similitudes*. This unit was not found among the Dead Sea Scrolls, but was part of the much later Ethiopic version of *1 Enoch*. Within that document, the *Parables* comprise chapters 37–71. Boccaccini argues that the *Parables* represent a continuation of the Enochic tradition after the "parting of the ways" among Essenes between the remaining Enoch group and those who went to Qumran.[83] If so, it may help to explain whether the *Parables* are a link in the chain of anti-imperial religious texts that led to the Gospel of Jesus Christ. For it is within this text that at least two crucial theological transformations occur. First, the "Son of Man" takes on a human face and is identified with the "messiah." Second, this person, also known as the "Chosen One," will render definitive judgment against "the kings of the earth" leading to the gathering of the righteous to live eternally in peace and justice.

It is impossible definitively to date *Parables'* composition. The world's most dedicated scholar of the Enochic material, George Nickelsburg, has settled on a date in the first decades of the first century CE, "on the grounds that Mark, the Q source, and the apostle Paul knew a form of the son of man tradition that we find in the *Parables* but not in Daniel 7."[84] However, another leading Enoch scholar, Michael Knibb, argues for a date later in the first century CE.[85] At stake is whether the *Parables* were influential on the New Testament or were a parallel or even later development. Walter Wink insists on a pre-date because of the sharp contrast in *Parables'* and the gospels' portrayal of the Son of Man, as we'll explore shortly. He writes that *Parables'* figure "is still heavenly, virtual, potential. It is not incarnate in a person or community."[86] However one answers this question, it is clear that *Parables* provides witness from outside the New Testament to hope in the God of Israel's final and definitive triumph over human empire via the victory of the Messiah Son of Man.

---

81. See, e.g., Hollander and De Jonge, who note the likely compositional history of the *Testaments* stretching from the Hasmonean era to the second century CE; see also Boccaccini (1998), 138–44, placing the *Testaments* ideologically between the Enochic and Qumran traditions.

82. Collins (1999), 83–85 (*Sibylline Oracles*); 199–202 (*Wisdom of Solomon*). For recent discussion of the book of Wisdom's provenance, see Grabbe (2004b), 87–95. Because of the Alexandrian perspective of these texts, they are not discussed in this volume.

83. Boccaccini (1998), 144–49.

84. Nickelsburg (2007b), 47.

85. Knibb (2007).

86. Wink (2001), 58.

The unit is called *Parables* because of the use of Ethiopic *mesale,* roughly synonymous with Hebrew *mashal,* both of which can be translated into Greek as *parabolē.*[87] It doesn't refer to a pithy anecdotal story as with Jesus' parables in the synoptic gospels, but rather to a prophetic, figurative discourse, akin to the "oracles" of Balaam at Numbers 23:17.[88] *Parables'* oracular discourses are tightly linked with the Enochic *Book of the Watchers.*[89] Central is Enoch's vantage point in "the confines of the heavens" (39:3) from where he received his visions.

Parables deeply rewards close engagement. The visions overflow with powerful, beautiful imagery that conveys God's judgment on empire and its supporters and celebration of the rewards in store for God's righteous. Its message to God's people amid Roman oppression — whether in Judea or elsewhere within the empire — expresses deep hope in the Creator's triumph over all that impedes the fullness of life and joy for people and all of creation.

Parables explicitly and repeatedly equates "sin" with imperial oppression. A few verses illustrate:

When [the Lord of Spirits'] hidden things are revealed to the righteous,
the sinners will be judged,
and the wicked will be driven from the presence of the righteous and
    chosen.
And thereafter, it will not be the mighty and exalted who possess the
    earth . . . (38:3–4a)

And then the kings and mighty will perish,
and they will be given into the hand of the righteous and holy,
and from then on, no one will seek mercy for them from the Lord of
    Spirits,
for their life will be at an end. (38:5–6)

And this son of man whom you have seen —
he will raise the kings and the mighty from their couches,
and the strong from their thrones.
He will loosen the reins of the strong,
and he will crush the teeth of the sinners.
He will overturn the kings from their thrones and their kingdoms,
because they do not exalt or praise him,
Or humbly acknowledge when the kingdom was given to them.
    (46:4–5)

In those days, downcast will be the faces of the kings of the earth,
and the strong who possess the earth, because of the deeds of their
    hands.

---

87. E.g., Ps. 78:2 (LXX 77:2).
88. See also Ezek. 17:2; 20:49; Knibb (2007), 48–49.
89. VanderKam (2007b), 86–90, shows numerous such links.

For on the day of their tribulation and distress they will not save
themselves....
(48:8; see also 53:5; 55:5; 56:5–8; 62:1–6, 9–12; 67:8–10)

Nowhere in *Parables* is there a sense of priestly squabbling over details
of ritual purity found in some of the Dead Sea Scrolls. The "righteous"
and "sinners" are sharply delineated as those who trust either in the creative power of "the Lord of Spirits" or in the mighty works of their own
hands. There is no specific connection here with Roman actions, as we saw
in *Psalms of Solomon*. Rather, *Parables* condemns the essence of imperial
power: the false claim to divine authority over people and the earth that
causes widespread suffering and poverty.

Similarly, people are called "righteous" for doing but one "work": offering praise and blessing to the Lord of Spirits rather than to the kings and
mighty of the earth. Their prayer is joined with the prayer of the "righteous
angels":

And there I saw another vision — the dwelling of the holy ones,
and the resting places of the righteous.
There my eyes saw their dwellings with his righteous angels
and their resting places with the holy ones.
And they were petitioning and interceding
and were praying for the sons of men.
And righteousness was flowing like water before them,
and mercy like dew upon the earth;
thus it is among them forever and ever. (39:4–5)

And all the righteous and chosen were mighty before [the Lord of
Spirits] like fiery lights.
And their mouths were full of blessing,
And their lips praised the name of the Lord of Spirits. (39:7)

And after this I saw thousands of thousands
and ten thousand times ten thousand

— they were innumerable and incalculable —
who were standing before the glory of the Lord of Spirits. (40:1)

In these days the holy ones who dwell in the heights of heaven were
uniting with one voice,
and they were glorifying and praising and blessing the name of the
Lord of Spirits,
and were interceding and praying in behalf of the blood of the
righteous that had been shed...
(47:2; see also 48:1; 58:2–6; 61:9–12; 62:13–16)

Similar imagery resounds through the book of Revelation, linking the
"holy ones" on earth with those in heaven. Whoever the "Enoch people"

were, they must have been a small minority over against the empire and its supporters, both in Rome and in Jerusalem. The vision of unity with the countless multitude "on the other side of the veil" was meant to inspire strength of purpose and commitment despite their minority status.

Parables' presentation is not simply a static portrait of condemned kings and joyous righteous ones. At the heart is the appearance of the Son of Man as God's definitive agent. The initial appearance takes up where Daniel 7 left off:

> There I saw one who had a head of days,
> and his head was like white wool.
> And with him was another, whose face was like the appearance of a
> man;
> and his face was full of graciousness like one of the holy angels.
> And I asked the angel of peace, who went with me and showed me all
> the hidden things, about that son of man . . .
> And he answered me and said to me,
> This is the son of man who has righteousness,
> and righteousness dwells with him.
> And all the treasuries of what is hidden he will reveal;
> for the Lord of Spirits has chosen him,
> and his lot has prevailed through truth in the presence of the Lord of
> Spirits forever. (46:1–3)

This Son of Man is not simply a revealer of hidden treasures. The text continues to describe several specific elements of his divine mission. We saw above his task of "overturning" kings and the mighty. This negative function, though, is just a preliminary component of his larger role.

> He will be a staff for the righteous,
> that they may lean on him and not fall;
> And he will be the light of the nations,
> and he will be a hope for those who grieve in their hearts.
> All who dwell on the earth will fall down and worship before him,
> and they will glorify and bless and sing hymns to the name of the
> Lord of Spirits. (48:4–5)

> He has preserved the portion of the righteous,
> for they have hated and despised this age of unrighteousness;
> Indeed, all its deeds and its ways they have hated in the name of the
> Lord of Spirits.
> For in his name they are saved,
> and he is the vindicator of their lives. (48:7)

The Son of Man, a.k.a. the Chosen One, is given a role that Isaiah linked to the "shoot" from "the stump of Jesse" (Isa. 11:1–2) and Sirach reserved for the torah:

And in him dwell the spirit of wisdom and the spirit of insight,
and the spirit of instruction and might. (49:3)

Sabino Chialà notes that by "giving the Son of Man certain prerogatives, the text stresses his 'messianic' nature, an element absent from the book of Daniel."[90] Further, his functions combine and extend those seen in *Book of the Watchers* assigned to the four named angels.[91] In Daniel and *Book of the Watchers*, God's victory remained hidden, visible and known only to Enoch and to those who received his book. In *Parables*, however, the Chosen One will be apprehended by the agents of empire, but it will be too late:

And there will stand up on that day all the kings and the mighty and
the exalted and those who possess the earth.
And they will see and recognize that he sits on the throne of his
glory....
And pain will come upon them as (upon) a woman in labor...
and they will be terrified and will cast down their faces,
and pain will seize them when they see that son of man sitting on the
throne of his glory.
And the kings and the mighty and all who possess the earth
will bless and glorify and exalt him who rules over all, who was
hidden. (62:3–6)

...And they will say,
"Would that we might be given respite,
that we might glorify and praise and make confession in the presence
of your glory. (63:5)

Our hope was on the scepter of our kingdom
and <throne of> our glory.
But on the day of our affliction and tribulation it does not save us..."
Now they will say to themselves,
"Our lives are full of ill-gotten wealth,
but it does not prevent us from descending into the flame of the
torture of Sheol."
And after that their faces will be filled with darkness and shame in
the presence of that son of man;
and from his presence they will be driven. (63:7–8, 10–11)

We hear a transformed echo of Third Isaiah's vision of kings coming to Jerusalem to offer tribute and praise (Isa. 60, 62). But the Enoch tradition is not interested in a restored and glorified Jerusalem served by the world's kings. Instead, *Parables* presents a vision of *a world without human kings at all.*

---

90. Chialà, 161.
91. Nickelsburg (2001), 45.

Finally, the Chosen One will complete his mission by gathering the righteous to share in the glory of his reign. We hear echoes of Daniel 12 brought to fulfillment in this passage:

> In those days, the earth will restore what has been entrusted to it,
> and Sheol will restore what it has received,
> and destruction will restore what it owes.
> For in those days, my Chosen One will arise,
> and choose the righteous and holy from among them,
> for the day on which they will be saved has drawn near.
> And the Chosen One, in those days, will sit upon my throne...
> and the faces of all the angels in heaven will be radiant with joy,
> and the earth will rejoice,
> and the righteous will dwell on it
> and the chosen will go upon it. (51:1–5)

> And they will raise one voice,
> and they will bless and glorify and exalt
> with the spirit of faith and with the spirit of wisdom,
> and with (a spirit of) long suffering and with the spirit of mercy,
> and with the spirit of judgment and peace and with the spirit of
>   goodness.
> And they will all say with one voice,
> "Blessed (is he), and blessed be the name of the Lord of Spirits forever
>   and ever." (61:11)

> And the Lord of Spirits will abide over them,
> and with that son of man they will eat,
> and they will lie down and rise up forever and ever. (62:14)

The sevenfold spirit blessing is the antithesis of empire's promises. It completely bypasses the torah covenant tradition, with its "promised land" and "holy city," envisioning simply the unity of those of whatever place and origin who gather in table fellowship with the Son of Man in the reign of the Lord of Spirits.[92]

Parables closes with a midrashic expansion of the description of Enoch's departure in Gen. 5:24 (*1 En.* 70–71). Enoch, "while he was living," is taken up into the presence of the Son of Man (70:1). He is shown the secrets of heaven and the home of the angels. Then there is a surprise twist. A mysterious figure[93] tells Enoch: "*you* are that son of man who was born for righteousness and righteousness dwells on you" (71:14). How can that be? What is the text trying to convey in identifying Enoch with the Messiah Son

---

92. Cf. Kvanig, 109.
93. Nickelsburg and VanderKam, 95, note the ambiguity: Is it an angel or the Lord of Spirits who speaks to Enoch at *1 En.* 71:4–17?

of Man? Andrei Orlov explores the tradition of the "heavenly counterpart," rooted in Jacob's wrestling experience (Gen. 32:24–30). Orlov notes

> Enoch's description reveals a contrast between the two identities of the visionary: the earthly Enoch ("a human being created just like yourselves") and his heavenly counterpart ("the one who has seen the Face of God"). Enoch describes himself in two different modes of existence: as a human being who now stands before his children with a human face and body and as a celestial creature who has seen God's face in the heavenly realm.[94]

Orlov suggests that for *Parables*' audience, this suggested that the "one with a pen" took up the authority of the heavenly counterpart across the succeeding generations, to continue to lead the faithful to trust in the heavenly victory of the Messiah Son of Man.[95] The sense of a heavenly counterpart to the earthly human being prepares for the understanding of Jesus as the embodied Son of Man in the gospels, who brings God's victory to earth, as it is in heaven.

With *Parables,* we can hear that the New Testament gospels were not the first, or at least not the only, texts from the first century CE to offer a universal vision of God's kingdom of peace and justice for all people. It is understandable that the upholders of Jerusalem and its temple would not include *1 Enoch* in their canon, just as it is understandable that they would similarly reject the gospels and their Jesus who referred to himself as "Son of Man" and was enthroned in crucifixion and resurrection as an alternative Messiah. It is now time to turn to that gospel to see how it proclaims and embodies the religion of creation and liberation that has stood against empire from the beginning.

---

94. Orlov, 135. He also notes (139) the Jacob/Enoch links via the use of the name Uriel for the "angel of the presence," also known as "Phanuel" (*1 En.* 70:9, 13), meaning "face of God," akin to "Peniel" at Gen. 32:21.

95. Ibid., 144.

PART IV

From Easter to the Eschaton:
Jesus' Fulfillment
of the Religion of Creation
and Defeat
of the Religion of Empire

Chapter Twenty

Enlightenment and Empire
READING JESUS FROM THE *LOCUS IMPERII*
IN THE LIGHT OF THE RESURRECTION

The coming of Rome gradually pressed Palestine into an imperial vise. It took almost exactly a century for the pressure to build enough to crush Jerusalem. The Romans managed to hold the tensions between their own military and economic domination on the one hand, and popular resistance on the other, in balance throughout much of the Mediterranean territory that they controlled, but, eventually, not in Palestine. The long history of the "two religions" was pressed into this short space, demanding a definitive answer to the question, "Is God on our side?" The outcome transformed Jerusalem and the world forever.

Thanks to Josephus, we know something not only about textual responses to this pressure, but also embodied ones: messianic, prophetic, and other movements inspired in varying degrees by the legacy of resistance to empire.[1] New Testament scholars, perhaps surprisingly, had long seemed to ignore this evidence for pre-Christian resistance to Rome. The reason lies deep in the often unexamined political and ideological presuppositions of many scholars since the Enlightenment. Recent decades have begun to reverse the pattern of previous centuries. We now stand ready to take full account of all the available evidence in seeking to understand the implications of the revolution begun by Jesus. Before we do so, it will help to situate our approach within this paradigm shift in New Testament studies.

Philosopher Charles Taylor has traced the movements over the past five hundred years that have taken us from the "age of enchantment" and into what he calls "a secular age."[2] Several aspects of this gradual and steady shift are directly relevant to how we read the New Testament. First, the development of independent, "reasoned" thought, unthreatened by institutional church authority (that was backed up by the power of the state) allowed inquiry into otherwise "forbidden" questions about Jesus and the New Testament. Rather than taking the biblical texts as "givens" that supported

---

1. See Horsley and Hanson, Horsley (1993b) for a descriptive analysis of these movements.
2. Taylor (2007).

theological developments over the previous fifteen hundred years, scholars began to ask how the texts came to be, what the relationship was between the "Jesus of history" and the "Christ of faith," and countless similar questions.[3] This questioning has not ceased, resulting in, among other things, a series of "quests for the historical Jesus."

Second, the Enlightenment invited inquiry in a "scientific" form that sought to achieve "objective" knowledge of the world, including history. This involved putting aside any "subjectivity" of the investigator, including religious stance, social location and personal history. In practice, this largely meant that scholars were Protestant,[4] socially privileged men, and mostly of German cultural formation. All of these factors greatly influenced the results of what became known as "historical criticism," but that influence remained largely unconscious and unexamined until very recently.

Finally, New Testament studies, having investigated the historical forms and "settings in life" of the texts, then tended to extract the *kerygma* (message) from the texts' own historically and socially localized contexts. This transformed the texts into containers of "universal" religious principles applicable to all peoples in all times and places in the same way. "Truth" was understood to be independent of the transitory situation in which it was discovered. The concrete and specific worlds of Jesus and the New Testament were no more important than the Greek worlds of Plato and Aristotle. The important truths could be removed from their historical context like a seed from a shell.

The Jesus who emerged from this process often resembled, if unconsciously, the imagination of the investigator. Since many of the scholars had inherited the German culture's Lutheran hostility to "the Jews,"[5] they "discovered" a Jesus whose "Jewishness" was irrelevant (at best) and a Christianity that had "replaced" Judaism. Since most if not all of the interpreters sat comfortably among the elite of the Western, imperialized world, Christianity, too, could find a home amid empire without being threatened by or threatening empire throughout history.[6] A parallel development took place in the scholarly understanding of the apostle Paul and his purposes in

---

3. See generally Wright (1992).

4. The Catholic Church, of course, resisting the Reformation, also resisted the Enlightenment transformation of New Testament studies, not officially joining the movement until the 1943 papal encyclical, *Divino Afflante Spiritu,* affirmed and expanded in the Vatican II text *Dei Verbum.* For a more recent statement of the Catholic approach to biblical studies, see the Pontifical Biblical Commission's 1993 document, "The Interpretation of the Bible in the Church," accessible at *http://catholicbibleresources.net/ChurchDocs/PBC_Interp.htm.*

5. Recently even the passionately anti-Nazi martyr, Lutheran theologian and pastor Dietrich Bonhoeffer, has been shown to have been infected by this legacy; see the sensitive discussion of these challenging questions in Haynes.

6. For the work of a towering figure from the last stages of this period, see Bultmann. His "existential" approach "de-mythologized" Jesus and the New Testament, rendering Christianity as a set of "answers" to a series of philosophical, if personal, questions. Bultmann was a German Lutheran who spent the entire Nazi period in Germany, although he, like Bonhoeffer, was a member of the "Confessing Church," which stood against Hitler. In his scholarship, his personal cultural context had no more relevance than did Jesus' own. See also Shawn

forming "churches" and writing letters to them. He became the "apostle to the Gentiles"[7] in the sense of turning from "Jew" to "Christian" and leaving behind all of who he was to found a "new religion." The "religion" to which Paul sought to "convert" people was purely "spiritual" and utterly disconnected from either the Roman world of his time or the sociopolitical context of any later readers' times.

The Nazi Holocaust of the Jews was one of several factors that began the process of unmasking the illusions and self-deceptions of this perspective. Suddenly, people began to notice how replete with anti-Jewish rhetoric New Testament scholarship was. In the 1960s, the attack on the old paradigm continued from new angles: postwar changes in the understanding of language and textuality led to "deconstruction" and "postmodernism."[8] In Pauline studies, Krister Stendahl's programmatic 1963 essay, "The Apostle Paul and the Introspective Conscience of the West," demolished many prevailing assumptions about who and what Paul and his message were and called scholars to what has been an ongoing paradigm shift.[9] The women's movement challenged patriarchal assumptions both about who "counted" as scholars and the role of men in the Bible's world.[10] Liberation theology, beginning in Latin America and spreading around the globe, began to "see" the suffering of the poor and oppressed and the parallels between Jesus' Palestinian context and that of marginalized peoples today.[11] This movement has included the oppression of people within the United States, such as African Americans.[12] This has led many in the first world to ask challenging questions about how to interpret and to *follow* Jesus from a privileged position *within* empire.[13] These movements were joined in the 1990s by the "turn to the subject," wherein the interpreter's own "social location" was recognized as an unavoidable component of one's stance as a biblical interpreter.[14] Finally, the development of "postcolonial" interpretation has explored the ongoing legacy of European colonial dominance.[15]

Kelley's analysis of the anti-Jewish elements of Bultmann's work and his relationship with the Nazi-sympathizing philosopher Martin Heidigger; Kelly, 129–64.

7. Recall Neil Elliott's observation (2008), 46, that to speak of "the Gentiles" rather than "the nations" is to "confuse social analysis with ideology."

8. For the effects of the new understanding of language and texts on New Testament studies, see Moore (1992).

9. Stendahl; see the discussion in chapter 26.

10. Feminist biblical scholarship has produced a mountain of challenging texts. Key early works include Schüssler Fiorenza (Harvard's Krister Stendahl Professor of Divinity) (1983 and 1988, the programmatic presidential address to the Society of Biblical Literature); Radford Reuther; Schneiders (1986).

11. E.g., Cardenal; for a first world liberationist approach to ancient Israel, see Gottwald (1979); for a global collaboration of liberationist Bible scholars, see Gottwald and Horsley.

12. The foundational work of "black liberation theology" is Cone; for African American biblical interpretation, see, e.g., Felder, Blount, et al.; Callahan.

13. A landmark is Stringfellow; see also Wylie-Kellerman; Myers (1988 and 1994), which laid the groundwork for my own work and that of many others.

14. Segovia and Tolbert (1995 and 2000).

15. E.g., Sugirtharajah; Segovia (2000).

These movements have totally transformed New Testament scholarship, although resistance from defenders of empire and domination continue.[16] Recent decades have witnessed tremendously productive research into the actual cultural context of Jesus and the New Testament generally, works to which this book is greatly indebted. Most recently, the scholarly community has begun to explore an element which may seem obvious, but which had been largely ignored: the towering reality of the Roman Empire and its world-shaping influence on everything that took place in the Mediterranean region in the first century of our era. Probably no one has single-handedly done more to promote this work than Richard Horsley, who for more than twenty years has engaged in collaborative and multidisciplinary investigation into the ways in which the Roman Empire has shaped the New Testament.[17]

My approach to the New Testament must be distinguished from two other approaches that I see as oddly parallel to each other. Both stem from the same misguided attempt to maintain an "objective" stance. At one end are the various forms of biblical literalism often grouped under the rubric, "fundamentalism." As we saw in Part I, these interpretations often seek the "truth" of the Bible within an unexamined set of assumptions grounded in Enlightenment thinking about "facts" and "science." For instance, consider the struggle to "prove" that the earth is only six thousand years old, based on taking the numbers in Genesis literally as "facts." Just as Genesis was not written to respond to Darwin, so Jesus' "miracles" do not need "defending" against the "threat" of secular science.[18] Rather, the stories of Jesus' powerful acts must be engaged from within the cultural context of their writers, neither "debunked" or defended from within a different cultural understanding of knowledge and truth.

The perhaps unlikely interpretive parallel to literalist fundamentalism is the pseudo-scientific work of the so-called "Jesus Seminar," a group of scholars as renowned for their publicity stunts to garner mainstream media attention as for what they have actually written.[19] The premise of their work is that the "real" sayings and deeds of Jesus can be separated from the "legends" and other accretions found in the canonical gospels. Their work is, in many ways, as old as Thomas Jefferson's eighteenth-century attempt to

---

16. E.g., Kim, relying heavily on Bryan, presents a broadside attack on the "anti-empire" movement within New Testament studies.

17. See the numerous bibliographic entries for Horsley. Elisabeth Schüssler Fiorenza (2007) has challenged this work to be more inclusive of feminist criticism. Needless to say, the work of uncovering and critiquing scholarly assumptions continues.

18. This kind of fundamentalism, ironically, works both ways, leading many supposed "scientists" to criticize or reject the Bible and "Christianity" because of lack of conformity to scientific forms of "proof"; e.g., the "new atheists" such as Dawkins.

19. For example, the Seminar gained notoriety for its procedure of voting on which parts of the gospels express the "authentic" sayings of Jesus; see Funk and Hoover. See, also, e.g., the 1996 *Time* magazine cover story featuring the Jesus Seminar, accessible at *www.time.com/time/magazine/article/0,9171,984367,00.html.*

cut out all the miracles and other "supernatural" events from the New Testament to reveal the "real" Jesus.[20] If their argument were to be made in a modern courtroom, it would be dismissed out of hand. For one thing, all of the gospels' quotations attributed to Jesus would be legally "hearsay" (since it is the evangelists' testimony, not the "direct" word of Jesus) and thus inadmissible in a trial seeking to determine the truth of what Jesus actually said. For the lesser purpose of simply determining whether Jesus "actually" made a given statement or performed a given act, there is a woefully insufficient store of "data" from which to make a "scientific" case. That two or three of the gospels agree about Jesus' words or actions proves nothing at all about "what Jesus really said" or did.[21] Finally, the approach fails to take seriously the New Testament as *literary texts* with their own integrity. In other words, the Jesus Seminar approach is simply fundamentalism turned on its head: the yearning to ground "truth" in "facts" is identical in both cases. Both approaches radically misunderstand the nature of the New Testament witness.[22]

One could simply ignore the entire phenomenon if it were not both prolific and a serious cause of confusion.[23] Further, since a number of the Jesus Seminar texts present a Jesus who stood against the Roman Empire, we must see how the approach used in this book differs radically from that of authors such as John Dominic Crossan, whose recent *God and Empire* touches on themes close to those of this book.[24]

My reading of New Testament texts differs from both kinds of fundamentalism in three major ways. First, it *takes seriously the canonical form of each complete text* — gospel, epistle, or apocalypse — as the basis from which the Christian message can be discerned. There are important reasons, as we'll explore, for writing and preserving "gospels" and letters rather than collections of sayings, in conveying both the continuity of Jesus with Israel's journey and his proclamation and embodiment of something radically new. To attempt to separate the "real" Jesus from the "myth" is to replicate in a new way the method of earlier scholars such as Bultmann.

Second, the interpretation in this chapter comes out of an openly committed stance of Christian discipleship. Attempting to understand Jesus

---

20. The "Jefferson Bible" can be read at numerous sites online.

21. For example, one would hardly try to argue that because Exodus and Deuteronomy agree on certain words or deeds of Moses, that this proves that Moses "really" said or did such things.

22. This same principle applies to the equally misguided campaign of Bart Ehrman and others to show how Jesus has been "misquoted" by the New Testament authors, e.g., Ehrman (2009). For a light-hearted critique, see the interview with Ehrman by Steven Colbert, accessible at *www.colbertnation.com/the-colbert-report-videos/224128/april-09-2009/bart-ehrman.*

23. See, e.g., Crossan (1993). For a strong critique, see Johnson (1997). For a response from the Jesus Seminar to its critics, see Miller (1999). See also the clarifying exchange between N. T. Wright and Crossan on the topic of Jesus' resurrection (Stewart 2006) and between Wright and the more moderate Seminar member Marcus Borg on Jesus more generally (Borg and Wright [2000]).

24. Crossan (2008).

"scientifically" with the rational mind alone almost guarantees that one will not "get it."[25] As Jesus says himself to people of a similar ilk in his own time, "I thank you, Father, Lord of heaven and earth, because you have hidden these things from the wise and the intelligent and have revealed them to infants" (Matt. 11:25; also Luke 10:21). This does not mean, of course, "checking our minds at the door" and denying what we *can* learn through clear thinking about the past. It *does* mean, as scholar Richard Hays has forcefully and passionately argued, that one can "have ears to hear" the Gospel only from a place of authentic trust in the power of God at work in and through Jesus. In a programmatic essay, Hays writes:

> We interpret Scripture rightly only when we read it in light of the resurrection, and we begin to comprehend the resurrection only when we see it as the climax of the scriptural story of God's gracious deliverance of Israel.[26]

Hays's perspective is hardly arbitrary. It matches the criterion provided many times in the New Testament. For example, in John's Gospel, the narrator responds to Jesus' statement, "Destroy this temple, and in three days I will raise it up": "After he was raised from the dead, his disciples remembered that he had said this; and they believed the Scripture and the word that Jesus had spoken" (John 2:19, 22). Throughout Mark, the disciples are utterly clueless, but the possibility of their comprehending Jesus' mission lies in their listening to the voice from the empty tomb, " . . . he is going ahead of you to Galilee; there you will see him, just as he told you" (Mark 16:7). Similarly, Paul tells the Corinthians, "My speech and my proclamation were not with persuasive words of wisdom, but with a demonstration of the Spirit and of power, so that your faith might rest not on human wisdom but on the power of God" (1 Cor. 2:4–5).

The paradigmatic expression of this principle is found in the story of the Road to Emmaus (Luke 24:13–32). Because the question of our interpretive method is so central to what follows, we must enter into this story before we explore the New Testament's anti-imperial message of trust in the Creator God of Israel.[27]

The story begins after Peter has investigated the women-disciples' crazy[28] story about an empty tomb and a wild message from two men in dazzling clothes about "rising again." Sure enough, Peter found, the tomb was empty, but what did it mean? It's not clear whether the Emmaus walkers know of Peter's experience, but they've heard the women's story and were apparently getting some distance to try to figure it all out, not to mention getting out of

---

25. For a biblical scholar's recent argument that "faith" and "reason" "are like oil and water, things that do not mix and should not be confused," see Hendel.

26. Hays (2003), 216.

27. See Myers (2006) for a reading of the Emmaus story from a similar perspective.

28. Greek *leros* (24:11, NRSV: "idle tale") is derived from a medical term connoting delirium caused by fever; Green, 839, n. 14.

harm's way in case the same authorities come after *them*. Was the messianic story over or not?

Of course, Jesus had told them on the way up to Jerusalem what was going to happen. Listen to a piece of his forewarning in light of our previous chapters: "...everything that is *written about the Son of Man by the prophets* will be accomplished" (18:31). We know that this means, in particular, the word about the "Son of Man" in Daniel 7 and Enoch's *Parables*. When Jesus was done warning them, though, we hear: "But they understood [*sunēkan*] nothing about all these things, what he said was hidden [*kekrummenon*] from them, and they did not know [*eginōskon*] what was said" (18:34). When they finally arrived in Jerusalem, Jesus lamented the fate of the city: "If you, even you, had only known [*egnōs*] on this day the things that make for peace! But now they are hidden [*ekrubē*] from your eyes" (19:42). The verbs for "know" and "hide" are paired in both places. Jerusalem and the disciples are in the same condition! The third verb in 18:34, "understand," is used subsequently only once in Luke: as the narrator tells us about the disciples in Jerusalem after the Emmaus pair had returned, "Then he opened [*diēnoigen*] their minds to understand [*sunienai*] the Scriptures" (24:45).

Thus, the frame of the Emmaus story already reveals the central point. Before the experience of the risen Jesus, the disciples — and the city — are in the dark. Afterward, the disciples' "minds are opened" to understand. The verb "to open" is repeated three times in Luke 24.[29] Ched Myers notes that it implies Jesus opening "faculties of perception that have been shut down by empire."[30] First, in v. 31, we hear that at the breaking of the bread in Emmaus, the disciples, "*eyes* were opened[31] [*diēnoichthēsan*] and they recognized him." That is step one: *seeing* the risen Jesus in one's midst. Second, in the next verse, they say, "Were not our *hearts burning* within us while he was talking to us on the road [lit., "in the way"], while he was opening [*diēnoigen*] the Scriptures to us?" Step two: *experiencing the fire* of the Scriptures being "opened" by the Risen One. Finally, step three, the *opening of minds to understand* the Scriptures.

In the heart of the Emmaus story, we see the "two religions" we've been exploring throughout this book in direct confrontation. The Risen Jesus is the judge of which is truly God's Word. The disciples, responding to Jesus' invitation, share their experience, based on the religion of empire that hoped for a military victory over the Romans, "inspired" by the Maccabees' victory over the Seleucids. But that dream has been dashed: "we *had been* hoping that he was the one to redeem Israel," they said (24:21). Jesus begins the process of turning their scriptural understanding inside out. His three-verse introduction says it all:

---

29. It is only used elsewhere in Luke to refer to "open" wombs (2:23).
30. Myers (2006), 65.
31. Recall the lambs who "opened their eyes" in *1 Enoch's Animal Apocalypse*; pp. 333–35.

Oh, how foolish you are, and how slow of heart to *believe all that the prophets have declared!* Was it not necessary that the *Messiah should suffer* these things and *then enter into his glory?"* Then *beginning with Moses and all the prophets, he interpreted*[32] *to them the things about himself in all the Scriptures.* (24:25–27; cf. 24:44)

The Risen Jesus provides the only reliable hermeneutical key to Christian interpretation of the Bible. The starting point is "all...the prophets." Those passionate critics of the people's persistent violation of the covenant are Jesus' first point of reference. The content of that message is about messianic suffering. Have we heard that before? We were given at least a hint in the combination of Isaiah's Suffering Servant and Daniel's *maskilim.* But neither was speaking of *messianic* suffering. Twice earlier in Luke, Jesus referred to the anticipated suffering of the Son of Man (9:22; 17:25). We find here the link made in Enoch's *Parables* equating Son of Man and Messiah. But the *Parables'* Messiah Son of Man was not said to "suffer." This is the central breakthrough that ultimately made this path through Scripture *Christian* and no longer *"Jewish."* It is the gospels — starting with Mark — that take the anti-imperial tradition to its "logical" conclusion in the death and resurrection of Jesus.

Finally, Jesus points toward a selective rereading of the entire scriptural tradition: *"the things about himself in all the Scriptures."* A naïve reading hears this suggesting that parts of the Bible were "predicting" Jesus, such as Isaiah's familiar foundation for Handel's *Messiah* at Isaiah 9:6–7. Jesus is not calling the disciples to pick verses here and there out of context that were somehow "secretly" about him, but *to find the continuing thread of the story that reaches this particular conclusion.* Paul had a similar method in mind when he explained to the Corinthians, "I handed on to you as of first importance what I in turn had received: that Christ died for our sins *in accordance with the Scriptures,* and that he was buried, and that he was raised on the third day *in accordance with the Scriptures"* (1 Cor. 15:3–4). There are no "magic verses" that Paul points to as "proof texts." Rather, Paul's own apocalyptic experience of the Risen Jesus led him to the same conclusion as the disciples on the road to Emmaus. He treats everything he knew and who he was before this experience as "crap" (Phil. 3:8; *skubula*). Only after *experiencing* God's world-shattering power to raise Jesus from the dead can one go back and truly comprehend the scriptural flow of salvation history.

The Jesus we find in the New Testament is neither philosopher nor sage; he is the embodiment of YHWH's authentic hopes and dreams for Israel. For all its internal diversity of form, language, and subject matter, the New Testament is absolutely consistent on this one foundational claim: *Jesus was*

---

32. Myers (2006), 61, notes the Greek verb (*diermēneusen*) means "translate": "Jesus is patiently translating this counterintuitive biblical wisdom into the plainest possible terms so these demoralized disciples can get it."

raised from the dead by the power of God and continues to live in and through the community of his followers. Any attempt to "make sense" of Jesus and/or the New Testament apart from a deep and abiding trust in the truth of this statement is doomed to fail. We "advanced" and sophisticated, twenty-first-century readers are in no different a position in this regard than the first disciples. Distanced, "objective" approaches may reveal interesting tidbits about the cultural context, use of language, and so forth but will never get to the heart of the matter.

There is one important corollary to this truth. The God of Daniel and Enoch was powerful, but his presence was far removed from the human, earthly struggle for justice, on "the other side of the veil" in heaven. Yes, God was engaged in the battle against the sinful empires that held God's people in bondage. But these and other apocalyptic authors depended on visionary experiences to reveal this power. Daily life did not seem to include encounters with God in the way ancestors like Abraham and Jacob had known. In the Word-made-flesh, though, this transcendent, powerful God became intimately bonded with human existence moment-to-moment. For instance, we hear Matthew explain Joseph's angelic dream encounter: "All this took place to fulfill what had been spoken by the Lord through the prophet: 'Look, the virgin shall conceive and bear a son, and they shall name him *Emmanuel*,' which means, 'God is with us'" (Matt. 1:22–23). What had meant for Isaiah the birth of King Hezekiah as the hoped-for bearer of YHWH's salvation is now transformed to the presence of God in Jesus, both in his earthly lifetime and in his ongoing, risen reality. From Easter forward, God is *with* God's people *in the flesh*.[33] This means that God's presence is always available to enlighten our reading of Scripture. Throughout Matthew, Jesus urges his disciples to come closer to him.[34] Those who remain at a distance call him "teacher,"[35] and he speaks to them in parables because "'seeing they do not perceive, and hearing they do not listen, nor do they understand" (Matt. 13:13, paraphrasing Isa. 6:9). Those who become part of his intimate household call him *Lord*: he speaks to them clearly and they understand.[36] In John's Gospel and in Paul, this is taken a further step, where Jesus speaks of disciples being *in* him[37] and Paul of being "*in* Christ."[38] The further one walks on this discipleship path *into* Christ,

---

33. Cf. Rev. 21:3, literally translated, "Behold, God's tent [*skēnē*] is with his people, and he will tent [*skēnōsei*] with them and they will be his peoples and God himself will be with them." Also John 1:14: "And the Word became flesh and tented [*eskēnōsen*] in us." The verb *skēnoō* is used only here in John's Gospel and in Revelation in the New Testament.

34. An important aspect of this in Matthew is moving with Jesus "into the house." See, e.g., 13:36; 17:25 and generally Crosby (2004).

35. E.g., 8:19; 12:38; 19:16; 22:24.

36. E.g., Matt. 9:28; 13:51.

37. E.g., John 15:5; 17:23. This is, of course, a central aspect of the Eucharistic passage in John 6:53–56, commanding disciples to "munch my flesh and drink my blood" to "abide in me and I in them."

38. Paul uses the term over seventy times.

the clearer the Word becomes. Again, this does not mean abandoning scholarly inquiry. It does mean, however, that scholarship alone cannot "hear"
the Gospel. Truth-revealing New Testament interpretation *requires* living in
the ongoing reality of God's immediate presence, known in the Risen Jesus.
Otherwise, we remain simply "scribes" or members of the "crowd."

Finally, the approach used here stands, like Mary in Luke's Gospel story
of the Annunciation (Luke 1:26–38), ready to *do* the Word of God as soon
as one *hears* what the Word is truly saying. In other words, a *commitment to
discipleship* is an essential aspect of the interpretive process. Specifically, this
means for me, and perhaps for most readers of this book, listening for the
Word while always being aware that our "home" is in the heart of empire.
We are the privileged, imperial elite, even if are struggling to make ends
meet. What Walter Wink has called "the domination system" (a.k.a., "the
world") works for *our* benefit.[39] This implies that the central call to me —
to us — is to "come out."[40] We listen to the New Testament not to consider
it, argue with it, or be amused by it, but to hear the Good News that leads
us from slavery to freedom, from darkness to light, from death to life.

I offer these methodological reflections here, rather than at the beginning of the book, because it is only with the New Testament that the
"two religions" we've been examining are finally and definitively separated.
Jesus and his followers are portrayed consistently rejecting the "religion of
empire" and its (false) gods in favor of the "religion of creation" and its one
God, YHWH, Creator of heaven and earth, Israel's liberating, wilderness
covenant-partner and "Father" of Jesus.[41] My hope is that the survey that
follows will illustrate the pattern that the reader's further engagement will
only make more clear.

---

39. Wink (1992).

40. For a systematic attempt to engage this call to radical discipleship through the use of
Mark's Gospel, see Myers (1994).

41. I am aware of the solid feminist reasons for eschewing such male language for God.
As I will show, I use it, as the New Testament writers do, not because God "is" "Father" and
not "Mother," but because in a world of imperially generated patriarchy, the claim that *God*
is "Father" stands in opposition to that claim being made by anyone else; see, e.g., Matt. 23:9,
where the denial of the right of any human to be called "father" comes as part of a series of
rejections of patriarchal authority and status. Note the parallel objection and parallel response
to the use of "Lord" for God and/or for Jesus.

Chapter Twenty-One

The Gospel of Jesus Christ against the Gospel of Empire

One of the most fruitful results of the paradigm shift in New Testament studies has been a wondrous outpouring of resources that shed light on the cultural contexts into which the Good News of Jesus Christ was proclaimed and lived. There are two "large" contexts that in turn could be broken down into many subcontexts. First, it is important to understand what life was like in *Palestine in the first century*.[1] This involves becoming aware of the relationships among individuals, families, and villages: the basic contours of "peasant economy,"[2] "honor and shame," and "reciprocity."[3] We cannot and need not explore these topics here, since others have done it well already.

The second large context is the Roman Empire. We've seen the people of God caught amid the snares of numerous systems of human domination across a thousand years: Solomonic, Philistine, Assyrian, Babylonian, Persian, Egyptian, Greek, and Hasmonean. The Roman Empire was the last in this series in the ancient world. When it began to collapse in the fifth century CE, it was not replaced as much as transformed, first into the Byzantine and later into the "Holy Roman" empires. As a result of this long continuity, there is an enormous deposit of remains available to study and from which we can learn. Of course, historical scholarship of the Roman Empire is nothing new; it was underway even before the Visigoths sacked Rome in 410 CE. However, much of that scholarship was done by writers themselves embedded within empire, such as the famous set penned by the British historian Edward Gibbon in the eighteenth century. That is, the Roman Empire was reflected upon by those *celebrating its accomplishments* and *lamenting its fall*. This is exactly what we'll find in the New Testament's book of Revelation, where the collapse of Rome is seen under the guise of the "fall of Babylon," and is lamented by the social elite (Rev. 18:9–19). However, its fall is celebrated by the "saints and apostles and prophets" (18:20), i.e., by the people of God under the reign of the Lamb and of God.

---

1. For good overviews, see Hanson and Oakman; Horsley and Hanson.
2. The term is often used by New Testament scholars in reference to the model developed by Gerhard Lenski; see Lenski.
3. E.g., Malina, DeSilva; Malina has produced an entire series of insightful "social-science commentaries" on individual gospels, Paul, and Revelation.

New Testament Timeline

	10	20	30	40	50	60	70	80	90	100

Events (upper band):

- Jesus crucified (c. 30)
- Saul in Arabia, travels to Damascus, converts from Pharisee to "apostle" (c. 35)
- Paul's first visit to elders at Jerusalem
- Paul and Barnabas build community in Antioch
- Paul's first missionary journey: Antioch, Cyprus, Pisidia, Lystra …Antioch
- Council at Jerusalem: Paul and Peter take separate paths (c. 50)
- Paul's 2nd missionary journey: Lystra, Phrygia, Galatia, Philippi, Thessalonika, Athens
- Paul's 3rd missionary journey: at Ephesus [53-56?] Paul winters at Corinth [57-58?]
- Paul arrested in Jerusalem
- Paul appears before Festus, delivered to Rome
- Paul under guard in Rome
- destruction of Jerusalem Temple [70]
- Beginning of development of urban Christianity within Roman culture (c. 80)
- Gospel of John, Revelation, Letters of John (c. 95)
- 1-2 Timothy/Titus (c. 100)
- Hebrews (?) (c. 80)
- Gospel of Matthew, Gospel of Luke, 1-2 Peter (?) (c. 85)

Lower band:

- Paul born in Tarsus, Cilicia (c. 10)
- ministry of John the Baptist; ministry of Jesus (c. 28)
- *childhood of Jesus*
- *periodic famines throughout Empire*
- *1 Thessalonians [c. 50]*
- *Philippians [c. 54-56]*
- *1 Corinthians [c. 55-57]*
- *2 Cor [c. 58?]*
- *Galatians [c. 57-58]*
- *Romans [c. 56-58]*
- *Philemon [?]*
- *Colossians [?]*
- *Ephesians [?]*
- *2 Thessalonians [?]*
- Gospel of Mark (c. 70)

Rulers:

- DEATH OF CAESAR AUGUSTUS [14 CE]
- REIGN OF TIBERIUS CAESAR [14-37 CE]
- PONTIUS PILATE, PROCURATOR IN JUDEA [26-36 CE]
- CALIGULA CAESAR [37-41]
- CLAUDIUS CAESAR [41-54]
- NERO CAESAR [54-68]
- VESPASIAN CAESAR [69-79]
- TITUS CAESAR [79-81]
- DOMITIAN CAESAR [81-96]

The scholarly shifts referred to in the previous chapter have led to historical interpretations that cast a more suspicious eye on the Roman Empire, and on empire in general.[4] Many helpful volumes, both by general historians and by New Testament scholars, have illuminated key aspects of the Roman Empire's ubiquitous presence in the lives of Jesus and his followers.[5] I hope this chapter will whet readers' appetites for more.

Many details of the Roman imperial context will emerge as we engage each of the major units of the New Testament. First, it may be helpful to summarize my position, given the emerging controversy over the claim that Jesus and the Gospel stood opposed to the Roman Empire. Jesus' mission was clearly not to "bring down" the Roman Empire in the traditional militaristic sense. At the same time, his goal was not to "spiritualize" political notions such as "kingdom" and "messiah" so as to render his followers either indifferent to "the world" or ineffective in participating in God's project of renewal and restoration. Finally, Jesus did not "inspire" his disciples to engage the empire's own social and political machinery in order to "reform" it. Rather, his purpose — as seen through a resurrection-oriented reading of the thousand-year long storyline we have followed — was to bring YHWH's ancient purpose for humanity to fruition: *the bringing forth of a people whose lives would be a light for others to show them how to live in true harmony (shalom) with God, one another and all creation.* This understanding of YHWH's purpose would have been obvious were it not for the persistent, powerful presence of the religion of empire claiming YHWH's authority, practiced by the Jerusalem temple, its priesthood, and its collaborators, among both the elite and ordinary people. In other words, Jesus, experiencing God's overwhelming love for him and for all creation, took up the sacred vocation of embodying YHWH's will by engaging in the two-part mission of denouncing the religion of empire and proclaiming as Good News the religion of God's immanent and abundant kingdom of peace, justice, love, and joy for all.

The question of whether Jesus stood against the Roman Empire *or* against the religious establishment thus frames the issue too narrowly and in a falsely dichotomous way. As we have seen, "from the beginning," religion and empire have worked hand in glove to generate oppressive worldviews incarnated in exploitative social, economic, and political structures. We cannot

---

4. For a clarification of terms and overview of the "logic" of historical empires from Rome to the U.S., see Münkler.

5. A sampling of recent work on the Roman Empire by nonbiblical scholars includes: Garnsey and Saller (economics); Huskinson (1999a) (culture, identity, and power); Zanker (role of visual imagery in Roman propaganda); Price (imperial cults); MacMullen (1966: dissent, 1981: social relations, 1983: paganism). Works by New Testament scholars include: Myers (1988: Mark's Gospel); Carter (2001a): Matthew's Gospel); Horsley (1997, 2000, 2004: Paul); Elliott (1994, 2008: Paul); Friesen; Howard-Brook and Gwyther (Revelation). To date, no full-scale work has been done on Luke-Acts from this perspective; cf. Cassidy (1978 and 1987) for early and preliminary studies and now Rowe (2009) on Acts. See also the programmatic series on Christian origins by Wright (1992, 1996a, and 2003). Cf. Moore (2006) for a sympathetic, but critical, review of this movement.

separate Jesus' denunciation of the Jerusalem elite from his rejection of the Roman Empire: they are one and the same.

The New Testament's final book, Revelation, loudly and insistently sings this song again and again. The image of the seductive whore "Babylon" and the destructive Beasts from land and sea cannot be reduced to simple ciphers for the Roman Empire. Rather, John of Patmos's vision reveals Rome simply to be the latest incarnation of the "Great City," first encountered in Genesis 10, and equated with such social formations as Sodom, Egypt, and Jerusalem (Rev. 11:8).[6] This "Babylon" is already "fallen," replaced by the manifestation of God's own "empire," the "holy city," New Jerusalem. Within this alternative reality, God's people are collectively *both* "priests" and a "kingdom" (Rev. 1:6; 5:10; 20:6) as they were always meant to be (Exod. 19:6).

Jesus reveals that all real power is from the Creator God, and that power, if allowed to flourish, generates the "blessing" of earthly abundance for all. There is no separation of "sacred" and "secular" realms. It is the seemingly endless attempt of humans to usurp God's unique authority that generates the counter-presence we have been calling "empire." The gospels portray a Jesus who sides consistently and definitively with the Creator/Liberator God and against the god(s) of empire. In this sense, those who would argue that Jesus' enemy was not "Rome" but what Paul calls "the principalities and powers" (e.g., Eph. 6:12) are correct. The enemy was no more limited to Pontius Pilate or Emperor Domitian than it is to particular individuals today exercising imperial authority. But this does *not* mean that the struggle is "only" spiritual. Rather, just as Jesus brought flesh to God's presence and expected his followers to do the same in his Name, so the "powers" are made flesh in the parade of fallen empires and their "inhabitants." Jesus stood up to oppose the specific incarnation of those powers that happened to "reign" in his time, but knew well that they were simply momentary manifestations of the "bigger" enemy. And in that historical moment, Jesus sought with all that was in him to inspire whoever "had ears to hear" to listen to his clarifying Word of hope that would lead others to follow in his footsteps. For this, he was brutally murdered by the representatives of empire. Again, there is no point in seeking to assign blame either to the Jerusalem or Roman authorities. In the end, they were on the same side. God was *not* on their side. God was on the side of Jesus.

Table 26 offers a schematic summary of the two "sides" of the battle in which Jesus engaged. The "themes" column is largely repeated from Table 1 in chapter 1, so readers can see how clearly Jesus sides with the religion of creation and against the religion of empire. In the following chapters, we'll look at sample texts that illustrate these elements, as well as the passages extracted out of context from the larger gospel that defenders of empire repeatedly cite to "prove" that Jesus either supported or was indifferent

---

6. Howard-Brook and Gwyther, 162–84.

Table 26: The "Two Religions" in the Gospels

Themes	Jesus	Supporters of Empire	Example of Jesus' Response to Empire's Claims
Source of "divine power"	YHWH, the "Sky Father," Creator of heaven and earth	YHWH *and/or* gods of empire	No power unless given from above
God's "home"	Amid God's people	In imperially sanctioned temples	Temple is coming down
Places of sacred encounter	River, mountain, wilderness, gatherings in Jesus' name, especially provision of hospitality and table fellowship	Temple and synagogue	Temple is "robbers' den"; synagogues are possessed by unclean spirits
Purpose of human life	Praise God joyously in gratitude for the gift of life	To serve the gods through loyalty (*pistis*, "faith") to empire	Trust in God and Jesus alone
Source of religious authority	Jesus	Priestly / scribal elite	Elite don't know Scriptures or power of God
Basic social structure	Egalitarian kinship	Hierarchical patronage	Jesus' family are those who hear the Word of God and do it; churches consist of "brothers and sisters"
Basic economic structure	Gift exchange	Money and debt	All debts forgiven (jubilee); God provides what people need as gift
Basic social architecture	House and village	Megalopolis	Babylon is fallen; discipleship communities in houses
Basic political structure	Kingdom / Lordship of God	Kingdom / Lordship of Caesar	Can't serve two masters
Relationship with unknown "others"	Healing all divisions	Generate and defend "borders" and "boundaries"	Crossing to "other side"; going to Samaria
Religious "obligations"	Love and praise of God and neighbor expressed in "right relationship" (justice), forgiveness and love of all	Rituals expressing loyalty to "patrons," both "divine" and human	It is not to be this way among you
Relationship with earth / land	Belongs to God; people are "tenants"	Belongs to king and those who can afford to buy it; others are tenants and slaves	Sell land and share proceeds
Relationship with "enemies"	Love them	Destroy them	Invite even Roman soldiers to participate in God's reign

to the power of Rome. The New Testament writers consistently call on the set of texts we've shown proclaimed the religion of creation. We hear repeated references to Genesis, Exodus, the prophets, and apocalyptic texts such as Daniel and *1 Enoch*. We virtually never hear from monarchy-supporting texts such as Joshua–Kings, except to parody their claims. The elite scribal "wisdom" literature, such as Proverbs, Qoheleth, and Sirach, are almost never quoted or implicitly cited. "Compromise" texts such as Deuteronomy and Leviticus are quoted selectively, always on behalf of creation and liberation and against human empire and domination. It is this kind of selectivity that the Risen Jesus opened the disciples to see and hear on the Road to Emmaus. It is the key to separating the God of Jesus from the god(s) of empire.

Chapter Twenty-Two

"The Beginning of the Good News of Jesus Christ"

THE GOSPEL OF MARK

The oldest of the canonical gospels is the one we know by the name of "Mark," although none of the gospels themselves claim specific authorship.[1] Ched Myers has argued convincingly that, contrary to earlier views that the gospel originated in Rome, the most likely provenance was Jerusalem amid the horrors of the Roman-Jewish War of 66–70 CE.[2] Its constant refrain of "at once"[3] echoes the urgency of responding to the sweep of Roman soldiers down from Galilee to recover control over Jerusalem after the "successful" rebellion of a coalition of Judean resisters. The central question facing the original audience was: What should we do when the Romans reach Jerusalem? Jesus' answer is shockingly specific: "when you see the desolating sacrilege set up where it ought not to be (let the reader understand), then those in Judea must flee to the mountains" (Mark 13:14). "Desolating sacrilege" recalls the book of Daniel[4] and expresses God's judgment on the imperial occupation of the temple. For Mark's audience, this certainly meant the presence of the Roman eagle brought by the invading army as an expression of their power and authority. Jesus tells his disciples not to defend Jerusalem, but rather, to run for the hills, like Lot escaping Sodom (Gen. 19:17). Jesus' disciples have no future with Jerusalem. As he tells them at the beginning of the chapter in the face of their awe at the grandeur of the Herodian building project: "Do you see these great buildings? Not one stone will be left here upon another; all will be thrown down" (Mark 13:2).

Jesus' condemnation of Jerusalem flows from the tradition of *1 Enoch*. Mark's Jesus combines Danielic and Enochic imagery in counseling the disciples amid the violent resistance to empire that rages around them. This message comes after twelve previous chapters in which Jesus systematically confronts the agents of empire while simultaneously trying to form

---

1. The attribution of authorship linking each gospel with an "apostle" was part of the imperial process of legitimation in the time of the emperor Constantine, to be explored in volume 2.

2. Myers (1988).

3. Greek *euthos* is used forty-one times in Mark of sixty times in the New Testament.

4. Dan. 9:27; 11:31; 12:11.

an alternative community that can see, hear and understand. Throughout Mark's narrative, tension between the two forces is palpable. A few examples illustrate the theme.

Mark's first verse announces the confrontation: "The beginning of the good news [*euangelion*] of Jesus Christ, the Son of God." The Greek noun, also translated "gospel," is found in the Septuagint only once (2 Sam. 4:10). There, the "good news" brought to David was that Saul was dead. For making this announcement, the messenger was killed.[5] The verb form (*euangelizō*) is less rare (used twenty-three times in the Septuagint). It is an important component of the message of Second and Third Isaiah,[6] as heard in this example:

> How beautiful upon the mountains are the feet of the messenger who announces peace, who *brings good news*, who announces salvation,[7] who says to Zion, "Your God reigns." (Isa. 52:7)

In Jesus' and Mark's time, it was also commonly used as part of the imperial claim to "bring good news." The gospel of Caesar was the Pax Romana, the "peace of Rome" provided by the gods, and embodied in the reign of the emperor. Mark begins by claiming his narrative to be the "beginning" of a counter-gospel, the heralding of one he calls both "messiah" (Christ) and "son of God." We saw that *Psalm of Solomon* 17 envisioned a new Davidic king as "messiah." The title "son of God" echoed royal claims in both Hebrew Scripture and the Roman world. In either context, it sought to provide divine legitimation for human kingship (e.g., Ps. 2). Mark provocatively starts his story by introducing the reign of a new divinely authorized king.

But, of course, traditional expectations are thoroughly subverted. Mark's story continues with Jesus coming to participate in John the Baptist's wilderness-based resistance movement. John is portrayed famously dressed in an "Elijah suit" (the leather belt, pointing back to 2 Kings 1:8), eating food provided directly by God (locusts and wild honey). Without a word, Jesus goes down into the water of the Jordan and comes up to see "the heavens torn apart." This is the third reference to Second/Third Isaiah in the first ten verses, here in fulfillment of Third Isaiah's prayerful plea amid the apparent victory of the Ezra-Nehemiah imperial restoration: "O that you would tear open the heavens and come down!" (Isa. 64:1). Jesus' apocalyptic experience includes a simple but empire-shattering message from "heaven": "You are my Son, the Beloved; with you I am well pleased." This knowledge

---

5. Although as we saw in Part II, this was part of the narrative cover-up of David's role in the fall of the house of Saul.

6. Found at Isa. 40:9; 52:7; 60:6; 61:1.

7. Hebrew, *yeshu'ah*, very close to the Hebrew for "Joshua" (*yehoshu'a*) thus, taken literally, "announces Jesus."

of being God's beloved is absolutely essential to both Jesus' and his disciples' capacity to proclaim and to live in radical resistance to the prevailing imperial ethos.[8]

Mark continues with Jesus' "immediately" being "driven" into the wilderness by the Holy Spirit. The brief summary of his sojourn there is wholly apocalyptic: tempted by "Satan" and with "the beasts" while served by angels. After this formational experience, Jesus bursts forth after John's arrest proclaiming the "good news of God" that "the kingdom of God has arrived" and that people should "repent" and "trust in the gospel" (1:15). Each of these phrases is important to Mark's message. The arrival of God's kingdom brings all the hopes of Second Temple resisters for the end of collaboration with empire to fulfillment and simultaneously announces the confrontation between the kingdom of God and any other "kingdom" that would claim divine authority. The call to "repent" (*metanoeite*[9]) invites people to perceive all of life differently, namely, from the perspective of God's inbreaking reign rather than that of imperial propaganda. Jesus constantly struggles with his disciples' seeming inability to "get it," despite their commitment to follow him (e.g., 4:13; 6:52; 7:18; 8:21; 9:32).

Before Mark's first chapter is over, Jesus has gone to the "synagogue" and confronted a man with an "unclean spirit" (1:21–29). *Never in the gospels does Jesus experience God in the synagogue.* Only unclean spirits are present in the synagogue. Mark says that people are amazed at his teaching, because Jesus, unlike the scribes, teaches with "authority." The synagogue is possessed by an "unclean spirit," which is the manifestation of the scribal collaboration with empire (e.g., 11:17–18; 12:38–44; 14:1ff.). It is this spirit that Jesus silences (1:25).

By the beginning of Mark 3, the sides have been taken. A politically and theologically unlikely conspiracy of Pharisees and Herodians[10] finds common cause in opposing Jesus (3:6). The only possible basis for these enemies to collaborate is their resistance to Jesus' indiscriminate invitation to participate in YHWH's direct reign. The rest of Mark plays out Jesus' ministry in the face of this combined resistance.

At the center of the Gospel is what Myers refers to as the "discipleship catechism" (Mark 8:22–10:52).[11] It comes on the heels of the second of Jesus' prophetic provisions of wilderness hospitality. Jesus has just warned the disciples to "beware of the yeast of the Pharisees and the yeast of Herod," precisely those we have seen conspiring. The dense disciples as yet have no clue, leading Jesus to berate them for their blindness, deafness, hardness of

---

8. A point made passionately and repeated by the popular spiritual writer Henri Nouwen, e.g., Nouwen (2002). For a selection of Nouwen's writings with an introductory essay by one of his friends, see Nouwen and Jonas.

9. The Louw-Nida lexicon defines it as "to change one's way of life as the result of a complete change of thought and attitude with regard to sin and righteousness" (41.52).

10. Recall pp. 357, 371–72.

11. Myers (1988), 236–88.

heart, and amnesia. The catechism is the prescription intended to heal their complete failure to perceive, i.e., to "repent" and trust in the Good News. It is framed by two healings of blindness (8:22–26; 10:46–52). After the initial healing of a blind person, Jesus takes the disciples to the north end of Galilee, far from the influence of Jerusalem, in the land historically associated with Jeroboam's rebellion and decentralized worship. Seán Freyne points out that choosing this locale shows that Jesus "was reluctant to become directly embroiled in the politics of urbanization and the damage that was being wrought to the fabric of village life."[12]

The distant outpost becomes the place in which Jesus challenges his disciples to recognize that his gospel radically opposes the religion of empire upon which they've been raised and in which they have placed their hopes. The disciples must initially have chosen to follow Jesus because of the harsh exploitation experienced by Galilean fishermen, whose catch was largely requisitioned by the Romans to supply mobile protein (i.e., salted fish) for the endless needs of the imperial army and for trade.[13] But given the verbal battle that ensues, it is clear that their hope was in a new Maccabee-like movement.

The key interaction that directly opposes the two perspectives is between Jesus and Peter. Jesus asks them all, "Who do you say I am?" Peter volunteers the response that we often perceive to be the "right" answer: "You are the messiah." Jesus' reply is immediate and strong: "he rebuked them and ordered them not to tell anyone" (8:30). In traditional scholarship, this is the so-called "messianic secret," Mark's supposed mysterious element that seems to undermine the public announcement of good news with which the narrative began. But understood within the dynamics of the two religions, there is no mystery or secret. Jesus sharply seeks to silence any association between his mission and Davidic kingship. In place of that (false) hope, he "began to teach them" a counter-story of the "Human One" (a.k.a. "the Son of Man") suffering rejection and death, only to "rise again." Rather than ask questions, Peter, we are told, "took *him* aside and began to rebuke *him*." Jesus' Gospel is not what Peter was hoping for. He takes it upon himself to stop Jesus from proclaiming such dangerous nonsense, saving Jesus' honor by doing it apart from the other disciples. But then, "turning and looking at his disciples, [Jesus] rebuked Peter and said, "Get behind me, Satan! For you are setting your mind not on divine things but on human things."

The rebuking has gone round and round. At stake is the nature of Jesus' mission and messiahship. The apocalyptic invocation of "Satan" reveals the need for Peter and the other disciples to get a "new mind," a *"metanoia-ed"* shift that will lead them to see, hear, and believe that Jesus' path, not Peter's, is God's "way out"[14] of empire. So after telling the crowd to "deny

---

12. Freyne (2004), 57.
13. Ibid., 51.
14. Recall the literal meaning of Greek *exodus*, "way out."

oneself" and "take up of one's cross," Jesus takes Peter, James, and John to a "high mountain apart, by themselves" (9:2). Just as Jesus' ministry was initiated by a time of deep listening to God in silence and solitude on the earth, so now the disciples' must experience the raw reality of God's presence confirming who Jesus is and the divine authority of his Word. The voice from the overshadowing cloud leads them to share in Jesus' initial encounter: "This is my Son, the Beloved; *listen* to him!"

The confrontation over and confirmation of Jesus' purpose (and thus, of the will of God), is grounded precisely in the question of which "religion" in the Bible is "true." To "listen" to Jesus is to accept and trust in *his* version of the scriptural story. Peter is wrong to hope for a Davidic warrior king. That is *not* YHWH's will. Rather, the path of Isaiah's Suffering Servant, embodied as we've seen in Daniel's *maskilim* and refracted through *1 Enoch*'s Messiah Son of Man, is the course Jesus takes and calls any who follow him to take. Sadly, Peter's resistance to this path continues all the way through Jesus' arrest and crucifixion. The only narrative suggestion of a possible reversal is his "remembering" after denying three times that he knew or understood or was even associated with Jesus. His cockcrow-triggered weeping may be the beginning of his "conversion" at last, confirmed by the voice of the "young man" in white at the tomb (16:7). But Mark gives Peter no easy out from his refusal to listen to the voice of God's Beloved.

Near the end of the discipleship catechism, Jesus challenges James and John over their request to "sit, one at your right hand and one at your left, in your glory" (10:37). Their request comes immediately after Jesus' third and final passion "portent."[15] After the previous portent, Jesus found his disciples arguing among themselves over which of them was "the greatest," leading Jesus to offer a lesson in servant leadership (9:31–37). Again, the yearning for imperial-like power and glory follows from a passion portent (10:33–34) and leads to another lesson in servant leadership (10:42–45). The contrast could not be clearer in both cases. Here, the point is made by twice implicating the "nations" (*ethnōn*) as those who practice the way Jesus teaches his disciples to resist. It is to the *ethnōn* that Jesus will be handed over (10:33), and it is among the *ethnōn* that "those whom they recognize as their rulers lord it over [*katakurieuousin*] them, and their great ones are tyrants over [*katexousiazousin*] them" (10:42). Both Greek verbs connote domination over others. The first is used for human control over animals (LXX, Gen. 1:28), but also specifically for imperial domination (Dan. 11:39; 1 Macc. 15:30). The second means literally "have authority over." Jesus must repeatedly teach his power-hungry disciples that being his followers means rejecting completely the ways that empire presents as "how things are."

From the end of the discipleship catechism to his crucifixion, Jesus continues his twin ministry of confronting the upholders of imperial religion

---

15. The term is from Myers (1988), 242, 260, 277.

while trying to strengthen and prepare his fledgling community to experience the full, raw brutality of empire lashing out against him. The last section of Mark begins with his enacted parable of condemnation of the temple in the form of the cursed fig tree "withered to the roots" (11:13–14, 20). Within this frame, he calls upon Third Isaiah's inclusive vision of a Jerusalem welcome to all who trust in YHWH (Isa. 56) while simultaneously echoing Jeremiah's divine judgment on the temple elite's imperial collaborators, who imagine their acts of exploitation of the poor and violence against the innocent are hidden from God's sight (Jer. 7). Unlike Isaiah or Jeremiah, though, Jesus does not hope for a purified temple. Rather, he replaces it with the gathered community of discipleship as a place of prayer and spring of divine mercy (11:23–25). He then proceeds one by one to dismantle the authority claims of each component of the temple elite: chief priest, scribes, Pharisees and Herodians, and Sadducees.

In the midst of these challenges is the famous incident involving "Caesar's coin."[16] The passage has become a virtual litmus test for both one's method of interpretation and one's understanding of the relationship between discipleship and citizenship.[17] I draw readers' attention to two details of the encounter. First, the questioners are the same conspiracy of Pharisees and Herodians who earlier had determined to destroy Jesus. Here, we are told explicitly that their question is intended to "trap him in what he said" (12:13). Jesus himself calls it a "test" (*peirazete*), recalling his encounters with Satan (1:13) and the Pharisees (8:11; 10:2). Thus, his response is not meant to engage an authentic question. Its purpose is simply to reveal the questioners' hypocrisy (12:15), just as throughout this section Jesus undermines the authority of each component of the temple elite.

Second, Jesus says, "Bring me a denarius and let me see it." This is the oft-ignored key to the passage: *Jesus does not traffic in the imperial coin.* It is not a matter of a fetishistic avoidance of an idolatrous object. Rather, Jesus, like the traditional religion that he embodies and brings to fulfillment, *rejects imperial economics altogether.* As we saw, the money economy began to flourish first within urban settings in the Persian Empire. The purpose of money has always been to enable trade with people with whom one is not in personal, kinship-like relationship. Jesus' discipleship community is a new *family* (3:32–35). It has no need for Caesar's or anyone else's coins (cf.

---

16. The only previous explicit reference to the Roman Empire in Mark is the Gerasene demoniac's statement of self-identity: "We are Legion," an unequivocal reference to the imperial army (5:9, 15). Despite the utterly unambiguous nature of the reference, some scholars continue to resist the narrative's claim that the people's captivity to Rome is embodied in the man who lives among the dead and cannot be restrained. See Moore (2006), 24–29, for a postcolonial reading of this passage; also Myers (1988), 192–94.

17. See, e.g., the writing of conservative Catholic bishop Charles Chaput, entitled *Render unto Caesar* (New York: Image, 2009). My informal research found ten books with that title or *Render to Caesar* at *amazon.com*. The scholarly literature on the question is immense.

Mark 6:8). Its "currency" is mutual gift.[18] Jesus' response to the icon[19] and inscription on the Roman coin has nothing at all to do with a supposed division of authority between "church" and "state," notions foreign to the ancient world. Nor does it have to do with "Christian citizenship" within an imperial context, the kind of "both / and" offered by the religion of Ezra-Nehemiah and the Hellenistic wisdom literature but rejected by Third Isaiah, *1 Enoch,* and others within the tradition of obedience to YHWH alone. The central purpose of this section of Mark's Gospel is to undermine the authority of those who benefit from dual allegiance to empire and temple. Jesus, opposed by the conspiracy of representatives of both, outfoxes them.

The series of challenges culminates with a bitter lesson about the cost of the temple's system to those long held up as the bellwethers of covenant obedience: widows. The degree to which churches today are enthralled by imperial religion can be seen in how this passage has been systematically abused in service to church fundraising campaigns, wherein people are urged to "sacrifice" like the widow, as if she is being held up as an example of piety. Rather, one can see in context that the widow is revealed as the victim of scribal hypocrisy and exploitation. In the verse immediately preceding the "lesson in sacrificial giving," we hear that scribes "devour widows' houses and for the sake of appearance say long prayers" (12:40). It takes quite a homiletic sleight of hand — or, putting it more charitably, discipleship blindness — to convert this victim of imperial injustice into a model for middle-class generosity.

Mark's Last Supper is a bittersweet farewell. Only the anonymous woman with the alabaster jar of ointment who anoints Jesus' head for his burial has a clue of what is to come. Despite Jesus' frequent admonitions to "stay awake," the disciples sleep through the arrival of the "strong man." We should not be surprised that when the arresting party arrives, *"all* of them deserted and fled" (14:50). Only Mark among the evangelists provides the symbolic presence of a naked young man, whose return, dressed in a white robe, signals the possibility of starting the story again from the experience of the empty tomb and the promise of an encounter with Jesus in Galilee, far from Jerusalem and its imperial collaboration.

Each detail of the First Gospel's crucifixion narrative contributes to the stark contrast between the two religions being portrayed throughout the story. Jesus is dressed and mocked as a king, executed alongside two village-based resisters.[20] The Jerusalem crowd, at the instigation of the chief priests, gladly takes up Pilate's offer to release the terrorist Barabbas rather than Jesus. The question is which of them is really "son of the father," Jesus, the

---

18. See also Myers (2001).

19. *eikōn,* which NRSV renders "head" at Mark 12:16, but rightly as "image" at Rev. 13:14–15.

20. The Greek *lēstēs* connotes a "social bandit" who would likely have been stealing from wealthy caravans of Jerusalem pilgrims to share among fellow villagers; see Horsley and Hanson, 52–85.

Beloved, or the murderous Barabbas (Heb., "son of the father"). Pilate is portrayed as a typical Roman procurator, protecting the Pax Romana by any means necessary. It is only the final apocalyptic inbreaking at Jesus' death that signals that empire has not had the last word, as divine darkness overshadows Jerusalem as it once did Pharaoh's Egypt (Exod. 10:21–22) and the curtain over the temple's Holy of Holies is torn in two "from above to below." Just as the story began with the tearing open of the heavens to reveal Jesus as God's Beloved Son, so now it comes to a close with the opposite effect: the revelation that the temple has been condemned "from above."[21]

Mark provides no resurrection encounter. It is only the women's willingness to witness, despite their "terror," that leaves open the possibility that God's victorious power over empire will be acknowledged and embraced. One of the great ironies of history is the construction of the Church of the Holy Sepulchre by the Emperor Constantine on the spot where the First Gospel proclaims of Jesus, the crucified: "he is *not* here" (16:6). From Genesis forward, we have seen cities, with temple and palace, built upon the foundation of the absence of YHWH, amid the imperial propaganda of divine authorization. That Mark's Gospel could be so blatantly reversed is a measure of how eagerly people continue to embrace the way of empire, even, blasphemously, in the name of Jesus.

---

21. The Greek *anōthen,* translated "from above," found only here in Mark, is used with similar double entendre at John 3:3, 7 and 19:11, 23.

Chapter Twenty-Three

"Strive First for the Kingdom of God"

MATTHEW'S GOSPEL

No one has done more to date in relating Matthew's Gospel to its Roman imperial context than Warren Carter. His excellent work has begun the process of hearing the Second Gospel in the way its first audience did, whether in Antioch in Syria, as traditionally understood,[1] or in any city throughout the Mediterranean. At the same time, Carter's work largely limits the question to specific connections between elements of Roman culture and politics and the Gospel. We will be considering here the wider question into which Carter's investigations are subsumed: How does Matthew portray Jesus siding with the religion of the Creator God of Israel against the imperial religion?

Matthew's Gospel's twenty-eight chapters contain about 90 percent of Mark's sixteen chapters. It also includes the material that scholars refer to as "Q" (from German, *Quelle,* "source"), which comprises the elements common to Matthew/Luke but not found elsewhere.[2] The final component of Matthew is the material unique to this gospel. This latter writing will be our focus. We will see how consistently this "Matthew material" affirms the scriptural texts within the creation/anti-empire tradition and subverts those in the Jerusalem/empire tradition. We will also see how, writing from within the people of Israel, Matthew presents a Jesus who incarnates the Messiah Son of Man in fulfillment of the apocalyptic hopes of the Enoch tradition.

Literally from its first words, Matthew's Gospel constructs its story in opposition to the dominant temple/empire story of his world. Numerous clues throughout the gospel combine to reveal the author to be writing from

---

1. Davies and Allison, 146–47, review numerous possibilities for the provenance of Matthew's Gospel, concluding that Antioch "remains no more than the best educated guess."

2. For an overview of Q from one of its leading scholars, see Kloppenborg (2008). There is a mountain of Q scholarship focused on Q as more "original" to Jesus than the canonical gospels. As such, Q has been very popular among members of the Jesus Seminar. The basic problem with this approach, of course, is that there is no such "thing" as Q. Not a single manuscript shred or literary reference to such a source has ever been found. Needless to say, the way of Jesus followed in the early churches was grounded not in the hypothetical Q, but in the actual gospels for which we have countless manuscripts and references. For a recent argument against Q, see Goodacre.

within the traditions of Israel rather than as an outsider from "the nations" like Luke.[3] The first sentence establishes this framework: "Book of genesis (*biblos geneseōs*)[4] of Jesus Christ, son of David, son of Abraham." The theme of new genesis is deeply embedded in the narrative. For the "insiders" of YHWH's people, it suggests the divine reestablishment of right relationship among God, humanity, and creation. For non-Israelites in the audience, it counters the Roman propaganda of the divinely ordained "golden age" of Augustus.[5]

The genesis theme returns near the end of Jesus' ministry. A rich young man walks away sad, unable to respond to Jesus' invitation to be "complete" or "mature" (*teleios*) by selling his possessions and giving the money to the poor. The disciples in turn are "greatly astounded" when Jesus offers the Markan cartoon image comparing the ease of a camel passing through the eye of a needle to that of a rich person entering God's kingdom (Matt. 19:24; Mark 10:24–25). But Matthew adds a new element to Mark's version:

> Truly I tell you, at the renewal of all things [*palingenesia*], when the Son of Man is seated on the throne of his glory, you who have followed me will also sit on twelve thrones, judging the twelve tribes of Israel. (19:28)

The term translated "renewal of all things" means literally "genesis again."[6] In Stoic philosophy, it referred to the rebirth of the world.[7] Matthew's context, however, is clearly not Greek philosophy, but apocalyptic wisdom. The imagery of the "Son of Man seated on the throne of his glory" comes directly from Enoch's *Parables*. Enoch's vision is made flesh in the community of discipleship that has the exalted Jesus as its king and lord rather than a human emperor. We thus see that the goal of the gospel from its first verse is to proclaim that in and through Jesus and his resurrection, God's just and peaceable kingdom comes down to earth, making it "genesis again."

There is another, more subtle way in which Matthew's unique first chapter recalls the Bible's opening book. Scholars so routinely speak of Genesis 1–2 as presenting "two stories of creation" that they often forget that this is nothing more than a modern construct based on two alleged "sources." The author of our gospel certainly had not heard of such a theory. His "book of genesis" parallels the opening chapters of Genesis. That is, Genesis starts with a "genealogy" of heaven and earth summarized at 2:4. It then continues

---

3. For a general overview of the question of who "Matthew" is, see Davies and Allison, 17–27.

4. The Greek phrase matches exactly the Septuagint translation of Gen. 2:4; the phrase is found elsewhere in the Greek Bible only at Gen. 5:1.

5. Carter (2005), 152–55.

6. Cf. Titus 3:5, the only other use of the term in the Greek Bible.

7. LSJ Lexicon, accessed online at *http://old.perseus.tufts.edu/cgi-bin/lexindex?entry=paliggenesi/a&display=Sgreek.*

with a "close up" version that focuses on the creation of the human as male and female. Matthew does the same thing: he begins with the genealogy[8] of Jesus, summarized with a marking of three sets of fourteen "generations" that flow from Abraham to "the Messiah" (1:17).[9] He then continues immediately with a "close up" version of the "birth [genesis] of Jesus the Messiah" (1:18, the only other use of the term in Matthew's Gospel).

We have seen how retelling the Genesis stories was at the heart of both 1 Enoch and Jubilees, texts challenging the relationship between the temple and empire during the Hellenistic era. Now, under the Roman Empire, Matthew continues the tradition and adapts it to his own understanding of God's kingdom irrupting into the world.

Another important element of the opening scenes of Matthew's counter-narrative is the role of dreams.[10] Both Enoch and Daniel were able to gain a divine perspective on imperial events by paying close attention to angelic voices within dreams. Matthew's first major character, Joseph, has four such encounters within the first two chapters (1:20; 2:13, 19, 22). His obedience to the angelic voice guided him and his family safely away from the clutches of Herod. His first dream guidance, though, provides a subtle, but key, critique of the prevailing torah/temple ethos that will be systematically elaborated by Jesus in the Sermon on the Mount. We are told that Joseph was a "righteous man," putting him in the company of Noah (Matt. 1:19; Gen. 6:9; 7:1).[11] But unlike Noah, whose pre-torah righteousness was important to the Enochic tradition, Joseph's righteousness is implied to be a matter of torah obedience. Such obedience to the law of Moses would have led him to divorce his pregnant fiancé. But the angelic dream leads him to a "higher" righteousness, one available directly to Israelites and others alike, independent of both torah and temple, as we see in the account of other recipients of dream guidance in Matthew.

Between Joseph's first and second dreams, the magi experience a collective dream. They are neither generic "wise men" as in some translations nor "kings" from "the Orient" as in the popular Christmas carol. They are specifically Persian royal officials, appearing in Daniel as imperial lackeys (e.g., 2:2, 10, 27).[12] They were well-known figures in the Greco-Roman world, although Roman intellectuals expressed contempt for their alleged powers of prediction.[13] The evangelist, however, paints his picture on a

---

8. "Genealogy" is an alternative translation of Greek, genesis, as so rendered in the NRSV, NIV, and NAB translations.

9. The three sets of fourteen also make six sets of seven, thus matching the six days of creation in Genesis.

10. Only Matthew in the New Testament uses Greek onar, "dream."

11. Gen. 6:9 LXX describes Noah as an anthrōpos dikaios, the only use of the term in the LXX about an actual person; the only other biblical use of the term is at Matt. 23:28; Joseph is described as ho anēr autēs dikaios, lit., "her man, righteous..." Noah's day is made an explicit topic at Matt. 24:37–38.

12. Horsley (1993a), 53–57.

13. Carter (2000), 74.

scriptural canvas: the gold- and frankincense-bearing visitors from the East embody the first stages of fulfillment of Isaiah 60, part of the counter-narrative to the Ezra-Nehemiah story of collaboration with Persia. They come because of a star, and leave because of a dream. The powerless minions of Nebuchadnezzar in Daniel 2 are transformed into obedient servants of the God of Israel.

There is a final opportunity to obey a divine dream at the end of the gospel, as Pilate's wife warns her husband as he sits on the judgment seat, "Have nothing to do with that righteous[14] one, for today I have suffered [*epathon*] a great deal because of a dream about him" (27:19). The only other "suffering" referred to in the gospel is that of Jesus (16:21; 17:12, 15). In contrast to Joseph and the magi, though, we hear nothing of Pilate's response to this warning. Instead, he listens to the voice of the chief priests, elders, and the Jerusalem crowd who cry out for Jesus' crucifixion. His attempt to wash his hands of the consequences of his choice rings hollow. Jesus' blood sticks to him and to the Roman Empire, in demonic alliance with the Jerusalemites, for all time.

Another theme in Matthew's Gospel not always recognized as part of the anti-empire message is Jesus' response to "disease." Matthew uses a number of Greek words to refer to the ill health cured by Jesus, which Jesus empowers his disciples to cure. Two words in particular are revealing. At the end of the first summary of his ministry, we hear:

> Jesus went throughout Galilee, teaching in their synagogues and proclaiming the good news of the kingdom and curing every disease [*nosos; also 8:17; 9:35; 10:1*] and every sickness [*malakia, also 9:35; 10:1*] among the people. So his fame spread throughout all Syria, and they brought to him all the sick, those who were afflicted with various diseases [*nosos*] and pains, demoniacs, epileptics, and paralytics, and he cured them. (4:23–24)

Matthew's use of both *nosos* and *malakia* draws attention to a specific Septuagint echo:

> He said, "If you will listen carefully to the voice of YHWH your God, and do what is right in his sight, and give heed to his commandments and keep all his statutes, I will not bring upon you any of the diseases [*noson*] that I brought upon the Egyptians; for I am YHWH who heals you." (Exod. 15:26)

> If you heed these ordinances, by diligently observing them... YHWH will turn away from you every illness [*malakian*]; all the dread diseases [*nosous*] of Egypt that you experienced, he will not inflict on you... (Deut. 7:15; cf. 28:59–60)

---

14. It is the final use of *dikaios* in Matthew, thus framing the entire gospel with the first use, the description of Joseph (1:9).

In other words, *nosos* signifies "Egypt disease," or more broadly, "empire disease."[15] On the one hand, it refers to the physical ailments that are a direct function of urban crowding, lack of sanitation, and epidemics caused by the relationship between surplus food and rats and other carriers of disease.[16] On the other, it points to the social oppression upon which empire is founded, including slavery and despair. We hear this latter connection made explicitly at Matthew's summary of Jesus' ministry that precedes the sending of the apostles to participate in Jesus' mission:

> Then Jesus went about all the cities and villages, teaching in their synagogues, and proclaiming the good news of the kingdom, and curing every disease [*nosos*] and every sickness [*malakian*]. When he saw the crowds, he had compassion for them, because they were harassed and helpless [*eskulmenoi kai errimmenoi*], like sheep without a shepherd. Then he said to his disciples, "The harvest is plentiful, but the laborers are few; therefore ask the Lord of the harvest to send out laborers into his harvest." (9:35–36)

The two words describing the state of the shepherdless people mean "troubled" and "thrown down," i.e., literally *oppressed*. Jesus' healing campaign has nothing to do with healing *isolated* cases of individual suffering, but of responding to the systemic pain that is the constant cost of empire. This connects us to Matthew's other use of *nosos*:

> That evening they brought to him many who were possessed with demons; and he cast out the spirits with a word, and cured all who were sick. This was to fulfill what had been spoken through the prophet Isaiah, "He took our infirmities and bore our diseases [*nosous*]." (8:16–17)

Jesus' healing ministry is interpreted as the incarnation of Second Isaiah's Suffering Servant (Isa. 53:4). As we saw in the discussion of Second Isaiah in chapter 15, the Servant embodied the consequences of Israel's sinful failure to abide by the covenant. Matthew again quotes from Isaiah's Servant poems at 12:18–21.[17] Jesus' mission is rejected by the temple/torah establishment and he thus turns to the nations. Carter writes that one of the key functions of the healing ministry is to "protest the current 'sick' imperial world and anticipate the yet-future, complete establishment of God's reign."[18]

Jesus' manifesto of God's reign follows immediately after the first summary. Perhaps no section of the New Testament has been both so commented

---

15. *Nosos* is used only eleven times in the LXX; see also Hos. 5:13 for a similar usage to those in Deuteronomy. It is also used eleven times in the New Testament, including Luke's parallels, Luke 4:40; 6:18; 7:21; 9:1; also Acts 19:12. The other use is Mark 1:34.

16. See Cohen (1991) and Mumford for the history of the physical illnesses caused by urbanization.

17. Quoting Isa. 42:1–4.

18. Carter (2000), 125.

on and so misunderstood as the Sermon on the Mount (Matt. 5–7). For many, it presents either an unlivable fantasy of perfect human behavior or, as for Martin Luther, a bar so impossibly high to cross that its purpose must be simply to turn people in desperation to God for salvation. But it was the young German Lutheran pastor Dietrich Bonhoeffer who was one of the first in the modern world to see the Sermon for what it is: a practical program for living in harmony with God and all humanity. His classic *The Cost of Discipleship* was published in 1937 amid Hitler's reign. A powerful recent documentary film on the life of Bonhoeffer reveals how shocking and transformative his approach to Jesus' message was for his students and fellow pastors.[19] Bonhoeffer, along with other ecumenical members of the "Confessing Church," incarnated his own insights in his attempt to resist the Nazi regime. The Confessing Church stood up in the face of the collaboration with Hitler made by many Lutheran pastors, and the Catholic Church through the infamous "Concordat."[20] *The Cost of Discipleship* remains an essential starting point for hearing the Sermon on the Mount from within empire.

More recent authors have built on Bonhoeffer's work and seen deeply into the anti-imperial stance of Jesus' teaching. Glen Stassen and David P. Gushee have shown how what have often been misread as paired antithesis ("You have heard it said . . . but I say to you") are actually a series of fourteen triads. Jesus first states the torah word of "Moses," then moves behind the legal prohibition to reveal the underlying cause of the prohibited behavior. Only then does Jesus state his "transforming initiative" to his disciples.[21] These triads fill in the Beatitudes with which the Sermon begins.

One example (5:21–26) illustrates the triadic pattern. The premise is that Jesus' disciples' "righteousness" or justice (*dikaiosunē*)" must exceed that of the "scribes and Pharisees" in order to "enter the kingdom of heaven" (5:20).[22] Jesus first recalls the torah prohibition, "you shall not murder" (5:21; Exod. 20:13; Deut. 5:17). The common misreading then sees Jesus prohibiting anger, which is both unhealthy and impossible advice. From this wrong starting point, one easily dismisses the entire sequence of teachings as misguided or impossible. However, what Jesus actually does is show the *cause of murder:* anger against a brother or sister that leads to insult (dehumanization) and begins the cycle of violence (5:22–23). *Rather,* Jesus says, "leave your gift there before the altar and go; first be reconciled to your

19. See *www.bonhoeffer.com/thefilm.htm* for background, video clips, and group study materials related to the film.

20. See generally Lewy.

21. Stassen and Gushee, 125–45; chart of the overall pattern is on p. 142. The chapter also has an excellent review of earlier approaches to the Sermon on the Mount. See also Stassen (2006).

22. Only Matthew links "scribes and Pharisees," presenting their collaboration as the reason for the people's inability to recognize what kind of obedience God really wants; see Matt. 23:13–39 for the harsh set of "woes" against them that leads to Jesus' lament over Jerusalem, whose house has been left "desolate" (23:38).

Table 27: Structure of the Sermon on the Mount

5:1–2:　Introduction: Jesus goes up the mountain

5:3–12:　The Beatitudes: honoring the poor and marginalized with one's life
5:13–16:　Salt and light: the power of small things to be transformative
5:17–20:　Jesus *fulfills* the law and the prophets, rather than abolishing it
　　　　　　(*framing with 7:12*)

5:21–48:　Jesus' Word regarding "justice"

　　　5:21–32: Part one: renouncing (male) power over others
　　　　　　5:21–26: Renouncing violence and anger that destroys others
　　　　　　5:27–32: Renouncing power over women
　　　5:33–48: Part two: renouncing public retribution and honor
　　　　　　5:33–37: Rejecting oaths
　　　　　　5:38–42: Rejecting retribution while maintaining personal dignity
　　　　　　5:43–47: Loving enemies
　　　5:48: Conclusion: be perfect / complete / mature (*teleioi*) as your heavenly
　　　　　　Father is

6:1–18:　Renouncing "justice" before people in favor of justice before God

　　　6:1:　　　Introduction
　　　6:2–4:　　Giving alms
　　　6:5–15:　Prayer
　　　6:16–18:　Fasting

6:19–34:　Renouncing worldly treasures

　　　6:19–21: Storing up treasure in heaven
　　　6:22–24: Being "single-eyed"
　　　6:25–34: Renouncing anxiety over life's necessities and trusting God instead
7:1–5:　Renouncing judgment over others
7:6:　Protecting Jesus' Word from being "trampled"
7:7–11:　Asking, searching, knocking: the means for living Jesus' Word
7:12:　The "Golden Rule" (*framing with 5:17*)

7:13–27:　Conclusion: discerning the path to life, truth, and wisdom

　　　7:13–14: Entering by the narrow gate
　　　7:15–23: Warning against false prophets
　　　7:24–27: The person who is wise is the one who hears and acts on Jesus'
　　　　　　words

7:28–8:1:　Jesus comes down the mountain

brother or sister, and then come and offer your gift" (5:24). The way of empire has always been to justify the escalation of the cycle of violence, as seen so tragically in the aftermath of 9/11. The Romans made an art of the kind of "scorched earth" policy that "taught a lesson" to people who would dare to resist imperial authority. Jesus reverses this completely. The reordering of priorities that places the reestablishment of just relationships among people before formal acts of worship echoes what the prophets so often said (e.g., Isa. 58; Amos 5; Mic. 6). Nothing is more urgent to God than the healing of broken relationships.[23]

The remainder of the Sermon continues in this way, systematically dismantling patterns of domination over others that have come to seem "divinely ordained," including male power over women. For those on the receiving end of domination, Jesus counsels what Walter Wink calls a "third way" between fight or flight. Wink has shown how the context of Matt. 5:38–42 is specific Roman practices over subjugated peoples.[24] In each instance, Jesus calls disciples neither to submit to oppression nor to fight back violently. Rather, he creatively offers ways to maintain one's dignity and even to shame nonviolently the would-be oppressor. For instance, the Roman soldier's "legal right" to impress a civilian to carry his heavy pack one mile was meant to make the oppression appear moderate in comparison with complete enslavement. The willingness to "go also the second mile" seizes the initiative from empire's agent and forces him to beg for his pack back rather than break the imperial law.

Matthew 5 ends with a word commonly mistranslated in a way that threatens to undermine this whole understanding of the Sermon: "Be perfect [*teleioi*], therefore, as your heavenly Father is perfect" (5:48). It is obviously impossible to "be perfect," and certainly not to be perfect as God is. But Jesus is not calling for perfectionism. Rather, *telios* ordinarily means "complete" or "mature," as we hear, for example, in Paul's word to the Corinthians: "Yet among the *mature* we do speak wisdom, though it is not a wisdom of this age or of the rulers of this age, who are doomed to perish" (1 Cor. 2:6).[25] The Sermon ends with two analogies that sum up the result of living the Sermon or resisting its message: that of good/bad fruit trees and that of a house built on sand or rock. The fruit tree comparison fits 5:48 exactly: the tree that bears fruit is not "perfect," but *mature*: it has grown into what God intended it to be, and now is providing food as gift for others. In the same way, disciples are to be fruit-bearers, building their "house" on a solid foundation. It is empire's house that is built on sand, guaranteeing that it will eventually collapse.

We note one further aspect of the Sermon's anti-imperial teaching. Matthew 6:19–34 addresses the question of true "treasure." Traditional

---

23. See also the two-volume work of Myers and Enns on this theme elsewhere in Matthew and the New Testament as well as in Christian practice.

24. Wink (1992), 175–94.

25. See also, e.g., 1 Cor. 13:10; 14:20; Eph. 4:13; Phil. 3:15.

misunderstandings of Jesus' message suggest that the contrast is between "worldly" wealth and postmortem reward "in heaven." Of course, we've seen all along that "heaven" does not refer to afterlife but to the realm of God's power and authority. The contrast is thus between the "rewards" of Caesar's false empire and those of God's authentic empire. The focus is on singleness of purpose[26] and direction: "no one can serve two masters/lords [kuriois]" (6:24).

The emperor, of course, was specifically referred to by the title "lord," a theme Paul countered directly at Philippians 2, as we'll see. The "lord" was the one at the top of the patronage system, the structure of loyalty/reward upon which the Roman Empire was built.[27] At the top, of course, were the emperor and his court. Below were layers of sharply divided and circumscribed classes, such as senators and equestrians. The Roman elite developed patron/client relationships with local elites in the provinces, just as each local elite did with people "below" them in their own cities. Through this process, networks of loyalty were created. The Latin word for the bond holding these relationships together is fide, rendered in Greek as pistis. We translate this into English as "trust" or "faith." To "trust" in the empire was to remain loyal in exchange for the provision of what one needed, especially national security under the rubric "salvation" (sōteria).

Matthew 6 establishes a community of discipleship grounded in a counter-loyalty to the true Lord: Israel's God, Creator of heaven and earth. It begins with the "Lord's prayer," itself a clear and sharp anti-imperial pledge of allegiance.[28] It calls on God as "father," a title also claimed by Caesar. It is God's name that is to be "hallowed," i.e., set apart as sacred. It is God's kingdom that one prays to come, "on earth as it is in heaven." It sets up the theme of treasure by calling on disciples to ask God for "daily bread." This recalls the manna episode (Exod. 16) and reminds hearers that one of the central "benefits" of empire has always been the provision of "bread." In the Roman world, this meant the annona, the dole provided first only of grain to Roman citizens, then later expanded to include olive oil and offered to all.[29] The prayer to rely exclusively and daily on God for food rejects the blandishments of imperial provision that would instill divided loyalty.[30] It ends with the call for mutual forgiveness, central to the understanding of "church" in Matthew 18.

---

26. The word translated by NRSV, if your eye is "healthy" (haplous), literally means "single," and is contrasted with poneros, "evil" (6:22). In other words, the single-eyed person keeps focused on the kingdom (6:33) while the evil-eyed person gazes around covetously and judgmentally at others.

27. On patronage, see generally Garnsey and Saller (1987) and their summary essay (1997).

28. See Ekblad (2008).

29. Perkins, 197–98.

30. Cf. Fyodor Dostoevsky's powerful parable of the willingness of people to exchange freedom in Christ for imperial bread in "The Grand Inquisitor" passage within The Brothers Karamazov.

It is the Creator God to whom Jesus directs disciples' attention in making his contrast between imperial and divine treasure. Birds do not practice surplus agriculture but are fed directly by God (6:26). Flowers do not manufacture clothing but "even Solomon in all his glory was not clothed like one of these" (6:28–29). Perhaps Jesus' satirical slap at empire is more obvious after our earlier engagement with the reign of Solomon. That is, Jesus says the most "glorious" of Israel's own kings was not as impressively clothed as a mere flower.

The point is driven home with Jesus explicitly contrasting his way and the way of "the nations, who strive for all these things" (6:32). Caesar's empire was a constant competition for the limited goods of status and honor. It led to being endlessly anxious (merimnaō, 6:25, 27, 28, 31, 34 [twice]) over having "enough." The way of God's empire, though, is a striving for *justice,* in which all one's needs are "given" (6:33).

Finally, Matthew's Gospel presents a series of *parables* designed to focus disciples' attention on the final outcome of the battle between God's empire and Caesar's empire. Repeatedly, apocalyptic language is drawn from the Enoch tradition. Consider, for example, the parable of the weeds and wheat that Matthew uniquely adds after retelling the Markan parable of the seeds and soils (Matt. 13:24–30, 36–43). Jesus interprets it to the disciples after leaving the crowd and going "into the house" (13:36). It is straightforward allegory, in which agricultural images correspond to an eschatological scenario in which the "children of the kingdom" are "planted" amid the "children of the evil one." At the "end of the age,"

> The Son of Man will send his angels, and they will collect out of his kingdom all causes of sin and all evildoers, and they will throw them into the furnace of fire, where there will be weeping and gnashing of teeth. Then the righteous will shine like the sun in the kingdom of their Father. Let anyone with ears listen! (13:41–43)

The imagery is almost precisely that of Enoch's *Parables* (1 En. 54:1–6; 58:3).[31] But, of course, for readers of Matthew's Gospel, the "Son of Man" is no longer an enigmatic figure, but has been embodied in Jesus.

Similarly, the final parable in Matthew is one frequently called on by those engaged in acts of solidarity with the poor, such as Catholic Workers and folks involved in "two thirds world" liberation movements: the story of the sheep and goats (25:31–46). Not always noticed is that the choice of sheep to symbolize those who care for Jesus echoes Enoch's *Animal Apocalypse* within *Dream Visions,* where the "sheep" escaped from the oppressive reign of the seventy shepherds to live within the house of the "Lord of the sheep." At the end of Matthew's parable, the sheep "inherit the kingdom" of Jesus'

---

31. Cf. Dan. 3:6 LXX; Van Henten notes the use of "furnace" (*kaminos*) in connection with the root for "to throw" (*ballō*) is only at Dan. 3:6 in the LXX, suggesting that Matthew is using the image here as a contrast with Daniel's "furnace."

Father, while the goats are sent into the "eternal fire prepared for the devil and his angels." The image of evil angels being punished in eternal fire is found also in the New Testament letter of Jude, where it is explicitly linked to the prophecy of "Enoch" (Jude 6–15; *1 En.* 67). The reason for the eternal punishment is behavior that is the inverse of that which causes such anxiety in Matthew 6. There, *striving for food and clothing* was rebuked as the way of "the nations." Here, it is *failure to provide food and clothing* to those in desperate need that is condemned. The contrast between the "two religions" could hardly be more sharp.

Neither *1 Enoch* nor Matthew's Gospel makes membership in God's kingdom a matter of ethnicity or place. Rather, inclusion is a result of practicing the justice toward others that becomes the treasure that God's people inherit. But Matthew, unlike *1 Enoch*, understands this to be taking place within the community of discipleship, which only Matthew among the evangelists refers to as *ekklēsia*, "church" (Matt. 16:18; 18:15–21). We will await our discussion of Paul to consider the cultural context of this term and how it points to communities in contrast with Roman imperial associations. It is this "church" that has the internal mission of practicing forgiveness and the external one of "mak[ing] disciples of all nations ... teaching them to obey everything that I have commanded" (28:19–20). As in the beginning, the Creator God continues to yearn for all people to recognize their solidarity as a single human family. It is Jesus' teaching, accompanied by his risen presence "with you always, to the end of the age" (28:20), that defeats the lies and violence of empire and enables it to be "genesis again."

Chapter Twenty-Four

Proclaiming Jubilee

LUKE'S GOSPEL AND
ACTS OF THE APOSTLES

The Third Gospel, and its companion, Acts of the Apostles, refer more specifically to Roman people and the empire than any other New Testament text.[1] The paired work has often been read as presenting a compromise between Christianity and the Roman Empire, and perhaps even an apologetic accommodation to Roman society.[2] A recent author who challenges the entire anti-imperial reading of the New Testament bases his claim largely on such an understanding of Luke's Gospel.[3]

The common foundation for this view is the (accurate) perception that Luke portrays some individual Romans as open to Jesus or as courteous to Christians. However, as we saw with Matthew's Gospel, the question of the text's anti-imperial stance cannot be answered simply by examining the author's portrait of explicitly Roman elements.

From the first chapter of the gospel to the end of Acts, Luke presents the Way of Jesus as the antithesis of the way of Rome. As C. Kavin Rowe puts it,

> No longer can Acts be seen as a simple apologia that articulates Christianity's harmlessness vis-à-vis Rome.... Rather, in its attempt to form communities that witness to God's apocalypse, Luke's second volume is a highly charged and theologically sophisticated political document that aims at nothing less than the construction of an alternative way of life — a comprehensive pattern of being — one that runs counter to the life-patterns of the Greco-Roman world.[4]

Like Mark and Matthew, Luke gives Jesus titles that otherwise belong to the emperor. But more than the previous evangelists, Luke systematically announces in and through Jesus the fulfillment of the biblical promise of

---

1. While most commentators agree that Revelation is the most vehemently anti-imperial text in the New Testament, it never mentions Rome explicitly.

2. See Walton for a review of recent perspectives; for a counter-perspective, see Cassidy, 34–35.

3. Kim.

4. Rowe (2009), 4.

jubilee: the great "fresh start" that releases debts of all kinds. He repeatedly mocks the pursuit of wealth and patronage relationships, lampooning or harshly criticizing those who have become rich at the expense of others. He presents the first, concrete response to the Pentecost outpouring of the Holy Spirit as the joyous, communal sharing of goods. His message, in fact, is perceived rightly as "a way of salvation" that is "not lawful for us as Romans to adopt or observe" (Acts 16:17, 21). His characters are frequently in jail for proclaiming this Way, threatened with, and sometimes receiving, harsh punishment. The survey of Luke's narrative below will show that, contrary to the view that Luke is somehow more "moderate," his gospel is as explicitly anti-imperial as any other. His Good News fulfills the same creation/liberation texts we have been exploring. Luke expects the Gospel to draw people from all social classes to form a new community in which hierarchies are leveled.

Luke's audience was most likely comprised of Roman citizens and others who had been formed in *paideia,* the educational and cultural system that produced elite members of urban society. *Paideia* "linked [the elite] with one another in a universal brotherhood," which combined with the patronage system to produce the basic social structure of Roman city life.[5] The gospel's vocabulary and sentence structure are at a level we might categorize as "collegiate." Luke's parables and other imagery fit the world of wealthy and powerful leaders of society: generals planning war; landowners with excess surplus; people planning huge banquets; business people with numerous debtors. Richard Pervo has shown how these elements, combined with a rather dark humor, were meant to provide "profit with delight" for young adults being formed to take their places among the elite, in accordance with manuals of instruction.[6] Luke's goal was to convince them that the Way of Jesus would actually provide what the empire promised but could not deliver: peace, justice, and abundance for all.

Luke, like Matthew, begins with a narrative of Jesus' birth. As different as Luke's infancy story is from Matthew's,[7] they share a basic theme: the birth of Israel's messiah is a threat to the imperial status quo. His opening chapters overflow with characters from the margins of Roman society who are portrayed as righteous before God. Thus, the contrast is immediately established between the empire's and God's ways of evaluating the quality of one's life.

One of Luke's favorite techniques is offering paired, male/female stories that present a destabilizing contrast. The first one of these pairs contrasts the priest, Zechariah, and the young woman, Mary. Both experience an encounter with the angel Gabriel, making an immediate connection with the Daniel and *1 Enoch* traditions. Zechariah, though, is rendered mute for

---

5. Miles (1999), 48.
6. Pervo.
7. For instance, Matthew's focus is on Joseph, Luke's is on Mary; Matthew has magi and Luke has shepherds; for an in-depth comparison, see Brown (1999); also Horsley (1993a).

his lack of faith, while Mary has "found favor with God" (1:1–20, 26–38). Zechariah is not a "villain," like many of the other male leaders in the gospel. His silencing provides him an opportunity to repent, which he does, and he becomes "filled with the Holy Spirit." Is Luke suggesting more broadly that male religious leaders need to be at least temporarily silenced so that women can speak and be heard?[8]

Between Zechariah's silencing and the freeing of his tongue, Luke narrates a familiar story, which ought to shock us with its bold radicality. The young Mary hastily takes a trip away from Nazareth in Galilee, apparently *by herself,* to visit a kinswoman in the Judean hill country. Elizabeth was also surprisingly pregnant, as Gabriel had told Mary. Everything about this "visitation" is culturally "wrong." First, that Luke places the narrative focus on an encounter between two women is itself destabilizing. How rarely biblical narrative has portrayed women in conversation![9] Second, Mary's solo adventure is unimaginable: for a young woman, betrothed in marriage, to take off alone would bring enormous dishonor on the family. Third, the exchange between the women is a "womb to womb" encounter, also unprecedented. Finally, Mary's Magnificat poetically proclaims God's salvation to consist of a radical reordering of society, where the powerful are brought down and the rich are sent away empty, while the lowly are lifted up and the hungry are filled. The words of her song weave together numerous biblical verses, but most especially, Hannah's song at the birth of Samuel (1 Sam. 2:1–10). Samuel, we recall, became the bridge figure between the judges and kings. His role included warning the people of the perils of kingship. Mary's song brings together numerous images from the psalms that speak of God's care and compassion for the lowly.[10] It serves as an overture to the ministry of Jesus and the outcome of God's mighty deeds in and through God's and Mary's son.[11]

The Magnificat is the first of numerous occasions where Luke proclaims God's ending of the old, unjust social order and the beginning of the new age of true *shalom* on earth.[12] Caesar Augustus exerts his authority by ordering a census that requires all to return to their hometowns. But Jesus' birth in a manger evokes an angelic "host" to proclaim God's glory and peace in place of the Pax Romana (2:13–14).[13] Soon thereafter, the infant Jesus is celebrated by a "just and devout" Israelite named Simeon. Three times in three verses (2:25–27), Luke tells us that Simeon is responding to the Holy

---

8. Cf. Dietrich (2004).

9. Leah and Rachel speak, but not happily (Gen. 30:14–15); Ruth and Naomi converse regularly. Are there any other female conversations in the Hebrew Scriptures?

10. Images echo, in order of usage, Ps. 69:30; 35:9; 136:23; 111:9; 103:17; 89:10; 68:1; 107:9; 98:3.

11. The Magnificat's other biblical echoes are from Deut. 10:21, Isa. 41:9 and Gen. 12:2–3.

12. Of the nineteen uses of the Greek *eirēnē* ("peace") in the synoptic gospels, fourteen are in Luke. See generally Swartley.

13. Brown, 415.

Spirit in coming to the child. His prayer of praise proclaims that in Jesus, "your salvation . . . [is] an apocalyptic light to the nations [au. trans., *phōs eis apocalupsin ethnōn*] and for glory to your people Israel" (2:30–32). Jesus' divine purpose is made clear right from the start of the gospel.

Once John and Jesus are grown, Luke provides another sharp contrast to set up Jesus' adult ministry. He names each of the imperial office holders, placing Herod and his brother Philip within the coterie of Roman agents, along with the Jerusalem high priests (3:1–2). But then Luke draws our attention away from the official power centers to the marginal space of the Jordan desert, where the Word of God comes to John, son of Zechariah. It is as if the CNN cameras switched suddenly from the White House to cover a rural street preacher. Luke's audience was well trained — as we are — to look to those "at the top" for "the news" we need to know. John's wilderness word calls Luke's hearers to be prepared to listen to new voices in surprising places to find the will of God.

John the Baptist issues a stern warning to those who come to him to avoid the "wrath to come" by "bear[ing] fruits worthy of repentance" (*metanoia*).[14] They cannot presume that having Abraham as a father is enough; that is, they cannot presume on the entitlements of birth, whether as ethnic "Jews" or, implicitly, as well-born Roman citizens. In particular, the fruit that John calls for is *economic justice:* sharing of clothes and food with "anyone who has none," not profiting off one's imperial authority as a tax collector or soldier (3:10–14).

Some have suggested that because John does not tell tax collectors or soldiers simply to give up their professions, he is accepting the basic Roman structure rather than undermining it. However, for tax collectors to "collect no more than the amount prescribed" would be to turn an already socially ostracized role into a nonprofit one. Similarly, for a soldier to forego the many opportunities to shake down conquered peoples would be to accept the payment provided by the imperial government and discourage long-term service.[15] Luke's narrative is not proposing a compromise, but rather, contains a "hidden transcript" that those "in the know" would recognize.[16] That is, if Luke were to show John demanding that people completely quit their imperial posts, his gospel would probably have been banned from distribution among his elite audience.[17] Instead of rendering his writing useless and putting his own life at risk, Luke develops an effective strategy for conveying his radical message by covering it with a thin veneer that shields

---

14. Two-thirds of the gospels' uses of the noun or verb for "repentance / repent" are found in Luke / Acts: thirteen in Luke, eleven in Acts, eight in Matthew, four in Mark, none in John.

15. See Alston for a detailed discussion of Roman army pay scales. Alston concludes: "In the imperial period, soldiers enjoyed a small surplus above subsistence" (122). It was the empire's inability to pay soldiers because of an insufficient tax base and high inflation that contributed substantially to its collapse in the coming centuries.

16. The term "hidden transcript" is from Scott (1992); see Horsley (2003) for application of the concept to New Testament texts.

17. See Miles (1999), 44, for Rome's severe retribution against dissenting literature.

some of its implications from prying eyes.[18] We see this strategy employed throughout Luke-Acts.

Sometimes, though, Luke's radicality breaks out into the open. He inserts just after Jesus' baptismal apocalyptic experience his own version of Jesus' genealogy. Matthew's takes Jesus back to Abraham, but Luke takes him back to Adam: Jesus is "son of humanity," not merely a child of Israel. At the same time, his genealogy comes to a blatantly anti-imperial conclusion: "son of God." Luke's audience would have immediately associated this title with the emperor, whether Claudius (who reigned at the time of the narrative) or Domitian (who reigned at the probable time of Luke's writing).[19]

Jesus, "full of the Holy Spirit," is then led by that Spirit into the wilderness, where he is confronted by the devil precisely over the meaning of this title (4:1–13).[20] The three temptations unmask the issues at the heart of empire: control of the food supply, worship of the source of the "kingdoms of the world," and "peace and security" (cf. 1 Thess. 5:3). The devil frames the first and third of his challenges with the conditional, "if you are the son of God...." In other words, "Caesar provides food and security in God's name; can you?" Jesus responds to both temptations by refuting the devil's premise. There is more involved in caring for people's true needs than simply guaranteeing bread and national security. The middle challenge is grounded in a startling claim. The devil shows him "all" the world's kingdoms and says that their glory and authority "has been given over to me." There is certainly not much veneer over this suggestion that the Roman Empire's power is in the devil's hands, a point also made by John of Patmos (Rev. 13). Jesus' response (from Deut. 6:13) gets at the core of the matter: the contrast between monotheism and polytheism. The devil does *not* ask for *exclusive* allegiance, but YHWH *does.*

Jesus leaves the devil and returns to Galilee, "filled with the power of the Spirit" (4:14). In his hometown of Nazareth, he turns to the text from Third Isaiah (61:1–2) and proclaims what is in effect his "mission statement":

> "The Spirit of the Lord is upon me, because he has anointed me to bring good news to the poor. He has sent me to proclaim release to the captives and recovery of sight to the blind, to let the oppressed go free, to proclaim the year of the Lord's favor...." Today this Scripture has been fulfilled in your hearing. (4:18–19, 21)

Jesus announces that the time has come for the "year of the Lord's favor," i.e., the jubilee year in which all things are begun anew, providing relief from

---

18. Recall the similar strategy suggested in chapter 9 for the author of the David/Solomon story.

19. Mowery, 102, 104.

20. Matthew also has a set of temptations by the devil, so this passage is not strictly "Lucan," but the details and place within Luke's narrative context make it an important initial component of Luke's anti-imperial stance, against those who argue that Luke is offering a watered down, compromised gospel.

the burden of what we might call "the four Ds": disease, debt, demons, and death. That this is the heart of Jesus' messianic ministry is reinforced when John the Baptist sends word from prison[21] to ask, "Are you the one who is to come, or are we to wait for another?" (7:20). Jesus' answer summarizes his ministry to date: "Go and tell John what you have seen and heard: the blind receive their sight, the lame walk, the lepers are cleansed, the deaf hear, the dead are raised, the poor have good news brought to them" (7:22). He then adds: "And blessed is anyone who takes no offense [*skandalisthe*] at me." John, like so many, is shown to have been "scandalized" by the kind of messiah Jesus has shown himself to be. He will not confront Rome on its own terms. Rather, he continues to liberate people from the various forms of imperial oppression, calling them into the new community of those who live by a different "gospel" than Caesar's.

We hear this message boldly proclaimed by Peter in Acts 3. Peter's transformation from frightened denier to courageous proclaimer reveals Luke's understanding of how the "power of the Holy Spirit" overcomes empire. Trust in the resurrection power available in and through the Holy Spirit banishes the fear through which empire maintains its "peace." Peter's speech directly accuses the people of Jerusalem of rejecting "the Holy and Righteous One" and killing "the Author of life, whom God raised from the dead" (3:14–15). But in spite of this horrible crime, he continues, the people are called to "Repent therefore, and turn to God so that your sins may be wiped out, so that times of refreshing may come from the presence of the Lord" (3:19–20). The double image of "wiping out" sins (i.e., blotting them out of the record)[22] and "times of refreshing"[23] conveys the invitation to begin again with a "clean slate" and a "fresh start."

The fulfillment of jubilee flows through Luke-Acts from beginning to end. One way Luke shows how this is concretely to take place is through paired stories that overcome boundaries between people established by either the imperial social order or Jerusalem's attitude toward "foreigners." For example, near the end of Jesus' long journey to Jerusalem (Luke 9–19), Luke pairs the story of the healing of a blind beggar with the "coming down" of the rich tax collector, Zacchaeus. The beggar is found sitting "beside the way" outside Jericho. His sight regained because of the saving power of his own faith, he follows Jesus into the city.

Immediately, the narrator shifts the focus to Zacchaeus. He is precisely the kind of person whom John the Baptist commanded to "collect no more" than necessary. Zacchaeus's "unclean" wealth has left him marginalized in

---

21. Although Luke 7:18 does not explicitly say that John was in prison as we hear at Matt. 11:2, Luke has told readers that John was in prison (3:20), and that Herod had beheaded him (9:9), so there is no reason to imagine that John was released between these two events.

22. *exaleiphō*; cf. Col. 2:14; Rev. 3:5.

23. *anapsuxeōs*, only here in the New Testament, means a "state of cheer and encouragement after a period of having been troubled or upset" or "relief from distressful, burdensome circumstances" (Louw-Nida 25.148, 22.35).

Judea, unless he abandons his Israelite heritage and seeks inclusion within the Roman community. But he has not chosen this path. Instead, because of his "shortness of stature" — a double entendre which emphasizes his lack of status as much as lack of physical height — he climbs a "sycamore tree" (*sukomorean*). Jeff Dietrich has shown how this tree is a "fake fig": from a distance, it looks like a tree that bears "good fruit," but upon close examination, its fruit is revealed to be small and bitter.[24] It is thus a symbol for Zacchaeus himself. We hear this echoed in his reply to Jesus' call to "hurry and come down" from the tree: "Look, half of my possessions, Lord, I will give to the poor; and if I have defrauded [*esukophantēsa*] anyone of anything, I will pay back four times as much." The term for "defraud" literally means, "fig informer," referring to people who curried favor with those above by tattling on others who illegally exported figs. Its meaning was quickly extended to any kind of extortion or false accusation.[25] Zacchaeus confesses his "false fig" stature and seeks to restore justice. Jesus in turn responds by announcing, "Today salvation has come to this house, because he too is a son of Abraham" (19:9). That is, salvation doesn't *come from* "above," but involves instead those *who are* "above" coming down and joining those who were "beside the way." Healed blind man and saved tax collector are now together in the new jubilee community of discipleship.

Another example of paired jubilee stories is Peter's encounter with the Roman centurion Cornelius (Acts 10). Cornelius is an officer and member of the "Italian cohort," an elite archery contingent.[26] His table-fellowship with Peter in Caesarea would be as shocking to his own peers as Luke tells us it is to Peter's peers in Jerusalem (Acts 11). Cornelius embodies Luke's hope for the conversion of members of the Roman elite in his audience. He has been a patron to the "whole Judean nation" but now is "baptized in the name of Jesus Christ" (10:22, 48). Peter suddenly "gets it," concluding with a strongly anti-imperial word:

> I truly understand that God shows no partiality, but in every nation anyone who fears him and is working for justice [au. trans., *ergazomenos dikaiosunen*] is acceptable to him. You know the message he sent to the people of Israel, announcing [*euangelizomenos*] peace by Jesus Christ — he is Lord of all. (10:34–36)

The claim that Jesus is "Lord of all" explicitly rejects the imperial claim of Caesar's lordship.[27] Peter's brief word interprets his encounter with Cornelius in familiar Isaian tones, for example:

---

24. Dietrich (2003).
25. *TDNT*, 1101.
26. Kroedel, 189.
27. Rowe (2005), 295, notes that Luke is the only one of the canonical gospel authors "to use the absolute *ho kurios* ['the Lord'] consistently and expansively for Jesus in his earthly career." See also Rowe (2009), 105–6.

> How beautiful upon the mountains are the feet of the messenger who announces peace, who brings good news [LXX, *euangelizomenos*], who announces salvation, who says to Zion, "Your God reigns." (Isa. 52:7)

> Peace, peace, to the far and the near, says YHWH; and I will heal them. (Isa. 57:19)

Although there is not a specific Enochic reference echoed in Peter's word, central to the entire Enochic book, especially the *Epistle of Enoch*, is the practice of justice as the criterion for membership in God's people. That justice is expressed in the breaking down of social barriers built up by empire and the restoration of a "level" playing field for all people.

Luke continues to present this theme in his sermon "on a level place" (6:17–49), the counterpart to Matthew's Sermon on the Mount. Unique to Luke's version is the series of "woes" that follow his beatitudes.[28] Here we find a more explicit echo from the *Epistle of Enoch*:

> But woe to you who are rich, for you have received your consolation. (Luke 6:24)

> Woe to you, rich, for in your riches you have trusted, from your riches you will depart, because you have not remembered the Most High in the days of your riches. (*1 En.* 94:8)

This theme appears again in the New Testament Letter of James (5:1–6). As John S. Kloppenborg notes, James's "catalogue of vices of the rich is remarkable for its resemblance to that of the *Ep[istle of]Enoch*."[29]

Luke's harsh polemic against the rich — the "winners" in the Roman economy — continues in a series of parables that reveal the arrogance and foolishness of those whose status is grounded in wealth. The first is about a landowner whose "problem" is an abundant agricultural surplus (12:16–20). Its only character is one whom the Romans would have honored as not only successful but prudent. But as Joseph Fitzmyer notes, the parable is Luke 9:25 — "What does it profit them if they gain the whole world, but lose or forfeit themselves? — "cast in narrative form."[30] Key to the lampooning portrait is the use of the first-person voice eleven times in three verses. Kenneth Bailey writes: "He trusts no one and has no friends or cronies with whom he can exchange ideas. We begin to get Jesus' picture of the kind of prison that wealth can build. He has the money to buy a vacuum and live in it."[31] In other words, he is like Zacchaeus "before." Unlike the tax collector, however, the man dies a "fool" (*aphron*). In the Septuagint, *aphron*

---

28. See also Luke 11:42–52, a series of woes addressed to Pharisees and lawyers, previously said as a combined group to have "rejected God's plan for themselves" by refusing to be baptized by John (7:30).

29. Kloppenborg (2003), 583.

30. Fitzmyer (1985), 971.

31. Bailey (Part 2), 65.

signifies "a person who rebels against God or whose practices deny God."[32] His self-enclosed wealth put him among those who, since Cain, turned their backs on God to live in a world of their own creation. In the end, when God's sovereignty is finally revealed, it is too late.

Another parable castigating the rich presents the man with poor Lazarus at his gate. It paints an all-too-realistic picture of the social chasm between those who dress in "purple and fine linen and who feasted sumptuously every day" and the poor, "covered with sores," licked by stray dogs, longing for the rich man's scraps. At death, though, the divide is reversed, with Lazarus "in the bosom of Abraham" and the rich man "tormented" and "in agony in these flames." George Nickelsburg notes that Luke's imagery of the chasm dividing sinners from the blessed is adapted from Enoch's *Book of the Watchers:*[33]

> Then I asked about all the hollow places, why they were separated one from the other. And he answered me and said, "These three were made that the spirits of the dead might be separated. And this has been separated for the spirits of the righteous, where the bright fountain of water is. And this has been created for <the spirits of the> sinners, when they die and are buried in the earth, and judgment has not been executed on them in their life. *Here their spirits are separated for this great torment,* until the great day of judgment, of scourges and tortures of the cursed forever, that there might be a recompense for their spirits." (*1 En.* 22:8–10, emphasis added)

Jesus' concluding comment that "If they do not listen to Moses and the prophets, neither will they be convinced even if someone rises from the dead" anticipates the hope of salvation experienced in the Emmaus story. Refusal to hear the scriptural story that Jesus proclaims and embodies leads the unrepentant rich into the fiery pit out of which there is no escape.

Yet another way Luke reveals the Gospel's overturning of the Roman social order is through his stories of inclusive table fellowship. Within the gospel, there are seven such scenes during Jesus' earthly lifetime, with the Emmaus meal an eighth that inaugurates the new age.[34] Within the Roman world, table fellowship exhibited and reinforced the carefully circumscribed social hierarchy. A parallel exclusivity was practiced by the Pharisees, keeping "sinners" away from the "righteous." Luke explodes both these perspectives, showing Jesus eating with tax collectors and other "sinners," and explicitly challenging the privileges of patronage.

For example, consider the Last Supper. For the second time in the gospel, the disciples, confronted with Jesus' prediction that the Son of Man will be betrayed, proceed to argue among themselves about "which one of them

---

32. E.g., Prov. 14:1; Jer. 4:22; Green, 491.
33. Nickelsburg (2003d), 566.
34. The table fellowship scenes are 5:29–39; 7:36–50; 9:12–17; 11:37–52; 14:1–24; 19:5–27; 22:14–38; 24:9–33.

was the greatest" (9:44–46; 22:22–24). Jesus' response strikes directly at the cultural assumption behind their dispute:

> But he said to them, "The kings of the nations lord it over [*kurieuousin*] them; and those in authority over them are called benefactors [*euergetai*]. But not so with you; rather the greatest among you must become like the youngest, and the leader like one who serves. For who is greater, the one who is at the table or the one who serves? Is it not the one at the table? But I am among you as one who serves. (22:25–26)

Luke adapts Mark's word for royal "lording"[35] and replaces Mark's "tyrants" (10:42: *katexousiazousin*) with the word for "patrons." Jesus' community is *not* to be organized around elite patronage. Jesus' Word rejects each element of the *paideia* in which his audience has been formed.

An earlier meal scene illustrates the social cost for the Roman elite in Luke's audience of following Jesus' Word. Jesus tells a story of a "great banquet" to which wealthy people are invited (14:16–24). Richard Rohrbaugh and Jerome Neyrey explain Luke's context:

> For many rich Christians their social position in elite circles was no doubt shaky enough that preparing a banquet for their peers might seem like a good way to solidify it. As a way of reassuring their friends that they had not broken faith with the system, they would invite only the right people.[36]

However, the guests each and collectively[37] offer transparently absurd excuses, designed to dishonor the inviter. The angry host orders his slaves first to go "into the streets and lanes of the town and bring in the poor, the crippled, the blind, and the lame," i.e., those for whom the message of jubilee *is* good news. When this is not sufficient to fill the banquet hall, the host tells the slave to go to the "narrow places" (*phragmous;* cf. 13:24), i.e., outside the town gates, to "compel" the lowest of the low to come in. Those furthest from the social center would be most suspicious of the motives of one of the elite calling them to table fellowship. For the banquet to be filled, these people's deeply socialized resistance must be overcome.

The story is followed by two illustrations of the social effect of not "counting the cost" (14:28) of discipleship before one begins. Both examples are from the context of the urban elite: building a tower and waging war. Being known as one who invites the poor into one's home — and thus has reneged on the social "given" of supporting the hierarchical patronage system — gets one cast out from "polite" society.[38]

---

35. Mark 10:42, *katakurieuousin*, followed by Matthew (20:25); cf. 1 Pet. 5:3.
36. Rohrbaugh and Neyrey, 146.
37. "But they all alike" (*apo mias*, 14:18), literally, "from one," reveals the conspiratorial nature of their refusal.
38. Cf. Luke 7:36–50.

Luke completes his warnings about the uncompromising nature of discipleship in the parable that precedes his entry into Jerusalem. The narrator explains Jesus' purpose in advance: "because he was near Jerusalem, and because they supposed that the kingdom of God was to appear immediately" (19:11). Like Mark's "widow's mite," the story of the "pounds" has been grossly misinterpreted by defenders of today's capitalist status quo as a lesson in "good investment." Within both Luke's narrative context and the Roman imperial cultural context, however, the parable is revealed for what it is: a sober warning against expecting immediate results when one confronts empire's injustice, other than the "result" of being rejected and punished.[39]

The opening scene is a thinly veiled retelling of Herod Archelaus's embassy to Rome in 4 BCE to seek imperial confirmation of his authority.[40] Local hostility to the Roman puppet is clearly expressed: "the citizens of his country hated him and sent a delegation after him, saying, 'We do not want this man to rule over us' " (19:14). For now, we hear nothing further about this protest. Instead, the parable turns to the slaves' actions with the money entrusted to them. The first two have produced enormous profits of 1000 percent and 500 percent, possible only through gross exploitation of the poor. This, of course, gains the nobleman's favor and each is rewarded with rule over a corresponding number of cities. The final slave, though, has resisted the nobleman's oppressive ways and taken the money out of circulation, at least temporarily. Further, he denounces his owner in strong terms: "You are a harsh man; you take what you did not deposit, and reap what you did not sow" (19:21). Not surprisingly, this bold act of resistance gains an equally strong rejoinder and the turning over of the money to the most "cooperative" of the slaves. The story ends with a gruesome twist: the nobleman orders the slaughter "in my presence" of those who resisted his reign. We now can hear another historical echo: that of the Hasmonean high priest Alexander Jannaeus's slaughter of eight hundred resisters to his own reign a hundred years earlier.[41] The point isn't to decide between these, or perhaps other, parallel historical cases. Luke warns his audience that regardless of the specific context, a harsh fate awaits those who choose to throw a spoke in the imperial wheel.

We see in all these examples that Luke is hardly offering a "compromise" with empire. His narrative thoroughly denounces every component of the imperial order and offers the Gospel as a diametrically opposed counter-Way. The empire, he warns, will certainly see it this way, too, and seek to dispose of any who would proclaim or embody this alternative Way. It is in his second volume, Acts of the Apostles, that Luke continues to hammer this point home.

---

39. My comments are derived from Herzog, 157–68.
40. Green, 676; Josephus, *JW*, 2.2.
41. See above p. 359.

Acts, more than any other biblical text, directly engages the Roman Empire. It ends with Paul under imperial house arrest in Rome, after a long series of spine-tingling adventures.[42] Recently, an enlightening series of books has highlighted many aspects of this Roman context.[43] Reading each scene in this light reveals how consistently and thoroughly Luke portrays the followers of the Way standing in opposition to the Roman imperial order. That some of the officials they encounter are less than thoroughly hostile does not evidence "compromise," but rather, the *possibility of conversion*. After all, many Roman historians and other intellectuals of Luke's time who were not Christians were highly critical of the exploitative and brutal nature of the empire. For example, we hear Tacitus place in the mouth of a conquered Briton, Calgacus, this bitter critique:

> Robbers of the world, having by their universal plunder exhausted the land, they rifle the deep. If the enemy be rich, they are rapacious; if he be poor, they lust for dominion; neither the east nor the west has been able to satisfy them. Alone among men they covet with equal eagerness poverty and riches. To robbery, slaughter, plunder, they give the lying name of empire; they make a desolation and call it peace.[44]

At the same time, Luke's portrait of Roman officials reveals them to be indifferent to violence in the streets (Achaian proconsul Gallio, 18:12–17), willing to torture to gain evidence (an anonymous chiliarch, 21:24), seeking to be bribed (Judean procurator Felix, 24:22–27), and beholden to the patronage system (Judean procurator Porcius Festus, 25:1–9). These portrayals are hardly designed to lead readers to be impressed with the representatives of Roman justice.

Acts shows the followers of the Way repeatedly under arrest, beaten, and threatened with death for their proclamation and behavior, both by the Jerusalem and Roman elites.[45] They respond throughout by maintaining their dignity, fearlessly and boldly standing firm in their positions, and embodying love of enemies. We find Peter so confident on the eve of his supposed execution that an angel has to strike him (*pataxas*; cf. 7:24; 12:23) to wake him up (12:7)!

This stance is a result of the disciples being filled with the Holy Spirit, starting with the Pentecost outpouring (Acts 2). Luke is not suggesting that the Holy Spirit had not been previously active in the world. We saw Jesus and others "filled with the Holy Spirit" earlier (e.g., Luke 1:67; 3:22; 4:1) and Luke also understands the Hebrew Scriptures to have been composed under that same influence (e.g., Acts 4:25; 7:51). The powerful, continuously present Spirit of God replaces the demonic spirits that animate empire, which

---

42. See Pervo for parallels between Acts and Greco-Roman adventure stories.
43. See Gill and Gempf, Winter and Clarke, and Rapske.
44. Tacitus, *Agricola*, 30.
45. E.g., arrested: 4:3; 5:18; 12:3; 21:33; beaten or flogged: 5:40; 16:22–24; 21:32–33; killed or threatened with killing: 7:58–60; 9:23–29; 12:2; 21:31; 23:12–35.

the disciples and apostles are charged with casting out (Luke 10:17; Acts 8:7; 16:16–18).

Above all, it is the Holy Spirit that enables people to take up the invitation to practice jubilee, as Jesus had preached and practiced. The first concrete response of those who receive the Pentecost Spirit is to interweave worship with an economic and social fresh start:

> They devoted themselves to the apostles' teaching and fellowship, to the breaking of bread and the prayers. Awe came upon everyone, because many wonders and signs were being done by the apostles. All who believed were together and had all things in common; they would sell their possessions and goods and distribute the proceeds to all, as any had need. Day by day, as they spent much time together in the temple, they broke bread at home and ate their food with glad and generous hearts, praising God and having the goodwill of all the people. (2:42–47a; also 4:31–35)

It is God's ancient vision — the fulfillment of the *metanoia* announced by John the Baptist (Luke 3:7–14) — made flesh, right under empire's nose. The Qumran community practiced a similar sharing of goods, but they did so, as did later monasteries, apart from the imperial economy. Luke, on the other hand, presents the new community's actions as a witness that inspires further defectors from empire's thrall: "And day by day the Lord added to their number those who were being saved" (2:47b).

"Being saved" is the term Acts uses for rejecting the "salvation" of the Pax Romana in favor of that which flows from the Pax Christi. It was Peter's exhortation to "save yourselves from this corrupt generation" (2:40) which generated the Pentecost response. We hear Peter proclaim later the radically anti-imperial announcement, "There is salvation in no one else, for there is no other name under heaven given among mortals by which we must be saved" (4:12; cf. 11:4; 16:30–31). It is this claim that is explicitly rejected as "not lawful for us as Romans to adopt or observe" in the Roman colony of Philippi (16:21).[46]

Acts, in fact, portrays the *impossibility of compromise* with empire's "salvation." Just after the second summary of the community's joyous sharing of goods (4:32–37), Luke narrates the story of Ananias and Sapphira, a married couple who sold a piece of property and, while laying some of it at the apostles' feet, held back part of the proceeds. Peter confronts Ananias at once:

> "Ananias," Peter asked, "why has Satan filled your heart to lie to the Holy Spirit and to keep back part of the proceeds of the land? While it remained unsold, did it not remain your own? And after it was sold,

---

46. See Oakes (2001) for the nature and history of Philippi, and the discussion of Paul's letter, pp. 461–71.

were not the proceeds at your disposal? How is it that you have contrived this deed in your heart? You did not lie to us but to God!" (5:3–4)

No one forced Ananias to join the Way, but to join is to be *completely in.* As Jesus said, one cannot serve two masters (Luke 16:13). Empire is almost always (at least implicitly) polytheistic, encouraging a "diversified portfolio" presented as simple prudence, then and now. Why put all one's eggs in one basket? But for radical monotheists within the tradition of Israel, one must love God with "all your heart, and with all your soul, and with all your strength, and with all your mind" (Luke 10:27; Deut. 6:5). If Jesus and his Way are the expression of YHWH's will, then one must be fully committed to seeking *only* that will and walking *only* that Way. The confrontation with Peter leads Ananias immediately to drop dead, with his wife falling in his footsteps (5:5–10).[47]

Luke's portrayal of the first communities of the Way is not a compromise, but it is also not an idealized fantasy. He shows the fledgling group struggling to discern God's will amid numerous pastoral challenges, including the assurance of adequate "daily bread" to people of a minority language (6:1–6); the question of the relationship between the law of Moses and the Gospel (15:1–31) and how to "translate" the Gospel so it can be heard by those from other starting points, such as indigenous religions (14:8–20) and Greek philosophy (17:15–33).

A particular example that has often baffled scholars is clarified by the approach we are using here. The so-called "Council of Jerusalem" begins with the question of circumcising people of "the nations" and ends with an agreement that is sent by letter with Paul and others (Acts 15:22–33). The conclusion of the council addressed to those "out of the nations" (*tois ex ethnōn*) is this:

> It has seemed good to the Holy Spirit and to us to impose on you no further burden than these essentials: that you abstain from what has been sacrificed to idols and from blood and from what is strangled and from fornication. If you keep yourselves from these, you will do well. (Acts 15:28–29; cf. 15:20)

Reading this as a question of partial withdrawal from the requirements of torah, interpreters have largely thrown up their hands. Alan Segal's comments are typical: "The apostolic decree, as Luke transcribes it, is neither exactly the laws of the resident sojourner nor the Noachian commandments; it is a peculiar, ambiguous mélange, perhaps even a combination of both."[48] However, why would the central, divinely mandated act of circumcision

---

47. The scene is clearly meant to be a darkly comic cautionary tale, rather than a literal description of events, given the absurd cultural impossibility of burying a man before informing his wife that he is dead.

48. Segal (1999), 13.

be rejected while a few obscure torah provisions were retained for non-Israelites? If we turn the question around, however, the decree makes perfect sense. Luke is not portraying the council imposing a few, seemingly random torah rules on foreigners, but indicating the *degree to which people imbedded in imperial behavior must withdraw in order to become "brothers and sisters" in the Way*. The set of behaviors does not designate three food rules and one sexual prohibition, but the *consistent expression of "coming out" from practices that mark inclusion within imperial society*.

Paul faces the theme of things sacrificed to idols and the related issue of blood in his first letter to the Corinthians (1 Cor. 8–10). At issue there for Paul was the same question Luke implies here: the appearance of wrongdoing if people committed to the Way are perceived as participating in imperial religion. Although Paul doesn't explicitly address "strangled" animals, the point is the same.[49] "Fornication" (*porneia*), is used consistently in anti-imperial texts as an expression of unholy "intercourse" not with women, but with imperial kings and merchants, as an expression of idolatry (e.g., 1 *En.* 8:2; 10:9; Rev. 9:20–21; 17:2; 18:3). In other words, the Council is calling people not out of "Judaism," but out of *empire*.

Most of all, Acts shows the apostles and disciples struggling with opposition from the Jerusalem temple supporters and other Judean-Roman collaborators. This is what ultimately leads to Paul's arrest and transport to Rome. It is no more a "purely religious" dispute than any other controversy in Luke-Acts. For example, we hear that when Paul and Silas arrive in Thessalonica, they enter a synagogue and present their understanding of the biblical Story as leading to the suffering and resurrection of the Messiah (recalling the risen Jesus on the Emmaus Road, Luke 24). Some "join" Paul and Silas, which leads the local Judeans to drag them before the city magistrates[50] and proffer highly political charges against them: "These people who have been subverting the empire[51] have come here also. . . . They are all acting contrary to the decrees of the emperor, saying that there is another king named Jesus" (17:67). A similar incident unfolds in Corinth, where Paul's Judean opponents seek to enlist the help of the Roman proconsul to thwart Paul's mission. It is not their "Jewishness" that is presented as problematic, but their collaboration with empire to hinder the progress of the Word of God. In other words, they are descendants of the Second Temple elite who had collaborated with the Persians and Greeks before the Romans. They refuse to accept the Good News that the religion of creation has defeated the religion of empire in the resurrection of the Messiah.

---

49. Witherington (1997), 454, explains that the practice of strangling, like the use of blood, sought to transfer the life energy (breath) of the sacrificed animal to the idol and, hence, to the people. Greek *pniktos* ("strangled") is never used in the LXX as part of torah or otherwise. The parallel Hebrew *machanaq* is found only at Job 7:15.

50. *politarchas*, a high-profile, imperial appointment; Horsley (1994), 421.

51. *oikoumenēn anastatōsantes*; the translation "subverting the empire" is provided by Johnson (1992), 307.

Saul / Paul's "conversion" is paradigmatic for this transformation, as we'll explore further in chapter 26. For now, we simply note that Paul's shift, according to Acts, is not from "Jew" to "Christian" but from defender of the establishment status quo to defender of the Way of Jesus as the fulfillment of "the promise made to our ancestors" (26:5–7).[52] Like the disciples on the Emmaus Road, Paul on the Damascus Road discovers that Israel's story was not intended to follow the Jerusalem-centered script, but rather the Genesis-Exodus-prophets narrative. He converts not to a "new" religion, but to the reality that the true religion in the name of YHWH has triumphed.

Paul spells this out clearly in his final defense before the Roman procurator Festus and the client king, Herod Agrippa (Acts 26). After summarizing his Damascus Road experience, Paul quotes the Risen Jesus telling him: "I will rescue you from your people and from the nations — to whom I am sending you to open their eyes so that they may turn from darkness to light and from the power of Satan to God" (26:17–18). Note that "your people" and "the nations" are presented as a united reality, just as those before whom Paul stands embodied the highest authority of both groups. It is to both that Jesus sends Paul, to "open their eyes" (recalling Enoch's *Animal Apocalypse*) to be turned from "the power of Satan to God." It is quite plain that "Satan," a.k.a. "the devil," is the source of empire's authority and of its collaborators (e.g., Luke 10:18; 22:3). The combination of apocalyptic images leads the procurator to tell Paul, "You are out of your mind." Paul ignores this, though, in one last attempt to lead the Judean king away from satanic glory and toward the light of God. Agrippa understands what is at stake, but demurs to the procedural question of Paul's legal fate (26:28–32).

Thus, Paul has both Roman and Judean officials refuse to take a stand on the truth of Paul's Gospel. Typical representatives of the elite, they look down upon someone whose passion leads him to risk his life for his beliefs. They shake their heads and turn Paul over to the soldiers for transfer to Rome. C. Kavin Rowe observes that "Luke's portrayal of the state vis-à-vis the Christian mission is a narratively complex negotiation between the reality of the state's idolatry and blindness — its satanic power — and the necessity that the mission of light not be misunderstood as sedition."[53] Luke does not present "the Way" as an attempt to overturn the Roman Empire directly, but rather, in the words of Dorothy Day, to "build a new civilization within the shell of the old."[54]

Luke ends his two volumes with the only narrated event that takes place in Rome in the New Testament. Paul undergoes many adventures at sea to get

---

52. The label "Christians" first appears at Acts 11:26 (see also 26:28) as a label given to "the disciples" by others. Rowe (2009), 130, observes that "insofar as the word Χριστιανοι (*Christiani*) appears in non-Christian sources with reference to events in the first century, it is uniformly a derogatory term." The term is never used in Paul's letters, being found elsewhere in the New Testament only at 1 Pet. 4:16, where it carries a pejorative overtone.

53. Rowe (2009), 88.

54. Ellsberg, 85.

there, with Luke portraying the boat journey as a metaphor for discipleship itself.[55] His arrival in the imperial capital is greeted by local Judean leaders, giving Paul one last chance to invite others to share in the Way of Jesus. Surprisingly, having followed Paul this far, Luke leaves him under house arrest in an apartment in Rome, where we are told he lived for two years. There is no confrontation with the emperor. We do not hear of Paul's final fate.[56] Acts could not reach a clear ending because the work of the Holy Spirit continued. Luke leaves the story open-ended, for readers to make flesh in their own lives.

---

55. Note the recurrent theme of "all in the boat" "being saved," 27:20, 24, 31, 34, 43, 44.

56. Only the apocryphal *Acts of Paul* narrates his beheading by the Romans at Nero's command.

Chapter Twenty-Five

"Savior of the World"
THE GOSPEL OF JOHN

The Gospel of John has often been misunderstood to be somehow "spiritual" and thus removed from the struggles of such "worldly" concerns as politics. It has been the least considered among the gospels by those exploring anti-imperial perspectives.[1] However, as I have written at length,[2] the Fourth Gospel's anti-imperial stance is the equal of the synoptic gospels, if expressed in different imagery and language. It does so while standing fully within the "religion of creation" that we have been exploring throughout this book.

The key to any understanding of John's Gospel is the prologue (1:1–18). Serving as a poetic overture, the opening verses present the themes and theological claims that unfold in the gospel narrative. The central section is the often mistranslated 1:12–13:

> But to all who received him,
> who trusted in his name,
> he gave power[3] to become children of God,
> who were born,
> not of blood or of
> the will of flesh or of
> the will of a man,
> but of God.

The metaphor of birth and rebirth flows throughout the gospel. It is, unfortunately, most familiar to readers because of the association with "born again Christians," for whom "accepting Jesus as personal lord and savior"

---

1. Recent efforts include Carter (2008) and Thatcher. Carter follows the traditional view that John's Gospel was composed in or for an audience in Ephesus. However, not only is there no internal evidence within the gospel to support this, John's language was clearly meant to appeal — and soon did appeal — to followers of Jesus throughout the Roman Empire. Whatever specific resonance John's Gospel may have had to the situation in Ephesus was quickly eclipsed by its "universal" anti-imperial message.

2. Howard-Brook [1994]; see also [1997] and Howard-Brook and Ringe (2003).

3. Richey, 69–82, has made a speculative but convincing argument for translating *exousia* in John's Gospel as "power" rather than "authority," based on its relationship to the Roman political meaning of Latin, *potestas,* as well as the way *exousia* is used narratively within John's Gospel.

is a once and done event, with little relationship to the rest of one's life or to the world "out there." The Gospel message, on its own terms, resists this kind of simplistic interpretation.

For the evangelist,[4] "birth" expresses both one's original creation by God and also one's commitment to follow Jesus, the full embodiment of that God, to the cross and beyond. Jesus' death is itself portrayed as a birth, seen in the blood and water flowing from his side[5] as a result of a Roman spear's penetration (19:34). His death releases the Spirit, a.k.a. the Advocate / Comforter (*paraklētos*), who accompanies disciples as they continue Jesus' mission of being "light" in the "darkness" of "the world."

But perhaps this is getting ahead of the story. Within the prologue, birth is portrayed as a *choice*. On one side is birth "out of God." On the other side are three alternatives. Each symbolizes an aspect of empire that Jesus comes into the world to oppose and call people out from. Each confrontation is dramatized in one of the major passages within the narrative.

Throughout the gospel, all distinctions between "us" and "them" in the traditional sense of "Israelites" and "nations" are erased. Instead, in solidarity with texts such as Third Isaiah and *1 Enoch,* John's Gospel presents the "us" and "them" not in "ethnic" terms but in terms of behavioral allegiance. One is either aligned with God or with the devil, a.k.a. "the evil one" (17:15, *tou ponērou*). One might characterize the gospel's approach as *"realized apocalyptic."* That is, what texts such as *1 Enoch,* Daniel, or the New Testament's Revelation present as visions of "the other side of the veil" (i.e., "heaven"), our evangelist shows embodied in people "on earth" (e.g., 17:4).[6] Thus, Jesus and those who would be his disciples are born "from above" (3:3, 7; cf. 19:11) or "from heaven" (3:31) while his opponents are "from below" (8:23) or "from earth" (3:31). Being "from below" is directly associated with being children of "the devil" (8:44; cf. 6:70; 13:2). Those who are "born from above" walk in truth (e.g., 8:32; 14:6) and love one another (e.g., 13:34; 15:12, 17), while those "born from below" are liars and murderers (8:44, 55), constantly seeking to kill Jesus (e.g., 5:18; 7:19; 8:37; 11:8) and threatening to kill his disciples (12:10; 16:2).

John's Gospel puts this contrast in the starkest possible terms. The approach is akin to Matthew's and Luke's question of serving two masters.

---

4. The gospel is traditionally associated with John, brother of James, sons of Zebedee. However, there is no real evidence for the personal identity of the author, nor the location from which he wrote. My earlier work was greatly influenced by the late twentieth-century's towering giant of John's Gospel scholars, the late Raymond Brown, in taking as a given the connection between the text and a specific group, the "Johannine community." However, more recent work by Richard Bauckham (1997) has led me to reconsider this association. Whatever particular relationship there may have once been between an individual author and a specific community was quickly subsumed into the gospel's availability and use by Christians throughout the Roman Empire. Given the paucity of solid evidence for either authorship or audience, it seems best to focus on questions for which we do have evidence to evaluate.

5. The Greek *pleuran* used at John 19:34 for Jesus' "side" matches the "rib" by which the "woman" was taken from Adam in the Septuagint of Gen. 2:21–22.

6. Cf. Carter (2008), 127–29.

The religion of empire is not simply "another way" for those who might "prefer" it, but a diabolic lie rooted in the sin of Cain (cf. 1 John 3:12).[7] That it purports — whether from a Roman- or Jerusalem-centered perspective — to be divinely ordained requires all the more a sharp and clear Word that reveals what the truth really is.

The three "not births" in 1:13 each express one pillar of this false religion that Jesus has come to destroy (cf. 2:19–21). The first is to be "born of blood" (*aimatōn*), literally plural, "bloods." This is an ancient idiom for "bloodshed,"[8] which refers to the use of "sacred violence" to bond people against a common enemy as a "scapegoat," a theme explored in detail by René Girard.[9] It is dramatized in the gospel's life-and-death struggle between Jesus and the "Judeans," his primary opponents, especially in the contrasting attitudes toward Lazarus in John 11–12.

It is essential that we clarify the question of who these opponents are and who they are not. The Greek *Ioudaioi* is commonly translated biblically as "Jews." Not surprisingly, in the post-Holocaust era, many Christians have been sensitive to the embarrassing and politically incorrect association between Jesus' opponents and Jews today that this translation generates. This has sometimes resulted in the alternative rendering "Jewish leaders" (CEV; NET Bible) or the "the Jews" (in quotes) as if the quotation marks somehow took away the anti-Jewish sting.

Both of these attempts completely miss the point, however. First, Shaye Cohen has shown how the term *Ioudaioi* had multiple meanings during the New Testament era, the primary of which was "Judeans," i.e., people from or in the geographic region of Judea.[10] Taking this further, Steve Mason shows that *Ioudaioi* never referred to members of a "religion" called "Judaism" but always to what Greek referred to as *ethnōs*, rendered "ethnic [group]" or "nation."[11] Second, within the specific narrative and ideological context of John's Gospel, *Ioudaioi* starts with this geographic sense but then builds up another, deeper meaning. The *"Ioudaioi"* are *anyone — whether among the elite or the lowly, whether ethnically/religiously "Jew" or "Greek" — who uphold the imperial status quo embodied by the Jerusalem temple.* Only when one consistently reads every use of the term in John's Gospel[12] this way, can one see clearly who Jesus' opponents are. His

---

7. The New Testament contains three "letters of John." The one known as "1 John" is most clearly connected with the gospel in use of language and in theological understanding.

8. See, e.g., Mic. 3:10; Hab. 2:12; Hos. 4:2; 1 Kings 2:5 (LXX).

9. The literature on the topic, and on Girard in particular, is enormous; see, e.g., Girard (1979 and 1989); also Bailie. Such sacred violence became a key component of the post-Constantinian church's persecution of "pagans" and "heretics"; see Gaddis.

10. Cohen (2001).

11. Mason, 33–56.

12. The term is found 195 times in the New Testament, 71 of which are in John's Gospel and only 17 in the synoptic gospels combined (it is found 79 times in Acts and 26 times in the Pauline writings). It is also found 213 times in the LXX in late texts, clustered in the books of Maccabees (124) and Esther (44).

battle is not against "the Jews," but against anyone who upholds the religion of empire, grounded as it is in lies and murder. From this perspective, one can hear what is at stake in Pilate's seemingly rhetorical question to Jesus, "I am not a Judean, am I?" (18:35). Of course, Pilate is not a "Jew," but he *would* be a "Judean" if he responds favorably to the chief priests' cry for Jesus' crucifixion.[13]

This recognition brings the heart of the Gospel home to readers throughout the ages, regardless of ethnicity or geography. "Judeans" are those who are "born of blood," i.e., whose religious identity is grounded in the murder of anyone who stands in opposition to empire. It is the identity from which Caiaphas counseled the chief priests and Pharisees, in the emergency Sanhedrin meeting that followed Jesus' raising of Lazarus (11:47–53). The evangelist takes us inside the conspiratorial backroom to overhear those whose "foul deeds" are done in darkness so as not to be exposed (3:19–21; cf. 7:7). Their political fear is brought into the light: "If we let him go on like this, everyone will believe in him, and the Romans will come and destroy both our place (*topon*, cf. Deut. 12:14ff., viz., "Jerusalem") and our nation (*ethnos*)." Their plea has nothing to do with God, but is simply a matter of holding on to the puppet power delegated by empire. That they identify themselves as an *ethnos* is itself a terrible confession: it is used throughout the Septuagint to translate Hebrew, *goyim*, "nations." Caiaphas' response makes explicit the essential principle of "sacred violence":[14] "You do not understand that it is better for you to have one man die for the people than to have the whole nation destroyed" (11:50). In seeking to activate the scapegoat mechanism, they reveal themselves to be loyal to the religion of empire (19:15). Regardless of geography or ethnicity, "Judeans" are those who depend on imperial violence and deceit to maintain their identity.

The second "not birth" is of "the will of flesh" (*sarx*). Translators face another seeming embarrassment here: the long history of Christian denial of "the flesh" in sexuality and, more generally, embodiment itself.[15] However, both the author of John's Gospel and Paul, as we'll see, use the term *sarx* in the same way: not to deny goodness of the body, but to symbolize humanity acting apart from God's Spirit. That is, the "true" human being, one who reflects the "image of God," is one in whom the "flesh" and God's Spirit are fully integrated (Gen. 1:27; 2:7). To be "born of flesh" echoes Cain's futile attempt to move "away from the presence of YHWH" (Gen. 4:16). We have seen this path followed throughout biblical history in the tragic cycle of imperial rising and falling, each one grounded in the same effort to "build" something lasting so as to "make a name" for the builders apart

---

13. Cf. the recent work by Kierspel, which purports to review all the theories about the identity of the *Ioudaioi* between 1972 and 2005 (13–59), but does not address the position I take here, as expressed more fully in my 1994 commentary.

14. See p. 196.

15. See Brown (1988).

from God. Each manifestation is doomed from the start, whether Tower of Babel or Jerusalem temple under imperial rule.

We see this "birth choice" dramatized both negatively and positively in John's Gospel. The encounter between Jesus and Nicodemus (John 3) challenges a "ruler of the Judeans" who is also a Pharisee to be "born again / from above" (*anōthen*) of "water and spirit." For Nicodemus, this would mean — as it did for another Pharisee, Saul / Paul — seeing all his worldly accomplishments as worthless and beginning life all over again "from above" (cf. Phil. 3:3–9). This challenge proves too much for him, though, despite what we later discover to be his "secret discipleship" (12:42–43; cf. 19:38). He will not "come out" as a follower of Jesus. He is last seen giving Jesus a royal burial rather than being found among the disciples who experience the Risen Jesus (19:38–42; 21:–14).

The positive response is found in the one born blind (John 9). He accepts Jesus' invitation to "wash in the pool . . . which means sent" after receiving from him symbols of new creation (Jesus' saliva mixed with soil; cf. 7:37–39, embodying Gen. 2:7). This leads to a series of challenges that result in his being thrown out of the synagogue,[16] only to be "found" by Jesus on the outside.[17] What Nicodemus, the man identified with the Jerusalem authorities, could not do, the former blind beggar can. The Way of Jesus is hard to embrace for those who have been richly rewarded by the imperial status quo, but is liberating joy for those who have been abandoned on the margins.

The final "not birth" is that of "will of a man" (*andros*). Some translations, seeking to use inclusive language because of the legacy of Christian sexism, render this something like "human will."[18] Ironically, this undercuts the evangelist's point: the Gospel is rejecting claims of identity grounded in various forms of *patriarchy*. The male-specific Greek word is only found in John's Gospel in a few places.[19] Elsewhere, the gospel uses the gender inclusive "human" (*anthrōpos*). When it refers specifically to males, it is largely drawing attention to the dominant role of men within the religion of empire. Jesus stands consistently against this kind of male power on which empire has always been founded.

This is dramatized in the gospel in four ways: two negative, one positive, and one that moves from negative to positive. The negative stories are of the Judeans' claim that "Abraham is our father" (8:33–58) and the implicit role of Caesar as father or "our man" among the Samaritans (4:16–18) and the Judean high priests (19:15). The positive expression is the role of

---

16. Greek, *aposunagōgos*, only here and John 12:42; 16:2 in the Bible.

17. This contrasts with Jesus' finding of the gospel's other healed person "in" the temple (5:14).

18. Cf. "a husband's will" (TNIV); "a husband's decision" (NET Bible); "human desires" (CEV, combining "will of the flesh" and "will of a man" into a single "not" birth).

19. 1:13; 1:30 (referring to Jesus); 4:16–18 (five times, referring to the Samaritan woman's "man") and 6:10 (referring to the five thousand "men" symbolic of a gathered army).

God as "Father" to Jesus and his disciples. The transformative story is the Samaritan shift from identity grounded in "our father Jacob" to worship of the universal Father of Jesus, culminating in the anti-imperial proclamation that Jesus is "truly Savior of the world" (4:42). At stake are questions of empire, ethnicity, and patriotism that highlight the contrast between "the two religions."[20]

The theme of rejecting ethnic descent from Abraham as the source of one's membership in YHWH's people is consistent among Matthew, Luke, and John, and will recur in the writings of Paul. It is not Abraham who is being rejected, however. As we hear Jesus tell the Judeans: *"If you were* Abraham's children, you would be doing what Abraham did, but now you are trying to kill me, a man who has told you the truth that I heard from God" (8:39–40). Their murderous desire makes them children of a different "father": the devil (8:44). The devil, under many names and guises, is the source of the religion of empire, recalling *1 Enoch's Book of the Watchers* and in line with the book of Revelation (Rev. 12–13).

Starting with Julius Caesar, Roman emperors claimed the title *parens patriae,* "father of the nation."[21] The claim to be "father(s) of the nation" continues across a wide range of cultures and periods. At stake is not only origin (birth) but allegiance (faith/loyalty). Jesus "outs" the Judeans for their loyalty to their "father," the devil. In a parallel way, Pilate outs the high priests in extracting from them the confession, "we have no king but Caesar" (19:15). In the background of this passover eve confrontation between Pilate and the high priests is the prayer in which one hears, "we have no king but you, O God."[22] In reality, the Jerusalem elite are loyal to neither Abraham nor YHWH. Their commitment is to "the evil one," embodied as "the ruler of this world" (12:31; 14:30; 16:11; 17:15).

On the other side of the balance is Jesus' encounter with a woman at a well in Samaria (John 4). We recall the history of Samaria and the Samaritans going back to the Deuteronomistic History's condemnation of the northern kingdom in general and in particular, the "mixed marriages" resulting from Assyrian relocation (2 Kings 17:24–41). This "us" versus "them" stance was taken up by Josiah and later by Ezra-Nehemiah. It continued with the building of a Samaritan temple on Mount Gerizim to rival the Jerusalem temple on Mount Zion, eventually destroyed by the Hasmonean John Hyrcanus around 129 BCE.[23] By Jesus' day, the divide between Judeans and Samaritans was so deep that pilgrims traveling to Jerusalem for the festival were reported to take the long way around across the Jordan valley rather than set foot on Samaritan soil. But for John's Gospel, it was "necessary"[24]

---

20. See also Reed, 95.
21. Kreitzer, 82.
22. Howard-Brook (1994), 412.
23. Josephus, *Ant.* 13.9.1; VanderKam (2004), 292.
24. The Greek *dei* generally expresses *divine* necessity, i.e., something that must be done according to God's will; e.g., in John's Gospel, 3:7; 9:4; 10:16; 20:9.

for Jesus "to go through Samaria" (4:4). The story, like most in John's Gospel, uses individual characters to represent social groups. The woman at the well embodies the Samaritans *as a people,* as we hear from her initial, first person *plural* comments which identify herself as a Samaritan and (wrongly, from readers' perspective) perceive Jesus to be a Judean. She continues in response to his seemingly cryptic comment about "the gift of God" and "living water" by invoking her national claim: "Are you greater than *our* father Jacob, who gave *us* the well, and with his sons and his flocks drank from it?" (4:12). The following exchange has seemed to some readers a disjointed series of non sequiturs. It is, in reality, a tightly coherent conversation that continues on the one question at issue between them: Who are God's people and where does God dwell?

In 4:16–18, we hear five times about "man" or "men." This has nothing to do with the woman's supposed flawed character or inability to "keep a man." Such misunderstandings only continue the patriarchal assumptions that the narrative is designed to undermine. That she is not an outcast among her people is made clear by their response later in the story to her word of witness, to which they respond by dropping their daily tasks and going out to the well to see the one she claims might be the Messiah (4:29–30). Rather, Jesus' question about her "man" is a matter of ascertaining her political-religious loyalty. That she claims to have "no man" is an expression of her/their rejection of the "fatherhood" of Caesar and the Romans, a historical detail backed up by Josephus's own account of the Samaritans at the time.[25] This stands in contrast to the "five men" who represent the peoples placed in Samaria by the Assyrians centuries earlier with whom the Samaritans *had* intermarried. This explains why the conversation then moves directly to the question of "which mountain" is the proper place on which to worship God: the woman understands exactly what the topic is and pushes it to the next level.

Jesus, as always speaking from the religion of creation, rejects totally the notion of a correct "place" for worship. His position implicitly recalls the experience of the Samaritans' "father," Jacob: "God was in this place and I didn't know it" (Gen. 28:16). Just as throughout Genesis YHWH could be known and worshiped anywhere and all people comprise one human family from the one Creator God, so Jesus seeks to lead the Samaritans to reject place and ethnicity as markers of holiness that would separate them from others.

The story's conclusion finds the Samaritan people welcoming Jesus and proclaiming him "truly Savior of the world" (4:40–42). Numerous Roman texts proclaimed emperors as "savior." The "world," of course, was what the empire claimed power over.[26] It parallels another title attributed to Jesus

---

25. Koester (1990), 675–77.

26. However, John's Gospel consistently uses the Greek *kosmos* rather than the word more commonly used in imperial parlance, *oikoumenē;* see, e.g., Luke 4:5, the "kingdoms of

within John's Gospel that was claimed by the emperor Domitian: "lord and God" (20:28).[27] The Samaritans, rejected outsiders from the perspective of the upholders of the religion of empire, are thus the first to recognize fully who Jesus is. Their shift from claiming a human father (Jacob) as the source of their identity to Jesus, the representative of the Creator God of Israel, exhibits precisely the transformation that the Judeans cannot make.

The question of Abraham and Jacob is part of the gospel's engagement with Genesis throughout the narrative. Its opening phrase, "in the beginning was the Word," echoes Genesis 1. Its opening scenes count out the first week of re-creation, culminating in the celebration of an outpouring of wine at a wedding in Cana of Galilee.[28] It is no accident that this experience of divinely provided abundance replaces the dryness of the Judean ritual jars, which Jesus orders to be filled (2:6–7). It is a symbol of the arrival of the messianic banquet, in which "mountains shall drip sweet wine" (Joel 3:18; Amos 9:13). But unlike Joel, John's Gospel does not place this amid the dwelling of YHWH "in Zion, my holy mountain" (Joel 3:17). Rather, it is fulfilled in the land of the former Israelites, in a place of natural fertility.[29]

Instead of celebrating Jerusalem as the goal of the messianic mission, Jesus immediately goes there to proclaim his opposition to his "Father's house" (*ton oikon tou patros*) having become a "buying and selling house" (*oikon emporiou*) (2:16).[30] The temple, rebuilt by Herod with Roman funding, is replaced by the living temple of Jesus' body. This is not a matter of "Christian" supersession of "Jewish" symbols, but of Jesus' proclamation and embodiment of the true religion of Israel against the urban, hierarchical, imperial counterfeit.

Another aspect of the Johannine Jesus' rejection of Jerusalem because of its accommodation to empire is his Word about *peace*. Within the Farewell Discourse (John 13–17), Jesus speaks twice of a peace that is radically different from that of "the world":

> Peace I leave with you; my peace I give to you. I do not give to you as the world gives. (14:27; cf. 20:19, 21, 26)

> I have said this to you, so that in me you may have peace. In the world you face persecution.[31] But take courage; I have conquered the world! (16:33)

---

the world" (*basileias tēs oikoumenēs*). *Kosmos* in John's Gospel becomes a technical term (used seventy-eight times) for the realm to which Jesus has come to embody God's Word, but which doesn't "know him" (1:10).

27. Jones, 112.

28. The days are sequenced at 1:29, 35, 39, 43; 2:1.

29. Cana was a center for worship of Dionysus, the Greek god of wine and feasting. The gospel implicitly rejects the impurity of this form of "earth worship" in favor of the proper focus on the God who has created the earth and all its abundance. For the relationship between Galilee and the Creator God, see Freyne (2004).

30. For John's Gospel's rejection of the imperial, money economy in favor of the divine, gift economy, see Howard-Brook (2009).

31. *thlipsis* literally means "pressure," i.e., the pressure to conform to the imperial order.

The "world's" peace is that maintained by the twin pillars of lies and violence, the tools already ascribed in John's Gospel to the devil. More specifically, in the gospel's time, this meant the Pax Romana. We must pause briefly to consider the nature of this "peace" so that we can clearly hear the contrast presented in the gospel.

The single, overarching claim of the Roman Empire was that it brought peace to the Mediterranean out of the long history of local warfare and imperial conquest that had plagued the region for centuries. Klaus Wengst writes:

> No war devastated the land and destroyed the cities: arts and crafts could unfold and agriculture developed; vines were grown even by the Rhine; trade and commerce flourished; new cities came into being, and old ones were redeveloped in splendor; the same law applied everywhere. We can understand why Aelius Aristides resorted to superlatives: "Cities now gleam in splendor and beauty, and the whole earth is arrayed like a paradise."[32]

This peace was proclaimed as a gift of "the gods." It could not have happened if the gods were not "with" Rome. The emperor Octavian, emerging triumphant from the Roman civil war, had unified the empire. He took up the title Augustus and became a visible, devout worshiper of the Roman gods. Cultural expressions of this victory were everywhere, in monuments, public inscriptions, patriotic ballads and poems, and in the material details of private life, such as cups, plates, and wall paintings.[33] The Roman philosopher Seneca put it like this: "For [Augustus] is the bond by which the commonwealth is united, the breath of life which these many thousands draw, who in their own strength would only be a burden to themselves and the prey of others if the great mind of the empire should be withdrawn."[34]

This would have been experienced differently by people living in the major cities of the empire, such as Rome, Alexandria, Antioch, and Ephesus, rather than in a hinterland such as Palestine. Wengst observes that a key principle of the Pax was "transferring war and its evil consequences to the periphery."[35] He notes that the poet Horace names this "with astonishing openness": the Pax "shall ward off tearful war, wretched plague and famine from the folk and from our sovereign Caesar, and send those woes against the Parthian and in the Briton."[36]

Jerusalem's elite, like the urban provincial elite throughout the empire,[37] had accepted this "peace" as a "divine gift." However, ordinary people did not see it this way, as is revealed by the constant acts of rebellion and

---

32. Wengst, 8.
33. Zanker.
34. Seneca, *De Clementia* I, 1.4.
35. Wengst, 18.
36. Quoted at ibid.
37. See e.g., Price for how these relationships worked in the province of Asia.

resistance reported by Josephus. Luke's Gospel has Jesus explicitly denounce Jerusalem's imperial collaboration as a matter of not knowing "the things that make for peace," which will lead, as with the first Jerusalem, to its downfall at the hands of enemy armies (Luke 19:42–44).

John's Gospel accomplishes the same result by a different route. We hear not only that Jesus "gives" peace differently from "the world," but also that Jesus *has conquered the world*. This statement is made before his death and resurrection, while speaking at the Last Supper. It is thus not the Passion events that first reveal this "conquest," but the very fact that Jesus stands in God's truth and embodies God's love rather than the lies and violence of the devil. The book of Revelation also speaks repeatedly within the messages to the churches of Asia of *present conquest* (e.g., Rev. 2:7, 11, 17, 26, 28; 3:5, 12, 21).

In both John's Gospel and Revelation, Jesus is "the Lamb."[38] One could hardly imagine an animal image less evocative of imperial might. It stands, as part of this gospel's "realized apocalyptic," in contrast to the predatory animals portrayed as embodiments of empire in Daniel and *1 Enoch*'s *Animal Apocalypse*. The "conquering Lamb" speaks of this contrast in his often misunderstood testimony before Pontius Pilate:

> Jesus answered, "My kingdom is not of this world [*ek tou kosmou*]. If my kingdom were of this world, *my underlings* [au. trans. *hupēretai*] would be fighting [*ēgōnizonto*] to keep me from being handed over to the Judeans. But as it is, my kingdom is not from here." (18:36, emphasis added)

The phrase *ek tou kosmou* is found thirteen times in John's Gospel, ten in the Farewell Discourse,[39] where Jesus repeatedly prepares his disciples to be *"in* the world" but not *"of* the world." Jesus is not contrasting an "earthly" kingdom with the "afterlife," but rather, *two sources of power*. From the beginning, people have sought to legitimize human power with claims to divine authority, developing throughout history versions of "the religion of empire." Jesus' kingdom is simply not another human power building project. It is, in contrast both to that of Rome and that of Jerusalem, a *truly* divinely authorized realm of power. Jesus illustrates this contrast with one simple, yet definitive criterion: kingdoms which are *ek tou kosmou* exert their power by "fighting"[40] for power rather than, as Jesus does: *loving to completion* (13:1).

This is further illustrated by two dramatic connections elsewhere in the gospel. The word translated above literally as "underlings"[41] is used

---

38. John 1:29, 36; thirty-one times in Revelation.

39. The only other use is 8:23.

40. The Greek *agōnizomai* can include nonviolent struggle / striving as well as violent fighting; cf. Luke 13:24; 1 Cor. 9:25; cf. Col. 1:29; 4:12; 1 Tim. 4:10. In context, however, it clearly envisions a physical fight to have Jesus released from Roman custody.

41. Sometimes misleadingly as, in NRSV, "police." The ancient world knew nothing like a modern "police force."

elsewhere in John's Gospel to refer to those who do the will of the Jerusalem elite (7:45–46; 18:3, 12, 18, 22; 19:6). It is these who engage in violence in defense of their own "kingdom." The other connection is at Jesus' arrest, where it was Simon Peter — who will momentarily deny being one of Jesus' disciples — who drew a sword and struck at the high priest's slave, only to be sharply admonished by Jesus (18:10–11). The conjoining of Peter's words and actions is key: his swordstroke is evidence that he was *not* at that moment a disciple of Jesus. It is only after this experience *and* Jesus' resurrection that Jesus, for the first time, calls Peter to discipleship (21:9). Only then is Peter "born of God" into Jesus' kingdom, one diametrically opposed to the kingdoms of "the world."

The choice of "birth" throughout the gospel expresses each person's response to the presence of the Light of God in and through Jesus, shining amid the darkness of empire. The gospel positions this set of contrasts at the heart of the prologue to highlight its goal: not to generate "Christology" but *discipleship*. As the narrator sums up at the hinge between resurrection stories, the gospel has been "written so that *you* may come to trust that Jesus is the Messiah, the Son of God,[42] and that through trusting *you* may have life in his name" (20:31).

The particularly Johannine phrase that expresses this gift is "eternal life" (*zōē aiōnion*).[43] It echoes one of only two Septuagint uses of the term, "Many of those who sleep in the dust of the earth shall awake, some to eternal life" (Dan. 12:2).[44] As with Daniel, the gospel's promise is not for "unending" life in the sense of a clock that ticks forever (whether on earth or in heaven). The term literally means, "life of the age." That is, Daniel's vision is of a world made right by God through the final destruction of all "beastly" empires and the rule of God through the Human One. John's Gospel claims that this promise has been fulfilled in and through Jesus, *now*. For example: "Amen, amen, I tell you, anyone who hears my word and believes him who sent me *has* eternal life, and does not come under judgment, but *has passed* from death to life" (John 5:24).[45] "Eternal" Rome's "Golden Age" proclaimed by its poets may be in the past, but the age of God's reign *has come* and is *here now*.[46]

To enable disciples to continue Jesus' proclamation and embodiment of the religion of creation, John's Gospel shows Jesus offering his disciples a "departure speech" that seeks to pass on his life to them as an "inheritance"

42. Richey, 97–103, discusses the use of this title in John's Gospel in opposition to the "Augustan ideology" of Caesar as "son of God."

43. Of twenty-five uses of *zōē aiōnion* in the gospels, seventeen are in John (of thirty-seven total in the New Testament). See also the useful discussion at Carter (2008), 204–27.

44. *Pss.Sol.* 3:12; see pp. 367–71.

45. See also 3:36; 6:47, 54. Note how the verses that follow 5:24 continue to express the fulfillment of Daniel 12:2, especially 5:24–29.

46. Levenson (2006) discusses the later rabbinic understanding of the "inextricably connected" experiences of personal resurrection and the restoration of Israel in "the World-to-Come," in which human beings have been re-created to render them fit for God's worldwide renewal (see esp. 223–24). John's Gospel understands this to be already fulfilled in the Word made flesh.

(John 13–17). The only thing that "happens" during this long Last Supper encounter is Jesus' washing of the disciples' feet. It is not, as often misunderstood, a last-minute lesson in "humble service," but a pointed preparation for the disciples' own persecution and rejection (15:18–16:4). Jesus tells them that he is doing this as an "example" (13:15, *hupodeigma*), recalling the Maccabees' "example" of how to die a noble death" (2 Macc. 6:27–28). It is intended to inculcate a deep and abiding intimacy among the disciples so that they will "know" and "love" one another as Jesus has known and loved them. It is by this mutual love that the world "will know that you are my disciples" (13:35). Apart from this ongoing intimacy, the disciples will certainly hide "in fear of the Judeans" (20:19) rather than proclaim the Gospel so that others might "have life in his name" (20:31).

John's Gospel, under the influence of Greek thought and imperial inclinations, eventually became used as a "proof" source for creedal statements designed to unify the newly "Christianized" Roman Empire under Constantine. However, on its own terms, it reveals a God whose power to create and to restore life trumps the Roman Empire and any other empire's death threats. Its Jesus, consistent with the one portrayed in the synoptic gospels, comes into the world to denounce claims that associate Israel's God with empire, and to lead people away from this darkness and death into the fullness of God's true Light and Life, which no empire can give nor take away.

Chapter Twenty-Six

"Christ the Power of God and the Wisdom of God"
PAUL'S COUNTER-IMPERIAL GOSPEL

With our consideration of the apostle Paul, we move simultaneously backward and forward in *time* in relation to the gospels. Paul's life and letters *precede* the writing of the canonical gospels, but, of course, *follow* the death and resurrection of Jesus (see "New Testament Timeline," p. 394). We also move a great distance *spatially,* as we consider Paul's thousands of miles traveling around the Mediterranean, proclaiming the Gospel, founding and building up communities "in Christ," which he called *ekklēsiai.* Finally, we also travel *culturally,* as we leave behind the homeland of "indigenous" Israelites and Judeans and engage the cities and countryside in which numerous local cultures had been overlaid in varying degrees with both Greek and Roman culture.

Chapter 20 considered the paradigm shift that has increasingly come to recognize the centrality of the Israelite / Judean and Roman cultural contexts of the New Testament. Nowhere is this more important than in the interpretation of Paul, the man and the letter writer. The simplistic, catechism-style formula that imagines a Jew named Saul who became a Christian and changed his name to "Paul" disappears entirely upon the most superficial examination of the actual situation.[1] To understand Paul's radically anti-imperial gospel requires listening to him speaking from deep within his "hybrid"[2] cultural context.

Pauline studies, as a subset of New Testament studies, has followed its own course in taking into account these "new" aspects of Paul's situation. The so-called "New Perspective"[3] began as an outgrowth of the 1963 landmark article by Krister Stendahl, "The Apostle Paul and the Introspective Conscience of the West."[4] Stendahl challenged the prevailing paradigm, in

---

1. See, e.g., Segal (1992) for a Jewish scholar's approach to the "apostolate and apostasy of Saul the Pharisee."
2. Cf. Bhabha (1994).
3. See "the Paul Page," which provides an enormous set of resources, both from the advocates of the "New Perspective" and its "neotraditionalist" critics, *www.thepaulpage.com/.*
4. Stendahl (1976).

which Paul was interpreted from the perspective of Martin Luther's personal struggle to achieve "justification" before God. Over the centuries, this approach led to the question of "faith versus works" taking center stage, with (the Protestant) Paul on the "side" of faith and the (Catholic) epistle of James allegedly on the side of "works."[5] Stendahl demolished this false dichotomy as a foundational misreading of the New Testament cultural context, and called for a thorough reexamination of Paul's writings in light of his Judean situation.

This new perspective was first developed in a landmark book by E. P. Sanders, *Paul and Palestinian Judaism*.[6] Sanders envisioned, within the variety of first-century practices, a core "Judaism" he called "covenantal nomism." However, as we have seen, especially in the immediately preceding chapters, there was no such thing as "Judaism" in the first century, but rather, there were a wide range of theologies and practices that we have shown to be attracted in different ways to the two poles of "imperial" and "creation" religion.[7]

A leading scholar who has pushed this New Perspective further into the soil of first-century Judaisms is N. T. Wright.[8] He has shown how Paul's theology stems from his rereading of the biblical story of Israel in light of his apocalyptic relationship with the Risen Christ, as portrayed both by Luke in Acts[9] and by Paul himself.[10] Far from "starting a new religion," Paul, as Luke reports him saying in Acts, has come to believe that in the life, death, and resurrection of Jesus the Messiah, "the promise made by God to our ancestors" has been fulfilled (Acts 26:6). Others have sought to push the New Perspective from various directions, while staying within the basic framework of Sanders's work.[11]

Wright has humbly acknowledged, however, that his own early work from the "New Perspective" had not taken into account the other key component of Paul's context: the Roman Empire.[12] It was the work of various scholars gathered under the leadership of Richard Horsley[13] that awakened Wright to the centrality of listening to *both* the "Jewish" and the Roman

---

5. Cf. Rom. 3–4 and James 2:14–26.
6. Sanders (1977).
7. See also Neusner et al. (1990) and Elliott (2000) for critiques of Sanders's attempt to find a "core" first-century Judaism.
8. See Wright (1993 and 2009).
9. Acts 9, 22, and 26 each present a version of Paul's "Road to Damascus" experience. The use of Acts to interpret Paul's letters is fraught with difficulties, given Luke's purposes in narrating the drama of the early church. My presentation in this chapter does not depend on Acts.
10. Gal. 1:12–16; cf. Eph. 3:5.
11. E.g., Campbell (2009), 412–68, who summarizes various perspectives before presenting his own.
12. Wright (2000).
13. Horsley (1997); see also the collections 2000a, 2000b, and 2000c and 2004) and Horsley's own work on 1 Corinthians (1998).

imperial contexts to understand Paul correctly. The collection *Paul and Politics* (2000), in which Wright is a contributor, was specifically addressed to responding to Stendahl's challenge from the perspective of empire.

Horsley's work has coincided with that of Neil Elliott, whose *Liberating Paul: The Justice of God and the Politics of the Apostle* (1994) dismantled the historical use of Paul "in the service of death" (e.g., as apologist for slavery and the repression of women) and began the process of listening anew to Paul as a staunch opponent of Roman claims to provide "salvation," "justice," "peace and security" and "Good News." Recently, Elliott has used this approach to reread parts of Paul's letter to the Romans.[14]

Not surprisingly, this approach has been challenged both from the "right" and from the "left." Conservatives have sought to "restore" the "spiritual" Paul concerned only with individual salvation who shows no interest in "politics" and counsels allegiance to governmental authority. At the other end of the spectrum, feminists such as Elisabeth Schüssler Fiorenza have challenged Horsley and Elliott for allegedly overlooking some of Paul's "reinscribing" of empire in the name of God/Jesus.[15] Further, some scholars continue to maintain a dichotomy between Paul's "Jewishness" as the "center" of his work (i.e., about "religious" questions) and the Roman imperial context (i.e., about "political" questions).[16]

Readers seeking to understand Paul generally and individual letters specifically cannot avoid taking these questions into account. One need not and should not pit Paul's "religion" against his "politics," nor his "Jewish" context against that of the Roman Empire. Similarly, it is a dead-end to position him as moving "away" from "Judaism" and "toward" a "Christianity" that is somehow unmoored from its biblical matrix. Rather, Paul, like the Gospel writers who followed him, came to see through his ongoing, apocalyptic relationship with Jesus Christ that the "true" religion of Israel was the one fulfilled by and in Jesus, i.e., the religion of the Creator God. Thus, his critique was always *both* against the ideas and people who support the Jerusalem-centered, imperially collaborating religion and the way of empire itself.

Seeking to provide a brief, synthetic picture of Paul's perspective is both risky and dangerous. Paul was not a "systematic theologian" offering a universal understanding of the implications of the death and resurrection of Jesus. In his own words, he sought to "become all things to all people, that

---

14. Elliott (2008).

15. Schüssler Fiorenza (2007); see also Clark Wire (1995); Castelli for feminist challenges to Paul's rhetoric of power before and apart from the work of Horsley and Elliott.

16. This is Campbell's (2009) perspective. His monumental book (over twelve hundred pages with notes) does an excellent job of taking down the wall of what he calls "Justification theory" brick-by-brick, but refers only obliquely to the actual political situation "on the ground" facing Paul's audience in Rome. His "apocalyptic" alternative to "Justification theory" barely engages the apocalyptic tradition we explored in Part III and gives little clue to what Paul's Gospel would mean concretely to his audience apart from the abstract ideas they might hold about what "salvation" is and "how" it happens.

I might by all means save some" (1 Cor. 9:22). This doesn't mean that he would water down the Gospel or compromise it to be popular. Rather, as we see Luke dramatize in Acts, Paul sought to "translate" the Gospel into terms understandable by specific audiences. He wrote in response to specific pastoral needs of local communities. Even in Romans, as many have pointed out recently,[17] Paul is responding to the specific challenge of following Jesus within the imperial capital during the reign of Nero.[18] Thus, any interpretation of Paul must take into account not only the general, overarching Judean and Roman contexts, but also the specific situation in the local place to which Paul is writing.

There is also the unavoidable issue of comprehensiveness. How can one claim "Paul's position" on a given issue without taking into account *all* of his writing? Given that two recent commentaries on, respectively, Romans and 1 Corinthians are each over a thousand pages,[19] such a task would exhaust even the most dedicated reader. However, it is also clear that the opposite approach, in which one or two texts are used to "prove" Paul's viewpoint, is unsupportable. For instance, the question of "Paul's attitude toward the Roman Empire in particular, or about governmental authority in general," often seems to begin and end with Romans 13:1–7. Whatever Paul might be saying in these few verses about the relationships among God, Rome, and the Christian community, it cannot be used as the hermeneutical box in which to contain all his other writings that exude such anti-imperial passion. Similarly, his texts that sound, to our ears, to be "anti-women,"[20] cannot alone overrule his ringing proclamation at Galatians 3:28, "There is no longer Judean or Greek, there is no longer slave or free, there is no longer male and female; for all of you are one in Christ Jesus." We must at least survey some kind of "representative sample" of his writings to be able to claim anything about the direction in which Paul was seeking to guide the first generation of Christians.

Finally, we must take some account of the vexed question of authorship. Virtually no modern scholar takes as a given Pauline "authorship" of all the New Testament texts that bear his name. Most would agree that a few such letters (1–2 Timothy; Titus) are demonstrably later than Paul's lifetime and express a perspective on many questions that is very different from that found in the undisputed Pauline letters.[21] However, some others, notably Colossians and Ephesians, occupy a middle ground in which scholarly disagreement is intense. For our purposes, it seems best to confine our

---

17. Elliott (2008); Wright (2002); Jewett (2007).
18. For a recent reexamination of the life and reign of this infamous emperor, see Champlin.
19. Jewett (2007); Thiselton.
20. E.g., 1 Cor. 11:2–16; 14:34–35; or the "household codes" at Eph. 5:21–33; Col. 3:18–4:1.
21. Cf. Tamez (2007) for a Latin American feminist reading of 1 Tim. as a struggle for power within early Christianity.

examination to those texts that are most likely to reveal Paul's own viewpoint. Readers are certainly encouraged to expand this study to test the thesis further.

Paul's "Conversion"

For I want you to know, brothers and sisters, that the Gospel that was proclaimed by me is not of human origin; for I did not receive it from a human source, nor was I taught it, but I received it through a revelation [*apokalupsis*] of Jesus Christ. (Gal. 1:11–12)

My speech and my proclamation were not with plausible words of wisdom, but with a demonstration of the Spirit and of power, so that your faith might rest not on human wisdom but on the power of God. (1 Cor. 2:4–5)

I know a person in Christ who fourteen years ago was caught up to the third heaven — whether in the body or out of the body I do not know; God knows — And I know that such a person — whether in the body or out of the body I do not know; God knows — was caught up into Paradise and heard things that are not to be told, that no mortal is permitted to repeat. (2 Cor. 12:2–4)

... as to the law, a Pharisee; as to zeal, a persecutor of the church; as to righteousness under the law, blameless. Yet whatever gains I had, these I have come to regard as loss because of Christ. More than that, I regard everything as loss because of the surpassing value of knowing Christ Jesus my Lord. For his sake I have suffered the loss of all things, and I regard them as crap [au. trans. *skubala*], in order that I may gain Christ and be found in him. (Phil. 3:5b–9a)

Indeed, to this very day, when they hear the reading of the old covenant, that same veil is still there [*anakaluptomenon*], since only in Christ is it set aside. Indeed, to this very day whenever Moses is read, a veil lies over their minds; but when one turns to the Lord, the veil is removed. (2 Cor. 3:14–16)

These brief passages reveal the essence of Paul's "conversion." From the moment of his first encounter with the Risen Christ, Paul remained in ongoing communion with his God and Lord, Jesus Christ. His writing is replete with the language of *intimate knowing*. The reality he named as being "in Christ" informed, shaped, and determined the goal of everything he said or did. Much like that of the disciples on the Emmaus Road, Paul's experience "converted" him to a radical, new understanding of Scripture and of God's means of reestablishing justice among God, people, and all of creation. As Alan F. Segal writes, "Mysticism in first-century Judea was apocalyptic, revealing not meditative truths of the universe but the disturbing news that God was about to bring judgment.... Paul is a first-century Jewish apocalypticist, and as such, he was also a mystic."[22]

Segal also makes an important link between Paul's experience and the Enoch tradition we've been exploring. Specifically, although Paul does not speak of Jesus as "the Son of Man," he does present his own spiritual experience in relation to Enoch's *Parables*. As Segal writes:

> *First Enoch* 71 gives us the experience of an adept undergoing the astral transformation prophesied in Dan. 12:2, albeit in the name of a pseudepigraphal hero.... Paul gives us the actual, confessional experience of the same spiritual event, with Christ substituting for the Son of Man.[23]

Segal, in considering how this central feature of Paul's life has often been ignored or downplayed among scholars, notes that the "scholarly reticence to ascribe spiritual experience to Paul may be rooted in theological embarrassment with the nonrational aspects" of the human person.[24] An implicit corollary is the scholarly hesitation to place the "converted" Paul where he belongs, among the apocalyptic advocates for God's inbreaking judgment on the imperial order and its collaborators in Jerusalem. Segal acknowledges that "ecstatic religion represents a peripheral strategy in first-century Judaism; it was an oblique attack against established order,"[25] but doesn't draw out the anti-imperial implications.

That task has been initiated by Neil Elliott, Richard Horsley, and others cited above. Both Elliott and Horsley begin from the same premise as Segal: that Paul's conversion was a thoroughly apocalyptic one. They then pick up where Segal left off, connecting Paul to the hopes and expectations of Israelites who had been marginalized because of their experience of a God whose reign stands over and against all human systems of dominating power. Horsley writes,

> the apocalyptic visionaries were able critically to demystify the pretensions and practices of the dominant imperial regime... [and] they insisted on the integrity and independence of their own society and its traditional way of life, over against attempts by the imperial regime to impose a dominant metropolitan culture and / or politics... were able, through their revelations, creatively to envision a future for their society in freedom and justice beyond their present oppression under imperial rulers and / or their local client rulers.

He then links this with Paul:

---

22. Segal (1992), 34.
23. Ibid., 47.
24. Ibid., 12. For a neurobiological approach to Paul's ecstatic religious experience, see Shantz.
25. Segal (1992), 15.

... the fundamental counterimperial agenda of Judean apocalyptic literature — martyr death and vindication, renewal of the people and divine judgment of imperial rulers — appear as the underlying structuring components of Paul's arguments.[26]

Elliott explains that, as a Pharisee,[27] Paul was already committed to an apocalyptic worldview. As we saw earlier, the Pharisees, in contrast to the Sadducees and other members of the Jerusalem aristocracy, had taken up the book of Daniel and its hope in bodily resurrection.[28] That perspective explained the brute fact of Roman rule as something allowed by God for a time for the sake of Israel's repentance, until God's judgment swept it away. Elliott writes that, before his conversion,

> Paul heard in the proclamation of the crucified messiah an apocalyptic announcement and thus a direct challenge to Rome. If one crucified by Rome had been vindicated by God — vindicated by being raised from the dead already — then the "time given to Rome" was at hand. The proclamation of the crucified was a declaration that the changing of the ages was at hand.
>
> The logic of the message would have been immediately clear. But Paul disagreed with its content, for reasons apparent enough to anyone with eyes to see: Pilate's vicious policies continued undisturbed....
>
> So the messianists were not only wrong about what time it was; they were dangerously wrong.... They threatened to provoke further violence from the Romans, thus aggravating Israel's misery.[29]

Paul's apocalyptic encounter with the Risen Christ utterly reversed this logic. Elliott continues: "in the cross Paul saw his own willingness to 'sacrifice' Jesus...to the violence of Rome, in order that the whole nation be 'saved' from that violence."[30] In this, he thought precisely like the Sanhedrin portrayed in John's Gospel, articulated in Caiaphas's infamous pronouncement of the need for a scapegoat.

Paul told the Galatians that, following his world-shattering experience, he "did not confer with any human being, nor did I go up to Jerusalem to those who were already apostles before me, but I went away at once into Arabia, and afterwards I returned to Damascus" (Gal. 1:16–17). Only after three years did he make a brief, two-week visit to Jerusalem and did not return again for another fourteen years. The decision to avoid Jerusalem underscores what becomes clear throughout his letters: that the heart of the meaning of what God had done in and through the death and resurrection of Jesus was *the final fulfillment of God's ancient plan to bring forth a people*

---

26. Horsley (2000b), 95, 98.
27. Perhaps surprisingly, Paul's reference to himself as a Pharisee at Phil. 3:5 is the oldest extant written reference to the Pharisees, predating Josephus's historical survey.
28. Josephus, *Ant* 18.1.3; Acts 23:6–8.
29. Elliott (1994), 170.
30. Ibid., 172.

through whom God's blessing would become available for all peoples. As N. T. Wright has argued, Paul's "Gospel," flowing out of his conversion and ongoing life "in Christ," expresses the "climax of the covenant."[31] His conversion meant that the long-awaited "end of exile" had finally taken place, and that the power of empire had been definitively broken. As we hear him say passionately to the church in Corinth:

> "At an acceptable time [*kairō dektō*, following LXX] I have listened to you, and on a day of salvation I have helped you." (quoting Isa. 49:8)

> Behold! Now is the *truly* acceptable time [*kairos euprosdektos*]; Behold! Now is the day of salvation! (2 Cor. 6:2)

The Isaiah passage that Paul declares to be fulfilled continues with an exuberant description of the joyous celebration that is to break out amid the movement out of Babylon and back home.[32] Paul's conversion leads him to write the final chapter in the story of God's journey with Israel, a chapter that reveals a tremendous "twist" in the narrative logic as Paul had previously understood it. Wright suggests that Paul's note of a long sojourn in Arabia and return to Damascus may be meant to invoke his shift in self-understanding from embodying Elijah's righteous "zeal" and violence to following Jesus in the role of Isaiah's Suffering Servant.[33] Whatever scriptural echoes may be heard in Galatians 1:13–17, it is abundantly clear that Paul's conversion meant the movement from persecutor to persecuted; from one who sought to destroy one's enemies to one who seeks to love them (e.g., Rom. 12:14–21). It moved him to a life of fearless and ceaseless effort, under the most brutal and harrowing of circumstances, oriented completely around a single goal: the announcement of God's victory and the incarnation of new, inclusive communities that would embody that Good News.

Forming and Nurturing Communities of the "Called Out" (ekklēsiai)

Paul refers to these communities "in Christ" as *ekklēsiai,* literally meaning "[the] called out." Only Matthew among the evangelists has Jesus use this term.[34] Apart from Acts and Revelation 2–3, Paul uses the term sixty-two of the remaining seventy-two times in the New Testament. It has a double resonance for Paul. On the one hand, it refers to the "assembly of YHWH" or "of Israel" named in Deuteronomy (but not elsewhere in the Pentateuch).[35] On the other hand, it was the term used by the Greeks to

---

31. Wright (1993).
32. See Hays (1989) for a full exposition of how Paul uses "echoes of Scripture" to convey much more than he actually writes.
33. Wright (1996b); 1 Kings 19.
34. Matt. 16:18; 18:17.
35. Deut. 4:10; 9:10; 18:16; 23:2–9; 31:30.

refer to the "assembly" of ancient Athens that gathered as the *demos* to do the city's work.[36]

Both of these ancient echoes can be heard in Paul's usage, but the meaning is also radically transformed as Paul applied it to the communities "in Christ" which God formed through parental care and nurture exercised through Paul. That is, the vocation of the "churches" is both to be the "Israel" of "the new age" inaugurated by the death and resurrection of Jesus the Messiah and to be the assembly of those "called out" from the Roman Empire, as Israel was called out from Egypt and Babylon. As Robert Jewett observes, "preaching the Gospel to establish faith communities, rather than force of arms or apocalyptic military miracles, is the means" by which God's justice is restored to the world.[37] Careful studies of Paul's letters reveal how clearly the apostle sees these new communities taking up Israel's religion of creation.

At the risk of redundancy, it is crucial that one hears clearly what Paul is *not* doing. He is not denouncing and replacing "Judaism" with "Christianity." He is not taking the concrete and specific provisions of the torah and "spiritualizing" them so that faithfulness is no longer about the stuff of daily life. He is not replacing a "torah of works" in which one "earns" God's approval with a "gospel of grace" in which God's approval is a gift.[38] All of these historical misunderstandings have been systematically refuted in light of the thorough "Jewishness" that Paul retained to the end of his life.[39] Rather, he is serving as an "angelic" herald of the Good News of the God of Israel: *the reign of sin and death, and the succession of empires in which that reign is embodied in "flesh," has been definitively broken by the power of God revealed through the death and resurrection of Jesus, the Messiah, Son of God, and true Lord of all.* The vocation of the *ekklēsiai* is to continue to bear witness to this Good News as "light to the nations" through their own embodiment of a radically different way, that of God's peace, justice, and love.

Paul's understanding of the purpose of these *ekklēsiai* shares John's Gospel's sense of what I called earlier "realized apocalyptic." That is, the churches are the earthly embodiment of the reality on "the other side of the veil" where God reigns. One clear example of this is Paul's frequent designation of church members as *hagioi*, i.e., "saints" or "holy ones."[40] In the Septuagint, *hagioi* is regularly used to refer to the heavenly beings that accompany YHWH, for example,

> Let the heavens praise your wonders, O YHWH,
> your faithfulness in the assembly of the *holy ones.*

---

36. See generally Howard-Brook (2001).
37. Jewett (2007), 143.
38. Campbell (2009).
39. E.g., Elliott (1994 and 2008); Wright (1997, 2002, and 2009).
40. E.g., Rom. 1:7; 1 Cor. 1:2; 2 Cor. 1:1; Phil. 1:1; Eph. 1:1; Col. 1:2.

> For who in the skies can be compared to YHWH?
> Who among the heavenly beings is like YHWH,
> a God feared in the council of the *holy ones*,
> great and awesome above all that are around him?
> (Ps. 88:6–8 [Eng. 89:5–7])

The *hagioi* are central to Daniel's vision of the reign of the Human One that follows after the destruction of the final beast: "the *hagioi* of the Most High shall receive the kingdom and possess the kingdom forever — forever and ever" (Dan. 7:18). For Daniel, the *hagioi* are the heavenly counterpart of the *maskilim*, the "wise" who stand firm in the face of the onslaught of the imperial "beasts." This sense continues in the Enoch *Parables*, where the *hagioi* "who dwell in the heights of heaven" intercede to the Lord of Spirits on behalf of the "righteous and holy and elect" on earth (47:2–48:1). As noted, for Paul, *Parables'* vision has become reality in and through Christ, and so the people who are now "in Christ" are themselves both "the righteous" and the "holy ones."

This is not a judgment on their moral qualities, as one might hear in the later sense of being "a saint."[41] Rather, it is an expression of the vocation of those who have "come out" from empire and committed, through baptism, to participate in the death and resurrection of the One who is now exalted above all else as "Lord."

To strengthen this vocational sense, Paul wrote occasional letters to the *ekklēsiai*. He knows, from his own experience, the ongoing challenge of living against empire in a public way. His criticism of Israel's failure to do this is no more "anti-Jewish" than was that of the great prophets of antiquity. Walter Brueggemann developed the now classic expression of the ongoing prophetic function as both "critical" and "energizing."[42] Paul was certainly critical of Israel's failures, as he was critical of the failures of the *ekklēsiai*, as we hear stated so strongly in 1 Corinthians. But he also pulled out all the stops to speak in a way that was not mere rhetoric or "persuasive words of wisdom" but rather, a "demonstration of spirit and power" (1 Cor. 2:4). It is this Spirit of God, as he says, that "energizes"[43] the various gifts given to the "holy ones" to carry out their vocation.

It is this Spirit, embodied in the baptized through the resurrection of Jesus, that enables the "veil" over Scripture to be removed so as to hear its true meaning and purpose (2 Cor. 3, esp. vv. 13–18). It is the same reality that was revealed on the Emmaus Road in Luke 24. It remains the key, more than any possible merely scholarly "insight," to understanding the truth embedded in the biblical narrative. Only through the energizing, empowering, clarifying presence of God's Spirit can even the most brilliant mind have "ears to hear" the apocalyptic Word. Paul continued to live by

---

41. See, e.g., Brown (1982).
42. Brueggemann (2001b).
43. 1 Cor. 12:11, NRSV; "are activated," Greek, *energei*.

this power throughout his life and committed every ounce of his energy to guiding others to this liberating encounter with the Risen Lord.

Paul's Gospel of the Victory of the Creator God over the Gods of Empire

The introduction to this chapter noted the outburst of scholarship in recent years which has shown how specific aspects of the Roman imperial order are echoed, only to be denounced, in Paul's letters. What has not been addressed as fully is how Paul's Gospel took sides with the Hebrew Scriptures' "religion of creation" and against its "religion of empire." Many of the traditional Pauline themes, heard through the perspective established throughout this book, come together as part of Paul's consistent understanding of how Jesus' death and resurrection brought the long biblical battle to a definitive conclusion. The discussion here can only suggest possibilities for closer engagement with Paul's writings.

One of the most misunderstood of Paul's messages is the one first challenged by Stendahl: the supposed antithesis between "law" and gospel understood as the contrast between "justification by works" and "by faith." N. T. Wright argues that it is not an abstract doctrine about how a person is "made right" (i.e., "justified") by God, but rather a redefinition of how one knows that a person is, right now, one of God's people. Key to Wright's conclusion is his interpretation of the Greek term, *pistis Christou*,[44] "not to human *faith* in the Messiah but to the *faithfulness* of the Messiah... to the divine plan for Israel." However, Jewett cautions that this interpretation "tends to lose sight of the social dimension of very early Christian usage" by which faith *in* Jesus expresses commitment to "participation as citizens in the realm of God's redeeming and righteous activity."[45]

Paul's understanding of the "divine plan for Israel" fulfilled in and through the death and resurrection of Jesus can be seen throughout his writings. It is nothing other than the Story that begins in Genesis and continues through Isaiah in the texts of the "religion of creation" we've been exploring. At each opportunity, Paul pounds home his passionate conviction that the apocalyptic event lifts the veil on Scripture and reveals once and for all time the true nature of Israel's God and of God's salvation.

Paul turns to Genesis again and again as his foundational source. In Galatians 3 and Romans 4, Abraham is Paul's faith hero. Paul twice quotes

---

44. Gal. 2:16; Phil 3:9.
45. Wright (2009), 112, emphasis in original. The so-called *pistis Christou* debate involves a technical grammatical argument beyond the purposes of this book; see, e.g., Hays (2001) for the argument that the term refers to the "faith *of* Jesus Christ" rather than "faith *in* Jesus Christ." See Campbell (2009) for an extended argument for interpreting it as the *"fidelity of Jesus Christ."* Jewett (2007), 276–77, who, recognizing that the answer could be "both" rather than "either/or," notes laconically, "it seems precarious to erect a theology on the interpretation of a case ending."

Genesis 15:6: "Abraham believed God, and it was reckoned to him as righteousness."[46] The immediate issue is the role of circumcision, a ritual that is not commanded by God until Genesis 17.

Three aspects of Paul's decision to ground his argument in Genesis 15:6 are important. First, Abraham's trust in YHWH comes *before* the initial covenant by which YHWH promises the land of Canaan as the specific expression of the earlier promise at Genesis 13:15. In fact, it comes even before the description at Genesis 15:18–21, where the land is specified as extending "from the river of Egypt to the Great River, the River Euphrates" and including the land of ten peoples already in the land of Canaan. Most discussions highlight Abraham's pre-circumcision trust, but take little notice of the land question.

Second, Abraham is neither "Israelite" nor "Jew," but is rather, a Babylonian called out of empire. Thus, his trust in YHWH stands for all those caught up within empire who trust in the interior Voice of the Creator God rather than the exterior mandates of "divine" kings. This establishes the primal basis for Paul's mission to the nations to become part of the newly redefined communities of the "called out."

Finally, and what is usually the focus of commentators, Abraham's trust in YHWH precedes the giving of the torah (law) through Moses on Mount Sinai. What Paul so adamantly objects to in claiming torah obedience as the basis for the recognition of one's membership in the people of God isn't that it is "legalistic." Rather, in continuity with earlier apocalyptic visionaries such as the authors of *1 Enoch*, Paul sees how torah has become an instrument for collaboration between the Jerusalem temple elite and the series of empires that have dominated God's people since the time of Babylon. In other words, he roots his radical, anti-imperial gospel in the scriptural narrative, beginning with YHWH's first call to "come out." It was Abra(ha)m's trust in this call that establishes his right relationship with the Creator God and launches the journey into a Promised Land free from imperial domination under the lordship of YHWH alone. Abraham thereby becomes the paradigm for those throughout the ages who hear this Word and do it.

That the battle over torah is part of the battle against empire can be seen in another attempt to call upon Abraham's faith, that of the defender of the torah-empire state, Ben Sirach. In his litany of "praise [of] famous men" (Sir. 44–50), he recalls Abraham as one who "kept the law of the Most High, and was taken into covenant with him" (44:20).[47] That is, Sirach reversed the Genesis text to suggest that Abraham was already a faithful torah adherent! Paul, unlike Sirach, takes the Genesis text on its own terms to underscore YHWH's original call out of empire, audible by

---

46. Each major term in the statement, here from the NRSV, has been the subject of intensive scholarly debate; see, e.g., Campbell (2009), 750–52; Jewett (2007), 310–12.

47. Witherington (2004), 49.

anyone anywhere who yearned to live in accordance with the ways of the Creator.

Paul's letter to the Romans emphasizes throughout the interconnectedness between the sinful oppressiveness of human empires and the effects on creation itself. The first chapter of Paul's letter contrasts the truth of the order of the Creator God with "the lie" of empire.[48] We hear this powerful, concise summary of this contrast:

> Ever since the creation [*ktiseōs*] of the world his eternal power and divine nature, invisible though they are, have been understood and seen through the things he has made. So they are without excuse; for though they knew God, they did not honor him as God or give thanks to him, but they became futile in their thinking, and their senseless minds were darkened. Claiming to be wise, they became fools; and they exchanged the glory of the immortal God for images resembling a mortal human being or birds or four-footed animals or reptiles. Therefore God gave them up in the lusts of their hearts to impurity, to the degrading of their bodies among themselves, because they exchanged the truth about God for the lie [*tō pseudei*] and worshiped [*esebasthēsan*] and served the creation [*tē ktisei*] rather than the Creator, who is to be praised forever! Amen. (1:20–25)

It is because of this "exchange of the truth about God for the lie" that the creation itself has been "in bondage" to empire. The word translated "worshiped" is closely related to *sebastos* (in Latin, *augustus*, the title Emperor Octavian took for himself). Robert Jewett notes "Paul's audience could scarcely have missed this allusion to the most prominent form of 'venerating the creature' in Rome."[49]

Creation's hope is that the "revealing [*apokalupsin*] of the children of God" will "set free" creation, which "has been groaning in labor pains until now" along with the children of God (Rom. 8:19–23).[50] In other words, it is the embodiment of the Creator's ways among the followers of Jesus that will put empire to an end and restore creation to its original, sacred state.[51] Paul's imagery anticipates the reversal of the "curse" in Genesis 3. As Jewett observes:

> In this powerful symbolization, humans trying to play God ended up ruining not only their relations with each other but also their relation

---

48. Elliott (2008), 77–83.

49. Jewett (2007), 171.

50. "Children of God" occurs five times in Romans, all in this section (8:14, 16, 19, 21; 9:8). See also Gal. 3:26; Phil. 2:15. It carries a very similar connotation to its use at John 1:12 and 11:52 (cf. 1 John 3:1, 10; 5:2), of people re-created by their withdrawal from empire and commitment to be "born" of God. The only other New Testament uses are Matt. 5:9 and Luke 20:36.

51. Ibid., 510, 512.

to the natural world. The Roman myth system claimed the exact opposite: that a ruler who plays god can restore the world to a paradisiacal condition by his piety and military dominance.... Paul's audience could well have thought about how imperial ambitions, military conflicts, and economic exploitation had led to the erosion of the natural environment throughout the Mediterranean world, leaving ruined cities, depleted fields, deforested mountains, and polluted streams as evidence of this universal human vanity.[52]

In the fulfillment of the religion of creation through the Gospel, however, creation's transformation happens from the bottom up, not the top down. Just as YHWH called a single man, Abram, out of Babylon to begin a process that would be blessing for "the nations," so now that promise reaches its fulfillment in the *ekklēsiai* that consist of the "children of God." Paul's Gospel is thus deeply ecological, linking creation's rebirth with humanity's.

Paul, of course, understands the apocalyptic "birth pangs"[53] to be an expression of the death and resurrection of Jesus, which began the process of undermining empire and revealing the Creator God's eternal reign. As he tells the Corinthian church: "Therefore, if someone in Christ: new creation!" (2 Cor. 5:17).[54] This "new creation" means that those "in Christ" are to live the Gospel of the Creator God in resistance to the way of the gods of empire, including the aspects of religious manifestations of Israel's historic understanding that Paul now can see clearly conflict with that Gospel. As he says to the *ekklēsia* in Rome: "Do not be conformed to this world, but be transformed by the renewing of your minds, so that you may discern what is the will of God — what is good and acceptable and mature [*teleios*]"[55] (Rom. 12:2).

What follows this exhortation is a litany of commands that individually and collectively reveal what this Gospel is to look like in practice. Christians are to see and experience one another as "one body in Christ," using their gifts "according to the grace given" for the sake of the life of the entire *ekklēsia* (cf. 1 Cor. 12, 14). Many commentators have noted how this image, in Romans and in 1 Corinthians, is designed to undermine the prevailing Stoic "fable of the body." As Halvor Moxnes writes, "the purpose of the fable was to make the plebeians repent and to realize that strife was dangerous to all. Thus, the fable was used by the most powerful group with the aim of restoring harmony."[56] Paul's use, in contrast, exhorts each member of the community to "love one another with mutual affection; in regard to honor prefer the others to yourselves."[57] (Rom. 12:10). Such a practice

---

52. Ibid., 513.
53. Romans 8:22, *sunōdinei;* Mark 13:8; 1 Thess. 5:3, *ōdinōn.*
54. There is no verb in the Greek text. Cf. Gal. 6:15.
55. Cf. 1 Cor. 2:6; 13:10; 14:20; Phil. 3:15.
56. Moxnes, 224.
57. Ibid., 225, provides this translation for the second clause of the quotation.

would undermine the hierarchical order upon which the Roman Empire was grounded.

Paul continues with admonitions that resonate with Matthew's Sermon on the Mount: "Bless those who persecute you...do not repay anyone evil for evil...never avenge yourselves...if your enemies are hungry, feed them..." (Rom. 12:14, 17, 19, 20). In other words, Paul's Gospel is far from some "Gnostic redeemer myth" presenting a Christ far removed from the one revealed in the gospels, but harmonizes with the evangelists' narratives. Of course, writing as he was to largely urban audiences, his metaphors often differed from the earthy imagery of Jesus as he is portrayed moving through Palestinian towns and villages. But the anti-imperial way of life into which he formed his *ekklēsiai* is identical to that of Jesus' own teachings.

One important difference, of course, is that Jesus is shown anticipating his death and resurrection, while Paul lives *in* that apocalyptic reality. This enables him to speak of God's victory as an act that puts Jesus Christ in a position of power and authority "above every name" (Phil. 2:9). He is, in direct opposition to the imperial claims for the emperor, the true Lord at whose name "every knee should bend, in heaven and on earth and under the earth" (Phil. 2:10). Peter Oakes writes,

> If Christ has replaced the Emperor as the world's decisive power then we are no longer in the established Graeco-Roman social world. Instead of a world under the high-status man, whose Roman Empire has commanded the hardening of an already stratified Mediterranean society into stone, the world is under a new lord.... One's position in Roman society is not a safe basis for confidence since Roman society is now no longer the social order commanded by one who rules.[58]

Each element of the Philippians "hymn" (Phil. 2:6–11) presents a form of lordship that completely overturns imperial notions of authority.[59] Paul offers it to the *ekklēsia* at Philippi, as he does all his "theology," to provide a model for their own lives: "Let the same mind be in you that was in Christ Jesus" (Phil. 2:5). It is a "mind" that is completely aligned in obedience to the Creator God, and not to any human authority or source of wisdom.

The antithesis between God's wisdom and various prevailing forms of human "wisdom" is a key theme in Paul's first letter to the Corinthians. Paul's message again offers an apocalyptic contrast to both Judean and Greek "wisdom." His purpose is not simply to trump competing worldviews, but to gauge them by the one criterion that matters: the death and resurrection of Jesus. He claims that "none of the rulers of this age understood" the reality of God's wisdom, proven by their crucifixion of "the Lord of glory" (1 Cor. 2:8). The opening chapters of 1 Corinthians relentlessly pound home this contrast, to set up Paul's series of pastoral responses to their

---

58. Oakes (2001), 206.
59. In addition to Oakes (2001), see Wright (2000).

ongoing embodiment of patronage status-seeking in place of the Gospel he
has taught them.

In so doing, he reveals his alignment with the radical anti-temple faction
of Judean thought that we have explored. For example, he tells them that
"*you* are God's temple," a subversive thing to write in the 50s, more than
a decade before the Jerusalem temple's destruction. His recognition of the
radicality of his statement can be heard in his words that follow: "If anyone
destroys God's temple, God will destroy that person. For God's temple is
holy, and you are that temple" (1 Cor. 3:16, 17). Paul knows well that
the Jerusalem temple was the centerpiece of the dominant Judean religion.
Yet his gospel, consistent with *1 Enoch* (and the New Testament gospels),
replaces the building with the human *ekklēsia*.

Paul's anti-Jerusalem temple stance is all the more radical given his perspective that his gospel of the "end of exile" is the fulfillment of the hopes
expressed in Second Isaiah and means the inclusion of the nations among
God's people. Consider, for example, this passage from Romans 10:11–16:

> The Scripture [Isa. 28:16] says, "No one who believes in him will be
> put to shame." For there is no distinction between Judean and Greek
> [as Gal. 3:28; Col. 3:11]; the same Lord is Lord of all and is generous to
> all who call on him. For, "Everyone who calls on the name of the Lord
> shall be saved." But how are they to call on one in whom they have
> not believed? And how are they to believe in one of whom they have
> never heard? And how are they to hear without someone to proclaim
> him? And how are they to proclaim him unless they are sent? As it is
> written [Isa. 52:7], "How beautiful are the feet of those who bring good
> news [*euangelizomenōn*, making the LXX's singular plural]!" But not
> all have obeyed the good news; for Isaiah says [Isa. 53:1], "Lord, who
> has believed our message?"

In 10:17–21, Paul continues with quotes from Psalm 19:4 and Deuteronomy 32:21, completing his argument with Isaiah 65:1–2. Paul interweaves
these texts as part of his explanation to the *ekklēsia* in Rome of why Israel
has not been rejected by God, but is being made "jealous" by the Word's
proclamation to the nations. In the course of his argument, we see how he
moves steadily through Isaiah.[60] Isaiah 52:7 continues, however: " ... who
announces salvation, who says *to Zion*, 'Your God reigns.' " As we saw in
chapter 15, Second Isaiah's call out of Babylonian Exile exhorts its audience to participate in the restoration of Jerusalem and the temple. Paul's
quote specifically omits this reference and those in Isaiah's following verses
to Zion/Jerusalem. This can hardly be an accident, given his quotation in

---

60. See also his use of earlier parts of Isaiah in Romans, e.g., 9:20 (Isa. 29:16; 45:9); 9:27
(10:22–33); 9:29 (1:9); 9:33 (28:16). Cf. Rom. 2:24 (Isa. 52:5); 3:15 (59:7–8).

his own next verse of Isaiah 53:1, just eight verses down in Isaiah's text from 52:7.[61]

Paul's use of Isaiah 53:1 links him with other Second Temple writers, such as Daniel and the New Testament evangelists, who interpreted God's response to the overwhelming injustice of empire in terms of the Suffering Servant. Paul not only sees this in the radical reversal revealed in Jesus' death and resurrection, but also sees himself — and all other Christians — called to continue to embody this stance until empire has completely collapsed. As we noted above, he has "converted" from the tradition of "zeal" manifested in "sacred violence" against enemies to that of suffering service, manifested in love of enemies. As he tells the Corinthian *ekklēsia*, "Be imitators of me, as I am of Christ" (1 Cor. 11:1). This admonition comes at the conclusion of his criticism of the Corinthians for seeking to parade their "freedom" as yet another occasion to gain status advantages over others. Rather, he tells them, "Let no one seek for themselves, but for the other" (1 Cor. 10:24). To imitate Paul who imitates Christ is to become servants to one another, willing to face rejection and persecution in the Roman world. As Isaiah's Servant and Jesus Christ were mocked by the upholders of imperial religion, so will all who choose to walk exclusively in the way of the Creator God.

Of course, for Paul, the essence of this is expressed in the oft-abused word, "love." Together, Paul uses the verb *agapaō* and the noun *agapē* nearly one hundred times.[62] It is the glue that holds together the God-given gifts and manifestations of the Spirit found within the *ekklēsia* (1 Cor. 12–14). As he says to the Galatians, in a close echo to the synoptic Jesus: "the whole law is summed up in a single commandment, 'You shall love your neighbor as yourself'" (Gal. 5:14). It is this individual and communal indwelling love of God that enables the *ekklēsiai* to live in radical opposition to the competitive self-seeking that characterizes the imperial way.

Our discussion of Paul's proclamation of an anti-imperial gospel, in continuity with the Genesis, prophetic and apocalyptic traditions of Israel, would not be complete if we did not at least acknowledge the existence of texts that have been cited as proof of Paul's collaboration with, rather than resistance to, the structures of imperial society. One is Romans 13 and the other is the set of so-called "household codes" calling for familial submission to patriarchal authority (Col. 3:18–22; Eph. 5:22–6:9).

Perhaps by listening to Paul in the order presented here rather than starting with Romans 13 as many do, we can hear that Paul's call for submission "to the governing authorities" is an anomaly rather than the heart of Paul's message. The passage has provoked a huge volume of commentary, perhaps revealing as much about the predispositions of interpreters as about

---

61. For Paul's ways of using Scripture, see Hays (1989).
62. This depends, of course, on which letters one attributes to Pauline authorship. The two words are used a combined 259 times in the New Testament.

Paul's actual intention.[63] We cannot engage Paul's overall theology of "the Powers"[64] nor the specific details of the cultural and narrative contexts of Romans 13. We can say, though, that whatever Paul meant to convey to the Christians at Rome in the 50s, it was *not* a general principle of subservience to imperial authority. How would such a conclusion explain Paul's own repeated resistance to Rome that led to imprisonments, beatings, and likely eventual execution?[65] Furthermore, we've seen how Paul's letters regularly insist on attributing to Jesus titles and authority that his audience would certainly have heard as "plagiarized" from Roman sources. Finally, we have explored how thoroughly Paul's Gospel instilled a worldview and way of life that would have been the opposite of "normal" attitudes and behavior.[66] The most likely explanation of Romans 13 is that it was a message addressed to specific concerns of Roman Christians under Nero.[67] That Paul never says anything like this to any of the other *ekklēsiai* is further evidence that it did not form a plank in his theological foundation.

The "household codes" in Colossians and Ephesians raise similar questions. Many have assumed that these letters do not express the mind of Paul, but rather of someone later seeking to begin the process of conforming Christian behavior to that of the Roman social order.[68] Others have attempted to play down what to our relatively emancipated ears sounds like blatant sexism into "love patriarchalism."[69] Thomas Yoder Neufeld has highlighted Ephesians' sense of "mutual subordination to Christ" between husbands and

---

63. See, e.g., Elliott (1997b) and (2008), 150–57; Jewett (2007), 780–803; Stringfellow (2004a); Winter (2002); Wright (2002).

64. See the landmark trilogy by Walter Wink (1984, 1986, 1992) on the "spirituality of the Powers."

65. Jewett (2007), 789, notes that Rom. 13 must be read in conjunction with Paul's words in the previous chapter: "Do not be conformed to this world, but be transformed by the renewing of your minds." Taubes, 52, observes how Rom. 13:1–7 is misunderstood without taking into account the surrounding verses: "Do not be overcome by evil, but overcome evil with good" (12:21) and "Owe no one anything except to love one another" (13:8).

66. Hardin, 85–147, building on the work of Winter (1994), 123–44, argues that Paul's polemic in Galatia is directed against local opponents who are seeking to have non-"Jewish" converts circumcised to provide legal cover under Roman law, i.e., to have followers of Jesus "pass" as "Jews" who participated in the imperial cult. Paul's passionate, angry resistance to those who would seek to enable public collaboration with Roman cult by Christians seems the opposite of what a broad reading of Rom. 13 would imply; cf. Rev. 2:9; 3:9, which may represent a similar situation in Smyrna and Philadelphia. Cf. Walsh and Keesmaat (2004) for a creative exposition of how Paul's message to the Colossians would have expressed a counter-imperial imperative.

67. Elliott (2008), 155, notes that Paul's statement that the "authority does not bear the sword idly" (13:4) would have challenged head-on Neronian propaganda that asserted that the sword has been "idled" during Nero's reign. Jewett (2007), 794, 803, argues that the passage was an expedient by Paul to garner patronal support for his proposed mission to Spain, while noting "the irony is particularly acute. . . . The mission would have no chance of extending its transformation of the sinful system of honor clear to the end of the known world without giving honor to whomever honor was due." He concludes, "Rom. 13:1–7 has provided the basis for propaganda by which the policies of Mars and Jupiter have frequently been disguised as serving the cause of Christ."

68. See, e.g., Schüssler Fiorenza (1983).

69. Lincoln, 355ff., offers a careful review of the literature on Ephesians.

wives that reorients the issue away from a one-way sense of domination and submission.[70]

Whether one can explain either letter's household code as consistent with Paul's otherwise radical sense of gender equality or must suggest a "reversion" or retreat from this radicality may again be putting too much weight on two brief texts amid Paul's larger written work. It may simply be that socially generated gender roles had not yet appeared to Paul as clearly to be functions of imperial structures of domination as they later came to be understood. But before we criticize Paul for "blindness," we must note how relatively recently our society has grappled with such long-established social roles and assumptions. It is unfair to expect that Paul, working in relative isolation, without the benefit of either generations of thoughtful and prayerful reflection or many "mature" companions in faith, could foresee every counter-imperial implication of his own gospel. It is perhaps ironic that letters written to address specific situations set in time and space have been held up both positively and negatively in the "culture wars" in our own time. I imagine that Paul would have more confidence than commentators sometimes do in the power of the Holy Spirit, present and active in love-based Christian communities throughout the ages, to guide people in such decisions rather than arguing endlessly over details of Paul's rhetoric and grammar.[71]

The larger pattern of Paul's writings and personal witness is clear, even if these few passages seem to muddy the waters. Paul was proposing no Gnostic redeemer myth nor a new religion divorced from his Judean roots. Rather, he was seeking to articulate and to embody what he understood to be an apocalyptic fulfillment of the core biblical message and of the long course of salvation history. The Exile had not truly ended with the coming of the Persians and the building of the second Jerusalem temple. Rather, it was the powerful act of Israel's God in the resurrection of Jesus that overturned an apparent imperial victory and turned it into the final victory of the Creator God's love for all of creation.

---

70. Yoder Neufeld, 279–89.

71. A similar point can be made about Paul's attitude toward "homosexuality." Suffice it to say that (1) Paul *never* addresses the question of mutually loving, voluntary relationships between partners of the same gender; and (2) the few Pauline texts that are enlisted on both sides of current debate must be considered with close attentiveness to the cultural context specific to each letter. For instance, Campbell (2009), 206–7, shows how interpreting Rom. 1:26–27 through the lens of "Justification theory" hopelessly distorts what those verses might actually be trying to convey.

Chapter Twenty-Seven

"Come Out, My People!"
THE BOOK OF REVELATION

Even commentators who resist acknowledging the anti-imperial thrust of the wider New Testament tend to accept that the book of Revelation expresses a vehement and urgent call to Christians to separate themselves from the seductive and beastly nature of the Roman Empire.[1] However, what many still seem to miss is that for John of Patmos — the seer whose apocalyptic vision is presented in the text — *Rome was simply the then-current manifestation of empire itself.*[2] His vision calls his audience in the *ekklēsiai* of the province of Asia to avoid Roman influence not because there is something unusually demonic about this particular empire. Rather, his book reveals the deeper truth: the Roman Empire was but one expression over the ages of "the great city," a biblical phrase referring to the social, political, and economic manifestation of a human system of power apart from the presence and guidance of the Creator God.

One of the great challenges to many readers today in hearing Revelation's radical call to God's people to "come out" of empire is the popular culture "noise" generated by the plethora of "end of the world" or "prophecy" readings not only of Revelation but of the Bible generally.[3] Such efforts do not take seriously the specific cultural contexts of ancient texts. Further, they utterly misread the purpose and function of apocalyptic writing. As we have seen, these narratives are neither predicting "the end of the world" in the sense of the demise of the space-time continuum, nor are they literally describing future events. Apocalyptic literature, from the Enoch tradition through Revelation, expresses a "God's eye" perspective on events "on the ground." This view from "the other side of the veil" is intended to encourage faithful resistance (*hupomenē*)[4] to empire and full trust in the reality of the Creator God's powerful reign.

Earlier apocalyptic texts such as 1 *Enoch* and Daniel offered visions of God's victory over imperial evil confined to the "heavenly" side of the

---

1. E.g., Moore (2006).
2. Much of this chapter draws on the more complete presentation in Howard-Brook and Gwyther.
3. See Howard-Brook and Gwyther, 3–18; see also Rossing.
4. Rev. 1:9; 2:2, 3, 19; 3:10; 13:10; 14:12; It is "translate[d]...correctly as 'resistance' and not 'endurance.' [It] is an active stance, implying engagement in history." Richard, 50.

veil. They inculcated trust in the God whose judgment would bring an end to empire, but did not envision a specific context in which this judgment would become manifest. With New Testament apocalyptic, however, as we've already seen in Paul, this promise has become reality in the death and resurrection of Jesus. John of Patmos's vision reveals how this tangible event has both brought the entire biblical Story to its conclusion and generated, in and through the *ekklēsiai*, "a kingdom and priests serving our God, and they will reign on earth" (Rev. 5:10; cf. Rom. 5:17).

Another struggle many have with Revelation is what appears to be a reversion to the God of violent "holy war" against God's enemies, after Jesus had taught and practiced *love* of enemies. John's vision is undeniably drenched in blood. God's victory over empire does not, in the short term, mean the conclusion of the violence perpetrated throughout the ages by the imperial "beasts." Key to understanding Revelation's portrayal of destruction and violence is its repeated representation of Jesus as the *Lamb*.[5]

The first time we hear Jesus as "Lamb" reveals John of Patmos's understanding of the relationship between "the two religions." John is standing within the heavenly throne room and sees a sealed scroll in the "right hand of the One on the throne." A fruitless search is made for one "worthy to open the scroll and break its seals," leading John to weep bitterly. However, one of the heavenly elders tells him, "Do not weep. See, the Lion of the tribe of Judah, the Root of David, has conquered, so that he can open the scroll and its seven seals" (Rev. 5:5). But when John looks he sees not a Lion but "a Lamb standing as if it had been slaughtered." What John *hears* ("Lion of the tribe of Judah...") expresses the biblical religion of empire, anticipating a warrior messiah who will win God's victory. When he actually *looks*, though, he sees the reality: a Lamb whose own death and resurrection embodies God's victory.[6]

We see this again in Revelation 7, where John *hears* that those sealed as God's servants are twelve thousand from each of the twelve tribes of Israel. This expresses the ethnically exclusive perspective of the Jerusalem elite and its supporters. But when John *looks*, he sees "a great crowd that no one could count, from every nation, from all tribes and peoples and languages" (7:4–9). The reality is not a restored tribal Israel, but a multicultural, multinational, multilinguistic multitude.[7] This vision follows from Third Isaiah and *1 Enoch,* where inclusion among God's people was grounded not in ancestry but in obedience to the Creator God. The religion of creation is again portrayed as triumphant over the religion of empire.

---

5. Only John 1:29, 36, refer to Jesus as "lamb" outside of Revelation, using Greek *amnos,* whereas Revelation always uses *arnion,* itself elsewhere in the New Testament only at John 21:5. There does not appear to be a substantive difference in meaning between these two terms.

6. Cf. Bauckham (1999), 215.

7. Sweet, 150–51.

John's apocalyptic vision of God's defeat of empire through the victory of the Lamb presents a "plot" that unfolds through the story of the two scrolls. The first of these scrolls, as we've seen, is in the hand of God and is sealed with seven seals. Only the crucified and risen Lamb is "worthy" to penetrate the mystery of the scroll, which is the Word of God. Readers are often led astray by equating what emerges from the Lamb's breaking of the seals with divine actions. The images of the "four horsemen" reveal, however, not God's actions, but *the imperial lies that prevent God's Word from being heard and known* by the "inhabitants of the earth."[8] The key to the imagery and thus, to understanding the violence portrayed, is to recognize that the *seals are not the scroll.* The seals express various ways in which empire generally and the Roman Empire in particular cast a "shroud" over the peoples within its influence.[9]

Thus, the violence that is unveiled is the empire's, not God's. Jesus' death and resurrection reveal the lies of imperial propaganda for what they are.

The scroll itself contains a series of seven "trumpet plagues." Each detail of John's imagery takes up elements of Hebrew Scripture.[10] There is indeed much violence in this part of the vision, and, as the "contents" of the scroll, we cannot write it off as the violence of empire. Key is the way the story of the trumpets ends:

The rest of humankind, who were not killed by these plagues:
Did not repent of the works of their hands or give up worshiping
    demons and idols of gold and silver and bronze and stone and
    wood, which cannot see or hear or walk.
And they did not repent of their murders or their sorceries
    [*pharmakōn*] or their fornication [*porneia*] or their thefts.
    (9:20–21)

The parallel phrasing underscores John's message: the outward worship of "the works of their hands" expresses the religious legitimation of the acts of empire.[11] Each of the four actions is shown to be a basic component of how *all* empires work. "Murder" names the violence against enemies by which empire maintains "peace." "Sorceries" are imperial illusions and propaganda by which people become confused about what's real. "Forni-cation" represents the unholy "intercourse" between the Roman elite and the local elite (cf. Rev. 18:9). Finally, "theft" unmasks empire's economic exploitation of the provinces (cf. 18:11–19). All of this is presented as "holy" through the imperial cult and the worship of local deities in support of

---

8. "Inhabitants of the earth" is used to refer to those enthralled to empire, Rev. 3:10; 6:10, 8:13, 11:10, 13:8, 12, 14; 17:2, 8.
9. Cf. Isa. 25:5.
10. For the way Revelation uses the biblical prophets, see Fekkes.
11. Cf. Isa. 2:8; 17:8; Jer. 1:16; 25:6–7; Mic. 5:13; also Ps. 115:3–9.

Table 28: The Seals on the First Scroll

Image	Meaning in Roman Empire	What Is Revealed
White horse, with mounted archer, conquering.	Parthian army, outside the eastern imperial boundary.	Empire does not control all the earth.
Red horse, permitted to "take peace from the earth" so that people "slaughter one another" with "a great sword" (*machaira*).	Civil war and capital punishment against those who resist imperial authority.	Imperial peace is constantly threatened by and threatening violence.
Black horse with scales, and the cry, "A quart of wheat for a day's pay [*denarius*], and three quarts of barley for a day's pay, but do no injustice (*adikēsēs*, au. trans.) to the olive oil and the wine!"	Huge agricultural estates (*latifundia*) run by the elite for profit are in competition with Rome's need to provide basic food to the hungry masses.	Imperial economics cannot provide abundance for all.
Pale green horse, ridden by Death and Hades, with power of sword, famine, and pestilence, and beasts of the earth.	The constant state of violence and suffering that makes up daily imperial life for most people.	God's judgment against empire is experienced in daily life.

Rome's authority.[12] The pattern extends all the way back to the beginning in ancient Babylon.

And yet, the passage ends with the *failure* of repentance. All of God's threats and plagues expressed in the trumpets did not break the imperial pattern that has dominated history. This failure leads immediately to a second scroll (Rev. 10). This one, unlike the first, is *open* and is given to John to "eat." It reveals another road to repentance, with the story of the "two witnesses" (Rev. 11). They are two churches[13] who offer prophetic testimony

---

12. See, e.g., Price, Friesen for how local religious worship in Roman Asia served to support the empire's authority.

13. The image of the witnesses as "two lampstands" (11:4) recalls the opening vision in which the Son of Man stands "in the midst of the lampstands," which are expressly named to be the seven churches to whom John is to write, 1:12–2:1. That there are "two" witnesses does not differentiate two from the seven, but fulfills the biblical requirement for more than one witness to sustain a charge of a violation of God's law, Deut. 19:15.

"in the street of the great city," but the "inhabitants of the earth," embodying the "beast from the abyss," rise up to kill them and then celebrate their
deaths. But the story does not end there: the "breath of life from God entered
them and they stood on their feet" (11:1). This re-creation (echoing Gen.
2:7) leads *some* of the celebrants to "give glory to the God of heaven."

The two scrolls tell the story of the "two religions." In the first scroll,
divine threats of violence fail to bring people to repentance (*metanoia*),
the "different mind" that leads people to "come out" of empire to live in
God's eternal reign. The second scroll tells the counter-story of the communal embodiment of the prophetic Suffering Servant, those followers of the
Lamb who accept violence rather than inflicting it, who speak God's truth
fearlessly regardless of consequences, and who trust in the God of Life to
triumph over death.

In the series of historical names given to "the Great City," John reveals
something that would have been shocking to many at the time, but should
not surprise readers who have followed the story of the two religions
throughout this book. We recall that the "Great City" first appeared in
Genesis 10, built by Nimrod, first warrior-king to face-off against YHWH
in the battle for authority and allegiance.[14] John was told that the "Great
City" was "called in the spirit [*pneumatikos*] Sodom and Egypt, where also
their Lord was crucified" (Rev. 11:8). As G. K. Beale notes, this "shows
that the city is not to be understood in a literal, earthly manner, but figu-
ratively through spiritual eyes.... The city is... any ungodly spiritual realm
on earth."[15] Its equation with traditional Israelite enemies such as Sodom
and Egypt is to be expected, but the "twist" is that the angel applies it to
Jerusalem. Indeed, Jeremiah had done likewise:

> For thus says YHWH concerning the house of the king of Judah: You
> are like Gilead to me, like the summit of Lebanon; but I swear that I
> will make you a desert, an uninhabited city. I will prepare destroyers
> against you, all with their weapons; they shall cut down your choicest
> cedars and cast them into the fire. And many nations will pass by this
> city, and all of them will say one to another, "Why has YHWH dealt
> in this way with that *great city*?" And they will answer, "Because they
> abandoned the covenant of YHWH their God, and worshiped other
> gods and served them." (Jer. 22:6–9)

In other words, when Jerusalem and Judah's royal elite practiced the religion of empire, YHWH treated them the same as any other empire doomed
to fall. John's vision, consistent with the apocalyptic condemnation of Jerusalem in the synoptic gospels, plays no favorites among empires and their

---

14. Its only recurrence other than those mentioned here is in the book of Jonah, where it
refers to Nineveh in the Assyrian Empire.

15. Beale, 592.

collaborators. Condemnation is not limited to foreign empires, nor is salvation limited to tribal Israel. All the "inhabitants of the earth" will be judged equally unless, in Paul's words to the *ekklēsia* at Philippi, they find their "citizenship in heaven" (Phil. 3:20).

John's understanding of these opposing futures is seen powerfully in the portraits of the fallen "whore," the "great city" Babylon and the emerging "bride," the "holy city" New Jerusalem (Rev. 17–18; 21–22; see Table 29). The Bible and related literature contain no starker contrast between the embodiments and fates of the "two religions" than John's picture. Babylon-as-empire is seductress and beast, with whom the "kings of the earth" "fornicate" (*porneia*, Rev. 18:3). It is "the best that money can buy," built on violence, economic exploitation and lies, and collapses because of its own rotten foundation. New Jerusalem-as-God's-kingdom is the bride of the Lamb. It is the pure gift of God. It has no need for temple or an elitist or hierarchical priesthood, for the Creator God is its temple and its citizens are all priests (21:22; cf. 20:6). It is no ascetic monastery, but radiates with the beauty and abundance of God's creation and the purified work of human hands (recalling the wilderness Mishkan, Exod. 25–40).

We are told at the beginning of Revelation that John is directed to address his written vision to seven *ekklēsiai* in the Roman province of Asia. What follows is no promise of pie-in-the-sky-when-you-die, but a spectacular expression of the reality, here and now, of what life in God's reign looks and feels like to those who embrace and live in it. The original recipients of the book were, like Daniel's *maskilim* or *1 Enoch*'s audiences, small communities of resistance that struggled to hold firm to the "eternal gospel" (Rev. 14:6) amid the seductions and threats of the Roman Empire. The "reality" all around them was the Pax Romana, emanating from the "eternal city," which proclaimed the gospel of Caesar.

It took — and continues to take — courage and faith, in short, *hupomenē*, not to give up on the hope of an alternative, a more real "reality" than the one packaged and sold by empire's marketing teams. Only by "coming out" further and further each day, moving steadily into life "in Christ," New Jerusalem, God's kingdom, can one truly know what is real, know who God is, and know how to live as joyous, loving members of God's intimate family.

Table 29: Babylon and New Jerusalem

Babylon	*New Jerusalem*
The Beast (17:3)	The Lamb (21:9 etc.)
The great prostitute (17:1)	The bride (19:7, 21:9)
Both prostitute and city	Both bride and city
Beast destroys Babylon (17:16)	Lamb marries the New Jerusalem (21:2, 9)
The great city (17:18, 18:16, 18:18–19)	The holy city (21:2, 21:10)
Practice of abomination and deception (17:4)	No abomination or deception (21:27)
Blood, murder (18:24)	Life, healing, no death (21:4)
Names not written in scroll (17:8)	Names written in book of life (21:27)
Name of Babylon on forehead (17:5)	Name of God / Lamb on forehead (22:4)
Clothed in scarlet and purple (17:4, 18:16)	Clothed in bright, clean linen (19:8)
All is for sale (18:12–13)	All is a gift (21:6; 22:7)
City an eternal smoking ruin (18:9, 19:3)	City an eternal splendid paradise (22:5)
No lamplight (18:23)	No need of lamplight; Lamb is lamp (21:23)
Wine of prostitution / blood (17:2, 18:3)	Water of life (22:1)
Nations intoxicated (18:3)	Nations healed (22:1)
Nations deceived and corrupted (19:2)	Nations walk in light (21:24)
City appropriates products of nations (18:12–13)	Nations bring glory and honor to city (21:26)
Weeping, wailing, mourning (18:11, 18:15, 18:19)	No tears or sorrow (21:4)
Sea as means of imperial trade (18:17, 18:19)	Sea is no more (21:2)
No more weddings (18:23)	The wedding of the Lamb (19:7)
Fruit is gone (18:14)	Fruit each month (22:2)
Gold, jewels, pearls as seductive (17:4)	Gold, jewels, pearls as constructive (21:11–21)
Seated on many waters (unstable) (17:1)	Built on 12 foundations (stable) (21:14–19)
Fallen (18:2); thrown down (18:21)	Coming down from heaven (21:10)
Foul and hateful birds and beasts (18:2)	Nothing unclean (21:27)
Dwelling of demons (18:2)	God dwells within (21:3)
Come out of her (18:4)	Come to see the bride (21:9)
Wrath of God (19:15)	Glory of God, radiance (21:11)
Babylon rules the kings of the earth (17:18)	God's servants reign over the city (22:5)

Conclusion

Hearing and Responding to God's Call: "Come Out, My People!"

History has made it very challenging to hear how clearly Jesus sided with the "religion of creation" against the "religion of empire." Gradually, the early churches became dominated by non-Israelites. The story of Israel's struggles and hopes for the inbreaking of authentic, divinely gifted world peace and justice became subsumed into more static understandings shaped by Greek philosophy. The biblical sense of the human being as earthly soil suffused with God's Spirit was replaced by a Platonic and Stoic sense of the rational mind reining in the animalistic body. Christian communities in which rich and poor were leveled into a shared abundance morphed back into the dominant structure of Greco-Roman urban life, with wealthy patrons providing handouts and "help" for those "below." A discipleship of equals became a hierarchy of offices and institutional authority. Renunciation of personal property was replaced by renunciation of the body, including the practice of celibacy.

Each of these overlapping changes led to the biggest transformation of all in the fourth century: the adoption of "Christianity" as the religion of the Roman Empire. Of course, the empire did not stop being an empire as a result of Constantine's "conversion" and Theodosius's edict mandating Christianity for all Roman citizens. Thus was born a startling oxymoron that has haunted true discipleship ever since: "imperial Christianity." How this process took place will be the subject of volume 2.

The outcome, of course, has been wars, economic exploitation, and countless varieties of domination "in the name of Jesus." In light of the journey we've made through this book, it should be easy to see that such manifestations could not ever truly be expressions of the Gospel of Jesus Christ. The history of Crusades and Inquisitions, of conquest and pillage under the apparent legitimation of "Christianity," has led to the hideous muddying and polluting of the crystal clear waters of New Jerusalem.

The legacy of this sinful perversion of the Gospel has deeply shaped American history as well. From before the nation's founding, European people on this continent have sought to claim the biblical God, the God of Jesus, for acts of genocide, theft, and environmental destruction. At the same time, there have been countless prophetic witnesses to the true God who have

473

resisted the imperial impulse at the heart of American history. Official narratives of our past tend to silence or diminish these voices, just as the imperial elite sought to silence Jesus and his first followers. We should not be surprised that we must do some digging to uncover the stories of the many holy women and men who dared to speak up and to embody the religion of creation in the Name of Jesus in the face of persecution and death. I hope to continue to tell the story of "the two religions" as they have been manifest in U.S. history in a future book.

We cannot undo history. We can, though, and must, unveil the lies of empire, especially when done in the holy Name of the Creator God, made flesh in Jesus and the people who bear his Name. We must not continue to allow the confusion between the "religion of creation" and the "religion of empire" to justify "Christian" war, racism, exploitation and other practices of domination and exclusion. "Christian" was first used as a pejorative label by the defenders of the imperial status quo to marginalize the followers of Jesus (Acts 11:26). As we hear spoken in the name of Peter:

> Yet if any of you suffers as a Christian, do not consider it a disgrace, but glorify God because you bear this name. For the time has come for judgment to begin with the household of God; if it begins with us, what will be the end for those who do not obey the Gospel of God? ... Therefore, let those suffering in accordance with God's will entrust themselves to a faithful Creator, while continuing to do good. (1 Pet. 4:16–17, 19)

If those of us today who claim the name "Christian" were truly following the Way of Jesus, the "name" would still be an object of reviling and persecution by the citizens of empire (cf. Matt. 5:10–12; John 15:18–16:4). But trusting in the power of the One who made us, who liberated the Israelites, who spoke through the prophets and apocalypticists, and who raised Jesus from the dead, we continue to offer our embodied witness to the reality of God's compassionate love for all people and all creation.

It is not too late to become the church Jesus died and rose to bring into being. Empire is already fallen and condemned. May we, this day, hear God's call to "*Come out, my people!*" and to move ever more completely into the abundant life given as gift by the Creator of us all.

Bibliography

Aberbach, Moses, and Leivy Smolar. "Aaron, Jeroboam, and the Golden Calves." *JBL* 8 (1967): 129–40.

Ackerman, Susan. "The Personal Is Political: Covenantal and Affectionate Love (*'āhēb, 'ahăbâ*) in the Hebrew Bible." *VT* 52, no. 4 (2002): 437–58.

Albertz, Rainer. *A History of Israelite Religion in the Old Testament Period.* Louisville: Westminster John Knox, 1992.

———. *A History of Israelite Religion in the Old Testament Period: From the Exile to the Maccabees.* Louisville: Westminster John Knox, 1994.

———. "The Social Setting of the Aramaic and Hebrew Book of Daniel." In *The Book of Daniel: Composition and Reception.* Vol. 1. Edited John J. Collins and Peter W. Flint, 171–204. Leiden: Brill Academic, 2001.

Alexander, Philip S. "The Evil Empire: The Qumran Eschatological War Cycle and the Origins of Jewish Opposition to Rome." In *Emanuel: Studies in Hebrew Bible, Septuagint, and Dead Sea Scrolls in Honor of Emanuel Tov,* ed. Shalom M. Paul, Robert A. Kraft, Lawrence H. Schiffman, and Weston W. Fields, 17–32. Leiden: Brill, 2003.

Alston, R. "Roman Military Pay from Caesar to Diocletian." *Journal of Roman Studies* 84 (1994): 113–23.

Alter, Robert. *The Art of Biblical Narrative.* New York: Basic Books, 1983.

———. *The Art of Biblical Poetry.* New York: Basic Books, 1987.

———. *Genesis: Translation and Commentary.* New York: W. W. Norton and Co., 1997.

———. *The David Story: A Translation with Commentary of 1 and 2 Samuel.* New York: W. W. Norton, 2000.

———. *The Book of Psalms: A Translation with Commentary.* New York: W. W. Norton, 2007.

Amit, Yairah. "The Sixth Century and the Growth of Hidden Polemics." In *Judah and the Judeans in the Neo-Babylonian Period,* ed. Oded Lipschits and Joseph Blenkinsopp, 135–51. Winona Lake, Ind.: Eisenbrauns, 2003.

Anderson, Benedict. *Imagined Communities: Reflections on the Origin and Spread of Nationalism.* New edition. London: Verso, 2006.

Antonelli, Judith. *In the Image of God: A Feminist Commentary on the Torah.* Lanham, Md.: Jason Aronson, 1997.

Arnold, Clinteon E. "Returning to the Domain of the Powers: *Stoicheia* as Evil Spirits in Galatians 4:3, 9." *NT* 38, no. 1 (1996): 55–76.

Ash, Paul S. "Jeroboam I and the Deuteronomistic Historian's Ideology of the Founder." *CBQ* 60 (1998): 16–24.

Assis, Elie. "To Build or Not to Build: a Dispute between Haggai and His People (Hag 1)." *ZAW* 119, no. 4 (2007): 514–27.

Atkinson, Kenneth. "On the Herodian Origin of Militant Davidic Messianism at Qumran: New Light From Psalm of Solomon 17." *JBL* 118, no. 3 (1999): 435–60.

———. *I Cried to the Lord: A Study of the Psalms of Solomon's Historical Background and Setting.* Leiden: Brill, 2004.

Aufrecht, Walter E., Neil A. Mirau, and Steven W. Gauley, eds. *Urbanism in Antiquity: From Mesopotamia to Crete.* JSOTSupp 244. Sheffield: Sheffield Academic Press, 1997.

Austin, J. L. *How to Do Things with Words.* 2nd ed. Oxford: Oxford University Press, 1976.

Avioz, Michael. "Reconsidering the Composition of the Story of Solomon's Dream at Gibeon (1 Kings 3:4–15)." *JBS* 6, no. 2 (2006): 1–6.

Bailey, Kenneth E. *Poet and Peasant and Through Peasant Eyes: A Literary-Cultural Approach to the Parables in Luke.* Grand Rapids: Eerdmans, 1983.

Bailie, Gil. *Violence Unveiled: Humanity at the Crossroads.* New York: Crossroad, 1995.

Barrack, William D. "The Eschatological Significance of Leviticus 26." *TMSJ* 16, no. 1 (2005): 95–126.

Barré, S.S., Michael L. "Textual and Rhetorical-critical Observations on the Last Servant Song (Isaiah 52:13–53:12)." *CBQ* 62 (2000): 1–27.

Barstad, Hans M. "After the 'Myth of the Empty Land': Major Challenges in the Study of Neo-Babylonian Judah." In *Judah and the Judeans in the Neo-Babylonian Period,* ed. Oded Lipschits and Joseph Blenkinsopp, 3–20. Winona Lake, Ind.: Eisenbrauns, 2003.

Barth, Fredrik, ed. *Ethnic Groups and Boundaries: The Social Organization of Culture Difference.* Prospect Heights, Ill.: Waveland Press, 1969.

———. "Introduction," in *Ethnic Groups and Boundaries: The Social Organization of Culture Difference,* ed. Fredrik Barth, 9–38. Prospect Heights, Ill.: Waveland Press, 1969.

Bar-Yosef, Ofer. "The Natufian Culture in the Levant: Threshold to the Origins of Agriculture." *Evolutionary Anthropology* 6, no. 5 (1998): 159–77.

Bar-Yosef, Ofer, and Richard H. Meadow. "The Origins of Agriculture in the Near East." In *Last Hunters — First Farmers: New Perspectives on the Prehistoric Transition to Agriculture,* ed. T. Douglas Price and Anne Birgitte Gebauer, 39–94. Santa Fe, N.Mex.: School of American Research Press, 1995.

Barzun, Jacques. *From Dawn to Decadence: 500 Years of Western Cultural Life, 1500 to the Present.* New York: HarperPerennial, 2001.

Bauckham, Richard, ed. *The Book of Acts in Its Palestinian Setting.* Grand Rapids: Eerdmans, 1995.

Bauckham, Richard. *2 Peter and Jude.* Word Biblical Commentary 50. Waco: Word Books, 1983.

———. *The Gospels for All Christians: Rethinking the Gospel Audiences.* Grand Rapids: Eerdmans, 1997.

———. *The Climax of Prophecy: Studies on the Book of Revelation.* Edinburgh: T. & T. Clark, 1999.

———. "The Early Jerusalem Church, Qumran, and the Essenes." In *The Dead Sea Scrolls as Background to Postbiblical Judaism and Early Christianity,* ed. James R. Davila, 63–89. Leiden: Brill, 2003.

Baumert, S.J., Norbert. *Woman and Man in Paul: Overcoming a Misunderstanding.* Collegeville, Minn.: Michael Glazier 1996.

Beale, G. K. *The Book of Revelation: A Commentary on the Greek Text.* New International Greek Testament Commentary. Grand Rapids: Eerdmans, 1998.

Bechtel, Lyn. "Rethinking the Interpretation of Genesis 2.4b–3.24." In *A Feminist Companion to Genesis,* ed. Athalya Brenner, 77–117. Sheffield: Sheffield Academic Press, 1993, 1997.

———. "Genesis 19: 1–11." In *Genesis: The Feminist Companion to the Bible.* Feminist Companion to the Bible, second series, ed. Athalya Brenner, 108–28. Sheffield: Sheffield Academic Press, 1999.

Beck, Norman A. *Anti-Roman Cryptograms in the New Testament: Symbolic Messages of Hope and Liberation.* New York: Peter Lang, 1997.

Becker, Adam H., and Annette Yoshiko Reed, eds. *The Ways That Never Parted: Jews and Christians in Late Antiquity and the Early Middle Ages.* Minneapolis: Fortress Press, 2007.

Bedenbender, Andreas. "The Place of the Torah in the Early Enoch Literature." In *The Early Enoch Literature,* ed. Gabriele Boccaccini and John J. Collins, 65–79. Leiden: Brill, 2007.

———. "Seers as Mantic Sages in Jewish Apocalyptic (Daniel and Enoch)." In *Scribes, Sages, and Seers: The Sage in the Eastern Mediterranean World,* ed. Leo G. Perdue, 258–70. Göttingen: Vandenhoeck & Ruprecht, 2008.

Bedford, Peter R. "The Neo-Assyrian Empire." In *The Dynamics of Ancient Empires: State Power from Assyria to Byzantium,* ed. Ian Morris and Walter Scheidel, 30–65. Oxford: Oxford University Press, 2009.

Bellwood, Peter S. *First Farmers: The Origins of Agricultural Societies.* Malden, Mass.: Blackwell Pub., 2005.

Ben Zvi, Ehud. "Who Wrote the Speech of Rabshakeh and When?" *JBL* 109, no. 1 (1990): 79–92.

Benjamin, Don C., and Victor H. Matthews. *Social World of Ancient Israel: 1250–587 BCE.* Peabody: Hendrickson, 2005.

Berger, Peter. *The Sacred Canopy: Elements of a Sociological Theory of Religion.* New York: Anchor, 1990.

Berger, Peter, and Thomas Luckmann. *The Social Construction of Reality: A Treatise in the Sociology of Knowledge.* New York: Anchor, 1967.

Bergsma, John S. "The Relationship between Jubilees and the Early Enoch Books (Astronomical Book and Book of the Watchers)." In *Enoch and the Mosaic Torah: The Evidence of Jubilees,* ed. Gabriele Boccaccini and Giovanni Ibba, 36–51. Grand Rapids: Eerdmans, 2009.

Berquist, Jon L. *Judaism in Persia's Shadow: A Social and Historical Approach.* Minneapolis: Fortress Press, 1995.

———. "Constructions of Identity in Postcolonial Yehud." In *Judah and the Judeans in the Persian Period,* ed. Oded Lipschits and Joseph Blenkinsopp, 53–66. Winona Lake, Ind.: Eisenbrauns, 2006.

———, ed. *Approaching Yehud: New Approaches to the Study of the Persian Period.* Atlanta: Society of Biblical Literature, 2007.

Beyerle, Stefan. "The Book of Daniel and Its Social Setting." In *The Book of Daniel: Composition and Reception.* Vol. 1. Ed. John J. Collins and Peter W. Flint, 205–28. Leiden: Brill Academic, 2002.

Bhabha, Homi K. *Nation and Narration.* Oxford: Routledge, 1990.

————. *The Location of Culture*. Oxford: Routledge, 1994.

Bilby, Kenneth. "Ethnogenesis in the Guianas and Jamaica: Two Maroon Cases." In *History, Power and Identity: Ethnogenesis in the Americas, 1492–1992*, ed. Jonathan D. Hill, 119–41. Iowa City: University of Iowa Press, 1996.

Bilde, Per, et al., eds. *Religion and Religious Practice in the Seleucid Kingdom*. Aarhus, Denmark: Aarhus University Press, 1990.

Birch, Bruce C. *Hosea, Joel, and Amos*. Westminster Bible Companion. Louisville: Westminster John Knox, 1997.

Bledstein, Adrien Janis. "Binder, Trickster, Heel, and Hairy-Man: Re-reading Genesis 27 as a Trickster Tale Told by a Woman." In *A Feminist Companion to Genesis*, ed. Athalya Brenner, 282–95. Sheffield: Sheffield Academic Press, 1993, 1997.

Blenkinsopp, Joseph. *Ezekiel*. Interpretation series. Louisville: Westminster John Knox, 1990.

————. *Sage, Priest, Prophet: Religious and Intellectual Leadership in Ancient Israel*. Library of Ancient Israel. Ed. Douglas A. Knight. Louisville: Westminster John Knox, 1995.

————. "The Judaean Priesthood during the Neo-Babylonian and Achaemenid Periods: A Hypothetical Reconstruction." *CBQ* 60 (1998): 25–43.

————. "Bethel in the Neo-Babylonian Period." In *Judah and the Judeans in the Neo-Babylonian Period*, ed. Oded Lipschits and Joseph Blenkinsopp, 93–107. Winona Lake, Ind.: Eisenbrauns, 2003.

————. *Judaism, the First Phase: The Place of Ezra and Nehemiah in the Origins of Judaism*. Grand Rapids: Eerdmans, 2009.

Blenkinsopp, Joseph, John J. Collins, Carol Meyers, and Leo G. Perdue, eds. *Families in Ancient Israel*. Family, Religion, and Culture. Louisville: Westminster John Knox, 1997.

Bloch-Smith, Elizabeth. "Israelite Ethnicity in Iron I: Archaeology Preserves What Is Remembered and What Is Forgotten in Israel's History." *JBL* 122, no. 3 (2003): 401–25.

Blount, Brian K., Cain Hope Felder, Clarice J. Martin, Emerson B. Powery, eds. *True to Our Native Land: An African American New Testament Commentary*. Minneapolis: Fortress Press, 2007.

Boccaccini, Gabriele. *Beyond the Essene Hypothesis: The Parting of the Ways between Qumran and Enochic Judaism*. Grand Rapids: Eerdmans, 1998.

————. *Roots of Rabbinic Judaism: An Intellectual History, from Ezekiel to Daniel*. Grand Rapids: Eerdmans, 2002.

————. "Response to Nickelsburg, 'The Epistle of Enoch and the Qumran Literature.'" In *George W. E. Nickelsburg in Perspective: An Ongoing Dialogue of Learning*. Vol. 1. Ed. Jacob Neusner and Alan J. Avery-Peck, 123–32. Leiden: Brill, 2003.

————, ed. *Enoch and Qumran Origins: New Light on a Forgotten Connection*. Grand Rapids: Eerdmans, 2005.

————, ed. *Enoch and the Messiah Son of Man: Revisiting the Book of Parables*. Grand Rapids: Eerdmans, 2007.

————. "Finding a Place for the Parables of Enoch within Second Temple Jewish Literature." In *Enoch and the Messiah Son of Man: Revisiting the Book of Parables*, ed. Gabriele, Boccaccini, 263–89. Grand Rapids: Eerdmans, 2007a.

Boccaccini, Gabriele, and Giovanni Ibba, eds. *Enoch and the Mosaic Torah: The Evidence of Jubilees*. Grand Rapids: Eerdmans, 2009.

Boccaccini, Gabriele, and John J. Collins, eds. *The Early Enoch Literature*. Leiden: Brill, 2007.

Boda, Mark J. "Oil, Crowns and Thrones: Prophet, Priest, and King in Zechariah 1:7–6:15." *JHS* 3 (2000–2001), accessed via *http://ra.tapor.ualberta.ca/cocoon/JHS/a022.html*.

———. "Terrifying the Horns: Persia and Babylon in Zechariah 1:7–6:15." *CBQ* 67 (2005): 22–41.

———. Review. "Diana Edelman, The Origins of the Second Temple: Persian Imperial Policy and the Rebuilding of Jerusalem." *JHS* 7 (2007), accessed via *www.arts.ualberta.ca/JHS/reviews/review268.htm*.

Bodley, John H. *Victims of Progress*. 3rd ed. Mountain View, Calif.: Mayfield, 1990.

Borg, Marcus J., and N. T. Wright. *The Meaning of Jesus: Two Visions*. San Francisco: HarperOne, 2000.

Boyarin, Daniel. *Intertextuality and the Reading of Midrash*. Bloomington: Indiana University Press, 1994a.

———. *A Radical Jew: Paul and the Politics of Identity*. Berkeley and Los Angeles: University of California Press, 1994b.

———. *Border Lines: The Partition of Judaeo-Christianity*. Philadelphia: University of Pennsylvania Press, 2006.

Boyd, Brian. "Agency and Landscape: Abandoning the 'Nature / Culture' Dichotomy in Interpretations of the Natufian and the Transition to the Neolithic." In *The Last Hunter-Gatherers in the Near East*. BAR International Series 1320. Ed. Christopher Delage, 119–36. Oxford: Hadrian Books, 2004.

Brenner, Athalya, ed. *A Feminist Companion to Genesis*. Sheffield: Sheffield Academic Press, 1993, 1997.

———. *Genesis: The Feminist Companion to the Bible*. Feminist Companion to the Bible, 1. Sheffield: Sheffield Academic Press, 1999.

Brett, Mark G., ed. *Genesis: Procreation and the Politics of Identity*. New York: Routledge, 2000.

———. "Earthing the Human in Genesis 1–3." In *Earth Story in Genesis*. The Earth Bible Series. Ed. Normal C. Habel and Shirley Wurst, 73–86. Cleveland: Pilgrim Press, 2001.

———. *Ethnicity and the Bible*. Boston: Brill Academic, 2002a.

———. "Interpreting Ethnicity: Method, Hermeneutics, Ethics." In *Ethnicity and the Bible*, ed. Mark G. Brett, 3–22. Boston: Brill Academic, 2002b.

Brettler, Mark. *The Book of Judges*. Old Testament Readings. New York: Routledge, 2001.

Briant, Pierre. "The Seleucid Kingdom, the Achaemenid Empire, and the History of the Near East in the First Millenium BC." In *Religion and Religious Practice in the Seleucid Kingdom*, ed. Per Bilde et al., 40–65. Aarhus, Denmark: Aarhus University Press, 1990.

Brown, Raymond. *The Birth of the Messiah: A Commentary on the Infancy Narratives in the Gospels of Matthew and Luke*. Anchor Yale Bible Reference Library. Updated edition. New Haven, Conn.: Yale, 1999.

Brown, Peter. *The Cult of the Saints: Its Rise and Function in Latin Christianity*. Chicago: University of Chicago Press, 1982.

———. *The Body of Society: Men, Women, and Sexual Renunciation in Early Christianity*. New York: Columbia University Press, 1988.

Browne, Nick, ed. *Francis Ford Coppola's The Godfather Trilogy.* Cambridge Film Handbooks. Cambridge: Cambridge University Press, 1999.

Brueggemann, Walter. *Genesis.* Interpretation: A Bible Commentary for Teaching and Preaching. Louisville: Westminster John Knox, 1982.

———. *Israel's Praise: Doxology Against Idolatry and Ideology.* Minneapolis: Fortress Press, 1988.

———. *First and Second Samuel.* Interpretation: A Bible Commentary for Teaching and Preaching. Louisville: Westminster John Knox Press, 1990a.

———. "The Social Significance of Solomon as a Patron of Wisdom." In *The Sage in Israel and the Ancient Near East,* ed. John G. Gammie and Leo G. Purdue, 117–32. Winona Lake, Ind.: Eisenbrauns, 1990b.

———. "At the Mercy of Babylon: A Subversive Rereading of the Empire" *JBL* 110, no. 1 (1991): 3–22.

———. "The 'Baruch Connection': Reflections on Jeremiah 43:1–7." *JBL* 113, no. 3 (1994a): 405–20.

———. *A Social Reading of the Old Testament.* Minneapolis: Fortress Press, 1994b.

———. *A Commentary on Jeremiah: Exile and Homecoming.* Grand Rapids: Eerdmans, 1998.

———. *Deuteronomy.* Abingdon Old Testament Commentaries. Nashville: Abingdon, 2001a.

———. *The Prophetic Imagination.* 2nd ed. Minneapolis: Fortress Press, 2001b.

———. *An Introduction to the Old Testament: The Canon and Christian Imagination.* Louisville: Westminster John Knox, 2003.

Brunt, P. A. "Laus Imperii." In *Imperialism in the Ancient World,* ed. P. D. A. Garnsey and C. B. Whittaker, 159–91. Cambridge: Cambridge University Press, 1978.

Bryan, Christopher. *Render to Caesar: Jesus, the Early Church, and the Roman Superpower.* Oxford: Oxford University Press, 2005.

Buell, Denise Kimber, and Caroline Johnson Hodge. "The Politics of Interpretation: The Rhetoric of Race and Ethnicity in Paul." *JBL* 123, no. 2 (2004): 235–51.

Bultmann, Rudolf. *Theology of the New Testament.* New York: Scribner, 1951.

Butler, Smedley D. *War Is a Racket.* Port Townsend, Wash.: Feral House, 2003.

Byrd, Brian F. "Reassessing the Emergence of Village Life in the Near East." *JAR* 13, no. 3 (2005): 231–90.

Callahan, Allen Dwight. *The Talking Book: African Americans and the Bible.* New Haven, Conn.: Yale University Press, 2008.

Callender, Jr., Dexter E. *Adam in Myth and History: Ancient Israelite Perspectives on the Primal Human.* Winona Lake, Ind.: Eisenbrauns, 2000.

Campbell, Douglass A. *The Deliverance of God: An Apocalyptic Rereading of Justification in Paul.* Grand Rapids: Eerdmans, 2009.

Capper, Brian, J. "The New Covenant in Southern Palestine at the Arrest of Jesus." In *The Dead Sea Scrolls as Background to Postbiblical Judaism and Early Christianity,* ed. James R. Davila, 90–116. Leiden: Brill, 2003.

Cardenal, Ernesto. *The Gospel in Solentiname.* Vol. 1. Maryknoll, N.Y.: Orbis Books, 1982.

Carr, David M. "The Politics of Textual Subversion: A Diachronic Perspective on The Garden of Eden Story." *JBL* 112, no. 4 (1993): 577–95.

———. *The Erotic Word: Sexuality, Spirituality, and the Bible.* Oxford: Oxford University Press, 2002.

―――. *Writing on the Tablet of the Heart: Origins of Scripture and Literature.* Oxford: Oxford University Press, 2005.

Carter, Warren. *Matthew and the Margins: A Sociopolitical and Religious Reading.* Maryknoll, N.Y.: Orbis Books, 2000.

―――. *Matthew and Empire: Initial Explorations.* Harrisburg, Pa.: Trinity Press International, 2001a.

―――. *John and Empire: Initial Explorations.* Harrisburg, Pa.: Trinity Press International, 2001b.

―――. "Resisting and Imitating the Empire: Imperial Paradigms in Two Matthean Parables." *Int* 56, no. 3 (2002): 260–72.

―――. "Are There Imperial Texts in the Class? Intertextual Eagles and Matthean Eschatology as 'Lights Out' Time for Imperial Rome." *JBL* 122, no. 3 (2003): 467–87.

―――. "Matthean Christology in Roman Imperial Key: Matthew 1:1." In *The Gospel of Matthew in Its Roman Imperial Context,* ed. John Riches and David C. Sim, 143–65. New York and London: T. & T. Clark, 2005.

―――. "Matthew's Gospel: An Anti-Imperial / Imperial Reading." *CTM* 34, no. 6 (2007): 424–33.

―――. *John and Empire: Initial Explorations.* Edinburgh: T. & T. Clark, 2008.

Casey, P. M. "Porphyry and the Origin of the Book of Daniel." *JTS* 27 (1976): 15–33.

Cassidy, Richard J. *Jesus, Politics, and Society: A Study of Luke's Gospel.* Maryknoll, N.Y.: Orbis Books, 1978.

―――. *Society and Politics in the Acts of the Apostles.* Maryknoll, N.Y.: Orbis Books, 1987.

―――. *Christians and Roman Rule in the New Testament.* New York: Crossroad, 2001.

Cassuto, Umberto. *A Commentary on the Book of Genesis.* Translated from the Hebrew by Israel Abrahams. 2 vols. Jerusalem: Magnes Press, Hebrew University, 1961–64.

Castelli, Elizabeth A. *Imitating Paul: A Discourse of Power.* Louisville: Westminster John Knox, 1991.

Cayley, David. *Ivan Illich in Conversation.* Toronto: Anasi, 1992.

Ceresko, O.S.F.S., Anthony R. "The Rhetorical Strategy of the Fourth Servant Song (Isaiah 52:13–53:12): Poetry and the Exodus–New Exodus." *CBQ* 56, no. 1 (1994): 42–55.

Champlin, Edward. *Nero.* Cambridge, Mass.: Harvard University Press, 2003.

Chaney, Marvin L. "Ancient Palestinian Peasant Movements and the Formation of Premonarchic Israel." In *Palestine in Transition: The Emergence of Ancient Israel,* ed. David Noel Freedman and David Frank Graf, 39–94. Sheffield: Almond Press, 1983.

―――. "Systemic Study of the Israelite Monarchy." *Semeia* 37, no. 1 (1986): 53–76.

Charlesworth, James H. *The Old Testament Pseudepigrapha.* Vol. 1. The Anchor Yale Bible Reference Library. New Haven, Conn.: Yale University Press, 1983.

―――. *The Old Testament Pseudepigrapha.* Vol. 2. The Anchor Yale Bible Reference Library. New Haven, Conn.: Yale University Press, 1985.

―――. "Can We Discern the Composition Date of the Parables of Enoch?" In *Enoch and the Messiah Son of Man: Revisiting the Book of Parables,* ed. Gabriele Boccaccini, 450–68. Grand Rapids: Eerdmans, 2007.

Chialà, Sabino. "The Son of Man: The Evolution of an Expression." In *Enoch and the Messiah Son of Man: Revisiting the Book of Parables,* ed. Gabriele Boccaccini, 153–78. Grand Rapids: Eerdmans, 2007.

Chow, John K. "Patronage in Roman Corinth." In *Paul and Empire: Religion and Power in Roman Imperial Society,* ed. Richard A. Horsley, 104–25. Philadelphia: Trinity Press International, 1997.

Clark Wire, Antoinette. *The Corinthian Women Prophets: A Reconstruction through Paul's Rhetoric.* Minneapolis: Fortress Press, 1995.

Coggins, Richard J. "Do We Still Need Deutero-Isaiah?" *JSOT* 80 (1998): 77–92.

Cohen, Mark Nathan. *Health and the Rise of Civilization.* New Haven: Yale University Press, 1991.

Cohen, Shaye J. D. "The Significance of Yavneh: Pharisees, Rabbis, and the End of Jewish Sectarianism." *HUCA* 55 (1984): 27–53.

———. *The Beginnings of Jewishness: Boundaries, Varieties, Uncertainties.* Berkeley: University of California Press, 2001.

———. *From the Maccabees to the Mishnah.* 2nd ed. Louisville: Westminster John Knox, 2006.

Cohn, Norman. *Cosmos, Chaos, and the World to Come: The Ancient Roots of Apocalyptic Faith.* New Haven, Conn.: Yale University, 1995.

Collins, John J. *Daniel, First Maccabees, Second Maccabees, With an Excursus on the Apocalyptic Genre.* New York: Michael Glazier, 1982.

———. *Daniel.* Hermeneia. Minneapolis: Fortress Press, 1994.

———. *The Scepter and the Star.* Anchor Bible Reference. New York: Doubleday, 1995.

———. *Jewish Wisdom in the Hellenistic Age.* OTL. Louisville: Westminster John Knox, 1997a.

———. *Apocalypticism in the Dead Sea Scrolls.* London and New York: Routledge, 1997b.

———. *The Apocalyptic Imagination: An Introduction to the Jewish Matrix of Christianity.* 2nd ed. New York: Crossroad, 1998.

———. *Between Athens and Jerusalem: Jewish Identity in the Hellenistic Diaspora.* 2nd ed. Grand Rapids: Eerdmans, 1999.

———. "Forms of Community in the Dead Sea Scrolls." In *Emanuel: Studies in Hebrew Bible, Septuagint, and Dead Sea Scrolls in Honor of Emanuel Tov,* ed. Shalom M. Paul, Robert A. Kraft, Lawrence H. Schiffman and Weston W. Fields, 97–122. Leiden: Brill, 2003.

———. "Response: The Apocalyptic Worldview of Daniel." In *Enoch and Qumran Origins: New Light on a Forgotten Connection,* ed. Gabriele Boccaccini, 59–66. Grand Rapids: Eerdmans, 2005a.

———. *Jewish Cult and Hellenistic Culture: Essays on the Jewish Encounter with Hellenism and Roman Rule.* Leiden: Brill, 2005b.

Collins, John J., and Peter W. Flint, eds. *The Book of Daniel: Composition and Reception.* Vol. 1. Leiden: Brill Academic, 2002.

Cone, James H. *A Black Theology of Liberation.* Maryknoll, N.Y.: Orbis Books, 1970.

Cook, Stephen L. *Prophecy and Apocalypticism.* Minneapolis: Fortress Press, 1995a.

———. "Innerbiblical Interpretation in Ezekiel 44 and the History of Israel's Priesthood." *JBL* 114, no. 2 (1995b): 193–208.

———. *The Social Roots of Biblical Yahwism.* Atlanta: SBL, 2004.

Coover Cox, Dorian G. "The Hardening of Pharaoh's Heart in Its Literary and Cultural Contexts." *Bibliotheca Sacra* 163, no. 651 (2006): 292–311.

Cornell, Stephen. "That's the Story of Our Life." In *We Are a People: Narrative and Multiplicity in Constructing Ethnic Identity*, ed. Paul Spickard and W. Jeffrey Burroughs, 41–53. Philadelphia: Temple University Press, 2000a.

———. "Discovered Identities and American Indian Supratribalism." In *We Are a People: Narrative and Multiplicity in Constructing Ethnic Identity*, ed. Paul Spickard and W. Jeffrey Burroughs, 98–123. Philadelphia: Temple University Press, 2000b.

Cox, Harvey. "The Market as God: Living in the New Dispensation." *Atlantic Monthly* 99, no. 3 (1999): 18–23; online at *www.theatlantic.com/issues/99mar/marketgod.htm*.

Crawford, Sidnie White. *The Temple Scroll and Related Texts*. Companion to the Qumran Scrolls. Sheffield: Sheffield Academic Press, 2000.

———. *Rewriting Scripture in Second Temple Times*. Studies in the Dead Sea Scrolls and Related Literature. Grand Rapids: Eerdmans, 2008.

Crenshaw, James L. *Old Testament Wisdom: An Introduction*. Louisville: John Knox, 1981.

Croatto, J. Severino. "A Reading of the Story of the Tower of Babel from a Perspective of Non-Identity: Gen. 11:1–9 in the Context of Its Production." In *Teaching the Bible: The Discourses and Politics of Biblical Pedagogy*, ed. Fernando F. Segovia and Mary Ann Tolbert, 203–23. Maryknoll, N.Y.: Orbis Books, 1996.

Crosby, Michael H. *House of Disciples: Church, Economics, and Justice in Matthew*. Eugene: Wipf and Stock, 2004.

Cross, Frank Moore. *Canaanite Myth and Hebrew Epic*. Cambridge: Harvard University Press, 1973.

———. *From Epic to Canon: History and Literature in Ancient Israel*. Baltimore: Johns Hopkins University Press, 1998.

Crossan, John Dominic. *The Historical Jesus: The Life of a Mediterranean Jewish Peasant*. San Francisco: HarperOne, 1993.

———. *God and Empire: Jesus against Rome, Then and Now*. San Francisco: HarperOne, 2008.

Cushman, Beverly. "The Politics of the Royal Harem and the Case of Bat-Sheba." *JSOT* 30, no. 3 (2006): 327–43.

Davies, Philip. *In Search of "Ancient Israel."* Sheffield: Sheffield Academic Press, 1995.

———. *Scribes and Schools: The Canonization of the Hebrew Scriptures*. Library of Ancient Israel. Ed. Douglas A. Knight. Louisville: Westminster John Knox, 1998.

Davies, W. D., and Dale C. Allison, Jr. *A Critical and Exegetical Commentary on the Gospel according to Saint Matthew*. 3 vols. Edinburgh: T. & T. Clark, 1989, 1991, 1997.

Davila, James R., ed. *The Dead Sea Scrolls as Background to Postbiblical Judaism and Early Christianity*. Leiden: Brill, 2003.

Davis, Ellen F. *Proverbs, Ecclesiastes, and the Song of Songs*. Westminster Bible Companion. Louisville: Westminster John Knox, 2000.

Davis, Ellen F., and Richard B. Hays, eds. *The Art of Reading Scripture*. Grand Rapids: Eerdmans, 2003.

Dawkins, Richard. *The God Delusion*. New York: Houghton Mifflin, 2006.

Dearman, J. Andrew. "My Servants the Scribes: Composition and Context in Jeremiah 36." *JBL* 109, no. 3 (1990): 403–21.

De Boer, Martinus C. "The Meaning of the Phrase τὰ στοιχεῖα τοῦ κόσμου in Galatians." *NTS* 53 (2007): 204–24.

Delage, Christopher, ed. *The Last Hunter-Gatherers in the Near East.* BAR International Series 1320. Oxford: Hadrian Books, 2004.

De Lange, N. R. M. "Jewish Attitudes to the Roman Empire." In *Imperialism in the Ancient World,* ed. P. D. A. Garnsey and C. B. Whittaker, 255–81. Cambridge: Cambridge University Press, 1978.

Dell, Katherine. "Scribes, Sages and Seers in the First Temple." In *Scribes, Sages and Seers: The Sage in the Eastern Mediterranean World,* ed. Leo G. Perdue, 125–44. Göttingen: Vandenhoeck & Ruprecht, 2008.

Dempsey, Carol J. "Micah 2–3: Literary Artistry, Ethical Message, and Some Considerations about the Image of Yahweh and Micah." *JSOT* 85 (1999): 117–28.

DeSilva, David A. *Honor, Patronage, Kinship, and Purity: Unlocking New Testament Culture.* Downers Grove, Ill.: Intervarsity, 2000.

Dever, William. "Archaeology, Urbanism, and the Rise of the Israelite State." In *Urbanism in Antiquity: From Mesopotamia to Crete,* ed. Walter E. Aufrecht, Neil A. Mirau, and Steven W. Gauley, 172–93. JSOTSS 244. Sheffield: Sheffield Academic Press, 1997.

———. *Who Were the Early Israelites and Where Did They Come From?* Grand Rapids: Eerdmans, 2006.

Dever, William G., and Seymour Gitin, eds. *Symbiosis, Symbolism, and the Power of the Past: Canaan, Ancient Israel, and Their Neighbors from the Late Bronze Age through Roman Palestina.* Winona Lake, Ind.: Eisenbrauns, 2003.

Diamant, Anita. *The Red Tent.* New York: Picador, 1998.

Dietrich, Jeff. "Looking for Jesus in All the Wrong Places." *Catholic Agitator* 33, no. 8 (2003): 4–5.

———. "The Annunciation to Mary and the Silence of the Patriarchs from A to Z." *Catholic Agitator* 34, no. 7 (2004): 1–2.

Dodson, Derek S. "Dreams, the Ancient Novels, and the Gospel of Matthew: An Intertextual Study." *PRSt* 29, no. 1 (2002): 39–52.

Doob Sakenfeld, Katharine. *Ruth.* Interpretation. Louisville: Westminster John Knox, 1999.

Douglas, Mary. *Jacob's Tears: The Priestly Work of Reconciliation.* Oxford: Oxford University Press, 2004.

Douglass, James. *JFK and the Unspeakable: Why He Died and Why It Matters.* Maryknoll, N.Y.: Orbis Books, 2008.

Duff, Paul B. "The March of the Divine Warrior and the Advent of the Greco-Roman King: Mark's Account of Jesus' Entry into Jerusalem." *JBL* 111, no. 1 (1992): 55–71.

Duncan-Jones, Richard. *Structure and Scale in the Roman Economy.* Cambridge: Cambridge University Press, 1990.

———. *Money and Government in the Roman Empire.* Cambridge: Cambridge University Press, 1994.

Duncan, David Ewing. *Calendar: Humanity's Epic Struggle to Determine a True and Accurate Year.* New York: Avon, 1998.

Dungan, David L. *Constantine's Bible: Politics and the Making of the New Testament*. Minneapolis: Fortress Press, 2006.

Dutcher-Walls, Patricia. "The Social Location of the Deuteronomists: A Sociological Study of Factional Politics in Late Pre-Exilic Judah." *JSOT* 52 (1991): 77–94.

———. *Narrative Art, Political Rhetoric: The Case of Athaliah and Joash*. JSOTSS 209. Sheffield: Sheffield Academic Press, 1996.

———. "The Circumscription of the King: Deuteronomy 17:16–17 in Its Ancient Social Context." *JBL* 121, no. 4 (2002): 601–16.

———. *Jezebel: Portraits of a Queen*. Collegeville, Minn.: Liturgical Press, 2004.

Dyck, Jonathan E. "The Ideology of Identity in Chronicles." In *Ethnicity and the Bible*, ed. Mark G. Brett, 89–116. Boston: Brill Academic, 2002.

Dykstra, Laurel. *Set Them Free: The Other Side of Exodus*. Maryknoll, N.Y.: Orbis Books, 2002.

Edelman, Diana. "Ethnicity and Early Israel." In *Ethnicity and the Bible*, ed. Mark G. Brett, 25–55. Boston: Brill Academic, 2002.

———. *The Origins of the "Second" Temple: Persian Imperial Policy and the Rebuilding of Jerusalem*. London: Equinox Publishing, 2005.

Ehrman, Bart. *Jesus, Interrupted: Revealing the Hidden Contradictions in the Bible (And Why We Don't Know about Them)*. New York: HarperCollins, 2009.

Eisenbaum, Pamela. "Paul as the New Abraham." In *Paul and Politics: Ekklesia, Israel, Imperium, Interpretation*, ed. Richard A. Horsley, 130–45. Harrisburg, Pa.: Trinity Press International, 2000.

———. "A Remedy for Having Been Born of Woman: Jesus, Gentiles, and Genealogy in Romans." *JBL* 123, no. 4 (2004): 671–702.

Eisenberg, Evan. *The Ecology of Eden: An Inquiry into the Dream of Paradise and a New Vision of Our Role in Nature*. New York: Vintage, 1999.

Ekblad, Bob. *Reading the Bible with the Damned*. Louisville: Westminster John Knox, 2005.

Ekblad, Eugene Robert. *Isaiah's Servant Poems According to the Septuagint: An Exegetical and Theological Study*. Leuven: Peeters, 1999.

———. *A New Christian Manifesto: Pledging Allegiance to the Kingdom of God*. Louisville: Westminster John Knox, 2008.

Elliott, Mark Adam. *The Survivors of Israel: A Reconsideration of the Theology of Pre-Christian Judaism*. Grand Rapids: Eerdmans, 2000.

Elliott, Neil. *Liberating Paul: The Justice of God and the Politics of the Apostle*. Maryknoll, N.Y.: Orbis Books, 1994.

———. "The Anti-Imperial Message of the Cross." In *Paul and Empire: Religion and Power in Roman Imperial Society*, ed. Richard A. Horsley, 167–83. Philadelphia: Trinity Press International, 1997a.

———. "Romans 13:1–7 in the Context of Imperial Propaganda." In *Paul and Empire: Religion and Power in Roman Imperial Society*, ed. Richard A. Horsley, 184–205. Philadelphia: Trinity Press International, 1997b.

———. "Paul and the Politics of Empire: Problems and Prospects." In *Paul and Politics: Ekklesia, Israel, Imperium, Interpretation*, ed. Richard A. Horsley, 17–39. Harrisburg, Pa.: Trinity Press International, 2000.

———. "The Apostle Paul's Self-Presentation as Anti-Imperial Performance." In *Paul and the Roman Imperial Order*, ed. Richard A. Horsley, 67–88. Harrisburg, Pa.: Trinity Press International, 2004.

————. *The Arrogance of Nations: Reading Romans in the Shadow of Empire.* Minneapolis: Fortress Press, 2008.

Ellsberg, Robert, ed. *Dorothy Day: Selected Writings.* Maryknoll, N.Y.: Orbis, 2005.

Ellul, Jacques. *The Technological Society.* New York: Vintage, 1967.

————. *The Meaning of the City.* Grand Rapids: Eerdmans, 1970.

————. *Anarchy and Christianity.* Grand Rapids: Eerdmans, 1988.

————. *Reading for Being: A Meditation on Ecclesiastes.* Grand Rapids: Eerdmans, 1990.

Emberling, Geoff. "Ethnicity in Complex Societies: Archaeological Perspectives." *J. Arch. Research 5,* no. 4 (1997): 295–344.

Embry, Brad. "The Psalms of Solomon and the New Testament: Intertextuality and the Need for a Re-Evaluation." *JSP* 13, no. 2 (2002): 99–136.

Endres, John C. *Biblical Interpretation in the Book of Jubilees.* Washington, D.C.: Catholic Biblical Association of America, 1987.

Engberg-Pedersen, Troels, ed. *Paul in His Hellenistic Context.* Minneapolis: Fortress Press, 1999.

Eskenazi, Tamara Cohn. *In an Age of Prose: A Literary Approach to Ezra-Nehemiah.* SBLMS 36. Atlanta: Scholars Press, 1988.

————. "The Missions of Ezra and Nehemiah." In *Judah and the Judeans in the Persian Period,* ed. Oded Lipschits and Joseph Blenkinsopp, 509–29. Winona Lake, Ind.: Eisenbrauns, 2006.

Eskenazi, Tamara C., and Kent H. Richards, ed. *Second Temple Studies.* Vol. 2: *Temple and Community in the Persian Period.* JSOTSS 175. Sheffield: JSOT Press, 1994.

Eskenazi, Tamara C., and Eleanore P. Judd. "Marriage to a Stranger in Ezra 9–10." In *Second Temple Studies.* Vol. 2: *Temple and Community in the Persian Period.* JSOTSS 175. Ed. Tamara C. Eskenazi and Kent H. Richards, 266–85. Sheffield: JSOT Press, 1994.

Eslinger, Lyle. "Viewpoints and Point of View in 1 Samuel 8–12." *JSOT* 26 (1983): 61–76.

Evans, Craig A. "Mark's Incipit and the Priene Calendar Inscription: From Jewish Gospel to Greco-Roman Gospel." *Journal of Greco-Roman Christianity and Judaism* 1 (2004): 67–81.

Faust, Avraham. "The Rural Community in Ancient Israel during Iron Age II." *BASOR* 317 (2000): 17–39.

————. *Israel's Ethnogenesis: Settlement, Interaction, Expansion, and Resistance.* London: Equinox: 2007.

Fekkes III, Jan. "Isaiah and the Book of Revelation: John the Prophet as a Fourth Isaiah?" In *"As Those Who Are Taught": The Interpretation of Isaiah from the LXX to the SBL,* ed. Claire Matthews McGinnis and Patricia K. Tull, 125–44. Atlanta: Society of Biblical Literature, 2006.

Felder, Cain Hope. *Stony the Road We Trod: African American Biblical Interpretation.* Minneapolis: Fortress Press, 1991.

Ferguson, John. "Classical Civilization." In *Propaganda and Communication in World History.* Vol. 1: *The Symbolic Instrument in Early Times,* ed. Harold D. Lasswell, Daniel Lerner, and Hans Speier, 257–98. Honolulu: East-West Center, University of Hawaii, 1979.

Fewell, Danna Nolan. *Circle of Sovereignty: Plotting Politics in the Book of Daniel.* Nashville: Abingdon, 1991.

————. *Reading between Texts: Intertextuality and the Hebrew Bible*. Louisville: Westminster John Knox, 1992.

Fewell, Danna, and David Gunn. *Gender, Power, and Promise: The Subject of the Bible's First Story*. Nashville: Abingdon, 1993.

Finkelstein, Israel. "City-States to States: Polity Dynamics in the 10th–9th Centuries BCE. In *Symbiosis, Symbolism, and the Power of the Past: Canaan, Ancient Israel, and Their Neighbors from the Late Bronze Age through Roman Palestina*, ed. William G. Dever and Seymour Gitin, 75–84. Winona Lake, Ind.: Eisenbrauns, 2003.

————. *David and Solomon: In Search of the Bible's Sacred Kings and the Roots of the Western Tradition*. New York: Free Press, 2007.

Finkelstein, Israel, and Neil Asher Silberman. "Temple and Dynasty: Hezekiah, the Remaking of Judah, and the Rise of the Pan-Israelite Ideology." *JSOT* 30, no. 3 (2006): 259–85.

Finkelstein, Jacob J. "Early Mesopotamia, 2500–1000 B.C." In *Propaganda and Communication in World History*. Vol. 1: *The Symbolic Instrument in Early Times,* ed. Harold D. Lasswell, Daniel Lerner, and Hans Speier, 50–110. Honolulu: East-West Center, University of Hawaii, 1979.

Fishbane, Michael. *Biblical Interpretation in Ancient Israel*. Oxford: Oxford University Press, 1989.

————. *Biblical Text and Texture: A Literary Reading of Selected Texts*. Oxford: Oneworld Publications, 1998.

Fitzmyer, Joseph A. *The Gospel according to Luke, I–IX*. Anchor Bible. New York: Doubleday, 1981.

————. *The Gospel according to Luke, X–XXIV*. Anchor Bible. New York: Doubleday, 1985.

————. *The Acts of the Apostles*. Anchor Bible. New York: Doubleday, 1998.

Fox, Everett. *The Five Books of Moses*. New York: Shocken, 1995.

Fraade, Steven D. "Interpretive Authority in the Studying Community at Qumran." *JJS* 44, no. 1 (1993): 46–69.

————. "The Torah of the King (Deut. 17:14–20) in the Temple Scroll and Early Rabbinic Law." In *The Dead Sea Scrolls as Background to Postbiblical Judaism and Early Christianity,* ed. James R. Davila, 25–62. Leiden: Brill, 2003.

Frankfurter, David. "The Legacy of Jewish Apocalypses in Early Christianity: Regional Trajectories." In *The Jewish Apocalyptic Heritage in Early Christianity,* ed. James C. VanderKam and William Adler, 129–200. Minneapolis: Fortress Press, 1996.

Freedman, David Noel, and David Frank Graf, eds. *Palestine in Transition: The Emergence of Ancient Israel*. Sheffield: Almond Press, 1983.

Frend, W. H. C. "Jerusalem and Babylon. A Study into Augustine's 'City of God' and the Sources of His Doctrine of the Two Cities" by Johannes van Oort (review), *Vigiliae Christianae*, 45, no. 3 (1991): 298–302.

Freyne, Seán. "The Disciples in Mark and the Maskilim in Daniel: A Comparison." *JSNT* 16 (1982): 7–23.

————. *Jesus, a Jewish Galilean: A New Reading of the Jesus Story*. Edinburgh: T. & T. Clark, 2004.

Fried, Lisbeth S. "Cyrus the Messiah? The Historical Background to Isaiah 45:1." *HTR* 95, no. 4 (2002): 373–93.

———. "The 'am hā'āre̦ in Ezra 4:4 and Persian Imperial Administration." In *Judah and the Judeans in the Persian Period,* ed. Oded Lipschits and Joseph Blenkinsopp, 123–45. Winona Lake, Ind.: Eisenbrauns, 2006.

———. "The Land Lay Desolate: Conquest and Restoration in the Ancient Near East." In *Judah and the Judeans in the Persian Period,* ed. Oded Lipschits and Joseph Blenkinsopp, 21–54. Winona Lake, Ind.: Eisenbrauns, 2006.

Friedman, Jonathan. "Notes on Culture and Identity in Imperial Words." In *Religion and Religious Practice in the Seleucid Kingdom,* ed. Per Bilde et al., 14–39. Aarhus, Denmark: Aarhus University Press, 1990.

Friedman, Richard E. *The Hidden Book in the Bible.* San Francisco: HarperSan-Francisco, 1999.

———. *Who Wrote the Bible?* San Francisco: HarperCollins, 1989.

Friesen, Steven J. *Imperial Cults and the Apocalypse of John: Reading Revelation in the Ruins.* Oxford: Oxford University Press, 2006.

Frolov, Serge. "Succession Narrative: A "Document" or a "Phantom?" *JBL* 121, no. 1 (2002): 81–104.

Fukayama, Francis. *The End of History and the Last Man.* Reprint ed. New York: Free Press, 2006.

Funk, Robert W., and Roy W. Hoover. *The Five Gospels: The Search for the Authentic Words of Jesus.* Santa Rosa, Calif.: Polebridge Press, 1993.

Gaddis, Michael. *There Is No Crime for Those Who Have Christ: Religious Violence in the Christian Roman Empire.* Berkeley: University of California Press, 2005.

Gager, John G. *The Origins of Anti-Semitism: Attitudes toward Judaism in Pagan and Christian Antiquity.* Oxford: Oxford University Press, 1985.

Gammie, John G., and Leo G. Purdue, eds. *The Sage in Israel and the Ancient Near East.* Winona Lake, Ind.: Eisenbrauns, 1990.

Garcia Martinez, Florentino, ed. *Wisdom and Apocalypticism in the Dead Sea Scrolls and in the Biblical Tradition.* Leuven: University Press, 2003.

Garcia Martinez, Florentino., ed., W. G. E. Watson, trans. *The Dead Sea Scrolls Translated: The Qumran Texts in English.* 2nd ed. Leiden: Brill, 1997.

Garnsey, Peter, and Richard Saller. *The Roman Empire: Economy, Society, and Culture.* Berkeley: University of California Press, 1987.

Garnsey, P. D. A., and C. B. Whittaker, eds. *Imperialism in the Ancient World.* Cambridge: Cambridge University Press, 1978.

Garnsey, Peter D. "Patronal Power Relations." In *Paul and Empire: Religion and Power in Roman Imperial Society,* ed. Richard A. Horsley, 96–103. Philadelphia: Trinity Press International, 1997.

Garseil, Moshe. "Revealing and Concealing as a Narrative Strategy in Solomon's Judgment (1 Kings 3:16–28)." *CBQ* 64 (2002): 229–47.

Garseil, Moshe. "Revealing and Concealing as a Narrative Strategy in Solomon's Judgment (1 Kings 3:16–28)." *CBQ* 64 (2002): 229–47.

Gempf, Conrad. "Luke's Story of Paul's Reception in Rome." in *Rome in the Bible and the Early Church,* ed. Peter Oakes, 42–66. Grand Rapids: Baker Academic, 2002.

Georgi, Dieter. "God Turned Upside Down." In *Paul and Empire: Religion and Power in Roman Imperial Society,* ed. Richard A. Horsley, 148–57. Philadelphia: Trinity Press International, 1997.

Gill, David W. J., and Conrad Gempf, eds. *The Book of Acts in Its Graeco-Roman Setting.* Grand Rapids: Eerdmans, 1994.

Girard, René. *Violence and the Sacred.* Baltimore: Johns Hopkins University Press, 1979.

———. *Things Hidden since the Foundation of the World.* Trans. Stephen Bann and Michael Metteer. Stanford, Calif.: Stanford University Press, 1987.

———. *The Scapegoat.* Baltimore: Johns Hopkins University Press, 1989.

Glendinning, Chellis. *My Name Is Chellis and I'm in Recovery from Western Civilization.* Gabriola Island, B.C.: Catalyst Books, 2007.

Goldstone, Jack A., and John F. Haldon. "Ancient States, Empires, and Exploitation." In *The Dynamics of Ancient Empires: State Power from Assyria to Byzantium,* ed. Ian Morris and Walter Scheidel, 3–29. Oxford: Oxford University Press, 2009.

Goodacre, Mark. *The Case against Q: Studies in Markan Priority and the Synoptic Problem.* Harrisburg, Pa.: Trinity Press, 2001.

Gordon, Richard. "The Veil of Power." In *Paul and Empire: Religion and Power in Roman Imperial Society,* ed. Richard A. Horsley, 126–39. Philadelphia: Trinity Press International, 1997.

Goulder, Michael. "Behold My Servant Jehoiachin." *VT* 52, no. 2 (2002): 175–90.

———. "Deutero-Isaiah of Jerusalem." *JSOT* 28, no. 3 (2004): 351–62.

Gottwald, Norman K. *The Tribes of Yahweh: A Sociology of the Religion of Liberated Israel, 1250–1000 BC.* Maryknoll, N.Y.: Orbis Books, 1979.

———. *The Hebrew Bible: A Socio-Literary Introduction.* Minneapolis: Fortress Press, 1985.

———. *The Politics of Ancient Israel.* Library of Ancient Israel. Louisville: Westminster John Knox, 2001.

Gottwald, Norman K., and Richard A. Horsley. *The Bible and Liberation: Political and Social Hermeneutics.* Maryknoll, N.Y.: Orbis Books, 1993.

Grabbe, Lester L. *Ezra-Nehemiah.* London and New York: Routledge, 1998.

———. "A Dan(iel) for All Seasons: For Whom was the Book of Daniel Important?" In *The Book of Daniel: Composition and Reception.* Vol. 1. Ed. John J. Collins and Peter W. Flint, 229–46. Leiden: Brill Academic, 2002.

———. *A History of the Jews and Judaism in the Second Temple Period.* Vol. 1: *Yehud: A History of the Persian Province of Judah.* London and New York: T. & T. Clark, 2004a.

———. *Wisdom of Solomon.* London and New York: T. & T. Clark, 2004b.

———. "The Parables of Enoch in Second Temple Jewish Society." In *Enoch and the Messiah Son of Man: Revisiting the Book of Parables,* ed. Gabriele Boccaccini, 386–402. Grand Rapids: Eerdmans, 2007.

Green, Joel B. *The Gospel of Luke.* NICNT. Grand Rapids: Eerdmans, 1997.

Gruen, Erich S. *Heritage and Hellenism: The Reinvention of Jewish Tradition.* Berkeley: University of California Press, 2001.

Gruenwald, Ithamar. "Apocalypticism and the Religion and Ritual of the 'Pre-Sinaitic' Narratives. In *Enoch and Qumran Origins: New Light on a Forgotten Connection,* ed. Gabriele Boccaccini, 148–51. Grand Rapids: Eerdmans, 2005.

Haas, Christopher. *Alexandria in Late Antiquity: Topography and Social Conflict.* Baltimore: Johns Hopkins University Press, 1997.

Habel, Norman C., and Shirley Wurst, eds. *Earth Story in Genesis.* The Earth Bible Series. Cleveland: Pilgrim Press, 2001.

Hall, Jonathan M. *Ethnic Identity in Greek Antiquity.* Cambridge: Cambridge University Press, 1997.

Halliday, M. A. K. "Anti-Languages." *American Anthropologist* 78, no. 3 (1975): 570–84.

Halpern, Baruch. "Levitical Participation in the Reform Cult of Jeroboam I." *JBL* 95, no. 1 (1976): 31–43.

———. "Centralization Formula in Deuteronomy." *VT* 31, no. 1 (1981a): 20–38.

———. *The Constitution of the Monarchy in Israel.* Chico, Calif.: Scholars Press, 1981b.

———. "Jerusalem and the Lineages in the Seventh Century BCE: Kinship and the Rise of Individual Moral Liability." In *Law and Ideology in Monarchic Israel.* JSOTSS 124. Ed. Baruch Halpern and Deborah W. Hobson, 11–17. Sheffield: JSOT Press, 1991.

———. "Why Manasseh Is Blamed for the Babylonian Exile: The Evolution of a Biblical Tradition." *VT* 48, no. 4 (1998a): 473–514.

———. "The New Names of Isaiah 62:4: Jeremiah's Reception in the Restoration and the Politics of Third Isaiah." *JBL* 117, no. 4 (1998b): 623–43.

———. *David's Secret Demons: Messiah, Murderer, Traitor, King.* Grand Rapids: Eerdmans, 2004.

Halpern, Baruch, and Deborah W. Hobson, eds. *Law and Ideology in Monarchic Israel.* JSOTSS 124. Sheffield: JSOT Press, 1991.

Hanson, K. C., and Douglas E. Oakman. *Palestine in the Time of Jesus: Social Structures and Social Conflicts.* 2nd ed. Minneapolis: Fortress Press, 2008.

Hardin, Justin K. *Galatians and the Imperial Cult: A Critical Analysis of the First-Century Social Context of Paul's Letter.* Tübingen: Mohr Siebeck, 2008.

Hardwick, Lorna. "Concepts of Peace." In *Experiencing Rome: Culture, Identity and Power in the Roman Empire,* ed. Janet Huskinson, 335–68. New York: Routledge, 1999.

Harrison, C. Robert, "Qoheleth among the Sociologists." *Bib.Int.* 5, no. 2 (1997): 160–80.

Hasel, Michael G. "Israel in the Merneptah Stela." *BASOR* 296 (1994): 45–61.

Hayden, Brian. "A New Overview of Domestication." In *Last Hunters–First Farmers: New Perspectives on the Prehistoric Transition to Agriculture,* ed. T. Douglas Price and Anne Birgitte Gebauer, 273–99. Santa Fe, N.Mex.: School of American Research Press, 1995a.

Hayes, John. *Amos, the Eighth-Century Prophet: His Time and His Preaching.* Nashville: Abingdon, 1988.

Haynes, Stephen R. *The Bonhoeffer Legacy: Post-Holocaust Perspectives.* Minneapolis: Fortress Press, 2006.

Hays, J. Daniel. "Has the Narrator Come to Praise Solomon or to Bury Him: Narrative Subtlety in 1 Kings 1–11." *JSOT* 28, no. 2 (2003): 149–74.

Hays, Richard B. *Echoes of Scripture in the Letters of Paul.* New Haven: Yale University Press, 1989.

———. *The Faith of Jesus Christ: The Narrative Substructure of Galatians 3:1–4:11.* 2nd ed. Grand Rapids: Eerdmans, 2001.

———. "Reading Scripture in Light of the Resurrection." In *The Art of Reading Scripture,* ed. Ellen F. Davis and Richard B. Hays, 216–38. Grand Rapids: Eerdmans, 2003.

———. *The Conversion of the Imagination: Paul as Interpreter of Israel's Scripture.* Grand Rapids: Eerdmans, 2005.

Heen, Erik M. "Phil. 2:6–11 and Resistance to Local Timocratic Rule." In *Paul and the Roman Imperial Order,* ed. Richard A. Horsley, 125–53. Harrisburg, Pa.: Trinity Press International, 2004.

Hendel, Ronald. "Mary Douglas and Anthropological Modernism." *JHS* 8 (2008): 1–11.

———. "Farewell to SBL: Faith and Reason in Biblical Studies." *BAR* 36, no. 4 (2010).

Hengel, Martin, James H. Charlesworth, and Doron Mendels. "The Polemical Character of the 'On Kingship' in the Temple Scroll: An Attempt at Dating 11Q Temple." *JJS* 37 (1986): 28–38.

Hengel, Martin, with Daniel P. Bailey. "The Effective History of Isaiah 53 in the Pre-Christian Period." In *The Suffering Servant: Isaiah 53 in Jewish and Christian Sources,* ed. Bernd Janowski and Peter Stuhlmacher, 75–146. Grand Rapids: Eerdmans, 2004.

Henry, Caleb. "Joab: A Biblical Critique of Machiavellian Tactics." *WTJ* 69 (2007): 327–43.

Henze, Matthias. "The Parables of Enoch in Second Temple Literature: A Response to Gabriele Boccaccini." In *Enoch and the Messiah Son of Man: Revisiting the Book of Parables,* ed. Gabriele Boccaccini, 290–98. Grand Rapids: Eerdmans, 2007.

———. "Daniel and Jubilees." In *Enoch and the Mosaic Torah: The Evidence of Jubilees,* ed. Gabriele Boccaccini and Giovanni Ibba, 52–66. Grand Rapids: Eerdmans, 2009.

Hermisson, Hans-Jürgen. "The Fourth Servant Song in the Context of Second Isaiah." In *The Suffering Servant: Isaiah 53 in Jewish and Christian Sources,* ed. Bernd Janowski and Peter Stuhlmacher, 16–47. Grand Rapids: Eerdmans, 2004.

Herring, George C. *From Colony to Superpower: U.S. Foreign Relations since 1776.* Oxford History of the United States. Oxford: Oxford University Press, 2008.

Herzog, William. *Parables as Subversive Speech: Jesus as Pedagogue of the Oppressed.* Louisville: Westminster John Knox, 1994.

Heym, Stephen. *The King David Report.* Evanston, Ill.: Northwestern University Press, 1998.

Hiebert, Theodore. *The Yahwist's Landscape: Nature and Religion in Early Israel.* Minneapolis: Fortress Press, 2008.

Hill, Jonathan D., ed. *History, Power, and Identity: Ethnogenesis in the Americas, 1492–1992.* Iowa City: University of Iowa Press, 1996a.

———. "Introduction: Ethnogenesis in the Americas, 1492–1992." In *History, Power, and Identity: Ethnogenesis in the Americas, 1492–1992,* ed. Jonathan D. Hill, 1–19. Iowa City: University of Iowa Press, 1996b.

Hillers, Delbert R. *Micah.* Hermeneia. Minneapolis: Fortress Press, 1984.

Himmelfarb, Martha. "Temple and Priests in the Book of the Watchers, the Animal Apocalypse, and the Apocalypse of Weeks." In *The Early Enoch Literature,* ed. Gabriele Boccaccini and John J. Collins, 219–35. Leiden: Brill, 2007.

Hirshman, Marc. *A Rivalry of Genius: Jewish and Christian Biblical Interpretation in Late Antiquity.* Albany: SUNY Press, 1996.

Hitchner, Robert Bruce. "Olive Production and the Roman Economy: The Case for Intensive Growth in the Roman Empire." In *The Ancient Economy,* ed. Walter Scheidel and Sitta Von Reden, 71–83. New York: Routledge, 2002.

Hobsbawm, Eric, and Terence Ranger, eds. *The Invention of Tradition*. Cambridge: Cambridge University Press, 1983.

Hogenhaven, Jesper. "The Prophet Isaiah and Judaean Foreign Policy under Ahaz and Hezekiah." *JNES* 49, no. 4 (1990): 351–54.

Hoglund, Kenneth G. *Achaemenid Imperial Administration in Syria-Palestine and the Missions of Ezra and Nehemiah*. Atlanta: Scholars Press, 1992.

Hölbl, Günther. *A History of the Ptolemaic Empire*. London and New York: Routledge, 2001.

Hollander, H. W., and M. De Jonge. *The Testaments of the Twelve Patriarchs: A Commentary*. Leiden: Brill, 1997.

Hope, Valerie. "The City of Rome: Capital and Symbol." In *Experiencing Rome: Culture, Identity, and Power in the Roman Empire*, ed. Janet Huskinson, 63–94. New York: Routledge, 1999.

Hopkins, Keith. "The Political Economy of the Roman Empire." In *The Dynamics of Ancient Empires: State Power from Assyria to Byzantium*, ed. Ian Morris and Walter Scheidel, 178–204. Oxford: Oxford University Press, 2009.

Horden, Peregrine, and Nicholas Purcell. *The Corrupting Sea: A Study of Mediterranean History*. Malden, Mass.: Blackwell, 2000.

Horsley, G. H. R. "The Politarchs." In *The Book of Acts in Its Graeco-Roman Setting*, ed. David W. J. Gill and Conrad Gempf, 419–32. Grand Rapids: Eerdmans, 1994.

Horsley, Richard A. "*Pneumatikos* vs. *Psychikos* Distinctions of Spiritual Status among the Corinthians." *Harvard Theological Review* 69, no. 3/4 (1976): 269–88.

―――. *The Liberation of Christmas: The Infancy Narratives in Social Context*. New York: Continuum, 1993a.

―――. *Jesus and the Spiral of Violence: Popular Jewish Resistance in Roman Palestine*. Minneapolis: Fortress Press, 1993b.

―――. *Galilee: History, Politics, People*. New York: Continuum, 1995.

―――, ed. *Paul and Empire: Religion and Power in Roman Imperial Society*. Philadelphia: Trinity Press International, 1997.

―――. *1 Corinthians*. Abingdon New Testament Commentaries. Nashville: Abingdon, 1998.

―――, ed. *Paul and Politics: Ekklesia, Israel, Imperium, Interpretation*. Harrisburg, Pa.: Trinity Press International, 2000a.

―――. "Krister Stendahl's Challenge to Pauline Studies." In *Paul and Politics: Ekklesia, Israel, Imperium, Interpretation*, ed. Richard A. Horsley, 1–16. Harrisburg, Pa.: Trinity Press International, 2000b.

―――. "Rhetoric and Empire — and 1 Corinthians." In *Paul and Politics: Ekklesia, Israel, Imperium, Interpretation*, ed. Richard A. Horsley, 72–102. Harrisburg, Pa.: Trinity Press International, 2000c.

―――, ed. *Hidden Transcripts and the Arts of Resistance: Applying the Work of James C. Scott to Jesus and Paul*. Atlanta: SBL, 2003.

―――, ed. *Paul and the Roman Imperial Order*. Harrisburg, Pa.: Trinity Press International, 2004.

―――, ed. *Christian Origins: A People's History of Christianity*. Vol. 1. Minneapolis: Fortress Press, 2006.

―――. *Scribes, Visionaries, and the Politics of Second Temple Judea*. Louisville: Westminster John Knox, 2007.

————. *Revolt of the Scribes: Resistance and Apocalyptic Origins.* Minneapolis: Fortress, 2010.

Horsley, Richard A., and John S. Hanson. *Bandits, Prophets and Messiahs: Popular Movements in the Time of Jesus.* San Francisco: Harper and Row, 1985.

Howard-Brook, Wes. *Becoming Children of God: John's Gospel and Radical Discipleship.* Maryknoll, N.Y.: Orbis Books, 1994.

————. *John's Gospel and the Renewal of the Church.* Maryknoll, N.Y.: Orbis Books, 1997.

————. *The Church before Christianity.* Maryknoll, N.Y.: Orbis Books, 2001.

————. "Hunger for Bread amid the Ruins." *Celebration* 38, no. 7 (2009): 3–5.

Howard-Brook, Wes, and Anthony Gwyther. *Unveiling Empire: Reading Revelation Then and Now.* Maryknoll, N.Y.: Orbis Books, 1999.

Howard-Brook, Wes, and Sharon Ringe, eds. *The New Testament: Introducing the Way of Discipleship.* Maryknoll, N.Y.: Orbis Books, 2003.

Hurston, Zora Neale. *Moses, Man of the Mountain.* San Francisco: Harper Perennial, 2008.

Huskinson, Janet, ed. *Experiencing Rome: Culture, Identity, and Power in the Roman Empire.* New York: Routledge, 1999a.

————. "Elite Culture and the Identity of Empire." In *Experiencing Rome: Culture, Identity, and Power in the Roman Empire,* ed. Janet Huskinson, 95–124. New York: Routledge, 1999b.

Ingram, Doug. *Ambiguity in Ecclesiastes.* New York: T. & T. Clark International, 2006.

Isager, Signe. "Kings and Gods in the Seleucid Empire." In *Religion and Religious Practice in the Seleucid Kingdom,* ed. Per Bilde et al., 79–90. Aarhus, Denmark: Aarhus University Press, 1990.

Jacobsen, Thorkild. *The Treasures of Darkness: A History of Mesopotamian Religion.* New Haven, Conn.: Yale University Press, 1976.

James, Paula. "The Language of Dissent." In *Experiencing Rome: Culture, Identity, and Power in the Roman Empire,* ed. Janet Huskinson, 277–304. New York: Routledge, 1999.

Janowski, Bernd. "He Bore Our Sins: Isaiah 53 and the Drama of Taking Another's Place." In *The Suffering Servant: Isaiah 53 in Jewish and Christian Sources,* ed. Bernd Janowski and Peter Stuhlmacher, 48–74. Grand Rapids: Eerdmans, 2004.

Janowski, Bernd, and Peter Stuhlmacher, eds. *The Suffering Servant: Isaiah 53 in Jewish and Christian Sources.* Grand Rapids: Eerdmans, 2004.

Janzen, J. "The Character of the Calf and Its Cult in Exodus 32." *CBQ* 52, no. 4 (1990): 597.

Japhet, Sara. "The Supposed Common Authorship of Chronicles and Ezra-Nehemiah Investigated Anew." *VT* 18 (1968): 330–63.

————. "Conquest and Settlement in Chronicles." *JBL* 98, no. 2 (1979): 205–18.

————. *The Ideology of the Book of Chronicles and Its Place in Biblical Thought.* Frankfurt am Main/New York: P. Lang, 1989.

————. *I and II Chronicles.* Louisville: Westminster John Knox, 1993.

————. "Composition and Chronology in the Book of Ezra-Nehemiah." In *Second Temple Studies.* Vol. 2: *Temple and Community in the Persian Period.* JSOTSS 175, ed. Tamara C. Eskenazi and Kent H. Richards, 189–216. Sheffield: JSOT Press, 1994.

———. "Periodization: Between History and Ideology, The Neo-Babylonian Period in Biblical Historiography." In *Judah and the Judeans in the Neo-Babylonian Period*, ed. Oded Lipschits and Joseph Blenkinsopp, 75–89. Winona Lake, Ind.: Eisenbrauns, 2003.

———. *From the Rivers of Babylon to the Highlands of Judah: Collected Studies on the Restoration Period.* Winona Lake, Ind.: Eisenbrauns, 2006.

———. "People and Land in the Restoration Period." In *From the Rivers of Babylon to the Highlands of Judah: Collected Studies on the Restoration Period,* 96–116. Winona Lake, Ind.: Eisenbrauns, 2006a.

———. "Periodization between History and Ideology II: Chronology and Ideology in Ezra-Nehemiah." In *Judah and the Judeans in the Persian Period*, ed. Oded Lipschits and Joseph Blenkinsopp, 491–508. Winona Lake, Ind.: Eisenbrauns, 2006b.

———. "Postexilic Historiography: How and Why?" In *From the Rivers of Babylon to the Highlands of Judah: Collected Studies on the Restoration Period,* 303–30. Winona Lake, Ind.: Eisenbrauns, 2006c.

———. "The Temple in the Restoration Period: Reality and Ideology." In *From the Rivers of Babylon to the Highlands of Judah: Collected Studies on the Restoration Period,* 183–232. Winona Lake, Ind.: Eisenbrauns, 2006d.

Jensen, Derrick. *Endgame.* Vol. 1: *The Problem of Civilization.* New York: Seven Stories Press, 2006a.

———. *Endgame.* Vol. 2: *Resistance.* New York: Seven Stories Press, 2006b.

———. *How Shall I Live My Life? On Liberating the Earth from Civilization.* Oakland: PM Press, 2008.

Jernielity, Thomas J. *Satire and the Hebrew Prophets.* Louisville: Westminster John Knox, 2002.

Jewett, Robert. "Response: Exegetical Support from Romans and Other Letters." In *Paul and Politics: Ekklesia, Israel, Imperium, Interpretation,* ed. Richard A. Horsley, 58–71. Harrisburg, Pa.: Trinity Press International, 2000.

———. "The Corruption and Redemption of Creation: Reading Rom. 8:18–23 within the Imperial Context." In *Paul and the Roman Imperial Order,* ed. Richard A. Horsley, 25–46. Harrisburg, Pa.: Trinity Press International, 2004.

———. *Romans: A Commentary.* Hermeneia. Minneapolis: Fortress Press, 2007.

Jobling, David. *1 Samuel.* Berit Olam Series. Collegeville, Minn.: Liturgical Press, 1998.

Jobling, David, Peggy L. Day, and Gerald T. Sheppard. *The Bible and the Politics of Exegesis.* Cleveland: Pilgrim Press, 1991.

Johnson, Luke Timothy. *Acts of the Apostles.* Sacra Pagina. Collegeville, Minn.: Liturgical Press, 1992.

———. *The Real Jesus: The Misguided Quest for the Historical Jesus and the Truth of the Traditional Gospels.* San Francisco: HarperOne, 1997.

Johnstone, William. "The Use of Leviticus in Chronicles." In *Reading Leviticus: A Conversation with Mary Douglas.* JSOTSS 227. Ed. John A. Sawyer, 243–55. Sheffield: Sheffield Academic Press, 1996.

Jones. Brian W. *The Emperor Domitian.* New York: Routledge, 1993.

Kates, Judith A., and Gail Twersky Reimer, eds. *Reading Ruth: Contemporary Women Reclaim a Sacred Story.* New York: Ballantine, 1996.

Keeley, Lawrence H. "Protoagricultural Practices among Hunter-Gatherers." In *Last Hunters–First Farmers: New Perspectives on the Prehistoric Transition to Agriculture*, ed. T. Douglas Price and Anne Birgitte Gebauer, 243–72. Santa Fe, N.Mex.: School of American Research Press, 1995.

Kelley, Shawn. *Racializing Jesus: Race, Ideology and the Formation of Modern Biblical Scholarship*. New York: Routledge, 2002.

Kessler, John, "Building the Second Temple: Questions of Time, Text, and History in Haggai 1:1–15." *JSOT* 27, no. 2 (2002): 243–56.

———. "Diaspora and Homeland in the Early Achaemenid Period: Community, Geography, and Demography in Zechariah 1–8." In *Approaching Yehud: New Approaches to the Study of the Persian Period*, ed. Jon L. Berquist, 137–66. Atlanta: Society of Biblical Literature, 2007.

Kierspel, Lars. *The Jews and the World in the Fourth Gospel: Parallelism, Function, and Context*. Tübingen: Mohr Siebeck, 2006.

Killebrew, Ann E. *Biblical Peoples and Ethnicity*. Atlanta: SBL, 2005.

Kim, Seyoon. *Christ and Caesar: The Gospel and the Roman Empire in the Writings of Paul and Luke*. Grand Rapids: Eerdmans, 2008.

King, Philip J., and Lawrence E. Stager. *Life in Biblical Israel*. Library of Ancient Israel. Louisville: Westminster John Knox, 2002.

King, Robert H. *Thomas Merton and Thich Nhat Hanh*. New York: Continuum, 2003.

Kinsler, Ross, and Gloria Kinsler. *The Biblical Jubilee and the Struggle for Life*. Maryknoll, N.Y.: Orbis Books, 1999.

Kinzer, Stephen. *Overthrow: America's Century of Regime Change from Hawaii to Iraq*. New York: Times Books, 2007.

Kitchen, Kenneth A. "Egyptian Interventions in the Levant in Iron Age II." In *Symbiosis, Symbolism, and the Power of the Past: Canaan, Ancient Israel, and Their Neighbors from the Late Bronze Age through Roman Palestina*, ed. William G. Dever and Seymour Gitin, 113–32. Winona Lake, Ind.: Eisenbrauns, 2003.

Kittel, Gerhard, and Gerhard Friedrich, eds. *Theological Dictionary of the New Testament* (one volume abridged). Grand Rapids: Eerdmans, 1985.

Klawans, Jonathan. *Impurity and Sin in Ancient Judaism*. New York: Oxford University Press, 2000.

Kloppenborg, John S. "Response to 'Revisiting the Rich and the Poor in 1 Enoch 92–105 and the Gospel according to Luke.'" In *George W. E. Nickelsburg in Perspective: An Ongoing Dialogue of Learning*. Vol. 2. Ed. Jacob Neusner and Alan J. Avery-Peck, 572–85. Leiden: Brill, 2003.

———. *Q, the Earliest Gospel: An Introduction to the Original Stories and Sayings of Jesus*. Louisville: Westminster John Knox, 2008.

Knauf, Ernst Axel. "Bethel: The Israelite Impact on Judean Language and Literature." In *Judah and the Judeans in the Persian Period*, ed. Oded Lipschits and Joseph Blenkinsopp, 291–349. Winona Lake, Ind.: Eisenbrauns, 2006.

Knibb, Michael A. "The Book of Enoch in the Light of the Qumran Wisdom Literature." In *Conflicted Boundaries in Wisdom and Apocalypticism*, ed. Benjamin G. Wright III and Lawrence M. Wills, 193–210. Atlanta: Society of Biblical Literature, 2005a.

———. "The Apocalypse of Weeks and the Epistle of Enoch." In *Enoch and Qumran Origins: New Light on a Forgotten Connection*, ed. Gabriele Boccaccini, 213–19. Grand Rapids: Eerdmans, 2005b.

————. "The Structure and Composition of the Parables of Enoch." In *Enoch and the Messiah Son of Man: Revisiting the Book of Parables*, ed. Gabriele Boccaccini, 48–64. Grand Rapids: Eerdmans, 2007.

Knoppers, Gary N. *Two Nations under God: The Deuteronomistic History of Solomon and the Dual Monarchies*. Vol. 1: *The Reign of Solomon and the Rise of Jeroboam*. Atlanta: Scholars Press, 1993.

————. "David's Relation to Moses: The Contexts, Content, and Conditions of the Davidic Promises." In *King and Messiah in Israel and the Ancient Near East*. JSOTSS 270. Ed. John Day. Sheffield: Sheffield Academic Press, 1998.

————. *Nehemiah and Sanballat: The Enemy Without or Within?* In *Judah and the Judeans in the Fourth Century BCE*, ed. Oden Lipschits, Gary N. Knoppers, and Rainer Albertz, 305–31. Winona Lake, Ind.: Eisenbrauns, 2007.

Koch, Klaus. "History as a Battlefield of Two Antagonistic Powers in the Apocalypse of Weeks and in the Rule of the Community." In *Enoch and Qumran Origins: New Light on a Forgotten Connection*, ed. Gabriele Boccaccini, 185–99. Grand Rapids: Eerdmans, 2005.

Koester, Craig. "'The Savior of the World' (John 4:42)." *JBL* 109, no. 4 (1990): 665–68.

————. *Symbolism in the Fourth Gospel: Meaning, Mystery, Community*. 2nd ed. Minneapolis: Fortress Press, 2003.

Koester, Helmut. "Imperial Ideology and Paul's Eschatology in 1 Thessalonians." In *Paul and Empire: Religion and Power in Roman Imperial Society*, ed. Richard A. Horsley, 158–66. Philadelphia: Trinity Press International, 1997.

Kolarcik, S.J., Michael. "The Sage behind the Wisdom of Solomon." In *Scribes, Sages, and Seers: The Sage in the Eastern Mediterranean World*, ed. Leo G. Perdue, 245–57. Göttingen: Vandenhoeck & Ruprecht, 2008.

Korsak, Mary Philip. *At the Start: Genesis Made New: A Translation of the Hebrew Text*. New York: Doubleday, 1992.

————. "Genesis: A New Look." In *A Feminist Companion to Genesis*, ed. Athalya Brenner, 39–52. Sheffield: Sheffield Academic Press, 1993, 1997.

Kramer, Paul A. *The Blood of Government: Race, Empire, the United States, and the Philippines*. Chapel Hill: University of North Carolina Press, 2006.

Kramer, Samuel Noah. *The Sumerians: Their History, Culture, and Character*. Chicago: University of Chicago Press, 1963.

————. *Sacred Marriage Rite: Aspects of Faith, Myth, and Ritual in Ancient Sumer*. Bloomington: Indiana University Press, 1970.

Kratz, Reinhard G. "Ezra — Priest and Scribe." In *Scribes, Sages, and Seers: The Sage in the Eastern Mediterranean World*, ed. Leo G. Perdue, 163–88. Göttingen: Vandenhoeck & Ruprecht, 2008.

Kreitzer, Larry Joseph. *Striking New Images: Roman Imperial Coinage and the New Testament World*. Sheffield: Sheffield Academic Press, 1996.

Kroedel, Gerhard. *Acts*. Augsburg Commentary on the New Testament. Minneapolis: Augsburg, 1986.

Kvanvig, Helge S. "The Son of Man in the Parables of Enoch." In *Enoch and the Messiah Son of Man: Revisiting the Book of Parables*, ed. Gabriele Boccaccini, 179–215. Grand Rapids: Eerdmans, 2007.

————. "Enoch Judaism — A Judaism without the Torah and the Temple?" In *Enoch and the Mosaic Torah: The Evidence of Jubilees*, ed. Gabriele Boccaccini and Giovanni Ibba, 163–77. Grand Rapids: Eerdmans, 2009.

Lasine, Stuart. "Jehoram and the Cannibal Mothers (2 Kings 6:24–33): Solomon's Judgment in an Inverted World." *JSOT* 50 (1991): 27–53.

———. "Reading Jeroboam's Intentions: Intertexuality, Rhetoric, and History in 1 Kings 12." In *Reading between Texts: Intertextuality and the Hebrew Bible*, ed. Danna Nolan Fewell, 133–52. Louisville: Westminster John Knox, 1992.

———. "The Ups and Downs of Monarchical Justice: Solomon and Jehoram in an Intertexual World." *JSOT* 59 (1993): 37–53.

———. "The King of Desire: Indeterminacy, Audience, and the Solomon Narrative." *Semeia* 71 (1995): 85–118.

———. *Knowing Kings: Knowledge, Power, and Narcissism in the Hebrew Bible*. Atlanta: SBL, 2001.

Lasswell, Harold D., Daniel Lerner, and Hans Speier, eds. *Propaganda and Communication in World History*. Vol. 1: *The Symbolic Instrument in Early Times*. Honolulu: East-West Center, University of Hawaii, 1979.

Layton, Robert H. "Hunter-Gatherers, Their Neighbors, and the Nation State." In *Hunter-Gatherers: An Interdisciplinary Perspective*, ed. Catherine Panter-Brick, Robert H. Layton, and Peter Rowley-Conwy, 292–321. Cambridge: Cambridge University Press, 2001.

Lease, Gary. "Mithra in Egypt." In *The Roots of Egyptian Christianity*, ed. Birger A. Pearson and James E. Goehring, 114–29. Minneapolis: Fortress Press, 1997.

Lemche, Niels Peter. *The Israelites in History and Tradition*. Louisville: Westminster John Knox, 1998.

Lenski, Gerhard E. *Power and Privilege: A Theory of Social Stratification*. Chapel Hill: University of North Carolina Press, 1984.

Leuchter, Mark. "Jeroboam the Ephratite." *JBL* 125, no. 1 (2006): 51–72.

Leveen, Adrianne. *Memory and Tradition in the Book of Numbers*. Cambridge: Cambridge University Press, 2008.

Levenson, Bernard M. "The Reconceptualization of Kingship in Deuteronomy and the Deuteronomistic History's Transformation of Torah." *VT* 51, no. 4 (2001): 511–34.

Levenson, Jon D. "Who Inserted the Book of the Torah?" *HTR* 68, nos. 3–4 (1975): 203–33.

———. *Sinai and Zion: An Entry into the Jewish Bible*. San Francisco: HarperSanFrancisco, 1985.

———. *Resurrection and the Restoration of Israel: The Ultimate Victory of the God of Life*. New Haven, Conn.: Yale University Press, 2006.

Levine, Baruch A. "The Clan-Based Economy of Biblical Israel." In *Symbiosis, Symbolism, and the Power of the Past: Canaan, Ancient Israel, and Their Neighbors from the Late Bronze Age through Roman Palestina*, ed. William G. Dever and Seymour Gitin, 445–53. Winona Lake, Ind.: Eisenbrauns, 2003.

Levinskaya, Irina, ed. *The Book of Acts in Its Diaspora Setting*. Grand Rapids: Eerdmans, 1996.

Lewy, Guenter. *The Catholic Church and Nazi Germany*. Cambridge: De Capo Press, 2000.

Lincoln, Andrew T. *Ephesians*. WBC 42. Waco: Word, 1990.

Linker, Damon. *The Theocons: Secular America under Siege*. New York: Anchor, 2007.

Lipschits, Oded. "Demographic Changes in Judah between the Seventh and the Fifth Centuries BCE." In *Judah and the Judeans in the Neo-Babylonian Period,* ed. Oded Lipschits and Joseph Blenkinsopp, 323–76. Winona Lake, Ind.: Eisenbrauns, 2003.

———. "Where Is the 'Myth of the Empty Land' to be Found? History versus Myth." In *Judah and the Judeans in the Neo-Babylonian Period,* ed. Oded Lipschits and Joseph Blenkinsopp, 55–74. Winona Lake, Ind.: Eisenbrauns, 2003.

Lipschits, Oded, and Joseph Blenkinsopp, eds. *Judah and the Judeans in the Neo-Babylonian Period.* Winona Lake, Ind.: Eisenbrauns, 2003.

Lipschits, Oded, and Manfred Oeming, eds. *Judah and the Judeans in the Persian Period.* Winona Lake, Ind.: Eisenbrauns, 2006.

Lipschits, Oded, Gary N. Knoppers, and Rainer Albertz, eds. *Judah and the Judeans in the Fourth Century BCE.* Winona Lake, Ind.: Eisenbrauns, 2007.

Lloyd, Alan B. "Nationalist Propaganda in Ptolemaic Egypt." *Historia: Zeitschrift für Alte Geschichte* 31, no. 1 (1982): 33–55.

Longman, Tremper. *The Book of Ecclesiastes.* NICOT. Grand Rapids: Eerdmans, 1997.

Loring, Eduard, with Heather Bargeron. *The Festival of Shelters: A Celebration of Love and Justice.* Atlanta: Open Door Community, 2009.

Lovin, Robin W. *Reinhold Niebuhr and Christian Realism.* Cambridge: Cambridge University Press, 1995.

Lowery, Richard H. *Sabbath and Jubilee.* Understanding Biblical Themes. Atlanta: Chalice Press, 2000.

Maccoby, Hyam. "Holiness and Purity: The Holy People in Leviticus and Ezra-Nehemiah." In *Reading Leviticus: A Conversation with Mary Douglas.* JSOTSS 227. Ed. John A. Sawyer, 153–70. Sheffield: Sheffield Academic Press, 1996.

MacMullen, Ramsay. *Enemies of the Roman Order: Treason, Unrest, and Alienation in the Empire.* Cambridge: Harvard University Press, 1966.

———. *Roman Social Relations, 50 B.C. to A.D. 284.* New Haven, Conn.: Yale University Press, 1981.

———. *Paganism in the Roman Empire.* New Haven, Conn.: Yale University Press, 1983.

———. *Christianizing the Roman Empire (A.D. 100–400).* New Haven, Conn.: Yale University Press, 1986.

———. *Christianity and Paganism in the Fourth to Eighth Centuries.* New Haven, Conn.: Yale University Press, 1999.

———. *The Second Church: Popular Christianity A.D. 200–400.* Atlanta: Society of Biblical Literature, 2009.

Malina, Bruce. *The New Testament World: Insights from Cultural Anthropology.* 3rd ed. Louisville: Westminster John Knox, 2001.

Mann, Michael. *The Sources of Social Power.* Vol. 1: *A History of Power from the Beginning to AD 1760.* Cambridge: Cambridge University Press, 1986.

Manning, Richard. *Against the Grain: How Agriculture Has Hijacked Civilization.* New York: North Point Press, 2005.

Mason, Steve. "Jews, Judaeans, Judaizing, Judaism: Problems of Categorization in Ancient History." *Journal for the Study of Judaism* 38 (2007): 457–512.

Master, Daniel M. "State Formation Theory and the Kingdom of Ancient Israel." *JNES* 60, no. 2 (2001): 117–31.

Mayer, Henry. *All on Fire: William Lloyd Garrison and the Abolition of Slavery.* New York: W. W. Norton, 2008.

Mazar, Amihai. *Archaeology of the Land of the Bible: 10,000–586 BCE.* Anchor Bible Reference Library. New York: Doubleday, 1992.

———. "Remarks on Biblical Traditions and Archaeological Evidence Concerning Early Israel." In *Symbiosis, Symbolism, and the Power of the Past: Canaan, Ancient Israel, and Their Neighbors from the Late Bronze Age through Roman Palestina,* ed. William G. Dever and Seymour Gitin, 85–98. Winona Lake, Ind.: Eisenbrauns, 2003.

McConville, J. G. "King and Messiah in Deuteronomy and the Deuteronomistic History." In *King and Messiah in Israel and the Ancient Near East.* JSOTSS 270. Ed. John Day. Sheffield: Sheffield Academic Press, 1998.

McGinnis, Claire Matthews, and Patricia K. Tull, eds. *"As Those Who are Taught": The Interpretation of Isaiah from the LXX to the SBL.* Atlanta: Society of Biblical Literature, 2006.

McKeown, James. *Genesis.* Grand Rapids: Eerdmans, 2008.

McKibben, Bill. *The End of Nature.* New York: Anchor, 1990.

Mead, James K. "Kings and Prophets, Donkeys and Lions: Dramatic Shape and Deuteronomistic Rhetoric in 1 Kings XIII." *VT* 49, no. 2 (1999): 191–205.

Meadowcroft, Tim. "Exploring the Dismal Swamp: The Identity of the Anointed One in Daniel 9:24–27." *JBL* 120, no. 3 (2001): 429–49.

Melugin, Roy F., and Marvin A. Sweeney, eds. *New Visions of Isaiah.* Atlanta: Society of Biblical Literature, 1996.

Mendels, Doron. *The Rise and Fall of Jewish Nationalism: Jewish and Christian Ethnicity in Ancient Palestine.* New York: Doubleday, 1992.

Mendelsohn, Isaac. *Slavery in the Ancient Near East: A Comparative Study of Slavery in Babylonia, Assyria, Syria, and Palestine, from the Middle of the Third Millennium to the End of the First Millennium.* New York: Oxford University Press, 1949.

Meyers, Carol. *Discovering Eve: Ancient Israelite Women in Context.* New York: Oxford University Press, 1988.

———. "Gender Roles and Genesis 3:16 Revisited." In *A Feminist Companion to Genesis,* ed. Athalya Brenner, 118–41. Sheffield: Sheffield Academic Press, 1993, 1997.

———. "Material Remains and Social Relations: Women's Culture in Agrarian Households of the Iron Age." In *Symbiosis, Symbolism, and the Power of the Past: Canaan, Ancient Israel, and Their Neighbors from the Late Bronze Age through Roman Palestina,* ed. William G. Dever and Seymour Gitin, 425–44. Winona Lake, Ind.: Eisenbrauns, 2003.

Meyers, Carol L., and Eric M. Meyers, "Jerusalem and Zion after the Exile: The Evidence of First Zechariah." In *Sha'arei Talmon: Studies in the Bible, Qumran, and the Ancient Near East presented to Shemaryahu Talmon,* ed. Shemaryahu Talmon, Michael A. Fishbane, Emanuel Tov, Weston W. Fields, 121–35. Winona Lake, Ind.: Eisenbrauns, 1992.

Meyers, Eric M. "The Crisis of the Mid-fifth Century B.C.E. Second Zechariah and the 'End' of Prophecy." In *Pomegranates and Golden Bells: Studies in Biblical, Jewish, and Near Eastern Ritual, Law, and Literature in Honor of Jacob Milgrom,* ed. Jacob Milgrom, David Pearson Wright, David Noel Freedman, Avi Hurvitz, 713–24. Winona Lake, Ill.: Eisenbrauns, 1995.

Middleton, J. Richard. *Liberating Image: The Imago Dei in Genesis 1.* Grand Rapids: Brazos Press, 2005.

Miles, John A., Jr. "Laughing at the Bible: Jonah as Parody." *Jewish Quarterly Review* 65, no. 3 (1975): 168–81.

Miles, Richard. "Communicating Culture, Identity, and Power." In *Experiencing Rome: Culture, Identity, and Power in the Roman Empire,* ed. Janet Huskinson, 29–62. New York: Routledge, 1999.

Milgrom, Jacob. *JPS Torah Commentary: Numbers.* Philadelphia: Jewish Publication Society, 1990.

Milgrom, Jacob, David Pearson Wright, David Noel Freedman, and Avi Hurvitz, eds. *Pomegranates and Golden Bells: Studies in Biblical, Jewish, and Near Eastern Ritual, Law, and Literature in Honor of Jacob Milgrom.* Winona Lake, Ill.: Eisenbrauns, 1995.

Miller, J. Maxwell, and John H. Hayes. *A History of Ancient Israel and Judah.* Philadelphia: Westminster Press, 1986.

Miller, Robert D. "Identifying Earliest Israel." *BASOR* 333 (2004): 55–68.

Miller, Robert J. *The Jesus Seminar and Its Critics.* Santa Rosa, Calif.: Polebridge Press, 1999.

Minette de Tillesse, Caetano. "The Conquest of Power: Analysis of David and Solomon's Accession Histories." In *Perspectives on Hebrew Scriptures: Comprising the Contents of the Journal of Hebrew Scriptures,* ed. Ehud Ben Zvi, 46–49. Piscataway, N.J.: Gorgias Press, 2006.

Mirau, Neil A. "The Social Context of Early Iron Working in the Levant." In *Urbanism in Antiquity: From Mesopotamia to Crete,* ed. Walter E. Aufrecht, Neil A. Mirau, and Steven W. Gauley, 99–115. JSOTSS 244. Sheffield: Sheffield Academic Press, 1997.

Moberly, R.W.L. "Preaching for a Response? Jonah's Message to the Ninevites Reconsidered." *VT* 53, no. 2 (2003): 156–68.

Modrzejewski, Joseph M. *The Jews of Egypt.* Princeton, N.J.: Princeton University Press, 1997.

Moore, Stephen D. *Literary Criticism and the Gospels: The Theoretical Challenge.* New Haven, Conn.: Yale University Press, 1992.

———. *Empire and Apocalypse: Postcolonialism and the New Testament.* Sheffield: Sheffield Phoenix Press, 2006.

Morgan, Teresa. *Literate Education in the Hellenistic and Roman Worlds.* Cambridge: Cambridge University Press, 1998.

Morgenstern, Mira. *Conceiving a Nation: The Development of Political Discourse in the Bible.* University Park: Pennsylvania State University Press, 2009.

Morris, Ian, and Walter Scheidel, eds. *The Dynamics of Ancient Empires: State Power from Assyria to Byzantium.* Oxford: Oxford University Press, 2009.

Mowery, Robert L. "Son of God in Roman Imperial Titles and Matthew." *Biblica* 83 (2002): 100–110.

Moxnes, Halvor. "The Quest for Honor and the Unity of the Community in Romans 12 and in the Orations of Dio Chrysostom." In *Paul in His Hellenistic Context,* ed. Troels Engberg-Pedersen, 203–30. Minneapolis: Fortress Press, 1999.

Mumford, Lewis. *The City in History: Its Origins, Its Transformations, and Its Prospects.* New York: Harcourt, Brace, and World, 1961.

Münkler, Herfried. *Empires.* Malden, Mass.: Polity Press, 2007.

Munro, Natalie D. "Zooarchaeological Measures of Hunting Pressure and Occupation Intensity in the Natufian." *Current Anthropology* 45 Supplement (2004) S5–S33.

Myers, Ched. *Binding the Strong Man: A Political Reading of Mark's Story of Jesus.* Maryknoll, N.Y.: Orbis Books, 1988.

———. *Who Will Roll Away the Stone?: Discipleship Queries for First World Christians.* Maryknoll, N.Y.: Orbis Books, 1994.

"...*and distributed it to whoever had need.*" *The Biblical Vision of Sabbath Economics.* Washington, D.C.: Tell the Word Press, Church of the Savior, 2001.

———. "Anarcho-Primitivism and the Bible." In *Encyclopedia of Religion and Nature,* 56–58. London: Continuum, 2005.

———. "Easter Faith and Empire: Recovering the Prophetic Tradition on the Emmaus Road." In *Getting on Message: Challenging the Christian Right from the Heart of the Gospel,* ed. Peter Laarman, 51–67. Boston: Beacon Press, 2006.

Myers, Ched, and Elaine Enns. *Ambassadors of Reconciliation: New Testament Reflections on Restorative Justice and Peacemaking.* Maryknoll, N.Y.: Orbis Books, 2009a.

———. *Ambassadors of Reconciliation: Diverse Christian Practices of Restorative Justice and Peacemaking.* Maryknoll, N.Y.: Orbis Books, 2009b.

———. "Brief Notes on the Genesis Creation and Fall Story." In *New Proclamation Commentary on Season of Creation, A: Land Sunday,* ed. David M. Rhoads. Minneapolis: Fortress Press, 2010.

Najman, Hindy. "Interpretation as Primordial Writing: Jubilees and Its Authority Conferring Strategies." *JSJ* 30, no. 4 (1999): 379–410.

Nakanose, Shigeyuki. *Josiah's Passover: Sociology and the Liberating Bible.* Maryknoll, N.Y.: Orbis Books, 1993.

Nelson, Hilde Lindemann. *Damaged Identities, Narrative Repair.* Ithaca, N.Y.: Cornell University Press, 2001.

Nelson, Richard D. "Josiah in the Book of Joshua." *JBL* 100, no. 4 (1981): 531–40.

Neusner, Jacob. *The Midrash: An Introduction.* New York: Jason Aronson, 1994.

———. *Judaism and the Interpretation of Scripture: Introduction to the Rabbinic Midrash.* Peabody, Mass.: Hendrickson, 2004.

Neusner, Jacob, and Alan J. Avery-Peck, eds. *George W. E. Nickelsburg in Perspective: An Ongoing Dialogue of Learning.* Vol. 1. Leiden: Brill, 2003a.

———. *George W. E. Nickelsburg in Perspective: An Ongoing Dialogue of Learning.* Vol. 2. Leiden: Brill, 2003b.

Neusner, Jacob, William S. Green, and Ernest Frerichs, eds. *Judaisms and Their Messiahs at the Turn of the Christian Era.* New York: Cambridge University Press, 1990.

Nevett, Lisa, and Phil Perkins. "Urbanism and Urbanization in the Roman World." In *Experiencing Rome: Culture, Identity, and Power in the Roman Empire,* ed. Janet Huskinson, 213–44. New York: Routledge, 1999.

Newsom, Carol A. *The Self as Symbolic Space: Constructing Identity and Community at Qumran.* Leiden: Brill, 2004.

Nickelsburg, George W. E. *1 Enoch 1: A Commentary on the Book of 1 Enoch Chapters 1–36, 81–108.* Hermeneia: A Critical and Historical Commentary on the Bible. Minneapolis: Fortress Press, 2001.

————. "The Epistle of Enoch and the Qumran Literature." In *George W. E. Nickelsburg in Perspective: An Ongoing Dialogue of Learning.* Vol. 1. Ed. Jacob Neusner and Alan J. Avery-Peck, 105–22. Leiden: Brill, 2003a.

————. "Religious Exclusivism: A Worldview Governing Some Texts Found at Qumran." In *George W. E. Nickelsburg in Perspective: An Ongoing Dialogue of Learning.* Vol. 1. Ed. Jacob Neusner and Alan J. Avery-Peck, 139–61. Leiden: Brill, 2003b.

————. "Response to Gabriele Boccaccini." In *George W. E. Nickelsburg in Perspective: An Ongoing Dialogue of Learning.* Vol. 1. Ed. Jacob Neusner and Alan J. Avery-Peck, 101–4. Leiden: Brill, 2003c.

————. "Revisiting the Rich and the Poor in *1 Enoch* 92–105 and the Gospel according to Luke." In *George W. E. Nickelsburg in Perspective: An Ongoing Dialogue of Learning.* Vol. 2. Ed. Jacob Neusner and Alan J. Avery-Peck, 547–71. Leiden: Brill, 2003d.

————. "Wisdom and Apocalypticism in Early Judaism: Some Points for Discussion." In *Conflicted Boundaries in Wisdom and Apocalypticism,* ed. Benjamin G. Wright III and Lawrence M. Wills, 17–38. Atlanta: Society of Biblical Literature, 2005a.

————. "Response: Context, Text, and Social Setting of the Apocalypse of Weeks." In *Enoch and Qumran Origins: New Light on a Forgotten Connection,* ed. Gabriele Boccaccini, 234–41. Grand Rapids: Eerdmans, 2005b.

————. "Enochic Wisdom and Its Relationship to the Mosaic Torah." In *The Early Enoch Literature,* ed. Gabriele Boccaccini and John J. Collins, 81–94. Leiden: Brill, 2007a.

————. "Discerning the Structure(s) of the Enochic Book of Parables." In *Enoch and the Messiah Son of Man: Revisiting the Book of Parables,* ed. Gabriele Boccaccini, 23–47. Grand Rapids: Eerdmans, 2007b.

Nickelsburg, George W. E., and James C. VanderKam. *1 Enoch: A New Translation.* Minneapolis: Fortress Press, 2004.

Noth, Martin. *The History of Israel.* 2nd ed. New York: HarperCollins, 1960.

Nouwen, Henri J. M. *Life of the Beloved: Spiritual Living in a Secular World.* New York: Crossroad, 2002.

Nouwen, Henri J. M., and Robert A. Jonas. *Henri Nouwen: Writings Selected with an Introduction by Robert A. Jonas.* Maryknoll, N.Y.: Orbis Books, 1998.

Nutton, V. "The Beneficial Ideology." In *Imperialism in the Ancient World,* ed. P. D. A. Garnsey and C. B. Whittaker, 209–21. Cambridge: Cambridge University Press, 1978.

Oakes, Peter. *Philippians: From People to Letter.* SNTSMS. New York: Cambridge University Press, 2001.

————, ed. *Rome in the Bible and the Early Church.* Grand Rapids: Baker Academic, 2002a.

————. "God's Sovereignty over Roman Authorities: A Theme in Philippians." In *Rome in the Bible,* ed. Peter Oakes, 126–41. Grand Rapids: Baker Academic, 2002b.

————. "Re-mapping the Universe: Paul and the Emperor in 1 Thessalonians and Philippians." *JSNT* 27, no. 3 (2005): 301–22.

Oakley, Francis. *Kingship: The Politics of Enchantment.* Madden, Mass.: Blackwell, 2006.

Oblath, Michael D. "Of Pharaohs and Kings — Whence the Exodus?" *JSOT* 87 (2000): 23–42.

O'Brien, William. "The Things Kings Do." *The Other Side* 35, no. 1 (1999).

Odell, Margaret S. *Ezekiel.* Smith and Helwys Bible Commentary. Macon, Ga.: Smyth and Helwys, 2005.

Olley, John W. "Pharaoh's Daughter, Solomon's Palace, and the Temple: Another Look at the Structure of 1 Kings 1–11." *JSOT* 27, no. 3 (2003): 355–69.

Olson, Daniel C. " 'Those Who Have Not Defiled Themselves with Women': Revelation 14:4 and the Book of Enoch." *CBQ* 59, no. 3 (1997): 492–510.

———. "Historical Chronology after the Exile according to *1 Enoch 89–90.*" *JSP* 15, no. 1 (2005): 63–74.

Ong, Walter. *Orality and Literacy.* 2nd ed. New York: Routledge, 2002.

Oppenheim, A. Leo. *Ancient Mesopotamia: Portrait of a Dead Civilization.* Chicago: University of Chicago Press, 1977.

———. "Neo-Assyrian and Neo-Babylonian Empires." In *Propaganda and Communication in World History.* Vol. 1: *The Symbolic Instrument in Early Times,* ed. Harold D. Lasswell, Daniel Lerner, and Hans Speier, 111–44. Honolulu: East-West Center, University of Hawaii, 1979.

Orlov, Andrei A. "The Heavenly Counterpart to Moses in the Book of Jubilees." In *Enoch and the Mosaic Torah: The Evidence of Jubilees,* ed. Gabriele Boccaccini and Giovanni Ibba, 131–44. Grand Rapids: Eerdmans, 2009.

Owen, Paul, and David Shepherd. "Speaking Up for Qumran, Dalman, and the Son of Man: Was Bar Enasha a Common Term for 'Man' in the Time of Jesus?" *JSNT* 81 (2001): 81–122.

Pàmias, Jordi. "Dionysus and Donkeys on the Streets of Alexandria: Eratosthenes' Criticism of Ptolemaic Ideology." *Harvard Studies in Classical Philology* 102 (2004): 191–98.

Panella, Clementina, and André Tchernia. "Agricultural Products Transported in Amphorae: Oil and Wine." In *The Ancient Economy,* ed. Walter Scheidel and Sitta Von Reden, 173–89. New York: Routledge, 2002.

Panter-Brick, Catherine, Robert H. Layton, and Peter Rowley-Conwy, eds. *Hunter-Gatherers: An Interdisciplinary Perspective.* Cambridge: Cambridge University Press, 2001.

Pardes, Ilana. *The Biography of Israel: National Narratives in the Bible.* Berkeley and Los Angeles: University of California Press, 2000.

Parpola, Simo. "Assyria's Expansion in the 8th and 7th Centuries and Its Long-Term Repercussions in the West." In *Symbiosis, Symbolism, and the Power of the Past: Canaan, Ancient Israel, and Their Neighbors from the Late Bronze Age through Roman Palestina,* ed. William G. Dever and Seymour Gitin, 99–111. Winona Lake, Ind.: Eisenbrauns, 2003.

Paul, Shalom M., Robert A. Kraft, Lawrence H. Schiffman, and Weston W. Fields, eds. *Emanuel: Studies in Hebrew Bible, Septuagint and Dead Sea Scrolls in Honor of Emanuel Tov.* Leiden: Brill, 2003.

Pearson, Birger A., and James E. Goehring, eds. *The Roots of Egyptian Christianity.* Minneapolis: Fortress Press, 1997.

Perdue, Leo G. "Wisdom and Apocalyptic: The Case of Qoheleth." In *Wisdom and Apocalypticism in the Dead Sea Scrolls and in the Biblical Tradition,* ed. Florentino García Martínez, 231–58. Leuven: University Press, 2003.

————. *The Sword and the Stylus: An Introduction to Wisdom in the Age of Empires.* Grand Rapids: Eerdmans, 2007.

————, ed. *Scribes, Sages and Seers: The Sage in the Eastern Mediterranean World.* Göttingen: Vandenhoeck & Ruprecht, 2008.

Perkins, Phil. "Power, Culture, and Identity in the Roman Economy." In *Experiencing Rome: Culture, Identity and Power in the Roman Empire,* ed. Janet Huskinson, 183–212. New York: Routledge, 1999.

Pervo, Richard I. *Profit with Delight: The Literary Genre of the Acts of the Apostles.* Minneapolis: Fortress Press, 1987.

Pfoh, Emanuel. "On Israel's Ethnogenesis and Historical Method." *HLS* 7, no. 2 (2008): 213–19.

Piovanelli, Pierluigi. " 'A Testimony for the Kings and the Mighty Who Possess the Earth': The Thirst for Justice and Peace in the Parables of Enoch." In *Enoch and the Messiah Son of Man: Revisiting the Book of Parables,* ed. Gabriele Boccaccini, 363–79. Grand Rapids: Eerdmans, 2007.

Pixley, George. "Micah — A Revolutionary." In *The Bible and the Politics of Exegesis,* ed. David Jobling, Peggy L. Day, and Gerald T. Sheppard, 53–60. Cleveland: Pilgrim Press, 1991.

————. *Exodus: A Liberation Perspective.* Maryknoll, N.Y.: Orbis Books, 1987.

Polaski, Donald C. "*Mene, Mene, Tekel, Parsin:* Writing and Resistance in Daniel 5 and 6." *JBL* 123, no. 4 (2004): 649–69.

————. "What Mean These Stones? Inscriptions, Textuality, and Power in Persia and Yehud." In *Approaching Yehud: New Approaches to the Study of the Persian Period,* ed. Jon L. Berquist, 37–48. Atlanta: Society of Biblical Literature, 2007.

Polley, Max E. *Amos and the Davidic Empire: A Socio-Historical Approach.* New York and Oxford: Oxford University Press, 1989.

Polzin, Robert. *Moses and the Deuteronomist.* Bloomington: Indiana University Press, 1980.

————. *Samuel and the Deuteronomist.* Bloomington: Indiana University Press, 1989.

————. *David and the Deuteronomist.* Bloomington: Indiana University Press, 1993.

Postgate, J. N. *Early Mesopotamia: Society and Economy at the Dawn of History.* London and New York: Routledge, 1994.

Premnath, D. N. *Eighth Century Prophets: A Social Analysis.* Atlanta: Chalice Press, 2003.

Price, S. R. F. *Rituals and Power: The Roman Imperial Cult in Asia Minor.* Cambridge: Cambridge University Press, 1985.

Price, T. Douglas and Anne Birgitte Gebauer. "New Perspectives on the Transition to Agriculture." In *Last Hunters–First Farmers: New Perspectives on the Prehistoric Transition to Agriculture,* ed. T. Douglas Price and Anne Birgitte Gebauer, 3–19. Santa Fe, N.Mex.: School of American Research Press, 1995a.

Price, T. Douglas, and Anne Birgitte Gebauer, eds. *Last Hunters–First Farmers: New Perspectives on the Prehistoric Transition to Agriculture.* Santa Fe, N.Mex.: School of American Research Press, 1995b.

Pyper, Hugh S. "Judging the Wisdom of Solomon: The Two-Way Effect of Intertextuality." *JSOT* 59 (1993): 25–36.

Quinn, Daniel. *Beyond Civilization: Humanity's Next Great Adventure.* New York: Three Rivers Press, 2000.

Ramsaran, Rollin A. "Resisting Imperial Domination and Influence: Paul's Apocalyptic Rhetoric in 1 Corinthians." In *Paul and the Roman Imperial Order,* ed. Richard A. Horsley, 89–102. Harrisburg, Pa.: Trinity Press International, 2004.

Rapske, Brian. *The Book of Acts and Paul in Roman Custody.* Grand Rapids: Eerdmans, 1994.

Redditt, Paul L. "Israel's Shepherds: Hope and Pessimism in Zechariah 9–14." *CBQ* 51, no. 4 (1989): 631–42.

———. "Nehemiah's First Mission and the Date of Zechariah 9–14." *CBQ* 56, no. 4 (1994): 664–78.

———. "Daniel 11 and the Sociohistorical Setting of the Book of Daniel." *CBQ* 60, no. 3 (1998): 463–74.

———. "Daniel 9: Its Structure and Meaning." *CBQ* 62, no. 2 (2000): 236–49.

Reed, David. "Rethinking John's Social Setting: Hidden Transcript, Anti-language, and the Negotiation of the Empire." *BTB* 36, no. 3 (2006): 93–106.

Rendtorff, Rolf. "Is it Possible to Read Leviticus as a Separate Book?" In *Reading Leviticus: A Conversation with Mary Douglas.* JSOTSS 227. Ed. John A. Sawyer, 22–35. Sheffield: Sheffield Academic Press, 1996.

———. *"The gēr in the Priestly Laws of the Pentateuch."* In *Ethnicity and the Bible,* ed. Mark G. Brett, 77–87. Boston: Brill Academic, 2002.

Rendtorff, Rolf, and Robert A. Kugler, eds. *The Book of Leviticus: Composition and Reception.* Supplements to Vetus Testamentum. Atlanta: Society of Biblical Literature, 2006.

Richard, Pablo. *Apocalypse: A People's Commentary on the Book of Revelation.* Maryknoll, N.Y.: Orbis Books, 1995.

Riches, John, and David C. Sim, eds. *The Gospel of Matthew in Its Roman Imperial Context.* New York and London: T. & T. Clark, 2005.

Richey, Lance Byron. *Roman Imperial Ideology and the Gospel of John.* CBQMS 43. Washington, D.C.: Catholic Biblical Association of America, 2007.

Rieger, Joerg. *Christ and Empire: From Paul to Postcolonial Times.* Minneapolis: Fortress Press, 2007.

Rieterer, Friederich V. "The Sociological Significance of the Scribe as the Teacher of Wisdom in Ben Sira." In *Scribes, Sages, and Seers: The Sage in the Eastern Mediterranean World,* ed. Leo G. Perdue, 218–44. Göttingen: Vandenhoeck & Ruprecht, 2008.

Rives, James. "Religion in the Roman World." In *Experiencing Rome: Culture, Identity, and Power in the Roman Empire,* ed. Janet Huskinson, 245–76. New York: Routledge, 1999.

Rosenberg, Emily. *Spreading the American Dream: American Economic and Cultural Expansion 1890–1945.* New York: Hill and Wang, 1982.

Rosenberg, Joel. *King and Kin: Political Allegory in the Hebrew Bible.* Bloomington: Indiana University Press, 1986.

Rosenblatt, Jason P., and Joseph C. Sitterson, eds. *"Not in Heaven": Coherence and Complexity in Biblical Narrative.* Bloomington: Indiana University Press, 1991.

Rossing, Barbara R. *The Rapture Exposed: The Message of Hope in the Book of Revelation.* New York: Basic Books, 2005.

Rowe, Kavin C. "Luke-Acts and the Imperial Cult: A Way through the Conundrum?" *JSNT* 27, no. 3 (2005): 279–300.

———. *World Turned Upside Down: Reading Acts in the Graeco-Roman Age.* Oxford: Oxford University Press, 2009.

Rowley-Conwy, Peter. "Time, Change, and the Archaeology of Hunter-Gatherers: How Original is the 'Original Affluent Society'?" In *Hunter-Gatherers: An Interdisciplinary Perspective,* ed. Catherine Panter-Brick, Robert H. Layton, and Peter Rowley-Conwy, 39–72. Cambridge: Cambridge University Press, 2001.

Rudman, Dominic. "Is the Rabshakeh Also among the Prophets? A Rhetorical Study of 2 Kings XVIII 17–35." *Vetus Testamentum* 50, no. 1 (2000): 100–110.

Radford Ruether, Rosemary. *Sexism and God-Talk: Toward a Feminist Theology.* Boston: Beacon, 1983.

Sacchi, Paolo. *Jewish Apocalyptic and History.* JSPSS 20. Trans. William J. Short, O.F.M. Sheffield: Sheffield Academic Press, 1990.

———. *The History of the Second Temple Period.* JSOTSS 285. Sheffield: Sheffield Academic Press, 2000.

———. "History of the Earliest Enochic Texts." In *Enoch and Qumran Origins: New Light on a Forgotten Connection,* ed. Gabriele Boccaccini, 401–7. Grand Rapids: Eerdmans, 2005.

Sahlins, Marshall. *Stone Age Economics.* Piscataway, N.J.: Aldine/Transaction, 1972.

Saldarini, Anthony J. *Pharisees, Scribes, and Sadducees in Palestinian Society.* Grand Rapids: Eerdmans, and Livonia, Mich.: Dove, 2001.

Sale, Kirkpatrick. *After Eden: The Evolution of Human Domination.* Durham, N.C., and London: Duke University Press, 2006.

Salvesen, Alison. "The Trappings of Royalty in Ancient Hebrew." In *King and Messiah in Israel and the Ancient Near East.* JSOTSS 270. Ed. John Day. Sheffield: Sheffield Academic Press, 1998.

Sanders, E. P. *Paul and Palestinian Judaism: A Comparison of Patterns of Religion.* Minneapolis: Fortress Press, 1977.

Sarna, Nahum. *Understanding Genesis.* New York: Schocken, 1970.

———. *JPS Torah Commentary: Genesis.* Philadelphia: Jewish Publication Society, 1989.

———. *Exodus: The Traditional Hebrew Text with the New JPS Translation.* JPS Torah Commentary. Philadelphia: Jewish Publication Society, 1991.

———. *Exploring Exodus: The Origins of Biblical Israel.* New York: Schocken, 1996.

Sawyer, John F. A., ed. *Reading Leviticus: A Conversation with Mary Douglas.* JSOTSS 227. Sheffield: Sheffield Academic Press, 1996.

Schäfer, Peter. *Judeophobia: Attitudes toward the Jews in the Ancient World.* Cambridge: Harvard University Press, 1998.

Schallenberg, Angeline Falk. "One in the Bond of War: The Unity of Deutero-Zechariah." *Didaskalia* 12, no. 2 (2001): 101–15.

Scham, Sandra. "The Days of the Judges: When Men and Women Were Animals and Trees Were Kings." *JSOT* 97 (2002): 37–64.

Scheidel, Walter, and Sitta Von Reden, eds. *The Ancient Economy.* New York: Routledge, 2002.

Schenker, Adrian. "Jeroboam's Rise and Fall in the Hebrew and Greek Bible." *JSJ* 39 (2008): 367–73.

Schiffman, Lawrence H. "The Pharisees and Their Legal Traditions according to the Dead Sea Scrolls." *DSS* 8, no. 3 (2001): 262–77.

Schneider, Tammi J. *Judges: Studies in Hebrew Narrative and Poetry.* Berit Olam. Collegeville, Minn.: Liturgical Press, 2000.

Schneiders, Sandra M. *Women and the Word: The Gender of God in the New Testament and the Spirituality of Women.* New York: Paulist Press, 1986.

———. *Written That You May Believe: Encountering Jesus in the Fourth Gospel.* 2nd rev. ed. New York: Crossroad, 2003.

Schofield, Alison, and James C. VanderKam. "Were the Hasmoneans Zadokites?" *JBL* 124, no. 1 (2005): 73–87.

Schöpflin, Karin. "Jotham's Speech and Fable as Prophetic Comment on Abimelech's Story: The Genesis of Judges 9." *SJOT* 18, no. 1 (2004): 3–22.

Schottroff, Luise. "The Creation Narrative: Genesis 1:2–24a." In *A Feminist Companion to Genesis,* ed. Athalya Brenner, 24–38. Sheffield: Sheffield Academic Press, 1993, 1997.

Schüssler Fiorenza, Elisabeth. *In Memory of Her: A Feminist Theological Reconstruction of Christian Origins.* New York: Herder and Herder, 1983.

———. "The Ethics of Biblical Interpretation: Decentering Biblical Scholarship." *JBL* 107, no. 1 (1988): 3–17.

———. *Revelation: Vision of a Just World.* Minneapolis: Fortress Press, 1991.

———. *Rhetoric and Ethic: The Politics of Biblical Studies.* Minneapolis: Fortress Press, 1999.

———. "Paul and the Politics of Interpretation." In *Paul and Politics: Ekklesia, Israel, Imperium, Interpretation,* ed. Richard A. Horsley, 40–57. Harrisburg, Pa.: Trinity Press International, 2000.

———. *The Power of the Word: Scripture and the Rhetoric of Empire.* Minneapolis: Fortress Press, 2007.

Schwartz, Seth. *Imperialism and Jewish Society: 200 B.C.E. to 640 C.E.* Princeton: Princeton University Press, 2004.

Scott, James C. *Weapons of the Weak: Everyday Forms of Peasant Resistance.* New Haven, Conn.: Yale, 1987.

———. *Domination and the Arts of Resistance: Hidden Transcripts.* New Haven, Conn.: Yale, 1992.

Scott, James M. "The Chronologies of the Apocalypse of Weeks and the Book of Jubilees." In *Enoch and the Mosaic Torah: The Evidence of Jubilees,* ed. Gabriele Boccaccini and Giovanni Ibba, 67–81. Grand Rapids: Eerdmans, 2009.

Seeley, David. "The Background of the Philippians Hymn (2:6–11)." *JHC* 1 (1994): 49–72.

Segal, Alan F. *Paul the Convert: The Apostolate and Apostasy of Saul the Pharisee.* New Haven, Conn.: Yale University Press, 1992.

———. "Universalism in Judaism and Christianity." In *Paul in His Hellenistic Context,* ed. Troels Engberg-Pedersen, 1–29. Minneapolis: Fortress Press, 1999.

Segovia, Fernando. *Decolonizing Biblical Studies: A View from the Margins.* Maryknoll, N.Y.: Orbis Books, 2000.

Segovia, Fernando, and Maryann Tolbert, eds. *Reading from This Place.* Vol. 1: *Social Location and Biblical Interpretation in the United States.* Minneapolis: Fortress Press, 1995.

———. *Reading from This Place.* Vol. 2: *Social Location and Biblical Interpretation in Global Perspective.* Minneapolis: Fortress Press, 2000.

Seitz, Christopher. *Theology in Conflict: Reactions to the Exile in the Book of Jeremiah.* BZAW 176. Berlin: de Gruyter, 1989.

————. "You Are My *Servant,* You Are the Israel in Whom I Will Be Glorified": The *Servant Songs* and the Effect of Literary Context in Isaiah." *CTJ* 39, no. 1 (2004): 117–34.

Seow, Choon-Leong. "Linguistic Evidence and the Dating of Qohelet." *JBL* 115, no. 4 (1996): 643–66.

————. "Theology When Everything is Out of Control." *Int* 55, no. 3 (2001): 237–49.

————. "The Social World of Ecclesiastes." In *Scribes, Sages, and Seers: The Sage in the Eastern Mediterranean World,* ed. Leo G. Perdue, 189–217. Göttingen: Vandenhoeck & Ruprecht, 2008.

Shantz, Colleen. *Paul in Ecstasy: The Neurobiology of the Apostle's Life and Thought.* Cambridge: Cambridge University Press, 2009.

Shaper, Joachim. "The Jerusalem Temple as an Instrument of the Achaemenid Fiscal Administration." *VT* 45 (1995): 528–39.

Sharp, Carolyn J. "The Call of Jeremiah and Diaspora Politics." *JBL* 119, no. 3 (2000): 421–38.

Shea, Christopher. "Debunking Ancient Israel: Erasing History or Facing the Truth?" *Chronicle of Higher Education* 21 (November 1997).

Shepard, Paul. *Coming Home to the Pleistocene.* Washington, D.C.: Island Press, 1998.

Sherratt, Andrew. "Plough and Pastoralism: Aspects of the Secondary Products Revolution" (1981). In *Economy and Society in Prehistoric Europe,* by Andrew Sherratt, 158–98. Princeton, N.J.: Princeton University Press, 1997a.

————. "The Secondary Exploitation of Animals in the Old World," (1983). In *Economy and Society in Prehistoric Europe,* by Andrew Sherratt, 199–228. Princeton, N.J.: Princeton University Press, 1997b.

————. "Changing Perspectives on European Prehistory," (1997b). In *Economy and Society in Prehistoric Europe,* by Andrew Sherratt, 1–35. Princeton, N.J.: Princeton University Press, 1997c.

————. *Economy and Society in Prehistoric Europe.* Princeton, N.J.: Princeton University Press, 1997d.

Simon-Shoshan, Moshe. "The Tasks of the Translators: The Rabbis, the Septuagint, and the Cultural Politics of Translation." *Prooftexts* 27, no. 1 (2007): 1–39.

Smith, Abraham. *Comfort One Another: Reconstructing the Rhetoric and Audience of 1 Thessalonians.* Louisville: Westminster John Knox, 1995.

Smith, Anthony D. *The Ethnic Origins of Nations.* London: Blackwell, 1988.

————. *National Identity.* Reno: University of Nevada Press, 1993.

Smith, Christopher C. "Ἐκκλεῖσαι in Galatians 4:17: The Motif of the Excluded Lover as a Metaphor of Manipulation." *CBQ* 58, no. 3 (1996): 480–99.

Smith, Daniel L. *The Religion of the Landless: The Social Context of the Babylonian Exile.* Bloomington, Ind.: Meyer Stone, 1989.

Smith, Mark S. *The Early History of God: Yahweh and the Other Deities in Ancient Israel.* 2nd ed. Grand Rapids: Eerdmans, 2002.

Smith-Christopher, Daniel L. "The Mixed Marriage Crisis in Ezra 9–10 and Nehemiah 13: A Study of the Sociology of the Post-Exilic Judean Community." In *Second Temple Studies.* Vol. 2: *Temple and Community in the Persian Period.* JSOTSS 175. Ed. Tamara C. Eskenazi and Kent H. Richards, 243–65. Sheffield: JSOT Press, 1994.

————. "Daniel." In *New Interpreter's Bible.* Vol. 7. Nashville: Abingdon, 1996.

————. "Between Ezra and Isaiah: Exclusion, Transformation, and Inclusion of the 'Foreigner' in Post-Exilic Biblical Theology." In *Ethnicity and the Bible,* ed. Mark G. Brett, 117–42. Boston: Brill Academic, 2002a.

————. "Prayers and Dreams: Power and Diaspora Identities in the Social Setting of the Daniel Tales." In *The Book of Daniel: Composition and Reception.* Vol. 1. Ed. John J. Collins and Peter W. Flint, 266–90. Leiden: Brill Academic, 2002b.

Sneed, Mark. "Qohelth and His 'Vulgar' Critics." *The Bible and Critical Theory* 1, no. 1 (2004): 1–11.

Sommer, Benjamin D. "Allusions and Illusions: The Unity of the Book of Isaiah in Light of Deuter.-Isaiah's Use of Prophetic Tradition." In *New Visions of Isaiah,* ed. Roy F. Melugin and Marvin A. Sweeney, 156–87. Atlanta: Society of Biblical Literature, 1996.

Sparks, Kenton L. *Ethnicity and Identity in Ancient Israel: Prolegomena to the Study of Ethnic Sentiments and Their Expression in the Hebrew Bible.* Winona Lake, Ind.: Eisenbrauns 1998.

————. Review, "Israel's Ethnogenesis: Settlement, Interaction, Expansion, and Resistance." *RBL* (2008) accessed at *www.bookreviews.org/bookdetail.asp? TitleId=6334&CodePage=6334.*

Spickard, Paul, and W. Jeffrey Burroughs, eds. *We Are a People: Narrative and Multiplicity in Constructing Ethnic Identity.* Philadelphia: Temple University Press, 2000.

Spieckermann, Hermann. "The Conception and Prehistory of the Idea of Vicarious Suffering in the Old Testament." In *The Suffering Servant: Isaiah 53 in Jewish and Christian Sources,* ed. Bernd Janowski and Peter Stuhlmacher, 1–15. Grand Rapids: Eerdmans, 2004.

Stager, Lawrence E. "The Patrimonial Kingdom of Solomon, in *Symbiosis, Symbolism, and the Power of the Past: Canaan, Ancient Israel, and Their Neighbors from the Late Bronze Age through Roman Palestina,* ed. William G. Dever and Seymour Gitin, 63–74. Winona Lake, Ind.: Eisenbrauns, 2003.

Stassen, Glen H. *Living the Sermon on the Mount: A Practical Hope for Grace and Deliverance.* San Francisco: Jossey-Bass, 2006.

Stassen, Glen H., and David P. Gushee. *Kingdom Ethics: Following Jesus in Contemporary Context.* Downers Grove, Ill.: Intervarsity Press, 2003.

Steinberg, Naomi. "The Deuteronomic Law Code and the Politics of State Centralization." In *The Bible and the Politics of Exegesis,* ed. David Jobling, Peggy L. Day and Gerald T. Sheppard, 161–72. Cleveland: Pilgrim Press, 1991.

————. *Kinship and Marriage in Genesis: A Household Economics Perspective.* Minneapolis: Fortress Press, 1993.

————. "Social Scientific Criticism: Judges 9 and Issues of Kinship." In *Judges and Method: New Approaches to Biblical Studies,* ed. Gale A. Yee, 45–64. Minneapolis: Fortress Press, 1995.

Stendahl, Krister. "The Apostle Paul and the Introspective Conscience of the West." (1963) reprinted. *Paul among Jews and Gentiles and Other Essays,* ed. Krister Stendahl, 78–96. Minneapolis: Fortress Press, 1976.

Stephanson, Anders. *Manifest Destiny: American Expansion and the Empire of Right.* New York: Hill and Wang, 1995.

Sternberg, Meir. *The Poetics of Biblical Narrative Literature.* Bloomington: Indiana University Press, 1985.

————. "Double Cave, Double Talk." In *"Not in Heaven"*: *Coherence and Complexity in Biblical Narrative*, ed. Jason P. Rosenblatt and Joseph C. Sitterson, 28–57. Bloomington: Indiana University Press, 1991.

————. *Hebrews between Cultures: Group Portraits and National Literature.* Bloomington: Indiana University Press, 1999.

Stewart, Robert B., John Dominic Crossan, and N. T. Wright. *The Resurrection of Jesus: John Dominic Crossan and N. T. Wright in Dialogue.* Minneapolis: Fortress Press, 2006.

Strawn, Brent A. " 'A World under Control': Isaiah 60 and the Apadana Reliefs from Persepolis." In *Approaching Yehud: New Approaches to the Study of the Persian Period*, ed. Jon L. Berquist, 85–116. Atlanta: Society of Biblical Literature, 2007.

Stringfellow, William. *An Ethic for Christians and Other Aliens in a Strange Land.* Eugene, Ore.: Wipf & Stock, 2004a.

————. *Conscience and Obedience: The Politics of Romans 13 and Revelation 13 in Light of the Second Coming.* Eugene, Ore.: Wipf & Stock, 2004b.

Stuckenbruck, Loren T. *1 Enoch 91–108.* New York: Walter de Gruyter, 2007.

Stulman, Louis. *Jeremiah.* Abingdon Old Testament Commentaries. Nashville: Abingdon, 2005.

Sugirtharajah, R. S., ed. *Voices from the Margin: Interpreting the Bible in the Third World.* Maryknoll, N.Y.: Orbis Books, 1993.

Suter, David W. "Temples and the Temple in the Early Enoch Tradition: Memory, Vision, and Expectation." In *The Early Enoch Literature*, ed. Gabriele Boccaccini and John J. Collins, 195–218. Leiden: Brill, 2007.

Swartley, Willard. *Covenant of Peace: The Missing Peace in New Testament Theology and Ethics.* Grand Rapids: Eerdmans, 2006.

Sweeney, Marvin A. "The Critique of Solomon in the Josianic Edition of the Deuteronomistic History." *JBL* 114, no. 4 (1995): 607–22.

————. *King Josiah of Judah: The Lost Messiah of Judah.* New York: Oxford University Press, 2000a.

————. *The Twelve Prophets.* Vol. 2: *Micah, Nahum, Habakkuk, Zephaniah, Haggai, Zechariah, Malachi.* Berit Olam. Collegeville, Minn.: Michael Glazier, 2000b.

————. "The End of Eschatology in Daniel? Theological and Socio-political Ramifications of the Changing Contexts of Interpretation." *Bib.Int.* 9, no. 2 (2001a): 123–40.

————. *The Twelve Prophets.* Vol. 1: *Hosea, Joel, Amos, Obadiah, Jonah.* Berit Olam. Collegeville, Minn.: Liturgical Press, 2001b.

————. "A Reassessment of the Masoretic and Septuagint Versions of the Jeroboam Narratives in 1 Kings/3 Kingdoms 11–14." *JSJ* 38 (2007): 165–95.

Sweet, J. P. M. *Revelation.* Louisville: Westminster John Knox, 1979.

Talmon, Shemaryahu, Michael A. Fishbane; Emanuel Tov, and Weston W. Fields, eds. *Sha'arei Talmon: Studies in the Bible, Qumran, and the Ancient Near East presented to Shemaryahu Talmon.* Winona Lake, Ind.: Eisenbrauns, 1992.

Tamez, Elsa. "Hagar and Sarah in Galatians: A Case Study in Freedom." Trans. Gloria Kinsler. *Word & World* 20, no. 3 (2000): 265–71.

————. *Struggles for Power in Early Christianity: A Study of the First Letter to Timothy.* Maryknoll, N.Y.: Orbis Books, 2007.

Taubes, Jacob. *The Political Theology of Paul*. Stanford, Calif.: Stanford University Press, 2004.

Taylor, Charles. *A Secular Age*. Cambridge: Belknap Press, 2007.

Taylor, Jean Gelman. *Indonesia: Peoples and Histories*. New Haven, Conn.: Yale University Press, 2003.

Taylor, Joan E. *Jewish Women Philosophers of First-Century Alexandria: Philo's 'Therapeutae' Reconsidered*. Oxford: Oxford University Press, 2003.

Tellbe, Mikael. *Paul between Synagogue and State: Christians, Jews, and Civic Authorities in 1 Thessalonians, Romans, and Philippians*. Stockholm: Almqvist & Wiksell International, 2001.

Thatcher, Tom. *Greater Than Caesar: Christology and Empire in the Fourth Gospel*. Minneapolis: Fortress Press, 2009.

Thiselton, Anthony C. *The First Epistle to the Corinthians*. New International Greek Testament Commentary. Grand Rapids: Eerdmans, 2000.

Tigay, Jeffrey. *Deuteronomy*. JPS Torah Commentary. Philadelphia: JPS, 1996.

Tiller, Patrick. *A Commentary on the Animal Apocalypse of I Enoch*. Atlanta: Scholars Press, 1993.

———. "Israel at the Mercy of Demonic Powers: An Enochic Interpretation of Post-exilic Imperialism." In *Conflicted Boundaries in Wisdom and Apocalypticism*, ed. Benjamin G. Wright III and Lawrence M. Wills, 113–21. Atlanta: Society of Biblical Literature, 2005.

———. "The Sociological Settings of the Components of 1 Enoch." In *The Early Enoch Literature*, ed. Gabriele Boccaccini and John J. Collins, 238–55. Leiden: Brill, 2007.

Tracy, David. *The Analogical Imagination: Christian Theology and the Culture of Pluralism*. New York: Crossroad, 1981.

Trible, Phyllis. *God and the Rhetoric of Sexuality*. Minneapolis: Fortress Press, 1978.

Turner, Laurence. *Genesis*. Sheffield: Sheffield Academic Press, 1999.

Vanderhooft, David. "Babylonian Strategies of Imperial Control in the West: Royal Practice and Rhetoric." In *Judah and the Judeans in the Neo-Babylonian Period*, ed. Oded Lipschits and Joseph Blenkinsopp, 235–62. Winona Lake, Ind.: Eisenbrauns, 2003.

VanderKam, James C. *The Dead Sea Scrolls Today*. Grand Rapids: Eerdmans, 1994.

———. *Enoch: A Man for All Generations*. Columbia: University of South Carolina Press, 1995.

———. "1 Enoch, Enochic Motifs, and Enoch in Early Christian Literature." In *The Jewish Apocalyptic Heritage in Early Christianity*, ed. James C. VanderKam and William Aler, 33–101. Minneapolis: Fortress Press, 1996.

———. *The Book of Jubilees*. Sheffield: Sheffield Academic Press, 2001.

———. "Those Who Look for Smooth Things, Pharisees, and Oral Law." In *Emanuel: Studies in Hebrew Bible, Septuagint and Dead Sea Scrolls in Honor of Emanuel Tov*, ed. Shalom M. Paul, Robert A. Kraft, Lawrence H. Schiffman, and Weston W. Fields, 465–77. Leiden: Brill, 2003.

———. *From Joshua to Caiaphas: High Priests after the Exile*. Minneapolis: Fortress Press, 2004.

———. "Mapping Second Temple Judaism." In *The Early Enoch Literature*, ed. Gabriele Boccaccini and John J. Collins, 1–20. Leiden: Brill, 2007a.

————. "The Book of Parables within the Enoch Tradition." In *Enoch and the Messiah Son of Man: Revisiting the Book of Parables*, ed. Gabriele Boccaccini, 81–99. Grand Rapids: Eerdmans, 2007b.

————. "Recent Scholarship on the Book of Jubilees." *CBR* 6, no. 3 (2008): 405–31.

VanderKam, James C., and William Adler, eds. *The Jewish Apocalyptic Heritage in Early Christianity.* Minneapolis: Fortress Press, 1996.

VanderKam, James C., and Peter Flint. *The Meaning of the Dead Sea Scrolls.* London and New York: T. & T. Clark, 2002.

Van Der Toorn, Karel. "Scholars at the Oriental Court: The Figure of Daniel against Its Mesopotamian Background." In *The Book of Daniel: Composition and Reception.* Vol. 1. Ed. John J. Collins and Peter W. Flint, 37–54. Leiden: Brill Academic, 2002.

————. *Scribal Culture and the Making of the Hebrew Bible.* Cambridge: Harvard University Press, 2007.

Van Wolde, Ellen. *Stories of the Beginning: Genesis 1–11 and Other Creation Stories.* Harrisburg, Pa.: Morehouse, 1996.

————. "The Earth Story as Presented by the Tower of Babel Narrative." In *Earth Story in Genesis.* The Earth Bible Series. Ed. Normal C. Habel and Shirley Wurst, 147–57. Cleveland: Pilgrim Press, 2001.

Valeta, David M. "Court or Jester Tales? Resistance and Social Reality in Daniel 1–6." *PRSt* 32, no. 3 (2005): 309–24.

————. "The Book of Daniel in Recent Research (Part 1)." *CBR* 6A (2008): 330–54.

Van Henten, Jan Willem. "Daniel 3 and 6 in Early Christian Literature." In *The Book of Daniel: Composition and Reception.* Vol. 1. Ed. John J. Collins and Peter W. Flint, 149–69. Leiden: Brill Academic, 2002.

Venter, Pieter M. "Spatiality in Enoch's Journeys (1 Enoch 12–36)." In *Wisdom and Apocalypticism in the Dead Sea Scrolls and in the Biblical Tradition,* ed. Florentino García Martínez, 211–30. Leuven: University Press, 2003.

Verheyden, Joseph. "The Fate of the Righteous and the Cursed at Qumran and in the Gospel of Matthew." In *Wisdom and Apocalypticism in the Dead Sea Scrolls and in the Biblical Tradition,* ed. Florentino García Martínez, 427–49. Leuven: University Press, 2003.

Von Wolde, Ellen. *Stories of the Beginning: Genesis 1–11 and Other Creation Stories.* New York: Morehouse Group, 1996.

Wallace, Howard N. "Rest for the Earth? Another Look at Genesis 2:1–3." In *Earth Story in Genesis.* The Earth Bible Series. Ed. Normal C. Habel and Shirley Wurst, 49–72. Cleveland: Pilgrim Press, 2001.

Wallerstein, Immanuel. *The Modern World System: Capitalist Agriculture and the Origins of the European World Economy in the Sixteenth Century.* New York: Academic Press, 1974.

————. *World Systems Analysis: An Introduction.* Chapel Hill, N.C.: Duke University Press, 2004.

Walsh, Brian J., and Sylvia Keesmaat. *Colossians Remixed: Subverting the Empire.* Downers Grove, Ill.: Intervarsity Press, 2004.

Walton, Steve. "The State They Were In: Luke's View of the Roman Empire." In *Rome in the Bible and the Early Church,* ed. Peter Oakes, 1–41. Grand Rapids: Baker Academic, 2002.

Walzer, Michael. *Exodus and Revolution.* New York: Basic Books, 1986.

Wan, Sze-kar. "Collection for the Saints as Anticolonial Act: Implications of Paul's Ethnic Reconstruction." In *Paul and Politics: Ekklesia, Israel, Imperium, Interpretation,* ed. Richard A. Horsley, 191–216. Harrisburg, Pa.: Trinity Press International, 2000.

Wason, Paul K. *The Archaeology of Rank.* Cambridge: Cambridge University Press, 1994.

Wasserstein, Abraham, and David J. Wasserstein. *The Legend of the Septuagint: From Classical Antiquity to Today.* Cambridge: Cambridge University Press, 2006.

Watts, James W., ed. *Persia and Torah: The Theory of Imperial Authorization of the Pentateuch.* Atlanta: SBL, 2001.

Weatherford, Jack. *Savages and Civilization: Who Will Survive?* New York: Ballantine, 1995.

Weber, Timothy P. *On the Road to Armageddon: How Evangelicals Became Israel's Best Friend.* Grand Rapids: Baker Academic, 2005.

Weigel, George. *American Interests, American Purpose: Moral Reasoning and U.S. Foreign Policy.* Santa Barbara, Calif.: Praeger, 1989.

Weinbrot, Howard D. *Menippean Satire Reconsidered: From Antiquity to the Eighteenth Century.* Baltimore: Johns Hopkins University Press, 2005.

Wengst, Klaus. *Pax Romana and the Peace of Jesus Christ.* Minneapolis: Fortress Press, 1987.

Wenham, Gordon. *Word Biblical Commentary.* Vol. 1: *Genesis 1–15.* Waco, Tex.: Nelson Reference, 1987.

———. *Word Biblical Commentary.* Vol. 2: *Genesis 16–50.* Waco: Nelson Reference, 1994a.

———. *Leviticus.* New International Commentary on the Old Testament. Grand Rapids: Eerdmans, 1994b.

Werline, Rodney A. "*The Psalms of Solomon* and the Ideology of Rule." In *Conflicted Boundaries in Wisdom and Apocalypticism,* ed. Benjamin G. Wright III and Lawrence M. Wills, 69–87. Atlanta: Society of Biblical Literature, 2005.

Westermann, Claus. *Genesis 37–50: A Continental Commentary.* Minneapolis: Fortress Press, 1986.

———. *Genesis 1–11: A Continental Commentary.* Minneapolis: Fortress Press, 1994.

———. *Genesis 12–36. A Continental Commentary.* Minneapolis: Fortress Press, 1995.

White, Hugh. *Narration and Discourse in the Book of Genesis.* Cambridge: Cambridge University Press, 2003.

White, Marsha. "Naboth's Vineyard and Jehu's Coup: The Legitimation of a Dynastic Extermination." *VT* 44, no. 1 (1994): 66–76.

Whitelam, Keith W. "The Symbols of Power: Aspects of Royal Propaganda in the United Monarchy." *BA* 49, no. 3 (1986): 166–73.

Wiesehöfer, Josef. "The Achaemenid Empire." In *The Dynamics of Ancient Empires: State Power from Assyria to Byzantium,* ed. Ian Morris and Walter Scheidel, 66–98. Oxford: Oxford University Press, 2009.

Williams, Gary R. "Contextual Influences in Readings of Nehemiah 5: A Case Study." *Tyndal Bulletin* 53, no. 1 (2002): 57–74.

Williams, Margaret. "Jews and Jewish Communities in the Roman Empire." In *Experiencing Rome: Culture, Identity, and Power in the Roman Empire,* ed. Janet Huskinson, 305–34. New York: Routledge, 1999.

Williamson, H. G. M. "The Family in Persian Period Judah: Some Textual Reflections." In *Symbiosis, Symbolism, and the Power of the Past: Canaan, Ancient Israel, and Their Neighbors from the Late Bronze Age through Roman Palestina,* ed. William G. Dever and Seymour Gitin, 469–85. Winona Lake, Ind.: Eisenbrauns, 2003.

Wills, Lawrence M. *The Jews in the Court of the Foreign King: Ancient Jewish Court Legends.* Minneapolis: Fortress Press, 1990.

Wink, Walter. *Naming the Powers: The Language of Power in the New Testament.* The Powers. Vol. 1. Minneapolis: Fortress Press, 1984.

———. *Unmasking the Powers.* The Powers. Vol. 2. Minneapolis: Fortress Press, 1986.

———. *Engaging the Powers: Discernment and Resistance in a World of Domination.* The Powers. Vol. 3. Minneapolis: Fortress Press, 1992.

———. *The Human Being: Jesus and the Enigma of the Son of the Man.* Minneapolis: Fortress Press, 2001.

Winter, Bruce W. *Seek the Welfare of the City: Early Christians as Benefactors and Citizens.* Grand Rapids: Eerdmans, 1994.

———. "Roman Law and Society in Romans 12–15." In *Rome in the Bible and the Early Church,* ed. Peter Oakes, 67–102. Grand Rapids: Baker Academic, 2002.

Winter, Bruce W., and Andrew D. Clarke, eds. *The Book of Acts in Its Ancient Literary Setting.* Grand Rapids: Eerdmans, 1994.

Wise, Michael O. *A Critical Study of the Temple Scroll from Qumran Cave 11.* SAOC 49. Chicago: Oriental Institute of the University of Chicago, 1990.

———. "Dating the Teacher of Righteousness and the Floruit of His Movement." *JBL* 122, no. 1 (2003): 53–87.

Witherington, III, Ben. *Paul's Narrative Thought World.* Louisville: Westminster John Knox, 1994.

———. *Conflict and Community in Corinth: A Socio-Rhetorical Commentary on 1 and 2 Corinthians.* Grand Rapids: Eerdmans, 1995.

———. *The Acts of the Apostles: A Socio-Rhetorical Commentary.* Grand Rapids: Eerdmans, 1997.

———. *Paul's Letter to the Romans: A Socio-Rhetorical Commentary.* Grand Rapids: Eerdmans, 2004.

Wittenberg, Gunther. "Alienation and 'Emancipation' from the Earth: The Earth Story in Genesis 4." In *Earth Story in Genesis.* The Earth Bible Series. Ed. Normal C. Habel and Shirley Wurst, 105–16. Cleveland: Pilgrim Press, 2001.

Wood, Gordon S. *Empire of Liberty: A History of the Early Republic, 1789–1815.* Oxford History of the United States. Oxford: Oxford University Press, 2009.

Wright, III, Benjamin G., and Lawrence M. Wills, eds. *Conflicted Boundaries in Wisdom and Apocalypticism.* Atlanta: Society of Biblical Literature, 2005.

Wright, N. T. *The New Testament and the People of God.* Christian Origins and the Question of God. Vol. 1. Minneapolis: Fortress Press, 1992.

———. *Climax of the Covenant: Christ and the Law in Pauline Theology.* Minneapolis: Fortress Press, 1993.

———. *Jesus and the Victory of God.* Christian Origins and the Question of God. Vol. 2. Minneapolis: Fortress Press, 1996a.

———. "Paul, Arabia, and Elijah (Galatians 1:17)." *JBL* 115, no. 4 (1996b): 683–92.

———. *What Saint Paul Really Said: Was Paul of Tarsus the Real Founder of Christianity?* Grand Rapids: Eerdmans, 1997.

———. "Paul's Gospel and Caesar's Empire." In *Paul and Politics: Ekklesia, Israel, Imperium, Interpretation,* ed. Richard A. Horsley, 160–83. Harrisburg, Pa.: Trinity Press International, 2000.

———. "Romans." In *The New Interpreter's Bible: Acts-First Corinthians.* Vol. 10. Nashville: Abingdon, 2002.

———. *The Resurrection of the Son of God.* Christian Origins and the Question of God. Vol. 3. Minneapolis: Fortress Press, 2003.

———. *Paul: In Fresh Perspective.* Minneapolis: Fortress Press, 2009.

Wylie-Kellerman, Bill, ed. *A Keeper of the Word: Selected Writings of William Stringfellow.* Grand Rapids: Eerdmans, 1996.

Yee, Gale A., ed. *Judges and Method: New Approaches to Biblical Studies.* Minneapolis: Fortress Press, 1995.

Zanker, Paul. *The Power of Images in the Age of Augustus.* Ann Arbor: University of Michigan Press, 1990.

Zerzan, John. *Elements of Refusal.* Columbia, Mo.: CAL Press, 1999.

———. *Running on Emptiness: The Pathology of Civilization.* Los Angeles: Feral House, 2008.

Zevit, Ziony. "False Dichotomies in Descriptions of Israelite Religion: A Problem, Its Origin, and a Proposed Solution." In *Symbiosis, Symbolism, and the Power of the Past: Canaan, Ancient Israel, and Their Neighbors from the Late Bronze Age through Roman Palestina,* ed. William G. Dever and Seymour Gitin, 223–35. Winona Lake, Ind.: Eisenbrauns, 2003.

Zornberg, Avivah Gottlieb. *The Beginning of Desire: Reflections on Genesis.* New York: Image, 1996.

———. *The Particulars of Rapture: Reflections on Exodus.* New York: Image, 2002.

Texts and Reference

Archer, Gleason, R. Laird Harris, and Bruce Waltke, eds. *Theological Wordbook of the Old Testament.* Chicago: Moody Publishers, 1980.

Louw, Johannes P., and Eugene A. Nida, eds. *Greek-English Lexicon of the New Testament Based on Semantic Domains.* New York: United Bible Societies, 1988.

LSJ Lexicon, accessed online at *http://old.perseus.tufts.edu/cgi-bin/lexindex?entry=paliggenesi/a&display=Sgreek.*

Soncino Midrash Rabbah. The CD Rom. Judaic Classics Library. Distributed by Davka Corporation. Brooklyn: Soncino Press, 1983.

Index

agriculture
  as divine curse, 26–28, 57–58, 146
  manna as alternative to, 149–50
  origins of, 25
  relationship to famine, 55, 88–89
  relationship to origin of cities, 25, 34, 38
  relationship to patriarchy, 27
Albertz, Rainer, 336, 347, 348, 350
Alexander Jannaeus, 359, 367, 428
Alexander the Great, 288, 293, 294, 305, 358
Allison, Dale C., Jr., 407, 408
Ammonites, 65, 186, 253, 327
Anderson, Benedict, 209, 211
angels, 63–64, 79, 144, 177, 270, 306, 331–33, 341, 344, 375–79, 401, 409, 416–17, 419–20, 429, 470
Antiochus III (Seleucid king), 313, 333, 336, 338, 341, 343–44, 349–50, 353, 355, 357
Antiochus IV Epiphanes (Seleucid king), 314, 316, 319, 323–25, 329, 333, 335
Antipater (father of Herod the Great), 368, 371, 372
Antony, Mark, 371, 372
apocalyptic
  birth pangs, 460
  defined, 300–301
  as expression of resistance to empire, 301–9, 318–23, 348–54, 372–73, 421, 452–53, 466
  as mystical experience, 301, 451–52
  as not about "end of the world," 300, 466
  pseudepigraphal authorship of, 299–300

apocalyptic (continued)
  "realized apocalyptic," 436, 455, 461
  as subversive wisdom, 289, 301, 461–62
  Zoroastrian influence on, 287
Apsu (Babylonian deity), 17
Aristobulus (Hasmonean king), 359
Aristobulus II (Hasmonean king), 367–68
Asherah/Astarte, worship of, 162–63, 165, 185
Ashur (Assyrian deity), 173
Assyria and Assyrians, 172–74, 177–79, 182, 196, 227, 231, 255
Astarte (or Asherah), 158, 162–63, 165, 185–86
Atkinson, Kenneth, 370, 371
Augustus Caesar, 371–72, 408, 420, 443, 459

Ba'al, 148, 158, 162–65, 185, 326; see also Asherah/Astarte.
Babylon
  ancient (3rd–2nd millennium BCE), 51
  destruction of Jerusalem by, 15, 22, 51, 95, 198, 218–22, 308
  destruction by YHWH, 223
  as metaphor for empire, 34, 46, 396, 471
  neo (6th century BCE), 16–18, 22–23, 32, 43
Barzun, Jacques, 14
Bauckham, Richard, 436
Beale, G. K., 470
Bechtel, Lyn, 28, 62
Bellwood, 25–26, 27, 146
Bennett, William, 292

Bethel
  criticized by prophets, 167–70
  destroyed by Josiah, 80, 185–86
  site of Abraham's altar, 59
  site of Jacob's dream, 80
  site of Jacob's settlement, 84
  site of Jeroboam's shrine, 94,
    155–56, 158–60, 174, 206
Bilby, Kenneth, 205
Bledstein, Adrien Janis, 77, 78
Blenkinsopp, Joseph, 68, 158–59,
    183, 241, 259, 263–64, 268, 289
blessing, 7, 28, 53–54, 59, 68, 72–73,
    75, 77–78
blindness, as metaphor for turning
    away from God, 63, 238, 239,
    331–34, 401–2, 422–24, 439
Bloch-Smith, Elizabeth, 200, 201
Boccaccini, Gabriele, 218, 228, 242,
    288, 299, 308, 310–11, 313, 315,
    318, 324–25, 333, 336, 352, 354,
    365, 371, 373
Boda, Mark, 247–48
Bonhoeffer, Dietrich, 384, 412
Brett, Mark, 21, 252, 269
Brown, Raymond, 436
Brueggemann, Walter, 33, 110, 132,
    191, 215–16, 220, 456
Bultmann, Rudolf, 384–85

Caesarea, 372, 424
Caesar's coin, 404
calendar, resisting imperial control of,
    359–61
Calgacus, 429
Callender, Dexter, 230
Campbell, Douglass A., 449, 457, 465
Canaanites, 45, 55, 71, 74, 93, 134,
    148, 253, 327
Carroll, Lewis, 49
Carter, Warren, 407, 411, 435
Cassuto, Umberto, 20, 34
centurion(s), 424
Chialà, Sabino, 377

Christianity
  as religion of Roman Empire, 96,
    473
  as vague category, xiii–xiv, 6
church(es) (*ekklēsiai*), 417, 444, 451,
    454, 455, 463, 469
circumcision, 59, 72, 86, 202, 242,
    325, 431, 458, 464
cities, origins of, 36–43
clans (*mishpachot*), as basic kinship
    unit in Israel, 152, 167, 209, 262;
    see also kinship
Cohen, Shaye J. D., 264, 289, 356,
    437
Collins, John J., 299–300, 314, 346,
    348, 350, 356, 364, 370
Constantine, Emperor, 96, 160, 283,
    399, 406, 473
Cook, Stephen, 166, 169, 176–78,
    241–42
Coover Dox, Dorian, 147
covenant
  with Abraham, 59
  with house of David, 94, 95, 188
  at Sinai with Israel, 93, 144, 152–53
Cox, Harvey, 55
Crawford, Sidnie White, 366, 367
Crenshaw, James, 291–92
Croatto, Severino, 49–50
Cross, Frank, 158
Crossan, John Dominic, 387
crucifixion
  of Jesus, 403, 405–6, 410, 438,
    453, 461, 468, 470
  as Roman punishment, 359

Davies, W. D., 407, 408
Day, Dorothy, 433
Demetrius II (Seleucid king), 358
Demetrius III (Seleucid king), 359
desolating sacrilege (aka abomination
    that desecrates), 349, 399
Dever, William, 13, 106, 108–9, 166,
    200, 202, 204–5, 208
devil, 417, 422, 433, 436, 440, 444;
    see also Satan

Diadochoi (successors to Alexander the Great), 288, 306
disease(s)
caused by agriculture or empire, 25, 146, 149
healing of, 237, 410–11, 423
see also Egypt, diseases of
Douglas, Mary, 253, 254, 255, 273–75, 277
Douglass, James, 151
dreams and visions
as encounter with God, 79–80, 98, 131–32, 227–28, 301, 318, 329–30, 343, 348–51, 409–10
interpretation of, 341–44
Dutcher-Walls, Patricia, 161, 180
Dykstra, Laurel, 139

Ea (Babylonian deity), 17
Eden (garden of), 22–31, 57, 60, 76, 99, 225, 230–31
Egypt
as alternative to Babylon preceding the Exile, 173, 216, 218–24
conquest of, by Alexander the Great, 288
diseases of, 146, 149, 410–11; *see also* disease
as embodiment of "the great city," 396, 470
imperial control of Canaan (13th–10th centuries BCE), 199–204
as location of Yahwistic temple alternative to Jerusalem, 222
outcry against, 60
plagues on, 28, 146
protest against Hellenistic rule, 295
pyramids, 49
relationship with Solomon, 121, 131, 140, 209
as refuge from Davidic dynasty, 135–37
revolt against Persia, 260–61
as source of food, 55–56, 57, 64, 87–89, 149–50

Egypt (*continued*)
as symbolic expression of Jerusalem monarchy, 100, 139, 141–45
see also Ptolemaic empire
Ehrman, Bart, 387
Elliott, Mark Adam, 299, 300, 308, 351, 360, 448
Elliott, Neil, 327, 385, 449, 452, 453, 464
Ellul, Jacques, 36, 51, 309
Emberling, Geoff, 205
Embry, Brad, 368, 369
empire
defined, 7–8
as network of social power, 38–39
origins in Genesis, 45–46
origins in Middle East, 40
Eskenazi, Tamara, 249, 251–53, 258–59, 261, 263
Essenes
in Jerusalem, 357
at Qumran, 362
eternal life, 351, 445
ethnicity and ethnogenesis, 200–202, 205–6, 210–11
eschatology and postmortem judgment, 272, 307–8, 310, 376–78
Euphrates River, 22–23, 121, 193, 458

Faust, Avraham, 202, 210
Fewell, Danna Nolan, 337, 340, 343, 347
Finkelstein, Israel, 106–8, 172
fish, Roman Empire's appropriation of, 402
Fishbane, Michael, 49, 81
Fitzmyer, Joseph A., 425
flesh, as metaphor for human life apart from God, 438, 455
Flint, Peter, 362
footwashing, 446
foreigners and strangers
exclusion of, by empire, 61–63, 142, 242
hospitality to, 59, 416–17, 426–27

foreigners and strangers (*continued*)
  inclusion of, within God's people,
    68, 265, 270, 276, 282
  intermarriage with, 71–72, 86,
    134–35, 253–55, 270, 282, 361
Fraade, Steven D., 367
Frei, Peter, 283
Freyne, Seán, 402, 442
Fried, Lisbeth S., 237, 255

Genesis, book of
  as counter-story to *Enuma Elish*,
    18–20, 32, 35, 43, 45, 47–51, 60
  as counter-story to Ezra-Nehemiah,
    269–71
  as counter-story to *Gilgamesh Epic*,
    44
  opposition to cities, 36, 47–51,
    61–65
Gilgal, as site of origin of Israel's
    monarchy, 168–69
Girard, René, 196, 437
global economy, 18, 24, 161, 230
Godfather saga, 111, 115, 116
Golden Calf narrative, 156–59
Gottwald, Norman, 264, 385
Grabbe, Lester, 246, 259
Gruen, Erich, S., 141, 290, 296, 324,
    327, 340

Halliday, M. A. K., 51
Halpern, Baruch, 106, 108–9, 113–
    14, 130, 140, 174, 182, 209,
    235
Handel's *Messiah*, 390
Hardin, Justin K., 464
Hasel, Michael G., 199
Hasmonean dynasty, 288, 290, 296,
    314, 327, 334, 337, 355–71
Hayes, John, 119, 137
Haynes, Stephen R., 384
Hays, J. Daniel, 128
Hays, Richard, 388, 454, 457
Hendel, Ronald, 388
Heym, Stephen, 113–14

Hill, Jonathan D., 200, 201
Hittites, 70, 73, 75, 134, 193, 253
Höbl, Gunther, 293, 294, 313
Hobsbawm, Eric, 205
Hoglund, Kenneth, 260–63
Hollander, H. W., 373
holy ones, *see* saints
holy war, 195, 326–28, 467; *see also,*
    violence
Horace (Roman poet), 443
Horden, Peregrine, 25–26
Horsley, Richard, 301, 303, 306, 313,
    317, 320, 323–24, 335, 337, 343,
    346, 350–51, 386, 448–49, 452
hunter-gatherers, 24–26, 37
Hyrcanus II (Hasmonean king),
    367–68

interpretation of New Testament
  African American, 385
  commitment to discipleship as
    criterion, 392
  effect of Enlightenment, 383–84
  effect of Nazi holocaust, 385
  feminist, 385
  fundamentalism and, 386
  Holy Spirit as criterion, 456
  influence of Luther, 384–85, 448
  Jesus Seminar and, 386–87
  liberation theology and, 385
  postcolonial, 385
  resurrection of Jesus as criterion,
    388, 395, 456
  road to Emmaus as interpretive key,
    388–91
  Roman Empire and, 395–96,
    448–49
Isis, 294, 295; *see also* Serapis

Japhet, Sara, 249, 250, 278, 279–80,
    282
Jason (Hasmonean high priest),
    323–25, 333
Jebusites, 94, 134, 253
Jefferson, Thomas, 386–87

Jerusalem
  archaeological evidence for, 106–8
  as center for worship, 80, 132, 153,
    159, 162, 174, 185–87, 206–9,
    252, 280, 282–83, 317
  claimed by David, 94
  conquest and destruction of, by
    Rome, 368, 371–72, 399, 438
  criticized by apostles, 423, 462
  criticized by Jesus, 389, 399, 442
  criticized by prophets, 177, 197,
    229, 338, 354, 369
  destruction of, by Babylon, 15, 22,
    51, 95, 198, 218–22, 308
  with elite as collaborators with
    foreign kings, 172–74, 259–64,
    291, 310, 315, 318, 321, 323–24,
    363
  as "great city," 470
  Hellenistic influence on, 288–90,
    324, 350, 356
  as "holy city," 251–52, 354, 396,
    471
  New, 471
  rebuilt under Persian sponsorship,
    257–64, 284
  support for as criterion for can-
    onization of texts, 286, 302,
    354
  threatened by Assyria, 172–74;
  see also Ptolemaic dynasty; Roman
    empire; Seleucid dynasty; Temple,
    Jerusalem
Jesus Seminar, *see* interpretation of
  New Testament
Jewett, Robert, 455, 457, 459, 464
Jobling, David, 188, 189
John Hyrcanus (Jerusalem priest), 359,
  440
Jonathan (Hasmonean high priest),
  356, 357–58, 363
Jonge, M. De, 373
Josephus, 314, 356–57, 359, 367,
  368, 383, 441, 444
Joyce, James, 49

jubilee, 276–77, 352, 354, 419,
  422–25, 427, 430
Judaism
  as anachronistic label in ancient
    world, 5, 437
  core as "covenantal nomism," 448
  Enochic, 242, 288, 308, 365
  Rabbinic, 354
  relationship with "Hellenism,"
    289–90, 327
  as vague category, xiii–xiv
  Zadokite, 242, 288, 308
Judeans (*Ioudaioi*), as opponents of
  Jesus, 437–38
Julius Caesar, 440

Keesmaat, Sylvia, 464
Kessler, John, 248
Kierspel, Lars, 438
Killebrew, Anne, 203, 204, 208
Kingu (Babylonian deity), 17
kinship, as relationship among God's
  people, 54, 154, 167, 174, 189,
  206, 281, 404; *see also* clans
Kitchen, Kenneth A., 106, 137, 209
Klawans, Jonathan, 361
Kloppenborg, John S., 407, 425
Knibb, Michael, 319, 373
Knoppers, Gary, N., 102, 255
Kramer, Paul, A., 211
Kvanvig, Helge, 320

Last Supper (of Jesus), 405, 426, 444,
  446
Levenson, Jon, 144, 328, 329, 351,
  445
Leuchter, Mark, 136, 137
love
  of enemies, 148, 196, 413, 429, 454
  of family, 66, 68–69, 74, 316
  of foreign women, 134
  by God, 94, 170, 224, 236, 395,
    400–401, 403, 444
  of God, 265, 431
  of neighbor/one another, 275, 436,
    444, 446, 460, 463–64, 467

Malina, Bruce, 393
Mamre, 59, 84
Mann, Michael, 38–41
Marduk (Babylonian deity), 17–18,
    19, 35, 235, 346
Master, Daniel M., 210
Mayer, Henry, 265
Mazar, Amihai, 106
McBride, John, 3
Meadowcroft, Tim, 352
Menelaus (Hasmonean high priest),
    324, 333, 350
Menippean satire, 337–38
Merneptah stele, 199–200, 202, 203,
    205
Merton, Thomas, xiv
messiah(s)
    Cyrus as, 236, 247
    David as, 178, 190
    Enochic Son of Man as, 377–79,
        403
    Jesus as, 96, 390, 400, 402, 407,
        409, 419, 423, 432, 441, 445,
        448, 453, 455, 457
messianic age, 351
messianic hopes, 334, 364, 369–71,
    467
Meyers, Eric, 260, 272
Midian/Midianites, 135–36, 143, 178
midrash, 32, 44, 53, 57, 69, 70, 302,
    378
Miller, Maxwell, 119, 137
Mishkan (desert tabernacle)
    as alternative to Jerusalem temple,
        154–56
    as model for Jerusalem temple,
        273–75
Moabites, 65, 253
money, as part of imperial economy,
    246, 256, 309, 404
monotheism, 235, 422
Morgenstern, Mira, 88
mountain(s), as place of encounter
    with God, 68, 93, 143–44, 151–
    52, 164, 196, 240, 307, 403,
    413

Moxnes, Halvor, 460
Mumford, Lewis, 37–41
Münkler, Herfried, 7–8, 203, 395
Myers, Ched, 389, 390, 392, 399,
    401, 414

Najman, Hindy, 322, 361
Nakanose, Shigeyuki, 182–83
Nebuchadnezzar, king of Babylon,
    216, 217–20, 329, 335, 338–47,
    410
Nelson, Hilde Lindemann, 19
Nelson, Richard, 193
Nero (emperor), 450, 464
Nhat Hanh, Thich, xiv
Nickelsburg, George, 298–99, 300,
    302, 306, 319, 321, 363, 373,
    378, 426
Nile River, 23, 40, 88, 139, 142
Nouwen, Henri, 401

Oakes, Peter, 430, 461
Oblath, Michael, 138–39, 141
Octavian, see Augustus Caesar
Odell, Margaret, 227, 228, 231, 240
Origen, 302
Orlov, Andrei, 379

parables
    within Deuteronomistic History,
        125–31
    in time of Jesus, 416, 440, 425–46,
        428
passover
    as Jerusalem temple feast, 186–87,
        282
    as wilderness family feast, 187, 193
patronage system, 415, 419, 426, 429,
    462
peace
    as provided by empire, 85, 255
    as provided by God/Jesus, 85, 400,
        420, 422–25, 442–43, 444
    see also Roman Empire: Pax
        Romana
Perdue, Leo, 235, 284, 291–93

Persian empire, rule over province of Yehud (Judah), 246–48, 257–64
Pharisees, 357, 359, 365–67, 401, 404, 412, 426, 438, 439, 451, 453
Philistines, 99, 110, 113, 202, 205, 208
Philo of Alexandria, 222
plagues
  on Egypt, 28, 56, 146–47
  on empire, 468–69
Platonism, 141, 384, 473
Polaski, Donald, 347
Polley, Max E., 169
Polzin, Robert, 125–26, 189–90
Pompey (Roman general), 368–71
prophets and prophecy
  age of declared ended by Second Temple elite, 284, 296–97
  as critical of empire, 161–71, 176, 197
prostitution as metaphor for imperial intercourse/idolatry, 128–29, 228–29
Ptolemaic dynasty
  control of Jerusalem by, 307
  Hellenistic royal ideology of, 293–96
  origin of, 288
Purcell, Nicholas, 25–26

Q (putative source for Matthew and Luke's gospels), 407

Rambam (Maimonides), 53
Religion, defined, 4–5
Rendtorff, Rolf, 273
repentance (*metanoia*), 165, 223, 328, 336, 346, 354, 362, 365, 401–2, 420–21, 423, 453, 460, 468–70
resurrection
  Israelite hopes for, 319, 328, 351, 445
  of Jesus, 390, 423, 445, 448, 455, 460, 463, 465, 467–68; *see also* interpretation of New Testament

Richey, Lance Byron, 435, 445
Rohrbaugh, Richard, 427
Roman Empire
  collaboration with temple elite, 371–72
  conquest and control of Jerusalem, 367–69, 371–72
  paideia (educational system), 419
  parens patriae, doctrine of, 440
  Pax Romana, 400, 406, 420, 429, 430, 443, 471; *see also* peace
  resistance to, 370–71, 400, 405, 408, 414, 432
  savior, emperor as, 441; *see also* son of God
  social structure, 415, 461
Rowe, C. Kavin, 433
Rowley-Conwy, Peter, 25
Rudman, Dominic, 177

Sabbath Economics Collaborative, 276
Sadducees, 356–57, 359, 404, 453
Sahlins, Marshall, 24
saints (aka "holy ones"), 302, 307, 319, 375, 393, 455–56
Saldarini, Anthony J., 356, 359
salvation, 178, 238, 265, 267, 308, 334, 351, 354, 364, 371, 391, 400, 412, 415, 419, 421, 424, 426, 430, 449, 454, 457, 462
Samaria and Samaritans, 108, 129, 161, 167–71, 186, 246, 255, 261, 276, 282, 372, 439–42
Sanders, E. P., 289, 448
Sarna, Nahum, 61, 63, 73, 79, 81, 140
Satan, 401, 402, 404, 430, 433; *see also* devil
Schüssler Fiorenza, Elisabeth, 385, 386, 449
Schwartz, Seth, 356
secondary products revolution, 40–41
Segal, Alan, 431, 447, 451–52
Seitz, Christopher, 233, 238

Seleucid dynasty
  control of Jerusalem by, 313–15,
    323–24
  nonviolent resistance to, 328–29,
    343–51, 361
  origin of, 288
  violent resistance to, 325–27,
    333–34
Sennacherib, king of Assyria, 173, 177
Seow, Choon-Leong, 309–10
Serapis, 294, 295; *see also* Isis
servant of YHWH
  as Daniel's *maskilim*, 350–51, 354
  Isaiah's, 237–39
  Jesus as, 390, 403, 411, 454, 470
Shechem/Shechemites, 83, 85–87,
    122, 123
Shepard, Paul, 25, 39, 146, 196
shepherd(ess)
  as angelic patrons, 332–34
  herders of sheep/goats, 24, 72, 143,
    166, 419
  as symbol for kings, 178, 208, 236,
    239–40, 411
  YHWH as, 122
Sherratt, Andrew, 26, 27, 40
Shiloh, 136, 158, 189, 206
Silberman, Neil, 106–8, 172
Simon III (Hasmonean high priest),
    358
Smith, Anthony, 201, 210
Smith-Christopher, Daniel, 254, 263,
    288, 337, 340, 342, 344–45, 347,
    349, 352
Sneed, Mark, 311
Sodom, 57–58, 60–64, 229, 396, 399,
    470
Son of God
  as imperial title, 280, 445
  as title for Jesus, 96, 400, 422, 445,
    455
Son of Man
  in Daniel, 343
  in Enoch, 373–74, 376–79, 389–90,
    407–8, 416

Son of Man (*continued*)
  in New Testament, 349, 389–90,
    407–8, 416, 452, 469
Steinberg, Naomi, 57
Stendahl, Krister, 385, 447–49, 457
Sternberg, Meir, 13, 29, 63, 70–72,
    142
Stoicism, 408, 460, 473
Stulman, Louis, 215, 216, 218
Sumer, 41, 46
Sweeney, Marvin, 166–67, 169, 170,
    297, 337, 338
synagogue(s)
  expelled from, 439
  unclean spirit of, 401

tablets, heavenly (as source of divine
    wisdom), 154, 319, 360–61
Tacitus, 429
Tamez, Elsa, 450
Taylor, Charles, 383
technology, Genesis's judgment upon,
    31
Temple, Solomon's
  building of, 94, 129, 142, 280–81
  evidence for, 106–9
  "repair of" as metaphor for united
    monarchy, 180–83
  see also Mishkan
Tiamet (Babylonian deity), 17–18, 20
Tiglath-Pileser (Assyrian king), 172
Tiller, Patrick, 330, 331, 332, 333,
    334
timeline, New Testament, 394
torah
  book of, "found" under Josiah,
    183–85
  established under Second Temple,
    283–85
  four-source theory of origins, 103
  of the king (Deut. 17:14–20),
    101–2, 188, 193, 366
  and prophets as collective canon
    under Hasmoneans, 356
  opposition to by Enoch tradition,
    304

Tracy, David, 268
tree(s)
  cedar, 231, 235, 258
  cosmic, 231, 345–46
  fig, 117, 121, 161, 174, 176, 404
  food from (hunter-gatherers), 24
  fragrant, 307
  fruit, good or bad, from, 414
  green (as place of worship), 129
  knowledge of good and evil
    (wisdom), 26, 29, 57, 99, 307
  of life, 30, 31
  menorah as stylized, 144
  olive, 123
  sacred, 59
  sycamore, 424
twelve tribes of Israel
  in book of Exodus, 154
  in book of Joshua, 194–95
  lack of premonarchical existence,
    117–19
  relationship with twelve apostles of
    Jesus, 408
Turner, Lawrence, 50, 59, 62
Tyre, 155, 230, 246

Ur (Babylonian city), 51

Valeta, David M., 337–38, 344, 348
VanderKam, James, 358, 362
Van Der Toorn, Karel, 297
violence
  relationship with cities and empire,
    35–36, 43, 256–57, 445, 467–68
  as "redemptive," 111–12
  as "sacred," 70, 196, 437, 438,
    453
  types biblically approved, 147–48
  see also holy war
Wallerstein, Immanuel, 203

Walsh, Brian J., 464
Wason, Paul, K., 39
Watts, James W., 283
Wengst, Klaus, 443
Wenham, Gordon, 57, 273
Westermann, Claus, 35, 57, 60, 71
White, Hugh, 35
White, Marsha, 165
Wiesehöfer, Josef, 259
wilderness (desert) as place of
  encounter with God, 59, 96,
    143–45, 150, 164, 170, 269–70,
    274, 331, 364, 400, 401, 421
Williamson, H. G. M., 262
Wink, Walter, 18, 343, 373, 392, 414
wisdom
  apocalyptic, 289, 298–301, 303–9,
    318–23; *see also* apocalyptic
  royal, 288–89, 290–93, 315–18
  skeptical/ironic, 289, 309–11
  of Solomon, 98, 123–31, 141
Witherington, III, Ben, 432
world-systems theory, 203–4; see also
  Wallerstein, Immanuel
Wright, N. T., 387, 395, 448–49, 454,
  457
writing
  David-Solomon succession narrative
    as first biblical, 113–14
  origins of, 41–42

Yoder Neufeld, Thomas, 464

Zadokites, 158–59, 241–42, 247,
  284, 302, 308, 315, 333, 338,
  353, 356, 358, 361
Zerzan, John, 25
Zevit, Ziony, 285–86
Zornberg, Avivah Gottlieb, 53, 70
Zoroastrianism, 286, 287, 319